The Artist In Our Midst 2

Cambridgeshire, Essex, Norfolk & Suffolk

A SELECTION OF WORKS BY LEADING CONTEMPORARY EAST ANGLIAN ARTISTS
As featured in *Green Pebble Magazine*

A Green Pebble Publication
Edited by Ruby Ormerod

First published in Great Britain in 2010
Green Pebble Publications
Roos Hall Studio
Bungay Road
Beccles
Suffolk NR34 8HE
www.greenpebble.co.uk

ISBN 978-0-9558147-1-6

Edited and Designed by Ruby Ormerod
Cover Image: *March Wave Rolling (Detail) (2010)* © Maggi Hambling (P 6 - 9)
Printed by Breckland Print, Suffolk, United Kingdom

Green Pebble Magazine is dedicated to the visual arts in East Anglia

Contents

4   Foreword

6   Artists

174   Opinions

186   Galleries

192   Index

Foreword

By Michael Charles

Publisher, Green Pebble Publications

4

Leading psychologist Professor Michael S. Gazzaniga helped discover that the right hemisphere of the brain sees an image and can mobilize a nonverbal response to it, but can't talk about what it sees. In this book, *The Artist in Our Midst 2,* we seek to let the artists' works have pride of place and have extracted (sometimes with great difficulty) a verbal response from each artist to try to better communicate the artist's answer as to 'why they have created in the way they have'. We have also dug a little deeper to give you, the reader, a glimpse of the 'who' and the 'how' by letting you into some of the artists' working spaces: their studios.

The 'when and where', at least, are easy, I can answer that: it is East Anglia in 2010. This book contains a selection of works by some of the leading practicing artists in East Anglia, arguably in the country, at the beginning of the 21st century.

My mission in producing this book, and indeed in the other books and magazines published by *Green Pebble*, is to help the artists articulate their vision and in so doing help us, non artists, better appreciate their work and fraught career choice.

The life of an artist is so full of contradictions it could almost define the word. From the outset the visual artist - the person with heightened sensitivity and a tendency to introspection, private contemplation and lonely observation - learns that producing work does not alone pay the bills, but selling work does; so *splosh* they fall, those sensitive souls, into the cut-throat world of commerce.

On a mission to talk to a man, called by some the greatest artist alive and practicing in Norfolk, I telephoned to make an appointment. After the phone had rung for many times it was eventually answered by a frightened, frail and faltering voice. Like an aged and rotten twig, a vocal pike - pitched to fend off strangers - demanded: 'Who's there?' Needless to say my credentials as a journalist were wholly insufficient. However, as a student I eventually managed to exchange words with the gentleman, albeit at a distance by telephone.

This is the story I discovered:
All his life this man had wanted to practice his art, but fearful of financial oblivion he had elected to take a job that, even though it crippled his soul, earned him a salary that paid his bills. As and when the weekends and holidays came round, he then had such an outpouring of condensed creativity that his work was admired and, yes, even occasionally purchased. Nearing retirement and after a lifetime of meaningless labour for a pittance, he eventually gave up the day job, determined to devote his life, at last, to his art.

Elated, he bought materials, undertook to enter into various exhibitions and chatted animatedly to his friends about his plans.

And so we come to the *But*. Having recently quit his job, his ability to pay his bills depended upon his ability to create art. But creativity can be a fragile, illusive endeavour. Sometimes, fairy-like, it skitters out of view when you want it the most. Confronted with the harsh glare of day-to-day living, his creativity withered. He discovered, and late in his life too, that creativity does not easily get harnessed to be switched on and off on demand. So there he hunkered, demoralised, not wanting to face the world, not wanting to create, but wanting his painful experience to be known by others.

Other artists have told me of their delight in discovering a new style of their work is selling well. They press on, eagerly exploring the new style and happily banking the money from the increasing sales. Then one day they go into their studio with another new style on their minds, indeed it fills their minds, and with the old style forgotten they excitedly create only to find the market wants the old style and there are no buyers for this new work.

Confronted with this dilemma, some turn back and make more of the high selling work and earn the label 'commercial' and others forge on with this new outpouring of creativity to earn the title of 'self indulgent'. Some even have art for themselves and art for the buyers.

Some artists share the harsh commercial realities of marketing, pricing, selling, delivery, packaging (aka framing) by entrusting that side of their endeavour to one, or more commonly, several galleries and allow those professionals to deal with the left brain logical issues whilst they allow their right brain to create. However, other artists fail to find a suitable gallery to work with and plod off into the twilit world of small business all on their own.

All artists who make a living from their own innovative creativity have to be very tough minded. They may appear soft and fluffy on the edges, but make no mistake, they are toughened and have stories of how someone tried to rip them off or inveigle them into some dodgy scheme. The practicing serious artists who live amongst us and, in many cases whose work appear in these pages, deserve our respect, they are focused and experienced. Without their work the heritage we leave to our grandchildren would be thin and pale.

Just as our artists struggle with the right and left brain issues of creating and selling, so do we the viewers get pulled from pillar to post by art that is felt and art that is thought; heart and brain. In some circles, contemporary art and 'modern art' seem to have the same meaning, i.e., challenging art with a mission to mystify. Here in this book, contemporary art means art made by people of today and reflects the styles of art currently being produced and, contrary to what we could be excused for believing by watching television, it means art that is stimulating to the senses and not at all superficial.

Exasperated by the interminable debates about 'art', many of us stomp off for a bit of retail therapy. Often what we buy goes well beyond the purely functional and we pay for a huge degree of decoration and distinction. The closer we get to uniqueness the more we are willing to pay. The works in this book are 'unique' and many cost less than a Hermes coat or a Rolex watch. Most are made by a single, highly skilled exponent of their art, rather than mass produced by a production line in a distant country.

Clearly our society has difficulty in valuing the work of artists. This is no new phenomena, but maybe, in the end, it comes back to what I started with, and Professor Michael S. Gazzaniga's discovery that the artist has the greatest difficulty in describing what he does. Designer brands, on the other hand, pay handsomely for the very best advertising to persuade us to buy their products which will never be as unique as an original work from a leading artist, such as those in this book.

The artists' works illustrated in these pages represent much of the best available in East Anglia and, due to the stature of many of these artists, further afield as well. These artists are all actively and massively contributing to our heritage. Now is the time to cherish them.
- Michael Charles

Maggi Hambling CBE

Maggi Hambling's paintings of the sea show extraordinary vitality and brilliance of texture. They are amongst the best things she has done, and they are getting better and better.
- David Scrase, The Fitzwilliam Museum, Cambridge

Maggi Hambling CBE
Painter and Sculptor
Near Saxmundham, Suffolk

I am obsessed by the Suffolk sea. When I was seven I witnessed the Coronation fireworks exploding in the night sky above the sea at Aldeburgh. That sight sowed the seed for my sculpture, *Scallop*, many years later. Now I watch the waves approaching, gathering momentum, becoming solid for a second before dissolving. It's close to an orgasm.

For me the greatest artists are Rembrandt, Van Gough, Rothko, Rodin, Cy Twombly and Titian. Locally, the Constables in Christchurch Mansion (Constable beats Turner any day). Further afield my favourite galleries are the British Museum, the National Gallery, the Rodin Museum in Paris and of course the Museum of Modern Art in New York.

My ambition for my work is to keep at it in the hope of getting better and my challenges are philistines, interviewers and committees.

A great painting is alive, being created in front of you again and again. A photograph, however moving the subject, is a dead thing by comparison, it is history and very tame. It can never surpass its mechanical means of execution; there is no physical urgency. If my waves, whether in paint or bronze, break *for me*, I hope they will for others.

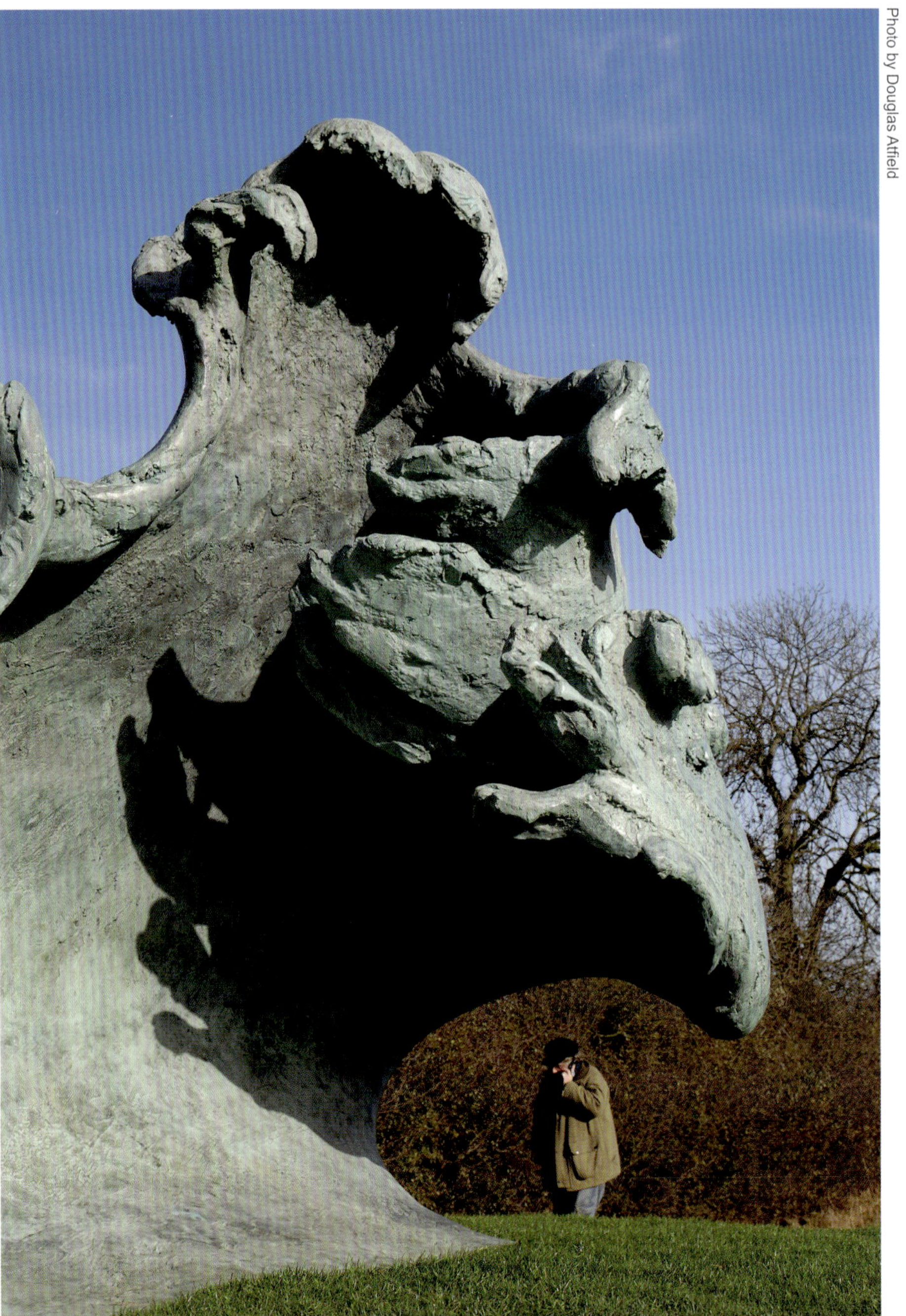

Rearing Wave, Detail (2009) Bronze 335 x 457 x 213cm

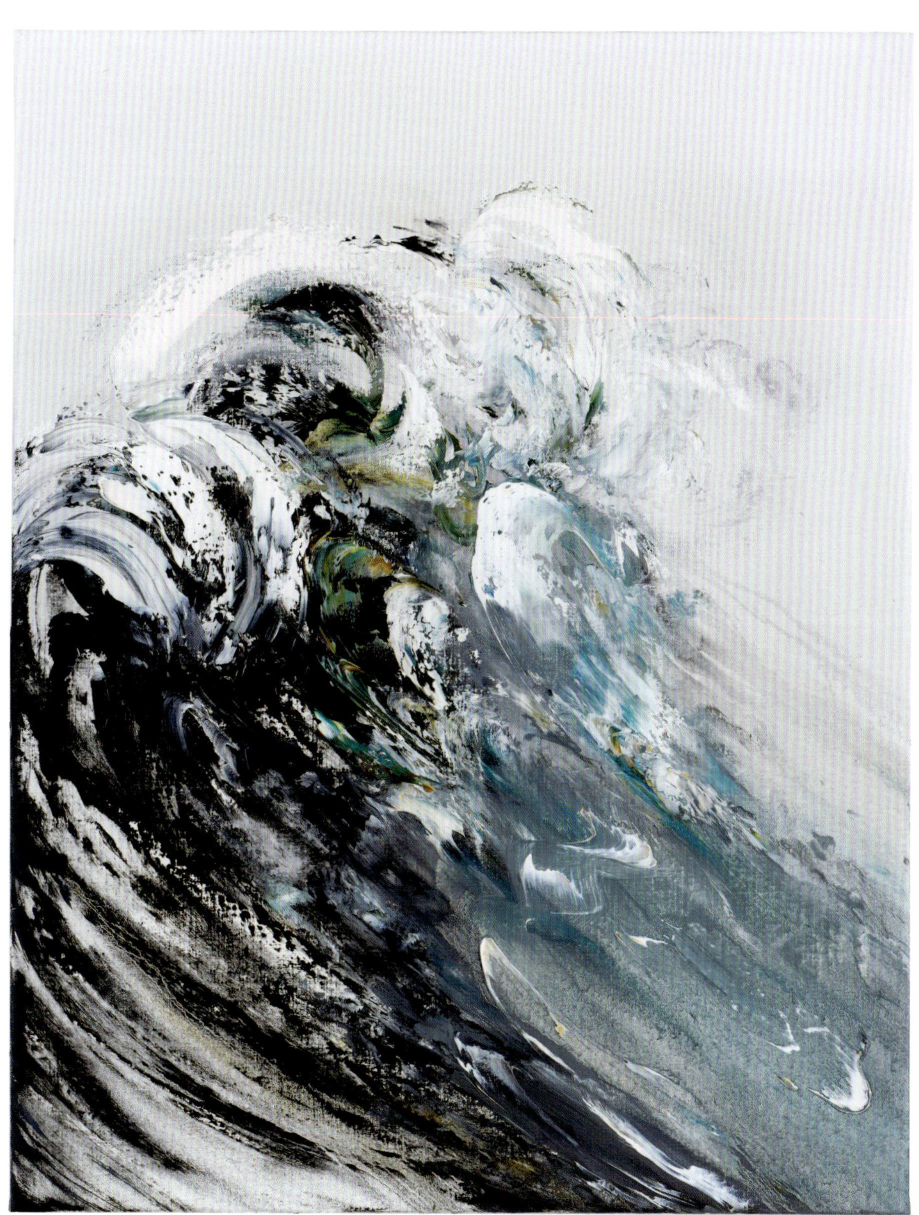

Rising Wave (2009) Oil on Canvas 122 x 91cm

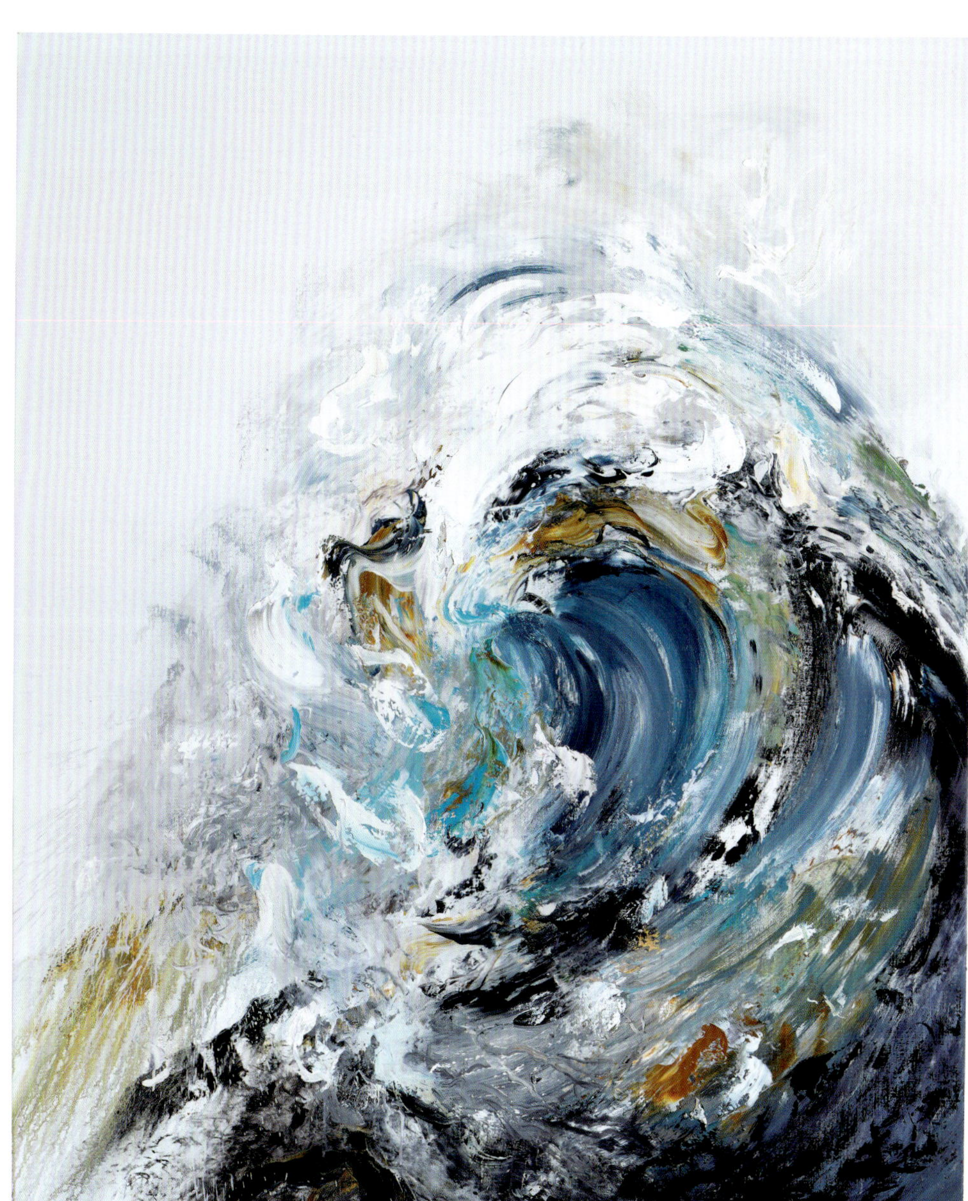

Summer Wave Tunnel (2009) Oil on Canvas 170 x 137cm

Maggi Hambling: Behind the Scenes

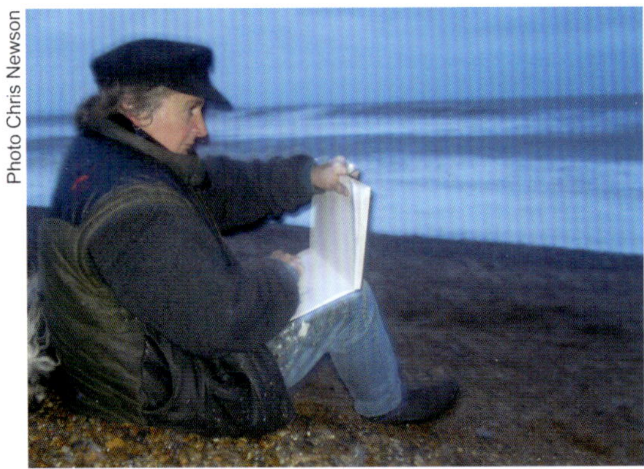

More about:

Maggi Hambling...

Educated-
East Anglian School of Painting 1960 onwards
Ipswich School of Art 1962 - 64
Camberwell School of Art 1964 - 67 Dip AD
Slade School of Fine Art 1967 - 69 H Dip FA

Accreditation-
Higher Diploma in Fine Art, Slade School of Fine Art, 1969

Honours-
Officer of the British Empire 1995
Commander of the British Empire 2010

Local Galleries Familiar With Artist's Work-
Christchurch Mansion, Ipswich
Fitzwilliam Museum, Cambridge
Snape Maltings Gallery, Snape, Suffolk

Collections (Open To The Public)-
British Museum, London
Tate Collection, London
National Portrait Gallery, London
Victoria and Albert Museum, London
Fitzwilliam Museum, Cambridge
Castle Museum, Norwich, Norfolk
Christchurch Mansion, Ipswich, Suffolk
Yale Center for British Art, USA
Australian National Gallery, Australia
Musée de la Main, Switzerland
Gulbenkian Foundation, Portugal

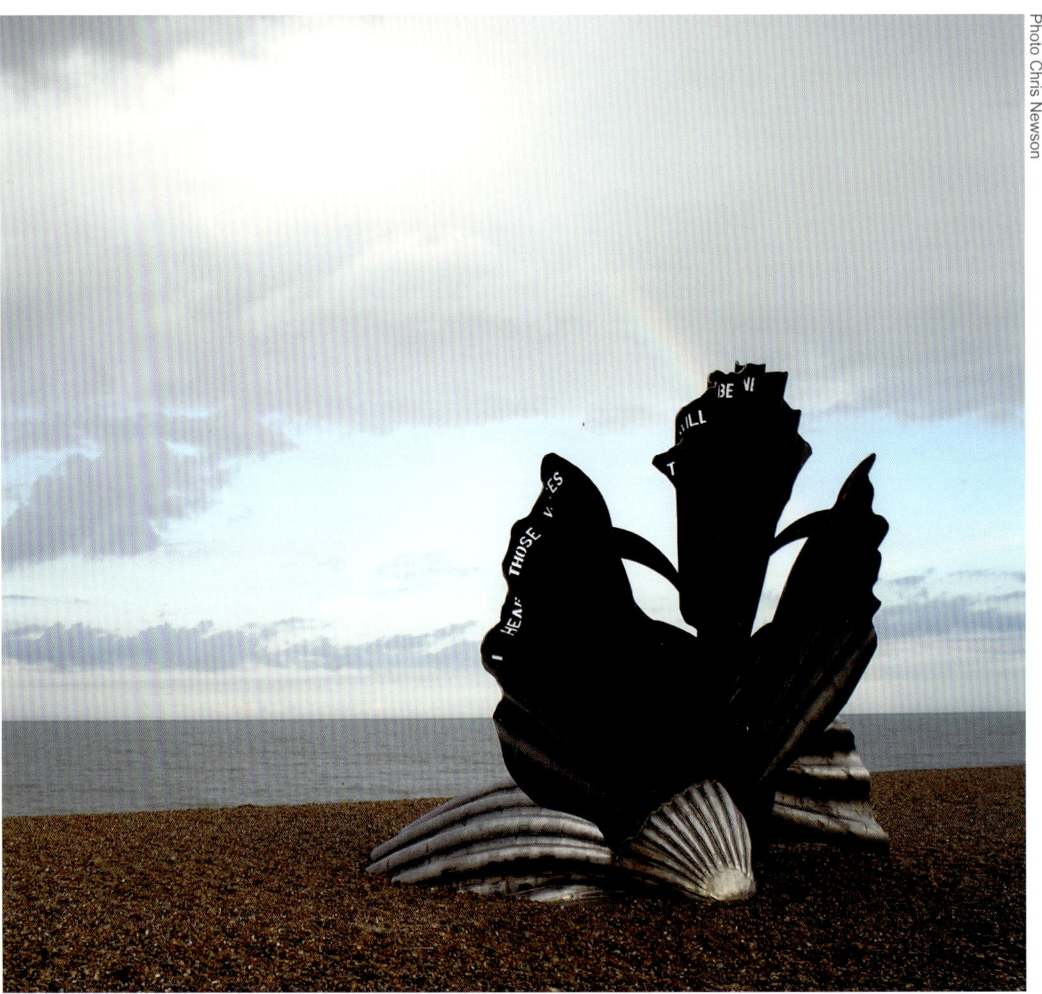

I make an early start before most people have risen, 5 am in summer and 6 am in winter, by going to the sea to make graphite drawings in the sketchbook. I draw the sea in any condition, but it's the moment of the waves breaking that I am really obsessed by.

I get back to the studio about an hour later and then work solidly, fuelled by coffee and cigarettes. My concentration is always on one piece at a time, but I often have half a dozen others around the walls, still cooking.

I hate interruptions and always enjoy the start of a new work and then descend into the pure hell of the middle section and finally, once the work is complete, I enjoy that for a moment. However, knowing when a painting or sculpture is finished is the trickiest bit of the whole business, and many are destroyed.

This Page Left: The Artist drawing, early morning
This Page Right: *Scallop (2003)* Stainless Steel
410 x 460 x 425cm
Opposite Page: The Artist in her studio with Lux

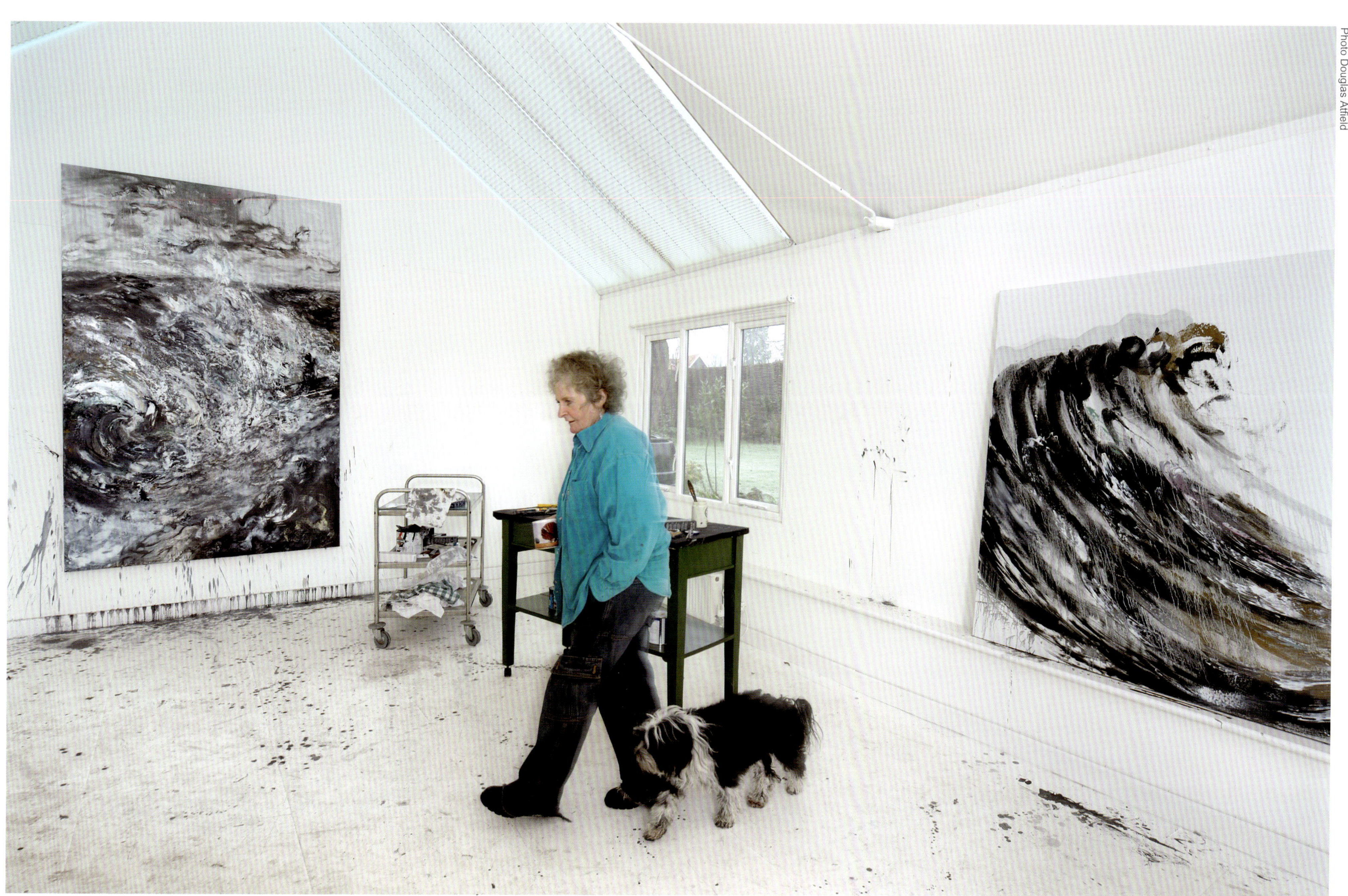
Photo Douglas Atfield

James Dodds

James Dodds is unique in his ability to paint shipping from the inside out. He makes us reassess both the tradition of marine painting from which he has emerged and the future direction the genre might take. Dodds' wooden boats are not so much represented as reconstructed on canvas, each rope and wooden joint scrupulously recorded, leading to paintings of great breadth and power.
- Messum's Fine Art, London

James Dodds
Painter, Printmaker
Wivenhoe, Essex

I feel uncomfortable making grand claims as to the intent or meaning of my work. On one level it is to earn a living and on another it is to explore, have a dialogue with the world around me with a wish to communicate and celebrate certain human values, and on a more personal level to find a state of grace only achievable through work.

Educated-
Royal College of Art, London
Membership of Local Art Societies-
Colchester Art Society
Honours-
Master of Art, Royal College of Art, London
Galleries Familiar With Artist's Work-
Messum's Fine Art, London
Bircham Gallery, Holt, Norfolk
Hayletts Gallery, Maldon, Essex
Collections (Open To The Public)-
Solidarnosc, University of Essex, Colchester, Essex
Website-
www.jamesdodds.co.uk
www.jardinepress.co.uk

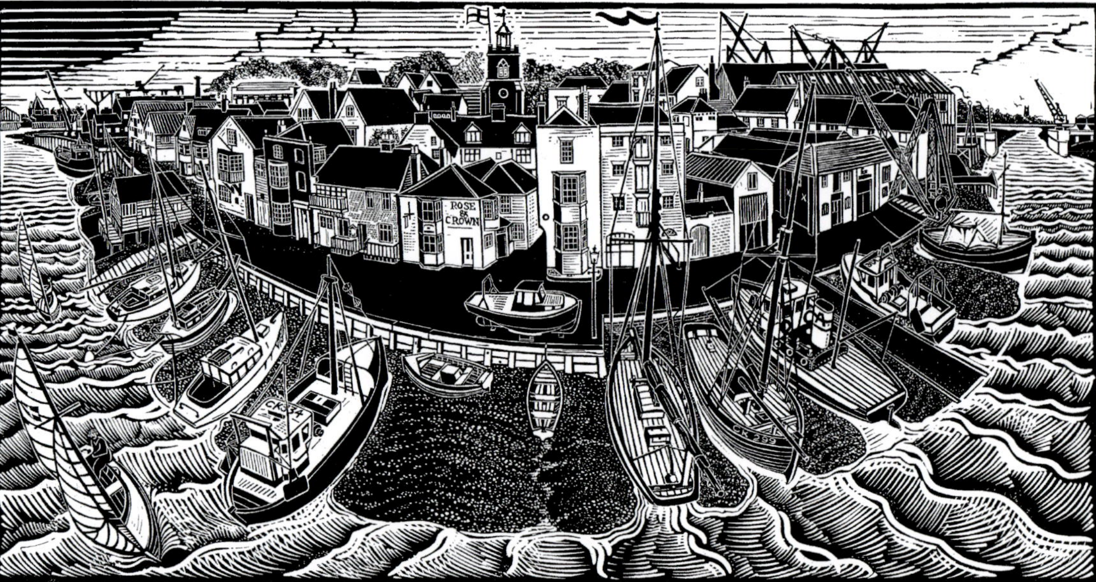

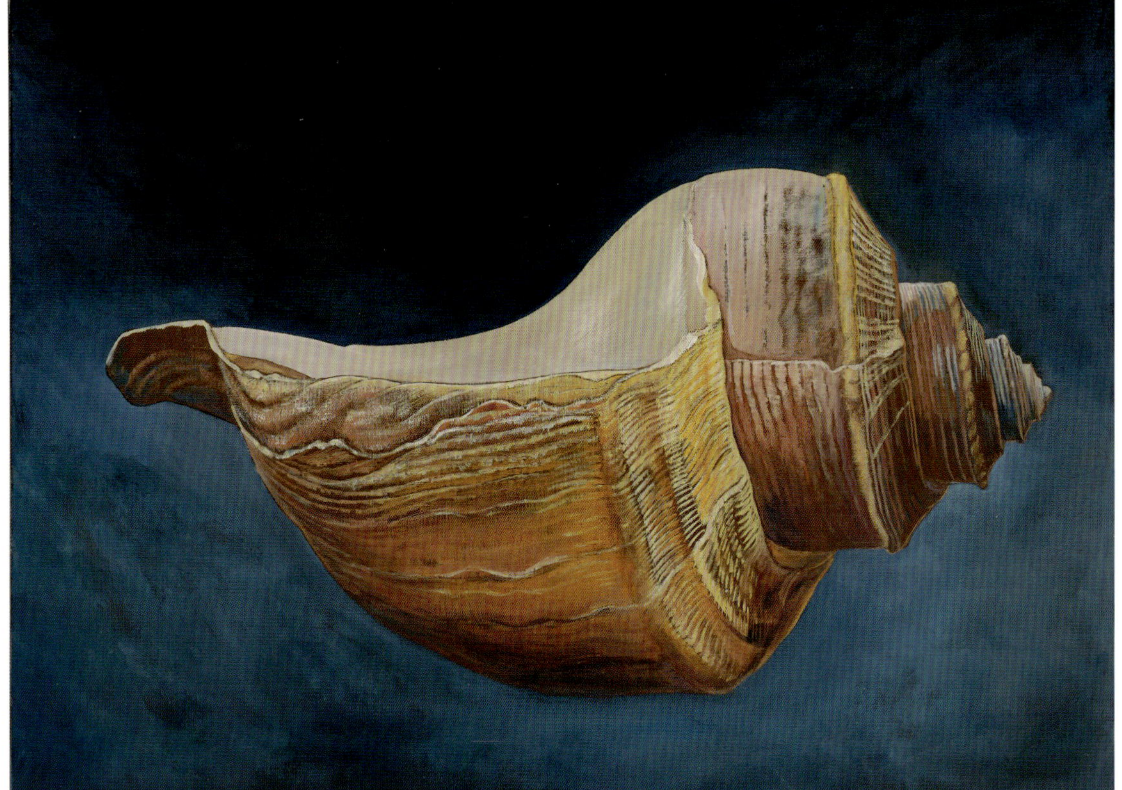

Top: *Wivenhoe Past and Present (1996)* Linocut 36 x 70cm **Bottom:** *Shell (2009)* Oil on Linen 61 x 81 cm

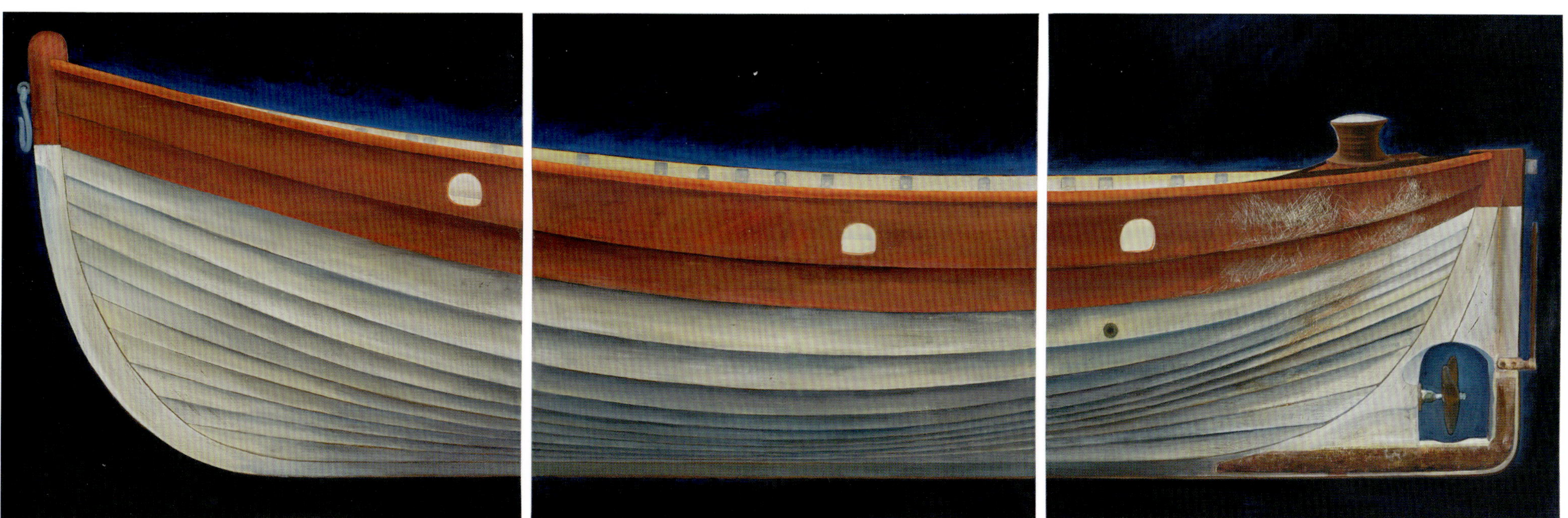

Salthouse Altarpiece (2008) Oil on Linen 90 x 270cm

Peter Baldwin NDD

Peter Baldwin paints pictures of deceptive simplicity with an underlying sophistication. When writing Artists in Britain Since 1945, *I surveyed the work of over 14,000 artists and now find that it is individualists like Peter, often producing small and quirky images, who linger in the memory.*
- David Buckman, **Writer and Journalist**

Peter Baldwin NDD
Painter
Sheringham, Norfolk

The work innovates within a modernist tradition, implied narratives and cryptic symbols engage with a personal language of form. The subject matter often involves the interface of land and sea, mystery and tension created beneath a serene and simplified surface. There is inevitably the tendency towards aspiring to a poetic condition, the work of Paul Nash and Michael Andrews are of particular interest in this respect.

Tree of Life is my contribution to Salthouse '10. The tree provides the symbolic context for the story in Genesis and the cross is seen as a pictogram of the tree. This interpretation celebrates the here and now involving joy, discovery and friendship. The artist standing at his appointed place, the trunk of the tree; he does nothing other than pass on what comes to him from the depths. He neither serves nor rules; he transmits.

Children on Wells Beach follows on. I wanted to develop a dialogical connection with the theme. I used the idea of a child doing a handstand. There is obvious physical energy, which also represents creative and energetic force. The use of the 'golden mean' in this context has direct connotations in terms of dynamics of nature.

Boy in a Tree is a further development of the theme. The tree is on the edge of the cliff. The subject of erosion, human interdependence and transcendence is apparent.

Educated- Norwich School of Art 1962
Membership of Local Art Societies-
Norwich Twenty Group
Galleries Familiar With Artist's Work-
Art 18/21, Norwich, Norfolk
Collections (Open To The Public)-
Havergate Island and *Pigman* Norwich Castle,
Norwich, Norfolk
Norwich Market, Sainsbury Centre for Visual Arts,
Norwich, Norfolk
Website- www.peter-baldwin.com

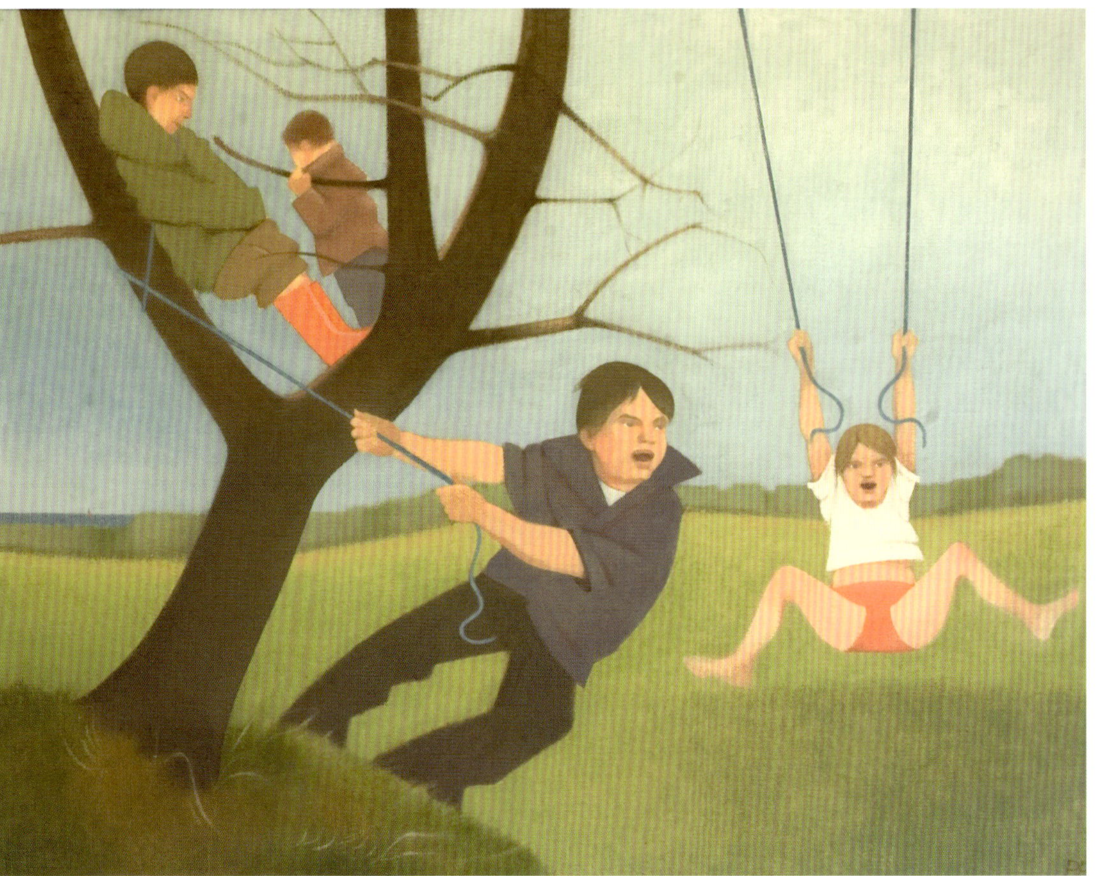

Tree of Life (2009) Oil 68 x 83cm

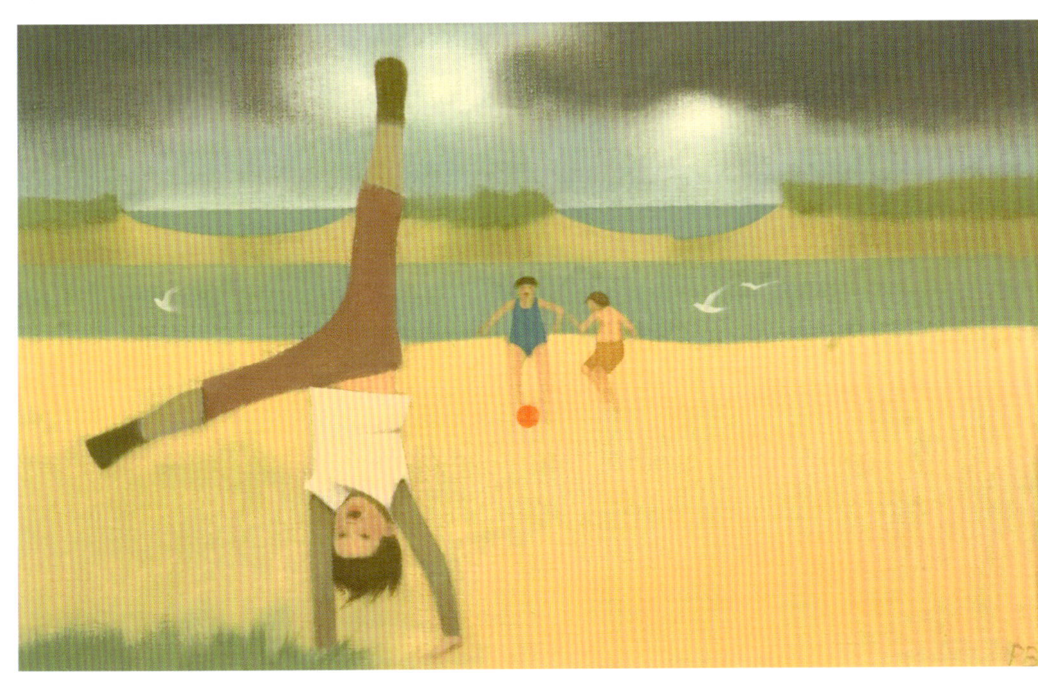

Children on Wells Beach (2009) Oil 34 x 48cm

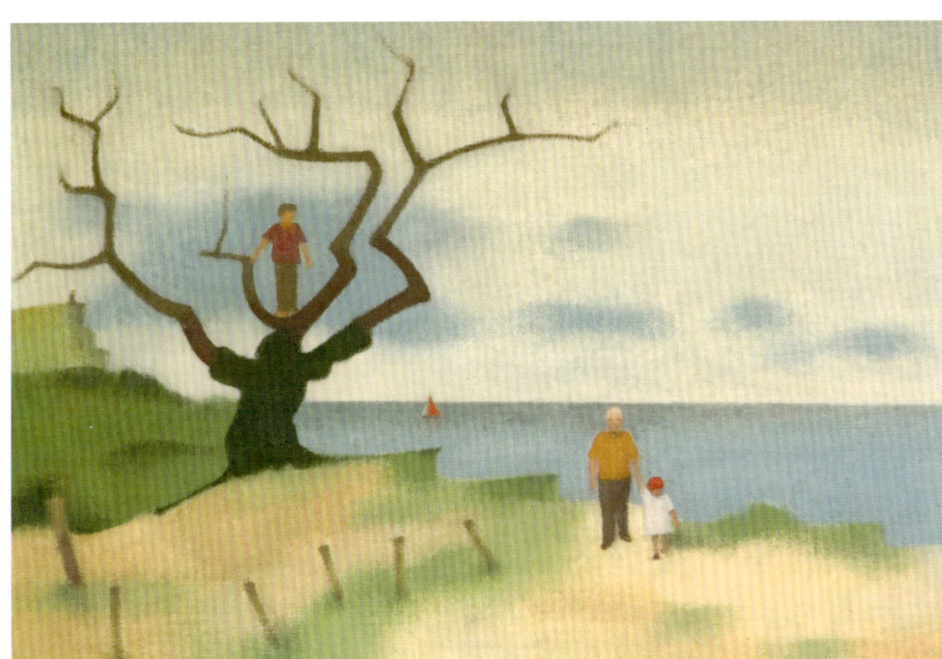

Boy in a Tree (2009) Oil 34 x 48cm

Tessa Newcomb BA (Hons)

At first sight Tessa Newcomb's delicate and lyrical paintings seem rooted in her native Suffolk and Norfolk countryside. However, through her unique sense of design and colour and an instinctive willingness to depart from the particular, they transport us into the elliptical and universal realm of poetry. At her best, she produces works that are both charming and decorative, that embody the spirit of place, but that still leave room for the viewer's imagination to discover, or invent, narratives of his or her own.
- Piers Feetham Gallery, London

Tessa Newcomb BA (Hons)
Painter
Wenhaston, Suffolk

I like painting people in the landscape; I like them moving around the landscape. And I like water when the light reflects off it. I tend to work on themes: birds, still lives, destinations. People love to think I am just in Suffolk, but I go abroad; Paris, Venice. However, I really know where I come from, I'm very definitely from around here.

I think my paintings look English, like Mary Feddon and Mary Potter. People love the mother connection (my mother was the artist Mary Newcomb) and I don't always terribly like it. Of course I learned from my mother, like you do an apprenticeship, but I paint more than my mother did. She thought more.

Winifed Nicholson made a beautiful picture of a blackbird in the snow. I liked it and the memory has filtered through to my painting of the *Blackbirds*, done in 1996 when the children were eight and nine and both had cats, Fatty and Thinny. I used to feed the cats from the frying pan. In the painting it's snowy and cold; the black birds came to clean up the remaining morsels of cat food still in the frying pan. Now the children have flown and those cats are replaced by Fluffy, but each spring there's a new family of blackbirds in my garden.

Telfer planting in the allotment. Telfer often wears his blue shirt when he is working in the allotment. Big men become gentle when sowing. He uses his index finger to tap seeds from the packet.

The tulips in *His Tulips* were based on the hilly allotment in Leiston. I admired the man's handiwork, especially the flowers planted in a pot and positioned purely for decorative purposes.

The image of the allotment in Southwold in *The Plot Unravelling* caught my imagination. Perhaps the man was getting behind with his work and had not cleared the allotment properly last autumn, so come the first good weather of the spring, he and his son went to the allotment to clear last year's old beans and fix the drainage. I loved the plastic sacks reflecting in the water.

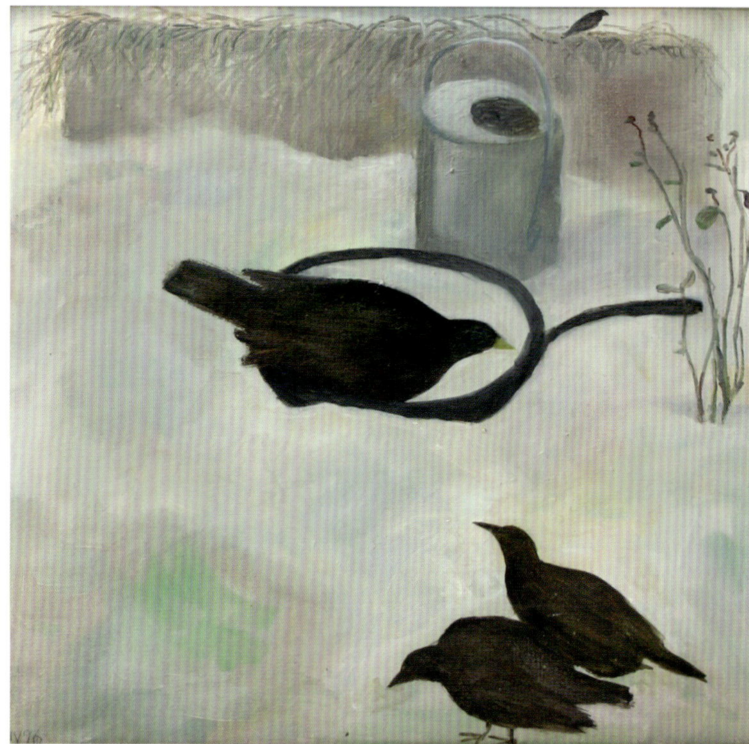

Black Birds (1996)
Oil on Canvas
25 x 25cm

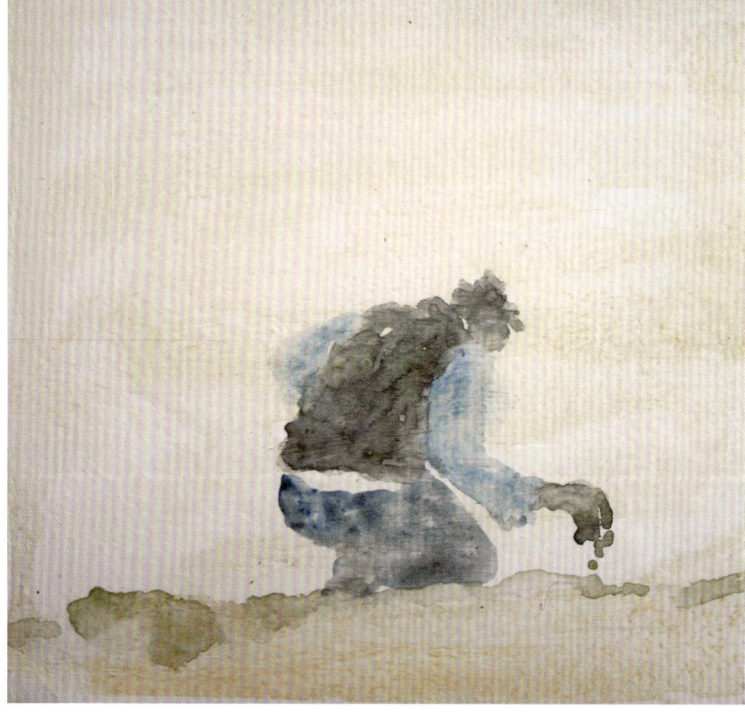

Telfer Planting In The Allotment (2010)
Watercolour
16 cm x 16.5cm

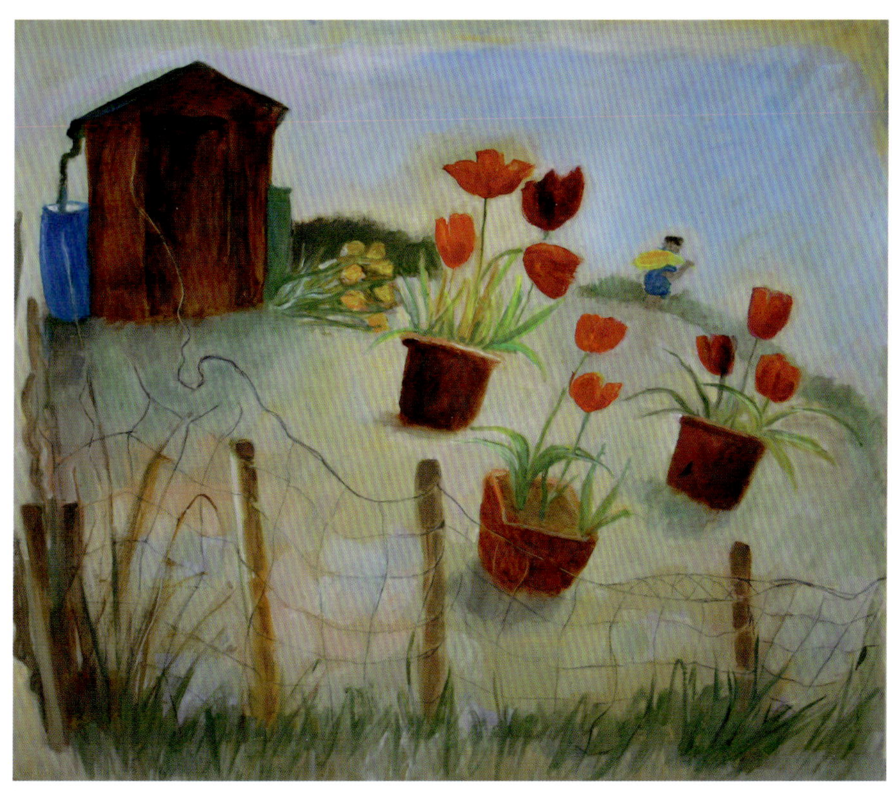

His Tulips (2010) Oil on Board 27 x 31cm

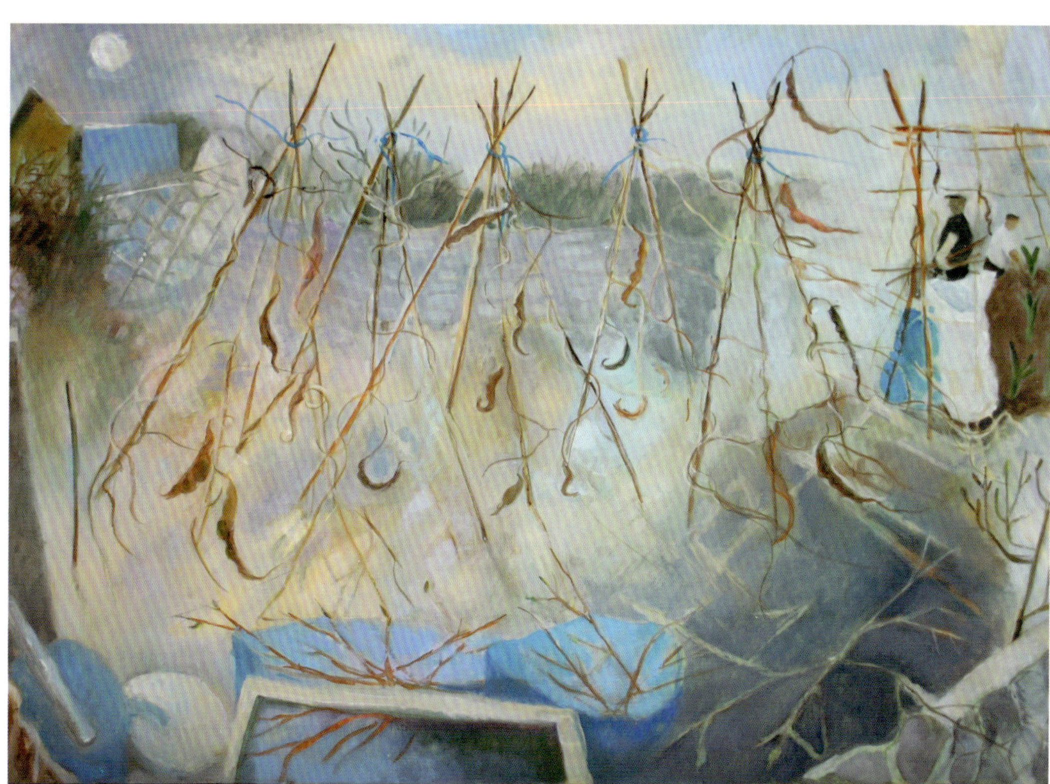

The Plot Unravelling (2010) Oil on Board 56 x 76cm

Tessa Newcomb: Behind the Scenes

More about:

Tessa...

Educated-
Bath Academy, BA Honours Degree in Fine Art
Wimbledon School of Art, Advanced Printmaking
Accreditation-
Bachelor of Art, Bath Academy of Art
Galleries Familiar With Artist's Work-
Cork Brick Gallery, Bungay, Suffolk
Strand Gallery, Aldeburgh, Suffolk
Crane Kalman Gallery, London
Piers Feetham, London
Publications-
Tessa Newcomb by Philip Vann, Sansom & Company
ISBN 978-1-904537-94-6
Collections (Open To The Public)-
Bradford Metropolitan Museum, Bradford
Whitworth Art Gallery, Manchester

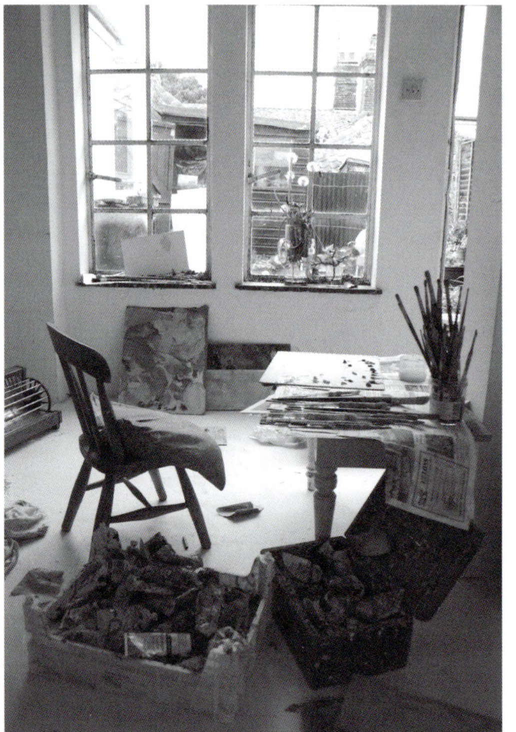

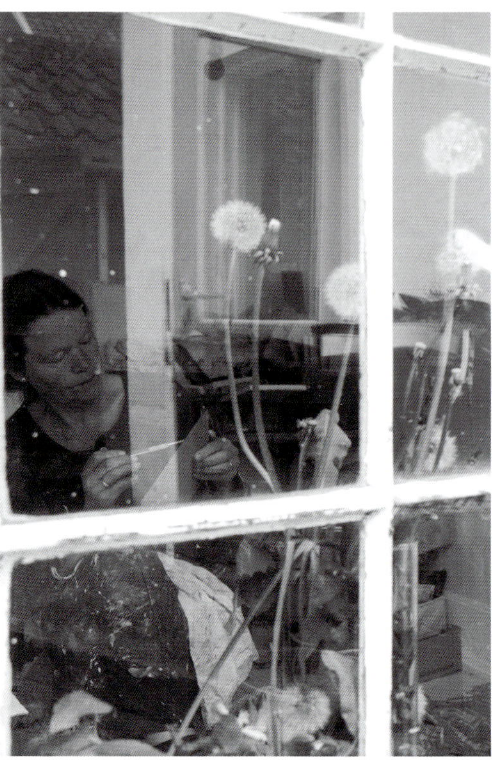

I've painted here in this same cottage for 29 years. Someone once asked me what the views from my cottage are. A backyard, it's ordinary but nice to me. The cottage is simple and an integral part of my life. Work is stored under chairs, in drawers, in sheds and in stacks against the wall.

My painting room is not grand enough to be called a studio. It's work-a-day, with not too much old stuff on the walls blocking new ideas. These new ideas are in little drawings I bring in. It feels safe in my studio, not overlooked, but it is cold so I have an electric fire (single bar) and Radio 3 as my constant companions. I like being here because I'm happy painting.

I paint in the small back room where the floor is bare concrete and the light pours in from the back yard. When the weather is warmer I have the back door open, but often it is closed and my small single bar electric heater keeps me vaguely warm, but I have to open the window every now and again to let the fumes of white spirit out. In the front room Radio 3 provides a constant cloud of sound, subtly influencing my mood and my thoughts as I select from my many boards' colour schemes to go with the emotional disposition of my current painting.

Tessa Newcomb: Behind the Scenes

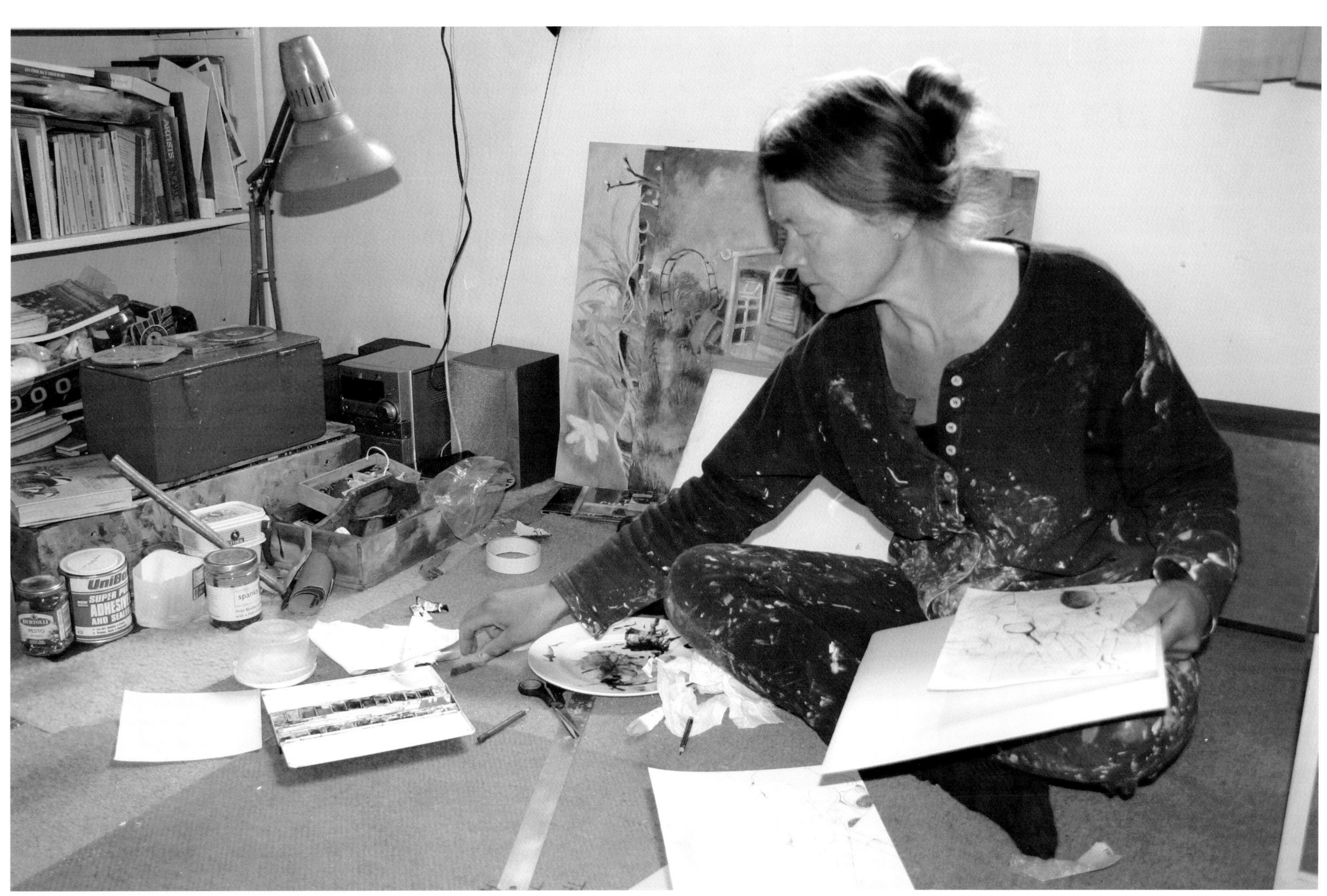

Maz Jackson

Maz Jackson
Painter
East Harling, Norfolk

I have spent a lifetime living and painting in Norfolk. Influenced by a childhood of visiting local churches and museums with my father, there is a direct link with the 15th century methods applied in my work. Mineral pigments, oak panels and gold leaf in my pieces are akin to those materials used by artists and craftsmen in medieval times when many of the beautiful East Anglican churches were built. Imagery is depicted with egg tempera on gilded oak panels following 15th century methods of Cennino d' Andrea Cennini.

Whilst travelling across *The Fens,* I realised we could be driving on top of the sea so I began to sketch the recurring goddess-woman underwater, underneath the Fens, her chalice-head a fecund pool emerging; her arms outstretched and feeling through the hillside edges, supporting the tribes of people either side on her fingers. The male sky-god looks on.

Guardian 3 is about male/female balance. Large blue male/god, sacred colour, strong protective, calm. Female, woman/goddess, red (no colour or creed, just passion and strength) supportive of all the tribes, the elders on her fingers..

Time. Egg tempera on a gilded, linen wrapped, gessoed oak post. Many recurring images are depicted on this piece: talking tribes, chalice-headed woman, burial mound landscape, fish and birds, the all-seeing eyes.

Educated- Norwich School of Art, BA (Hons)1976
Membership of Local Art Societies-
Norwich 20 Group, Norfolk
Bury St. Edmunds Art Society, Suffolk
Accreditation With National Art Societies-
Chair of British branch S.T.P. S.G.F.A.
Society of Egg Tempera Painters
Society of Graphic Fine Art
Honours-
Trevisan International Art, Pemio Ecole D'Este
Galleries Familiar With Artist's Work-
Cobbold & Judd, Hintlesham Hall, Suffolk
Chimney Mill Galleries, Bury St Edmunds, Suffolk
Doric Arts, Holt, Norfolk
Collections (Open To The Public)-
Untitled Detroit Museum of Art, Detroit, USA
Responsibility NY Arts Gallery Collection, Beijing, China
Lust Trevisan International Art, Ferrara, Italy
Website--www.mazjackson.eu

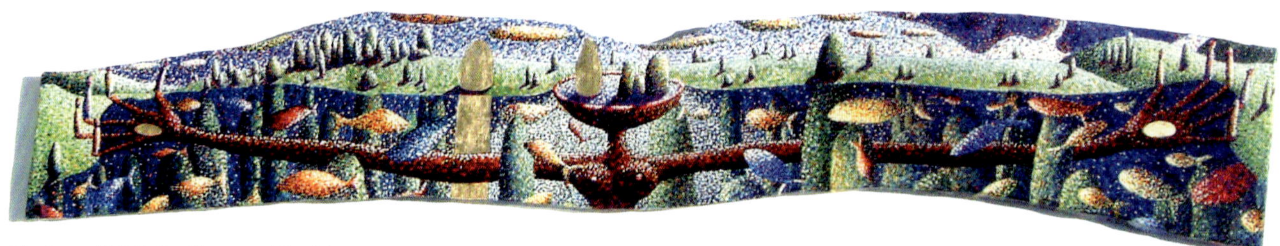

The Fens (2008) Egg Tempera 90 x 70cm

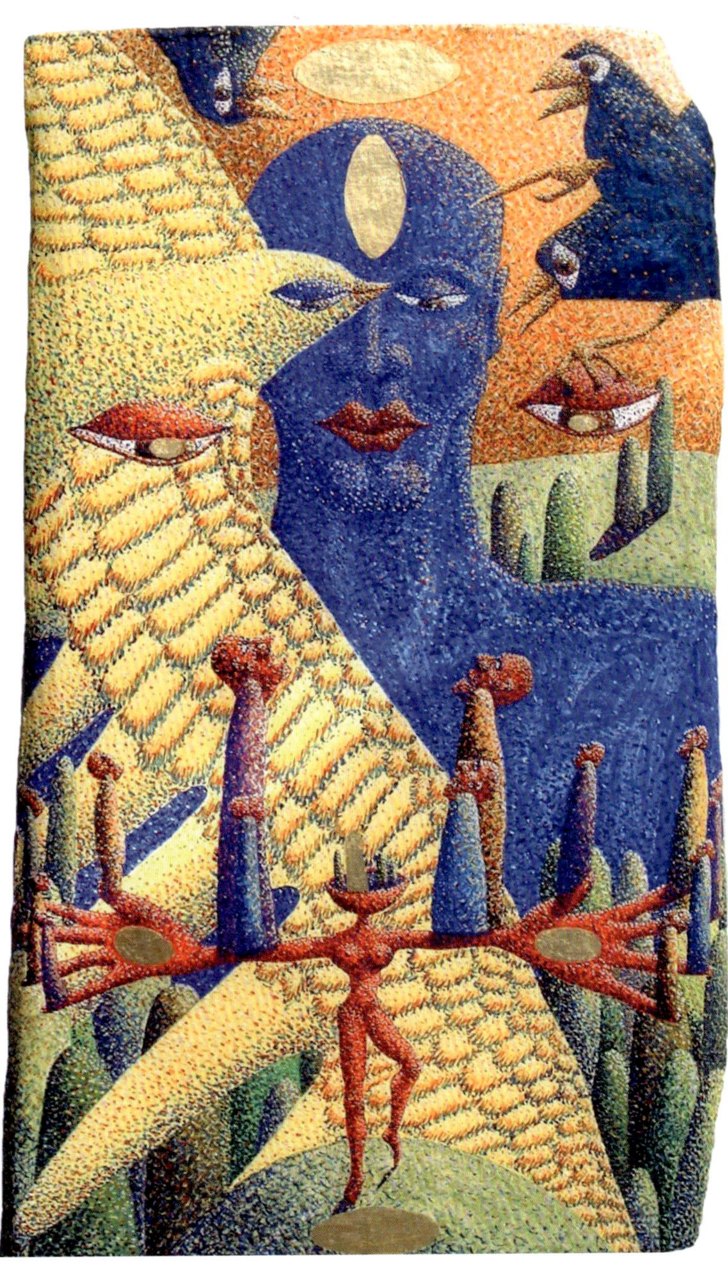

Guardian 3 (2008) Egg Tempera 70 x 41cm

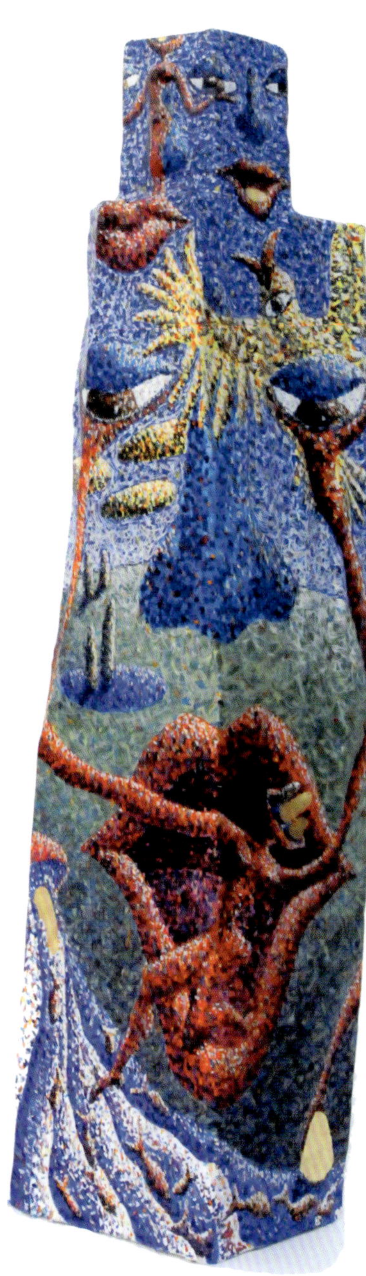

Time (2009) Egg Tempera 53 x 13 x 10cm

Pam Schomberg

Pam Schomberg
Ceramicist
Colchester, Essex

I will spend hours in museums. Not necessarily looking at ceramics, which of cause I do, but at all kinds of artefacts; textiles, weapons, armour, costumes, jewellery, being moved by the pure architecture and aesthetic shapes made, looking at pattern and colour combinations.

Besides being directly influenced by the ancient world, more recently it would be the exotic use of paint and colour of Gustav Klimt, and the strong forms produced by the potter Hans Coper.

Since childhood I have been fascinated by the ancient artefacts on display in Colchester Castle Museum and as a potter have felt their influence very strongly. Recently I am pleased to have been invited by the museum to have an exhibition of my work reflecting their collection, and *Open Bowl* is the first piece made towards the production of this body of work.

From my repertoire of forms, I think the *Jug* is my favourite. They're made in a variety of sizes and materials, both large stoneware and tiny porcelain. Many have comical character although this particular piece is quiet and elegant. The form and geometry work well, it has a nicely balanced handle and understated but harmonious proportions. It isn't often you get all these things right in one piece.

In contrast to the other two porcelain pieces, *Tall Pot* is built from stoneware clay. It is tall and chunky and made as part of a series of 'horned' pots. Despite the fact it seems to be dressed in a blue ball gown it feels masculine, perhaps influenced by drawings I have made of ancient helmets and armour.

Educated-
Sligo School of Art, Ireland
Colchester Institute School of Art, Essex 1985
Membership of Local Art Societies-
Suffolk Crafts
Anglian Potters
Accreditation With National Art Societies-
Society of Designer Craftsman
Galleries Familiar With Artist's Work-
Hayletts Gallery, Maldon, Essex
Alexander Gallery, Brighton
Cecilia Colman Gallery, St John's Wood, London
Collections (Open To The Public)-
Tea Service made for Crittall Windows as bursary prize,
on display in Braintree Museum, Essex
Website- www.pamschomberg.com

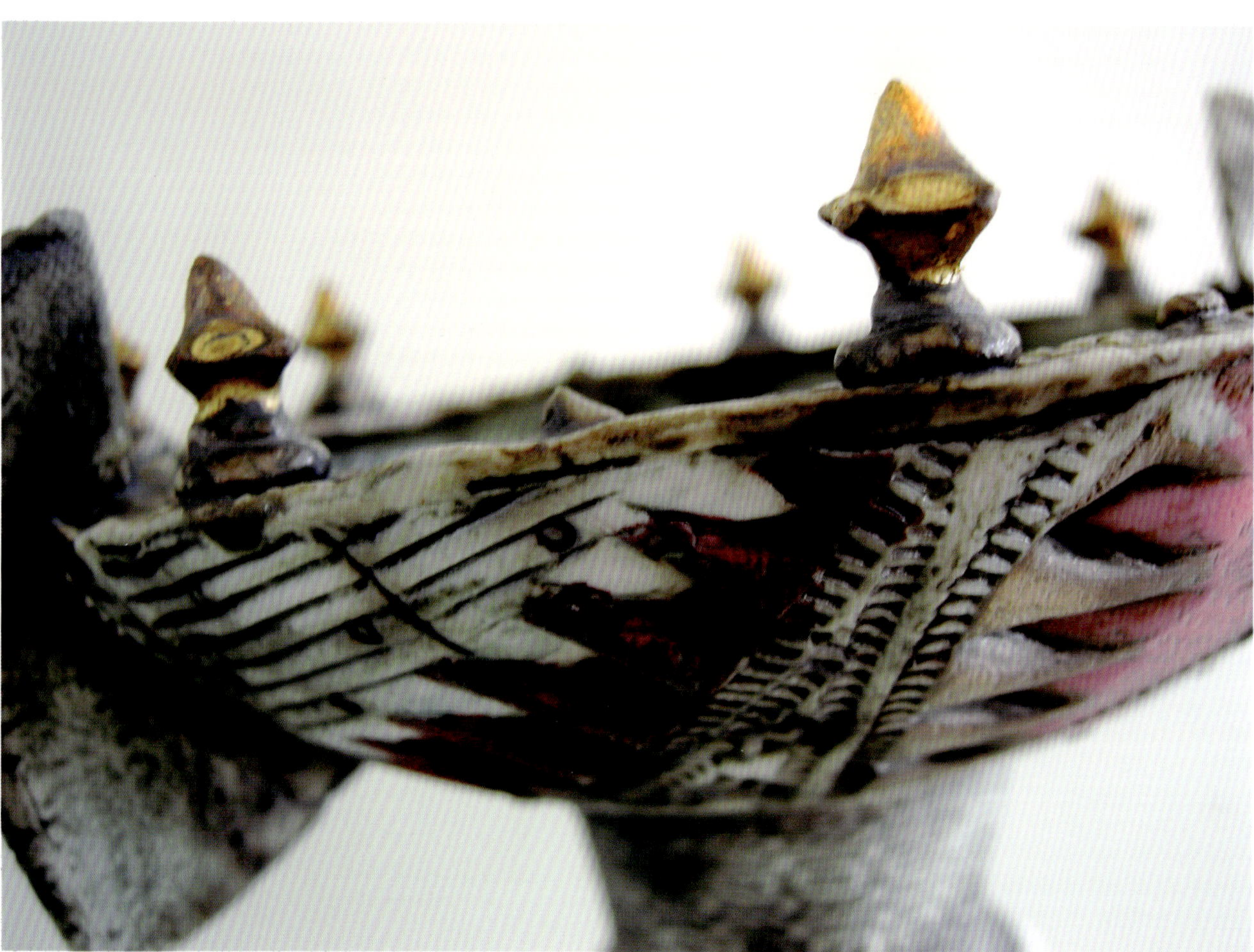

Open Bowl (2010) Porcelain 20 x 15cm

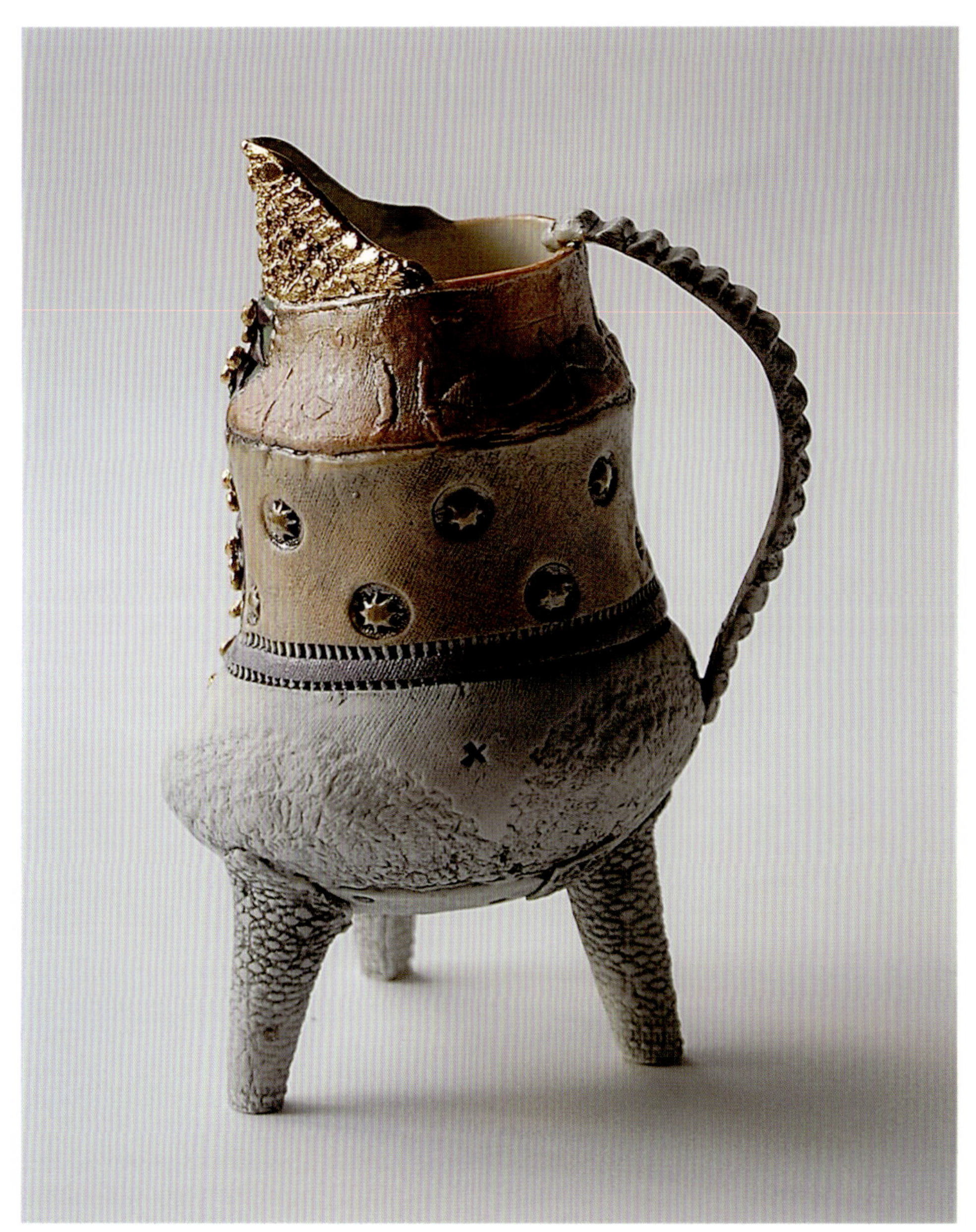

Jug (2009) Porcelain 15cm

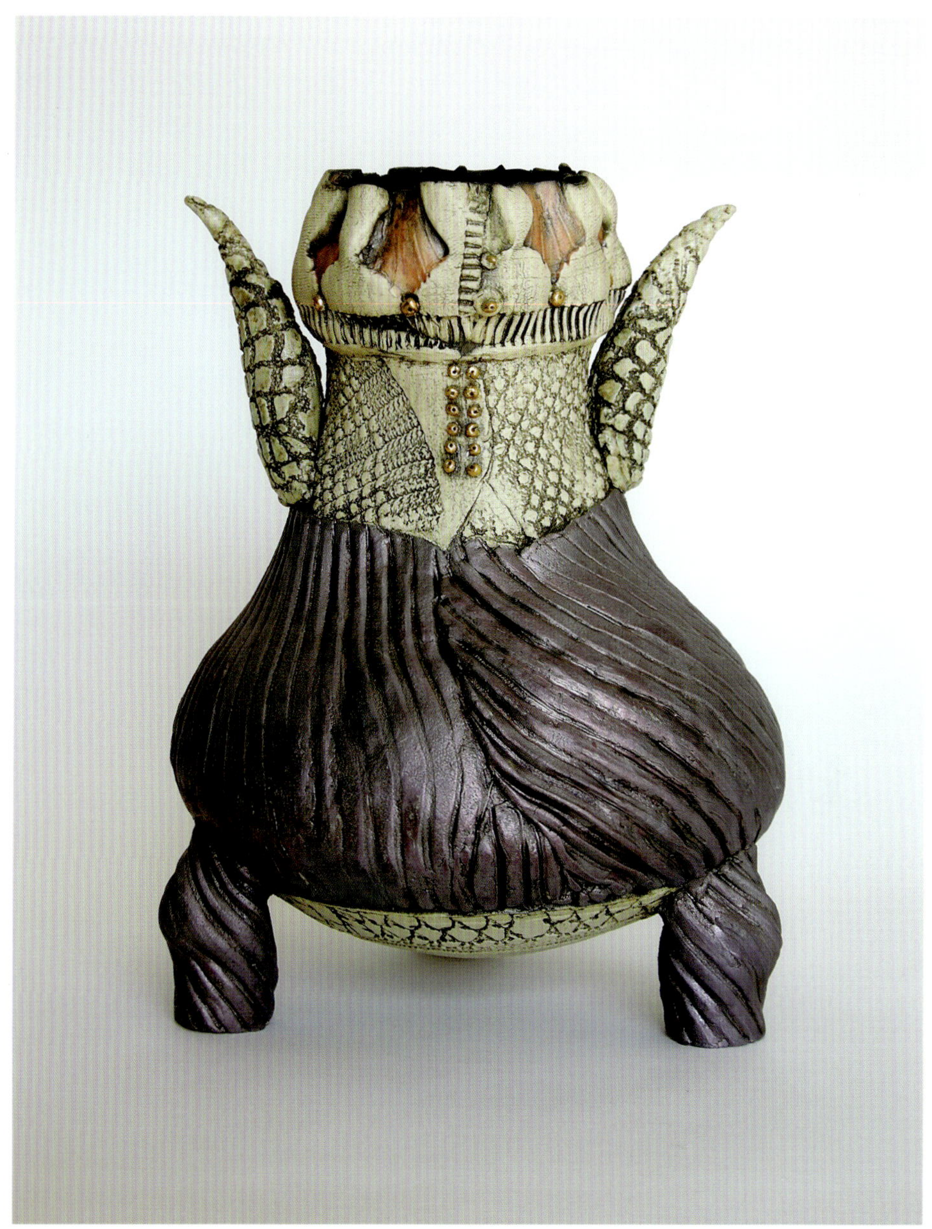

Tall Pot (2008) Stoneware 40cm

Chris Kendrick

Chris Kendrick has an eye for realistic detail and clarity in his work, which serve to act as a distillation of visual experience, literally holding up to the light qualities in objects and materials which for the most part are taken for granted in everyday life. His use of metallic objects – particularly copper – in some recent compositions has opened up new areas of exploration in his work.
- Norwich Frame Workshop, Norwich, Norfolk

Chris Kendrick
Painter
Norwich, Norfolk

I have an on-going obsession with the visual qualities which define objects and materials and the way we perceive them. What makes glass look like glass, or copper look like copper for example? What is it about the interaction of light and shadow and reflection, and the way our eyes perceive these, that enables us to make sense of the visual world around us? Moreover, how do I as an artist try to represent these qualities convincingly in paint?

I prefer as much as possible to work from life and still life allows me to do this most easily. Once arranged, objects don't have a tendency to move or require conversation. The greatest difficulty in this regard is the habit of some foodstuffs to putrefy and develop unpleasant odours over time. Especially fish.

I greatly admire the 'Pronk' style of artists who worked in the Netherlands in the 17th century; painters such as Willem Kalf and Jan de Heem. Kalf, in particular, often set his compositions of opulent items against dark backgrounds to create depth, and used quite a rich palette. In many instances the most ornate silver or glassware is merely suggested against the darkness with deceptively simple-looking, economic touches of paint, yet this creates a breathtaking whole. A technique I can only aspire to.

The starting point for the composition *Pears in Copper Bowl* was the contrast between the rather cool greens of the pears and the warm tones of the copper bowl. I had to set the viewpoint quite high to make the most of this, to show the pears and capture the highlights and reflections inside the bowl. I found the patterns of light reflected onto the red cloth quite fascinating too, almost like a bow wave in water.

Educated- Norfolk Institute of Art & Design 1993
Galleries Familiar With Artist's Work-
Llewellyn Alexander Ltd, Waterloo, London
Southwold Gallery, Southwold, Suffolk
Norwich Frame Workshop, Norwich, Norfolk
Website- www.chriskendrick.co.uk

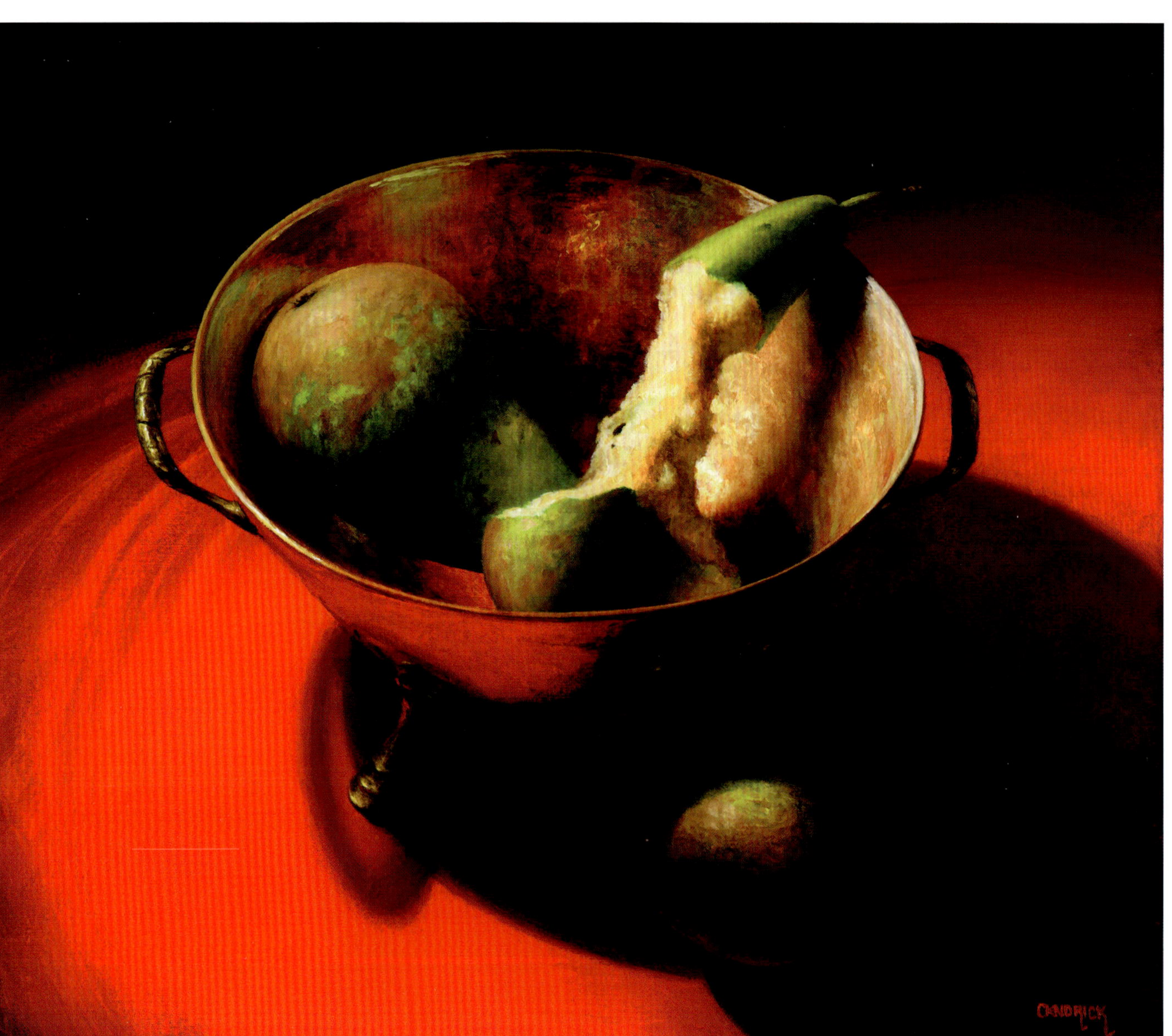

Pears in Copper Bowl (2010) Oil on Canvas Panel 23 x 22 cm

Deanna Tyson FRSA

Deanna Tyson's work can be awesome. Injustice, bigotry, greed, cruelty and other human traits that anger her are her subject matter, her targets; soft, beautiful materials and bright colours are her palette.
- **Williams Art, Cambridge**

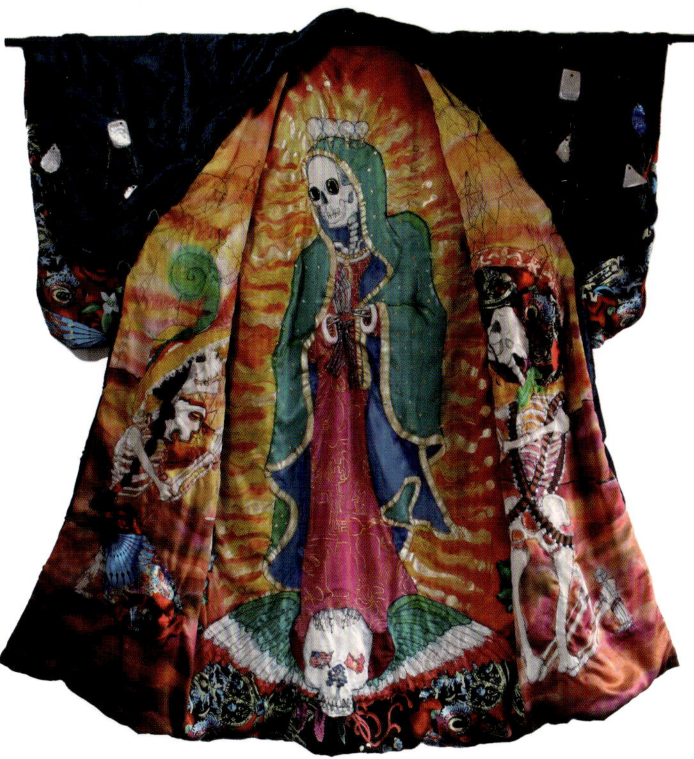

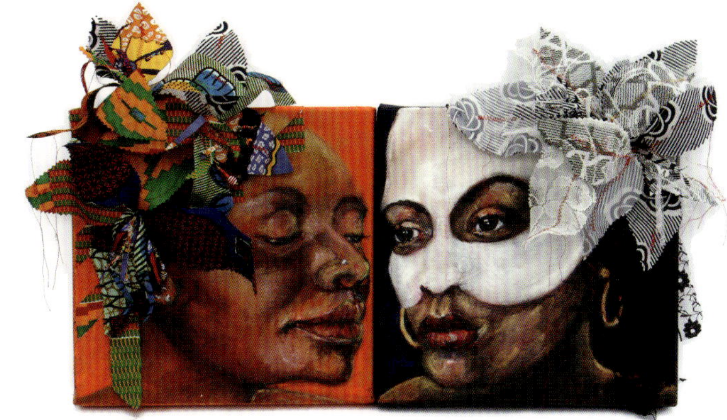

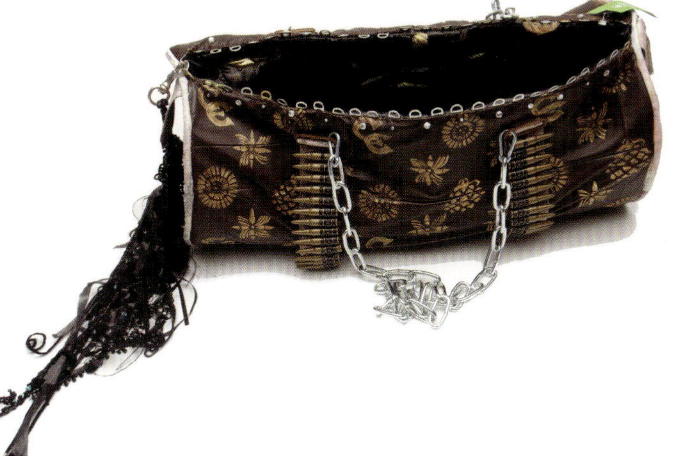

Deanna Tyson FRSA
Artist/Painter, Textiles
Fulbourn, Cambridgeshire

As with all artists, the world around me is my inspiration. My role as an artist is to respond to that world. Unfortunately my world tends to be filtered through the news media and current affairs and reflects the Human Condition. Conflict, corruption, energy consumption and pollution inform my current body of work.

Our Lady of Energy Consumption is a silk kimono inspired by a night flight over the sprawl of Mexico City whose light-spangled undulating hills glittered like an extravagant evening gown. What beauty, what energy consumption! My response, a holy shrine of a kimono spangled with talismanic energy symbols in which Day of the Dead figures genuflect for deliverance from the energy crisis. They pray to a dead Madonna of Guadalupe who only has eyes for her dead son.

Dee Dee Sings Billie. These portraits are a response to the music I love and that I play for inspiration whilst working. In them I hope to weave the shared and contrasting experiences of both jazz singers. Billie Holiday experiencing the dark side of white supremacy and having to suppress her African roots in order to work. Dee Dee Bridgewater free to trace her West African roots, delighting in her musical heritage and paying homage to the brave Lady Day.

Costing the Earth is a giant sized 'designer' bag made from a second hand Oxfam purchased faux-leather coat. Covered with logos of warfare and lined with masks quilted in African wax cloth, it is my metaphor for the exploitation of Africa's people and mineral resources by the Western World.

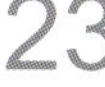

Educated- Newcastle University
Membership of Local Art Societies-
Cambridge Art Movement at Williams Art;
Cambridge Open Studios; Cambridge Design Collective
Accreditation With National Art Societies-
Fellow, Royal Society of Arts (RSA)
Member, Society of Designer Craftsmen (SDC)
Galleries Familiar With Artist's Work-
Williams Art, Cambridge; Primavera, Cambridge;
Buckenham Galleries, Southwold, Suffolk
Collections (Open To The Public)-
King Charles II Palace House, Newmarket, Suffolk
Website- www.deanna-tyson.com

From Top to Bottom:
Our Lady of Energy Consumption (2010)
Silk 150 x 140cm

Dee Dee Sings Billie (2010)
Dyptich 30 x 60cm

Costing The Earth (2009)
Mixed Media 40 x 100cm

Akiko Fujikawa

Akiko Fujikawa came to England decades ago and is a long-term resident of Burnham on Crouch, but she remains the most Japanese of print artists. Her apparently simple prints, using very few strong and contrasting flat colours, explore with some subtlety the complexities of human emotions and relationships.
**-Lawrence Smith, Formerly Keeper of Japanese
 Antiquities, The British Museum**

Akiko Fujikawa
Woodblock Printmaker
Burnham on Crouch, Essex

When my English husband first brought me to Essex, I particularly enjoyed the vision of freedom provided by the wide open spaces. At my home in Kyoto we are surrounded by mountains, which are very beautiful but nevertheless they deny the viewer sight of the horizon. Here, I relish the open space.

Only after my Mother died did I discover that she was a person of considerable artistic skill and very honoured to present an ornamental scroll to the Emperor. However, she continually took me to a number of art exhibitions, especially to see the work of Picasso. My husband was the respected art lecturer and practitioner Geoffrey Wickham and it was he who helped me to develop my artistic eye, whilst Mr Takeji Asano developed my ability to make woodblocks and, importantly, a clean line. The results of these great influences on me are an enduring love for the work of Pablo Picasso, Henri Matisse, Ben Nicholson, Paul Cezanne and Kurt Schwitters.

In general my ambition for my work is entirely personal. I experience a great sense of relief when I have completed a piece satisfactorily. There are three distinct stages to my work, the preliminary concept encapsulated by drawings, the woodblocks and then finally the prints; the finished piece being comprised of several coloured printed layers. Each stage has its challenges, sometimes physical, sometimes intellectual and sometimes emotional. The relief I feel once a piece is complete is for two reasons: one, I can now move on to the next piece; and two, it is the relief of a mother giving birth to a new child that is beautiful in her own eyes.

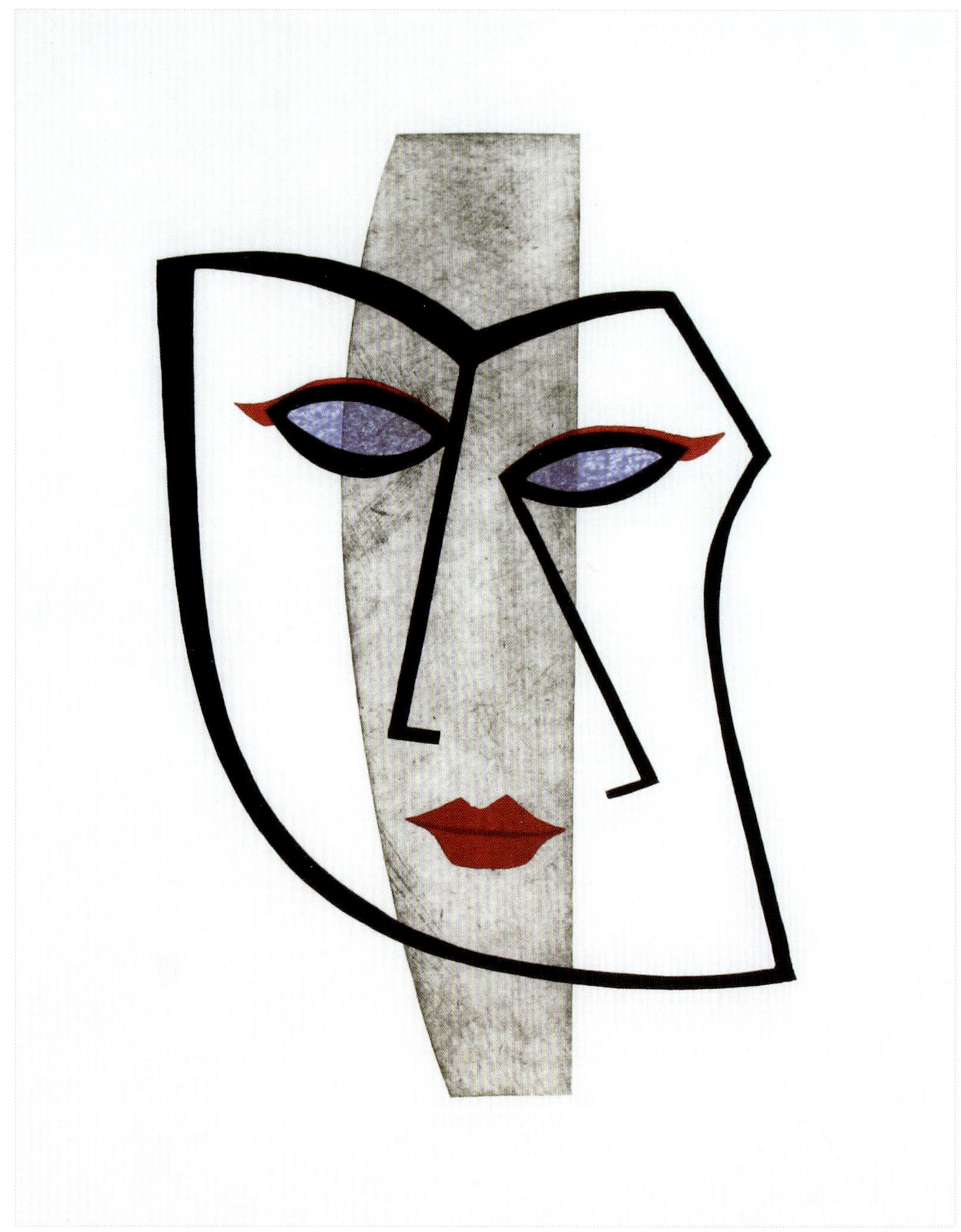

Ochobo (2010) Woodblock Print 36.5 x 29cm

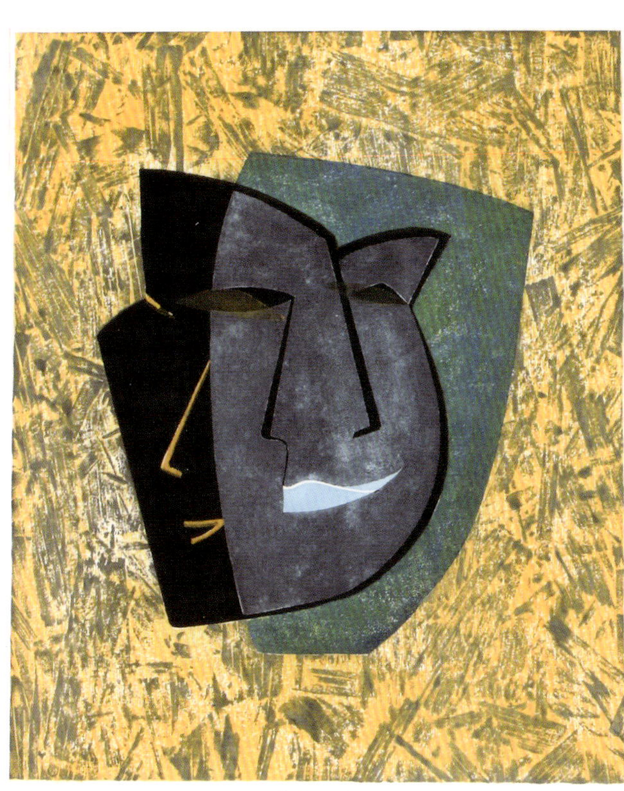

Watching Me (2010) Woodblock Print 36.5 x 29 cm

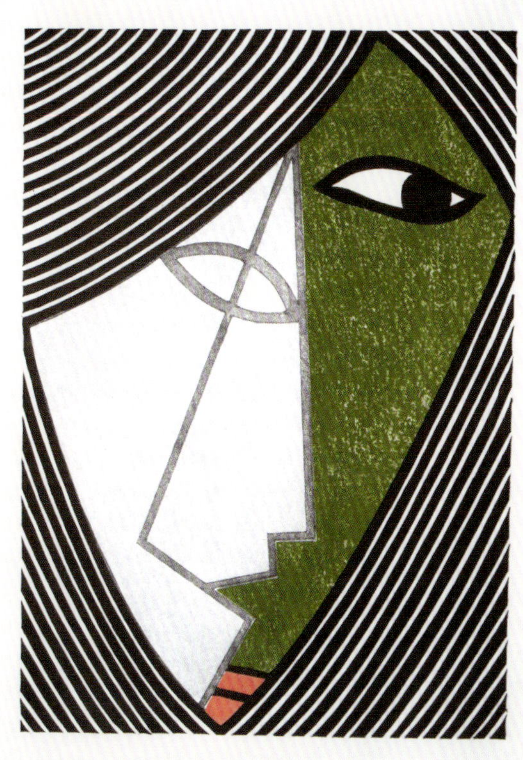

Were (1993) Woodblock Print 39 x 27cm

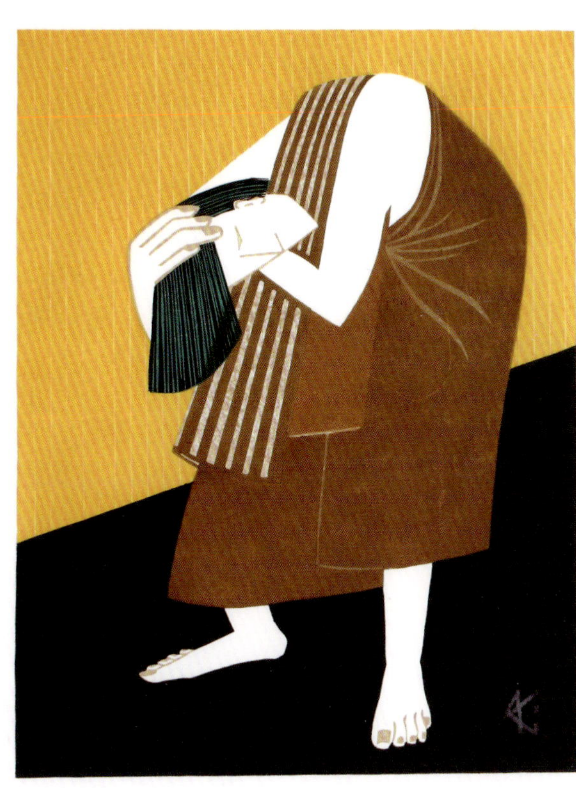

I Never Knew (2000) Woodblock Print 48 x 36cm

Akiko Fujikawa: Behind the Scenes

More about:

Akiko…

Educated-
Personally tutored by Mr Takejo Asano and Mr Katsuyuki Nishijima of Kyoto (1979 – 1985)

Galleries Familiar With Artist's Work-
Rickshore House, London
Ice House Gallery, London

Collections (Open To The Public)-
The British Museum, London
Braintree Museum, Braintree, Essex
Chelmsford Museum, Chelmsford, Essex

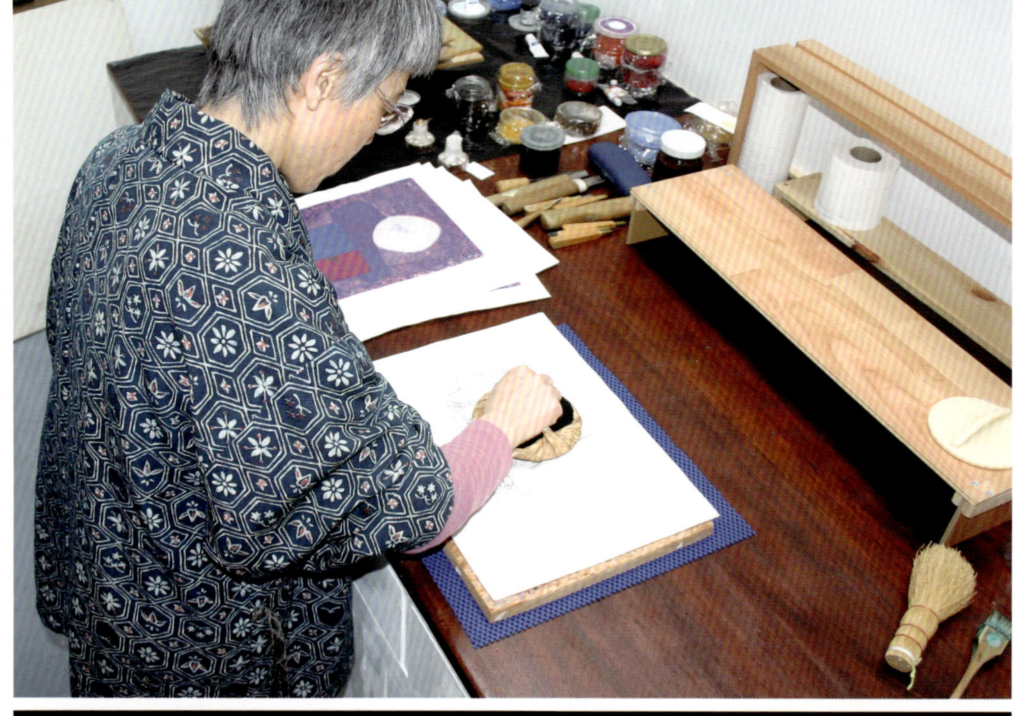

My studio is a converted chapel so I have a high ceiling (which lets in lots of light) and thick warm walls that keep the atmosphere calm and tranquil. I try to keep my studio clean and organised as the many stages to my work require a large amount of space where work can be kept at the right level of humidity without being creased or dirtied.

I like to start the day by getting all the chores out of the way, once that is done I can clear my mind and start creating. When I am working my senses are further stimulated by the pure smell of the Japanese solid ink I use. The smell is vaguely medicinal but also strongly charcoal. When I am working strongly I will sometimes speak out loud but largely I work silently and hate interruptions; I put the telephone on answer phone. I am very conscious of my health these days, so I always stop for meals as after my husband's death I spent several years being unwell, so now I am very careful with my health.

I can only work on one piece at a time and never use an image or a found item for my inspiration. It all comes from what I see and from my own mind. It can be the smallest hint of an image that may suggest itself in the dust on the ground that may spark my imagination and lead to me developing an idea.

I know the piece is finished when I experience the same level of passion at the end of a piece as I did at the beginning; when the layers of overlapped colour are correct. We cannot mix colour and have to rely on the overlapping colours.

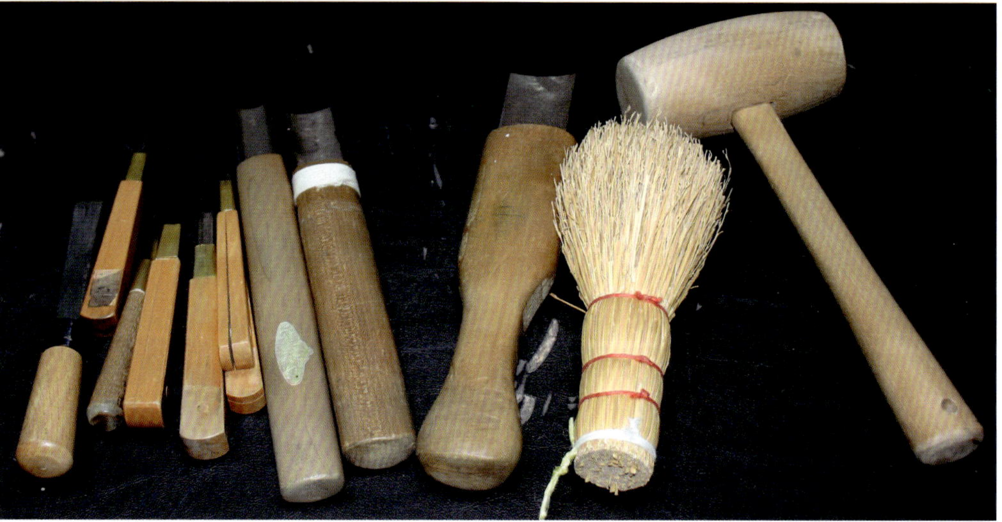

This Page: Akiko at work with her tools.
Opposite Page: Akiko in her studio, surrounded by her late husband's paintings.

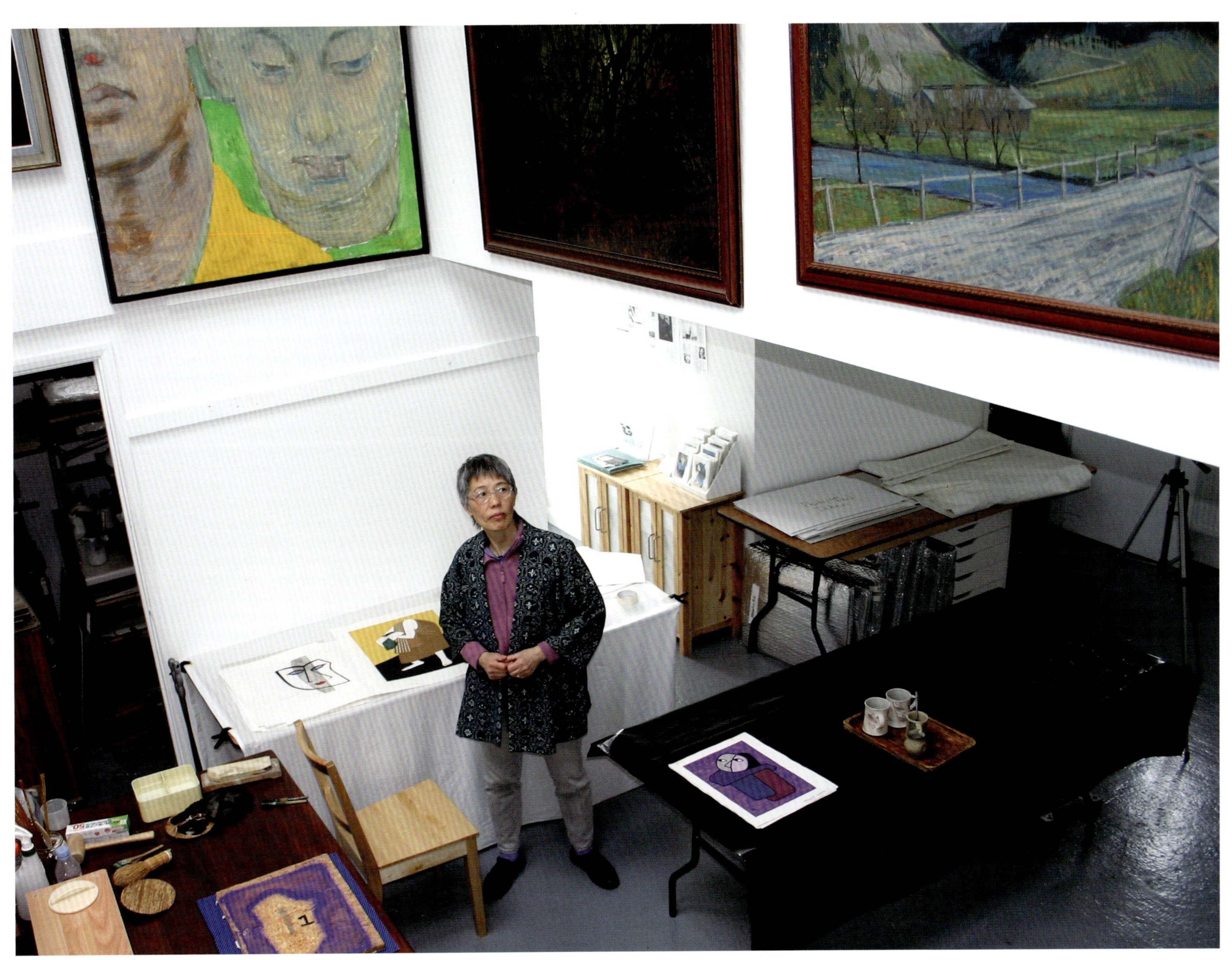

Christophe Gordon-Brown

Christophe Gordon-Brown's work is accessible through its simplicity and eye catching beauty. Once engaged you will be led into a more complex world where form, shape, edge, light, material and texture all collude to express something more thoughtful and challenging. There is playfulness and trickery too. Follow an edge and you are unlikely to predict its ending. Accept an understanding of a piece without proper scrutiny and you will have missed a sensitivity, a care or an intent which is being presented to you to think about. His work does not mimic the natural world, rather it is a fusion of all that we make with the more eternal and enduring objects that nature scatters at our feet.
- John Bacon, Collector

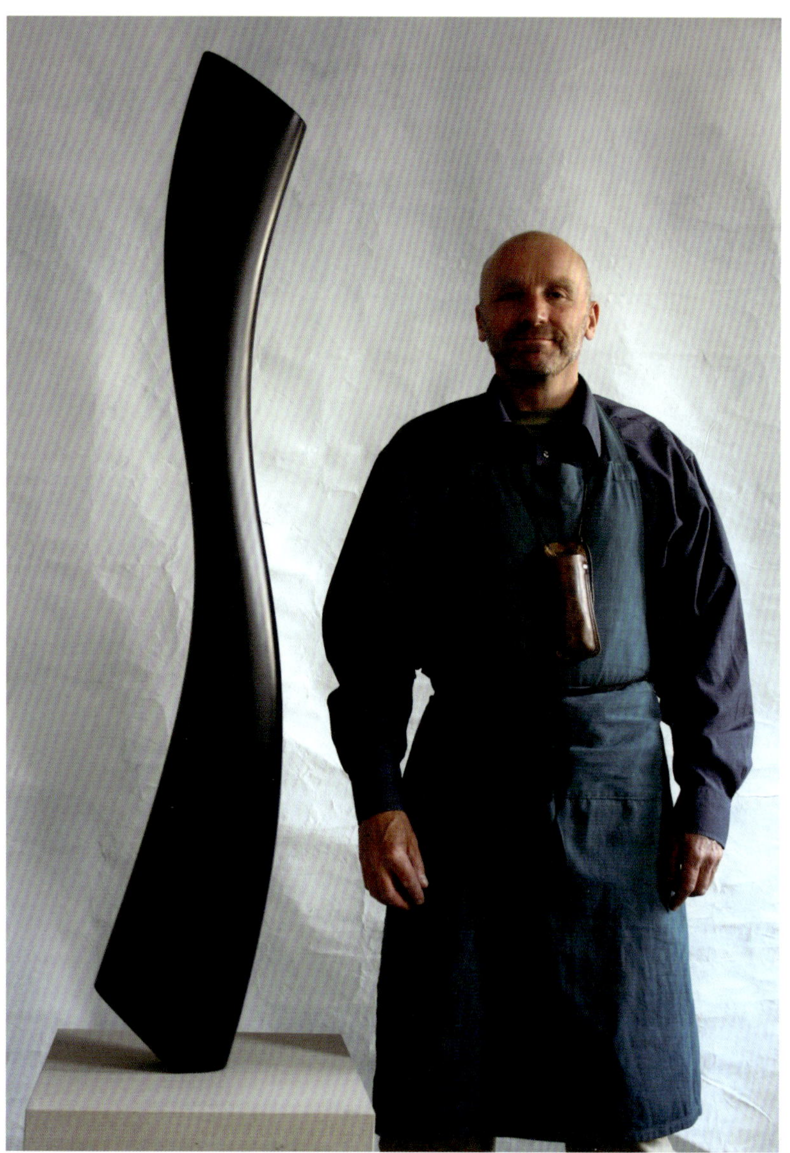

Christophe Gordon-Brown, with Commission for Beijing Shopping Centre
Slate (2009) Slate 160cm high

Christophe Gordon-Brown
Sculptor
Cambridge

The first ten years of my life were spent in Uganda. This had quite an effect on my creativity, mainly because of the sense of freedom a young person had there. Most of my life was out of doors, exploring, building dams and dens and other funny things a boy does. This teaches him initiative and creativity, because there's no entertainment provided, you had to find it and make it happen.

Also, because there were few boundaries such as walls, hedges, ditches, roads and rules, this gave a feeling of being able to roam where the fancy took you. So anything felt possible, as it were. Life and landscape were explored, and therefore you practised going into these unknowns – which is what one does as an artist.

My work is usually in stone. The search is for beauty. Simplicity is the governing concept. The curve symbolises the fluid and dynamic aspect; the straight line the structural and orderly. A correct balance between the two brings a tension that appears to mimic life itself. Too much chaos (curve) or too much rigidity (straight line) introduces an imbalance. Beauty seems to hover mysteriously between the two poles.

Educated- Loughborough College of Art and Design BA Silversmithing. Goldsmithing.
Website- www.cgb-sculpture.co.uk

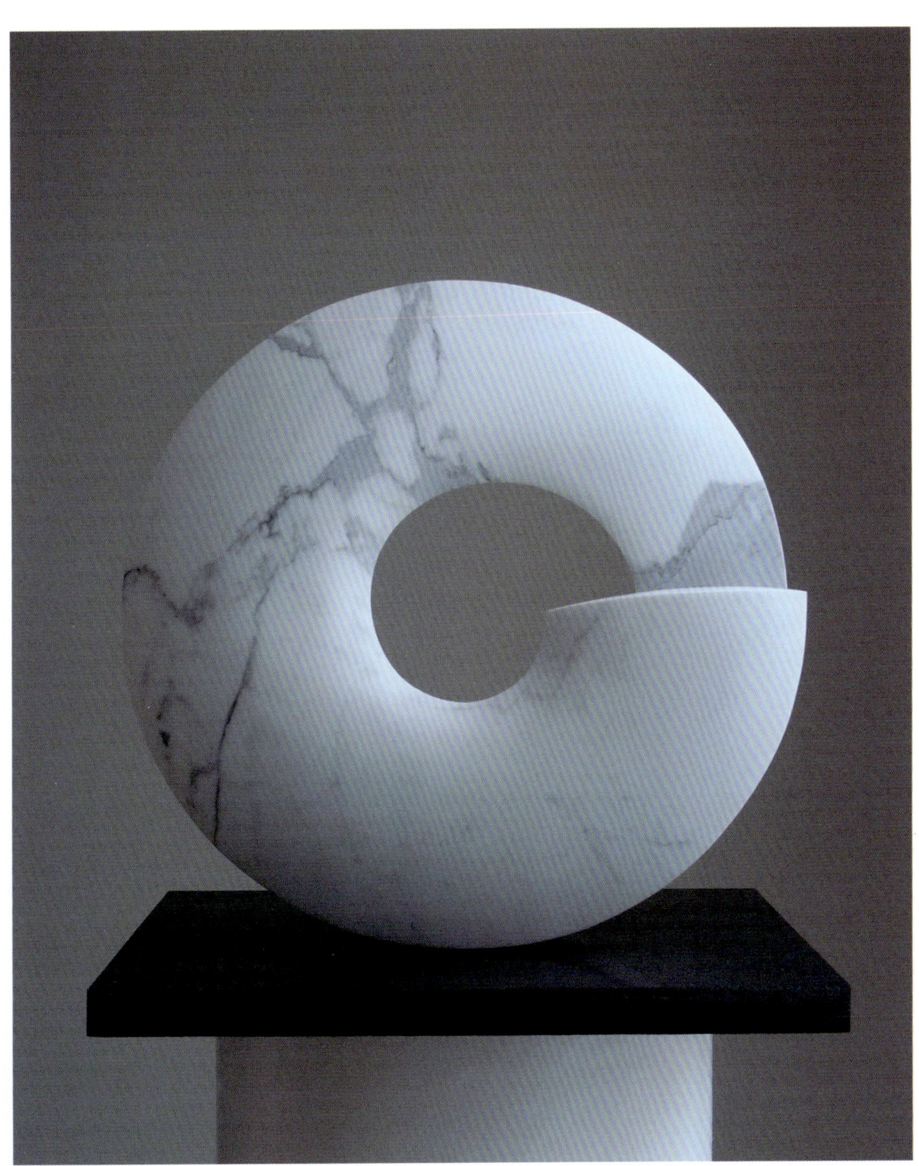

Spiral (2008) Marble 50cm diameter

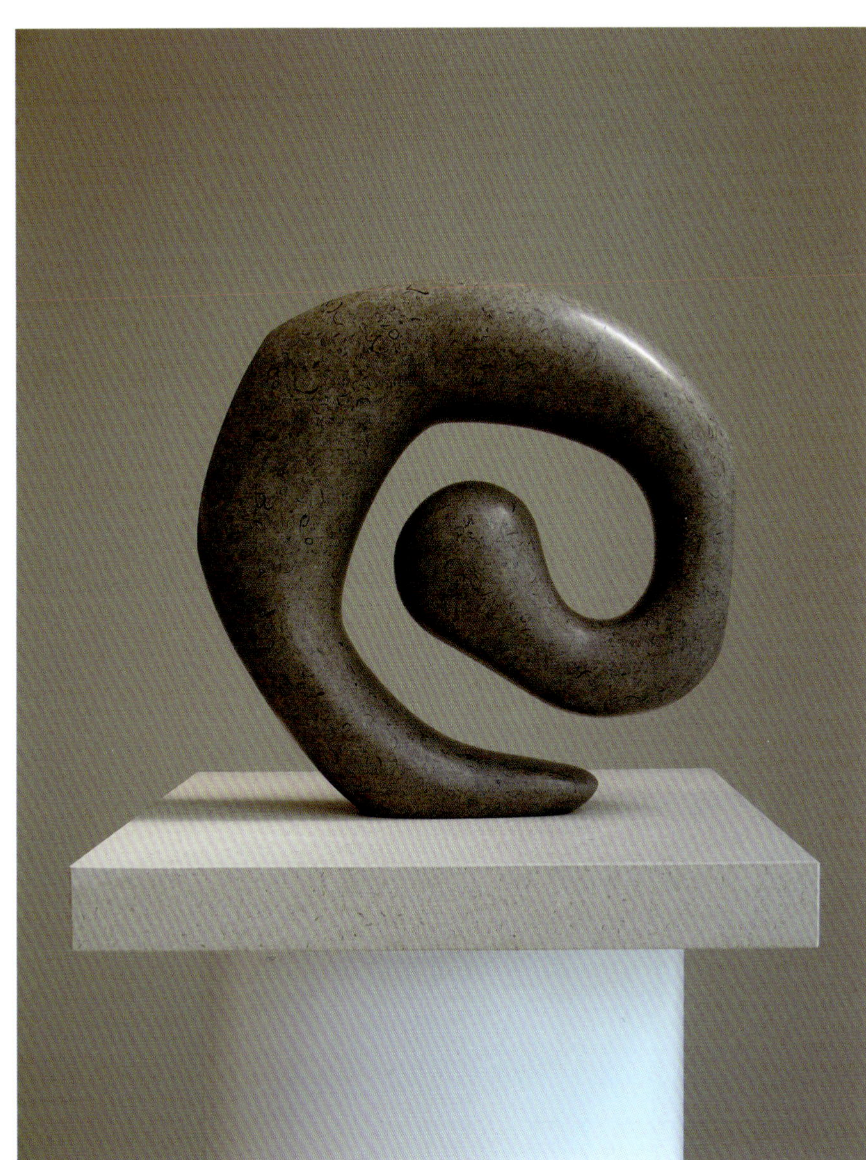

Yoga (2007) Purbeck Marble 47cm diameter

Mary Husted BA (Hons)

Imbued with references to visual and emotional memory, the works of Mary Husted emit a powerful resonance with their viewer. Mary's oeuvre consists of both abstract works and figurative pieces. Each can be seen to hold a narrative of her evolving personal history. It is hard not to be affected by the artists' honesty or drawn into the unfurling stories hidden beneath the layers of her art.
- New Hall Art Collection, Murray Edwards College, Cambridge

Mary Husted BA (Hons)
Fine Artist
Vale of Glamorgan, South Wales

Particular qualities of light engage me in a compelling way. These are the bedrock of my artistic sensibility. A sense of place, of 'being there', is an essential ingredient in my work, much of which has been landscape referenced. I also work with images connected to memory, often using old photographs to explore notions of time, place, narrative and identity. The most recent work responds to the finding of my long lost son, and takes the form of layered drawings in a three dimensional format.

In *Ghosts and Relics: Knitting Lessons* the work starts from a photograph of my twin sister and me taken in the 1950s. I like to change an image through interventions on a photocopier, then draw into it, layering on other materials to create an enigmatic image with hints of narrative, hoping to trigger a viewer's own memories of significant moments. The work refers indirectly to relinquishment and finding of my son.

Dissolve is constructed of layered drawings around three sides of a perspex box, so that the images can be viewed through each other; with the drawing I explore resemblances and differences. There are two images of my son, as a child and as a man, together with one of my own face as a young woman (taken from the only photograph I have of me with my infant son). The feathers refer to earlier work and the flight of a bird.

45 Years Of Separation depicts my son (the child I never knew) and the man I met two years ago. The fabric acts as a separating veil and this holds symbolic resonance for me.

Educated- South Glamorgan Institute of Higher Education 1990
Membership of Local Art Societies-
Butetown Artists, Cardiff Bay, Wales; The Welsh Group; Women's Arts Association, Wales
Collections (Open To The Public)-
Dreams, Oracles, Icons; Alliteration; and *Sea Table*
New Hall Art Collection, Murray Edwards College, Cambridge
Flotsam Newport Museum and Art Gallery, Newport, Gwent, South Wales
As Slowly as the Crocodile Walks, University of Glamorgan Art Collection, Trefforest, Mid Glamorgan, Wales
And Time Again, Australian National University, Canberra, Australia

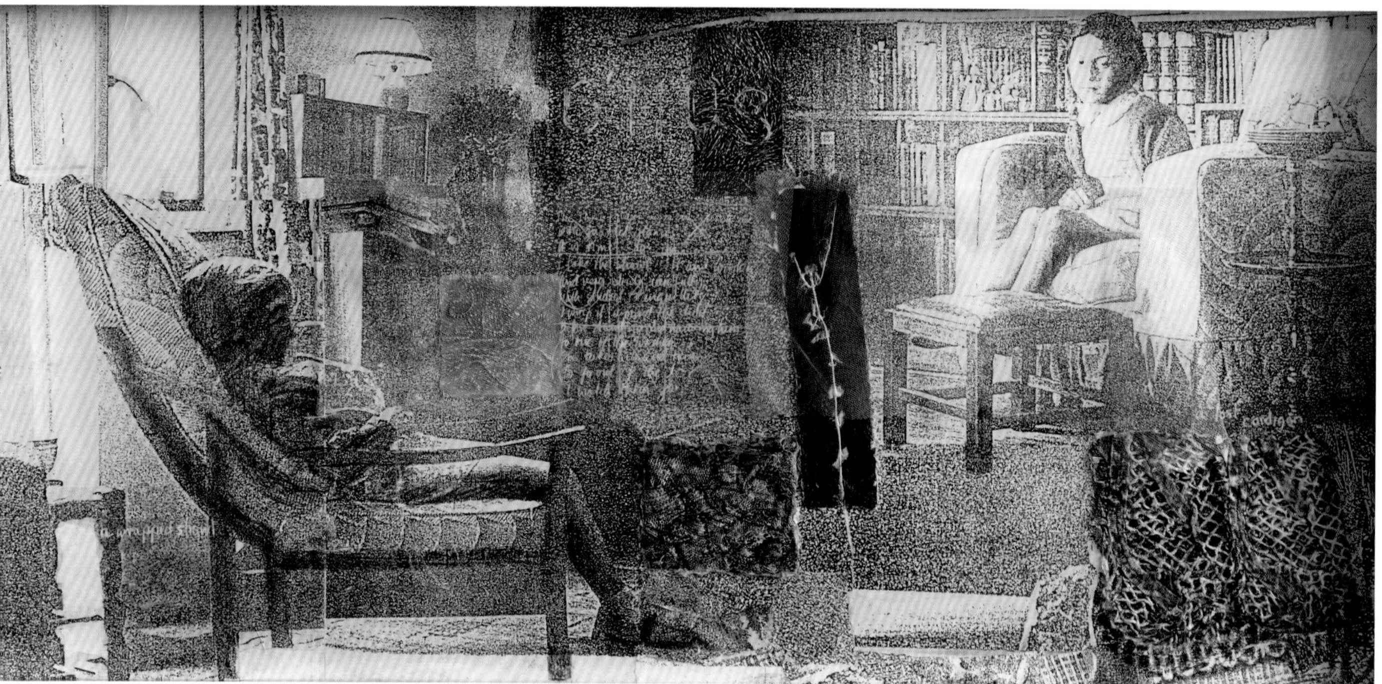

Ghosts and Relics: Knitting Lessons (2008) Mixed Media 63 x 35cm

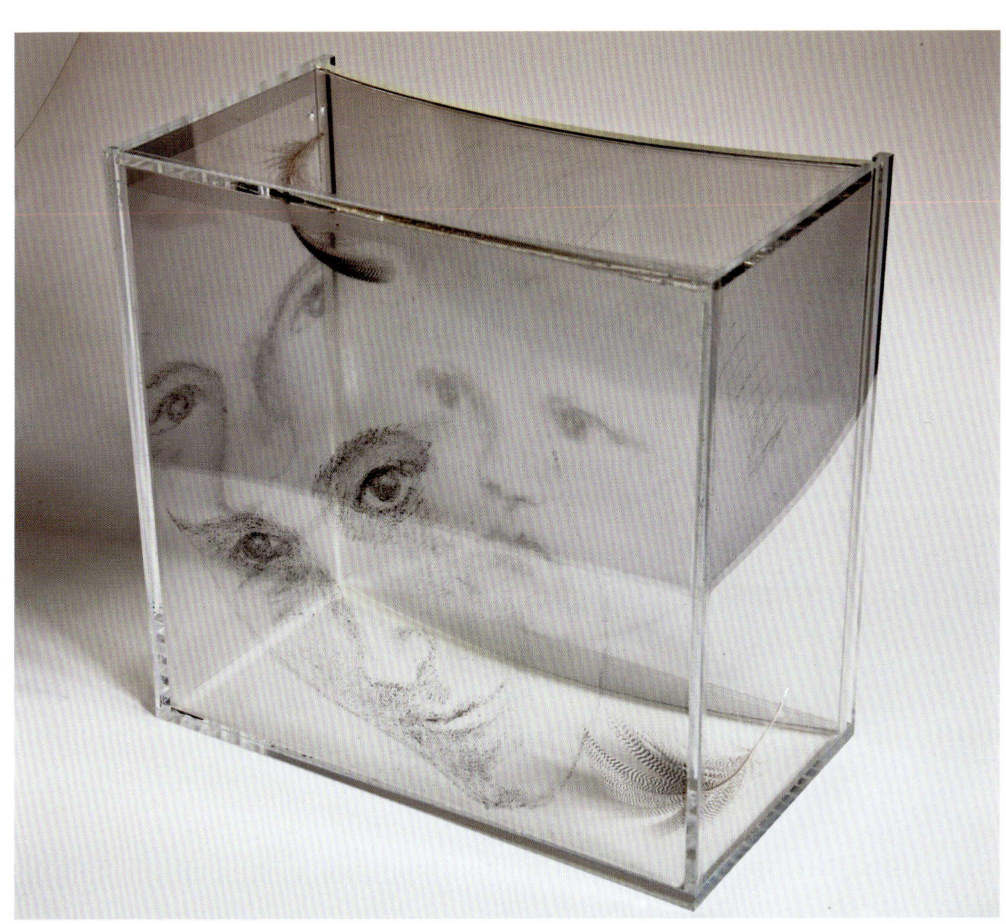

Dissolve (2009) Pencil On Clear Acetate with Feathers in Custom-Made Perspex Box 22 x 22 x 12cm

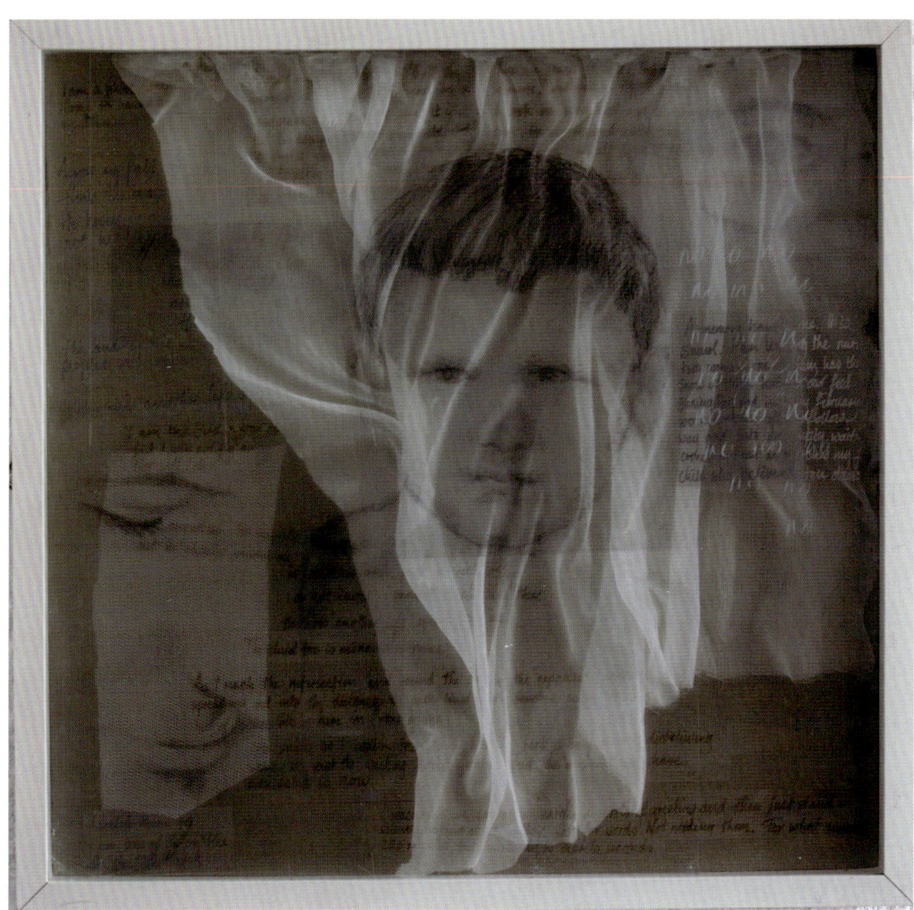

45 years of Separation (2009) Mixed Media in Boxed Frame with Fabric 52 x 52cm

Tolly Nason BA (Hons)

Tolly Nason's craftsmanship is impeccable. Her vision is highly original. Not just original but extremely beautiful, colourful, lively and life-enhancing.
- Sea Pictures Gallery, Clare, Suffolk

Tolly Nason BA (Hons)
Glass Artist and Photographer
Abington/Willingham, Cambridgeshire

My initial exposure to Glass Casting was as an assistant to Bertil Vallien at Kosta Boda in Sweden and this had a major impact on me. My work is heavily influenced by the material itself which takes on many contrasting forms within the scope of kiln casting.

The subject matter is rooted in my passion for the natural world but I often try to capture the essence of a life form in order to achieve simplicity within my sculpture. I work using my photography, sketchbooks and by studying museum specimens directly.

Creating the Galapagos finch beaks was to coincide with the 150th Anniversary of Darwin's *Origin of Species* and they were initially displayed by the Cambridge Museum of Zoology.

The beaks were an integral part of Darwin's Theory of Evolution and showing them 20x life-size in this way clearly demonstrates the variation in the sizes and shapes of the beaks which were adapting to differing environments. The pieces were lit from behind, the striking red glass contrasting with the pale exhibits. The beaks cross boundaries between science and art and seem to be engaging people across the disciplines.

This was my most ambitious project yet, starting with accurate dimensions from the actual finch skins in Cambridge, Tring and New York. I made clay positives, rubber moulds and used the lost wax process, followed by casting the glass and annealing for up to a month each. Finally they have been cold-worked by hand to achieve the final finish. A labour of love!

I was trying to capture the quality of the ancient little pate-de-verre pieces you see in museums with *Whimsicals*. The technique uses glass powders made into a paste and pressed onto the inside of a mould. Each piece requires a new mould to be carved out before packing the glass; practice and patience are essential.

Educated- Winchester School of Art, Hampshire 1999; Rhode Island School of Design, USA; Pilchuck Glass School, Seattle, USA
Membership of Local Art Societies- Cambridge Open Studios; Cam-creative; CAMBA (Cambridge Artists)
Local Galleries Familiar With Artist's Work-
Sea Pictures Gallery, Clare, Suffolk
Buckenham Galleries, Southwold, Suffolk
Primavera, Cambridge, Cambridgeshire
Collections (Open To The Public)- *Large Ground Finch Beak*; and *Warbler Finch Beak* Princeton University, USA
Website- www.thebowerhousegallery.com

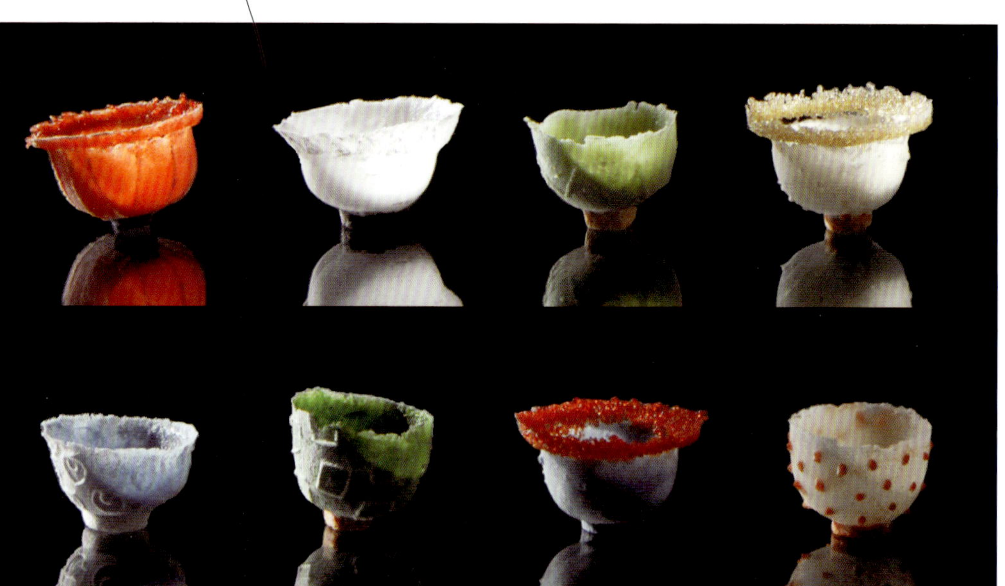

Whimsicals (2008) Pate-de-Verre 4cm

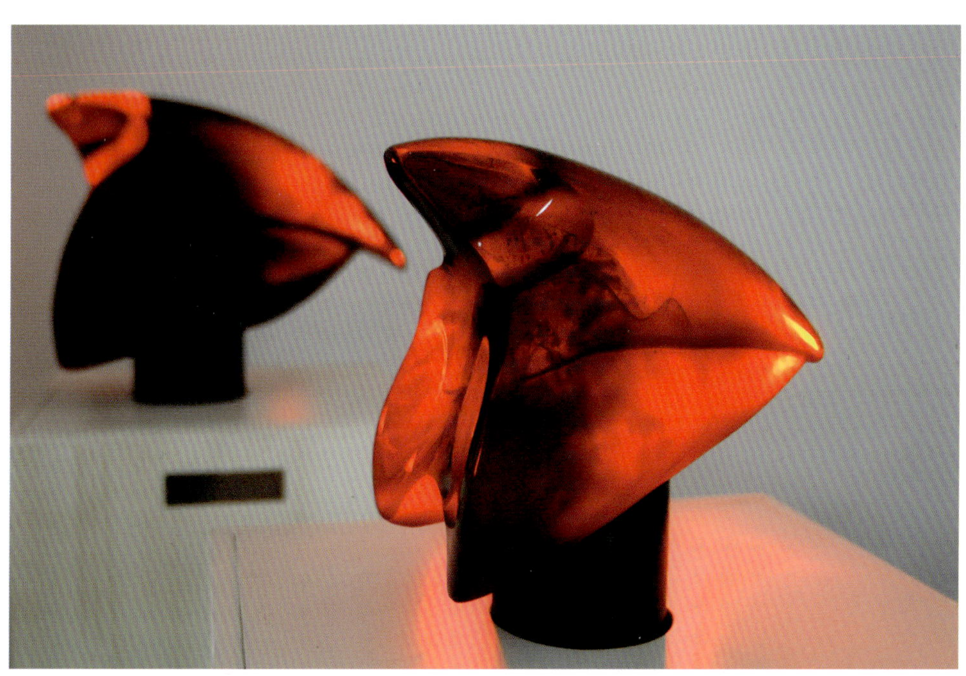

Seeing the Light: Finch by Finch (2009) (Detail) Cast Red Glass 20x Life-Size

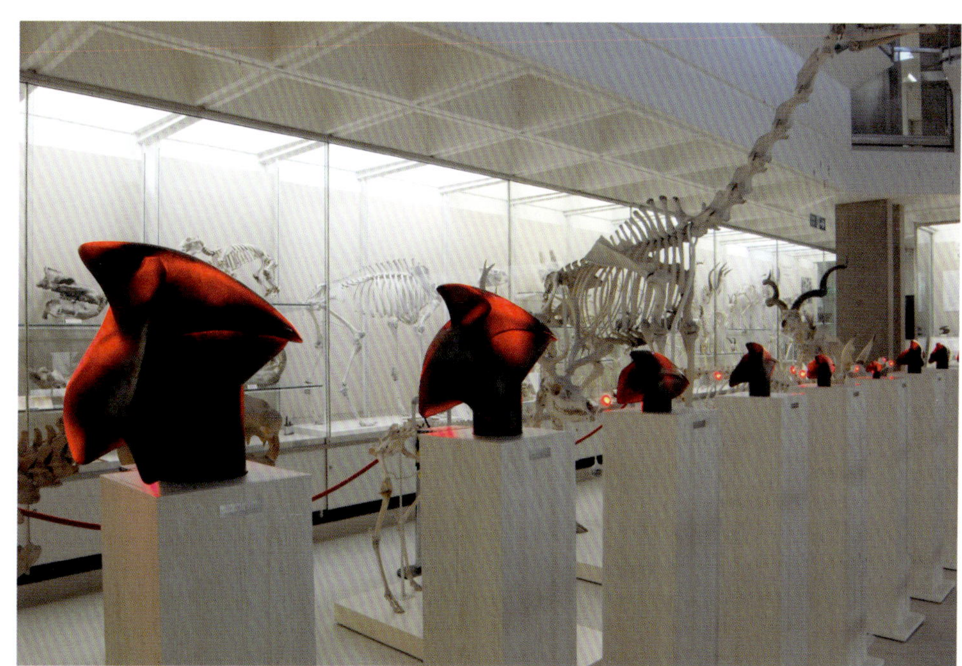

Seeing the Light: Finch by Finch (2009) Cast Red Glass 20x Life Size; Installation Spans 14 Metres.

Brian Whelan

Brian Whelan
Painter
Hanworth, Norfolk

On the Edge of the City: You can take the man out of the city but not the city out of the man. I'm compelled to paint London, the city of my birth, but from the safety of a Norfolk studio; as if memory proves to be the only way the vast subject matter can be put into a work of art. Something I could not manage when I lived in London.

A Table of Welcome: My first visit to East Anglia was in 1984 to meet artist Arthur Boyd at his studio in Suffolk. He made me feel very welcome. On the train back to London, I resolved to spend more time in the area. From that day on I associate East Anglia with all the pleasures of life: art, music, good food and drink, nature and friendship.

It took me seven years to unlearn seven years of art school training. Then I discovered the *Wenhaston Doom* in Suffolk; a stunning medieval painting of the last judgement that miraculously survived the Reformation. A door had opened into a room that I am still exploring.

I'm told medieval people read paintings in very much the same way we read a book. In galleries today, signs placed next to paintings explain them. *The Mystery of the Message* refers to the cognitive space between the viewer and a work of art, or to put it another way, the distance the pilgrim may have to travel before the journey gives up its meaning. Every figure, plant, animal, inanimate object and gesture in the painting points a way.

Holy City (22 Sept '09): The multi-perspectives and contradictory scales I employ in organising urban chaos are also employed in a series of paintings called Holy Cities. Inspired by frequent explorations of sacred spaces around the world, these paintings allow me to enjoy the pleasures of colour, decoration and design, without the burden of a narrative. The paintings can appear complex whilst I hope achieving harmony. The paintings take a long time to finish and I continue working on them until I can say, 'that is a city in which I would like to take a walk.'

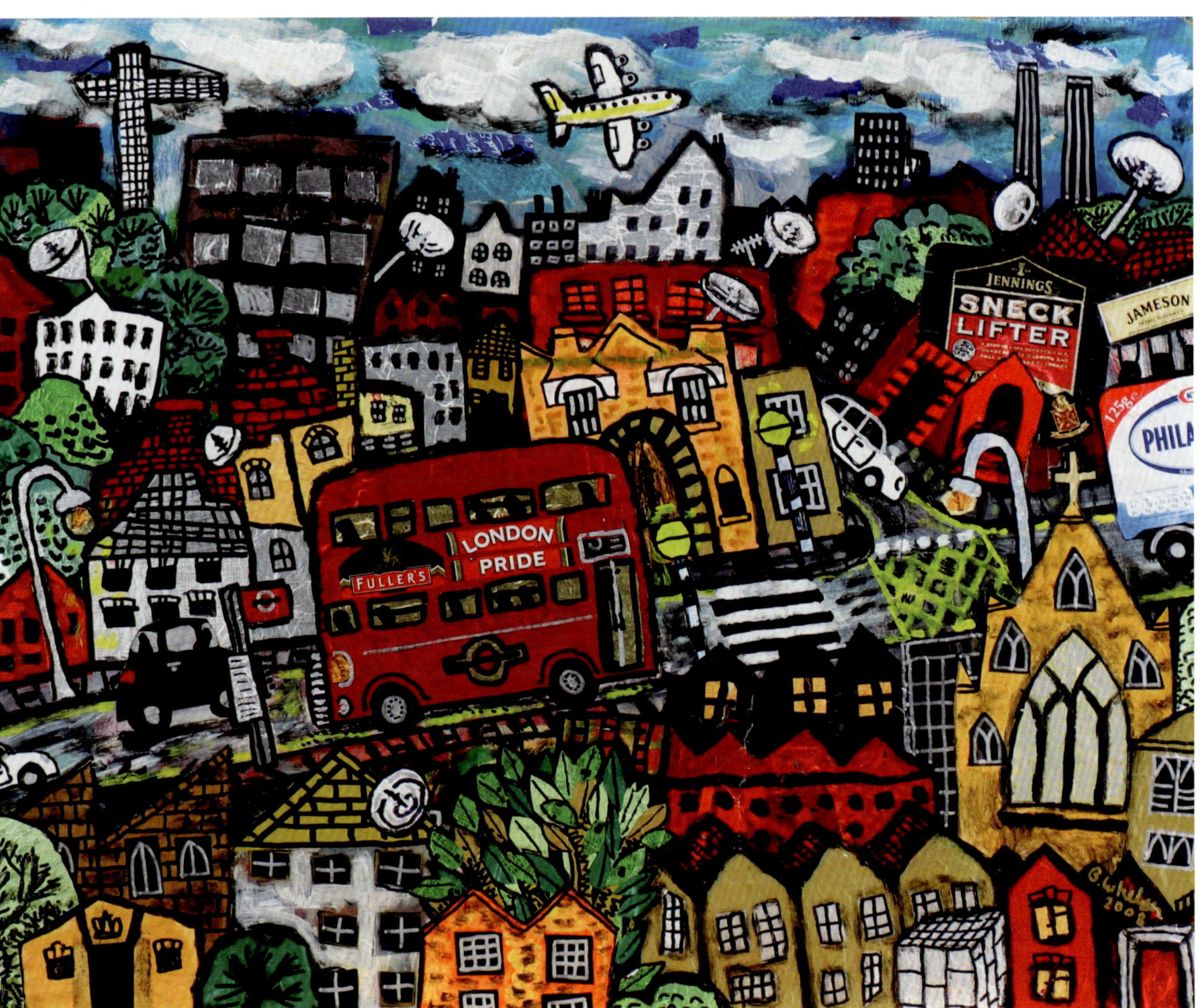

On the Edge of the City (2008) Mixed Media 56 x 69cm

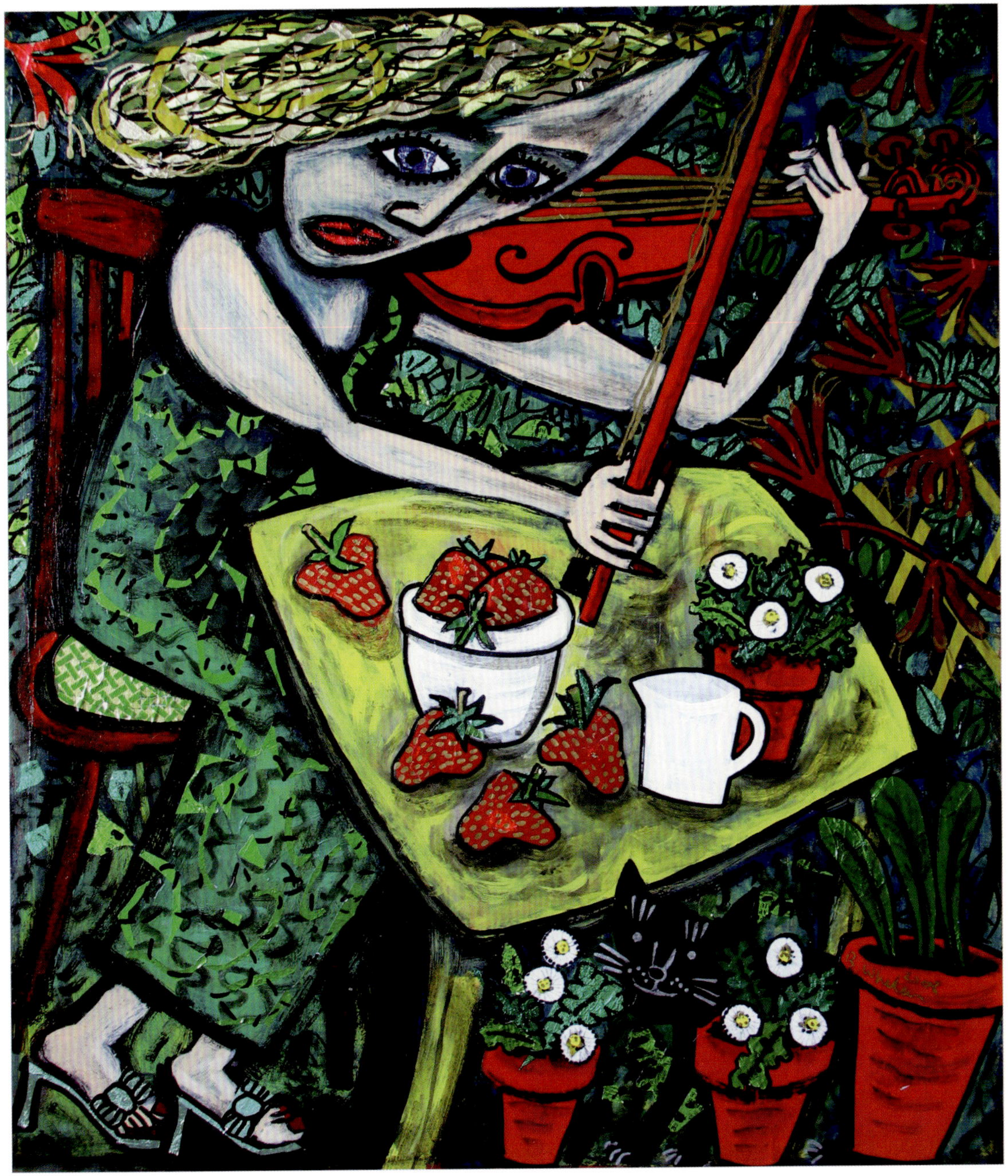

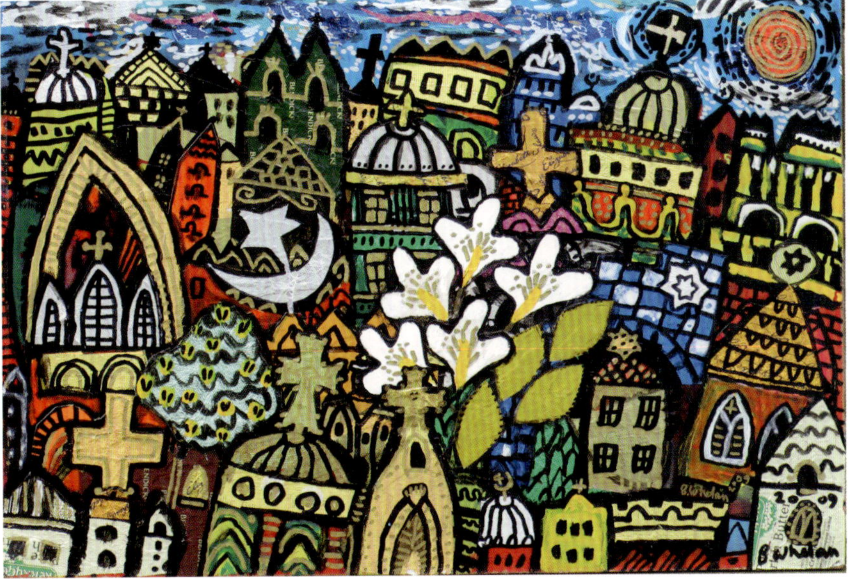

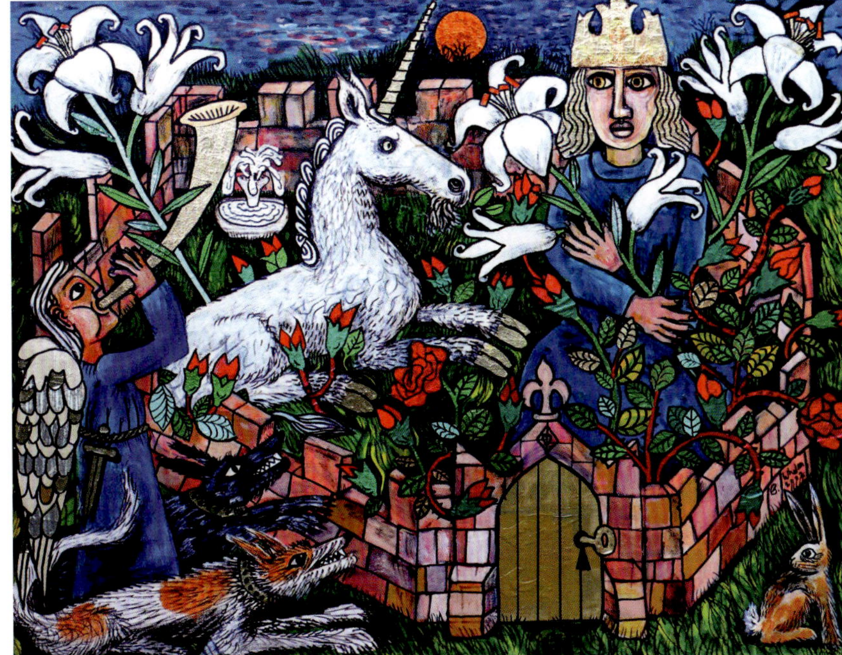

Left: *A Table of Welcome (2008)* Mixed Media 56 x 46cm; **Top Right:** *Holy City (22 Sept 2009)* Mixed Media 36 x 58cm; **Bottom Right:** *Mystery of the Message (2002)* Mixed Media 76 x 101cm

Brian Whelan: Behind the Scenes

More about:

Brian...

Educated-
Royal Academy of Arts, RA Diploma in Painting
and Drawing
Membership of Art Societies-
East Anglia Art Fund
Norfolk Contemporary Art Society
The Arts Club, Mayfair, London
Galleries Familiar With Artist's Work-
Thompson's Gallery, London
Doric Arts, Holt, Norfolk
St Giles Street Gallery, Norwich, Norfolk
Crome Gallery, Norwich, Norfolk
Wildwood Gallery, Bury St Edmunds, Suffolk
Website- www.brianwhelan.co.uk

For many years I worked in sheds at the bottom of gardens. Each shed bigger than the one before. The landlord of my last and biggest shed asked for it back and I was devastated.

Moving studios is a daunting experience if you have been painting all your life but it worked out for the best when we found these converted stables in North Norfolk.

I don't like to make a decision to go into the studio – I just want to find myself there – working. And this is how it happens, even before the morning coffee has brewed.

The ideas for paintings can come from anywhere but I have noticed they often come out of conversations with people in pubs, on the street, on a train, in a waiting room.

To say 'A painting is finished when I stop working on it' is flippant - but true. I seem to go through an initial excitement and when the insight or vision is passed and I am disappointed by my efforts, I put the work away and start something new. Rediscovered, the set-aside painting usually makes me think, 'Hey, that's not as bad as I'd thought!'

When I was younger I was always destroying my work or using the canvas over and over again. Arthur Boyd persuaded me to be more generous and patient with myself. I certainly have a lot more work around me now and find some of the paintings have taken years to finish.

I still get a kick out of seeing a painting framed. It is as though I am seeing it for the first time – back at that point when I first had the impulse to paint it.

This Page: Brian's new converted stables in North Norfolk; Detail from inside The Stables
Opposite Page: Brian's studio

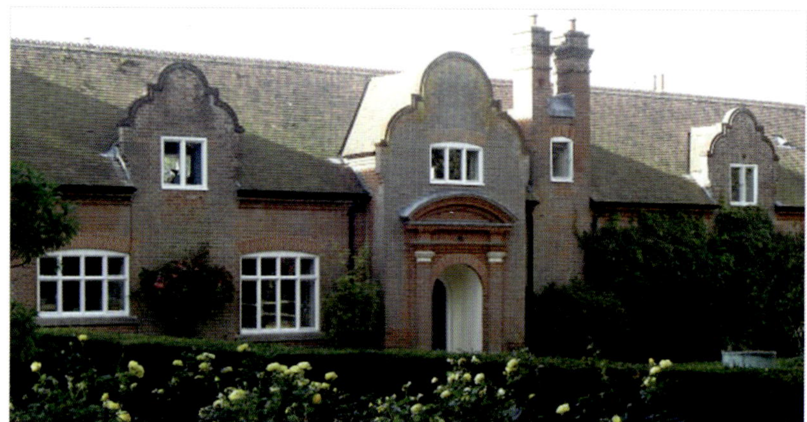

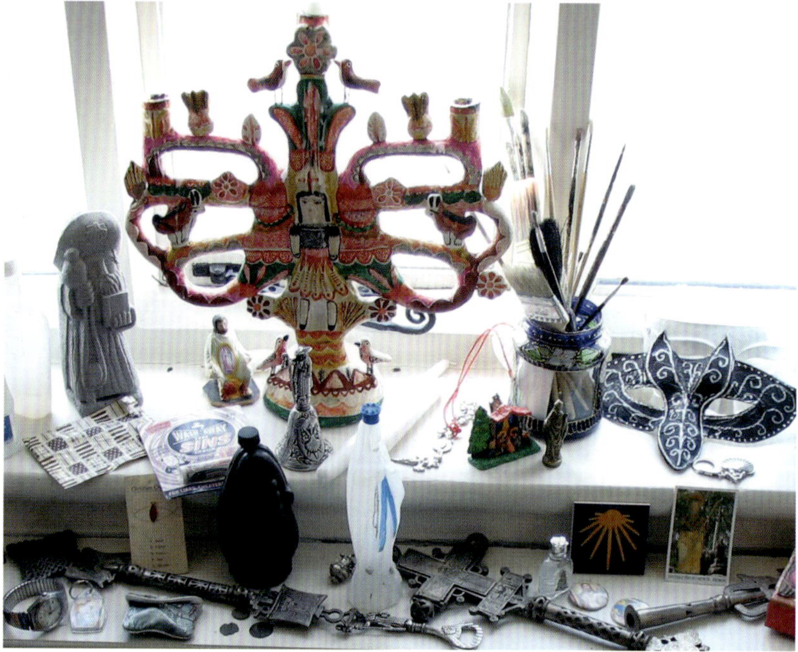

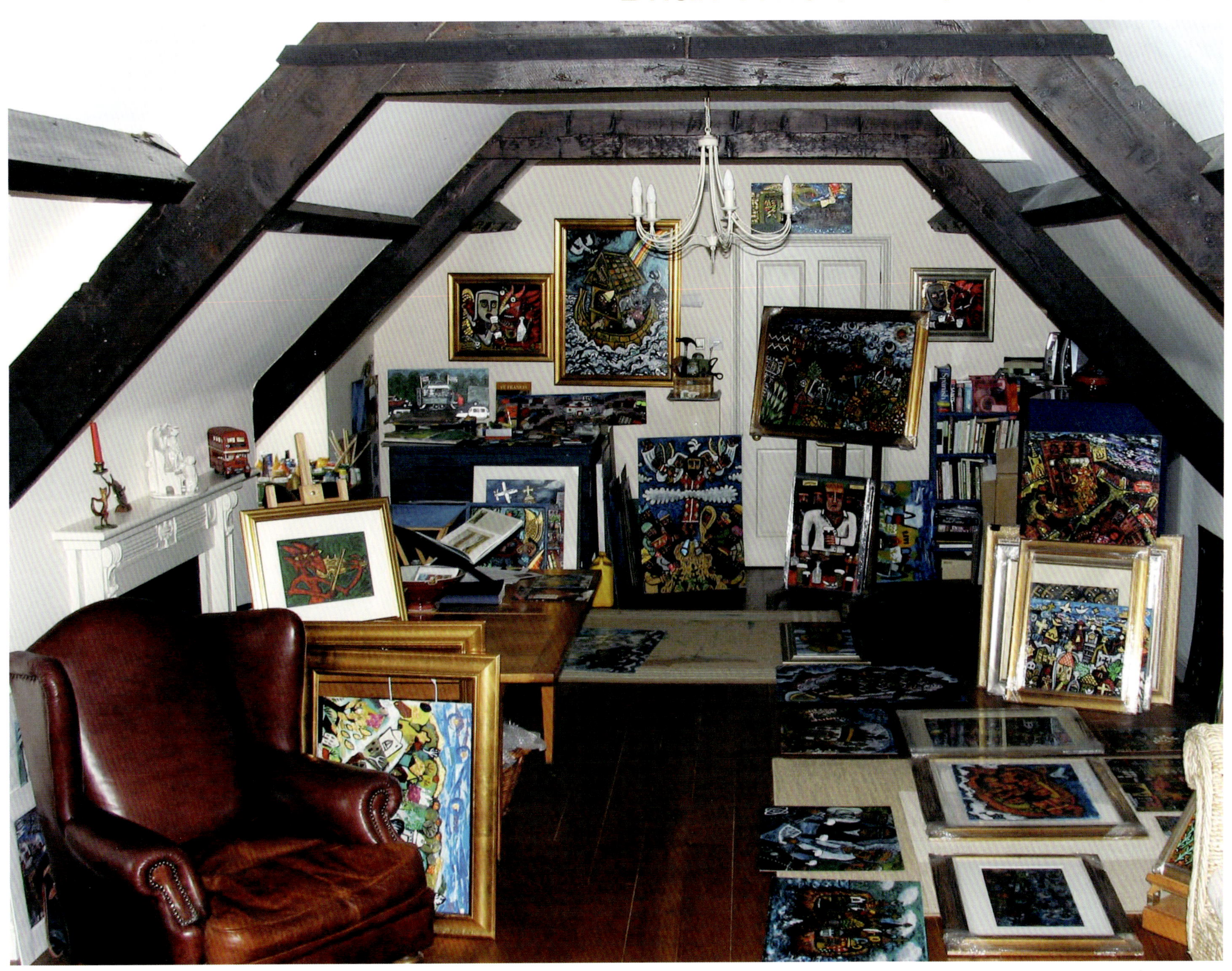

Beka Smith BA

Beka Smith is one of the finest portrait painters I have seen come through my gallery.
- Storm Fine Arts, Burnham Market, Norfolk

Beka Smith
Portrait Painter, London

Before I start the portrait, I try to get to know the sitter as well as possible. I talk to them and try to find out what interests them, their ideas on life, what they believe in, anything that is basic to their character. I am searching for clues as to what 'makes them tick' and I try to empathize with them.

Throughout the process of creating the portrait, I try to be as objective as possible. I am really just painting or drawing the shapes and tones I see in front of me. In an accurate representation of these, somehow the likeness of the person begins to emerge.

Having for some while been interested in the idea of costume and masquerade, alongside my love of character illustration, I have become fascinated by the idea of someone projecting a character conjured up from their imagination. In *Alter Ego,* the sitter has re-invented themselves, and as an artist I am responding by painting my interpretation of this. These portrayals move a step away from the recognized conventional idea of a portrait.

In the *Ego Alter Ego* series of deliberately unnamed paintings, I explore the multiple personas of my highly imaginative subjects as they perform their different roles. These paintings are a study of different aspects of self-perception.

Dr Leslie Wayper's portrait was originally commissioned by Fitzwilliam College, Cambridge, as a pencil sketch. On meeting him at his home, I was so struck by his character that I was compelled to undertake a separate painting, which took several months to complete. The final sitting was a few days before his death in 2006 at the age of ninety-three. I wanted to capture someone nearing the end of his life, a feeling of calm resignation as well as a sense of humour. His portrait was exhibited in the BP Portrait Awards 2006 and was voted third in 'The People's Choice.' A benefactor later purchased it for the college.

In the self-portrait *In a Different Light* I have tried to capture to some extent something of my own Alter Ego, a reflective aspect of my character that may not always be apparent, since I am more often perceived as an extrovert. I have aimed here at portraying a pensive and questioning mood, the direction of thought a little mysterious, perhaps, hinting at a more private side to my personality.

Educated- University of West of England, Bristol
Membership of Local Art Societies-
Second Floor Studios and Arts
Galleries Familiar With Artist's Work-
Storm Fine Arts, Cambridge
Website- www.bekasmith.com

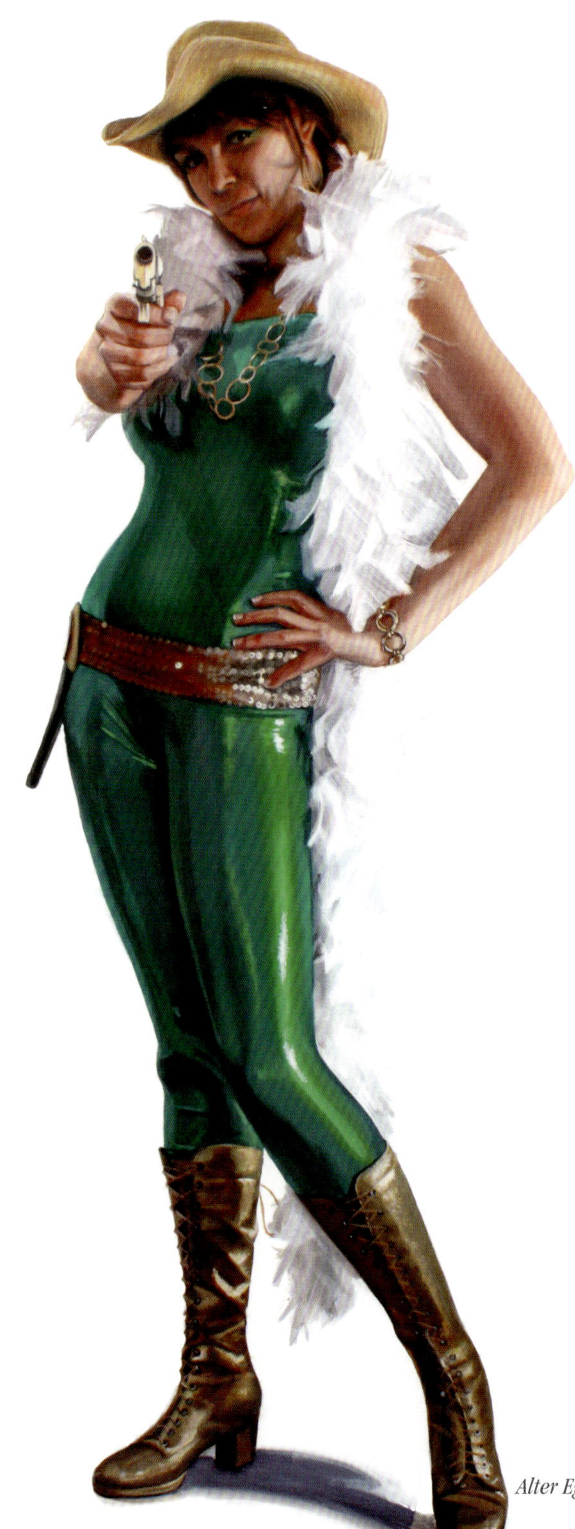

Alter Ego (2009) Acrylic on Canvas 120 x 60cm

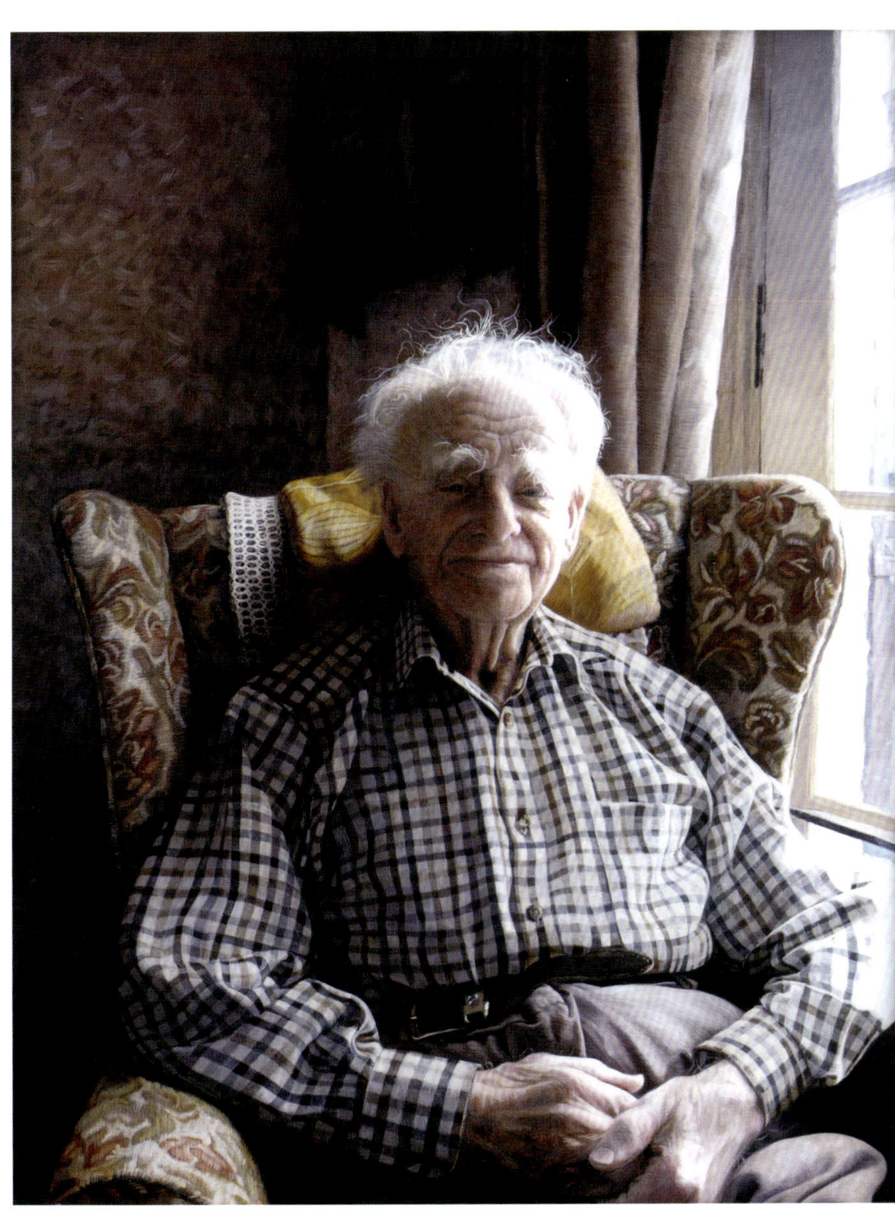

Portrait of Leslie Wayper (2006) Acrylic on Board 45 x 55cm

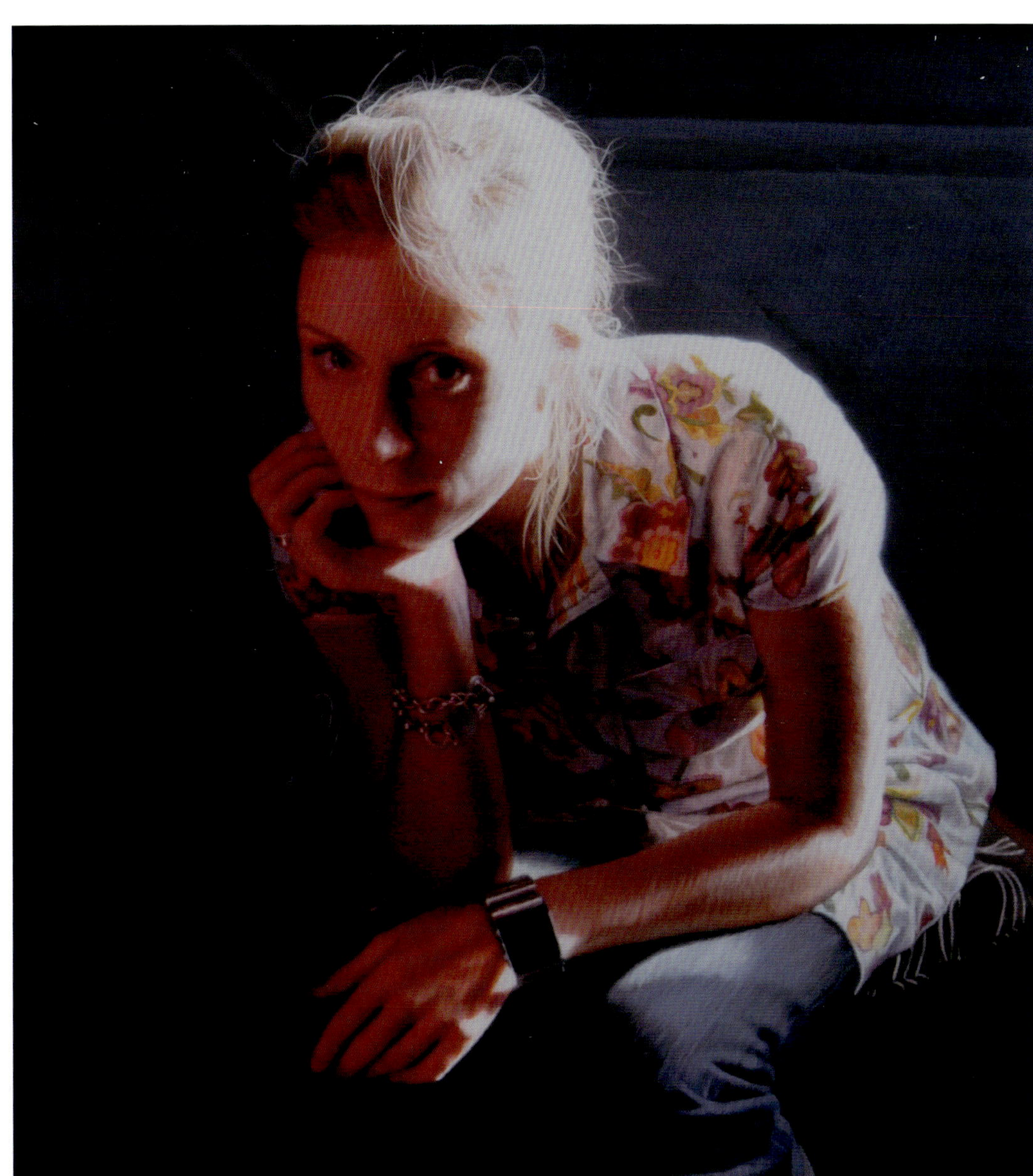

In a Different Light (Self Portrait) (2008) Acrylic on Board 45 x 55cm

David Morris MA

On entering the gallery for the first time, new visitors stop in their tracks when they see David Morris' photographs on the wall and are transfixed by the sheer quality and impact of his images.
- The Garden House Gallery, Cromer, Norfolk

David Morris MA
Photographer
Cromer, Norfolk

I'm an available light photographer, which means I work with whatever light I'm given. On that edge between just enough light and nothing you can find some really interesting images. For landscapes I prefer the extreme ends of the day. I'm also working on a protracted study of the world of bars and drinkers and here again the light is dramatic and extreme, but it's not all glum. I have a study of the mussel beds at Hunstanton which have all the lightness of Japanese silk paintings.

The Girl Who Never Smiled was a striking looking girl. I'd seen her a few times in the streets of the Navigli in Milan, but I never saw her smile – not once. I was in the Cape Town bar, a very popular place where I'd taken shots before - the owner Sergio makes it his business to know everyone else's whilst dispensing lethal measures of excellent wine. The girl came in but I had my back to her. I thought *now or never* and held the camera up in front of me, twisted it round back to front and fired.

With *Last of the Light*, I'd spent a useless day in perfectly wonderful light at Morston Quay and achieved absolutely nothing. On the way home I stopped for one final look down the coast; the light was extraordinary. I set the tripod up and realised it would need a very long exposure – nearly fifteen minutes in fact, but the results were remarkable, the camera recorded tones and shapes of which you were only dimly aware.

White beach huts Normandy. As you'd expect, the French do their beach huts with style. Just a little way along the coast the theme is pastel colours, here they opted for white. It was a case of almost too much light, overexpose and you would lose the detail in the white woodwork. The electric blue sky makes the drama. I've got a series of shots from here at different exposures. The effect of white beach huts devoid of any human presence is really quite strange and ethereal.

Educated- Central St Martins School of Art & Design, London
Honours- Professional Photographer of the Year, awarded in 2009 by *Professional Photographer of the Year* Magazine
Galleries Familiar With Artist's Work- Bircham Gallery, Holt, Norfolk; The Garden House, Cromer, Norfolk; The Galley@Horning, Horning, Norfolk
Website- www.davidmorrisphotographer.com

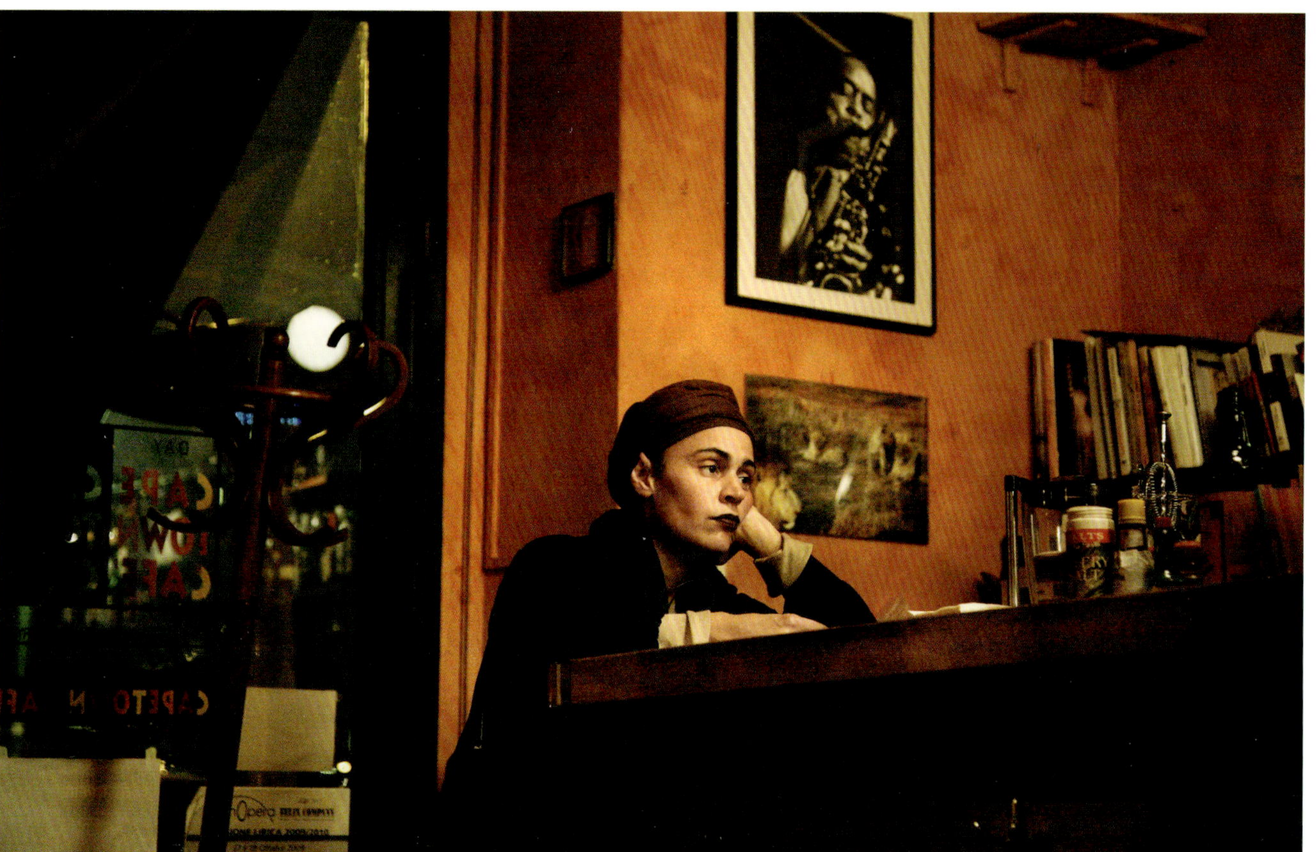

The Girl Who Never Smiled (2009) Photograph 39.5 x 60.4cm

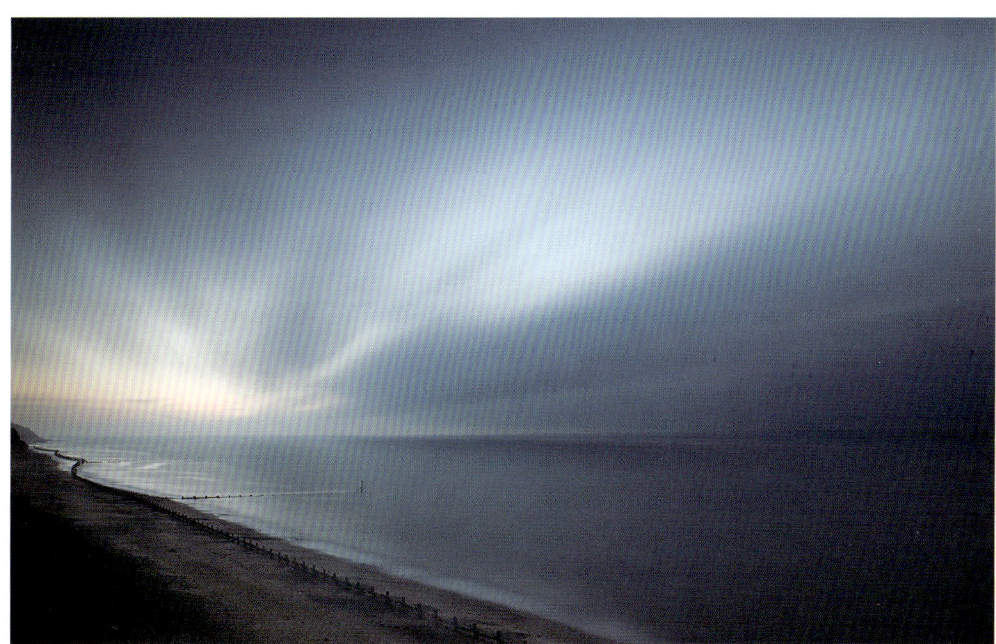

Last of the Light (2009) Photograph 39.5 x 60.4cm

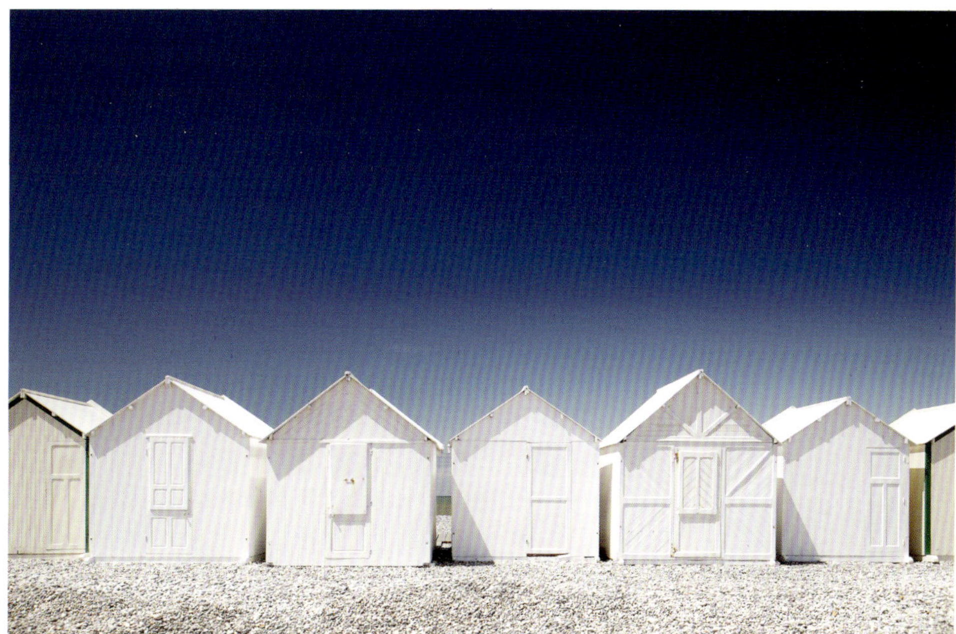

White Beach Huts Normandy (2009) Photograph 39.5 x 60.4cm

David Porteous-Butler

David Porteous-Butler
Painter
Milden, Suffolk

42

I am told I have a strength for capturing personality in portraits, and love to find the timeless scene to immortalise on canvas. I use a palette knife and a limited range of oil colours. My aim is to take the realms of traditional representational painting to new levels. Interpreting light through observation and impression, and conveying an emotional response to a subject, are the keystones of my work.

I love to find a group of people in a landscape involved in some activity. It's not always easy to secure a photograph but I never have a shortage of subject matter.

I am always happy to pop into the National Gallery to see my favourites, Claude Monet, Camille Pissaro and Alfred Sisley. When in Paris, I never miss a trip to the Musee D'Orsay.

The Late Sir Kyffin Williams was my greatest influence. He was a great supporter both when I was at school and much later when I decided to become a professional artist. I particularly value the power and simplicity of his images, coupled with his economical use of colour.

Having started so late in life as a painter I feel I have to work very intensively to achieve a substantial volume of work. Fortunately I have to make a living from painting so there is no conflict of interest. I feel my personal development is progressing well and am encouraged by the occasional 'wow!' from my London gallery.

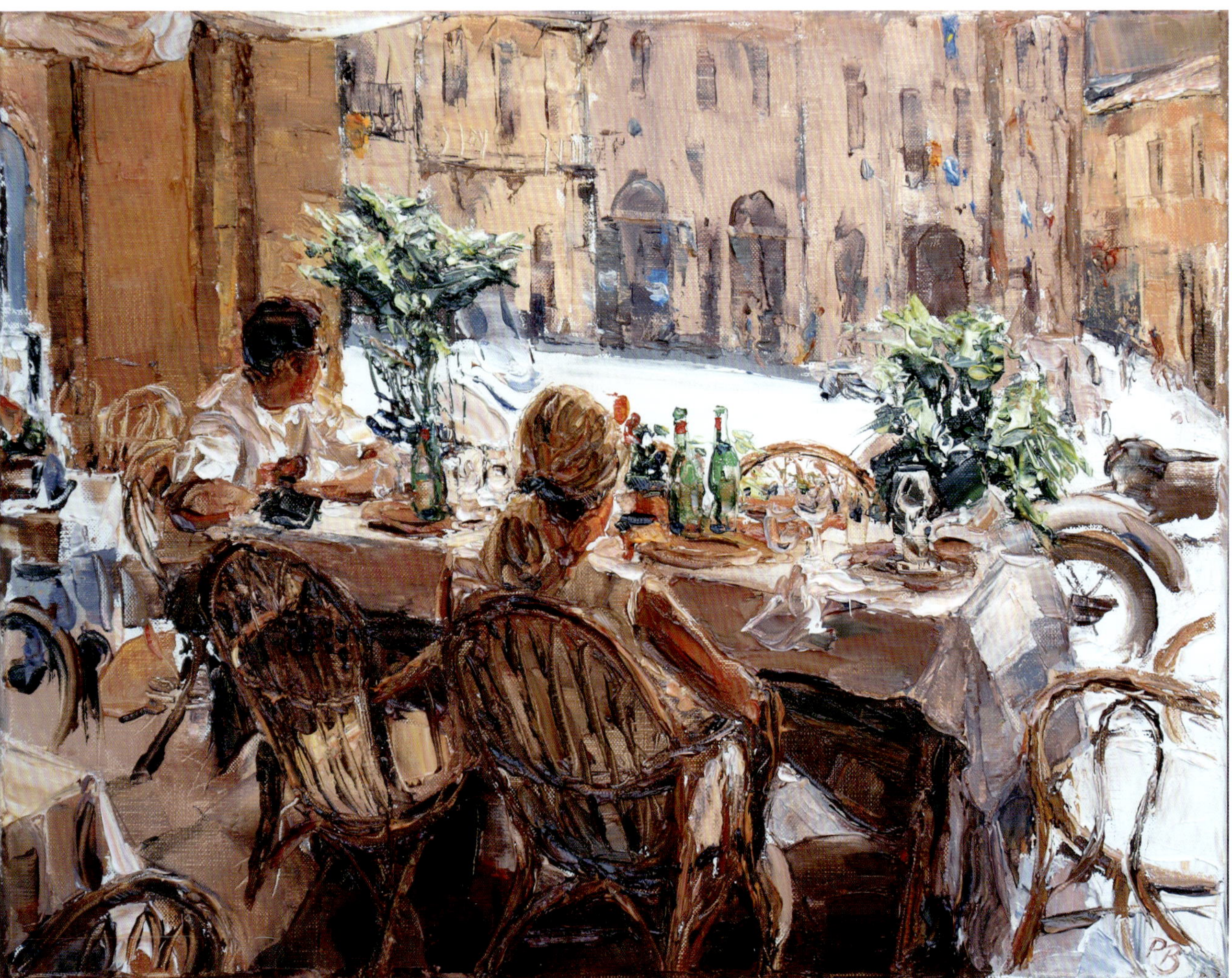

Lunch- Arezzo(2009) Oil on Canvas 40 x 50cm

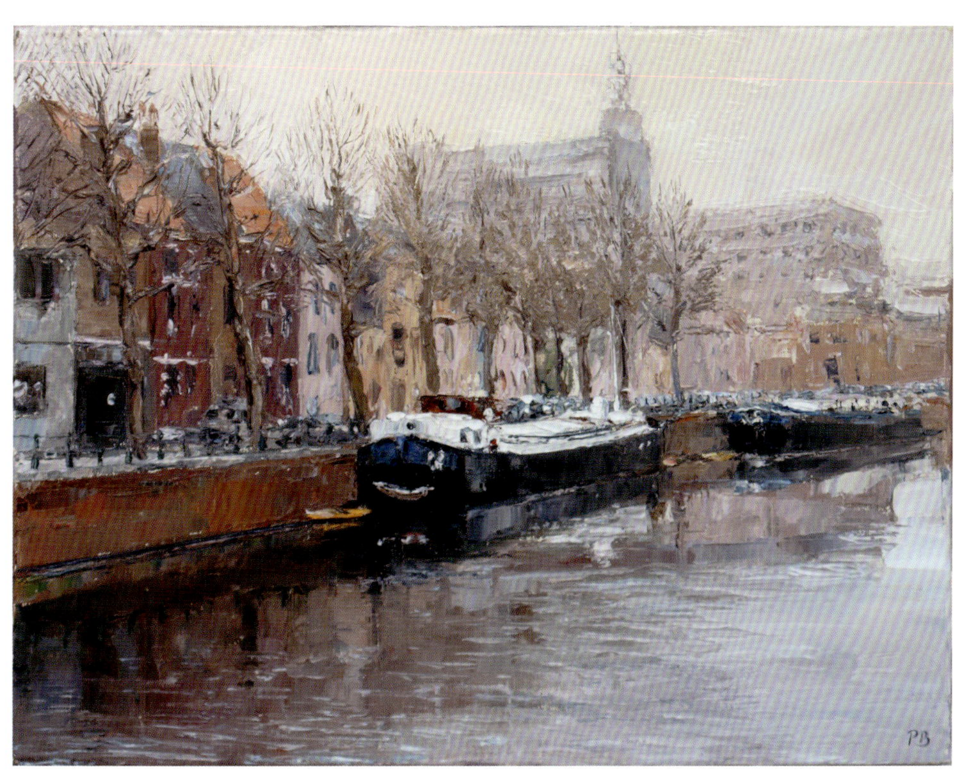

Barges- Ghent (2010) Oil on Canvas 40 x 50cm

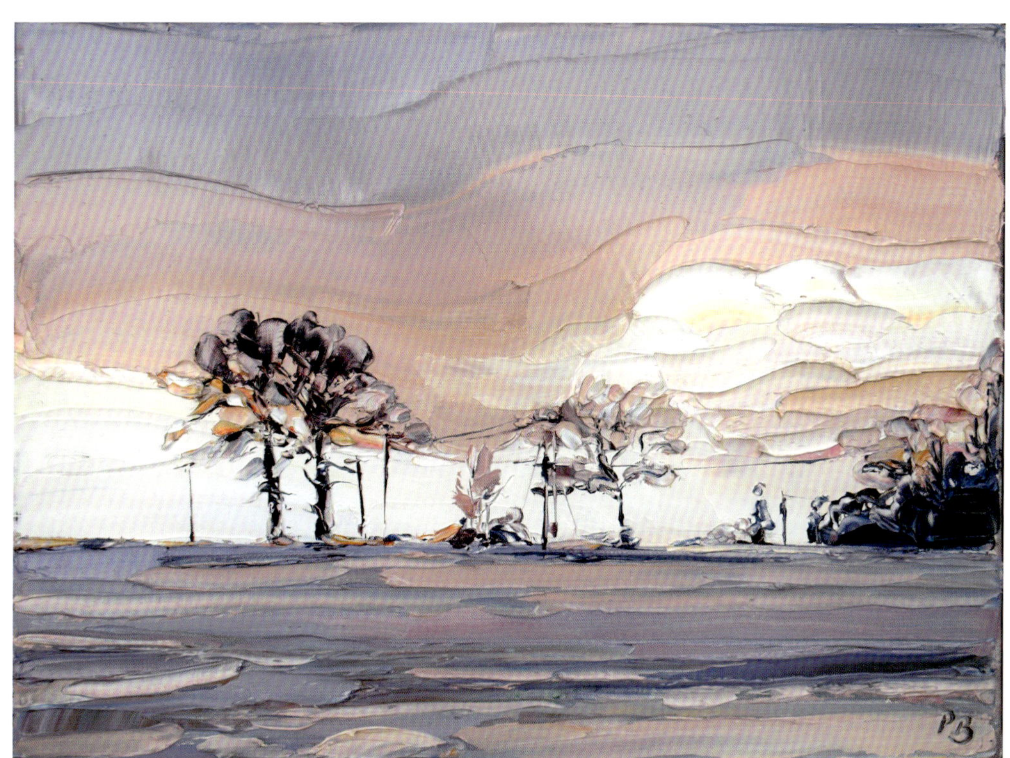

Winter- Milden (2008) Oil on Canvas 30 x 40cm

David Porteous-Butler: Behind the Scenes

More about:

David....

Educated- Highgate School, London
Galleries Familiar With Artist's Work-
Enid Lawson Gallery, London
Wren Gallery, Burford, Oxfordshire
Mandell's Gallery, Norwich, Norfolk
Collections (Open To The Public)-
Welsh National Library, Aberystwyth, Wales
Website- www.pbart.co.uk

My studio has almost perfect northern light from sliding doors facing up the garden towards the house. My working day is not complete without music. I have an excellent sound system but the only practical way of listening is to Radio 3. One day I shall find time to load my I-Pod so that I can listen to my vast library of recordings. There is a mezzanine 1st floor that has glass balconies either side that allows extra light to the south side of the main floor. My office is based here. Canvasses are stored against the wall but tend not to be there very long before they depart for my galleries. I only notice how little storage space I have when painting for a solo show!

My working day starts at 8.00am or earlier if the light allows. Although I have daylight lighting throughout the studio I don't like working with it unless absolutely necessary I finish at about 6 pm but sometimes have to return after supper to clear up or do office work

I stop for an espresso about 11.30am and lunch at 1.30pm. These breaks are essential just to relax and unwind a little.

I mostly work from photographs. The exception to this is portraits. I often make drawings of my subject and only after I have begun to understand my sitter do I take photographs. Eventually I expect I shall work exclusively from life. When I paint I use a large wall-mounted monitor for displaying photographs. I usually only work on one painting at a time but when I'm working on a portrait which can take days or weeks, I paint other work alongside.

The start of a painting often dictates the overall outcome and within the first hour I often get fired up with the knowledge that it's going to work out fine. Fortunately, only rarely does a painting fail entirely and have to be scraped off before drying. Because I'm working from a tangible image it's just a question of working through the process of applying paint correctly. Sometimes it goes better than others – that's life!

Studio work is a lonely business. It is much better to be alone with your thoughts and memories stimulated by a Beethoven quartet or a Bach cantata. There seems to be enough partitioning in my brain to allow both the input and output to function optimally. Then the telephone goes. Where is it this time? Under a Rag? Upstairs next to its twin? If it's a friend I'm delighted to be interrupted, if it's a cold-seller, I fume and spit.

It is always a pleasure to invite people to my studio. I find the evening most suitable so as not to interrupt the output but I'm secretly delighted to have a friend drop in. I even have a painter friend who works with me, mostly in silence but the company is tangible.

The Studio: David built the studio himself with the help of his great friend and professional builder, Andy Carr. It is made with a steel and lightweight block. With a traditional exterior cladding, the North facing wall is a series of U-Glass folding doors.

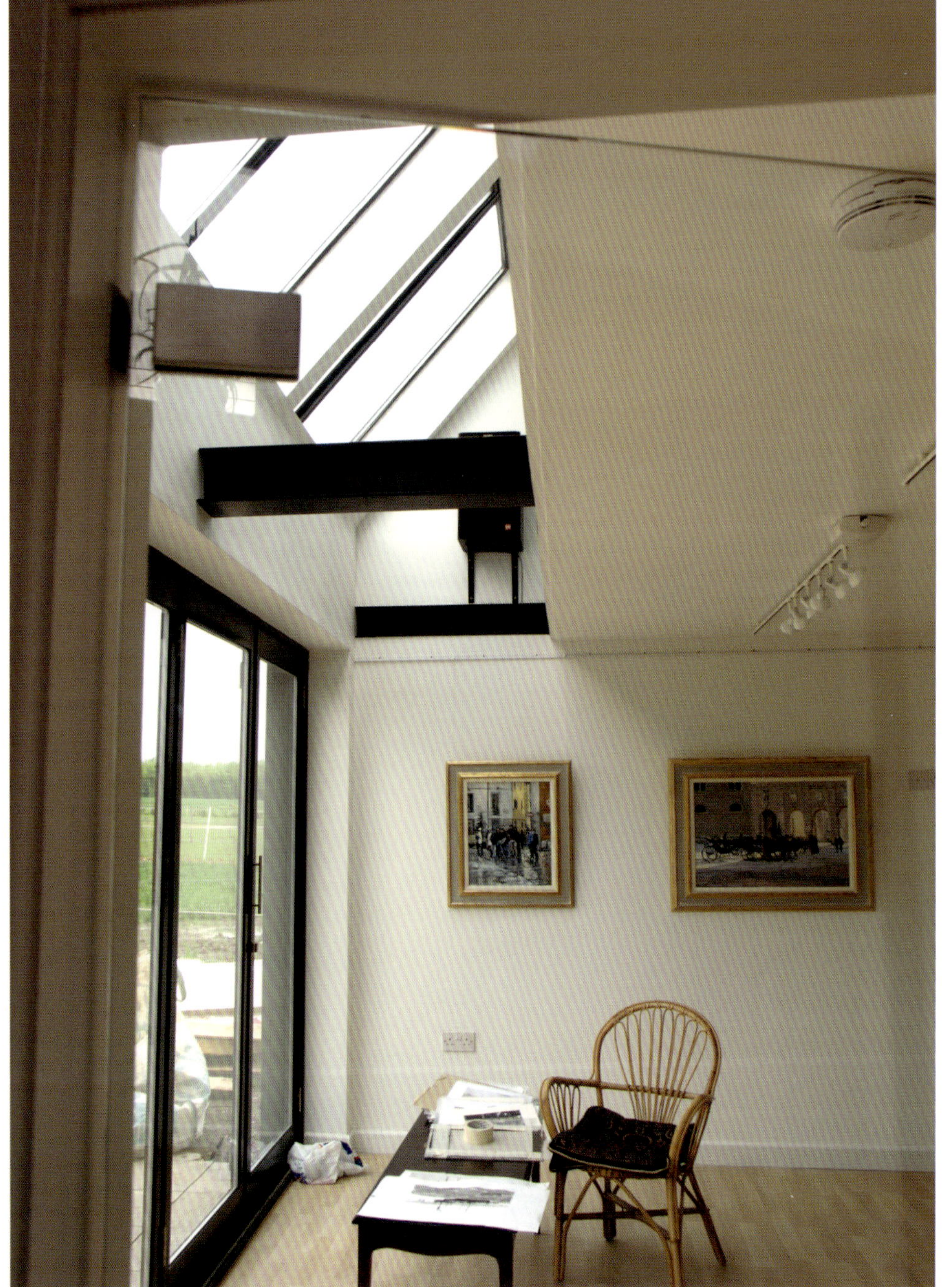

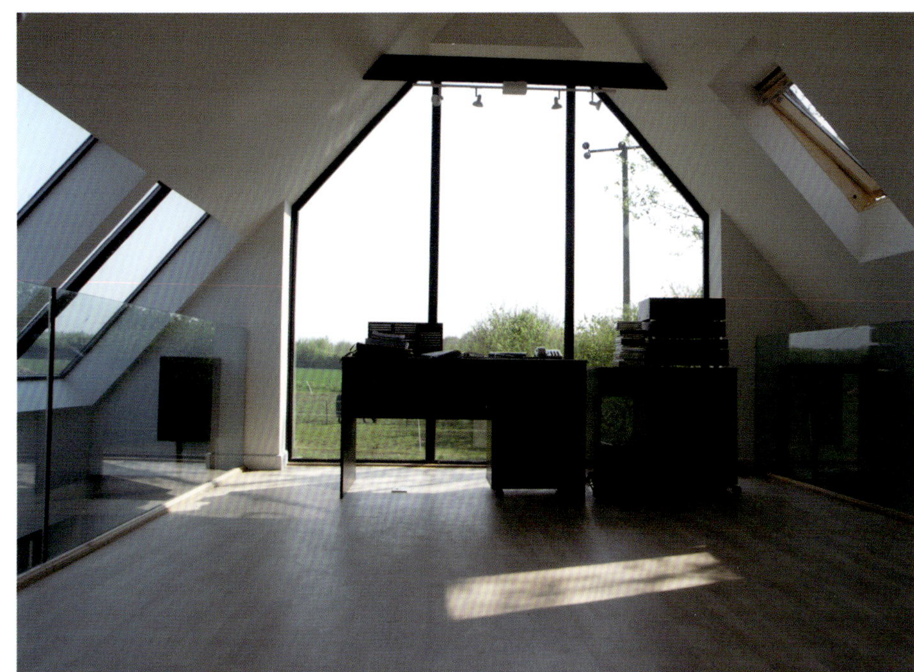

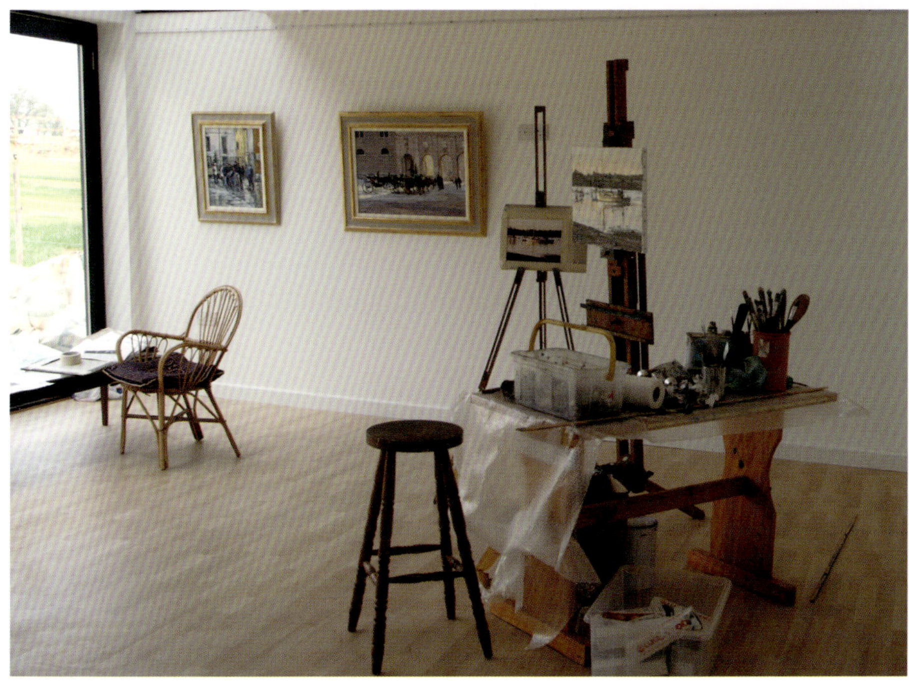

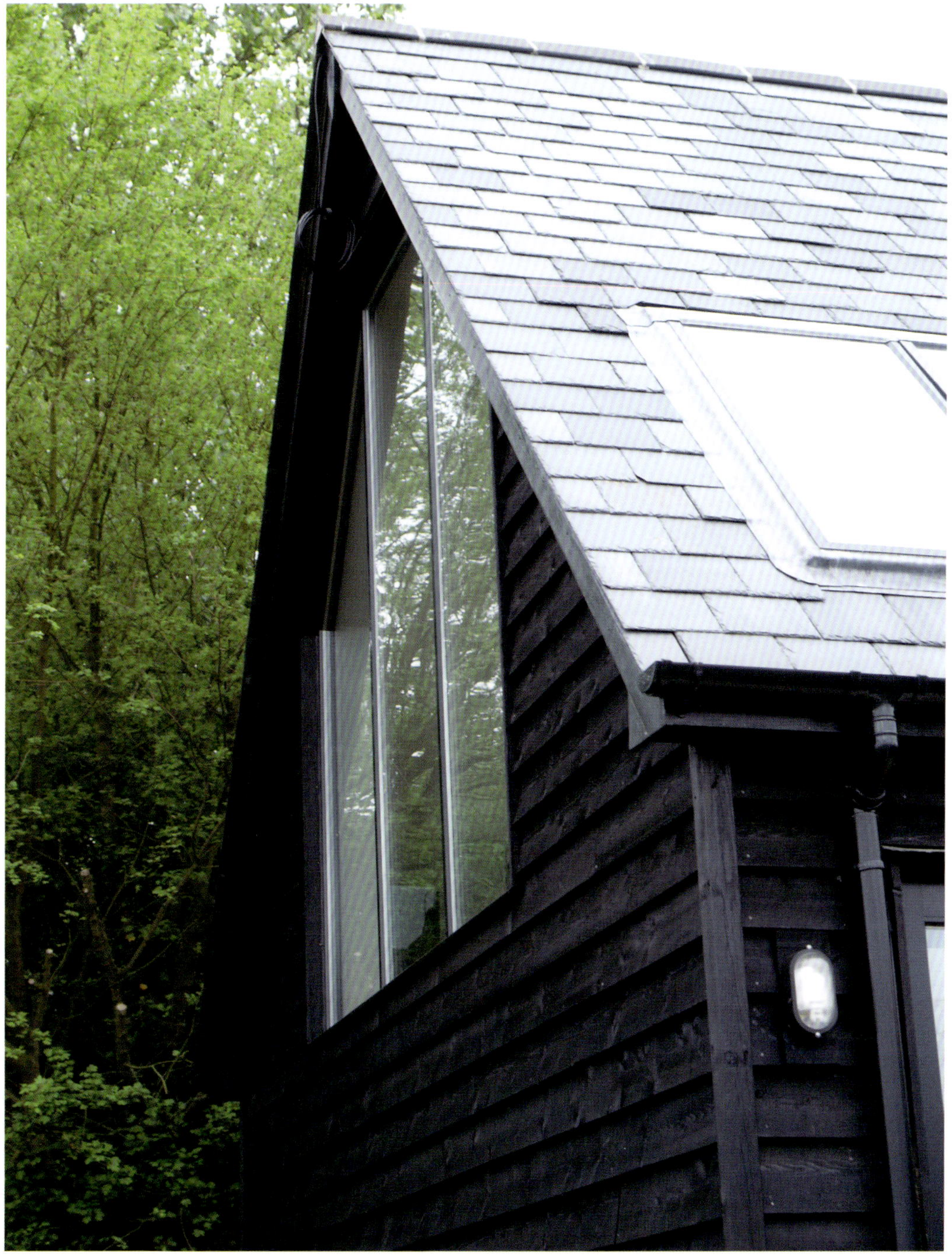

Jane German NDD, ATC

Jane's method of painting leaves one wondering how it is achieved: the subtle colours are muted yet luminous, with the paint worked into, rather than placed upon, the canvas. Recent works are sensual, sumptuous compositions of fruit, vegetables, pottery and fabrics, in the great tradition of the still life. Jane's work is sought after and collected, especially by those who share her love of the natural world.
- Harleston Gallery, Harleston, Norfolk

Jane German NDD, ATC
Painter
Starston, Norfolk

Humble realities: domestic animals, hedgerows, birds, a picking of fruit or vegetables, a favourite bowl, piece of fabric or found natural objects. These are the focus of my recent paintings. My garden, which overlooks the River Beck in Starston is bordered by hedges, beyond which Friesians graze in the water meadow. Over the years these cattle have featured in my work and last year this collection was exhibited at The Cut, Halesworth, entitled 'The Other Side of the Hedge'.

In *Cow, Hedge, Bryony,* I aim to elevate the familiar sighting of a cow through a hedge to an evocative composition of animal, branch and foliage, all of which are given equal importance in the painting. My composition fills the picture surface with forms. The black and white abstract pattern of the cow intermingles with the foliage, contrasting starkly, but at the same time in harmony with the subtle framework of the layed hedge.

My admiration for paintings by Dutch and Flemish masters and other European painters has fed my desire to explore more fully the tradition of the still life.

In *Quinces, Bowl, Leaves* I have taken familiar objects and dwelt on their elegance, simplicity and pure form. Quinces, with their jewel-like quality, nesting in a dark, insect-patterned bowl on a background of Autumn; a variety of objects brought together in an exotic slice of everyday life.

Educated- Loughborough College of Art
Membership of Local Art Societies-
Harleston & Waveney Art Trail
Norfolk Contemporary Art Society
Galleries Familiar With Artist's Work-
Cork Brick Gallery, Bungay, Suffolk
The Cut, Halesworth, Suffolk
Harleston Gallery, Harleston, Norfolk
Website- www.janegerman.com

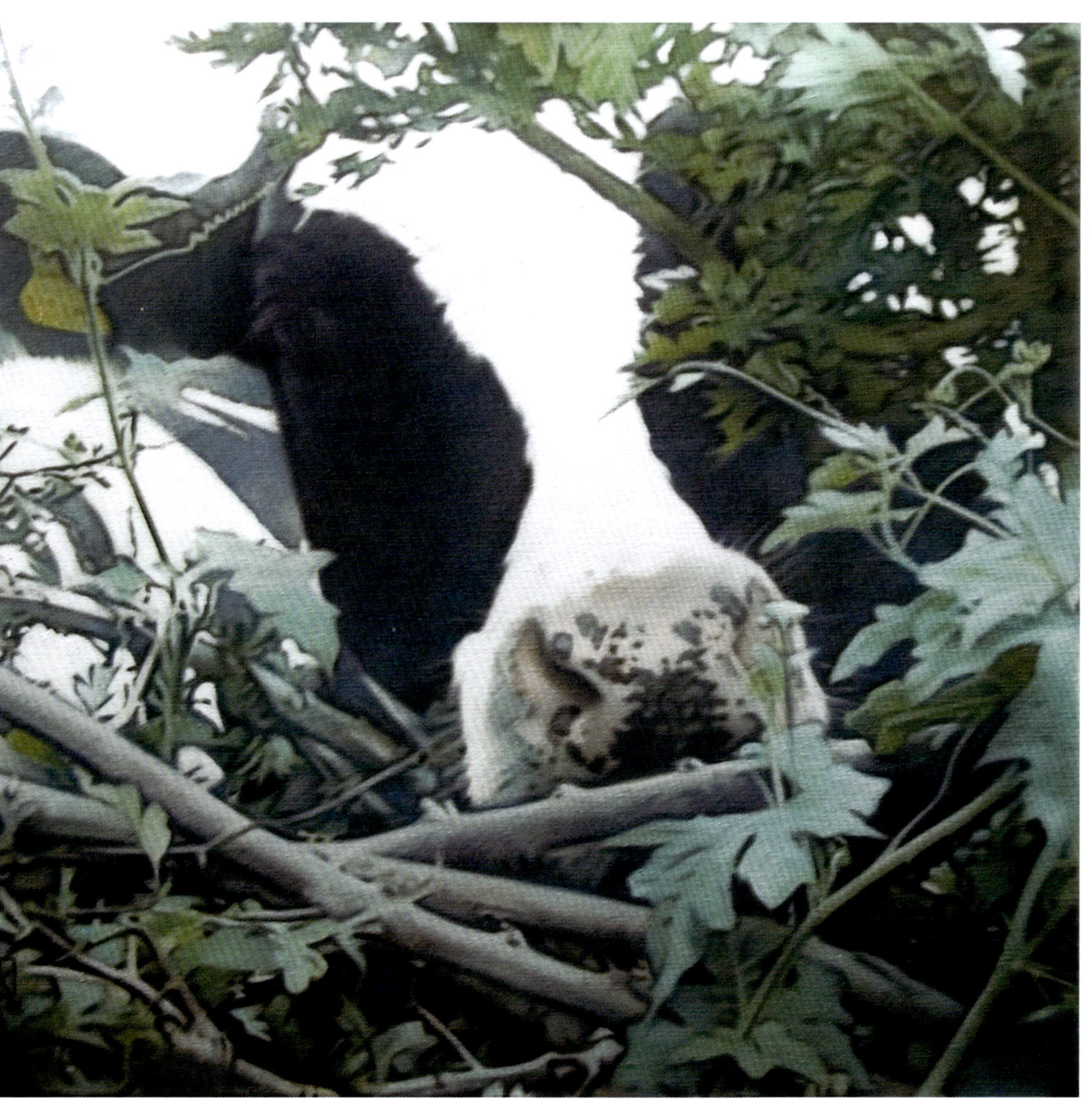

Cow, Hedge, Bryony (2009) Oil on Canvas 60 x 60cm

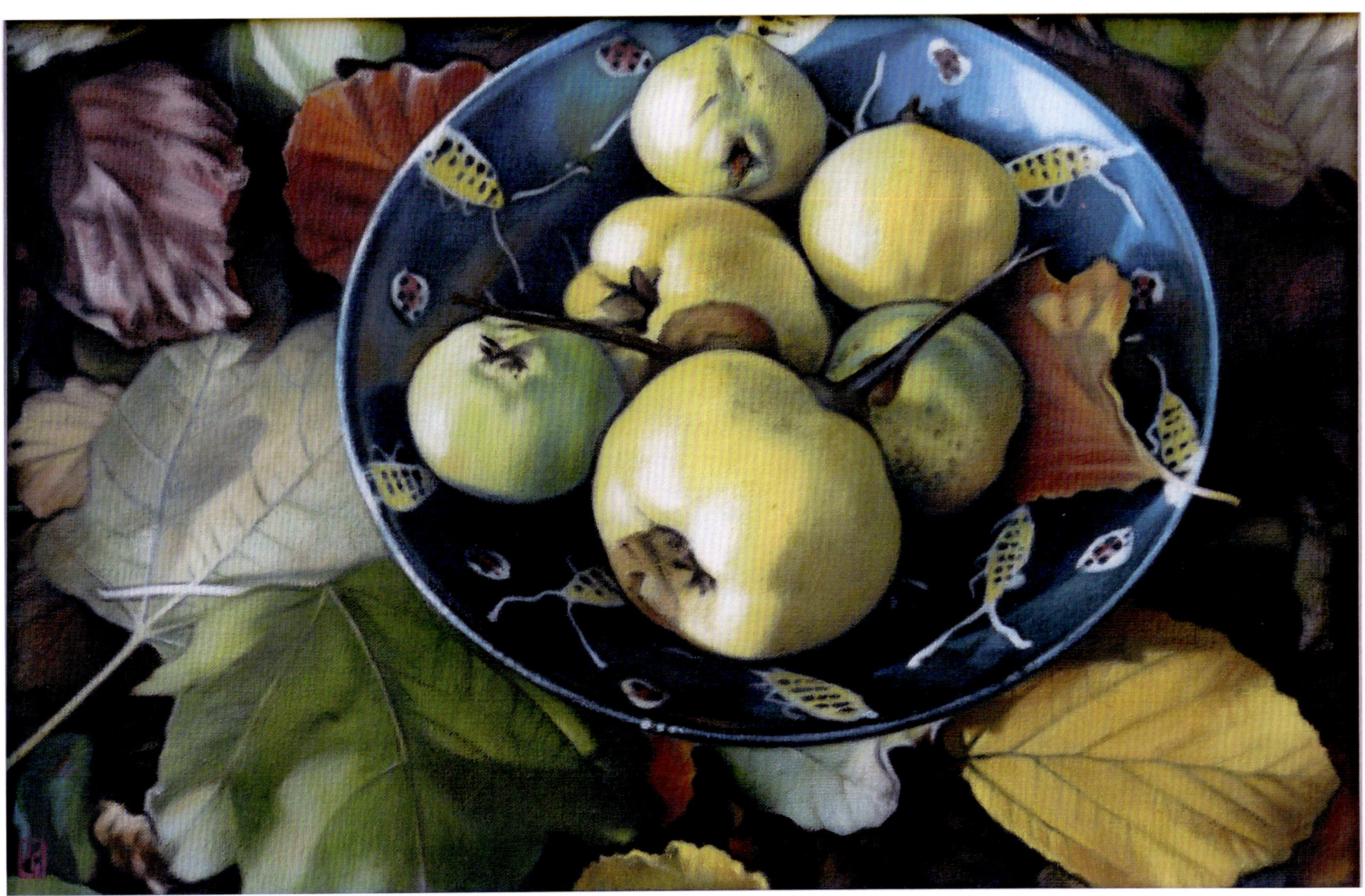

Quinces, Bowl, Leaves (2009) Oil on Canvas 40 x 60cm

Christine McKechnie NDD,SGFA

Christine's work is exceptional in the quality of her collage; one has to look hard to realise the pieces are not paintings or drawing. Making images and scenes using tiny scraps of paper, her talent is remarkable. Understated as an artistic medium, Christine takes collage to another dimension.
- Buckenham Galleries, Southwold, Suffolk

Christine McKechnie NDD, SGFA
Collage Artist
Southolt, Suffolk

I make water colour painted paper collages. I developed the technique in the United States in the late sixties when my oil paints and easel were impounded in a dock strike.

At the same time, being poor in an empty apartment, I made paper maché pots from the *New York Times*, and pieced quilts using fragments of Liberty lawn fabric brought from home, like the early settlers.

I hope that eventually my womanly skills will be recognised by a wider public.

I identify with Mary Delaney, a friend of Queen Charlotte, the wife of King George III. She embroidered her own court dresses, designed shell grottoes, and made botanic collages of plants collected abroad.

If God lives in Suffolk, he takes his holidays in Italy. *Amelia's Restaurant Montepecini* is a view from our holiday villa there. We used to walk to the nearby hill top village to have our supper at Amelia's restaurant.

Stream, Honister Pass, Lake District. I have gone to Seatoller in the Lake District annually, and the detailed drawing for this collage was done in stages before breakfast and a day's walking.

My daughter lived in Hong Kong for a while off Hollywood Road in the antique dealers' district. *Hong Kong At Night* is a view from her apartment.

Educated-
Kingston School of Art, London
Accreditation:
National Design Diploma (NDD), Kingston College of Art
Society of Graphics Art (SGFA)
Membership of Local Art Societies-
Artworks
Suffolk Open Studios
Website- www.christinemckechnie.co.uk

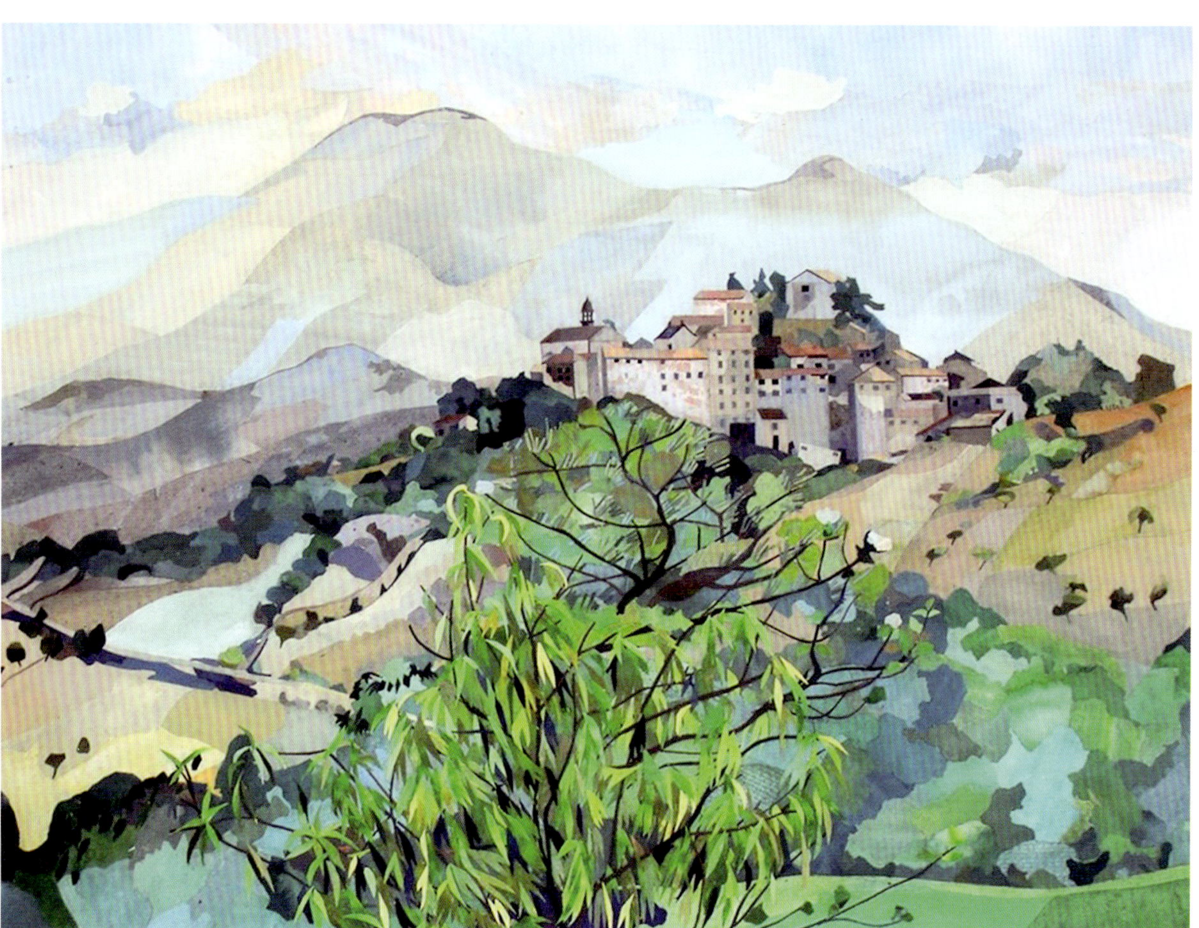

Amelia's Restaurant Montepecini (2002) Water Colour Painted Paper Collage 67 x 46cm

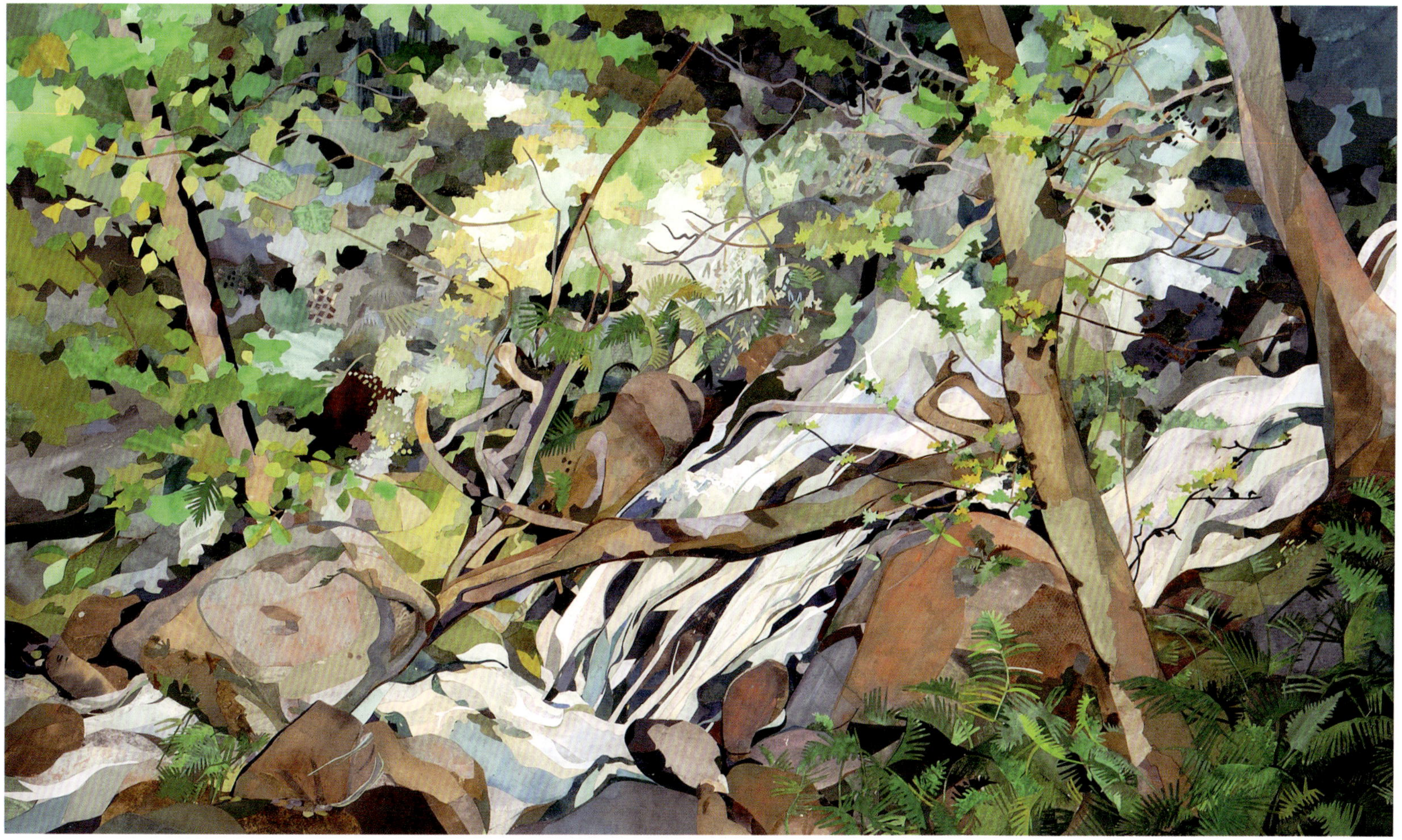

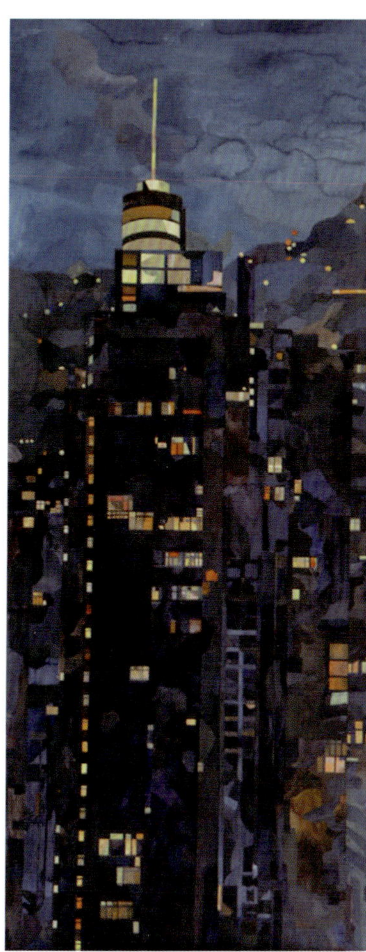

Stream, Honister Pass, Lake District (2000) Water Colour Painted Paper Collage 90 x 55cm

Hong Kong at Night (2010)
Water Colour Painted Paper Collage
37 x 78cm

Jonathan Trim

Jonathan's atmospheric landscapes expertly capture both the beauty of light and water in a variety of locations and the sense of emotion from being present in the moment.
- A2 Gallery, Wells, Somerset

Jonathan Trim
Painter
Leigh-on-Sea, Essex

My sketchbooks are the central inspiration for all my work. I carry one with me wherever I go. I spend a great deal of time walking and sketching in the landscape. The sketchbooks often contain notes about the sounds, smells and experiences of being in these locations. This working method creates for me deep feelings and a connection to the landscape.

The subsequent paintings are about these intense feelings of place, memory and existence.

Summer Stillness On The River Stour evokes the quiet solitude that can be found on the River Stour. The river catches the light and can be seen glistening through overhanging trees. It is also about the mystery of the riverbank. My practice is to create a foreground utilising materials found in the location. I have embedded these materials into the paint surface. These often include small stones, sand, crushed shells and small plant roots.

I have lived by the Thames Estuary all my life. It is an inspirational place for me with its ever-changing weather and skies. This presents a constant challenge for me. *Ebbing Tide Thames Estuary Chalkwell* shows an outgoing tide and the Kent coast seen across the river with the fields of Kent catching the light. The foreground shows the beach marked by countless footprints and above it all the sky marked with aircraft vapour trails.

East Anglia has always provided me with a rich source of subject matter. The reflective quality of light on water has been a constant fascination to me. *A Warm Day On The River* is about the wonderful light in the Stour valley. I often start these paintings out on location and finish them in the studio. The richly layered foreground gives way to the stillness and calm of a summer's day on the Stour.

Educated-
Leeds University (Huddersfield Polytechnic)
Post Grad Cert Art Education 1980
Membership of Local Art Societies-
Leigh Art Trail, Essex
Galleries Familiar With Artist's Work-
The Appleyard Gallery, Holt, Norfolk
Buckenham Galleries, Southwold, Suffolk
Back2thewall Gallery, Burnham-on-Crouch, Essex
Website- www.jonathantrim.com

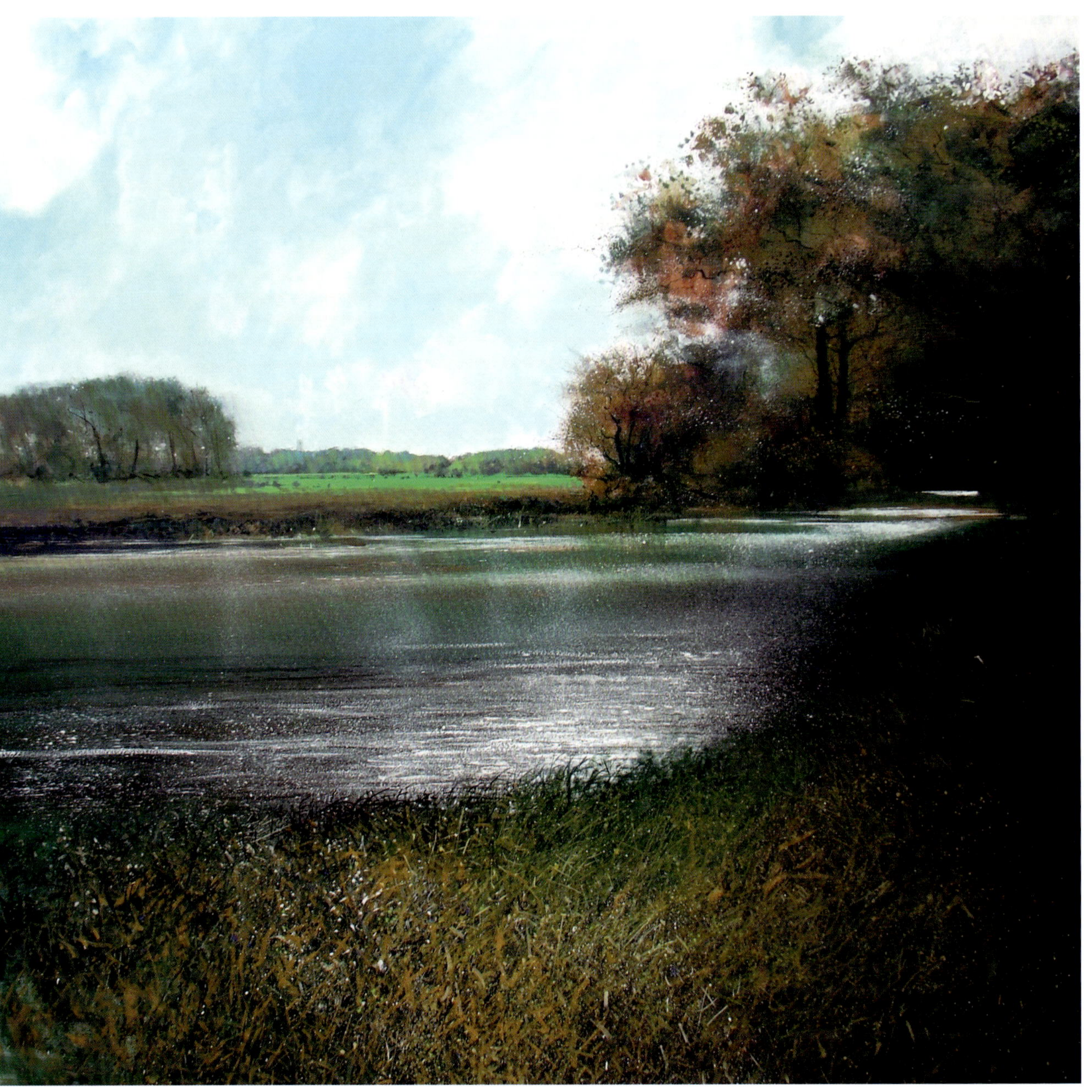

Summer Stillness On The River Stour (2010) Acrylic on Canvas 120 x 120cm

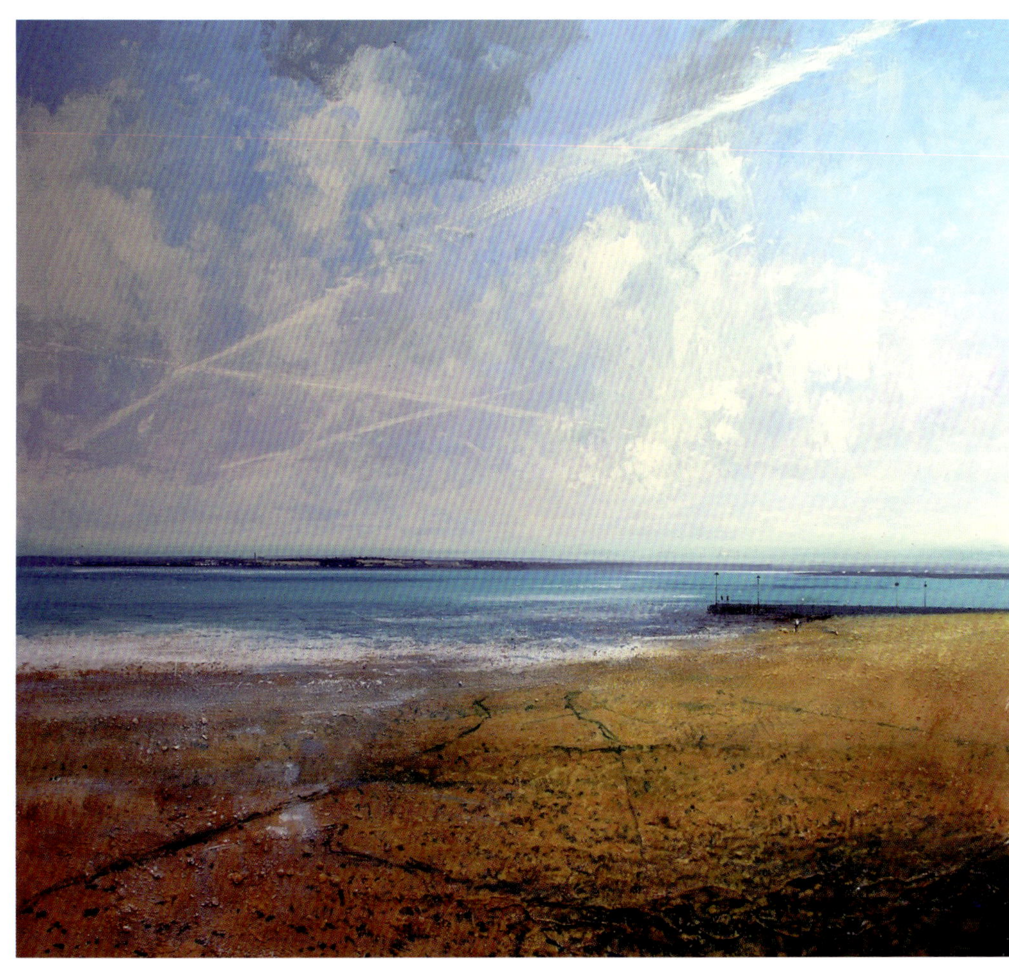

Ebbing tide Thames Estuary Chalkwell (2010) Acrylic on Canvas 120 x 120cm

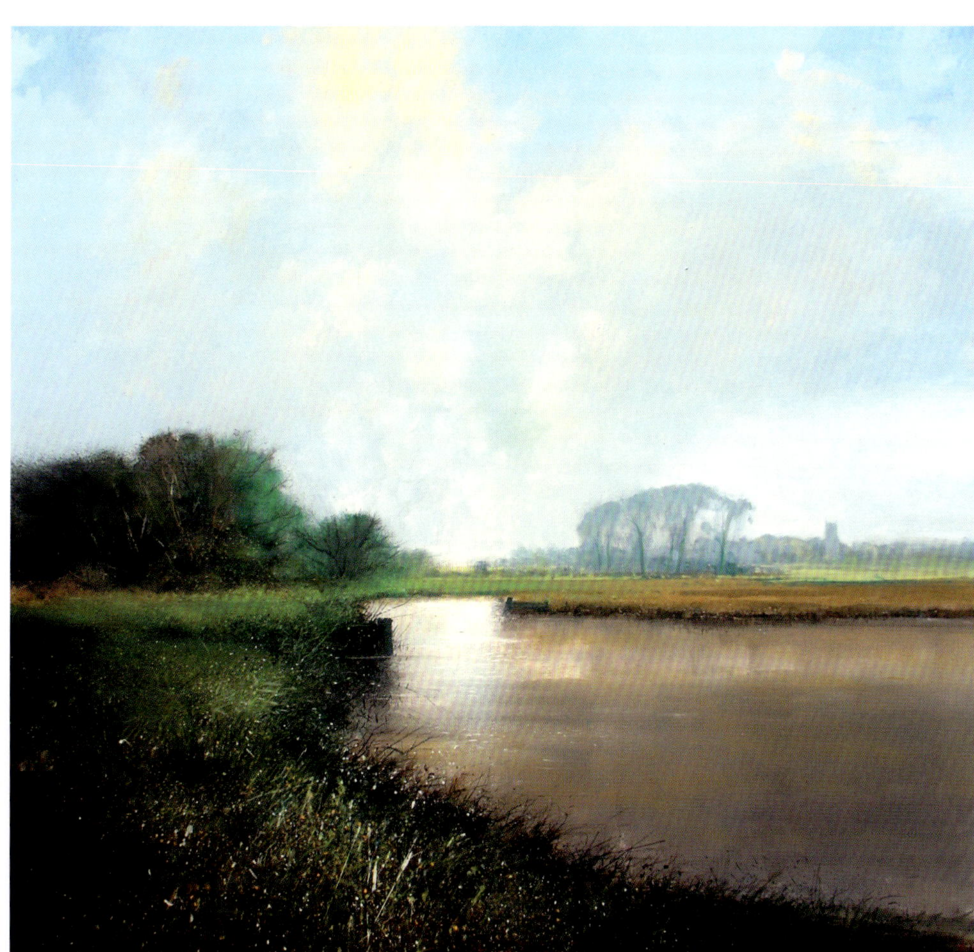

A warm day on the River (2010) Acrylic on Canvas 120 x 120cm

Mary Spicer BA

Mary Spicer BA
Painter
Ditchingham, Suffolk

Fields and footpaths surround me, always changing with light and weather, always posing questions and asking for a response. The Norwich School of Painters at the Castle Museum always help me in my search for a personal and contemporary understanding of landscape.

My last trips to London took in the latest David Tress exhibition, the Fleming Collection's show of Joan Eardley's work and the Courtauld Gallery - much inspiration to bring home.

In *Silent Twilight*, the snow created a blanket of silence. It had started to thaw but the sky still promised more. I walked for miles, taking photos and making hurried sketches. I've cycled past the red house hundreds of times and as dusk fell its warm colour glowed against the white snow, the fading light darkening the trees and hedgerows. Oil paint was the perfect medium for attempting to communicate what I had experienced.

Educated- Brighton Polytechnic, Faculty of Art and Design 1976
Membership of Local Art Societies-
The Norwich Twenty Group
Norfolk Contemporary Art Society
Galleries Familiar With Artist's Work-
John Russell Gallery, Ipswich, Suffolk
Cork Brick Gallery, Bungay, Suffolk

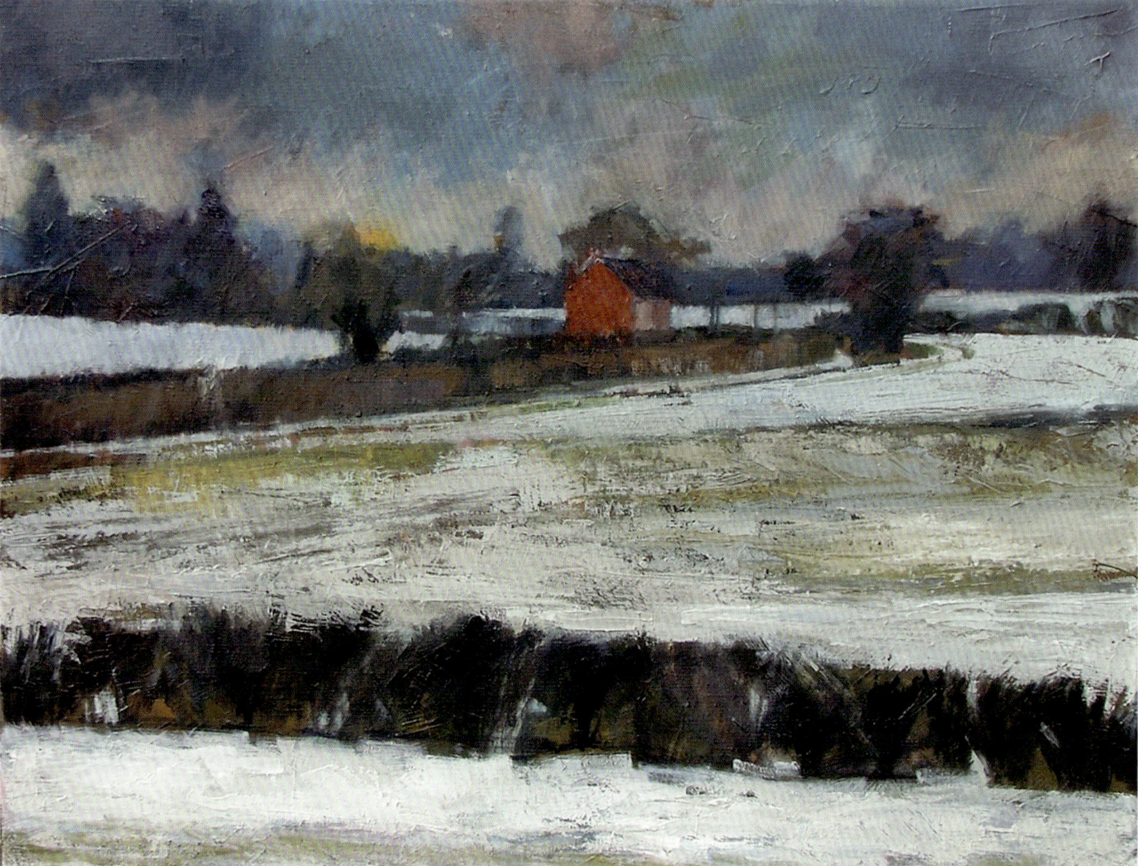

Silent Twilight (2009) Oil on Canvas 71 x 92 cm

Jennifer Mackay Windle PGE

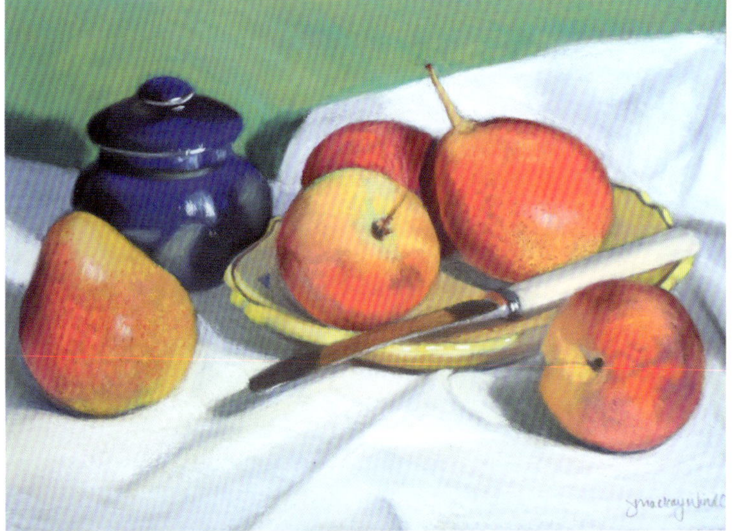

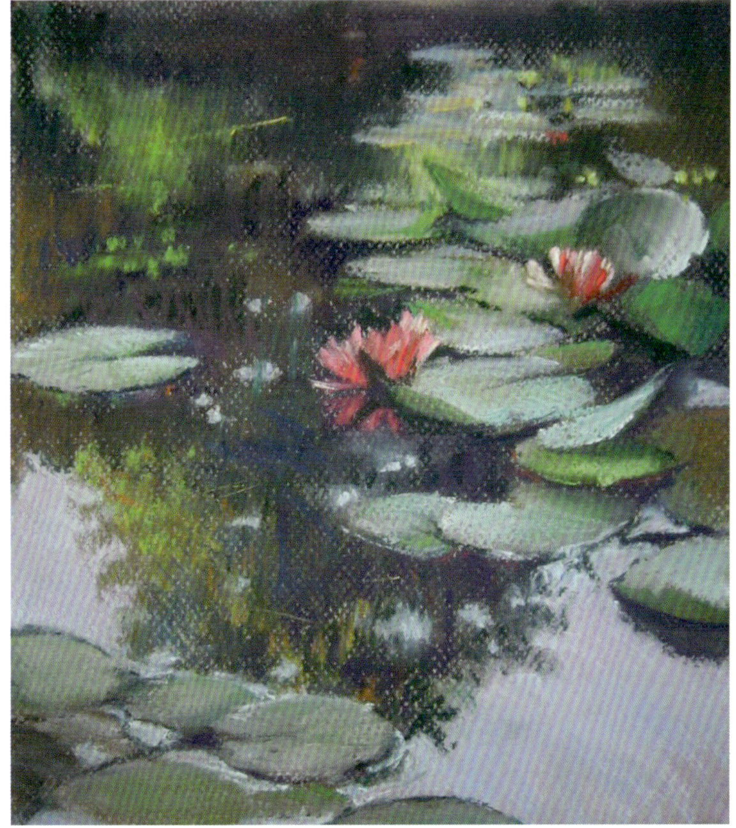

Top: *Still life with Pink Ladies and Knife (2008)* Pastel 22 x 24cm
Bottom: *Water Lilies, Evening at Giverny (2009)* Pastel 22 x 24cm

Jennifer Mackay Windle PGE
Painter
Leiston, Suffolk

My passion for painting comes from my emotional response to beauty, the effects of sunlight hitting a wheat field, intense colours of fruits and flowers or broad expanses of ocean and sky. Simple country villages in England and France also inspire me.

Significant influences on my style and subjects come from studying the great masters and the work of my great-great-great aunt, American Laura Coombs Hills (1859-1952), famous for her portraits and floral paintings in watercolour and pastel.

I want to describe the richness of colour, texture and form in a traditional way, emphasizing light and shadow dramatically. Pastels allow me to achieve this by the method of application, blending the pastel directly on the paper; vibrancy is maintained as the tones sparkle and complement one another. I trained as an oil painter but find pastels to be in my blood now and love creating with them. Portraits will be my next challenge.

Educated- Art Institute of Boston, Boston Massachusetts, USA
Membership of Local Art Societies-
East Suffolk Design and Fine Art Society (ESDFAS)
Accreditation With National Art Societies-
Pastel Guild of Europe
Galleries Familiar With Artist's Work-
Thompson's Gallery, Aldeburgh, Suffolk
Website- www.jennifermackaywindle.com

Doug Farthing MBE, AFAS, ISWA

Douglas's painting and drawing has a spontaneity that has come from a spirit to interpret and express the world around him. He records the conflict in the Middle East not just from a soldier's view but from an observer's view; the people, the land, everyday life in a very poor part of the world where violence can erupt at any moment.
- Mandell's Gallery, Norwich, Norfolk

Doug Farthing MBE, AFAS, ISWA
Painter
Lowestoft, Suffolk

I am inspired by all that I see, in particular the beauty within hardship.

I record war and the effects of war through my art. The landscape, people, equipment and soldiers - the emotions and the reality of a life.

Soldiers find themselves in a testing and exciting environment. I find it rewarding to draw the viewer into the situation, young men and women from both sides - the armies and civilian populations.

I feel great pleasure when, in my work, someone recognises a moment they have experienced in their own life.

Villagers look on as we inspect a well we hope to repair before leaving. The child in blue is so fascinated by me, as I am by him. In a heat of 43 degrees, the dust and extreme sunlight force me to work fast on the *Boy in Blue*. A light oil wash has been used for *Boy in Blue* and the natural wood of the ammo crate has been left raw to show the lightest lights. The texture of the crate somehow adds to the overall effect of this oil study.

A *Pony and Trap* pass us on the road to Peshawar. I love to work this way, picking up materials at hand; the cartridge box was emptied about two hours before and the rounds placed into my magazines. A quick drawing using Indian ink. Seizing the situation and moment, instant lights and dark capture the energy. Using this medium is second to none.

Quickly I capture the instant a soldier has been shot. The team behind close in with the enemy before returning to treat the soldier for his injuries. The *Drawing from War Diary: Man down, green zone Helmand, Afghanistan* encapsulates all that it is to be a soldier under fire – the energy, the momentum of moving forward. My aim is to place the viewer into a sudden life or death situation and to draw from them an emotion of fear combined with excitement.

The soldier injured on the ground in some ways may be the lucky one? The others are moving into unknown territory.

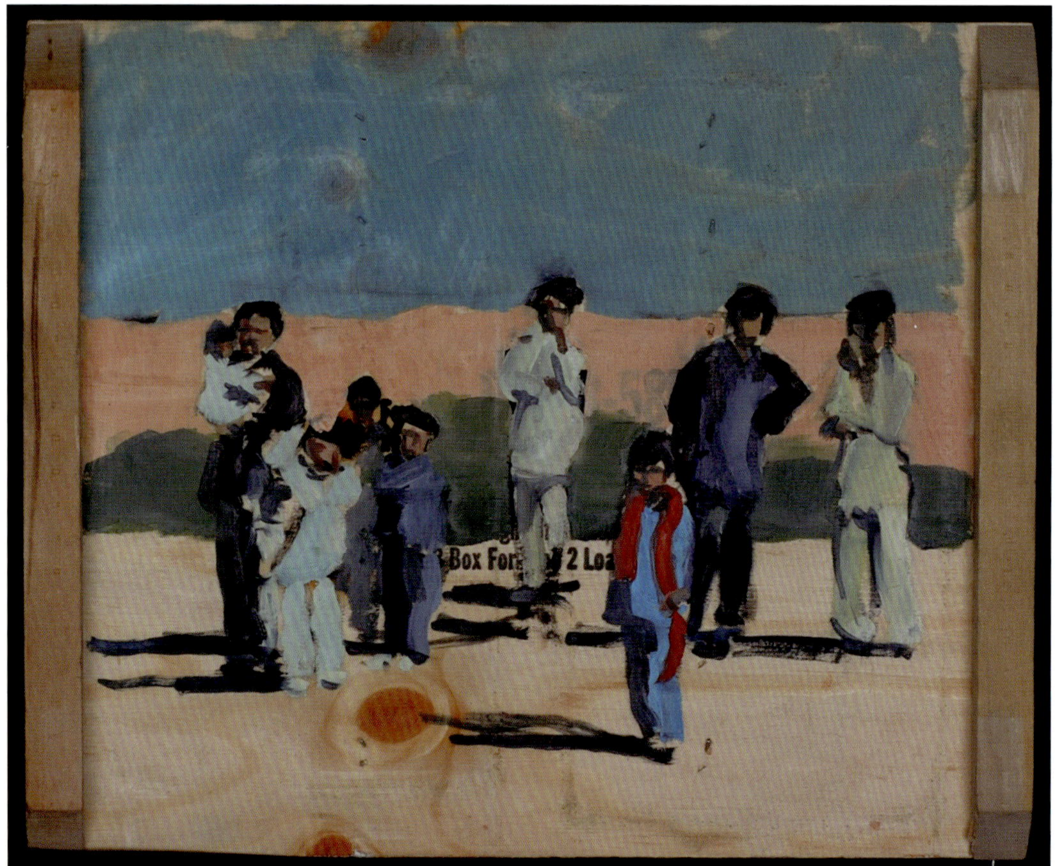

Boy in Blue (2010) Oil on Wood (Wooden Ammo Box) 31 x 36.5cm

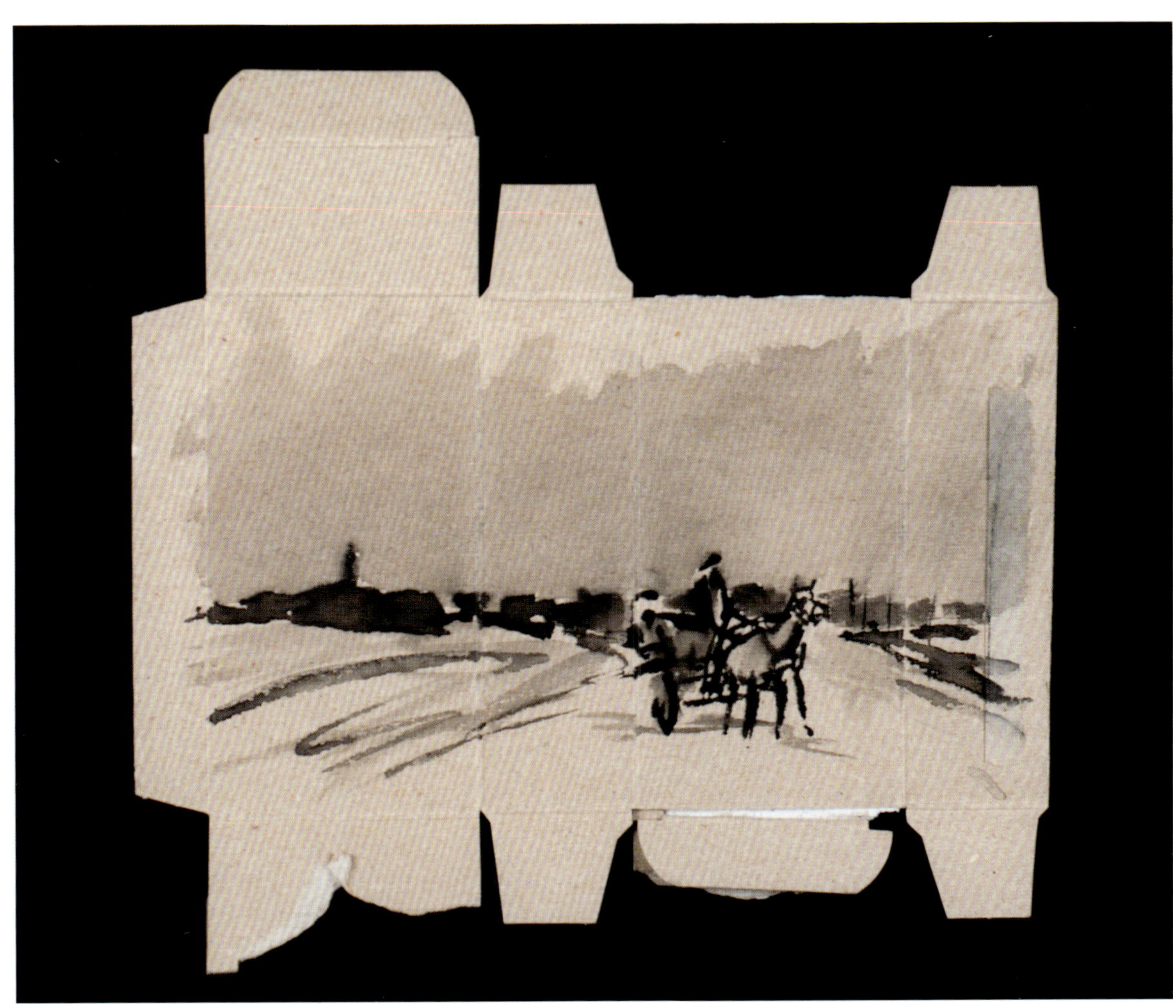

Pony and Trap (2010)
Indian ink on Cardboard (Cartridge Box) 10.5 x 17.5cm

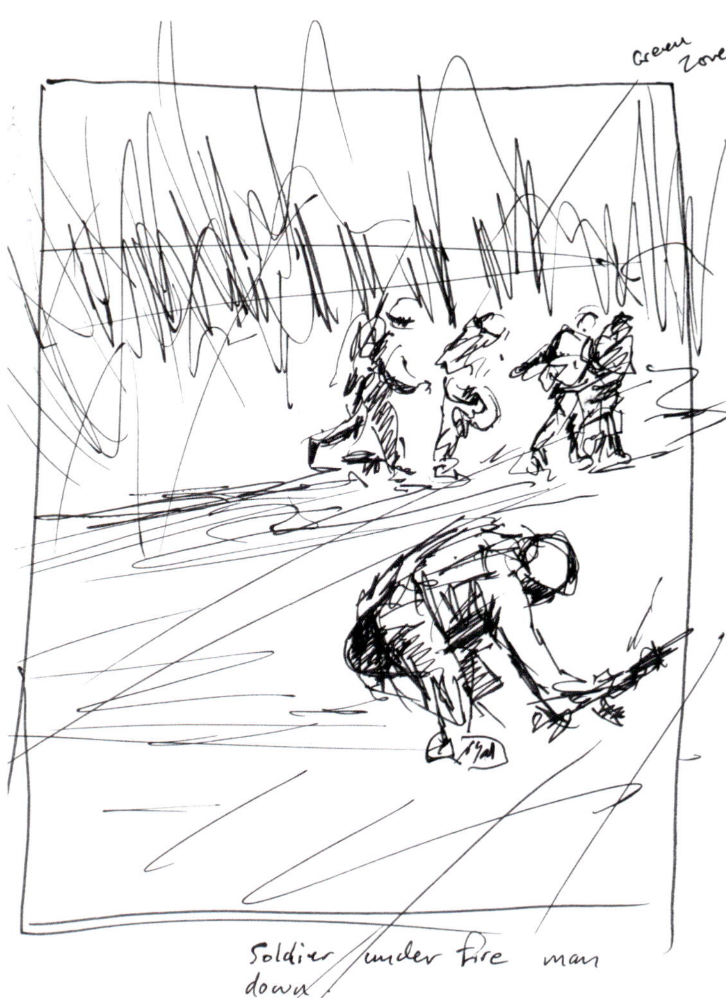

Drawing from War Diary: Man Down, Green Zone Helmand, Afghanistan (2010)
Pen on Paper 20.5 x 15cm

55

Doug Farthing: Behind the Scenes

More about:

Doug....

Educated- No formal art school tuition
Accreditation With National Art Societies-
AFAS Armed Forces Art Society
ISWA International Society of War Artists
Galleries Familiar With Artist's Work-
Mandell's Gallery, Norwich, Norfolk
Ferini Art Gallery, Pakefield, Suffolk
Collections (Open To The Public)-
The Fourth Man National Army Museum, London
Pump House Contact National Army Museum, London
3 PARA SFSG Afghanistan National Army Museum, London
Tank Park Iraq National Army Museum, London
Website- www.douglasfarthingart.com

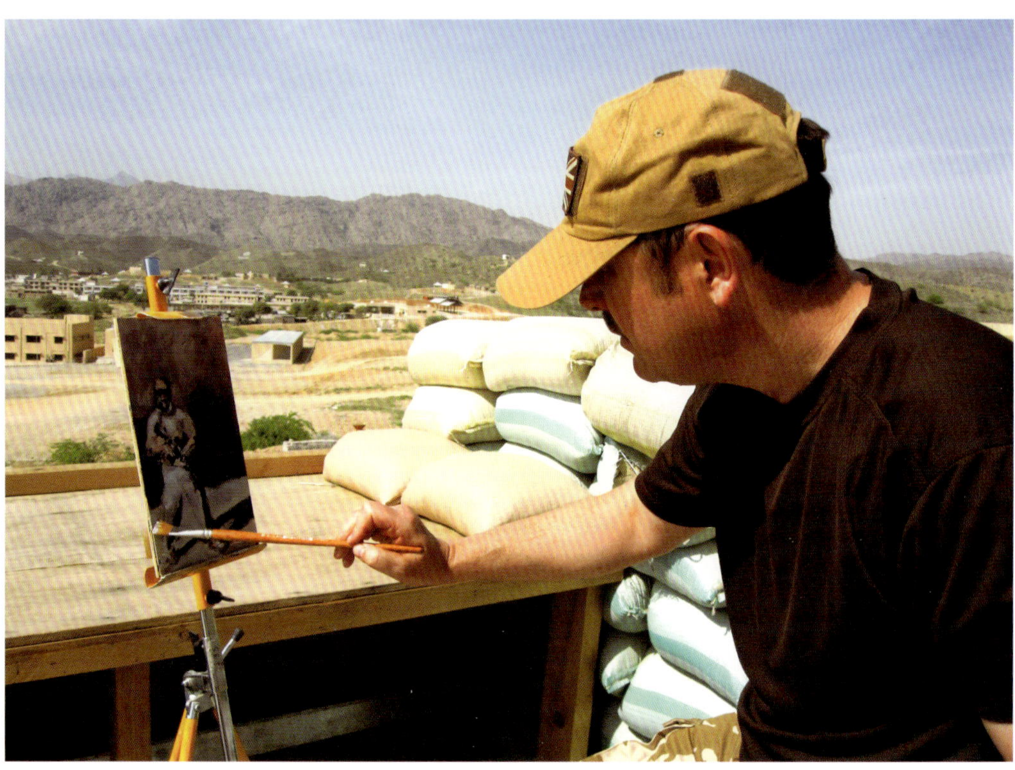

Mostly I will be away in a war zone, recording and painting everything I see. My studio at war is unpredictable - I've been in bombed-out buildings, on school rooftops, in bunkers and trenches.

When asked for commissioned work I'm often 'looked after', normally working in more comfortable surroundings, courtesy of a brigade commander.

All I require is the inspiration which I can find all over the battlefield; the hardships and austere environment aid my painting or sketches.

When working I will collect materials for the piece - this could be wooden ammo boxes, ration packs or just cardboard for my canvas. Or if I have time, I'll prepare a rabbit skin-cured canvas.

I'll produce many studies of the same subject finding, more often than not, the best composition by accident. I'll work, sometimes cleaning off the complete painting at the end of the day with turps.

My favourite pieces can happen in 10 minutes, after days at the easel.

I am always confident to succeed, and set myself up for success. Sometimes I find a weakness in my technical ability but this is soon overcome by hard work and trial and error. If it works, I will walk away - even if the piece is not finished. The next day I look again and generally I am happy to leave the painting alone. If not, it all comes off with turps and I'll start again.

This Page: Douglas painting
Opposite Page: Douglas in a war zone

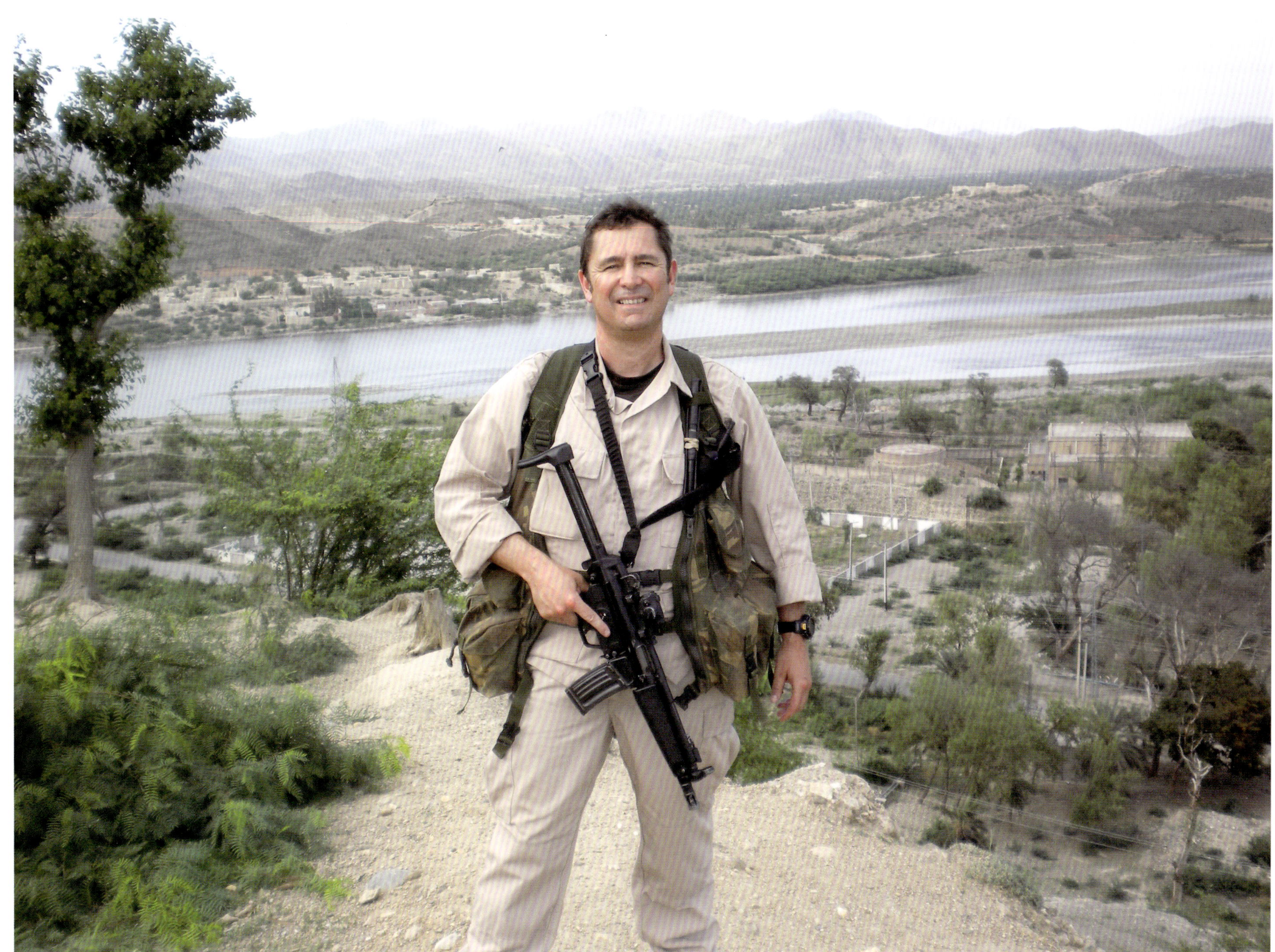

Nicola Slattery BA

Nicola expresses herself both through painting in acrylics and dry point prints. The subjects are fanciful and idiosyncratic; a source of an individual imagination. Her dry point prints - exquisitely engraved on a Perspex sheet, printed and hand coloured - are smaller but nonetheless as evocative and curious as the paintings. Living locally, it is always exciting to see Nicola's new productions.
- Cork Brick Gallery, Bungay, Suffolk

Nicola Slattery BA
Painter and Printmaker
Harleston, Norfolk

Described as 'haunting and surreal', I hope my work is like reading a random page in a gripping novel, you want to know more but instead of turning pages, you turn over your imagination.

A strong sense of narrative is my aim whilst never telling the whole story. Viewers share imagined moments portrayed in a picture but remain free to create their own beginnings and endings according to what they see. Ambiguity is deliberate.

In the painting *A House for Me,* I see the child in the picture anticipating the time when she must leave her childhood home. She hopes to have her own house in which she can create a secure home.

With my painting *Tipping the Balance*, I am expressing how many people feel when experiencing the legal system. Ordinary people can feel small and powerless and this judge appears to have the ability to tip the scales. I have no personal experience of this, it is just the impression I sometimes get from the news.

The painting *Good Company* symbolises a journey searching for peace and serenity. Perhaps it's about drifting towards sleep or maybe its about hoping for changes to happen in life. There are no oars or rudder on the boat, just a sheep for good company.

Educated- Coventry Art School 1986
Galleries Familiar With Artist's Work-
i2art, Saffron Walden, Essex
Cork Brick Gallery, Bungay, Suffolk
Cambridge Contemporary Art, Cambridge
Collections (Open To The Public)-
A Greek Tragedy Bedfordshire County Council, Bedfordshire;
Hel Norfolk Contemporary Art Society, Norwich;
Gathering Fish, Market Street; and *TrollCart* JD Wetherspoon plc, Gt. Yarmouth, Norfolk;
Happy Ever After Queen Elizabeth II Law Courts, Birmingham;
Beauty Knows No Pain Leicester Collection for Schools, Leicester;
Quietly Sleeping; Nurture and Grow Barlow Lyde & Gilbert, London
Website- www.nicolaslattery.com

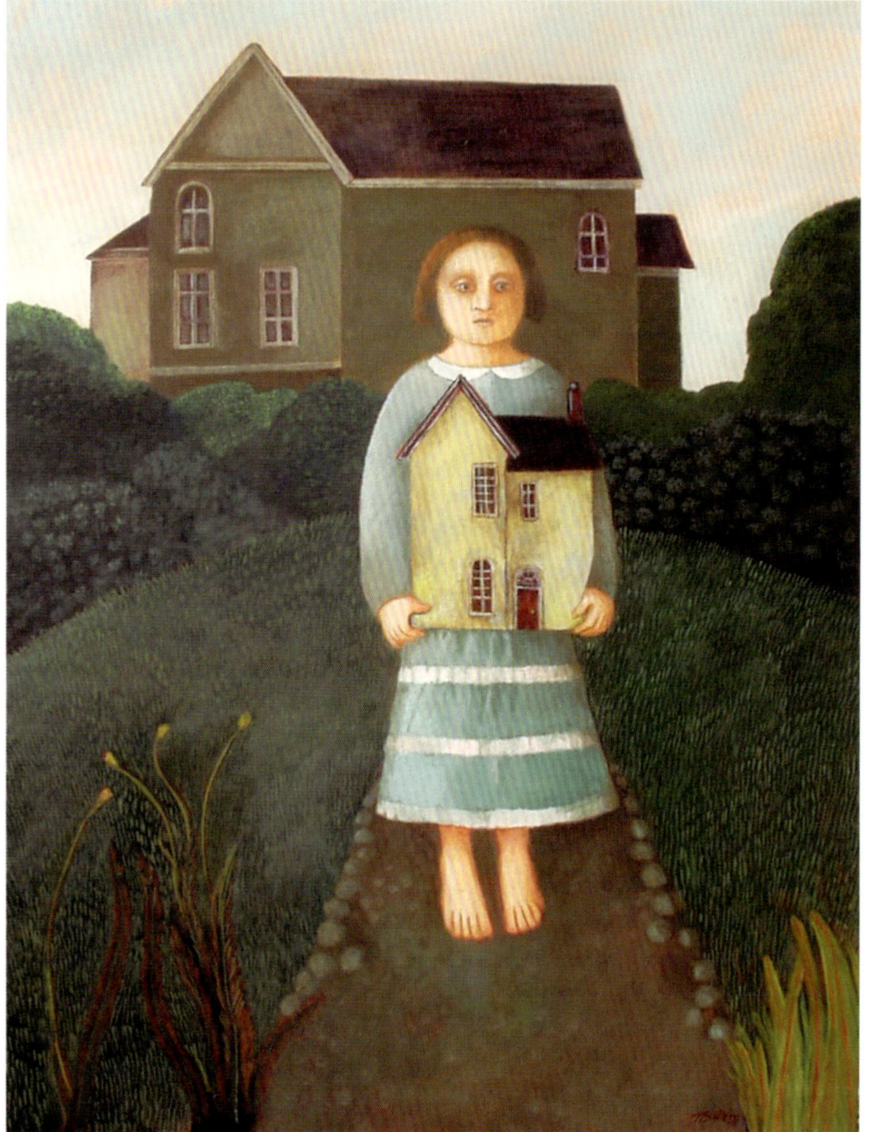

A House for Me (2010) Acrylic on Board 58 x 43cm

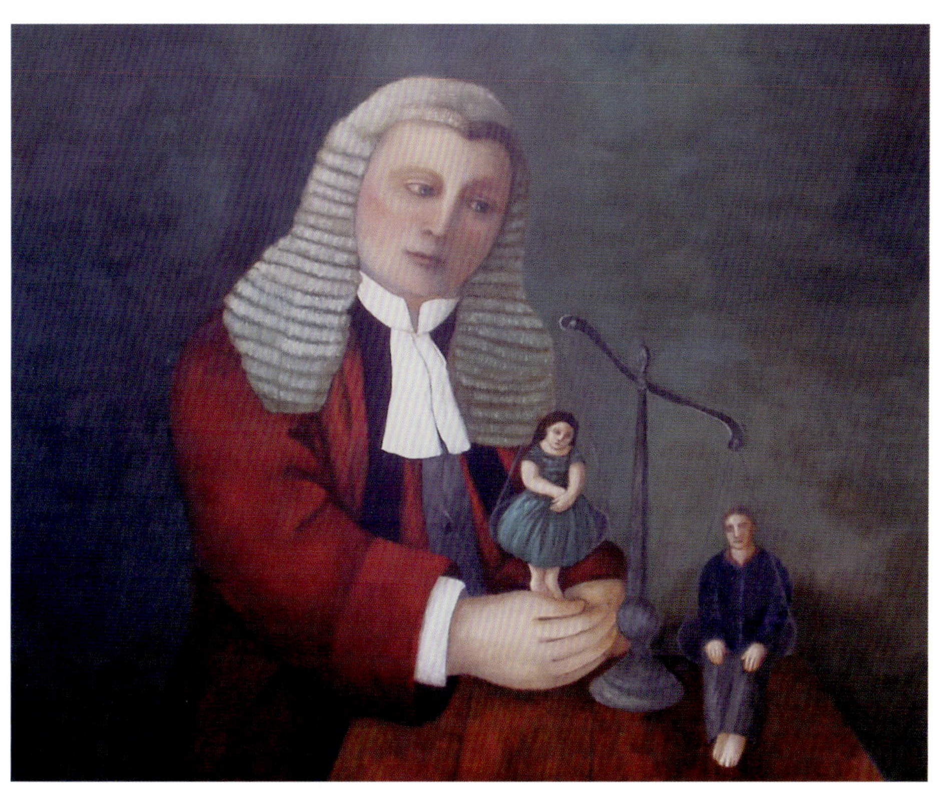

Tipping the Balance (2010) Acrylic on Board 60 x 70cm

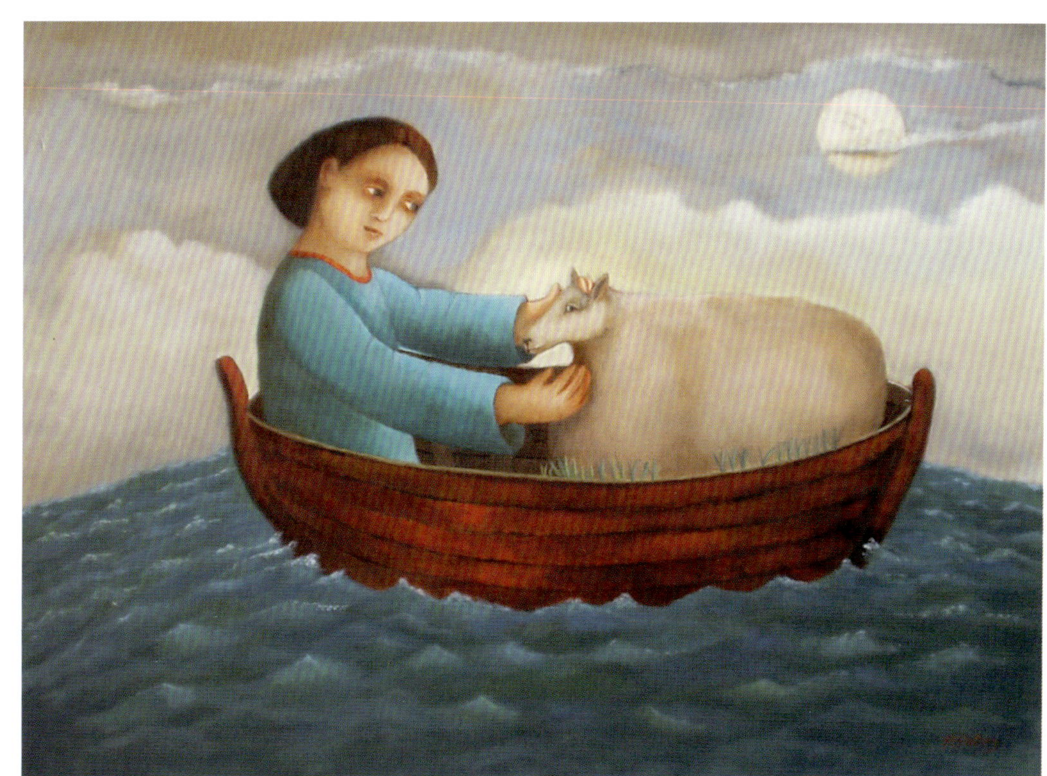

Good Company (2010) Acrylic on Board 46 x 61cm

Sarah Baddon Price BA (Hons)

The appeal of Sarah's work lies not just in the dichotomy she creates, but in the way that each piece feels complete but with the power to intrigue.
- The Frame Workshop, Ipswich, Suffolk

Sarah Baddon Price BA (Hons)
Painter
Ipswich, Suffolk

Each painting is a visual snapshot of a particular relationship, experience or journey; often with the title being suggestive of the source. Initially I cover the entire canvas with a chosen colour. Secondly I paint a horizon line, essentially creating a landscape which acts as a frame work within which I can create. At the onset, the end point is a complete unknown, spontaneously I draw with paint, then over-paint or sponge off all that is displeasing to my eye, whilst the rest remains. It is common practice for me to have to live with the painting in my peripheral vision for prolonged periods before the next 'move' reveals itself, it can be a time-consuming endeavour.

After Easter was painted after a trip to Scotland where I spent time hill walking with my two daughters. In essence it is a very feminine study both visually and metaphorically. The female figure evolved from quick sketches of tiny religious Goddess icons that caught my eye on a visit to the Sainsbury Centre prior to our departure – these were collected by Lady Sainsbury and are some of the oldest artefacts in the entire collection. The bowl represents another figure or vessel, in this case an absent friend. This painting is an exploration of the relationship/distance between these two elements.

Lewis is an abstract expressionist portrait of my son. The representational form of the yellow 'L' has been turned upside down; when he applies himself Lewis really can do things standing on his head. The painting, like the person, has a clear, bright surface resonance, juxtaposed by a concealed darker/deeper layer of passions which is closely guarded, only revealed by looking through the arrowslit, like those of ancient castles.

Interdict ostensibly represents the magnetism and dynamism present in a prohibited relationship. *Interdict* was painted during the aftermath of a painful separation. I deliberately selected an autumnal palette, offsetting this against vibrant blues. This painting handles one of my recurring themes where I explore the interconnection of two individual sculptural figures and at the same time create an over all portrait. Ephemeral expression provides an overview where art imitates life.

Educated- Winchester School of Art, BA (Hons) 1988
Galleries Familiar With Artist's Work-
The Frame Workshop & Gallery, Ipswich, Suffolk
The Pin Mill Studio, Ipswich, Suffolk
Website- www.sarahbaddonprice.co.uk

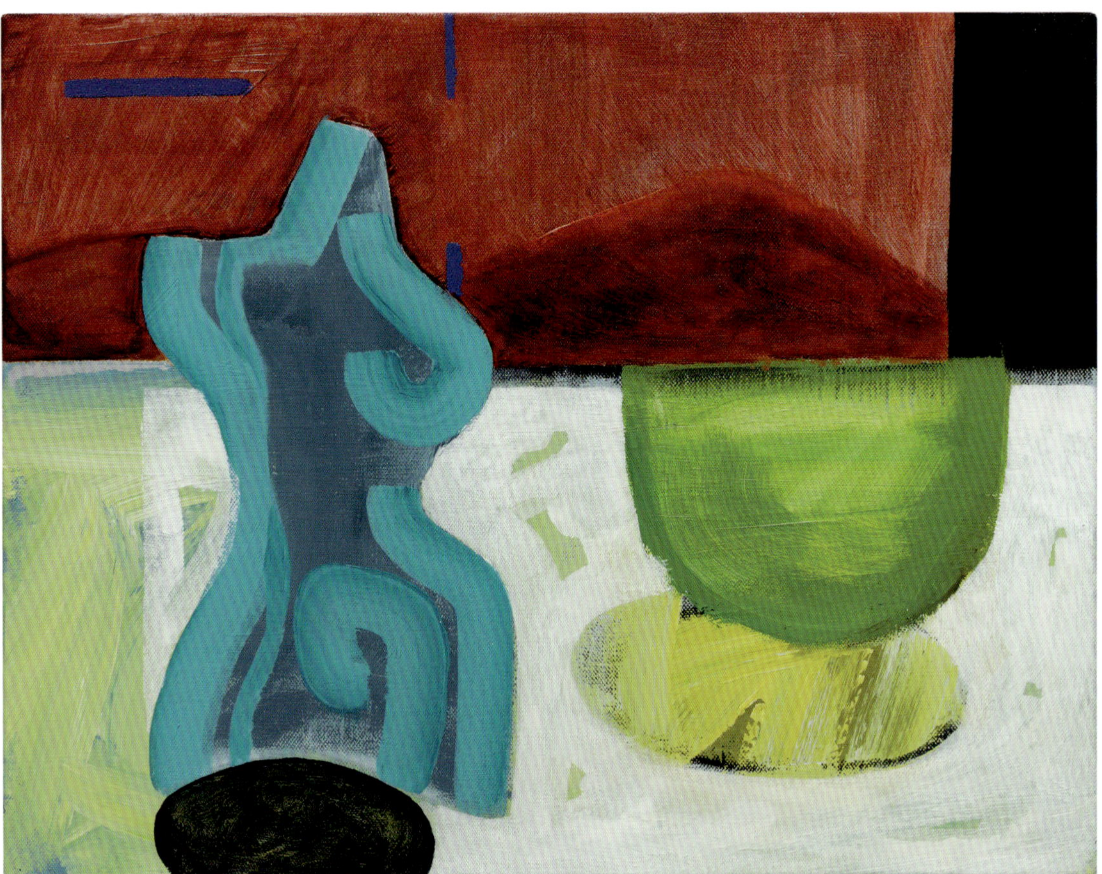

After Easter (2009) Acrylic on Canvas 41 x 51cm

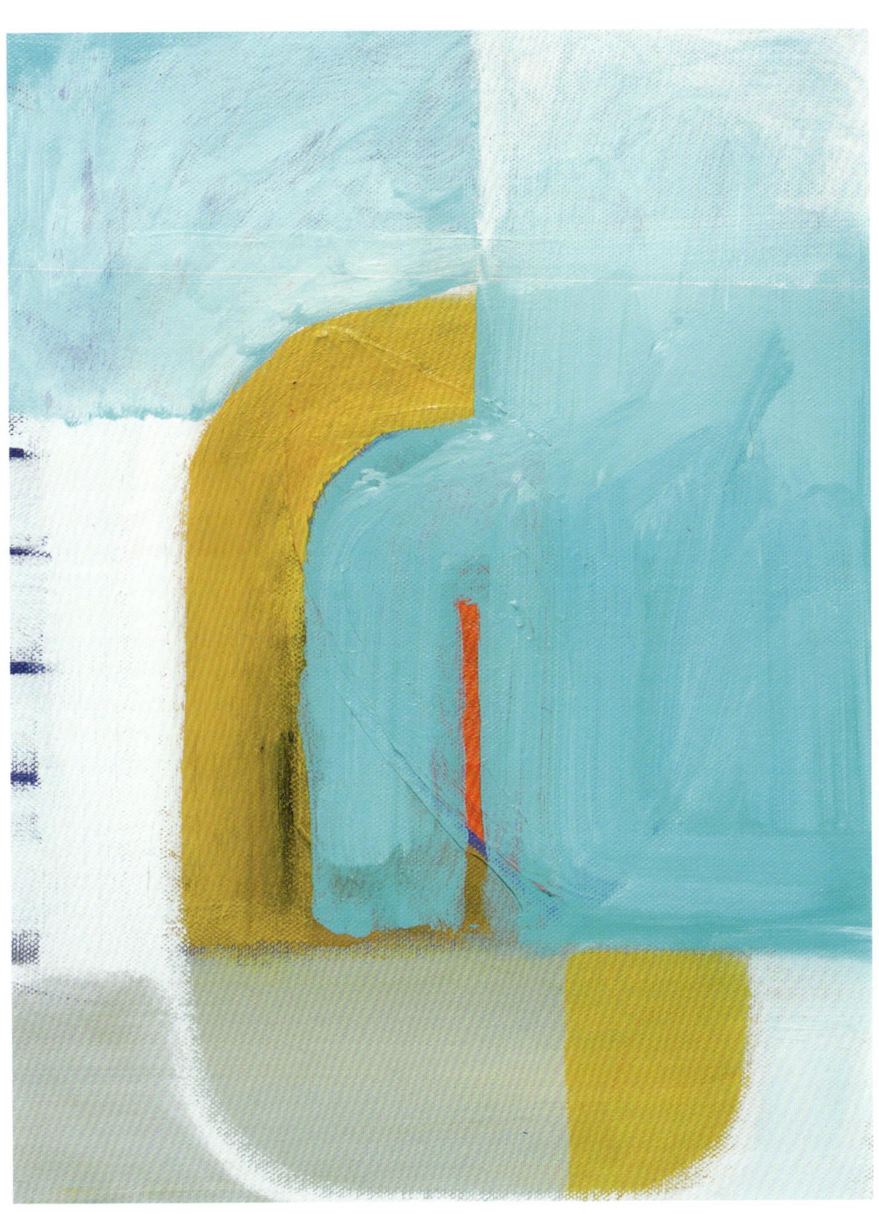

Lewis (2009) Acrylic on Canvas 35 x 25cm

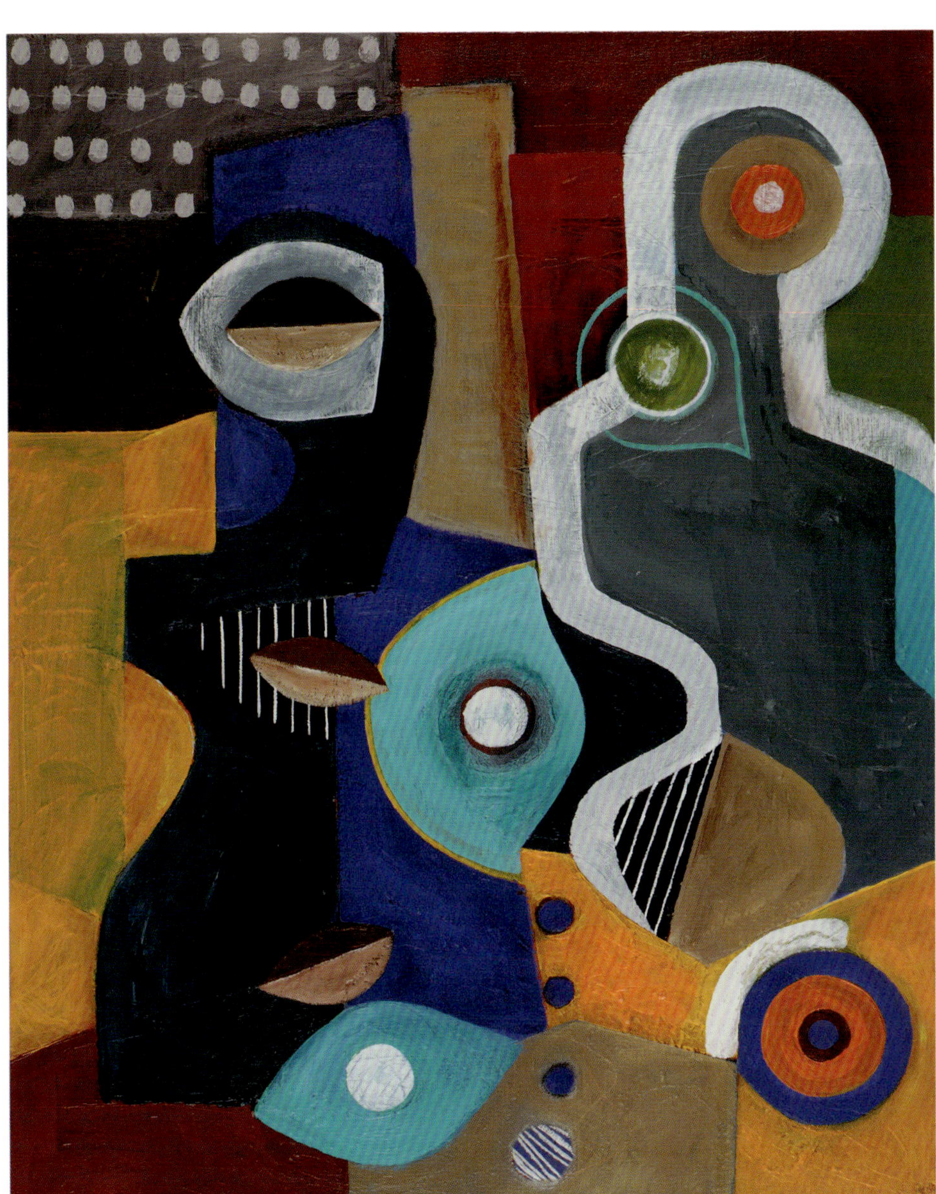

Interdict (2006) Acrylic on Canvas 90 x 70cm

Ruth McCabe

Ruth McCabe
Painter and Wire Sculptor.
Wenhaston, Suffolk

The grasses and wildflowers in my grandfather's meadow seemed, when I was very small, as tall as me. Their gentle, fragrant memory provides solace still, and may hint at the source of joyful connection I feel now with the Suffolk agricultural landscape which I love to paint in all seasons.

Animals have also always provided warm attachment figures and my affection for them materialises in paintings of the lovely weighty bodies of ewes. Artists who work towards abstraction and use colour beautifully are my inspiration.

June Garden is an abstract and much-loved painting which expresses my joy and gratitude for the zingy limes and soft rosiness of the June garden and for the indomitable return to a fullness of life that is so evident each year in the natural world.

My experience of human life is of too much wrongness, whether in the form of greed or unkindness. The wrens who have chosen to raise their chicks in our honeysuckle right now are, without knowing it, making life worthwhile.

I am very pleased with the free style of *Spring Surge*, a response to the relief that fine weather brought this Spring. I really felt part of a tremendous upsurge of energy and enjoyed making quick sweeps of paint over the surface. This painting depicts the Blyth Valley - the landscape on my doorstep - its colours and shapes are inside me in such a way that they just emerge.

Following on from *Coastal Landscape,* a bright, summery series in which I used strong colour, *In Shadow* was at first very red! But the more I worked with colour, the more the red felt wrong. It was hard to achieve a balance, something that I think reflects the struggle of winter: so dark and cold. What a relief to find the light, pleasing pale yellows balanced by shadowy blues.

Membership of Local Art Societies- Southwold Art Circle;
Suffolk Open Studios
Galleries Familiar With Artist's Work-
Buckenham Galleries, Southwold, Suffolk
Appleyard, Holt, Norfolk
Reunion, Felixstowe, Suffolk
Website-www.ruth-mccabe-artist.co.uk

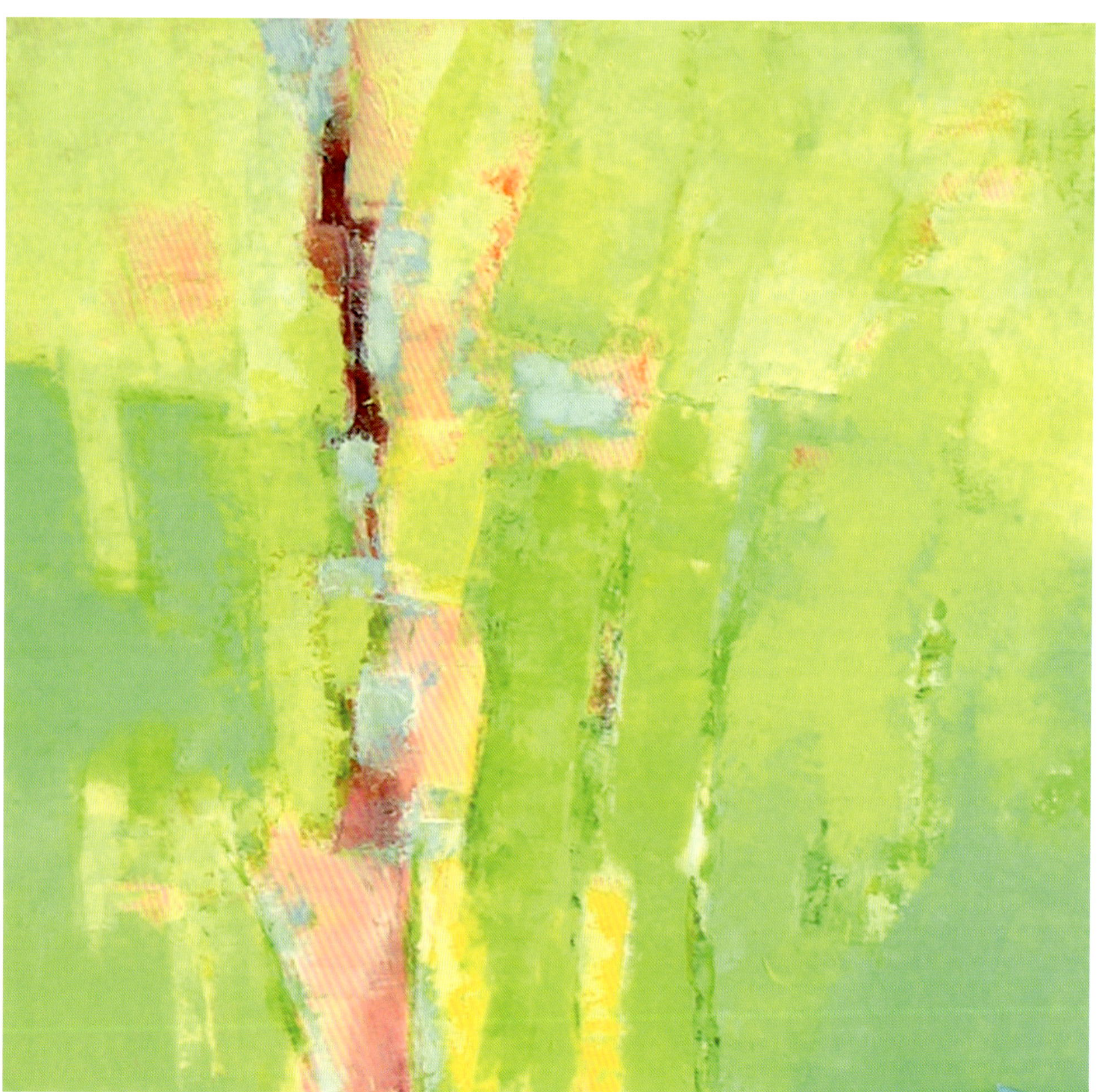

June Garden (2009) Oil on Canvas 40 x 40cm

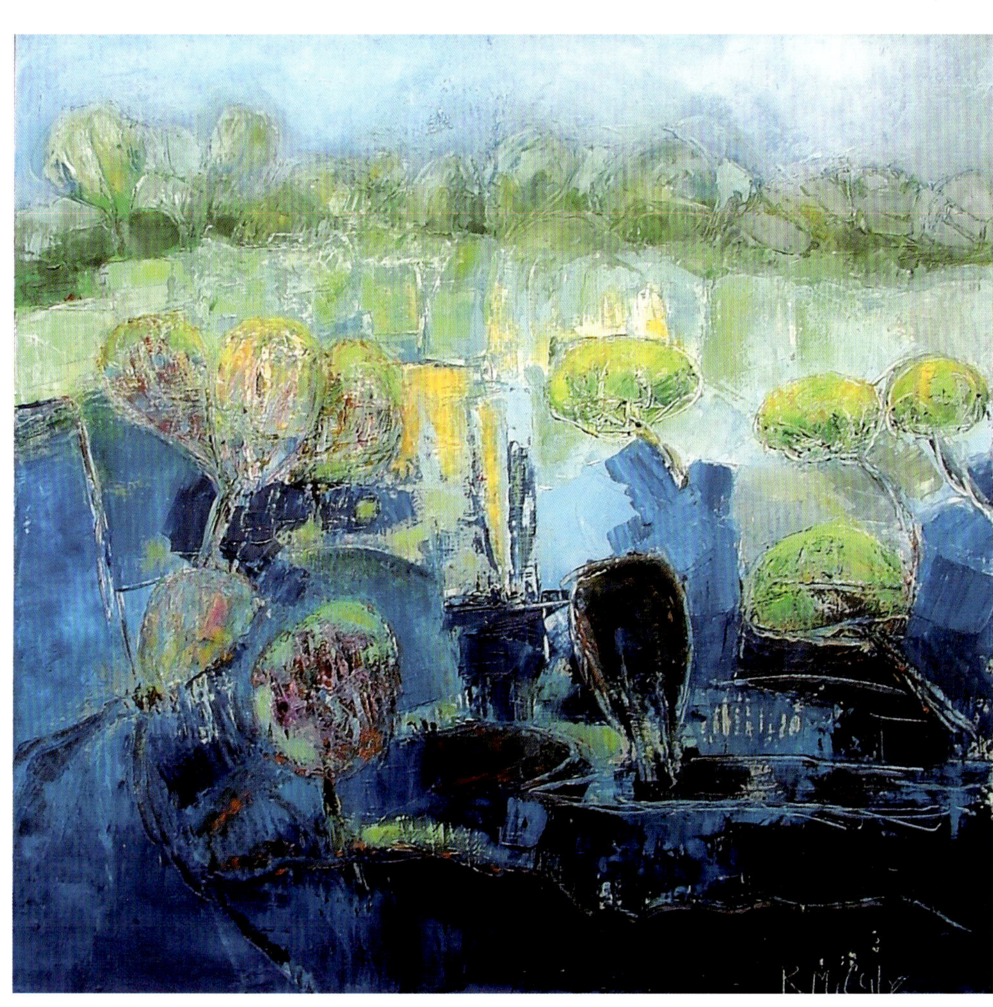

Spring Surge (2010) Oil on canvas 50 x 50cm

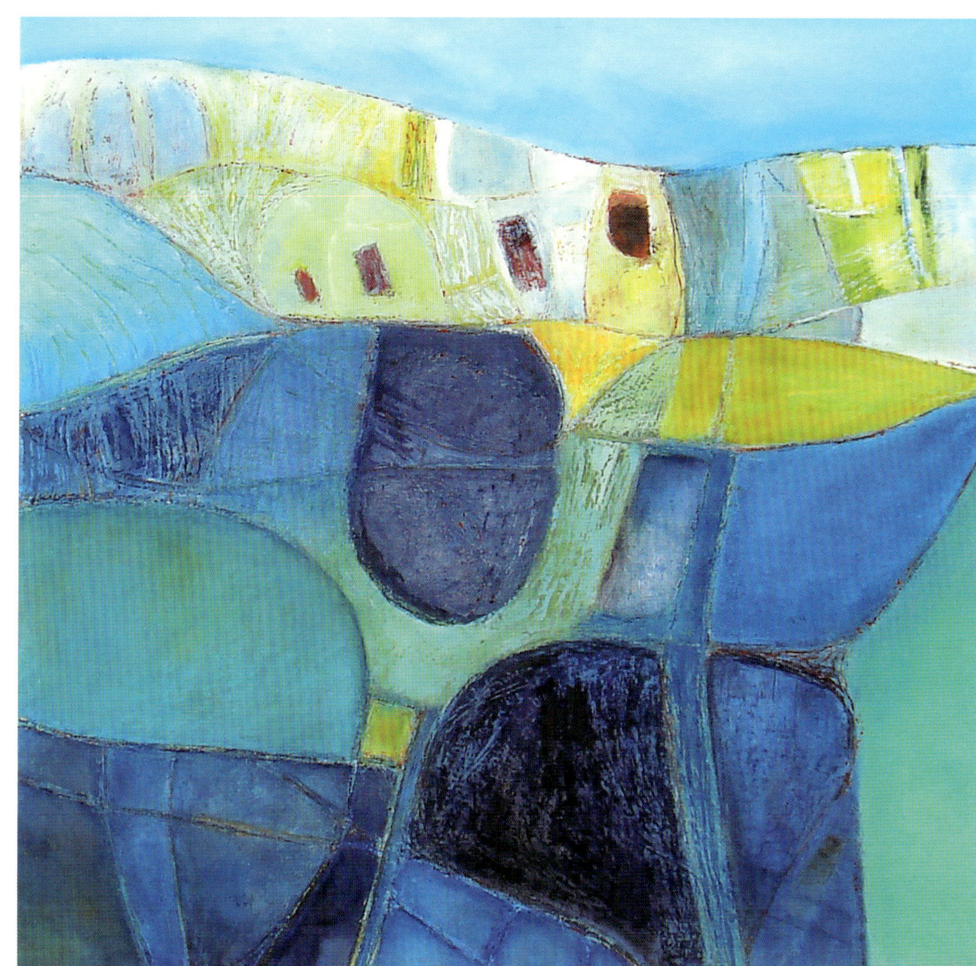

In Shadow (2010) Oil on Canvas 60 x 60cm

Tom de Freston

Tom de Freston
Painter
Cambridge

64

I am a contemporary history painter. My work draws from the grand art historical traditions of classical antiquity, the Italian Renaissance, the French Academy and Modernism. My references are resituated into dystopian environments, with a tendency for the tragic comic.

The Fitzwilliam Museum and the National Gallery are favourite haunts, with the works of Titian, Poussin and Rembrandt being particular favourites.

In *Jesus Christ, 'Nothing Martyrs Anymore'*, I want the work to feel like Michelangelo's *Last Judgement* has been devoured and then excreted in a new zombified form. A camp Jesus hovers amongst an apocalyptic mass of fallers whose grandeur is stripped by the geometry of their order; more 'William Morris wallpaper' than 'Milton's Fall of the Rebel Angels'. The foreground is littered with nods to Martyrs across History, all told in lurid, melodramatic reds.

Mr. Gandia uses the cold view of crime scene investigation photography.

Traditionally, painting has looked to depict dramatic moments in flux. In this case the moment of violent drama has clearly passed. Instead we are left to ask what has happened here, when and why? Our inability to find any answers or solutions is intended to leave us with a sense of emptiness.

Fallen Man gives a clear nod to Robert Capa's most iconic photograph. It is a work which examines the nature of tragedy in painting, the play between the illusion of a certain ideal and its inevitable failure.

'For all their challenging and sometimes disturbing flourishes, these canvasses invite us to recognise ourselves in them, in all our moments of heroism and vulnerability, triumph - and failure.'
Mike McCahill, *Sunday Telegraph*

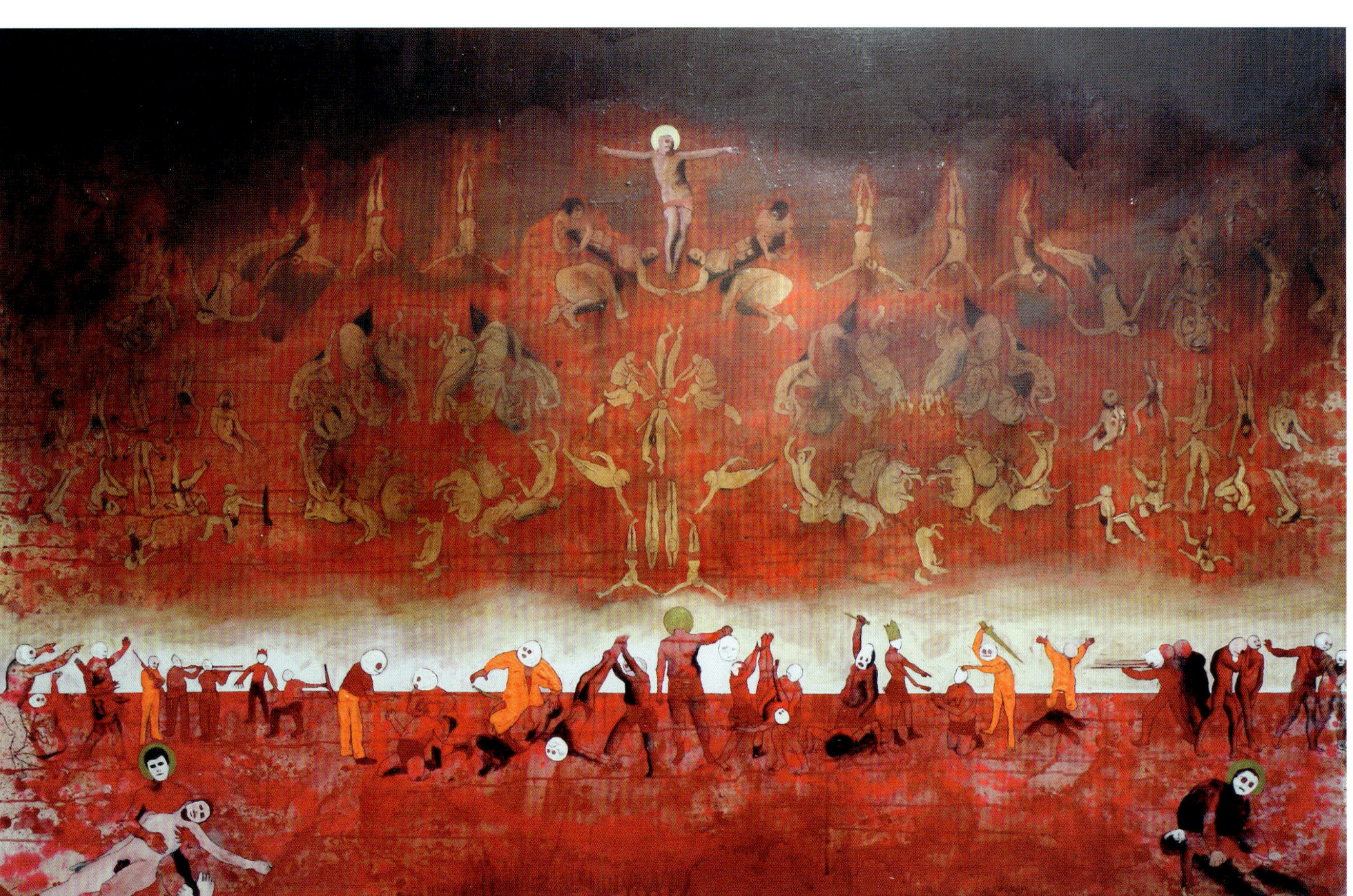

Jesus Christ: 'Nothing Martyrs Anymore' (2010) Oil on Canvas 183 x 123cm

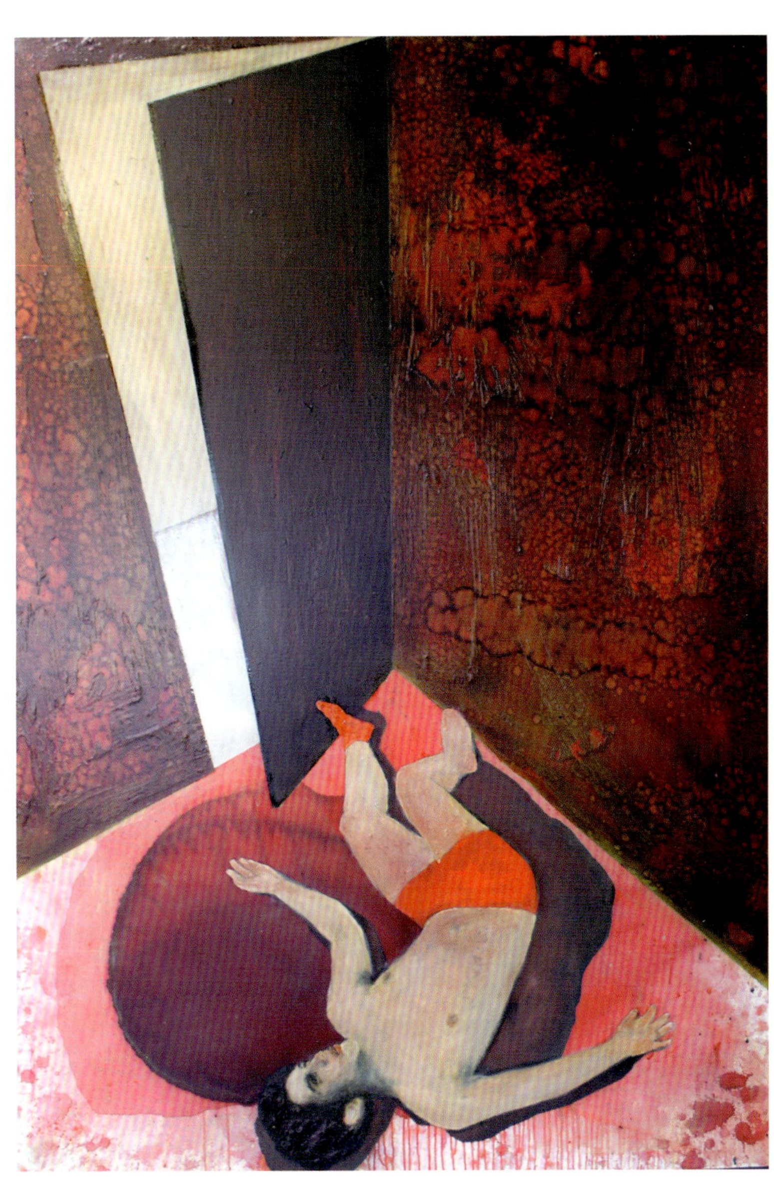

Mr. Gandia (2010) Oil on Canvas, 183 x 122cm

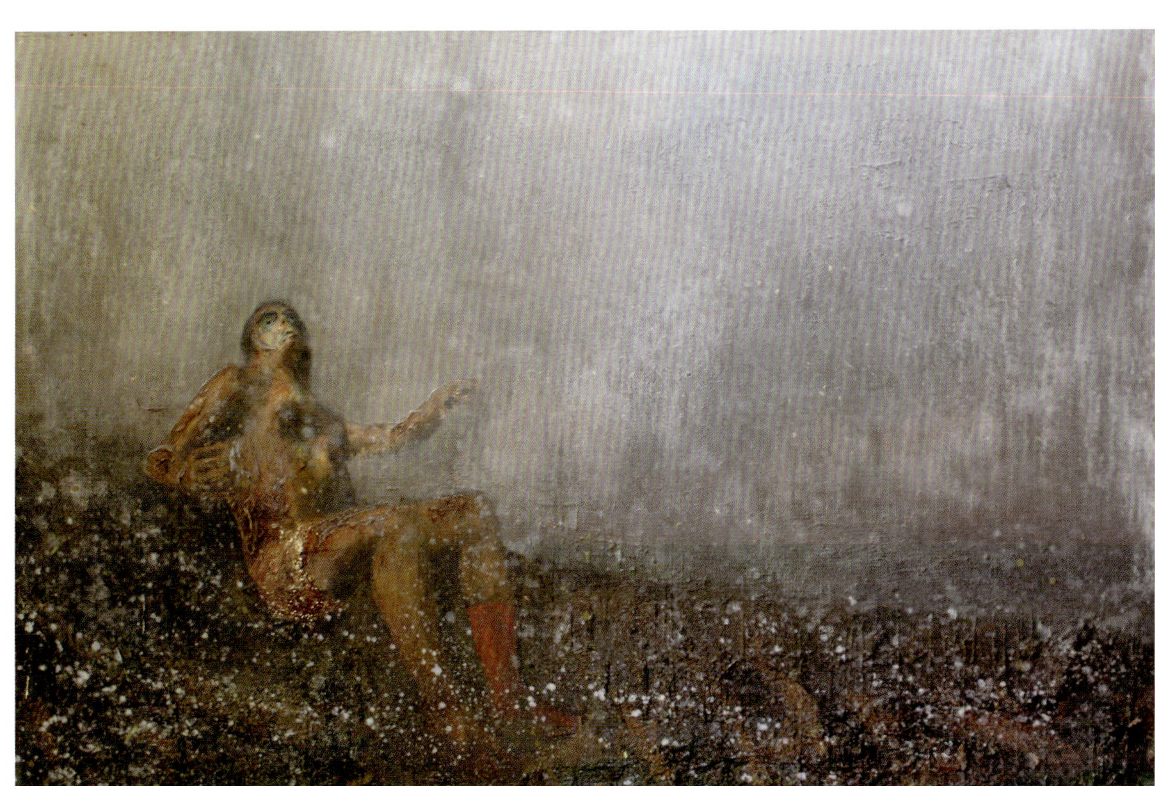

Fallen Man (2010) Oil on Canvas 183 x 122cm

Tom de Freston: Behind the Scenes

More about:

Tom....

Educated-
History of Art MA(Cantab) Cambridge University 2007
Fine Art LMU BA (Hons)
Honours-
Levy Plumb Visual Arts Residency,
Christ's College, Cambridge, September 2008
Artist in Residence, The Leys, Cambridge
Galleries Familiar With Artist's Work-
HRL Contemporary
Kettles Yard, Cambridge
Fitzwilliam Museum, Cambridge
Collections (Open To The Public)-
History Painting, Christ's College MCR, Cambridge
Website- www.tomdefreston.co.uk

I eat breakfast every day at 7.30 and enter the studio at 8 am. I stay until late. This routine is essential.

Multiple images, a few large paintings, a host of drawings, a handful of etchings and a new body of photographs will all be worked on during a typical week. This ensures I get directed by the work, so I remain a reader of my images rather than a dictatorial author.

I keep myself surrounded by a mountain of art books, found images, newspaper cuttings and piles of photos.

I use myself or other 'actors' to create photographic tableaux. These provide the basis for drawings, which lead into characters for new paintings.

A range of people visit the studio, their presence is never a distraction but instead opens an essentially honest discourse, one which the pretence of exhibitions and formal texts can never match.

I never get creative block, perhaps due to the organic manner in which my ideas evolve. I have always been highly prolific.

I see the studio as a home to a multiplicity of conversations between myself and the images; infinite yes and no decisions. The focus is on these tiny steps, not on the final destinations.

This Page: Tom as *David but no Goliath*
Opposite Page: Tom working on *The Wait of Flesh*

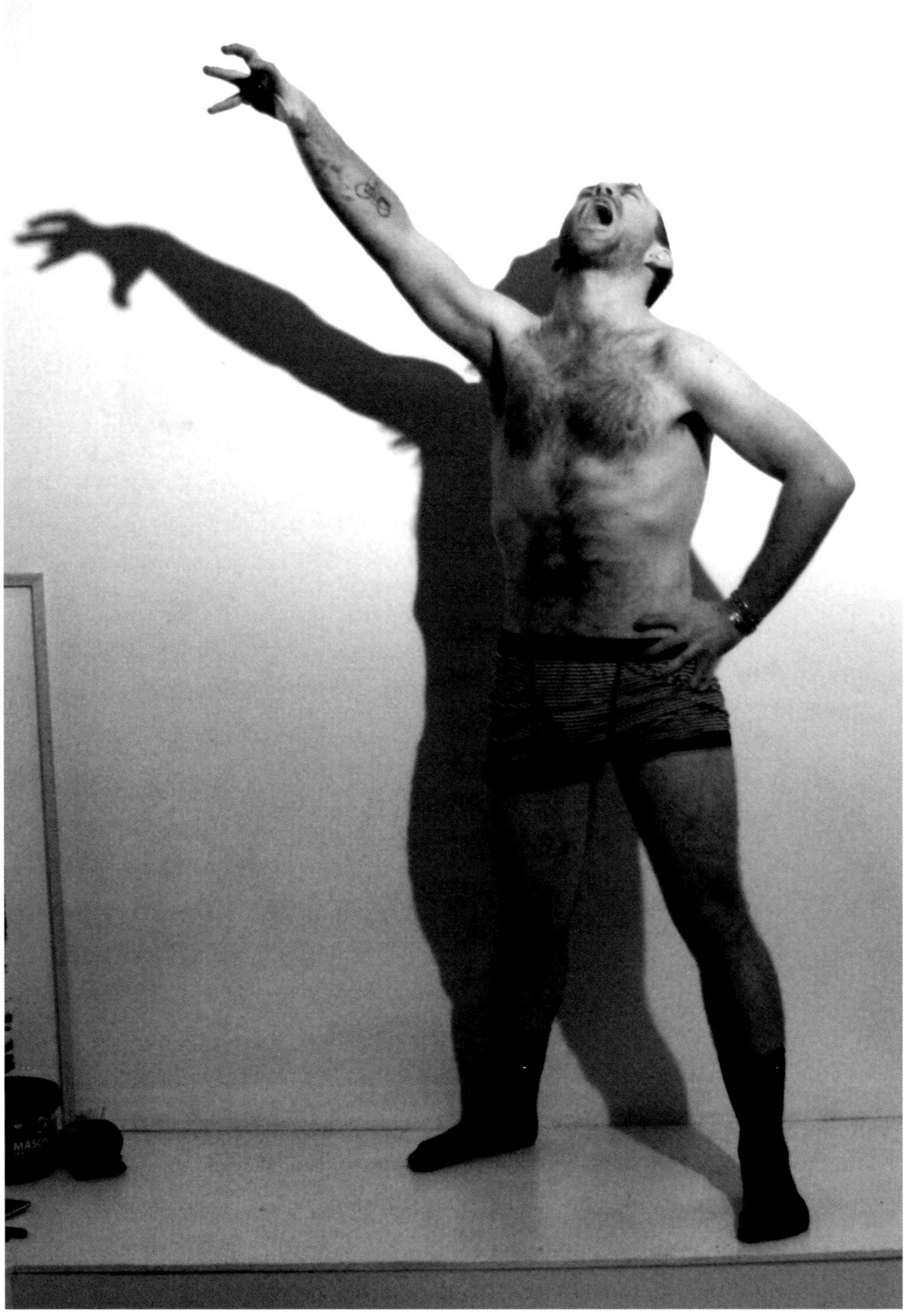

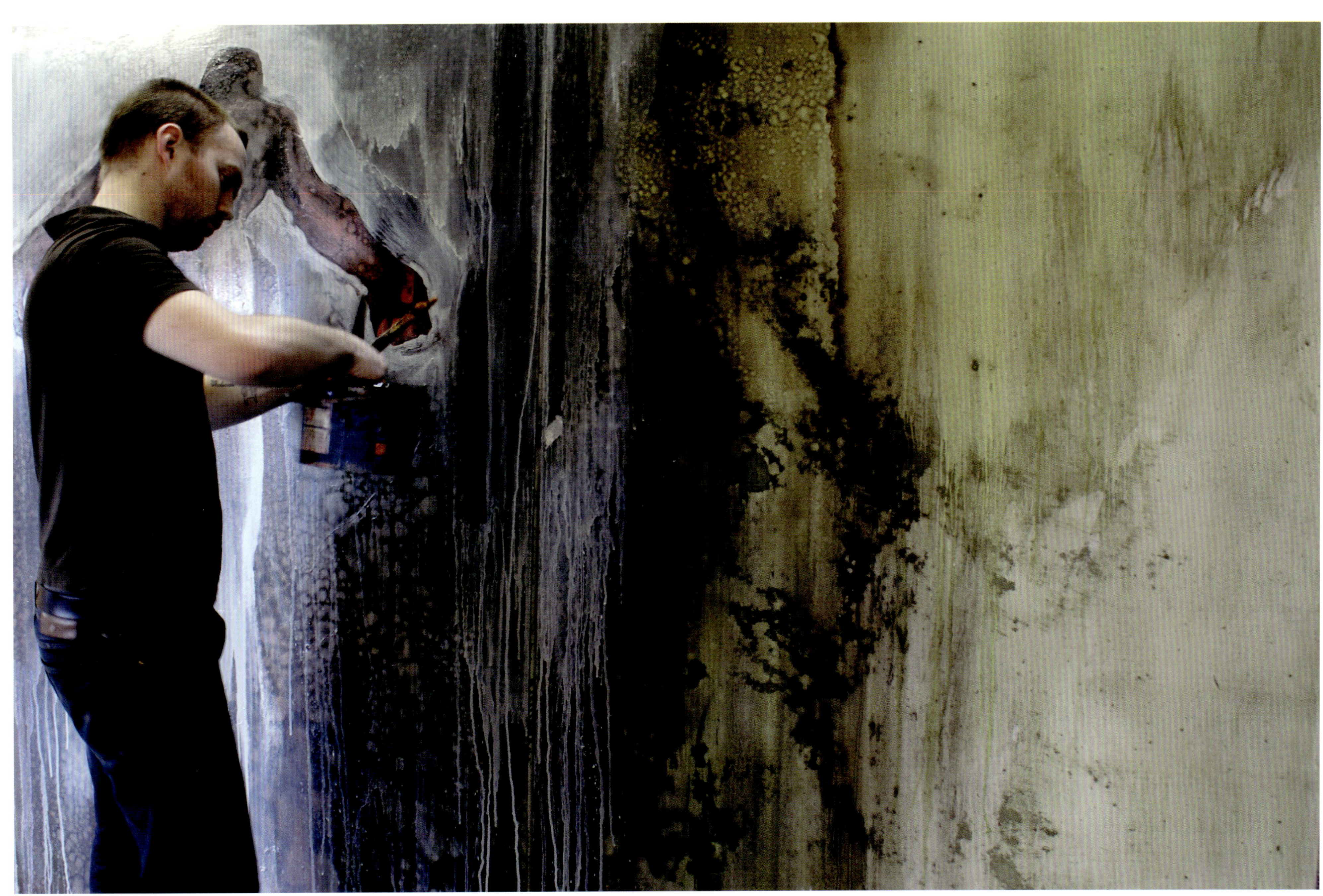

Gail de Cordova BA

Though seemingly abstract, Gail de Cordova's paintings evoke places, times, scents, breezes, seasons, memories...and one is at a loss to define exactly how these are communicated: they just are. Every work is different yet they are all unmistakably Gail's, so strong is her visual style.
-Williams Art, Cambridge

Gail de Cordova BA
Painter and Mixed Media Artist
Cambridge

I find my inspiration in nature and the natural world and how we connect with it at a deeper level. I work with both the detail - for example lichen on tree bark - and the wider picture, mists on distant hills.

At the moment I am part of Cambridge Arts Movement (CAM), an exciting new collective of local artists.

My ancestors came from Cordoba in Southern Spain (hence my name) and I have spent a lot of time in Spain. I wanted to convey the heat and vibrancy of Andalucia in *Andalucian Dream*. The red is meant to express this. I have always loved Matisse's *Red Studio*. Tone and colour create mood and emotion. For me this particular red sings with joy.

I had just returned from Sweden when I painted *Narnia*. I had an exhibition in a beautiful stately home, Gunnebo Slott, just outside Gothenburg. It was a truly magical place. Surrounding the house were lakes and silver birch woodlands and the light was ethereal. I was trying to capture this. The title arose when three people - two of them children - independently commented that the picture was like Narnia.

Nijar Nights is a very different painting from *Narnia* and much bigger. I had been staying in a little white village, Nijar, in Southern Spain, white-washed walls surrounded by mountains which became inky blue at night. I was also reading Tracy Chevalier's novel *Virgin Blue* at the time. It wasn't until a viewer commented that they felt the painting was like the blue of the Madonna that I realised that the book was also part of the painting.

Educated- Exeter College of Art and Design 1981
Membership of Local Art Societies-
Cambridge Arts Movement (CAM)
Galleries Familiar With Artist's Work-
Williams Art, Cambridge
Broughton House Gallery, Cambridge
i2 Art Gallery, Saffron Walden, Essex
Website- www.gaildecordova.com

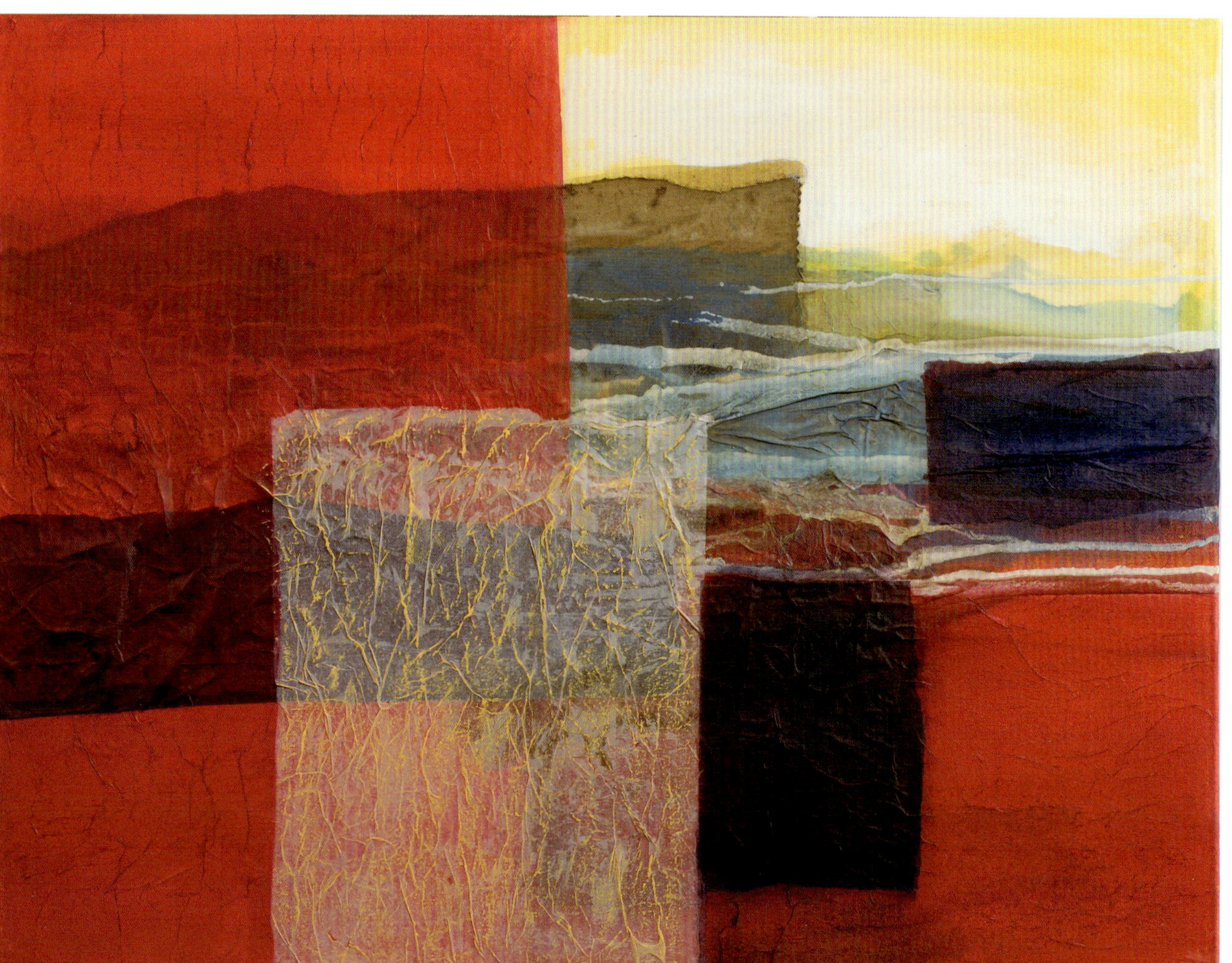

Andalucian Dream (2009) Mixed Media on Canvas 66 x 84cm

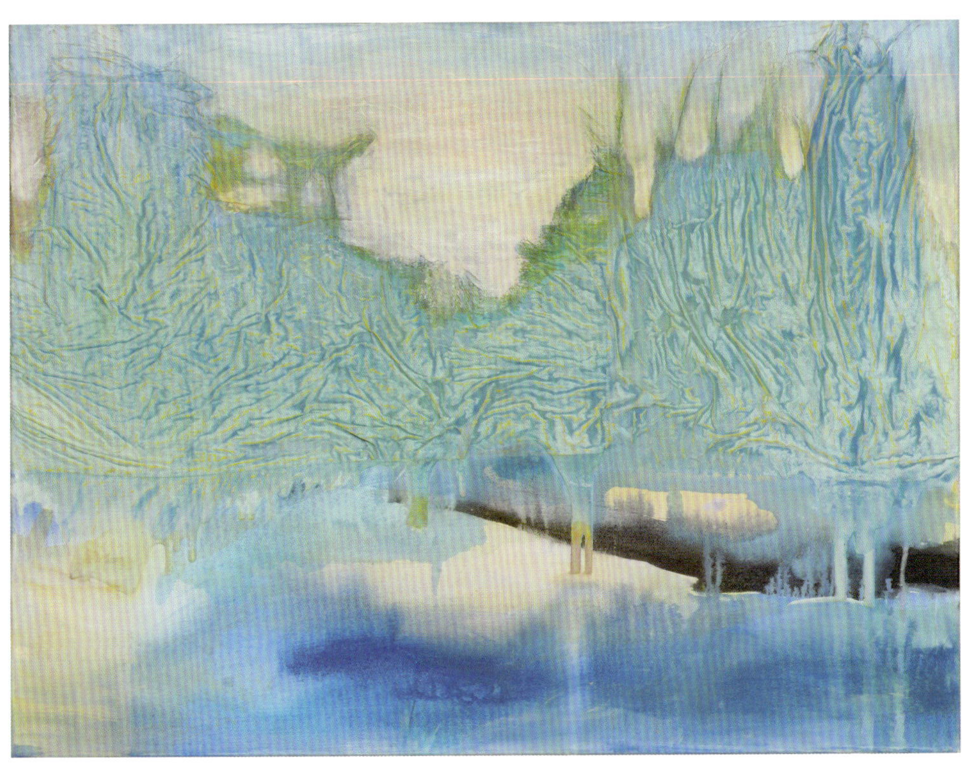

Narnia (2007) Mixed Media 66 x 84cm

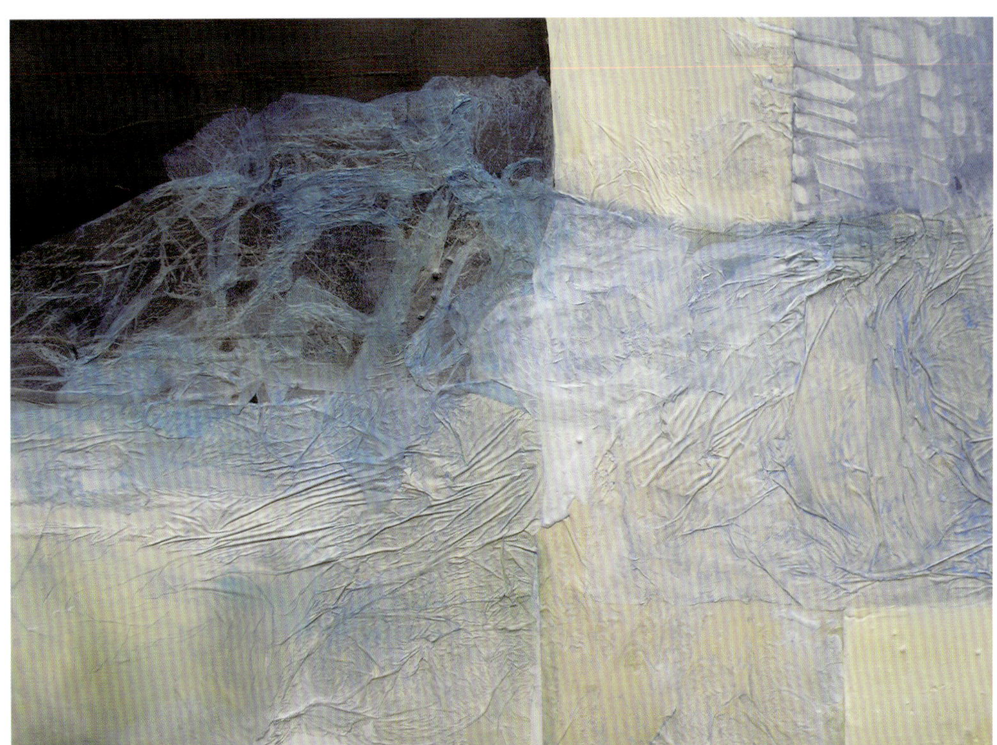

Nijar Nights (2006) Mixed Media 107 x 142cm

Chris Newson BA (Hons)

Chris's paintings are very emotive, strong and full of colour and texture, truly three-dimensional. They show the emotion he went through following a close bereavement, the love for his wife Heidi, and her work as a teacher. Other paintings show his relationship with Suffolk, golden fields and blue skies and the sometimes stormy coast, but all with Chris's inimitable use of textured paint. An exciting artist.
-The Old Printworks Gallery, Saxmundham, Suffolk

Chris Newson
Painter, Filmmaker
Saxmundham, Suffolk

I am very fortunate to have a two-room Victorian wash house for my studio (it's part of H.G.Crisp's Garden) which hunkers down at the back of a miniature town garden in Saxmundham. I like to start work early, 7.30 am. It's always cold in the studio but I am so absorbed in my work I soon forget the cold, even food. With my heavy metal music filling my ears I venture into the unknown with my paintings and lose all track of time.

I like to work on several canvases at the same time and my work is informed by Aubach and Van Gogh. But my most important influence is Maggi Hambling, who is not only a friend but also a very rigorous mentor.

Holding My Brother. My young brother died of cancer on Christmas Eve, 2008. Many of my paintings have been influenced by the love and the respect I have for him. His strength always radiated from him until the end. The only good thing to come out of the whole tragic affair was the fact that we got to say goodbye. As youngsters we were joined at the hip. I would have done anything to be able to drag him out of the ground. The cancer does not just affect the sufferer, it affects everyone who loves the sufferer. There is nothing that will ever be so bad that I cannot pull on the strength he has instilled in me.

Frustration. This is an experiment with paint. My friend and artist Jason Gathorne-Hardy bought me some large paint tubes. I was able to paint directly from squeezing the tube. After studying Aubach's work I was not afraid to use more paint in a square inch than most people use to paint a whole picture. It shows the frustration of how I was feeling that day. It's something I feel I can use to counsel myself through all the trials and tribulations of my life. The paint takes my pain and anger and manifests itself in my work.

Educated- Ipswich Performing Arts School
Galleries Familiar With Artist's Work-
RE+new, Woodbridge, Suffolk
The Old Print Works Gallery, Saxmundham, Suffolk
Website- www.chrisnewsonart.co.uk

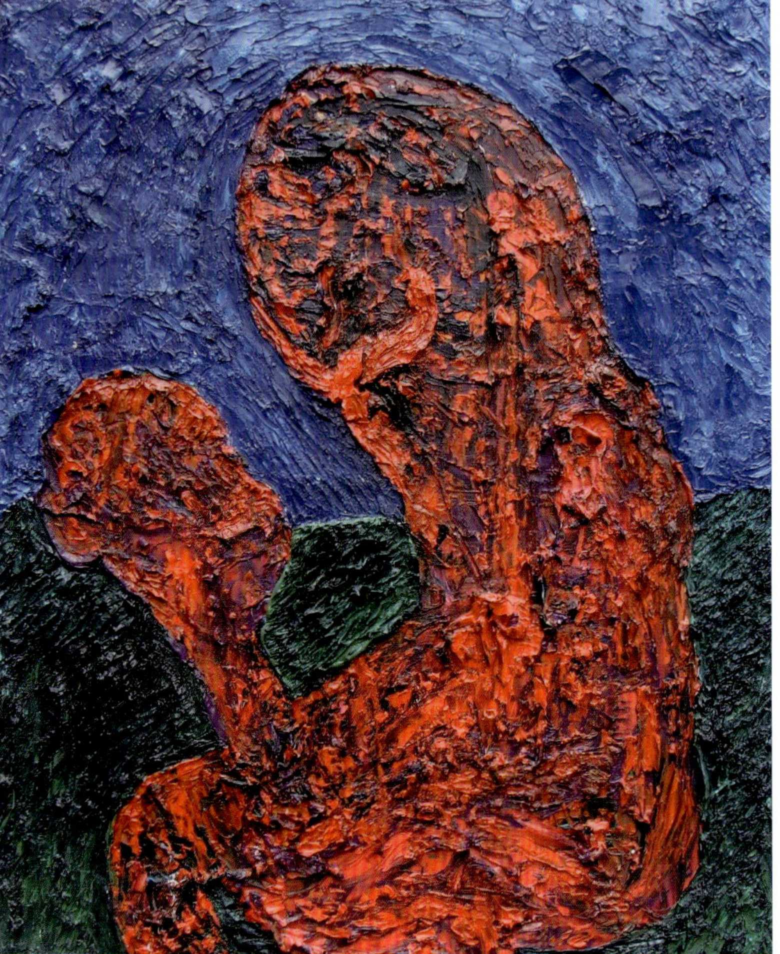

Holding My Brother (2009) Oil on Canvas 500 x 400cm

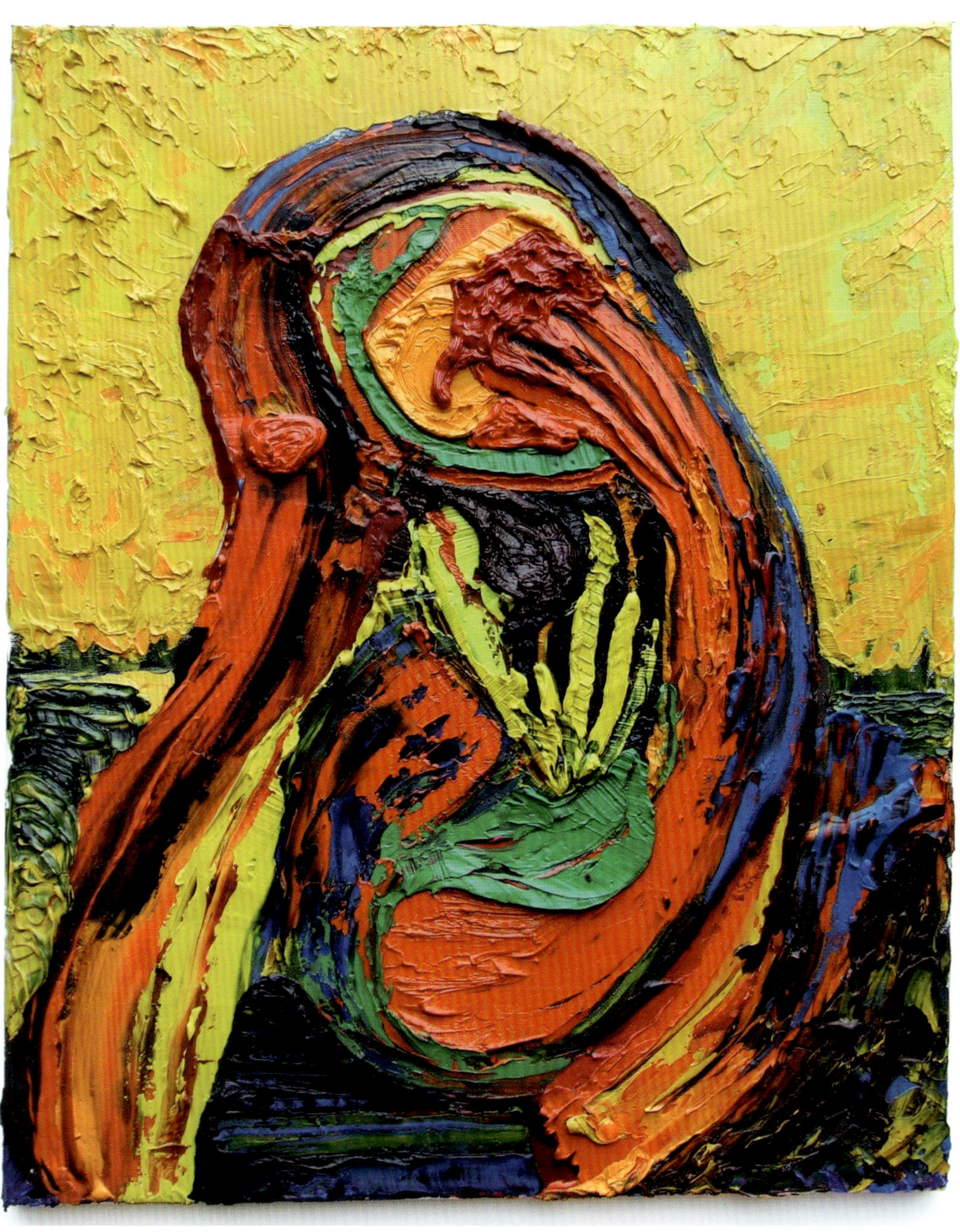

Frustration (2009) Oil on Canvas 500 x 400cm

Brüer Tidman ARCA

*Although Bruer's paintings are often erotic, always tender, one is not fixed on the subject but thrilled by the painting as a whole.- **Chappel Galleries**, **Chappel**, **Essex***

Brüer Tidman ARCA
Painter
Great Yarmouth, Norfolk

Over the past three decades I have drawn at and made works from the Norwich and Lowestoft Night Shelters; drawings and paintings in and of the Gt.Yarmouth Hippodrome Circus; and many other figurative works. The three works that appear in this book were made several years apart. The earliest is the *French Lady,* painted in the late seventies; I made several studies of her and also of other members of her family when we were all living in a dysfunctional 17th century farmhouse in North Norfolk.

She was the mother of the head of this family and had for many years been living on her own in a small house in rural France. The decision was made to sell her home and bring her to live in the farmhouse. She had never had a bath in her life, so the two eldest women in the house decided that she should have one. Her screams and shouts were terrific and could be heard all through the house. She suddenly understood: she had been brought to England to be murdered by drowning.

Although quite small, she was a fighter, and put up a fierce (French) resistance; so much so, the two women couldn't handle her and shouted down for my assistance. I immediately ran up the stairs and scooped her out of the bath. I learned later that she was certain that a miracle had been performed, and from that time on she genuinely thought of me as the village priest. Her appointed and favourite place to sit in this rather bare stone-floored house was by the Rayburn in the middle room, I being the only other person left in the farmhouse during the day. There I drew and painted, and obliged her by topping up her fire when needed, confirming her absolute conviction that I had been sent to save her from witches. She was a good sitter, whilst indulging in her favourite pastime of spitting on the floor. This work is just a straight forward study of her.

Twenty years later I painted *Beth in the Bedroom,* one of many of Beth Narborough. This painting now illustrates the cover of Robin Trower's latest record *What Lies Beneath*. Trower was a member of the famous Procol Harum, whose 1960s hit *A Whiter Shade Of Pale* rocketed to No.1 all over the world. Trower recognized something in this painting that connected with the music he was making. A quest by two artists working in different art forms for *What Lies Beneath*.

The *Illusionist* was finished this year. It is an idea of symbolism and abstraction forming the illusion of reality. The combination of elements – creativity, eternity, life forming, appearance forming – but also with the importance of chance. So, what lies beneath, stardust?

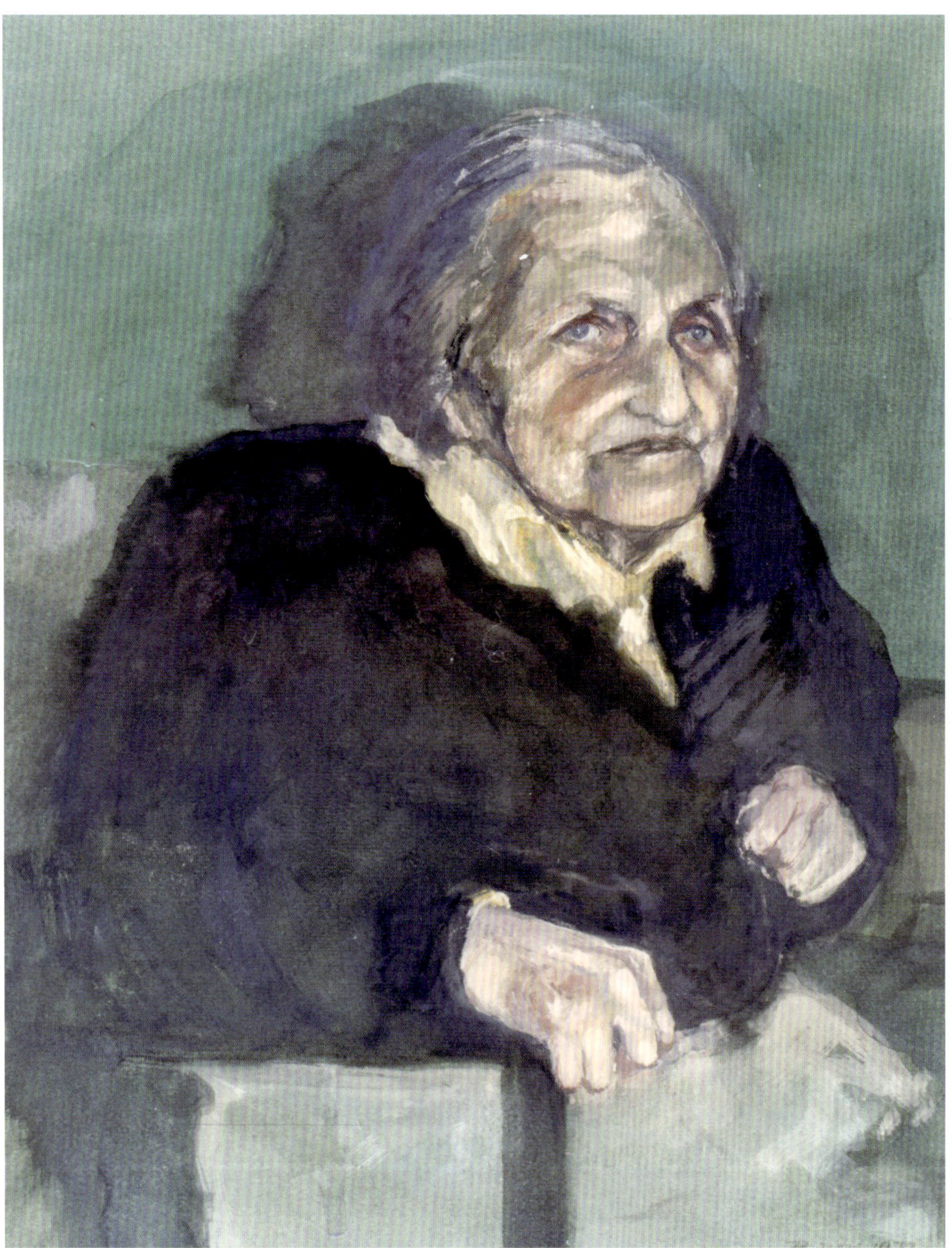

French Lady (1977) Mixed Media 35 x 30cm

Brüer Tidman ARCA

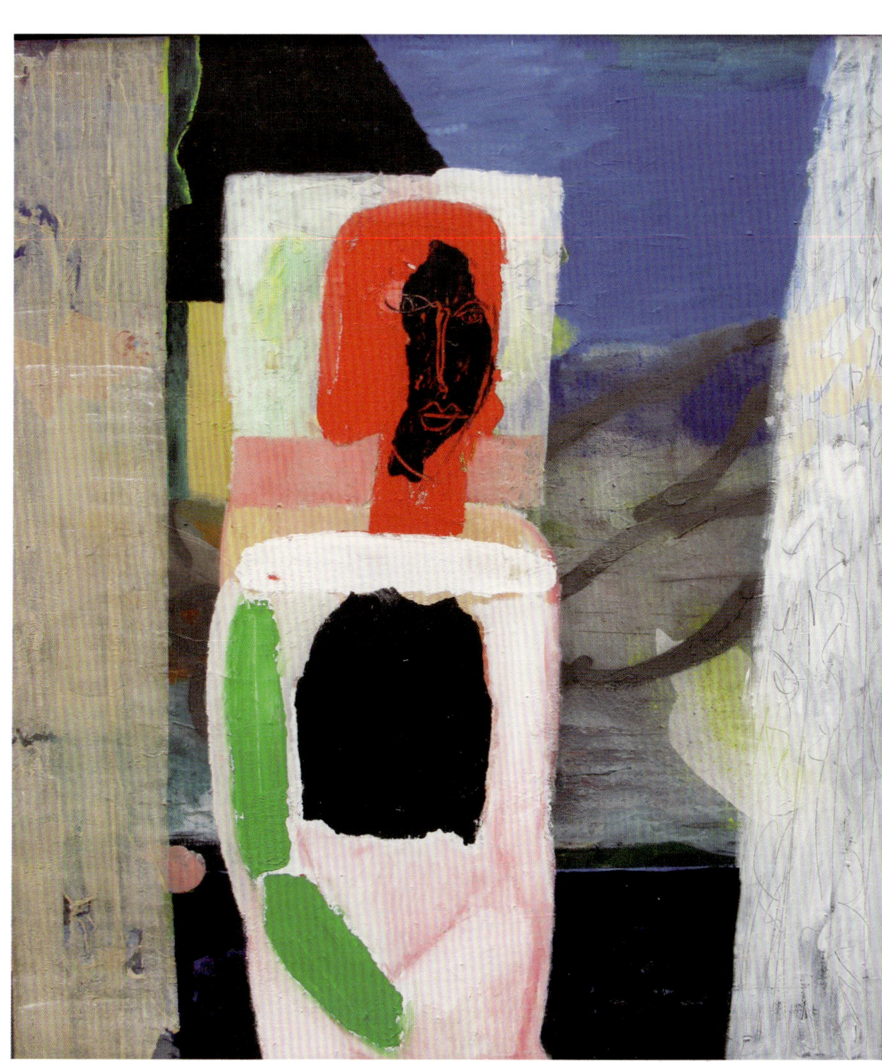

Beth In The Bedroom (1998) Acrylic and Mixed Media on Canvas 183 x 168cm

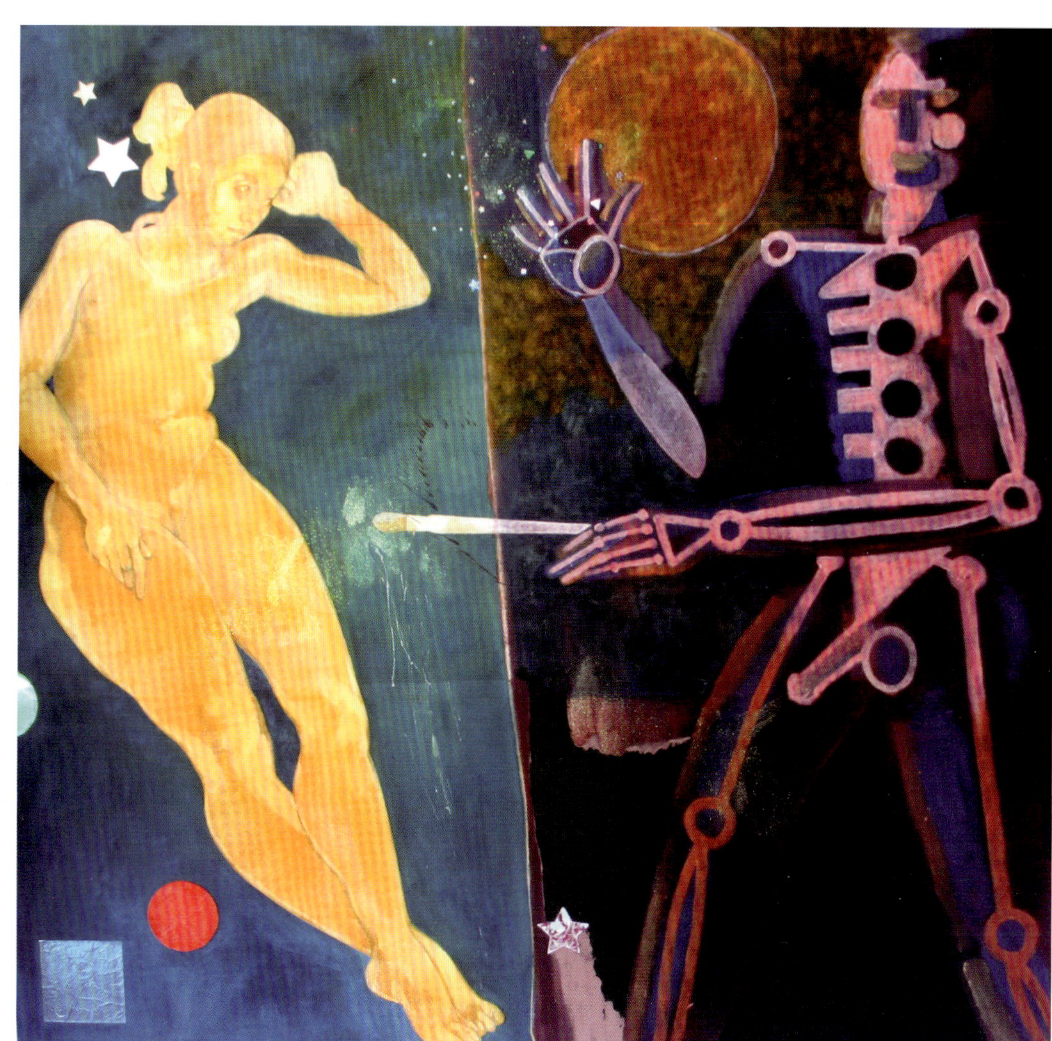

Illusionist (2010) Acrylic and Mixed Media on Canvas 183 x 183cm

Brüer Tidman: Behind the Scenes

More about:

Brüer....

Educated- Royal College of Art
Accreditation With National Art Societies-
Associate of the Royal College of Art
Galleries Familiar With Artist's Work-
School House Art Gallery, Wells-next-the-Sea, Norfolk
Norwich Castle, Norwich, Norfolk
Chappel Gallery, Chappel, Essex
Collections (Open To The Public)-
Norwich Castle, Norwich, Norfolk
The University of Essex, Colchester, Essex
The Imperial College of Science, London
Rijkers Art Collection, Netherlands
Website- www.bruertidman.com

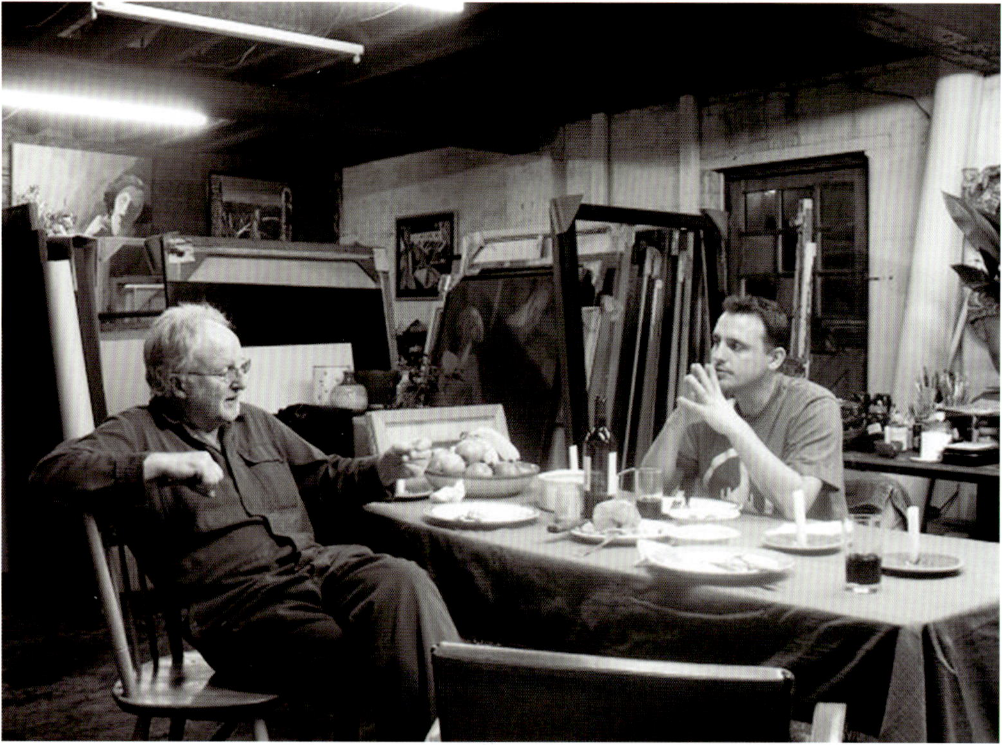

My studio is a large open space with thick wooden plank floorboards underfoot and humming neon lights above. The big old windows used to have fist sized 'ventilation' holes until recently when the old wooden frames were replaced with efficient white plastic ones. Seagulls nest and roost all around, their crazed calls a constant backdrop to my work.

I need the high ceilings as I work on large canvases, one at a time, and as and when the mood takes me – often all through the night. I am not far from my artist friends John Kiki, Emrys Parry, Bridget Heriz and Kate Coleman who pop in from time to time; and occasionally, as shown in the picture of my studio, one of my sons drops by and we descend into deep conversation.

This Page: Brüer and his son, Rueben
Opposite Page: Brüer's studio in the winter

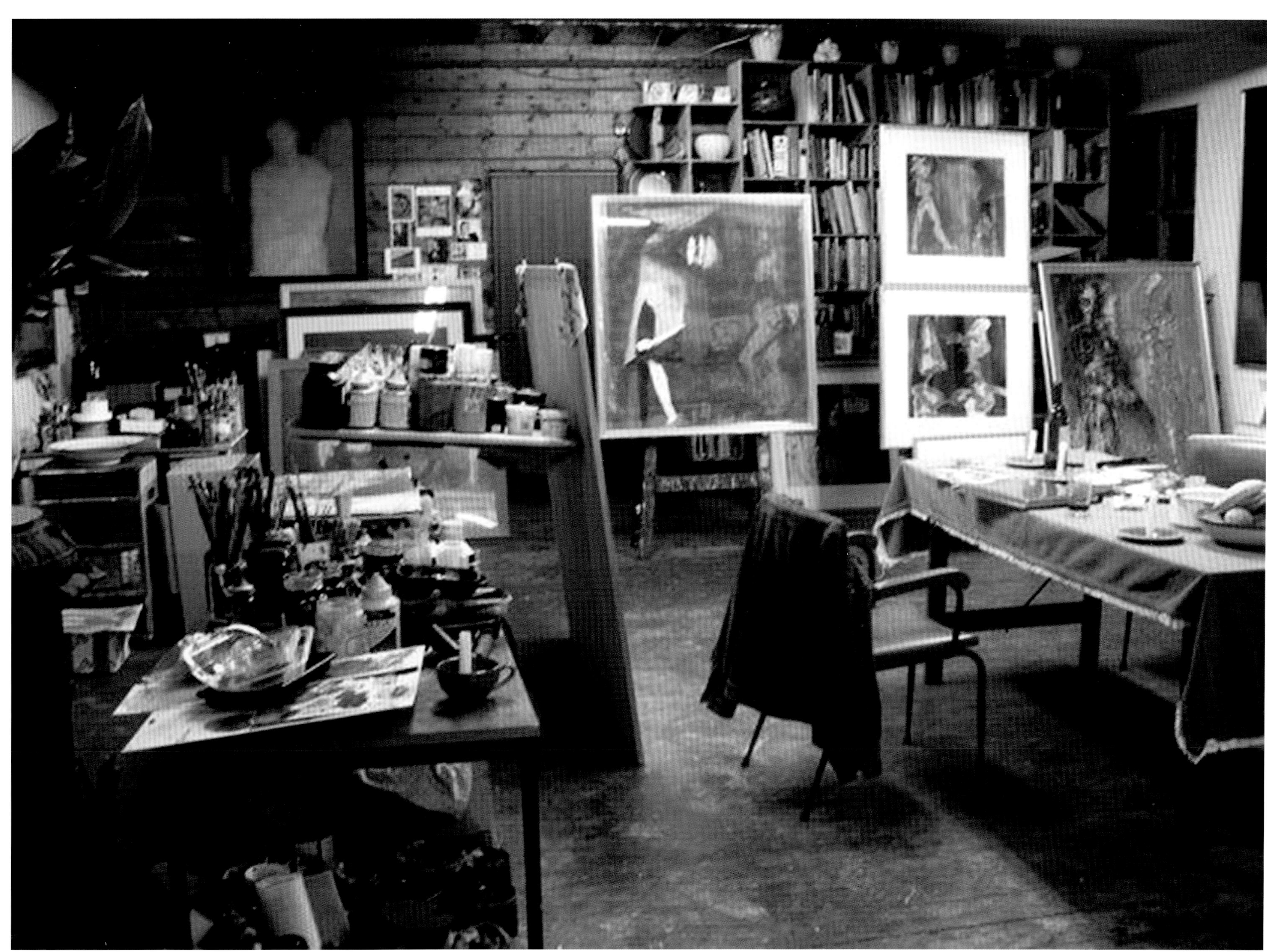

Dee Nickerson

Dee's pictures are distinctive in their style, using chalk pastels and acrylics. Her ladies stand, sit or busy themselves in the day-to-day routines of life. Dee likes to tell a story in her pictures, influenced by the weather, the seasons and the patterns and colours of nature. Her landscape paintings, often from memory, have a naive quality.
–Cork Brick Gallery, Bungay, Suffolk

Dee Nickerson
Painter
Harleston, Norfolk

Personal experience, observation and surroundings are my constant inspiration because I feel it is important to communicate an underlying truth based on something I am very familiar with.

My interest in looking at people, and seeing how others portray them, makes the National Portrait Gallery my favourite place to visit in London. With their bold story telling approach, Mary Feddon and Stanley Spencer are artists whose work I look at most. Both make the ordinary extraordinary.

I often use the experience of 'waiting' as a subject. Usually a person, I try to express how the observed outer stillness may conceal a number of thoughts and feelings beneath the surface. These I attempt to convey through choice of palette and the environment.

Looking For The Plough is a memory of the farm where I grew up during the 1960s. As today the place bears little resemblance to how it was then (the house renovated, buildings converted or demolished, ponds filled and small fields made into one), I want to record how I remember it. Using a map-like or bird's eye perspective, it shows my interest in pattern, both literal and metaphorical, and the relationship between nature and human endeavour.

In my most recent paintings, I have been developing a Matisse influence by choosing a very limited palette of almost primary colours (azure, vermillion, raw sienna) and black and white. Keen to maintain a child's view of the world in simplistic terms, I am hoping to recreate the feelings of new experiences: in *Beach Hut Retreat* and *Girl With Matisse Towel*, the excitement of visiting the beach.

Educated- Great Yarmouth College of Art & Design,
BTec Diploma in General Art and Design 1984
Membership of Local Art Societies-
The Harleston & Waveney Art Trail Collective,
Harleston, Norfolk
Accreditation With National Art Societies
Galleries Familiar With Artist's Work-
Cork Brick Gallery, Bungay, Suffolk
The Harleston Gallery, Harleston, Norfolk
The Southwold Gallery, Southwold, Suffolk

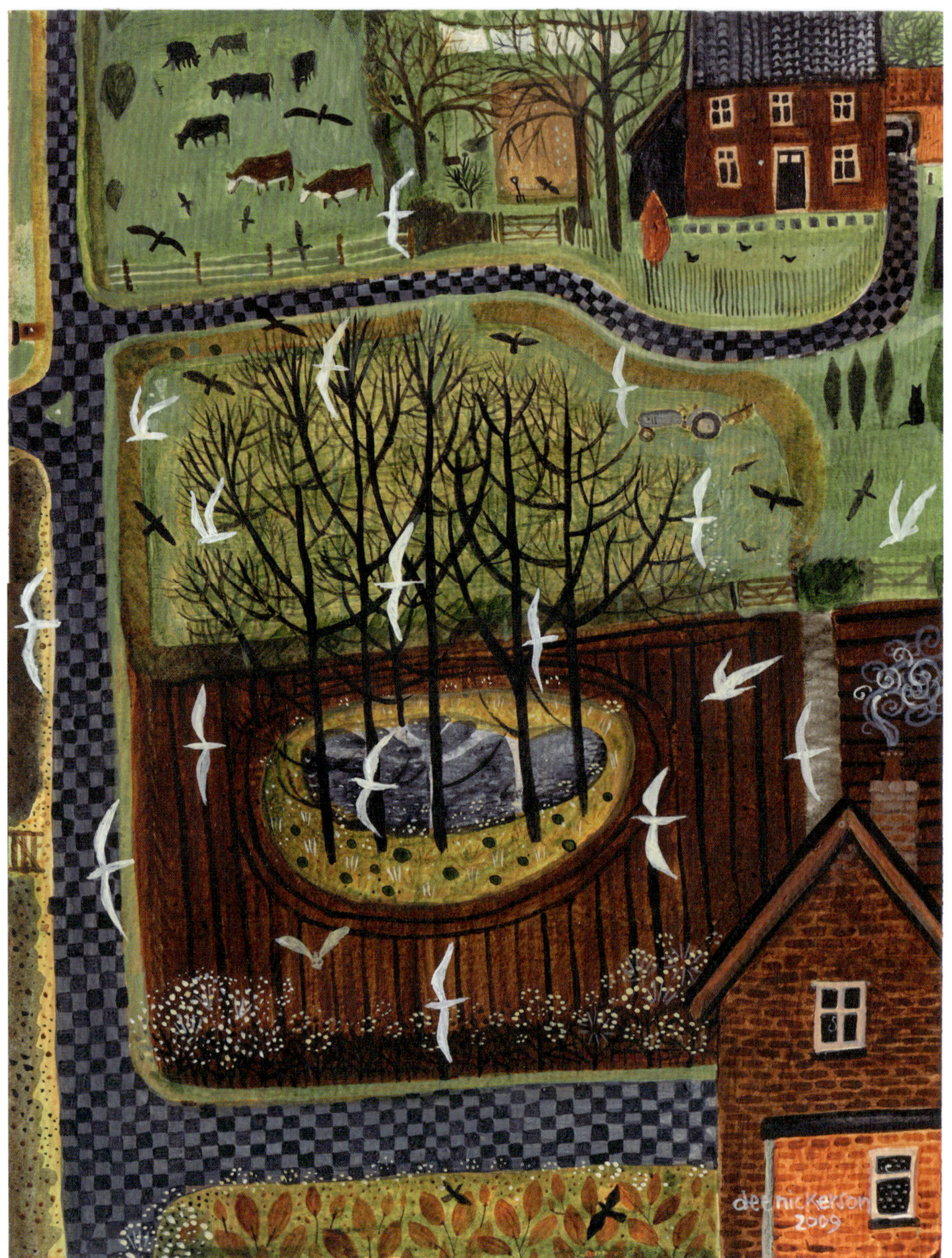

Looking For The Plough (2009) Acrylic on Paper, 28 x 20cm

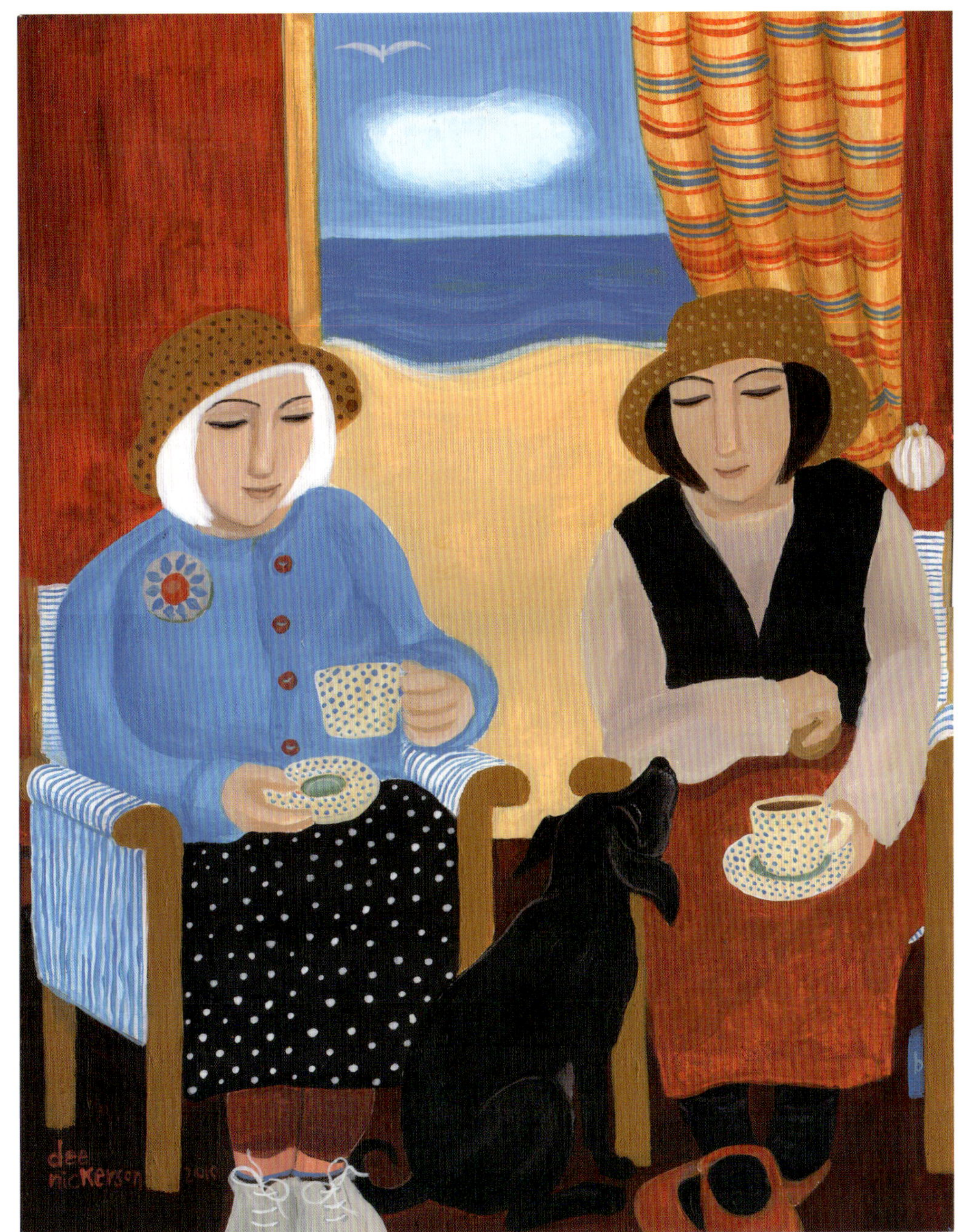

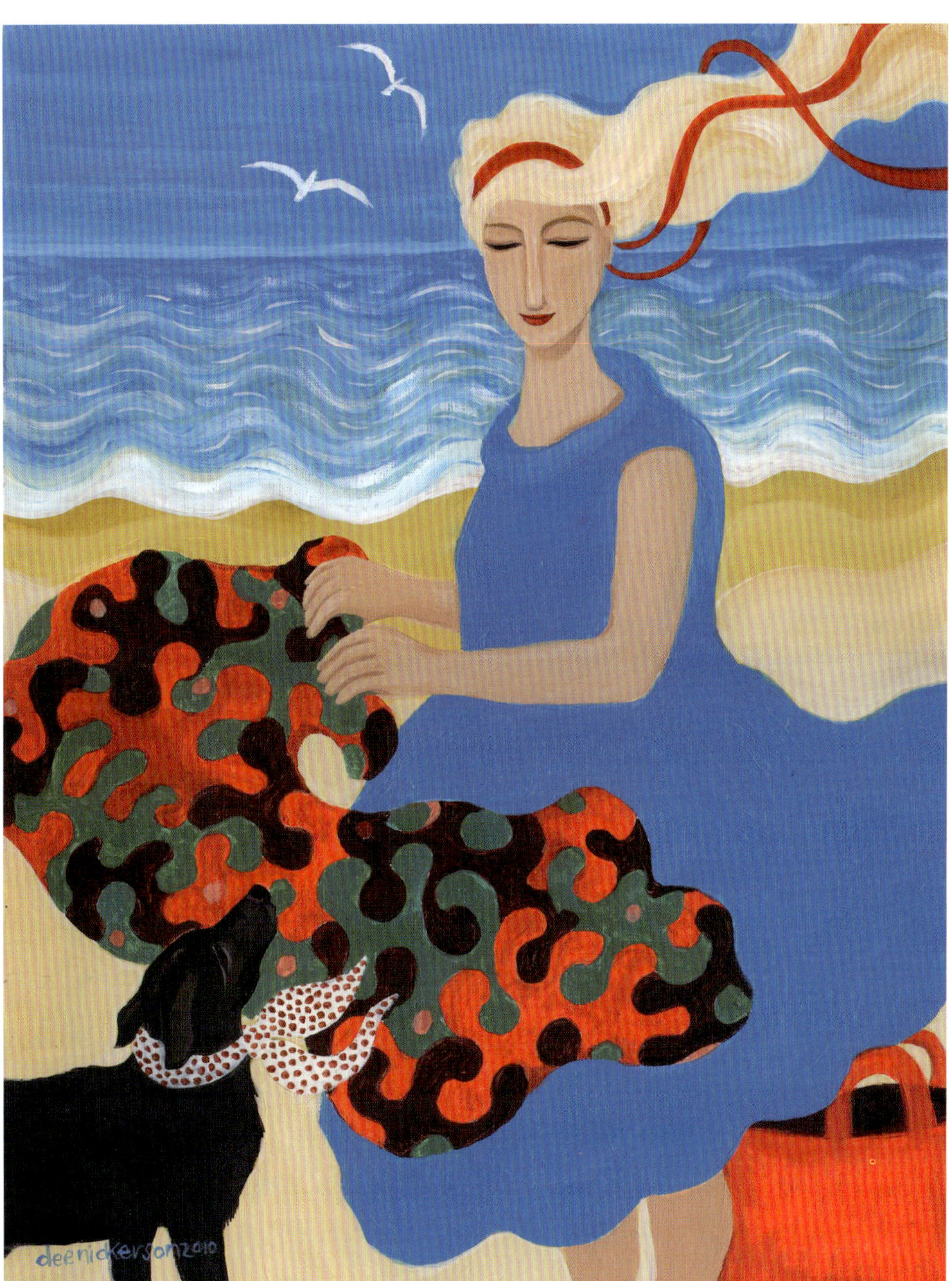

Beach Hut Retreat (2010) Acrylic on Paper 40.5 x 30.5cm

Girl With 'Matisse' Towel (2010) Acrylic on Canvas 40.5 x 30.5cm

Kit Wade

Kit Wade
Painter
Gresham, Norfolk

As a painter I am stimulated by 'curiouser and curiouser': why is this like that? Perhaps it was the class nature table in the early fifties, or the London Pride in my Grandad's yard, but the sum of it all is 'wow, look at that'. My overriding inspiration is the painter Ralph Lillford, for his expectations of endeavour and aspiration, the 30 hour day, and indefatigable spirit; Howard Hodgkin, Robert Rauschenberg, Peter Lanyon, John Sell Cotman, Lilian Colbourn, but first, Lillford.

What Know They of Harbours tells of returning to boats and havens, the optimism of the venture and relief at a safe return - a bit like embarking upon a painting; restraining the palette whilst trying to achieve the brilliance of the day. How to get a brighter blue than comes out of the tube? How to achieve that elusive sense of place so people know what it's like? Even if they've never been and for those who have been, to be transported back.

What a large, imposing building Binham Priory is, saturated with people's lives and such patterns. Working with glass recently has begun to alter the way I see a completed painting. All paintings are now a prelude to glasswork which may never happen. It's to do with finitely dividing up a 2D surface to share a feeling, a response to what I've seen, to get someone else to notice the colours and patterns rather than the technical, architectural stuff.

The *Hedge at Gresham* is a painting from my own collection, where sky and trees mesh together, where trees listen and watch over centuries - my 'old men of Norfolk' - where all that changes is the weather. I try to catch change in a fixed form, but never know if it's been captured until after the moment has gone.

Like the story about the seagull sandwich, you know when a painting is finished when you smile, and then you walk out of the pub!

Educated- Borough Road College, Isleworth
Membership of Local Art Societies-
North Norfolk Organisation for Visual Arts (NOVA)
Galleries Familiar With Artist's Work-
C21 Shop, Mundesley, Norfolk
Flint Gallery, Blakeney, Norfolk
Big Blue Sky, Wells next the Sea, Norfolk
Website- www.kit-wade.co.uk

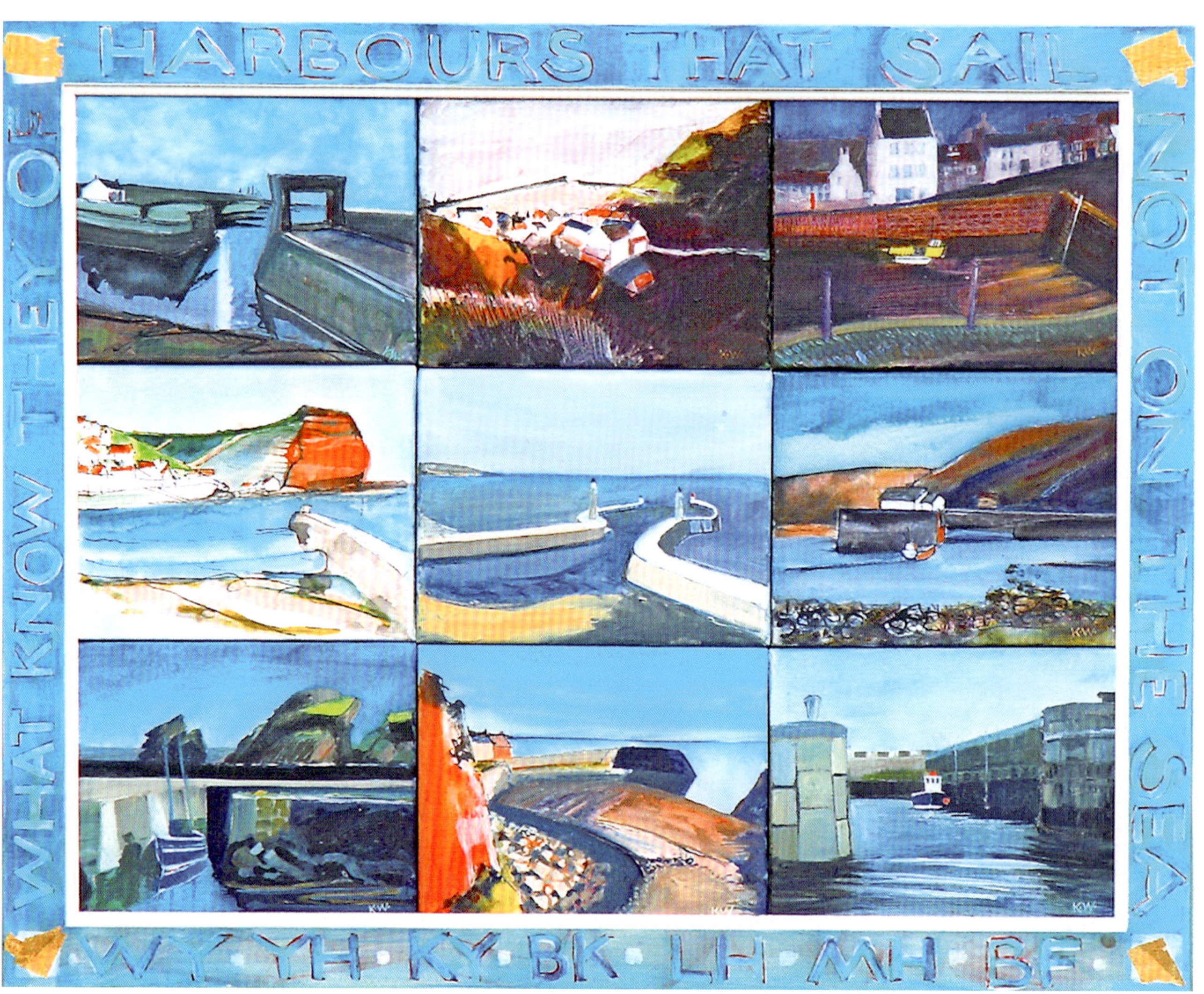

What Know They of Harbours (2006) Acrylic 84 x 100cm

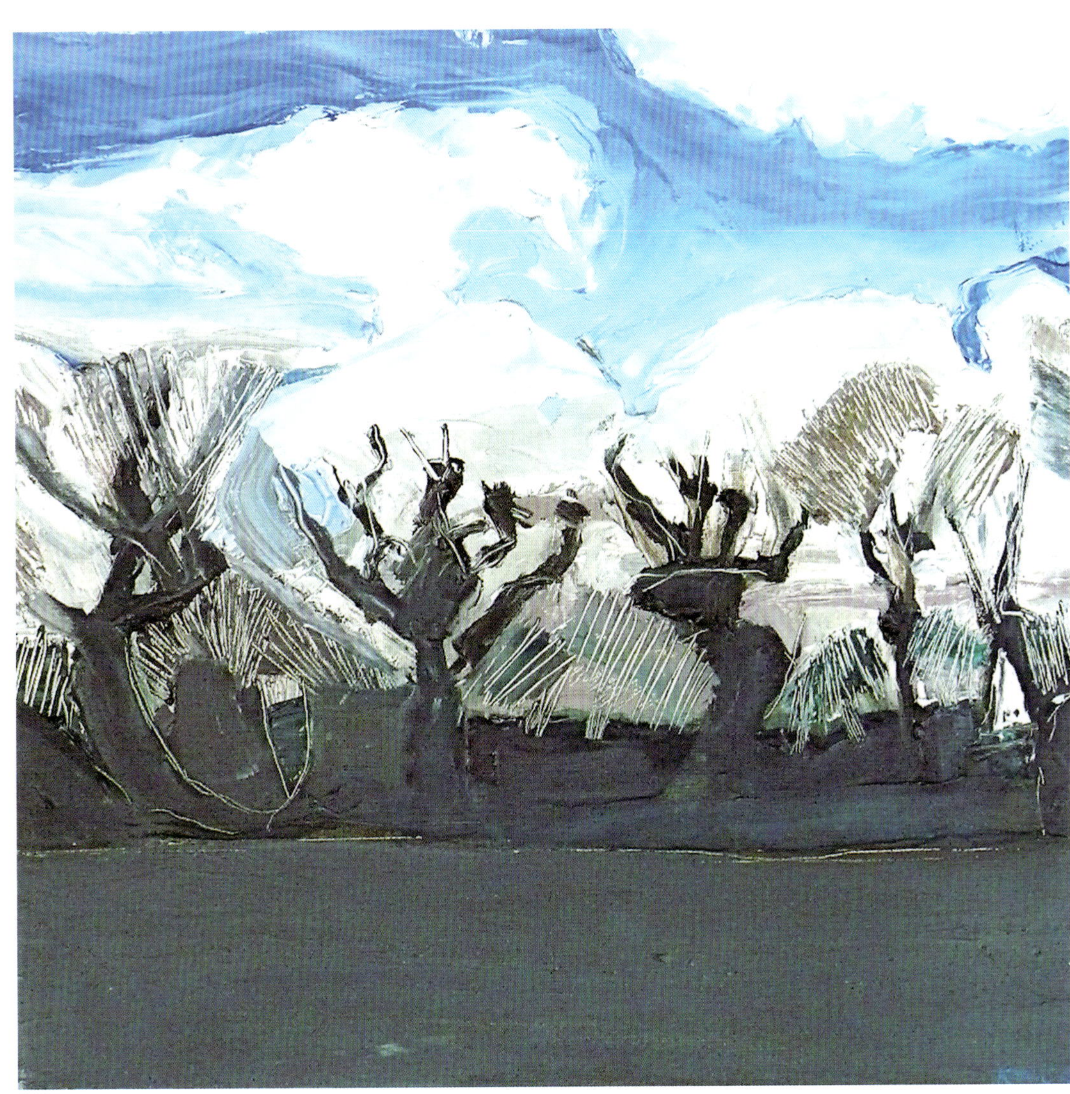

Hedge at Gresham (2004) Oil 40 x 40cm

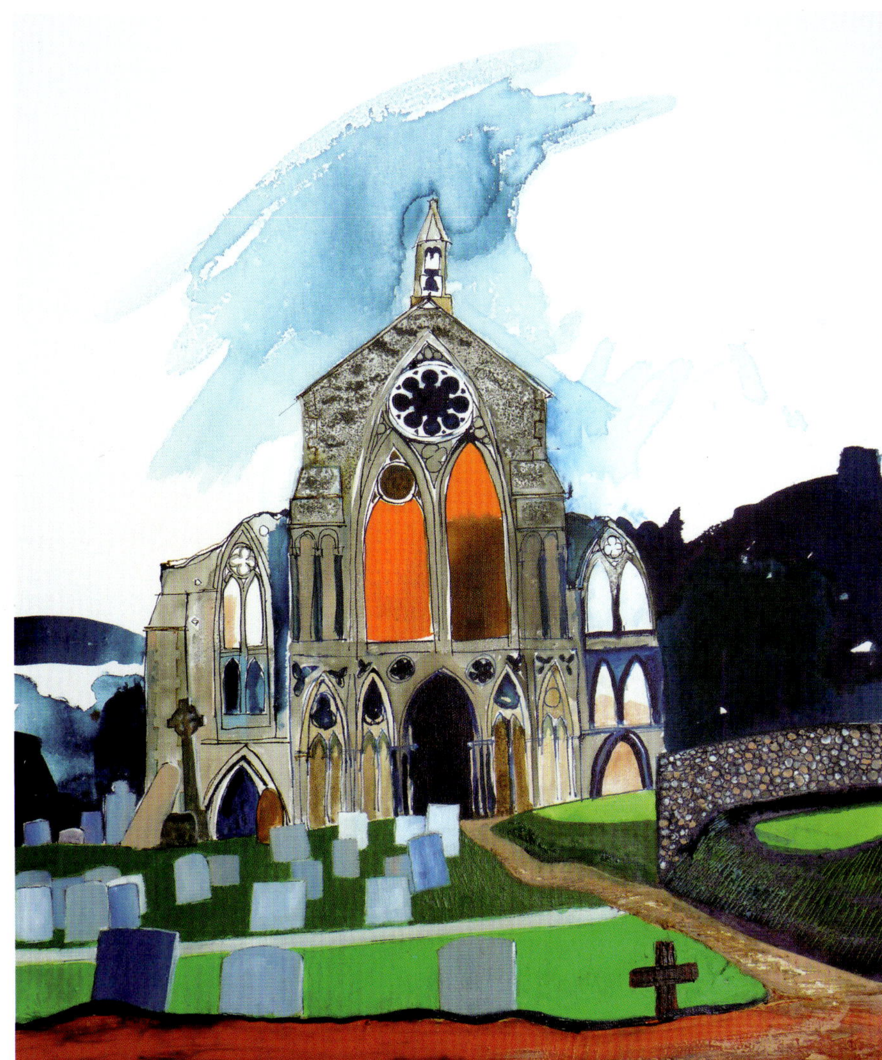

Binham Priory (2010) Mixed Media 60 x 50cm

Elizabeth James MA

Elizabeth's pictures, whether watercolour, acrylic or oil are created in an expressive style that portrays the atmosphere of a place and time rather than topographical detail. She demonstrates a continuing preoccupation with the horizon, with the division between the sky and the land always a focal point of the picture. The range of colours she uses reflects very well the shades often seen around the East Anglian coast and countryside.
- Reunion Gallery, Felixstowe, Suffolk

Elizabeth James MA
Painter
Stowmarket, Suffolk

Inspired by the East Anglian coast and countryside, with its vast stretches of unspoilt beaches and stunning skies, I work in a fluid, expressive style. My overall aim is to portray the atmosphere of a place rather than the topographical detail and to create work that draws the viewer in.

Known mainly for my watercolour paintings, I have begun experimenting with larger vibrant oil paintings and softer hued acrylics.

The image *Russet Leaves* depicts walking through the autumn woods gazing up through the myriad coloured leaves to the clear blue sky beyond.

Educated- Norwich University College of the Arts 2009
Membership of Local Art Societies- Suffolk Open Studios
Galleries Familiar With Artist's Work-
Reunion Gallery, Felixstowe, Suffolk
Website- www.elizabeth-james.com

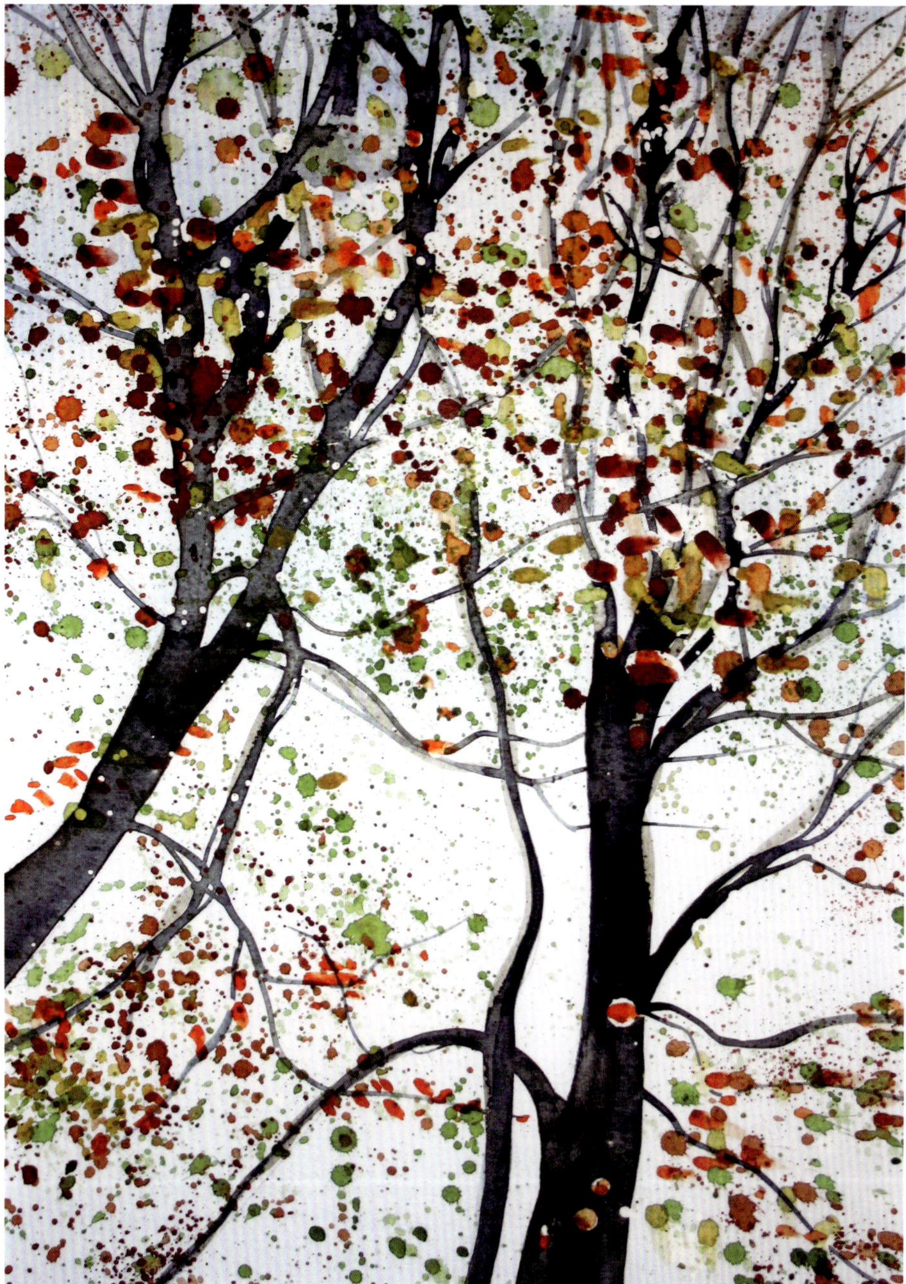

Russet Leaves (2010) Watercolour 51 x 41cm

Will Teather

Dawn in the Hinterlands (2009) Pastel on Panel 95 x 100cm

Will Teather
Painter, Pastel Artist
Norwich, Norfolk

My work takes some of its inspiration from magical realist writers such as Angela Carter and Gabriel Garcia Marquez. I enjoy the way that these authors blur the boundaries between reality and artifice through the absorption of folklore and the carnivalesque into their work. Hence, whilst my images often appear surreal, on closer inspection there is a sense in which they may in fact be staged for a theatre production.

Dawn in the Hinterlands has several underlying themes that I am still coming to understand. On one level it is simply about the series of artworks leaving behind the nightlit Aberdeen cityscapes where they originally began. Nonetheless, it could also be read as a motif for society's loss of innocence through industrialisation and sexual revolution: symbolised by the burlesque Goddess sat on the steam engine and the modern-day child running in front. The characters making a rather half-hearted attempt to halt the advance of the vehicle are Christina and Augustus from 'Nightmare Cafe,' a touring production that carries its own story beyond the frame.

Educated-
Chelsea College of Art and Design
Honours-
Trustee, Anteros Arts Foundation
Artist in Residence 2009, Anteros Art Centre
Staff Award, Norwich University College of the Arts
Galleries Familiar With Artist's Work-
Art 18/21, Norwich, Norfolk
Mandell's Gallery, Norwich, Norfolk
Norwich Assembly House, Norwich, Norfolk
Collections (Open To The Public)-
The Mannington & Wolterton Estate, Norfolk
Website- www.willteather.com

Jamie Andrews

Jamie's work never fails to ignite childlike enthusiasm. He zealously collects plasticky trinkets, charms, cracker toys, doll parts and fuzzy felts and embeds them in lashings of paint in the most intoxicating and vibrant colours. Jamie assembles narratives in boxes. Sometimes I can follow the story - a nursery rhyme or a political event perhaps - and sometimes I sense that Jamie is only revealing half the story! When the penny drops, I feel like I'm sharing the joke with him.
- Targetfollow, Norfolk

Jamie Andrews
Painter, Sculptor
Lowestoft, Suffolk

My work is about play in every sense of the word; mind games to tease the eye and engage the senses. Fed by an obsessive desire for the childish and childlike naïve innocence as viewed through the eyes of an adult's knowledge and experience, the work is far from puerile and often leads to challenging and thought-provoking images. I use found objects such as toys, gold and silver jewellery as symbols to connect with my audience in communicating a variety of messages.

10,000 men is a sculpture based on the old nursery rhyme *The Grand Old Duke of York*. Seven years in the making, it is exactly 10,000 toy soldiers painstakingly applied, one soldier to another, by dipping them in an acrylic blood pigment and then placing them together to slowly form a shape like a termite hill, its intention to reflect the pointless act of war and man's repeated endeavours to persist in it. Winner of the Al-turner-tive Turner prize, Liverpool 2007; and winner of the Bayer Prize, Norwich 2009.

Flick of a Switch was one of those paintings that just happened at the end of the day whilst cleaning up. A small piece of board that was used as a palette suddenly appeared as a cross whilst scraping the white paint from my trowel. Then placing two dolls' hands at either side, it became a crucifixion, a silver charm for a head. A pair of action man combat boots later and the crucifixion transformed into the explosion, that of a suicide bomber.

The painting *My God is Better Than Yours* resonates with playground teasing - 'Mine's Better Than Yours' but also has a more chilling message when related to current and past world conflicts. Embedded letters, apparently as artlessly placed as magnets on a fridge door, form words with an entirely adult meaning. The sugary smile on a doll's impassive pink face becomes a leer, peering disembodied from thick layers of bright acrylic paint that sings out like a stain glass window.

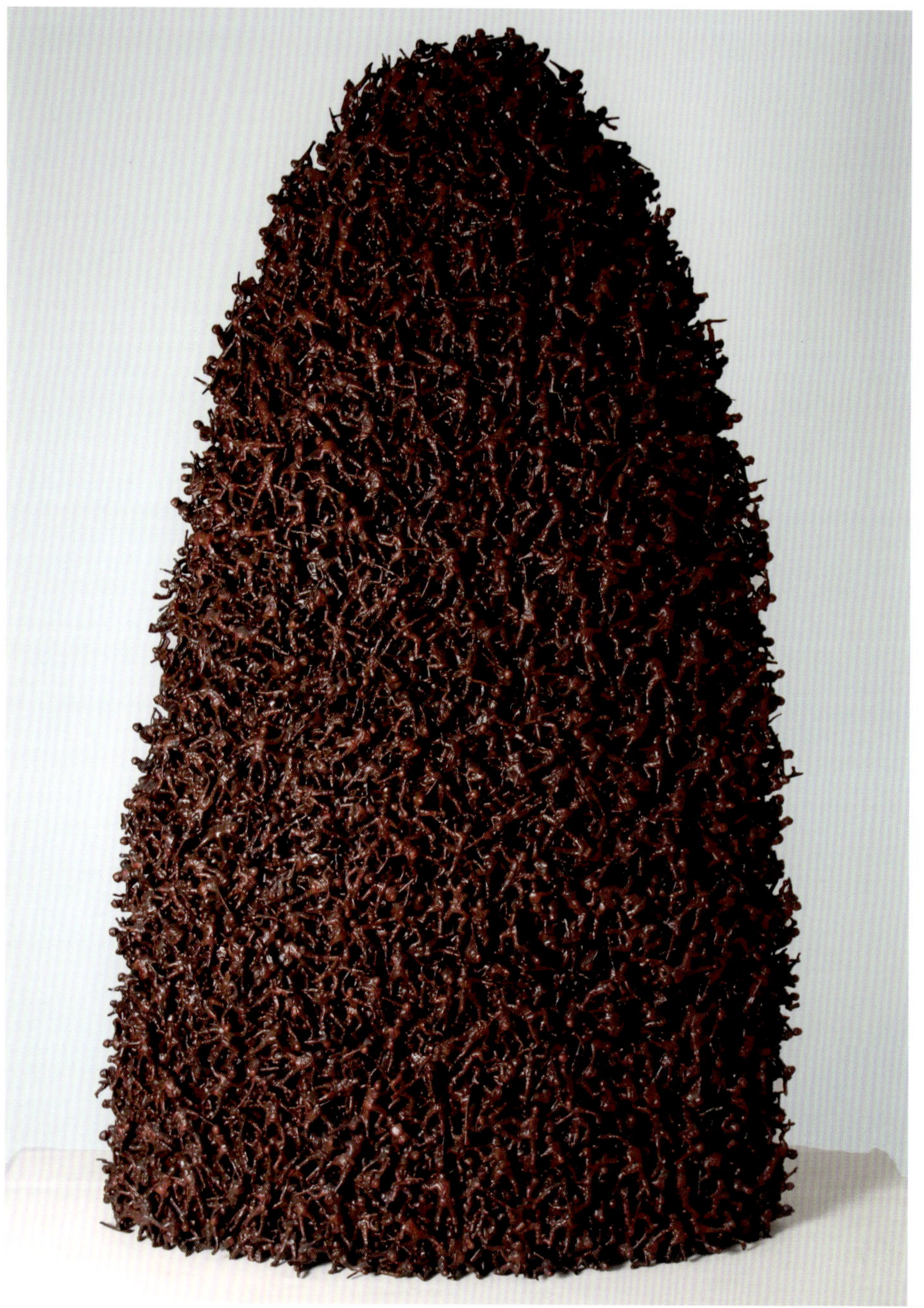

10,000 men (2007) Toy Soldiers and Acrylic Blood 112 x 66 x 24cm

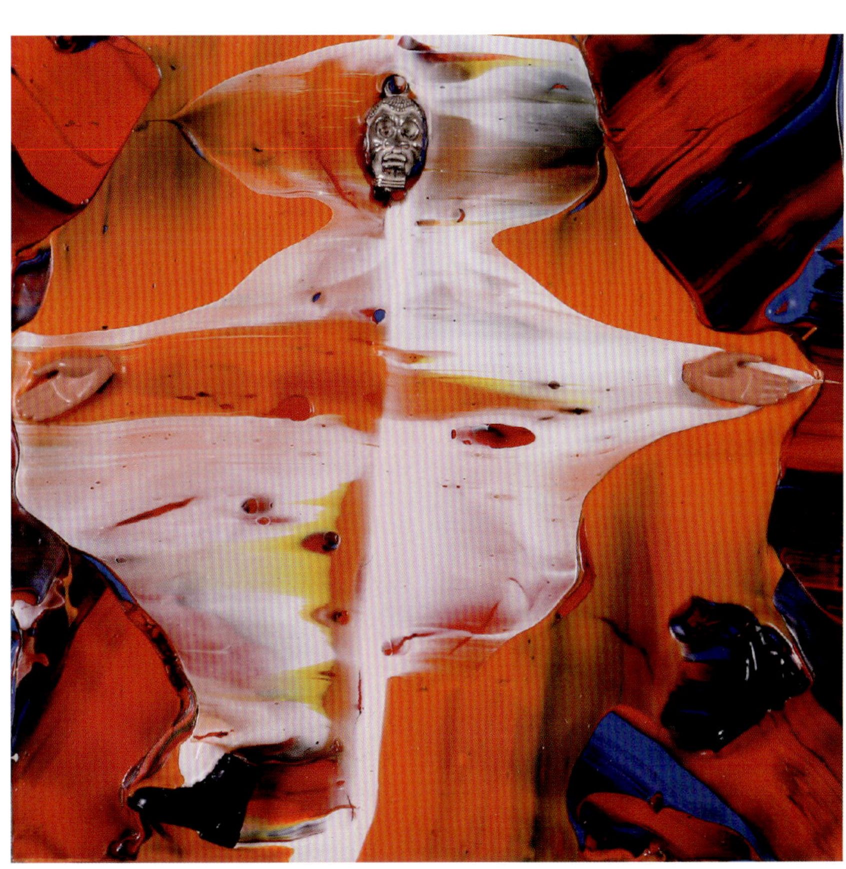

Flick of a Switch (2008) Silver Charm, Plastic and Acrylic Paint on Board 36 x 36cm

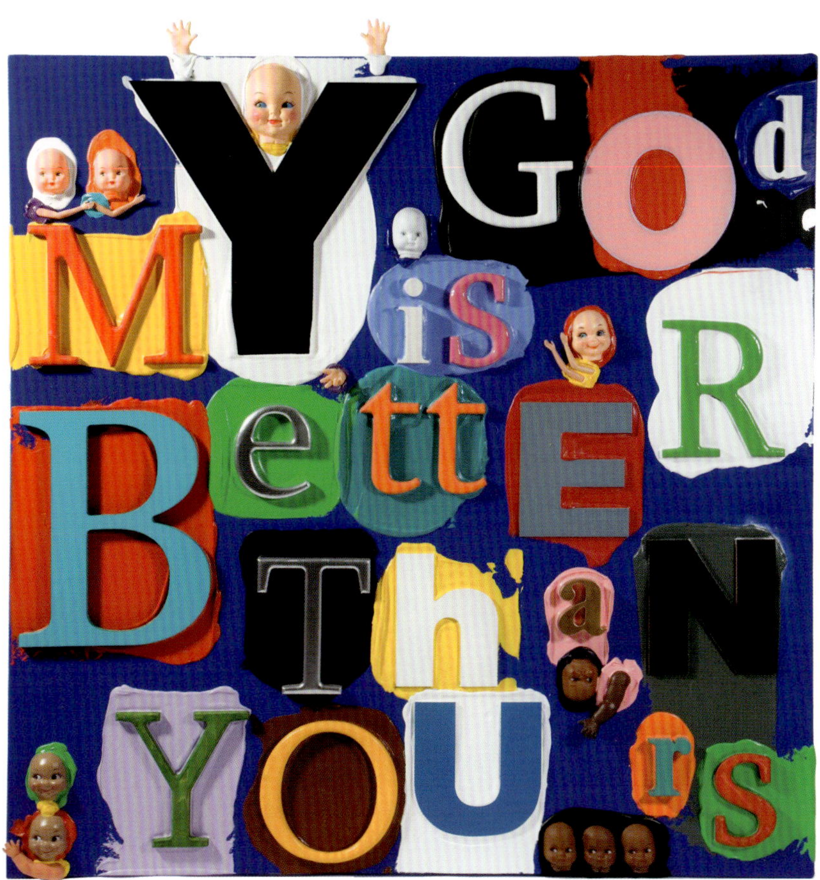

My God Is Better Than Yours (2009) Embedded Objects, Acrylic Paint on Canvas 143 x 143cm

Jamie Andrews: Behind the Scenes

More about:

Jamie....

Educated- No formal art school tuition
Galleries Familiar With Artist's Work-
Targetfollow, Norwich, Norfolk
Ferini Art Gallery, Lowestoft, Suffolk
Website- www.jamieandrewsart.com

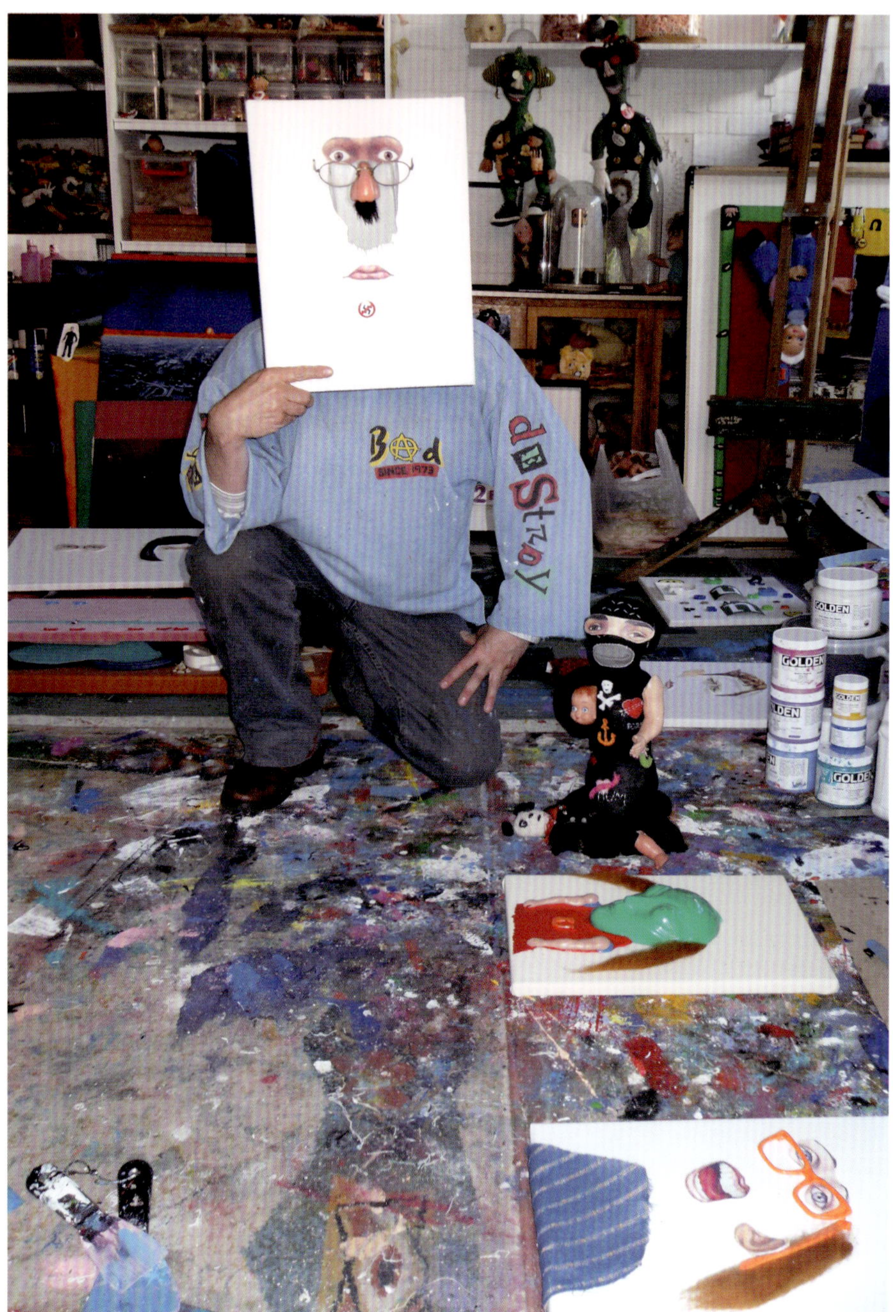

S et in the corner of a high walled Victorian garden, there lie two small fish ponds and the entrance to my studio. A child's name plaque hangs on the door, which simply reads, 'Jamie's Room'. This is the place of work, contemplation and above all, play. The wailing sounds of Public Image, Talking Heads, Iggy Pop and other such bands of the 70s and 80s resonate within, drowning out the sounds of traffic and the outside world. The studio resembles the bedroom of a teenager who refuses to tidy his room, reflecting my disorderliness. Boxes of toys and dolls' body parts fill the shelves whilst ongoing works spread out across the floor awaiting the next inspiration. What little floor space is visible has layers of paint and marks like an abstract expressionist work in itself, the tools for making these marks are often unconventional and lay scattered around the room: a builder's trowel, planks of wood and various objects still dripping with the paint from the night before. Completed works are perched on any available space in expectation of a final judgement, hoping for a frame, if not banished to a box or a bottom drawer.

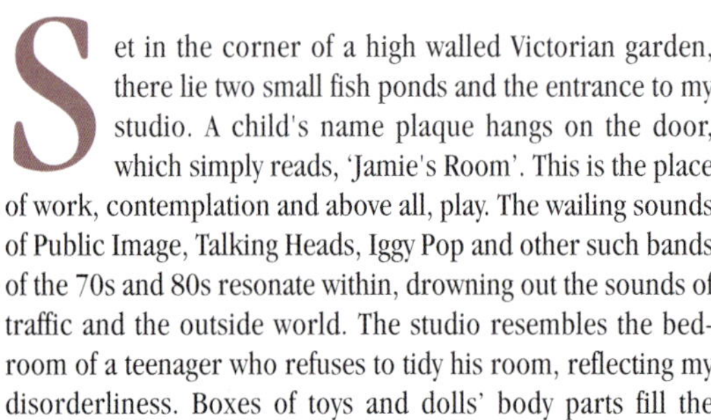

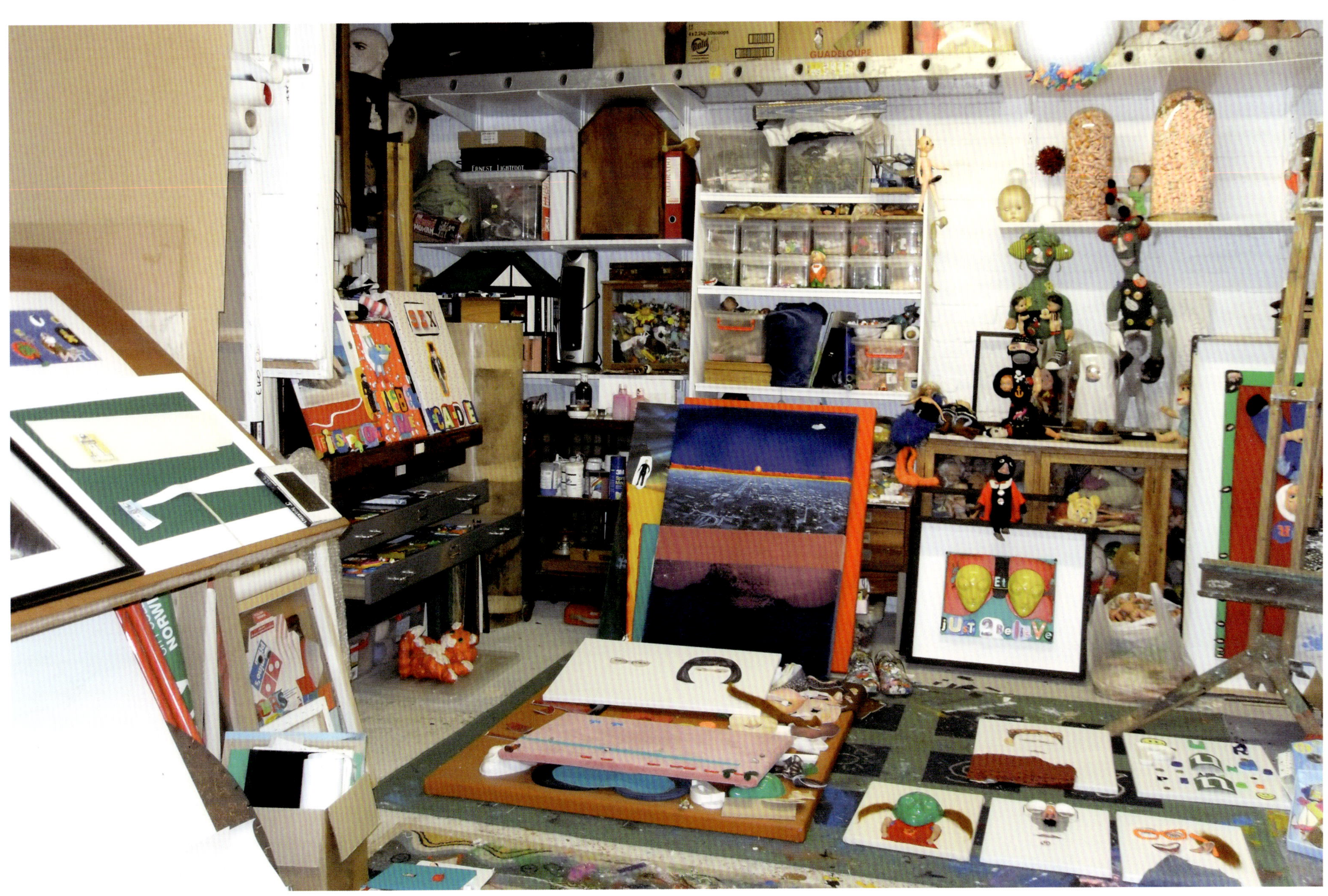

Tony White

The bold colours and graphic shapes in Tony's work attract immediate attention. His work tends to invoke an emotional response, with visitors responding to the 'hidden' elements in the work and intrigued by what they personally see in the juxtaposition of shapes and colours.
- The Riverslade Gallery, Saffron Walden, Essex

Tony White
Painter, Printmaker
Newport, Essex

My images typically contain areas of bold colour with an organic and sculptural sense inspired by biological, geological and celestial forms. I often return to the sun and moon, ice, rock and stone, and to sentinel trees. My style is informed by the shapes, textures and colours of Henry Moore at Perry Green, Barbara Hepworth, Wilhelmina Barnes-Graham, and prints of Terry Frost, Edward Bawden and Michael Rothenstein. The latter two from the Fry Art Gallery in Saffron Walden.

Blue Bossa seeks to capture in a simple form the strength and vibrancy of an event. A bold, striking and lasting impression, the type of which is often fleeting but memorable in nature. I would hope to evoke a spontaneous response, a `wow`, such as you might get when a spectacular moment occurs in life.

Silva-IV combines colour passages within and beyond the vertical elements and aspires to draw in the viewer to see what lies beyond. Symbolic of life`s events or acquaintances, spreading out in front and presenting choices and decisions in the way forward and in the people and places lost and found.

Bio-III, although appearing to be firmly rooted in my experience as a microbiologist, and echoing the organic shapes and structures that are found in bacterial forms, or the organelles of a cell under the microscope, explores the connections and relationships, rhythms and forms, that are found in life and music. The passages and flows, stops and starts, connections, barriers and resolutions of life`s jazz.

Educated-
No formal art school tuition
Advanced Printmaking Techniques, Curwen Print Study Centre
Membership of Local Art Societies-
Society of East Anglian Watercolourists (SEAW)
Cambridge Open Studios
Accreditation With National Art Societies
Galleries Familiar With Artist's Work-
Darryl Nantais Gallery, Linton, Cambridge
The Riverslade Gallery, Saffron Walden, Essex
Collections (Open To The Public)-
Bio-VI Museo della Carta e della Filigrana (Paper and Watermark Museum), Fabriano, Marche, Italy
Website- www.tonewhite.com

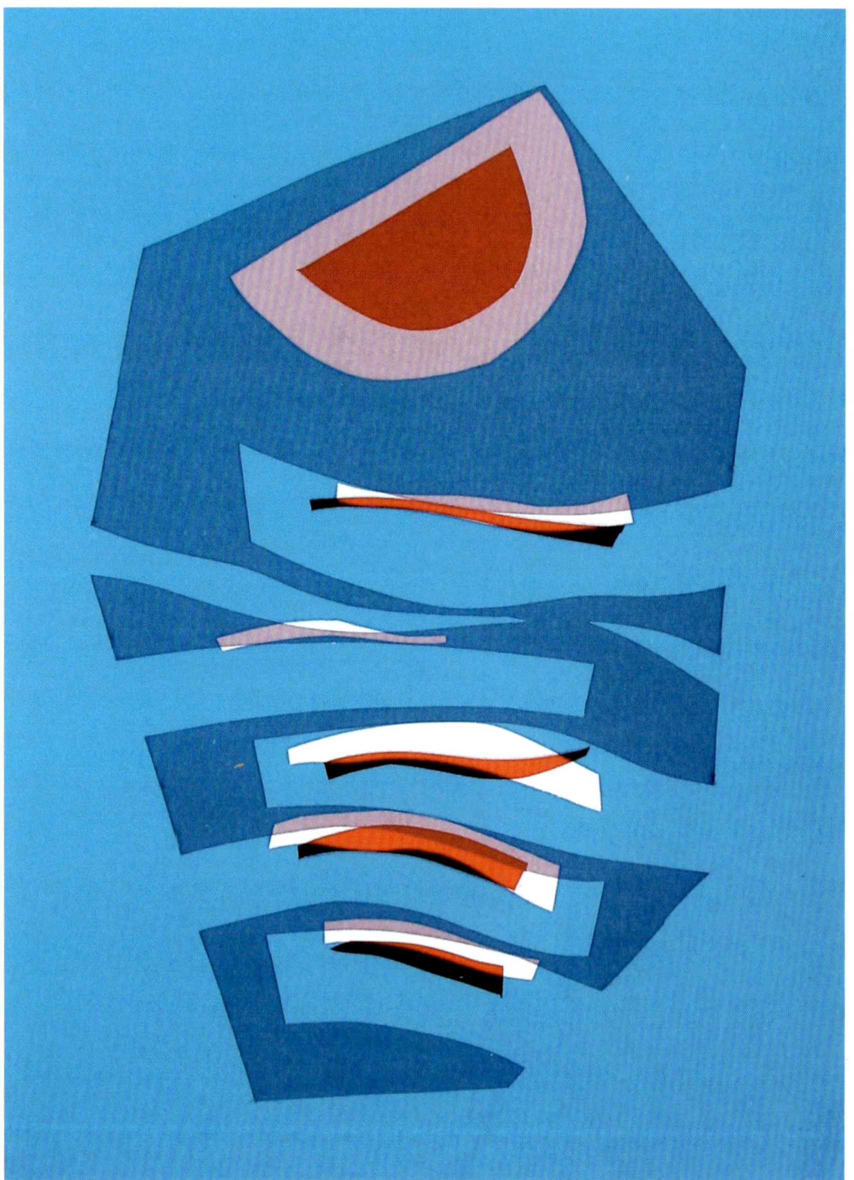

Blue Bossa(2009) Screenprint 35 x 26cm

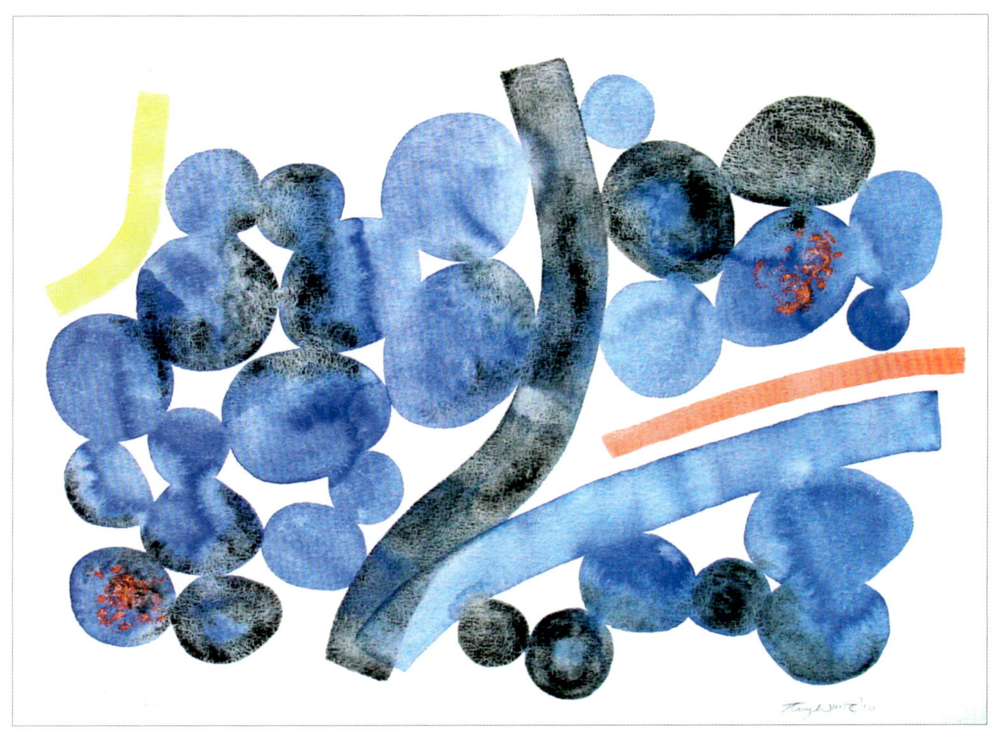

Bio-III (2010) Watercolour/Oil Pastel on Handmade Fabriano Paper 56 x 75cm

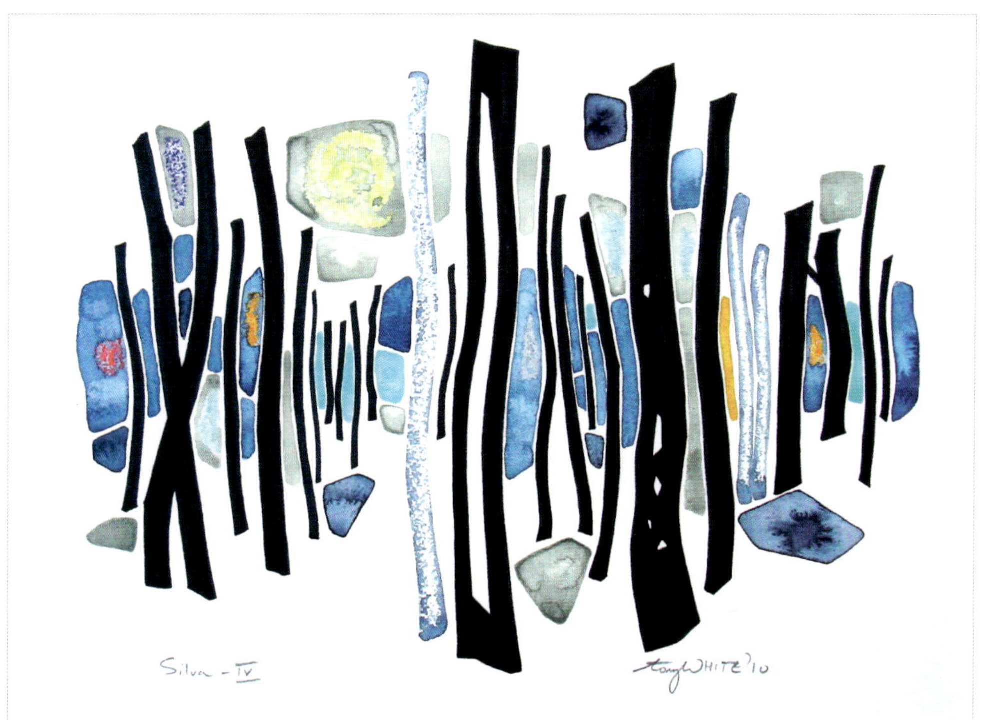

Silva-IV(2010) Watercolour/Oil Pastel/Black Pen 28 x 35cm

Robert Priseman

Robert Priseman
Painter
Wivenhoe, Essex

I enjoy the dialogue which exists between artists and takes place in a tangible sense through their work. British painters such as Michael Andrews, Frank Auerbach and Francis Bacon have a particular fascination for me, whilst past masters such as Friedrich, Goya, Poussin, Vermeer and Warhol offer limitless inspiration.

Electric Chair forms part of the 'No Human Way to Kill' project (in collaboration with Firstsite and the University of Essex Human Rights Centre) and depicts the electric chair at New York's Sing Sing Prison. It is the same chair that Andy Warhol used as a model for his iconic image and is based on a photograph supplied courtesy of the New York State Department of Correctional Services.

Dachau shows the interior of a small gas chamber located at the Dachau Concentration camp near Munich, Germany. It is one in a series of five paintings and six drawings which trace the developmental steps taken by the Nazis towards industrialised killing and was inspired in part by a painting by Luc Tuymans of the same name.

Galleries Familiar With Artist's Work-
Firstsite Contemporary Art, Colchester, Essex
The University of Essex Art Gallery, Colchester, Essex
Collections (Open To The Public)-
The Royal Collection, Windsor Castle
Wolverhampton Art Gallery
Derby Museums and Art Gallery
The University of Kent
Corpus Christi College, Cambridge
The University of Hull
Cranfield University
Lucas Industries
MFU Mutual
Sheffield Hallam University
Northern College
The Guggenheim, New York
Website- www.artfractures.com

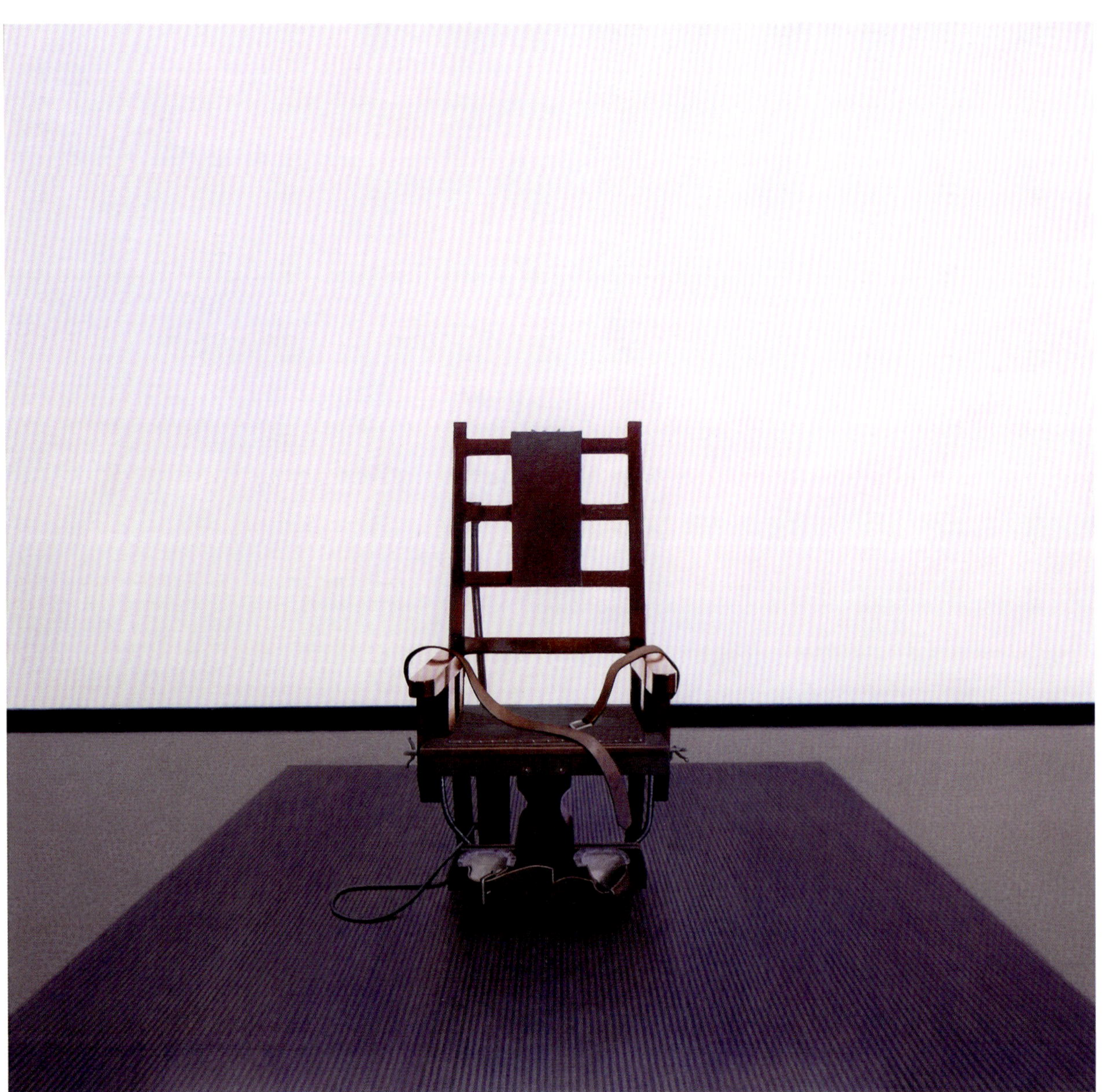

Electric Chair (2007) Oil on Linen 153 x 153cm

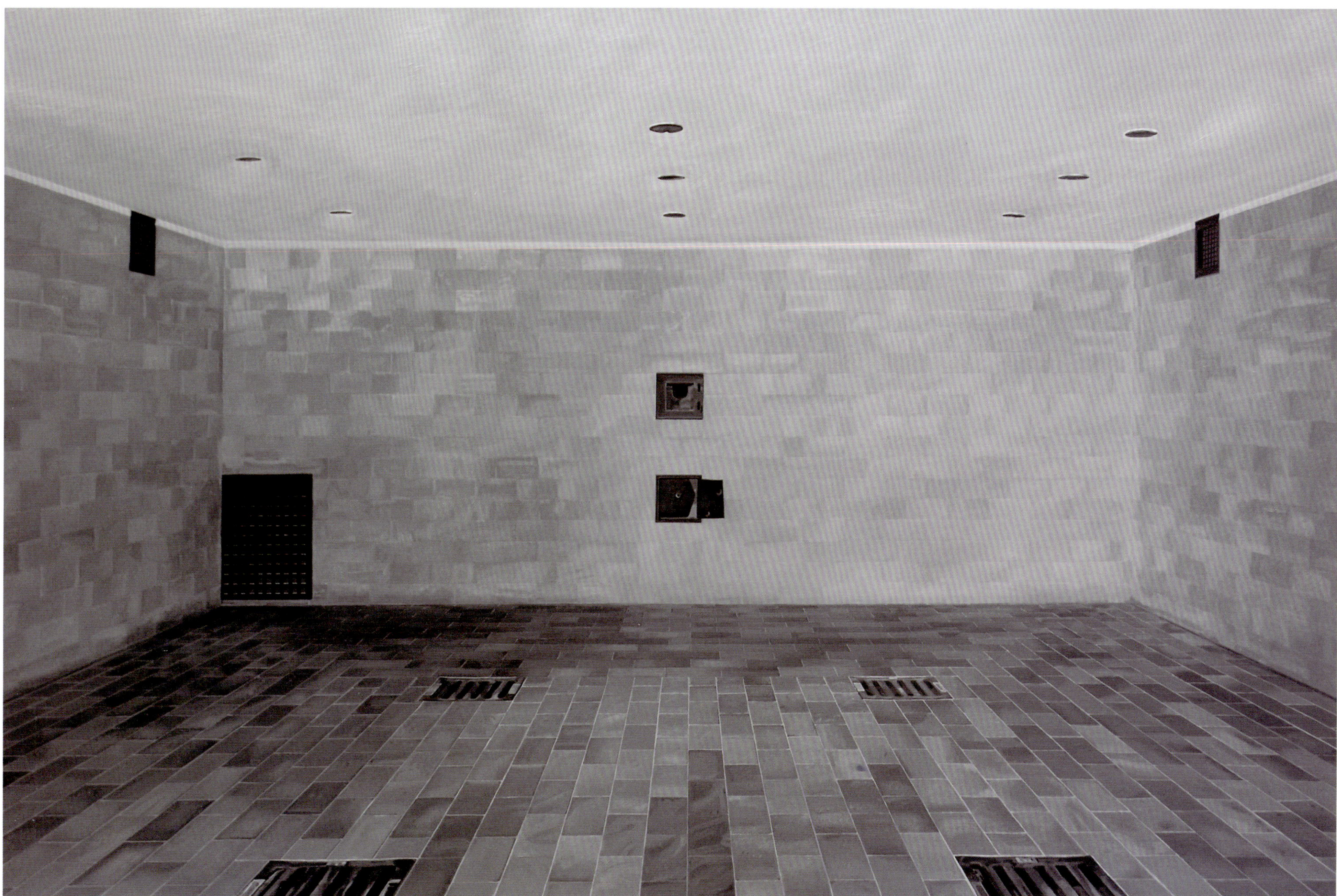

Dachau (2009) Oil on Linen 183 x 274cm

Susan Gunn BA (Hons)

Susan Gunn's largescale abstract gesso paintings evoke both fragility and resilience, featuring cracks and fissures on the surface which evolve during the drying process. At times visceral, at times radiating serenity, Gunn's emotive paintings evoke contemplation and display a transformative power on the spaces they inhabit. Each work displays balance and sensitivity to colour, composition and surface.
-ROLLO Contemporary Art, London

Susan Gunn BA (Hons)
Painter
Norwich, Norfolk

I find the work of Callum Innes inspirational. I was fortunate to be mentored by him for a year after being introduced by Amanda Geitner (Head of Collections at Sainsbury Centre for Visual Arts) in 2005 and visited his studio in Edinburgh. It was such a privilege to see inside the inner sanctum of such an important contemporary artist and this taught me how important the planning aspect of my kind of painting is. Formal lines and seemingly simple compositions are actually quite arduous to achieve and the tightrope between success and failure very fine.

I plan my paintings by drawing many layouts in my sketch book, the pages are graph paper. This enables me to plan the space and ratios each area covers in relation to the whole and mostly I work in series. Proportion and balance are important considerations. Colour can be a frivolous distraction, but I love colour so I tend to work in monochromes or limited combinations of colour.

Although my works are planned and geometrically strict, the aspect of my work that is unpredictable is the rate at which the gesso dries out and the cracks and fissures appear in the surfaces and sometimes overspill the strict geometry. This is the crux of the work really, the way my paintings develop have much to do with chance as well as hard work and meticulous planning; each piece is unique and cannot be copied or replicated, even by me. This is what excites me and I have been known to sneak back to my studio in the middle of the night to watch them as the fissures appear in the dried-out gesso like a parched riverbed.

The three pictures shown here are:
Dark Matter. I adore the black surface, it can appear reflective and aloof or absorbent, drawing, sucking you into it like a black hole as the light changes.
Ground Mineral 2009. The Prussian Blue I used to stain the white gesso, in this case, has reacted with the yellow tint in the oil to form the appearance of a verdigris green. There are also other dry pigments that have also been pressed into the surface.
Ground Neutral 2009. I often use Michael Harding's handmade paints, the Titanium White has a wonderfully fragile, bone white quality.

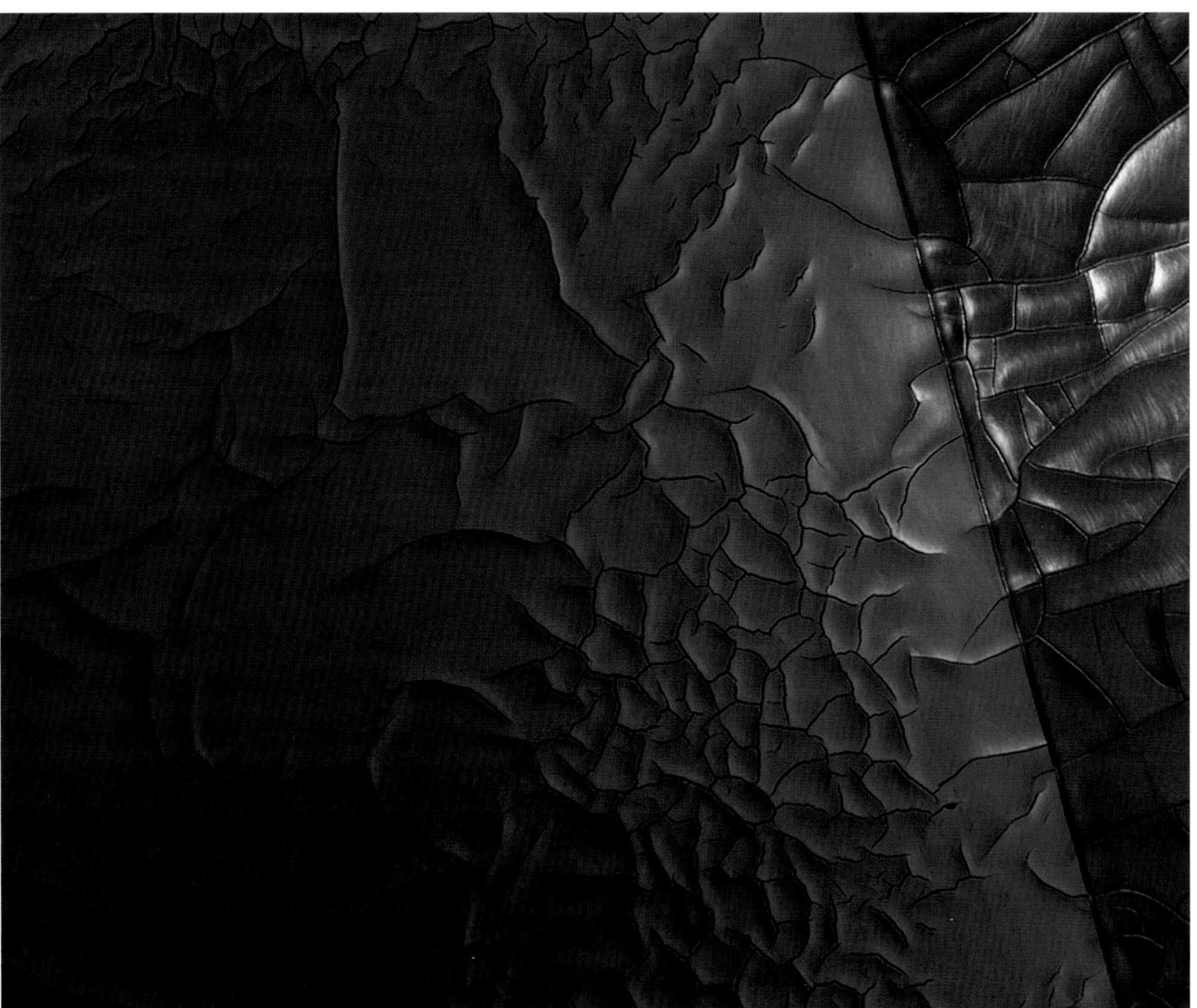

Dark Matter (Detail) (2007) Encaustic and Gesso on Canvas on Aluminium Supports 183 x 183 x 3.5cm

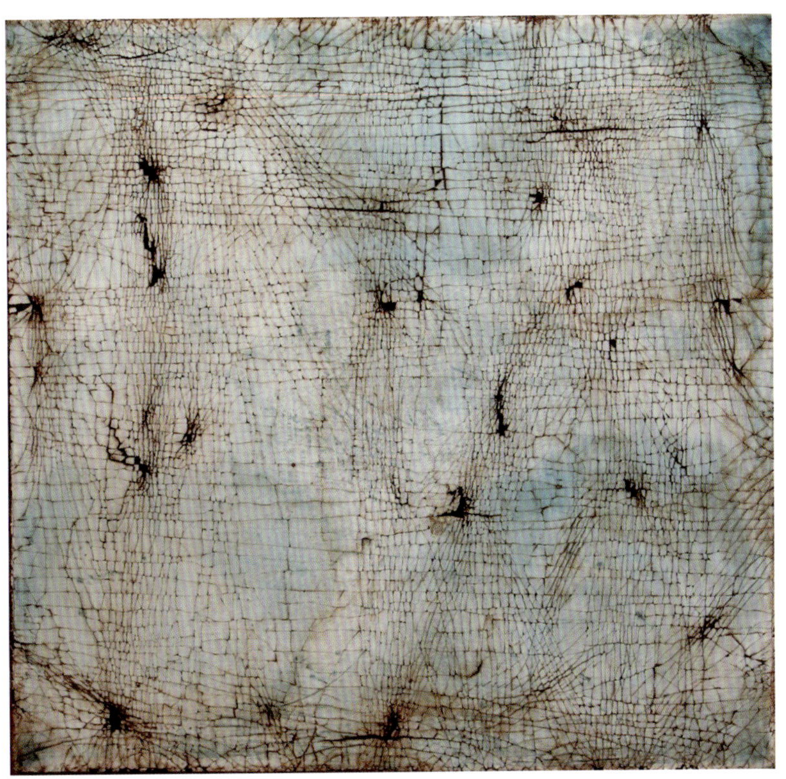

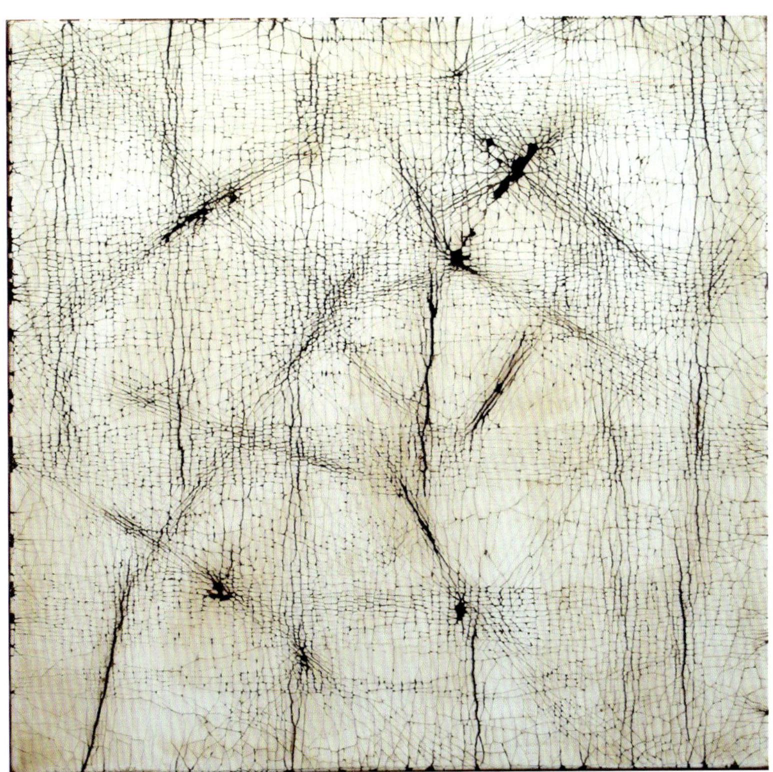

Ground Mineral (2009)
Encaustic and Gesso on Canvas on Aluminium Supports 50 x 50 x 4cm

Ground Neutral (2009)
Encaustic and Gesso on Canvas on Aluminium Supports 50 x 50 x 4cm

Susan Gunn: Behind the Scenes

More about:

Susan…

Educated- Norwich University College of the Arts
Membership of Local Art Societies-
Norfolk Contemporary Art Society
Outpost, Norwich, Norfolk
East Anglian Art Fund
Sainsbury Centre for Visual Arts
Honours-
Winner of the Bishops Art Prize 2003
Winner of the Sovereign European Painting Prize 2006
Galleries Familiar With Artist's Work-
Norwich Castle, Norwich, Norfolk
Rollo Gallery, London, London
Sainsbury Centre for Visual Arts, Norwich, Norfolk
Collections (Open To The Public)-
Arts Council England, East
Archant Collection, Norwich, Norfolk
The Sovereign Art Foundation, Hong Kong
Norwich Castle Museum & Art Gallery, Norwich, Norfolk
Sainsbury Centre Visual Arts, Norwich, Norfolk
Website- www.susangunn.co.uk

My studio is hidden inside a stable block and double garage that I have converted over the years to suit my practice. There is a workshop and mixing area where my structures are made and the gesso, paint and rabbit skin glue is mixed. This leads into an office and storage space and onto a larger working and drying space. It has no windows, which people find rather odd for an artist but it's well lit and insulated so the space stays warm in the winter and cool in the summer. Wall space is the premium and I enjoy the safe enclosed feeling inside.

My work sometimes spills outside in the summer unless it's too hot; it's great to hear the sound of the birds when I start work in the morning; the perennial return of the swallows that nest nearby is always a heart-warming occasion.

When I have been working on a painting for sometimes weeks or months, depending on the size, I am happy to finish and go onto the next idea. Sometimes the surfaces have to be disregarded as they break beyond stability. The more interesting pieces often provide some kind of struggle in the making and bringing round, and being able to rescue a piece is quite satisfying.

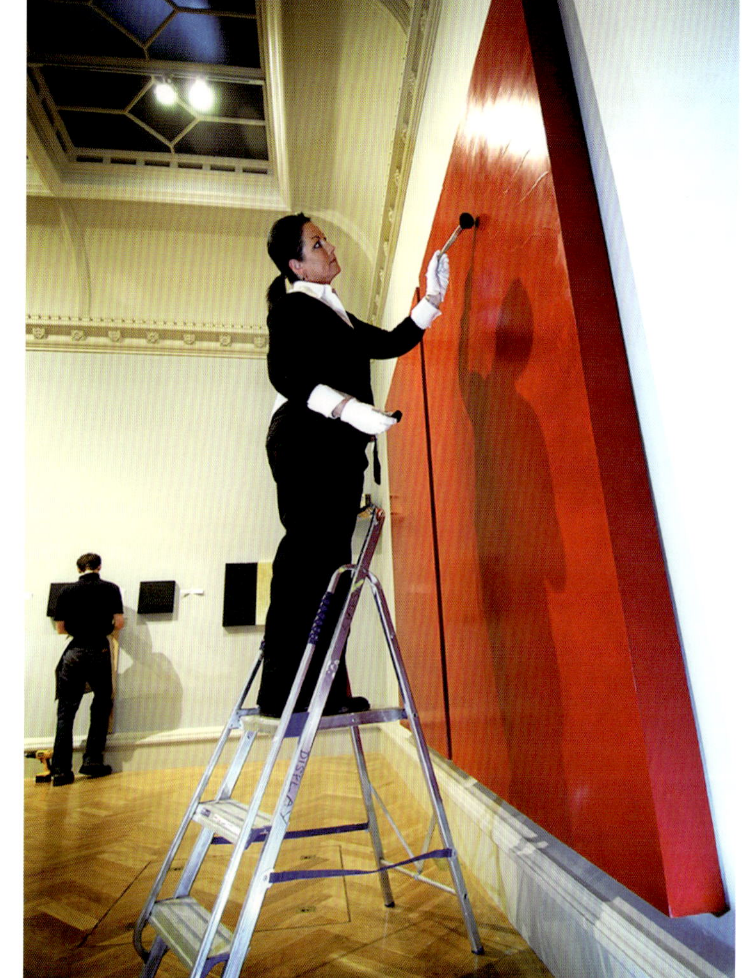

This Page: Susan on a ladder during installation at Norwich Castle Museum
Opposite Page: Susan's studio with numerous works in progress

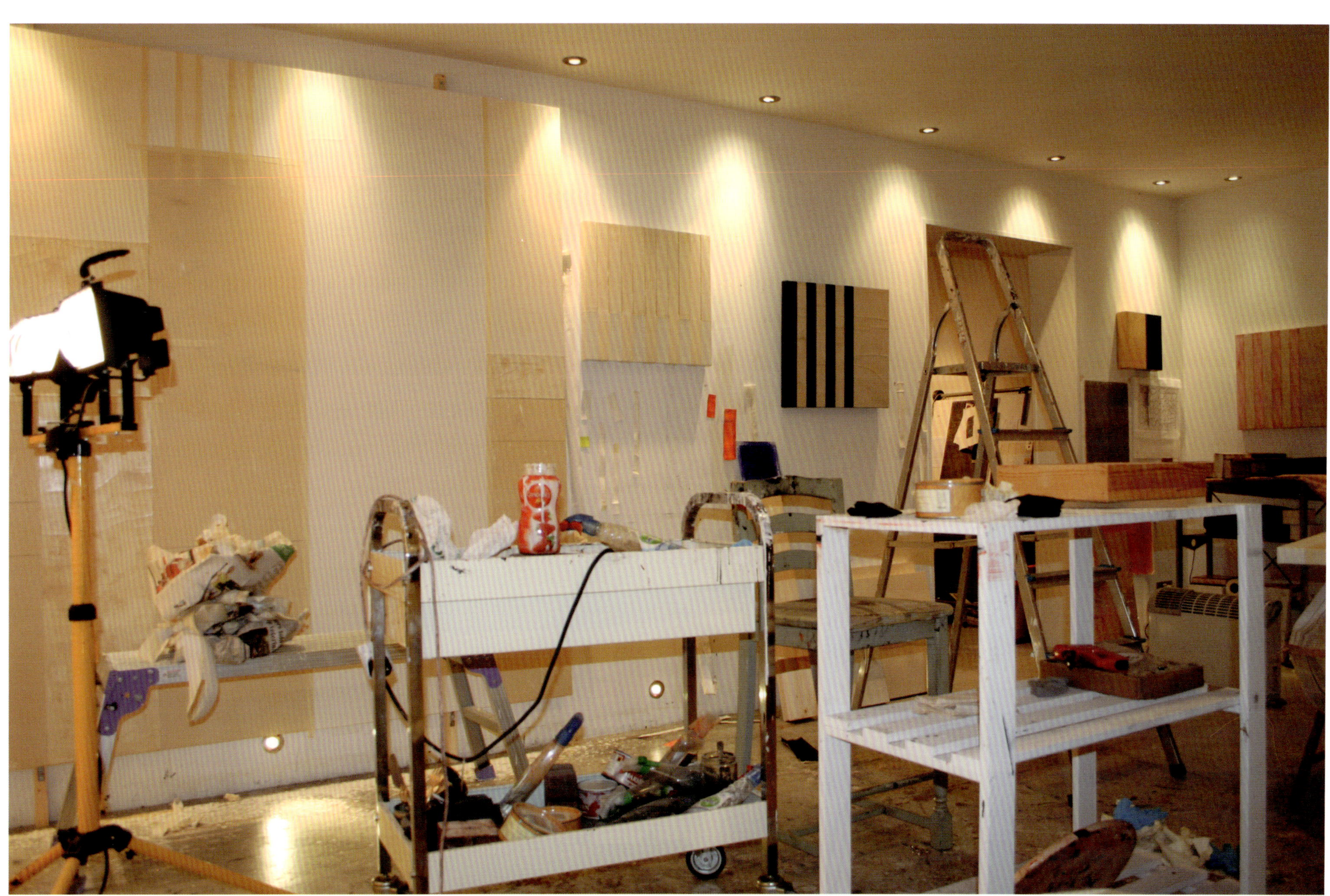

Gill Levin FRSA

Gill continues to pursue her dual career of artist and jazz musi-cian, and her painting echoes the sounds and harmonies of her music within a visual form. She has been painting for over sixty years and her work continues to excite and stimulate the viewer.
- Harleston Gallery, Harleston, Norfolk

Gill Levin FRSA
Painter
Needham, Norfolk

As a Londoner, I've been heavily inspired by the power station, the old docks and all the industrial works along the Thames, but living in Norfolk now, the skies, trees, grasses, and the Waveney are an added inspiration. I've always been intrigued by 'the spaces between', and that's why I have been able to use the demise of the West Pier, Brighton, as a huge source of work, as in *Under the Pier IX*. Industrial landscapes and cranes of all sorts have given me such pleasure to paint. They create wonderful shapes between horizontal and vertical lines and endless ideas for composition; I'm extremely particular about composition and always have been – I had such good teachers– in particular Prunella Clough.

Sky, land and water need to have vigour and movement because it's the wind, strong or gentle, that dictates the mood which I've tried to capture in *Stormy Sunset*. Now I am living in Norfolk permanently, I find the drama and light in the skies so exciting, especially the storms and the setting or rising sun, colouring and affecting the land. For this reason I connect the sky and the land rhythmically as though they are one, because of the effect each has on the other.

Now I'm living in the country, grasses, reeds and trees figure largely in my work, such as *Early Spring*; the spaces between and patches of light coming through are so compelling. The land-scapes and grass paintings are from imagination and memory, and so are more relaxing to paint than the industrial landscapes which are so detailed and specific. I tend to suit my style to the subject. The seasons are important to me and dictate the mood of each painting.

Educated- Chelsea School of Art, NDD 1956
Membership of Local Art Societies-
Norwich 20; Norfolk Contemporary Art Society;
Harleston and Waveney Art Trail, Norfolk
Accreditation With National Art Societies-
The Royal Society of Arts
Galleries Familiar With Artist's Work-
Harleston Gallery, Harleston, Norfolk; The Southwold Gallery, Southwold, Suffolk; The John Russell Gallery, Ipswich, Suffolk
Collections (Open To The Public)-
Landscape, Hereford College, Oxford, Oxfordshire
Miallet Contemporary Art Society, London
The Clown John Lewis Partnership, London
Factory Slough Picture Collection, Middlesex

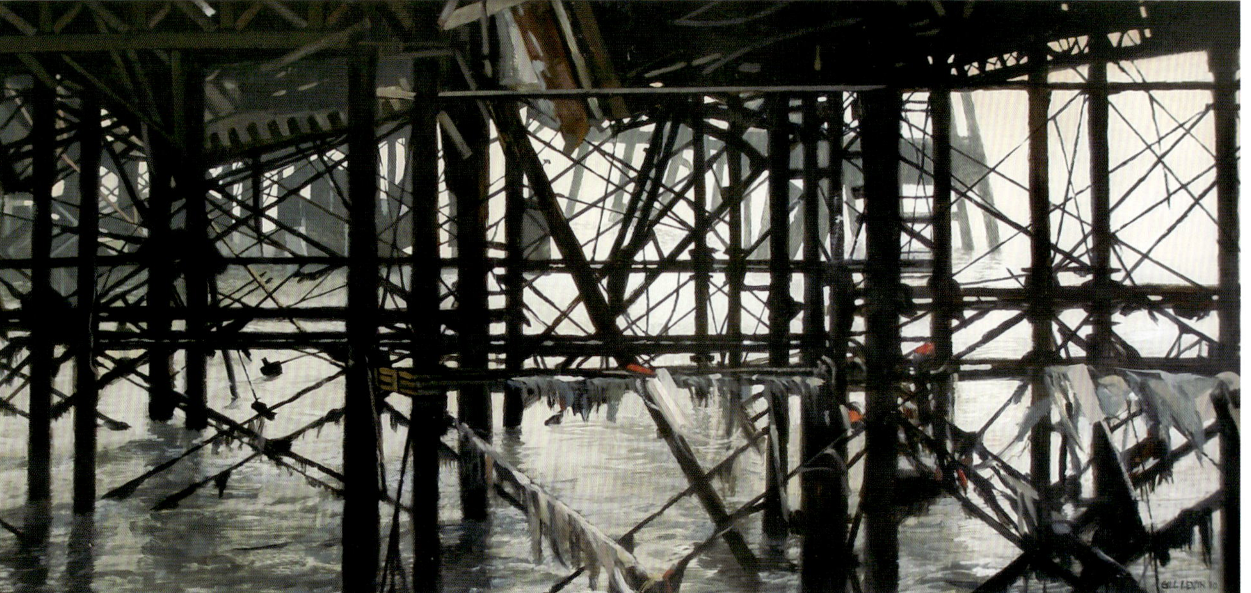

Under the Pier IX (2010) Oil on Board 46 x 92cm

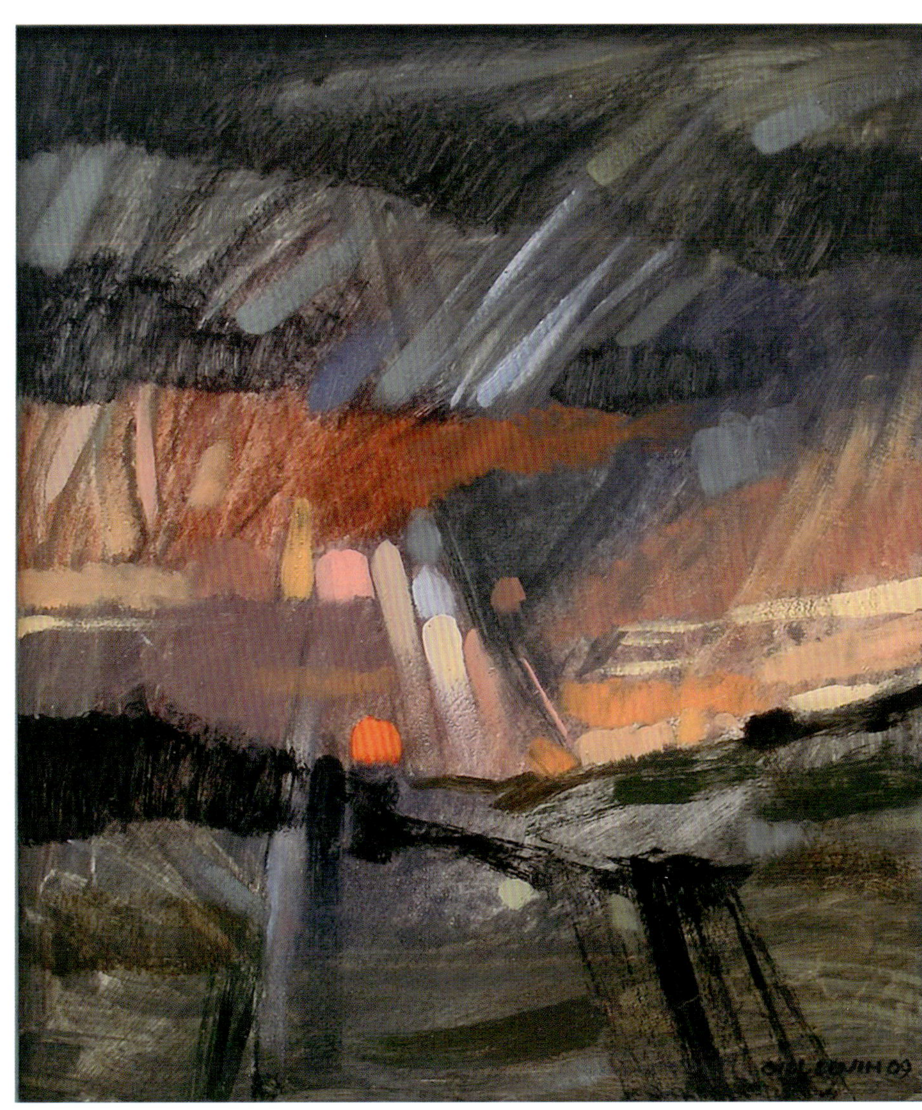

Stormy Sunset (2009) Oil on Board 35 x 30cm

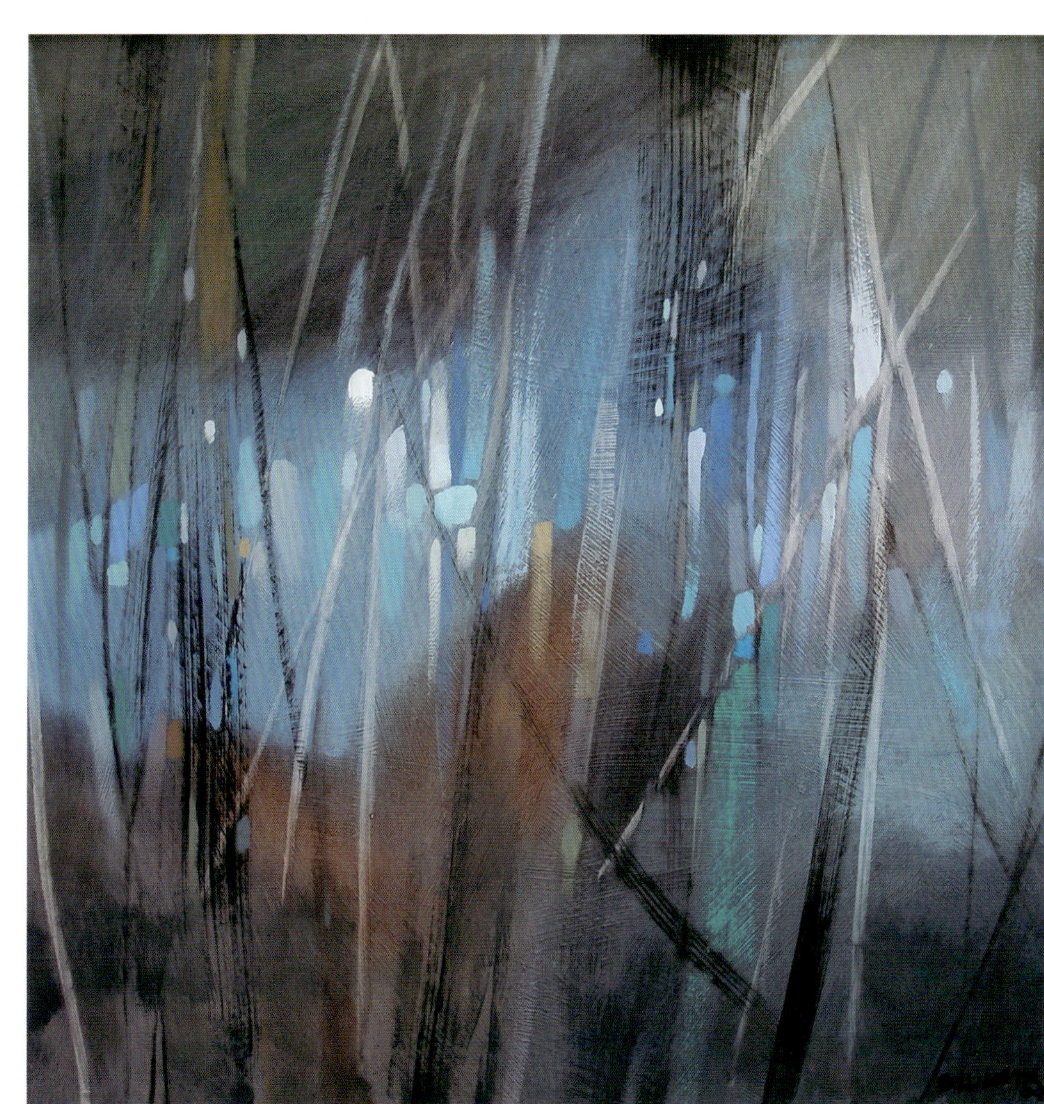

Early Spring(2009) Oil on Board 60 x 55cm

Jack Stephenson

Jack Stephenson
Painter
Middleton, Suffolk

I was trained in the early 1960s when it was still possible to learn the craft of painting from practising artists who themselves had been taught the secrets of the studio from an earlier generation of fine painters. The teachers who influenced me most were Ken Howard, Olwyn Bowey and David Tindle, all now RAs, and all painters in the British figurative tradition that has come down to us from Sickert and his followers.

Although my kind of painting could not be described as 'cutting edge' I feel strongly that it is still possible for a figurative artist to produce work that is, in its own way, lively, contemporary and relevant.

It has been with these thoughts in mind that I have developed an interest in the Conversation Piece with a view to bring it up to date and turn, what is essentially an 18th to 19th century form, into a mirror on the way we live now.

I am particularly fascinated by the potential of these group paintings to depict more than outward appearance; with effort and sensitivity it is possible to convey much more than that.

I run classes from my Theberton House studio where students are taught traditional painting techniques working from both the nude and the clothed model. I also give illustrated talks on the painters of the late 19th and early 20th century. Talks given so far have included Joaquin Sorolla y Bastida, Antonio Mancini, Sir William Orpen, Ben Nicholson, Walter Sickert and Anders Zorn.

It has long been my intention to intensify my concentration on painting from the nude and in recent months I have embarked on a new course of work which will eventually be shown in the Peter Pears Gallery in 2012.

Educated- Goldsmith's College,London
Membership of Local Art Societies- The Suffolk Group;
Southwold Art Circle
Website- www.portraitsfromlife.co.uk

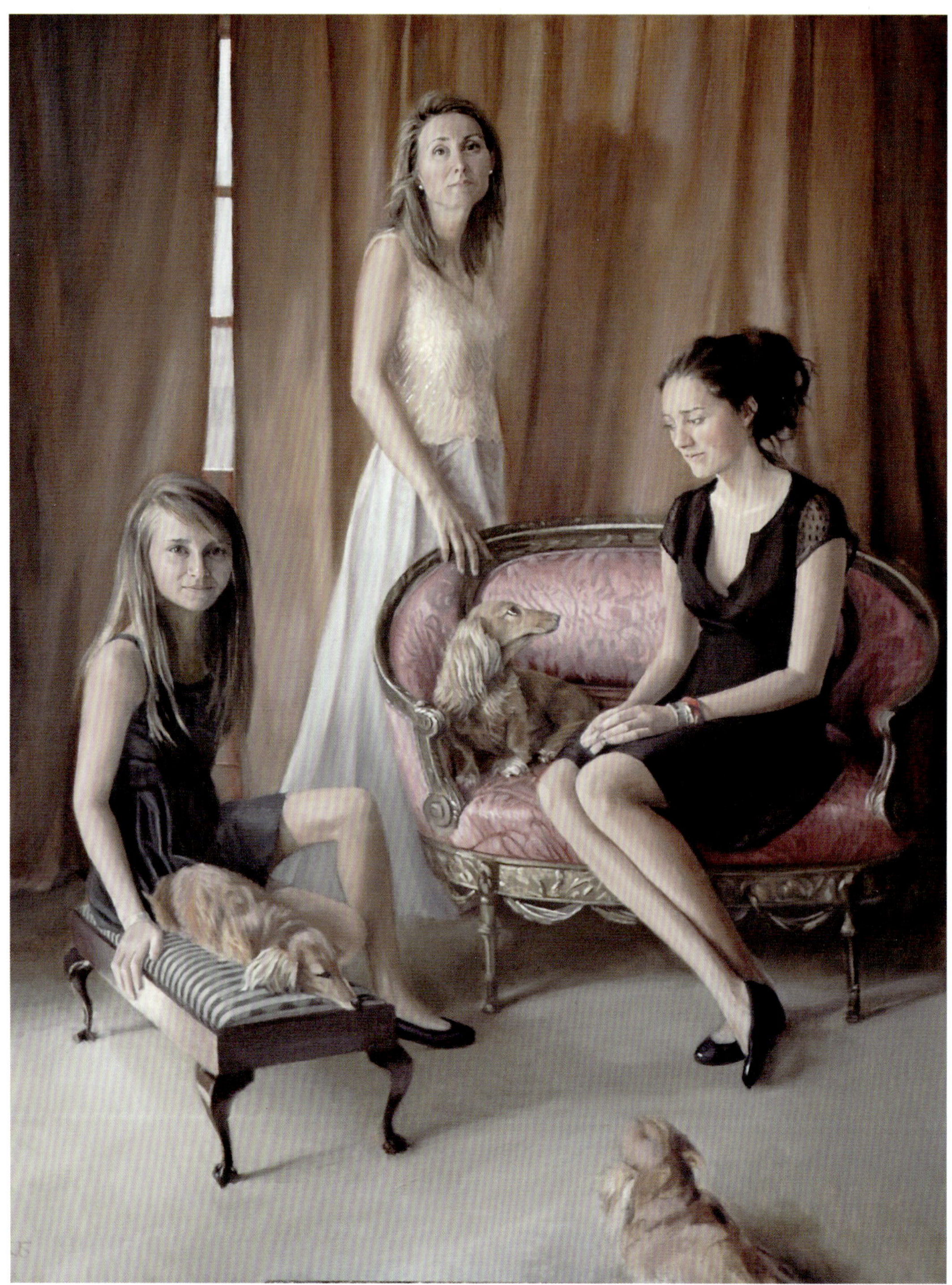

The Kendall Girls Oil on Linen 100 x 130cm

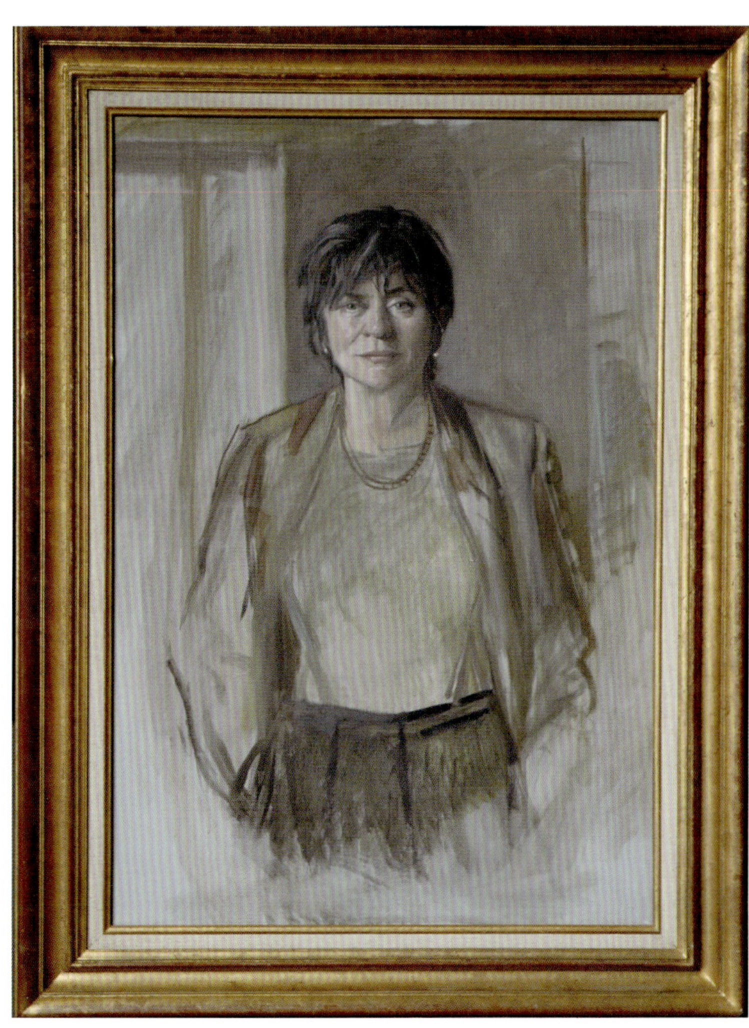

Diana Quick Oil on Linen 80 x 100cm

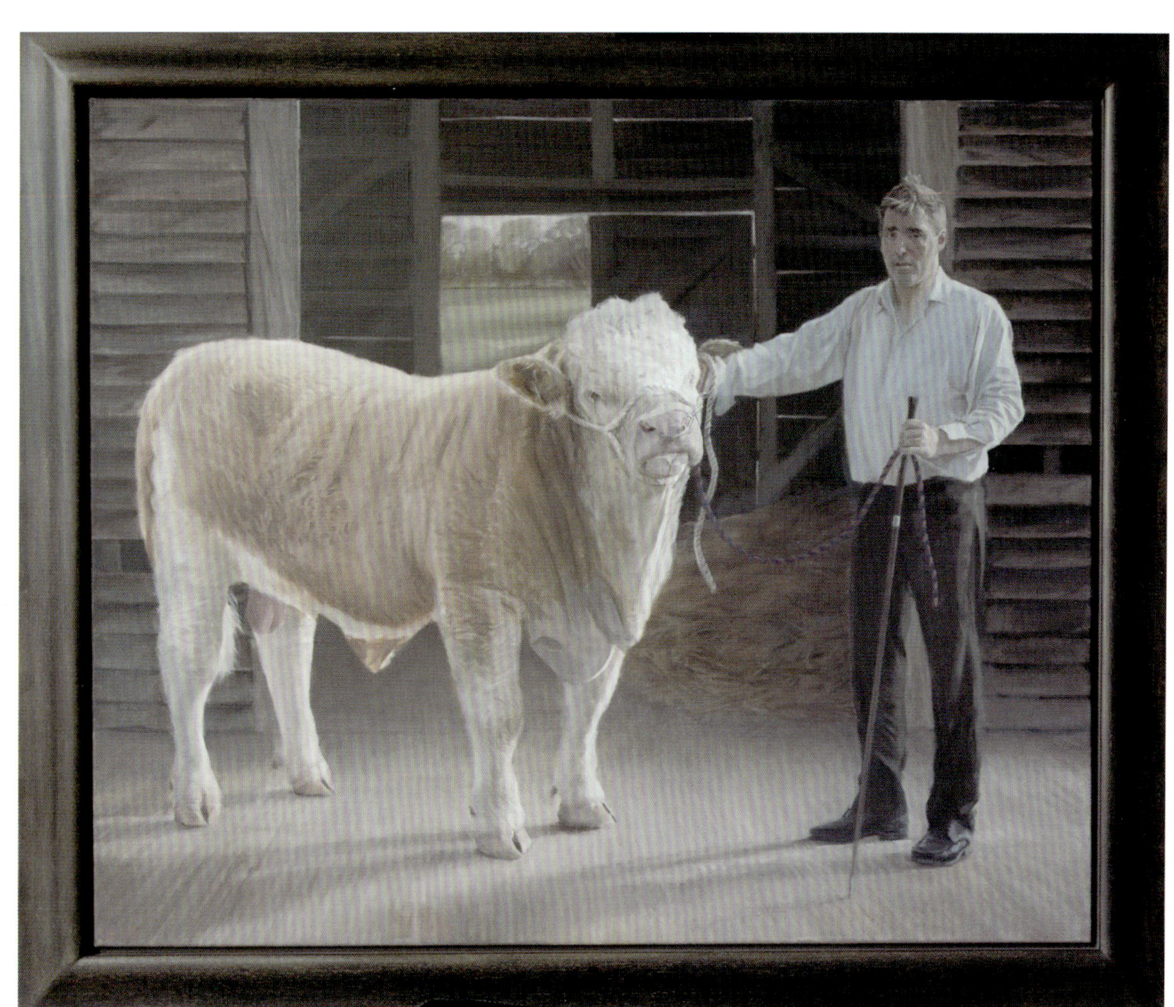

Victorious Oil on Linen 105 x 130cm

Honor Surie MA

*It's hard to distil any single aspect of Honor Surie's work that
makes it enduringly attractive. The secret is in the combination
of all the parts, including the subtle use of colour and texture,
which allows the viewer to feel and experience the subject and
breathe the Suffolk air.*
- Reunion Gallery, Felixstowe, Suffolk

Honor Surie (MA)
Painter, Sculptor
Woodbridge, Suffolk

I love the rivers, bordered with reeds, mud flats and reflected
lights and absorb the feeling of these areas. I look at local places,
draw them, and using this reference develop them into compositions that please me, which is why I find myself painting mainly
landscape. These ideas go onto canvas. I began painting with oils,
but at the moment I am using acrylics.

The work *Corn for Pheasants* depicts a corner of a field near
where I live. It makes a good composition in certain lights; I got
obsessed with it and did numerous paintings of the subject from
different angles.

I get hooked on a subject and work fanatically, making works
over and over again until I've exhausted it, but even then, years
later I may return to work on the same theme.

To me *Birds at Blythburgh* depicts the subtlety between mud
and water and the distance across the expanded river. I painted it
very quickly and knew when to stop - which is not always easy to
do. I strive to achieve the image I want with the minimum of
strokes, but I so often get carried away with details.

I think that *Down Butley River* captures the peace and calm of
a winter's evening, the location is another favourite place that I
could use constantly, painting each time, hopefully, a simpler
work. I really enjoy the constant challenge of striving towards
greater artistic satisfaction.

Educated- Norwich School of Art and Design 2000
Galleries Familiar With Artist's Work-
RE+new, Woodbridge, Suffolk
Buckenham Galleries, Southwold, Suffolk
Reunion, Felixstowe, Suffolk
Collections (Open To The Public)-
Tam Ipswich Borough Council, Suffolk
Hands and Dove Tuddenham Parish Council, Suffolk
Website- www.honorsurie.co.uk

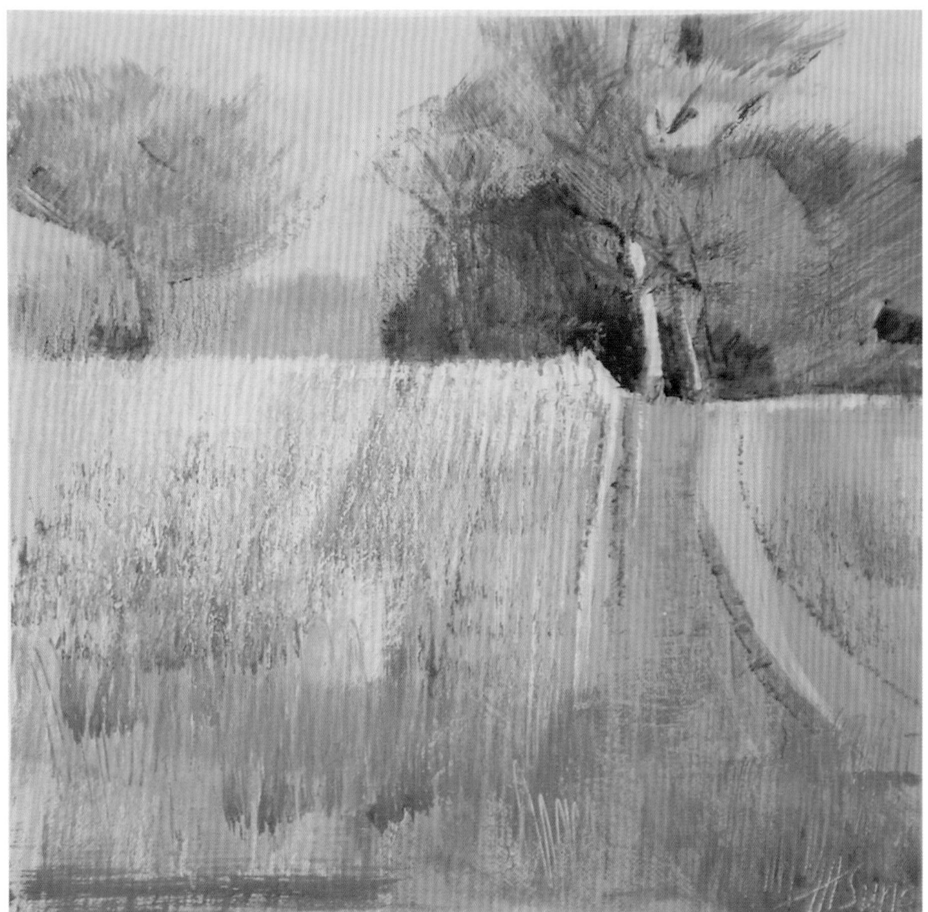

Corn for Pheasants (2010) Acrylic on Canvas 30 x 30cm

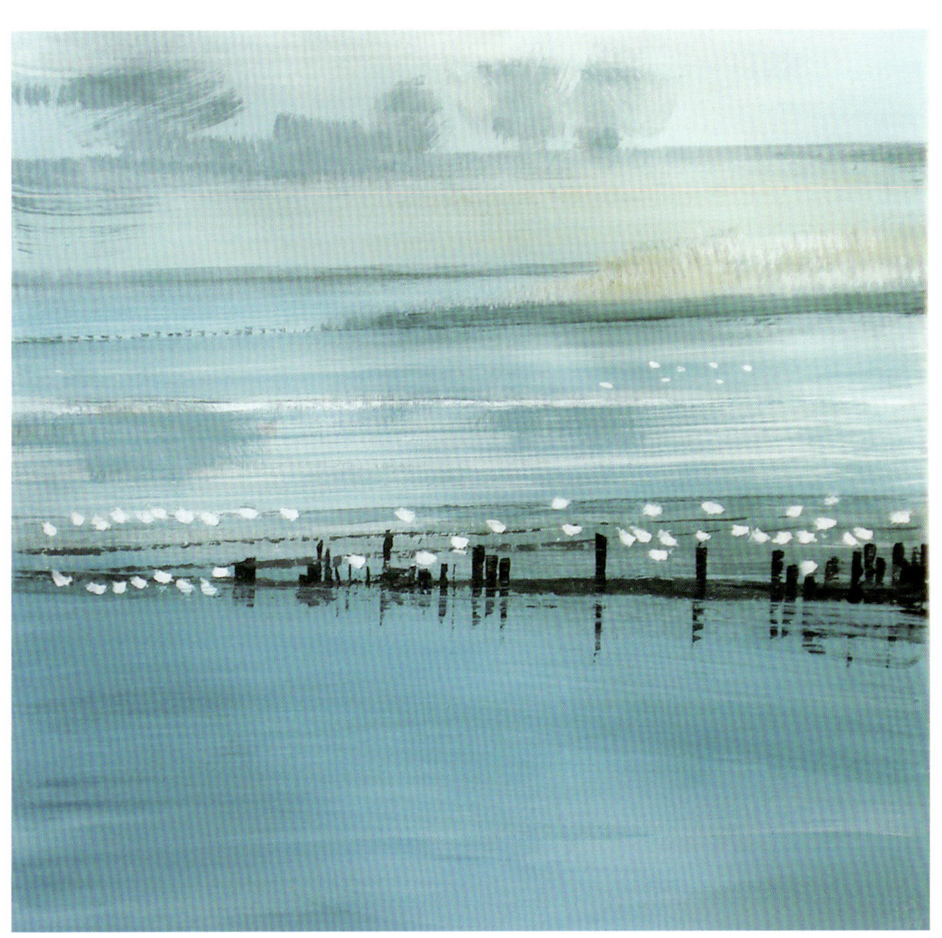

Birds at Blythburgh (2010) Acrylic on Canvas 60 x 60cm

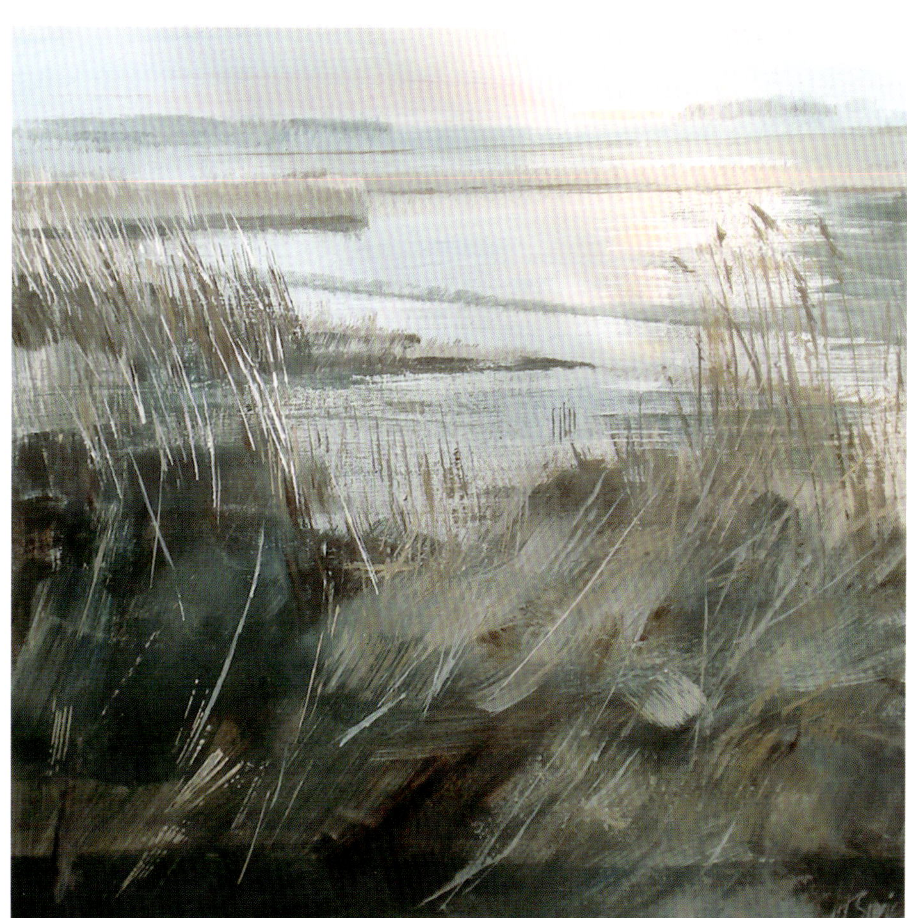

Down Butley River (2009) Acrylic on Canvas 60 x 60cm

Eleonora Knowland BA (Hons)

It is as if Eleonora wants us to remember a forgotten pleasure lying beneath her soft delicate pallet of oil colour.
- Digby Gallery at the Mercury Theatre, Colchester, Essex

Eleonora Knowland BA (Hons)
Painter
Eye, Suffolk

My work is inspired by landscape, more specifically the moments of colour and light in the landscape. I find the soft agricultural countryside breathtaking; which is best expressed by painting on curved canvasses.

3.24 Winter is an investigation into catching light early one winter's evening; thin layers of paint are built up to create a depth of colour. I stitch onto the canvas as part of the structure of the landscape. This can be in the form of lines or pleats or slashes; often representing field boundaries, rows of stakes or a line of trees. These marks are a visual punctuation in the paintings, creating tensions and responses. I hope my paintings lift viewers' spirits. There is no 'right' way to look at my work; my thoughts are not yours.

Staffa Island is my interpretation of an interesting geological rock formation of basalt columns off the coast of Scotland. I have created the form of the image with hand stitched lines before painting the canvas. The fantastic colours of the Gulf Stream were really inspiring, particularly as it rose and fell against the rocks. An idea of the bulk and downward drive of the island is what I was aiming to capture.

In the detail image of *Staffa Island* it is possible to see the stitched lines that form the columns. When working on a painting I find it very exciting as it nears the end. How do I know when it is finished? I feel a sense of joy, relief, calm and at the same time a strong emotional uplifting.

11.59 Summer is one of a series of paintings of sunlight glimpsed through trees. I have returned to this subject time and time again in an effort to express my understanding of the experience. In *11.59 Summer* I have used string applied to the canvas to signify the solidity of trees, then glazed layers of paint over these lines to create the glimpsed sunlight. The constant repainting of an idea is interesting as thoughts become refined at each attempt.

Educated- School of Art and Design, Colchester Institute
Membership of Local Art Societies-
Artworks, Suffolk; Nine Artists, East Anglia and London
Galleries Familiar With Artist's Work-
Buckenham Galleries, Southwold, Suffolk
Lesley Craze Gallery, Clerkenwell Green, London
Digby Gallery, Balkerne Gate, Colchester
Website- www.eleonoraknowland.co.uk

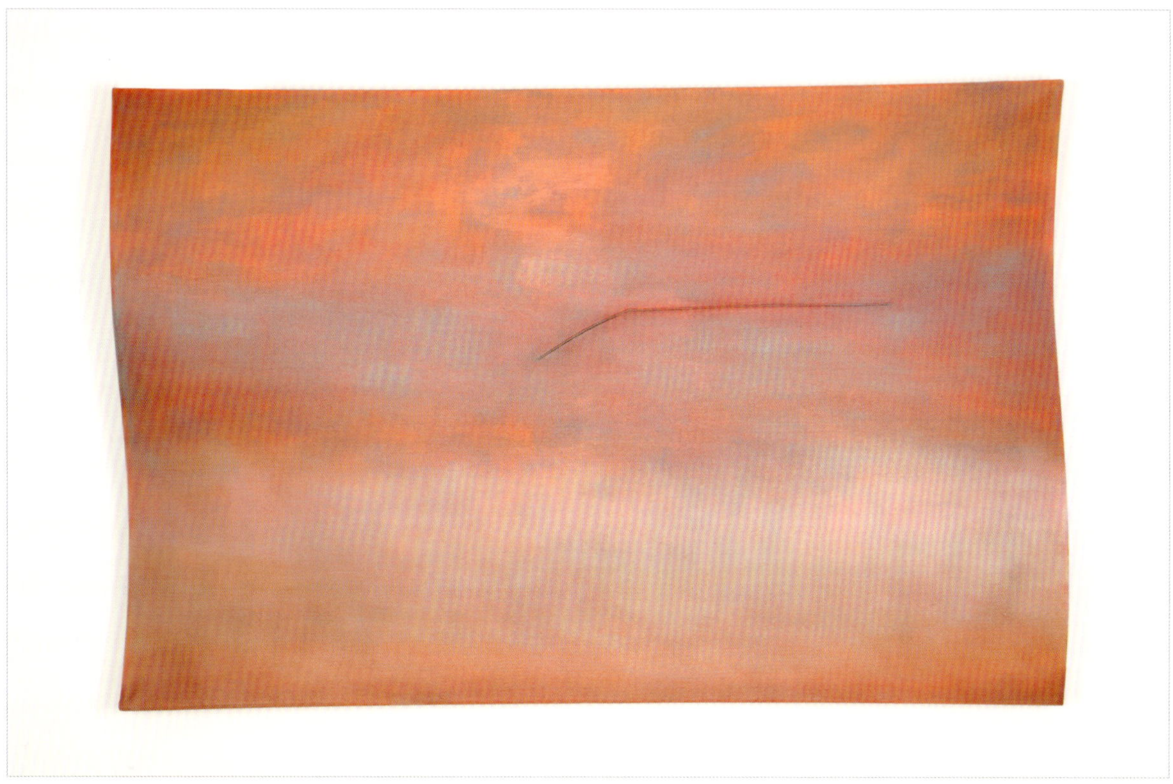

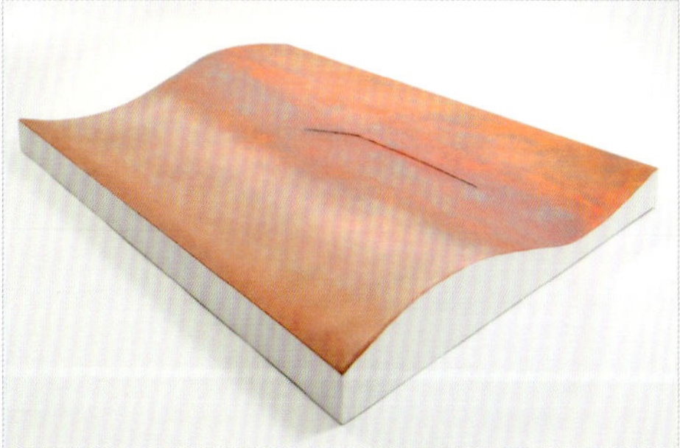

Above :
3.24 Winter (2008)
Oil on Curved Stitched Canvas
80 x 120cm
Left: At this angle it is possible to clearly see the curved canvas of *3.24 Winter (2008)*

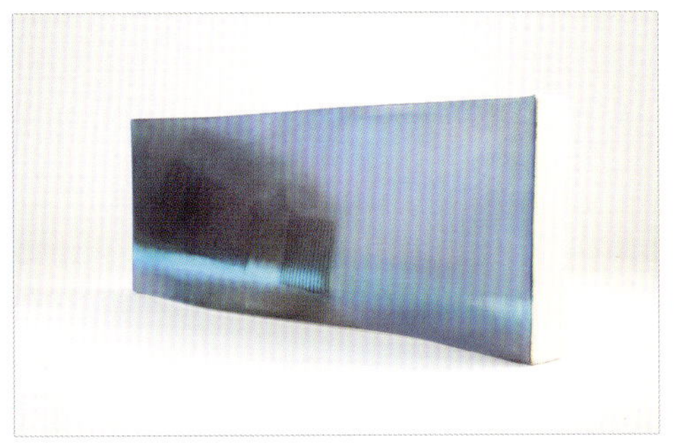

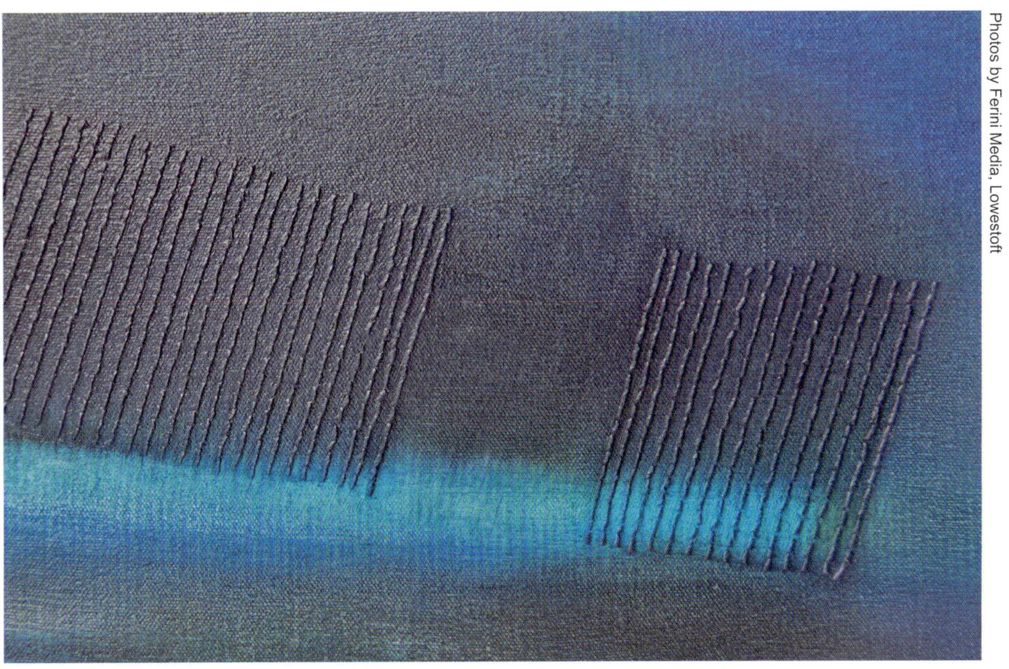

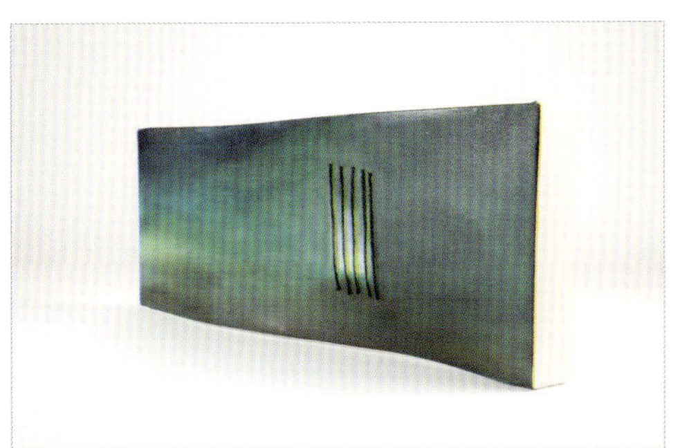

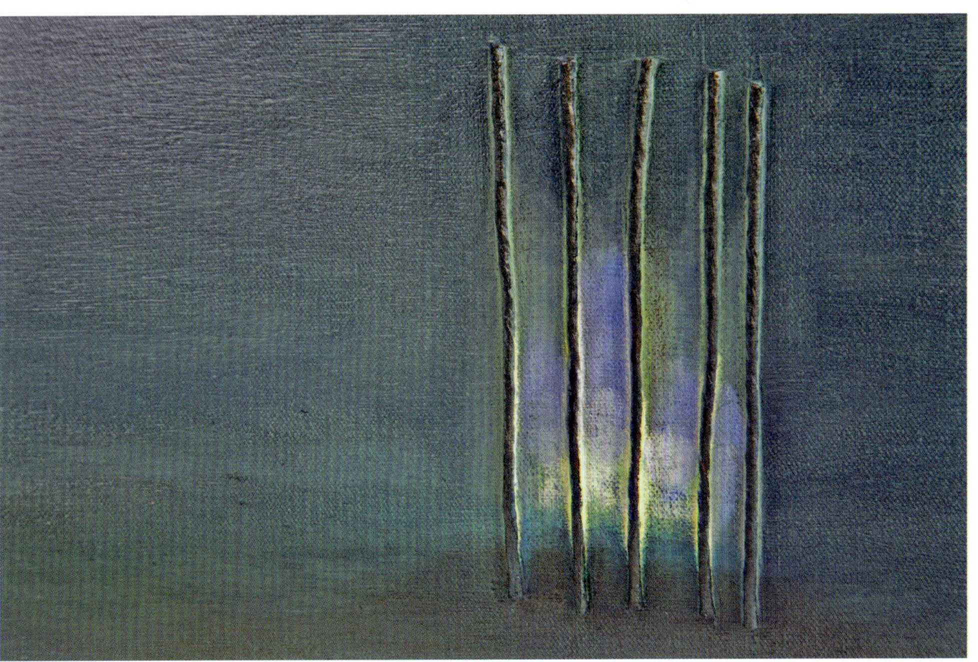

Above Left: Three-quarter view of *Staffa Island (2009)*
Oil on Curved, Stitched Canvas 18 x 50cm
Above Right: Detail from *Staffa Island (2009)*
Bottom Left: Three-quarter view of
11.59 Summer (2010) Oil on Curved Canvas 18 x 50cm
Bottom Right: Detail from *11.59 Summer (2010)*

Chris Hann Dip.AD, PGDFA (London)

Chris Hann Dip. AD, PGDFA (London)
Painter, Draughtsman, Installation Artist
Norwich, Norfolk

I'm a native of the Isle of Wight so the sea has always figured in my work. Between 1972 and 1982 the Norfolk landscape and seascape was my subject matter but a move to Cornwall changed my palette and I became preoccupied with boats, fishermen's cottages and the fishing industry. I visit St. Ives and Mousehole every year to make drawings and take photos which are a catalyst for further experiments and finished works done in the studio.

A continuous series of drawings exists in my sketchbooks of the rooftops and chimneys of fishermen's cottages in Mousehole and St. Ives. *St.Ives Nocturne No. 3* is a development of one of them. Many of the drawings are done by not looking at the paper – an attempt to portray the wonderful lack of town planning in the evolvement of these two fishing villages. I use oil pastel, pen and turps to create a feeling of memory and history.

Nearly all my paintings start with drawing – either taking a line for a walk or planning the composition formally. *After the Fishing* started as a formal drawing using the simplified shapes of fishing boats and their contents viewed from above, and using colour to push and pull the space in the painting. The square format was chosen to contradict the movement provided by the curves which travel through the image.

Pointwest started as a large drawing which exists in its own right and this is the second version which started life as a painting based on the wedge-shaped gap in Mousehole harbour. The title is meant to be literal, both boats pointing west and making reference to the fishing industry in Penwith and the brotherhood that has existed between the fishermen. The structure of the painting refers to displacement in the water.

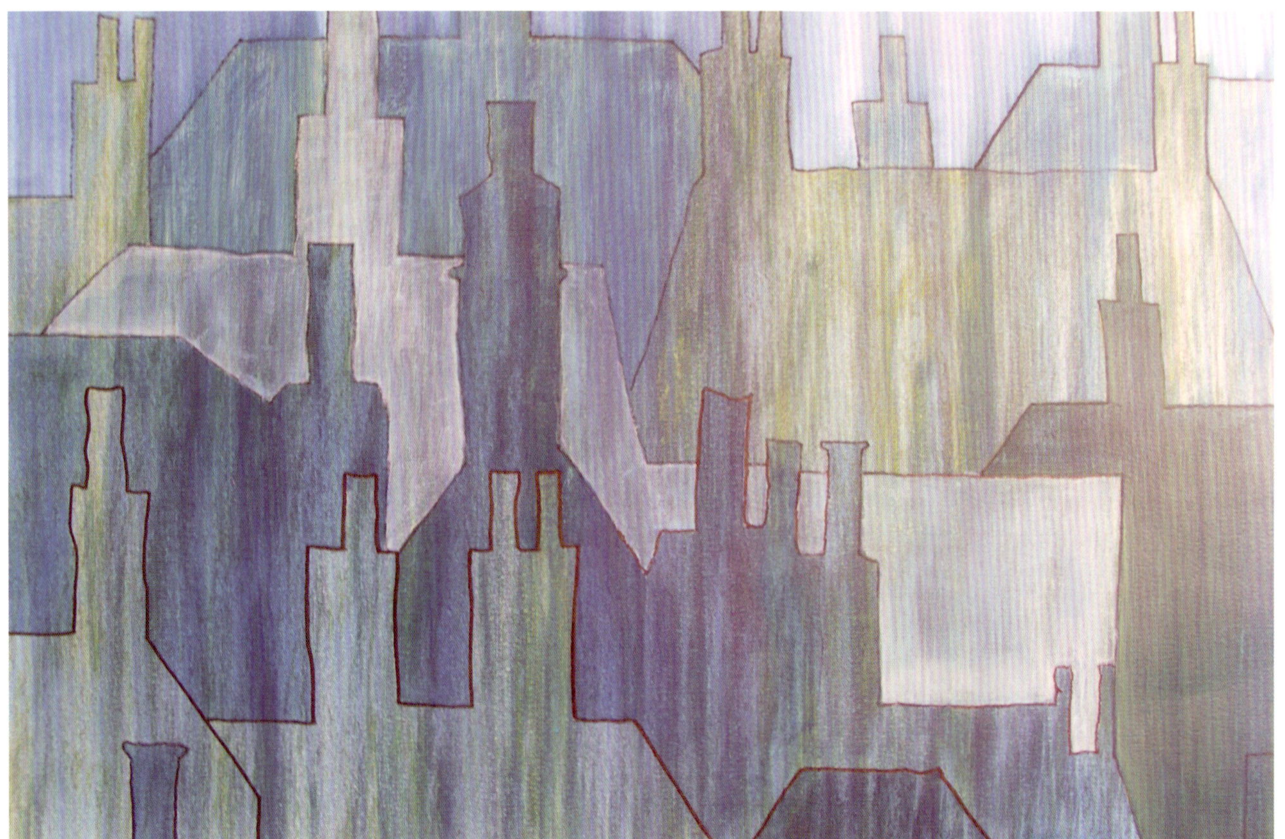

St.Ives Nocturne No. 3 (2010) Oil Pastel, Pen and Turpentine on Paper 56 x 37cm

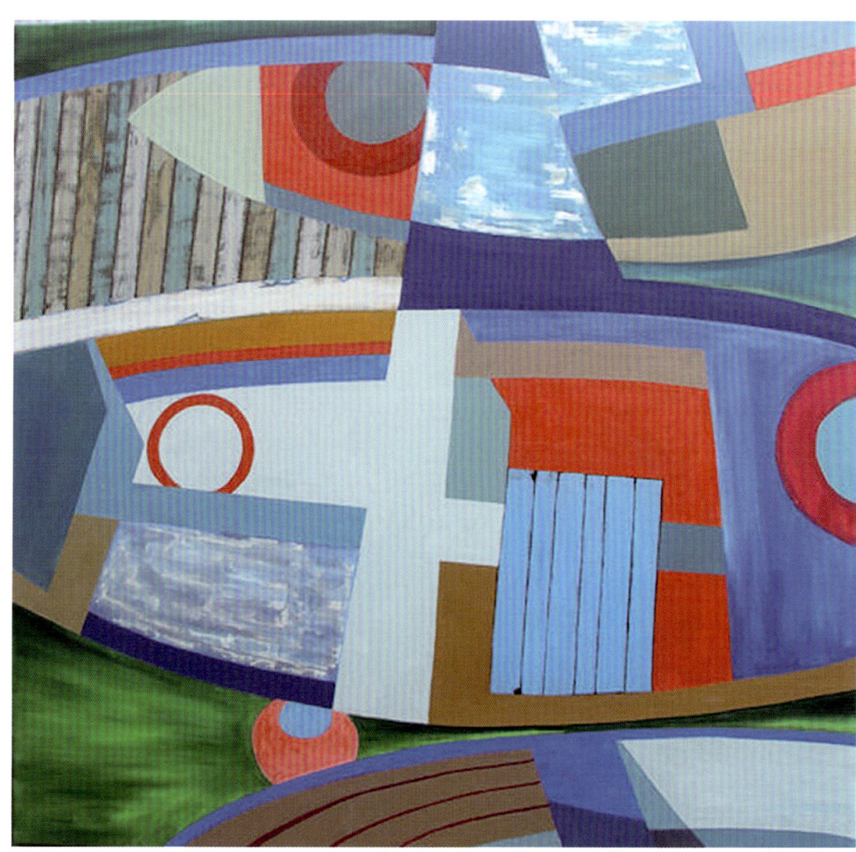

After the Fishing (2009) Oil on Canvas 80 x 80cm

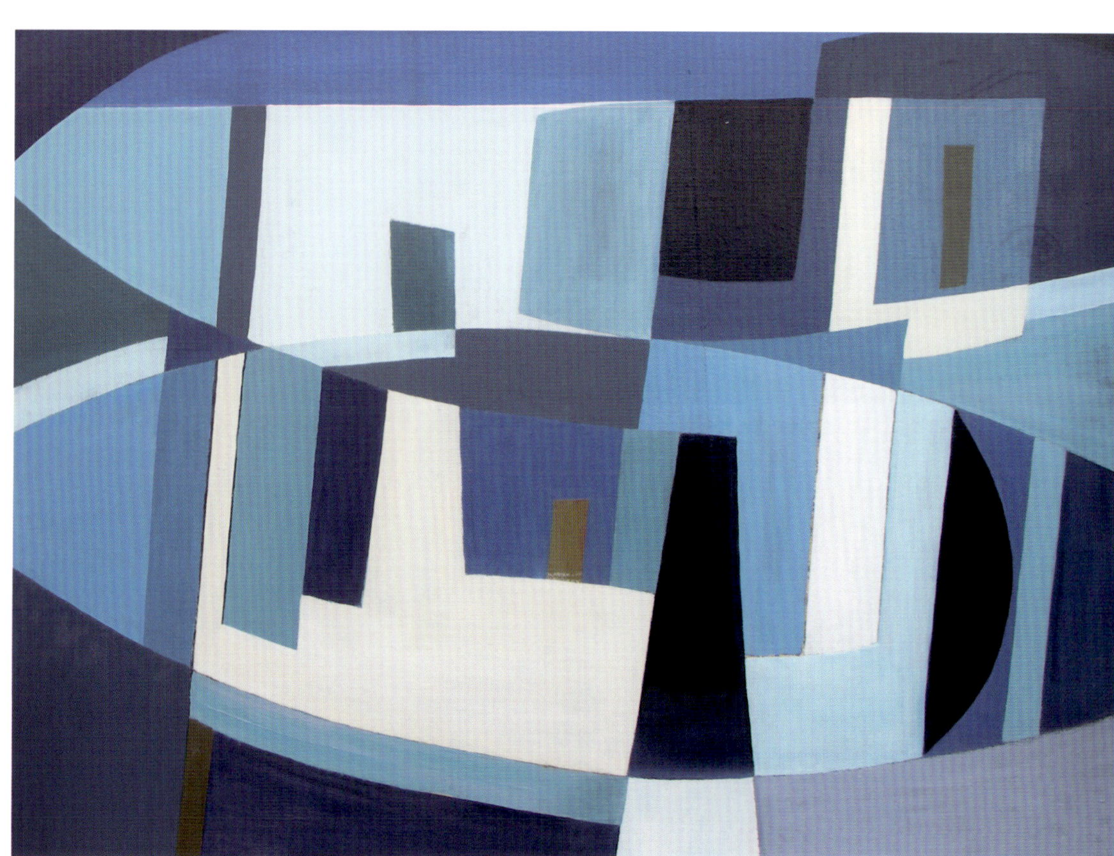

Pointwest (2009) Oil on Canvas 104 x 76cm

Chris Hann: Behind the Scenes

More about:

Chris…

Educated-
Slade School of Fine Art,
Postgraduate Diploma in Fine Art (London) 1970

Accreditation With National Art Societies -
Dip. AD from the Council For National Academic Awards
(CNAA) 1968; Postgraduate Diploma in Fine Art (PGDFA)
from University College London

Galleries Familiar With Artist's Work-
The Hatfield Hines Gallery, Holt, Norfolk

Collections (Open To The Public)-
Reclining Nude and *Stage Design*, Portsmouth Museum
and Art Gallery, Portsmouth, Hampshire

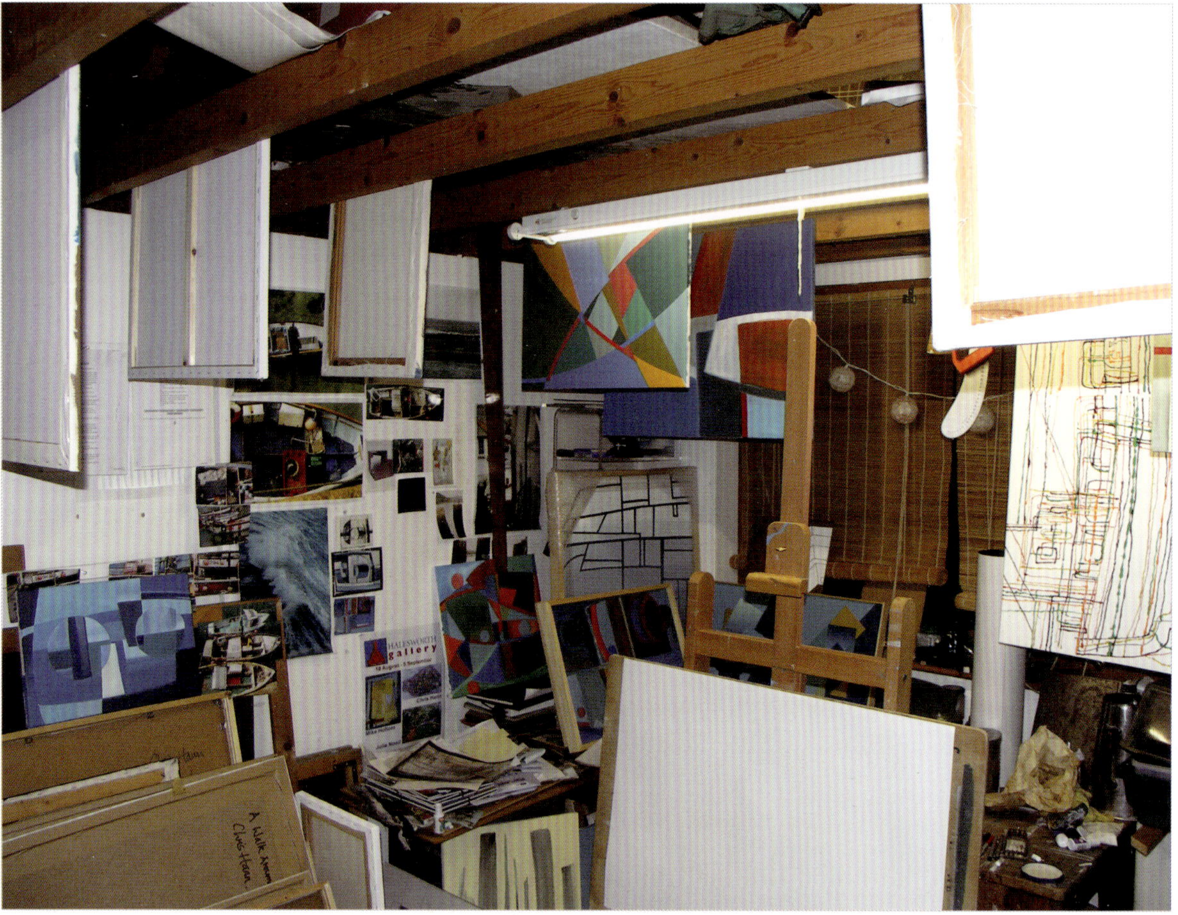

My studio is a brick built, pitch roofed building with windows on two sides, approximately 22' x 10' and situated in my back garden. I share it with my wife Hannah who is also a professional painter. There is plenty of storage in the roof space as well as an area on one side of the studio to store paintings. There is one heater, which is adequate to keep the studio warm in the winter, and a radio (Channel 4).

I surround myself with sketchbooks which are full of drawings from St. Ives, Mousehole, Newlyn and Penzance; places I visit every year. I also have a lot of photographs around the walls of boats and rooftops. A combination of these two references feeds my work. Drawing is a very important part of my practice but, unlike the drawing I did in the 70's which was mainly analytical and relied on tone, nearly all my drawing now is linear and much of it is done without looking at the paper. This is in contrast to my painting which is still influenced by American hard-edge painting, using flat, complementary and close-tone colour.

My subject matter is fishing boats and their contents, and the rooftops and chimneys of fishing cottages. I also have a passion for Mousehole harbour, particularly the wedge shape between the harbour walls which appears in a number of my works, sometimes as the thwart of a boat in perspective.

I have a good knowledge of the St. Ives artists and count Ben Nicholson as a favourite and an influence, as well as Terry Frost. I have done a lot of research into Cubism and have developed various methods related to Cubism that inform my work.

I often work on two to three paintings/drawings at a time and find that I can often resolve problems in one painting by working on another. If I cannot find a way forward, I normally start another work and then return a week or so later. Ideas and challenges are the most exciting part of my practice.

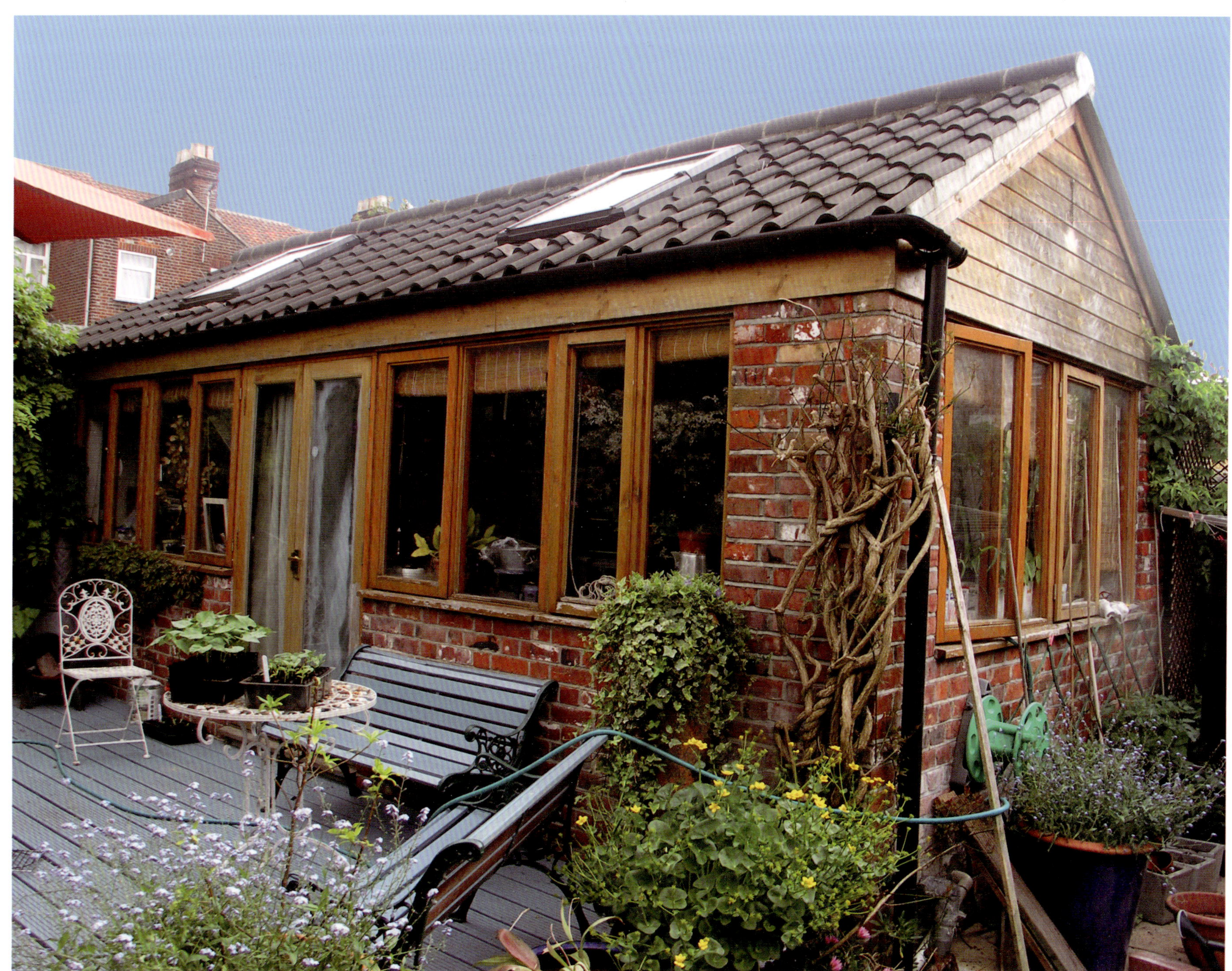

Tory Lawrence

Tory Lawrence
Painter
Rendham, Suffolk

Animals and the landscape have been my subjects for 30 years and 25 solo exhibitions. I have been inspired by artists of the Renaissance like Giovanni Bellini and Piero de Cosimo; particularly for their details in the distant land, and also the Dutch landscape painters (Salmon Ruisdael, Philips Koninck and Jan van Goyen). More recent artists such as Rothko of Cy Twombly make one think and want to return to the studio and paint.

For my current work (2010) I draw outside in my sketch book. Alone, sitting on a three-legged stool (which often collapses in the mud) and in silence, I concentrate on the colours and shapes of the subject. These are the best moments of being an artist.

Then I return to the studio, which is a large shed in the garden, and paint in oil from the drawings and memory. If I have been in front of the subject for an hour or more, I remember it very well and clearly.

Track to the Ridgeway came about when I returned to the Berkshire Downs where I had lived for 40 years, and drew this track leading up to the Ridgeway, the oldest road in England. In the studio the paint seemed to work itself and I left it in a raw state, unlike some paintings which might need more work a month or so later.

Covehithe is an extraordinary, strange and magical place, probably lucky not to be under the sea. In *Covehithe*, I aimed to portray the feeling of a lost world and ruined church, juxtaposed with the recently harvested corn field. Never satisfied with a painting, I just try to keep experimenting, until I can go no further

Educated- No formal art school tuition
Galleries Familiar With Artist's Work-
Cobbold & Judd, Hintlesham, Suffolk
The Town Hall Galleries, Ipswich, Suffolk
Collections (Open To The Public)-
River Deben in Winter (2010); Snow on a Ploughed Field, Rendham (2010); and *All Saints Church, Ramsholt (2010);* plus sketch book drawings for each, Council Borough Collection of Ipswich, Suffolk
Website- www.torylawrence.com

Track to the Ridgeway (2010) Oil on Board 227 x 292 cm

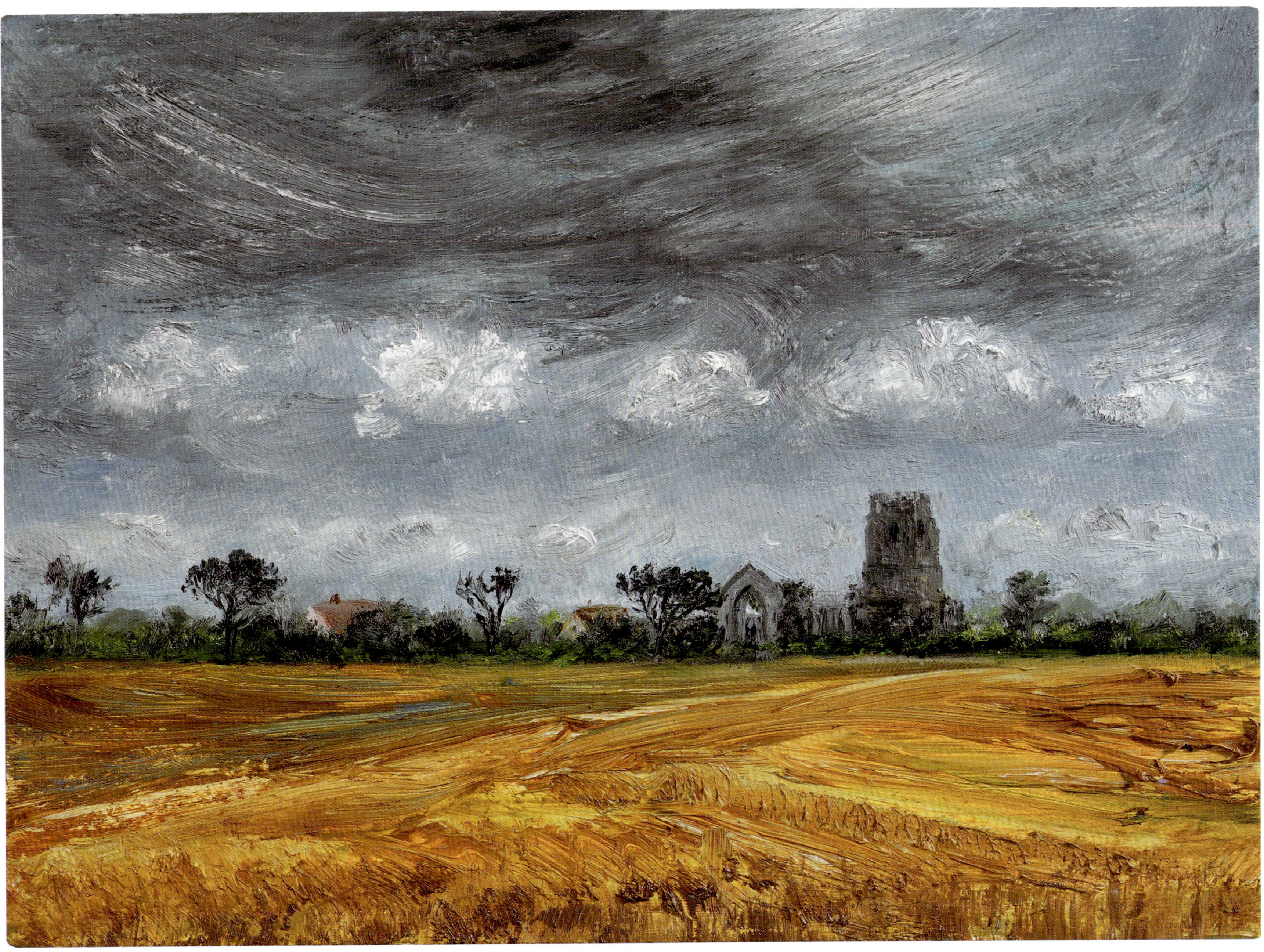

Covehithe (2009) Oil on Board 227 x 292 cm

Alyson Lomas BA (Hons)

Alyson Lomas
Painter
Framlingham, Suffolk

Since moving to Suffolk just over two years ago I have found the pace of life to be more conducive to my creativity and change in health. The rhythm of painting, the trickle, splash and spatter of brushstrokes bring remembered ideas and images to the surface as well as suggesting new developments.

The textures and colours of the Suffolk landscape are the inspiration for my semi-abstract paintings. The process begins with the fluid paint flow which creates its own rhythm and identity. Artists who have inspired me are Kurt Jackson, Barbara Rae, Ivon Hitchens and Helen Frankenhaler.

I aim to create a sensation of remembered responses to the landscape. The creative process is always a pull between colour, shape and textures, with each stage creating its own history as layer upon layer build a surface of glazes and colour changes.

The accidental nature of the painting stages can, at times, create a series of obstacles to be overcome. The initial trigger is, almost always, the interaction of vibrant colours. The resulting stages are challenging but full of rewarding discoveries. The time to stop is when I have a sense that the painting has its own sense of identity and, ideally, some of the spirit of the landscape.

Educated-
St Martin's School of Art
Liverpool University
Winchester School of Art
Galleries Familiar With Artist's Work-
Buckenham Galleries, Southwold, Suffolk
RE+new, Woodbridge, Suffolk
Collections (Open To The Public)-
Diversity, Arts Council, Holton Lee, Dorset
Woodlands, Council of Europe, Strasbourg, France
Website- www.alysonlomas.co.uk

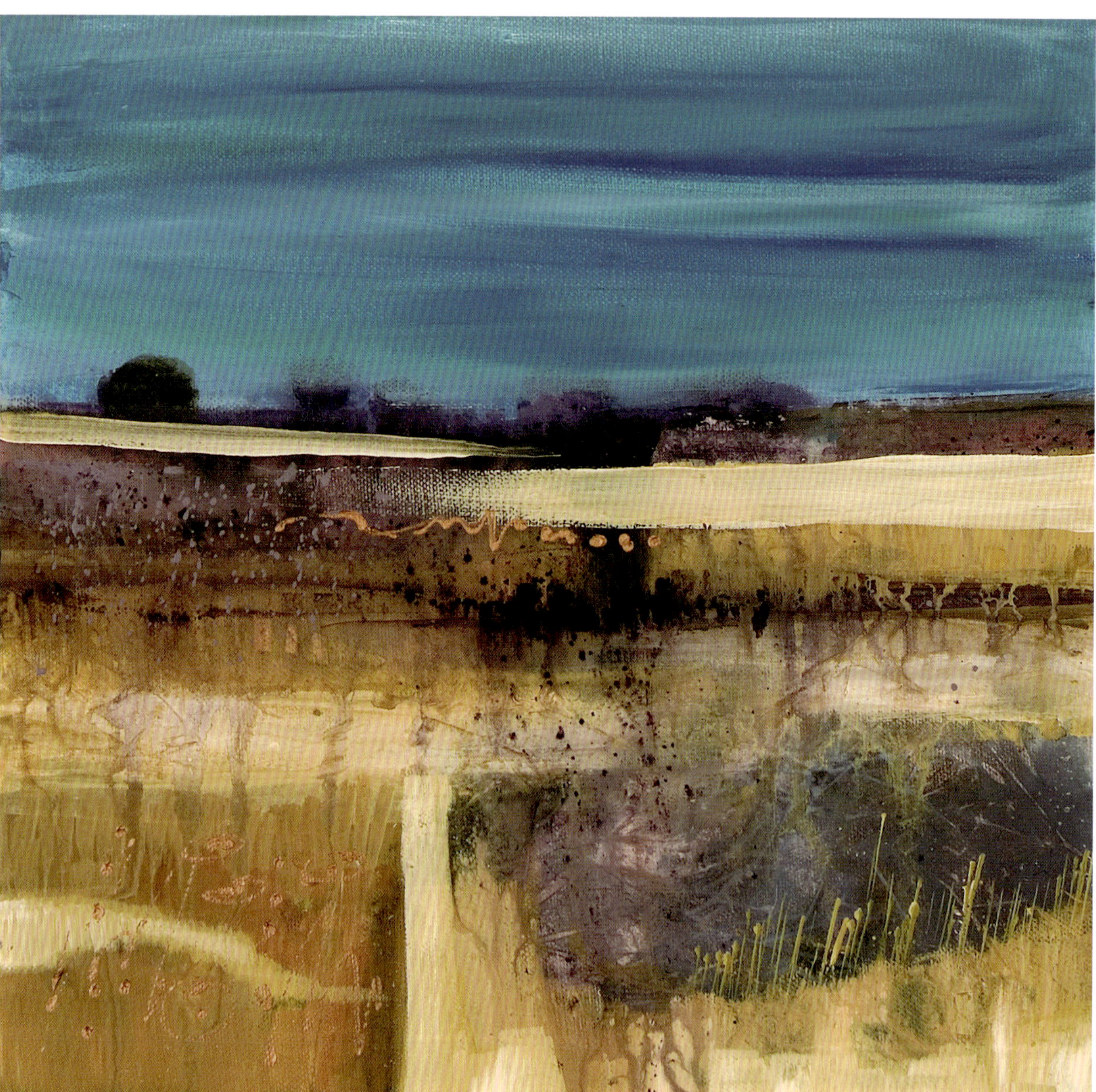

Lavender Fields (2009) Acrylic 30 x 30cm

Alyson Lomas BA (Hons)

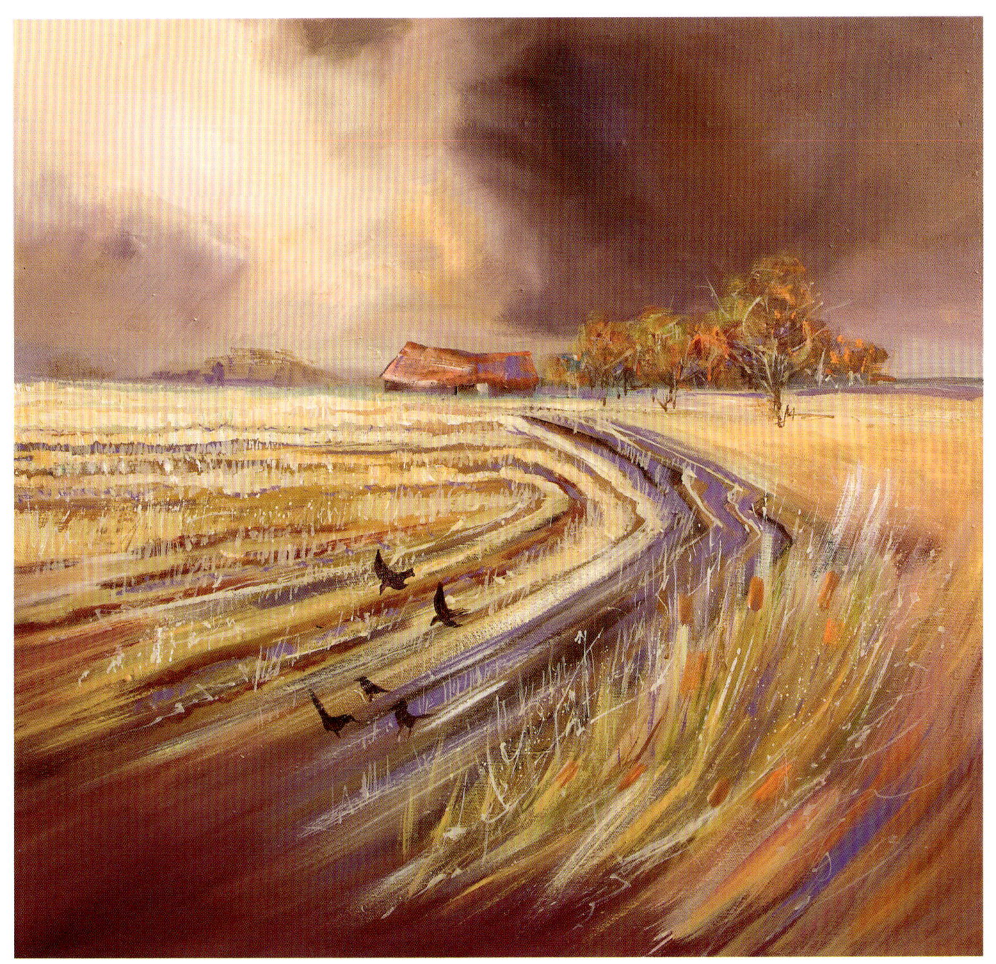

Morning Light 2 (2010) Acrylic 60 x 60cm

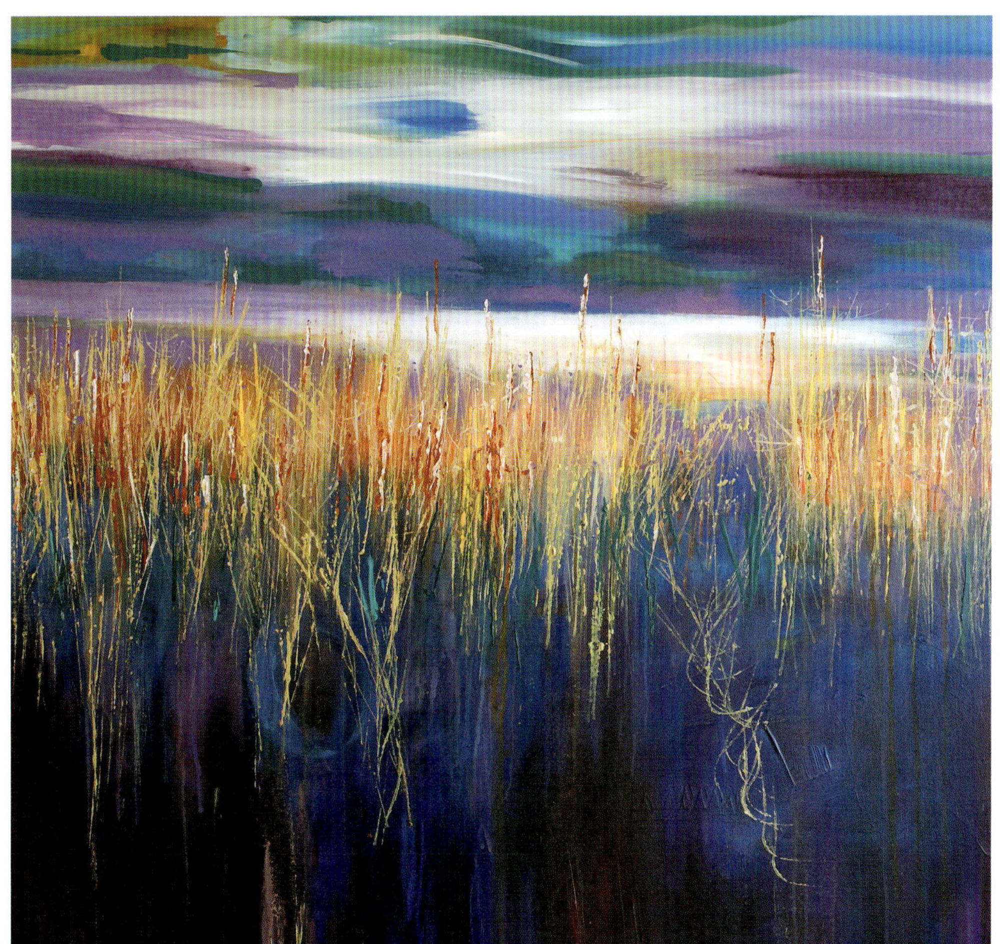

Marshland Reeds (2008) Acrylic 60 x 60cm

John Reay

There are artists who make a lot of noise about what they do, others who quietly beaver away with humility and professionalism, gaining a loyal band of supporters. Among the latter group I place John Reay, an acknowledged master of the modern East Anglian school. His paintings and pastels are notable for their enticing light and colour effects. His solo and mixed show appearances have included some of the most distinguished London and provincial galleries.
- David Buckman, Writer and Journalist

John Reay
Painter
Lowestoft, Suffolk

Having grown up in London, I have always loved the open spaces of the coast. So, having moved to East Anglia to attend Norwich Art School, I moved to Lowestoft to live near the sea after graduating. The local coastline, and figure painting have become the major themes of my work. The artists always in my mind are Edward Hopper, Georges Seurat, Balthus and Jan Vermeer. Each of these artists is concerned with particular qualities of light, stillness and pictorial geometry.

In my own work I try to create images of stillness and contemplation, as an antidote to the noise and busy-ness of our lives and of other media. In connection with this I have always been influenced by the work of sculptors, and often make small maquettes in clay to compliment my preparatory drawings and photography. The colour in my work is informed by the many small oil studies I make on the coast. Sometimes I exhibit these as an end in themselves, but most are kept, to work from in my larger studio paintings, as the subtle colour changes of the coast are often too ephemeral to memorise, and difficult to record accurately in any other way.

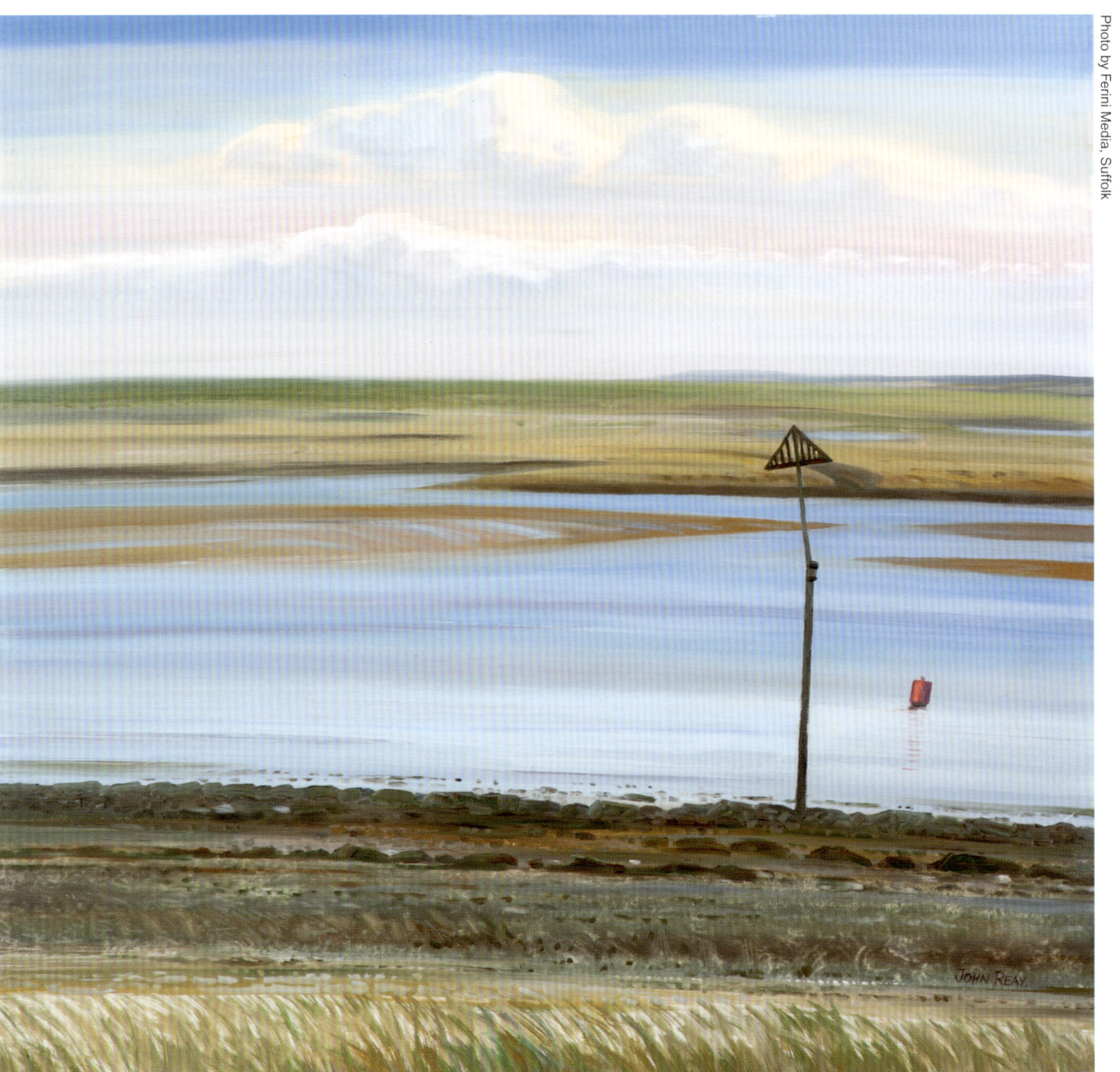

The Creek, Wells, Norfolk (2007) Oil 100 x 100cm

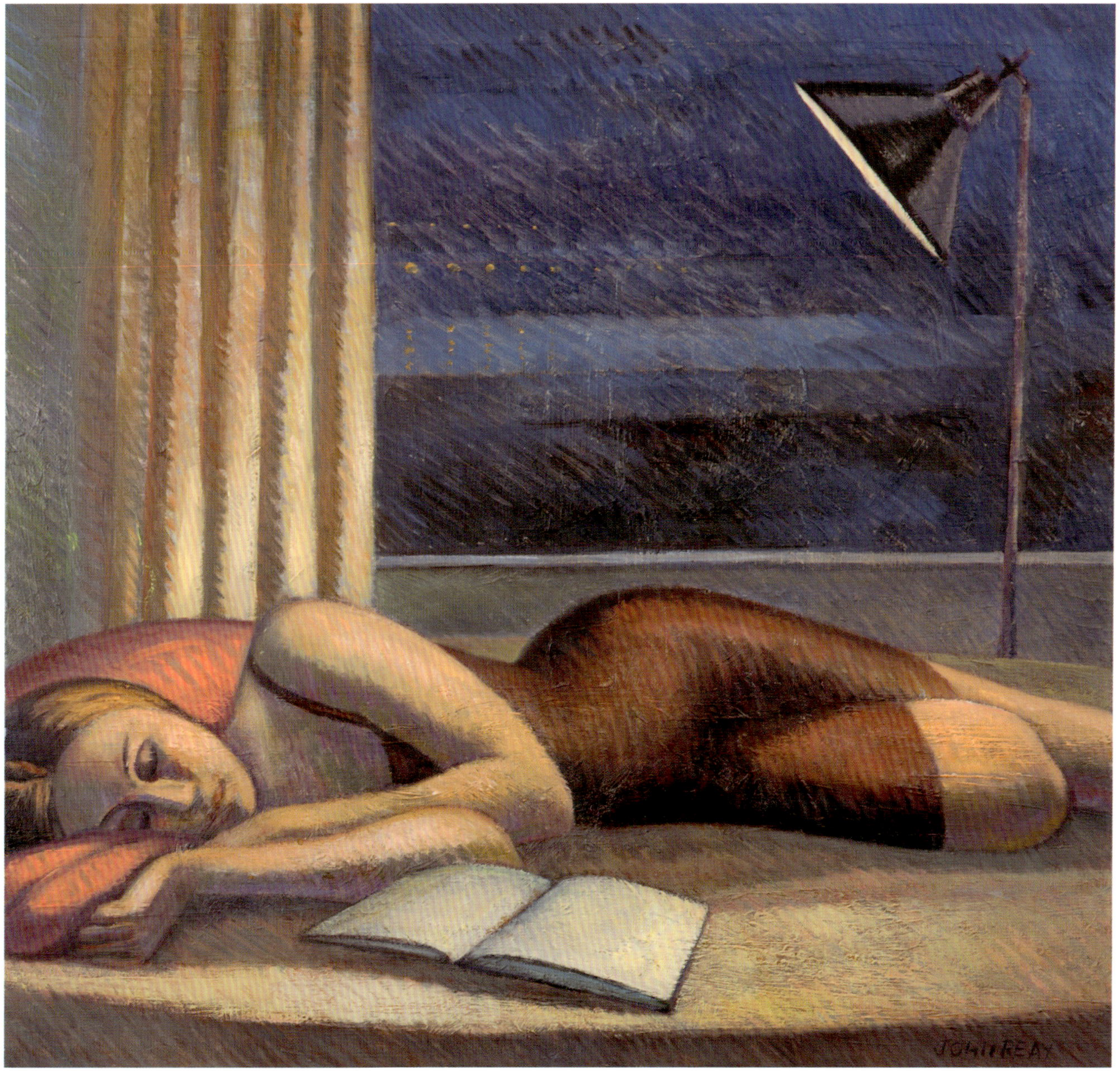

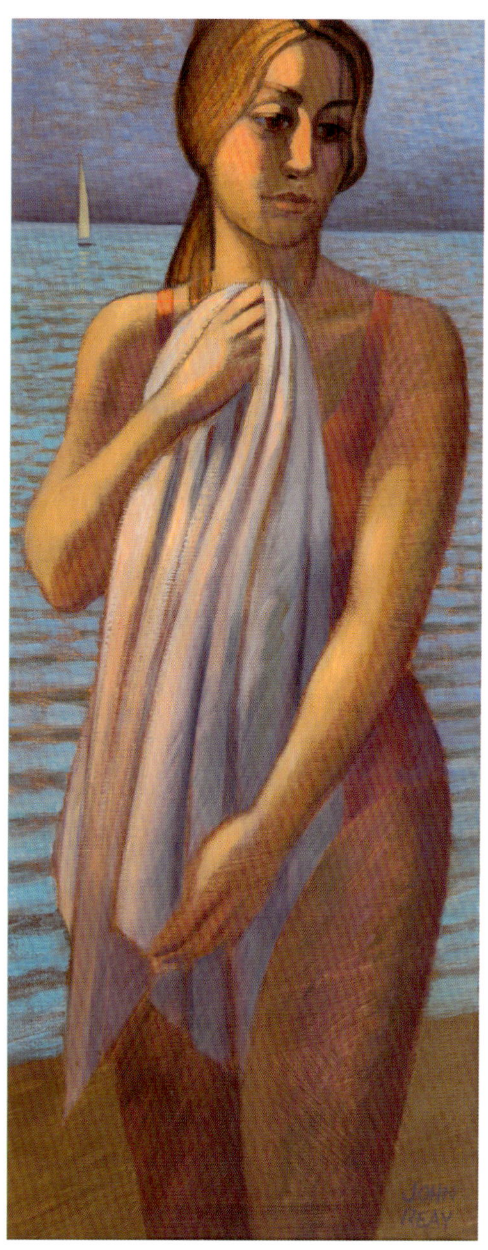

Sue Reading in Studio, Evening (2005) Oil 100 x 100cm

Bather in Red, Evening Light (2008) Oil 100 x 40cm

John Reay: Behind the Scenes

More about:

John…

Educated-
Norwich Art School, Norwich, Norfolk 1974
Galleries Familiar With Artist's Work-
Buckenham Galleries, Southwold, Suffolk
Ferini Art Gallery, Lowestoft, Suffolk
Thompson's Gallery, Aldeburgh, Suffolk
Collections (Open To The Public)-
Portrait of Joan, Doncaster Art Gallery, Doncaster, Yorkshire
Website- www.johnreay.co.uk

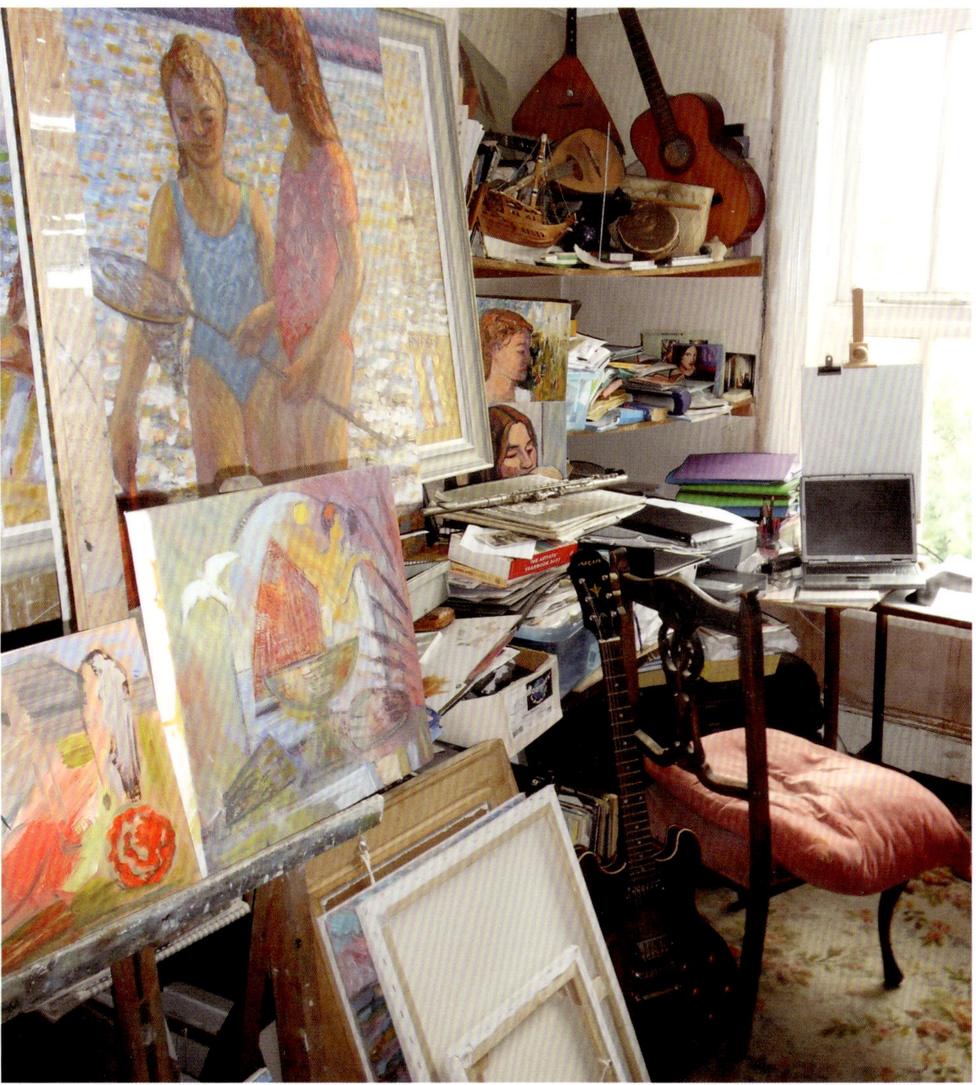

My studio is in my home, a large Victorian house in Lowestoft. The first floor has two large rooms knocked through to make one large studio space. The front end overlooks the railway line and inner harbour, facing south, and is bright and sunny . The other end faces north, overlooks the garden and has good light for painting.

As well as the usual clutter of an art studio, there are many musical instruments, and cats. I listen to music whilst working; classical music on Radio 3, or jazz CDs.

I often take breaks from painting for music practice, mainly saxes and flute, but also guitar or keyboard, to study harmony. The studio is also a place where my partner Sue likes to relax with the cats and read or listen to music. She models for me frequently and is the inspiration for my figure paintings.

My time is divided between work in the studio and part-time teaching, either in art or special needs education, both of which I have always enjoyed and found stimulating.

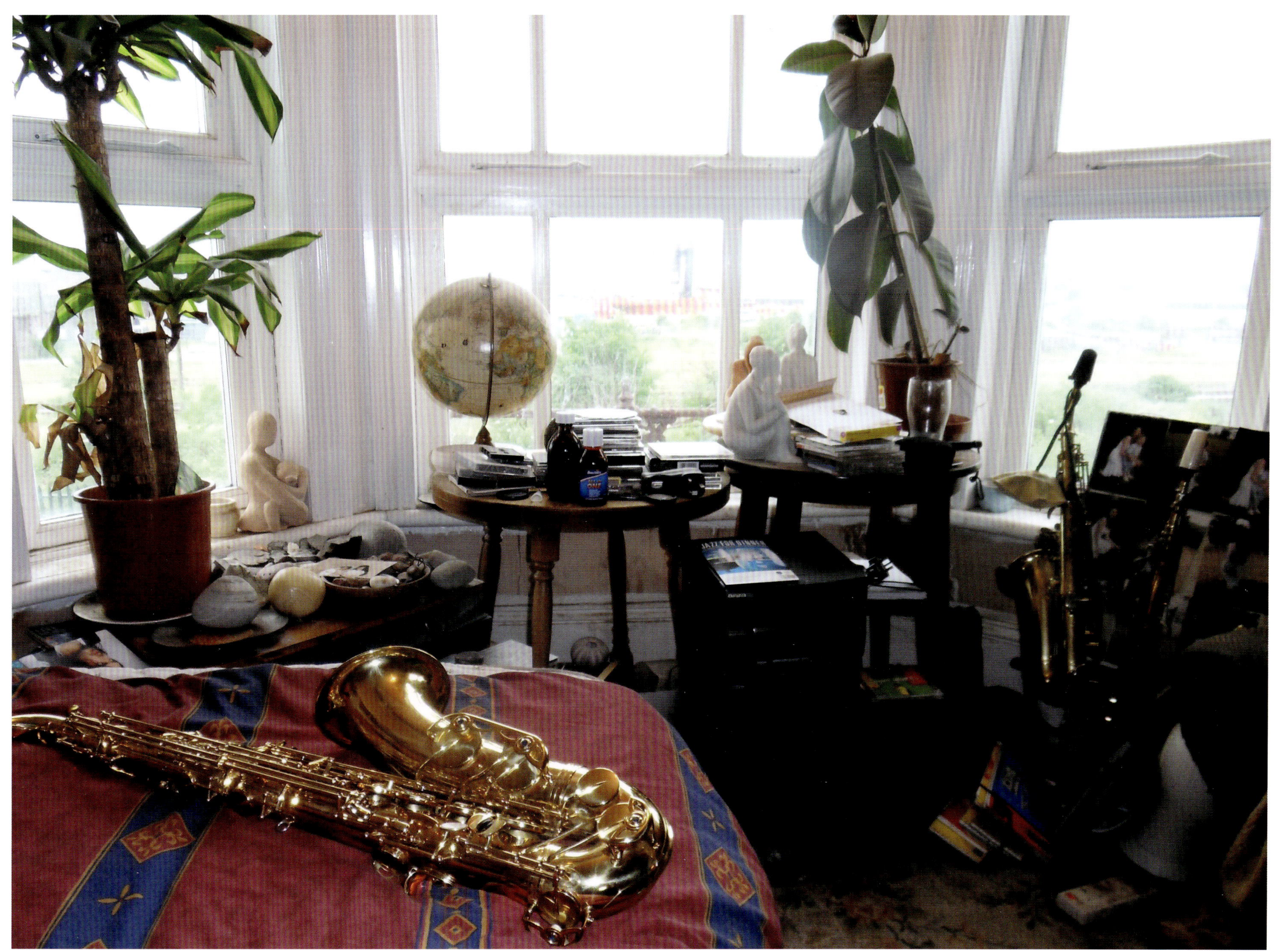

Doreen Abel

114

Doreen Abel
Painter
Beccles, Suffolk

In a world that can seem uncertain and even a little frightening - it is beauty that inspires my work.

I seek to express the gentleness of the female form in my latest series of pastel paintings, but I find the challenge of capturing the excitement and vibrance of the changing seasons requires a much bolder approach and then, out comes the pallette knife and the large canvas!

I am fortunate to have two daughters who are happy to pose for my pastel paintings. In the study, *Wedding Dreams* I have used the minimum of subtle pastel to portray this very private moment.

Edge of Winter was painted almost entirely in a single session, in direct response to waking up to a glorious dawn over fresh snow.

Fields of Gold depicts the warm glow of an autumn evening, which brought its own special magic and demanded to be painted.

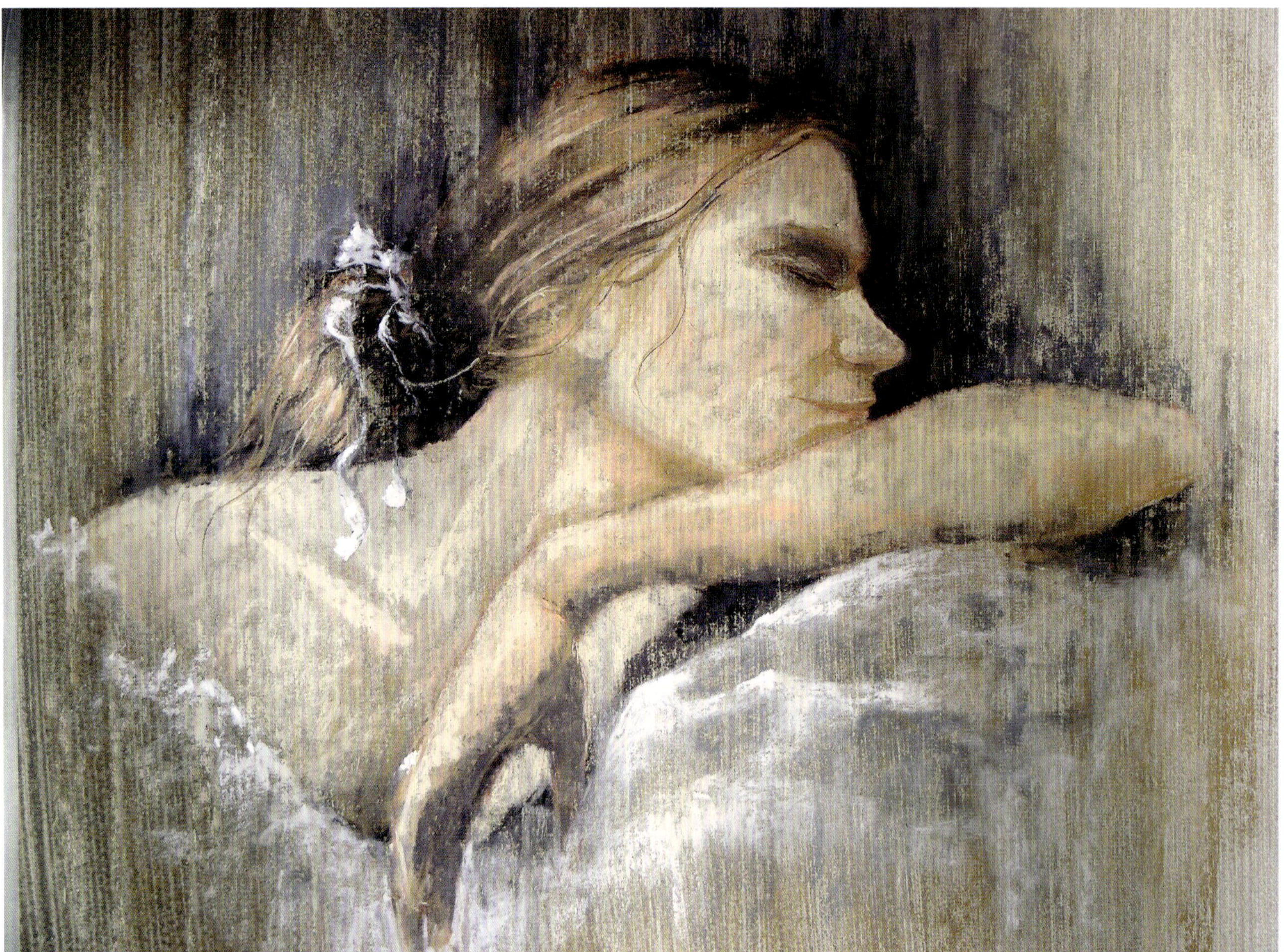

Wedding Dreams (2009) Pastel 45 x 45cm

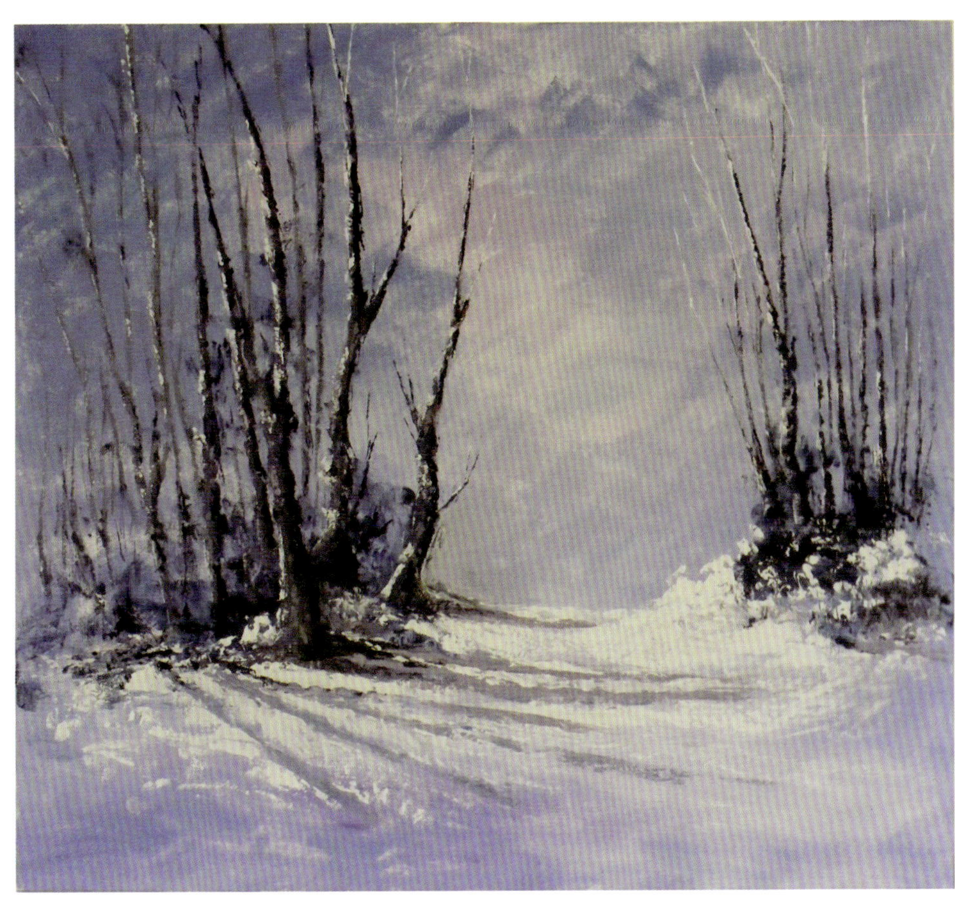

Edge of Winter (2009) Oil 100 x 100cm

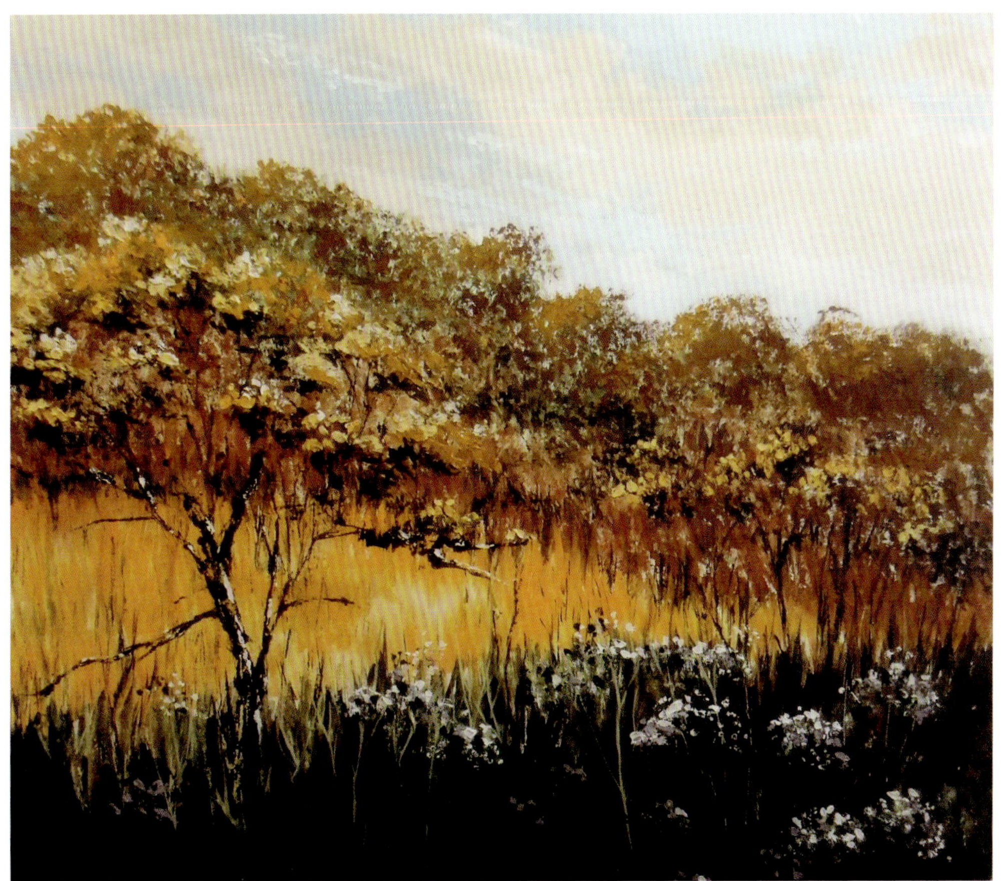

Fields of Gold (2009) Oil 90 x 90cm

Delia Tournay-Godfrey BA (Hons)

Whether a stormy seascape, Italian landscape or simple flower studies, Delia's painting possesses calm, poetic observation coupled with sensitive technique. Her painting has an uncomplicated quality with enviable light, sure brushwork; a clear vision cleanly painted in close tones.
- Chappel Galleries, Chappel, Essex

Delia Tournay-Godfrey BA (Hons)
Painter
Ipswich, Suffolk

I often spend hours searching for a painting that I am to do today. It is always recognisable when it reveals itself to me; a spark or bubble of excitement as I see a composition that will work as a painting. Seeing the right figure in the right setting depends on the shapes and colours they form at the time, and how this all relates to the edges of the support that I have with me to work on. Then the real struggle begins!

I suppose the most exciting paintings are when I see a setting; a crashing sea, a dark and threatening sky, the edge of a building in a certain light, and a figure appears to enliven the whole scene. It's then an absorbing process of observation and rapid paint application alongside critical pictorial selection; what to leave in, what to leave out, which colours to use. *Walk On A Stormy Day* is an example of this as two figures were struggling to leave the beach before the heavens opened. There was time enough to paint their essential characteristics so they look like real moving people, but no time to overwork the paint so it retains its character, remaining fresh and lively. The mood this little painting developed became very important to me, like a metaphor for the human condition.

Again with *Blustery Day, Aldeburgh Beach*, the waves crashing on the beach was a perfect backdrop for when this family walked along the water's edge, creating a particular moment in time that is immediately identifiable. Long after the figures have disappeared I am still trying to resolve the painting, so the figures will relate to the environment they are in and there is an overall tonal unity and colour harmony.

Early Evening Walk is a larger painting produced in my studio from a smaller work I had painted in my car. It was the culmination of a month of daily painting activity at Slaughden; of figures walking in that marvellous setting with its unique light; the ever-changing weather conditions creating the very typical colours and the beautiful atmosphere of Suffolk.

Educated- Suffolk College (University of East Anglia) 1996
Galleries Familiar With Artist's Work-
Chappel Galleries, Chappel, Essex
Snape Maltings Gallery, Snape, Suffolk
Strand Gallery, Aldeburgh, Suffolk
Website-www.deliatournay-godfrey.co.uk

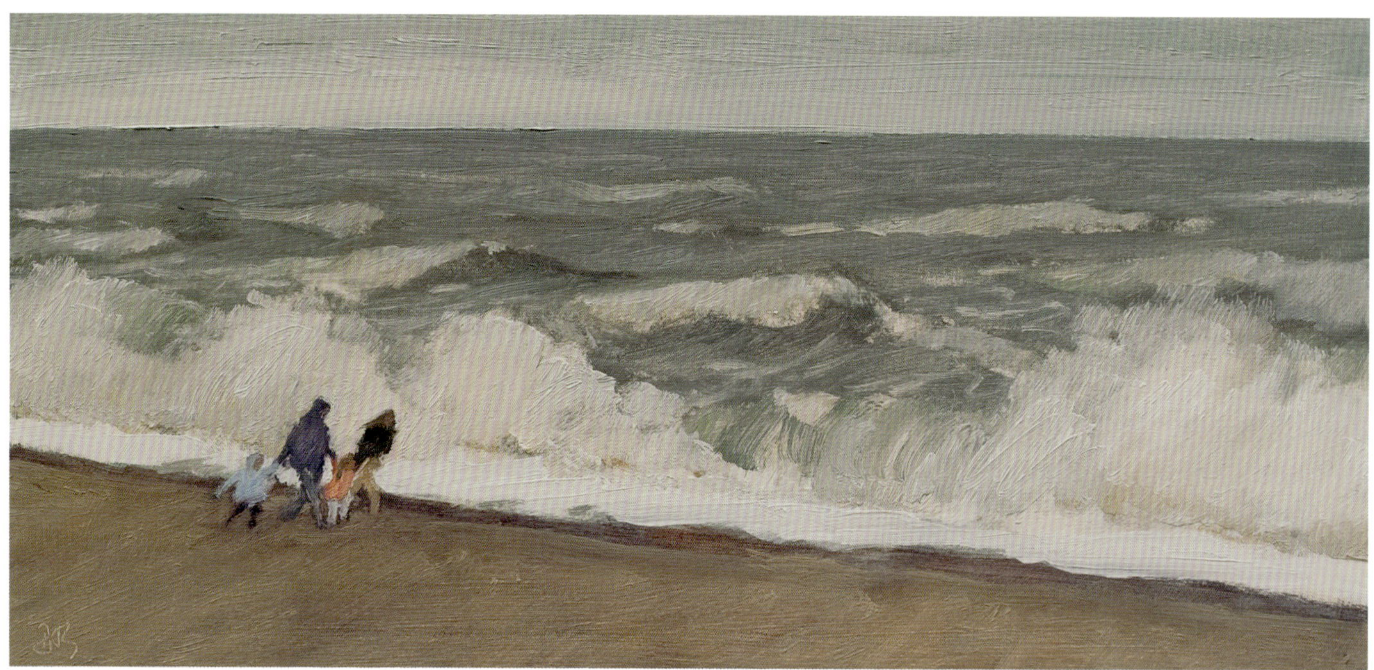

Blustery Day, Aldeburgh Beach (2009) Oil on Board 14 x 29cm

116

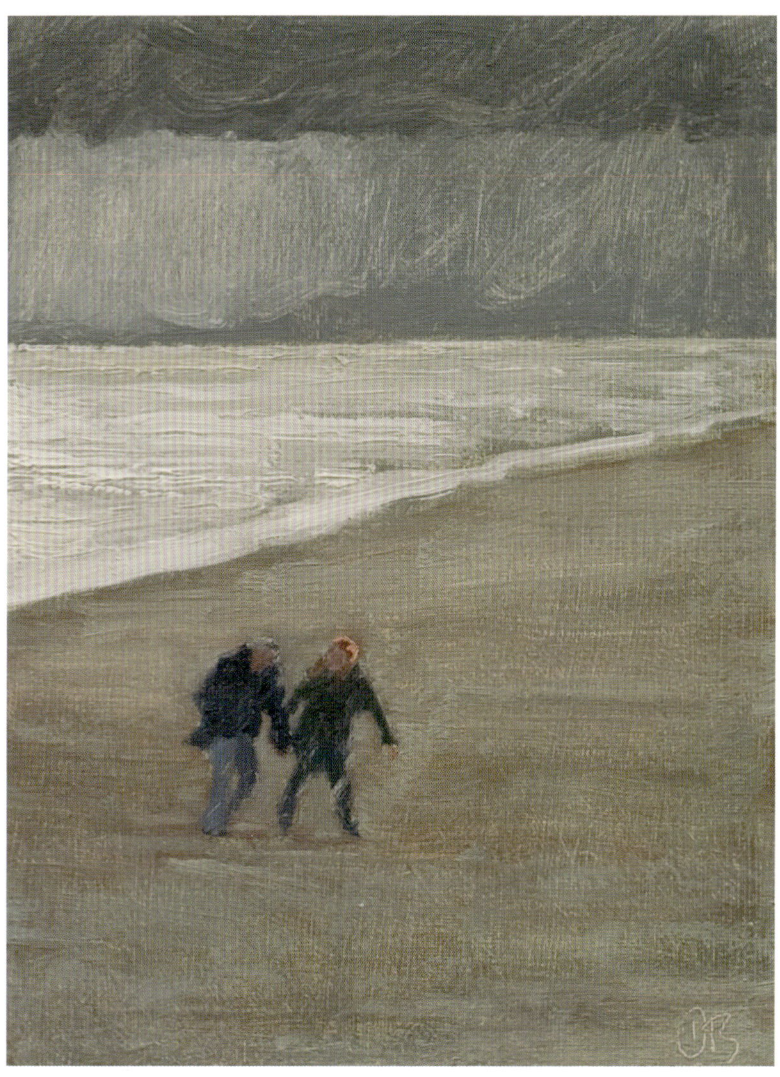

Walk On A Stormy Day (2009) Oil on Board 18 x 13cm

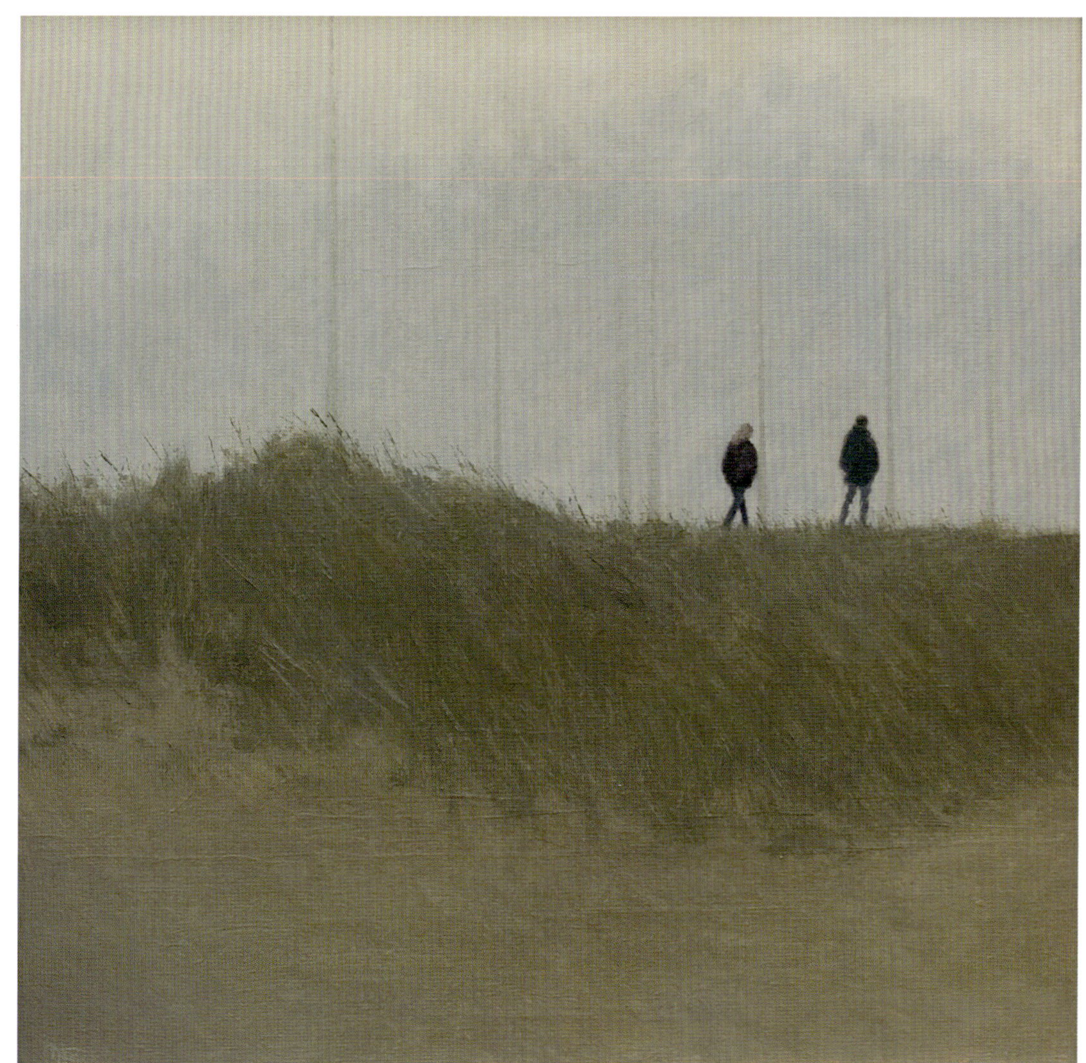

Early Evening Walk (2010) Oil on Canvas 59 x 58cm

Maureen Jordan SBA

Maureen Jordan SBA
Pastel Painter
Ipswich, Suffolk

I have always been interested in the effect of sunlight and spotlights on flowers, landscapes or figures. I find it fascinating that simple images can be incredibly different due to the variation in light level, light direction and reflections. All my work is a struggle to capture those variations and I'm constantly experimenting with vibrant pastels, sometimes mixing them with acrylics, textures and metallics to create stunning effects of bold colour and texture. To achieve these results I have been influenced by the wonderful work of Ken Howard - painting light - and John Blockley for his exciting colour and pastel textures.

For *English Lavender By The Sea,* a fellow artist and I had gone to the Norfolk lavender fields to sketch and photograph this and other views. I rarely draw in the countryside by myself as I feel very vulnerable, so my landscapes are usually done from photographs. This landscape is a large picture produced from pastel sketches I did that day. Eventually this image was produced as a large print by Castlebar Graphics.

My flower paintings can generally be divided into three categories. Large paintings, basically realistic garden scenes, as in the case of *Pansies under the Zantedeschia.* Small pictures, such as *Afternoon Daisies* and *Anemones on the Windowsill,* which are rather done on the spur of the moment - I cut some flowers, pop them into one of my many vases, jugs or a jam jar and just enjoy! And lastly, when I have time to play, I use mixed media, very loose and vibrant.

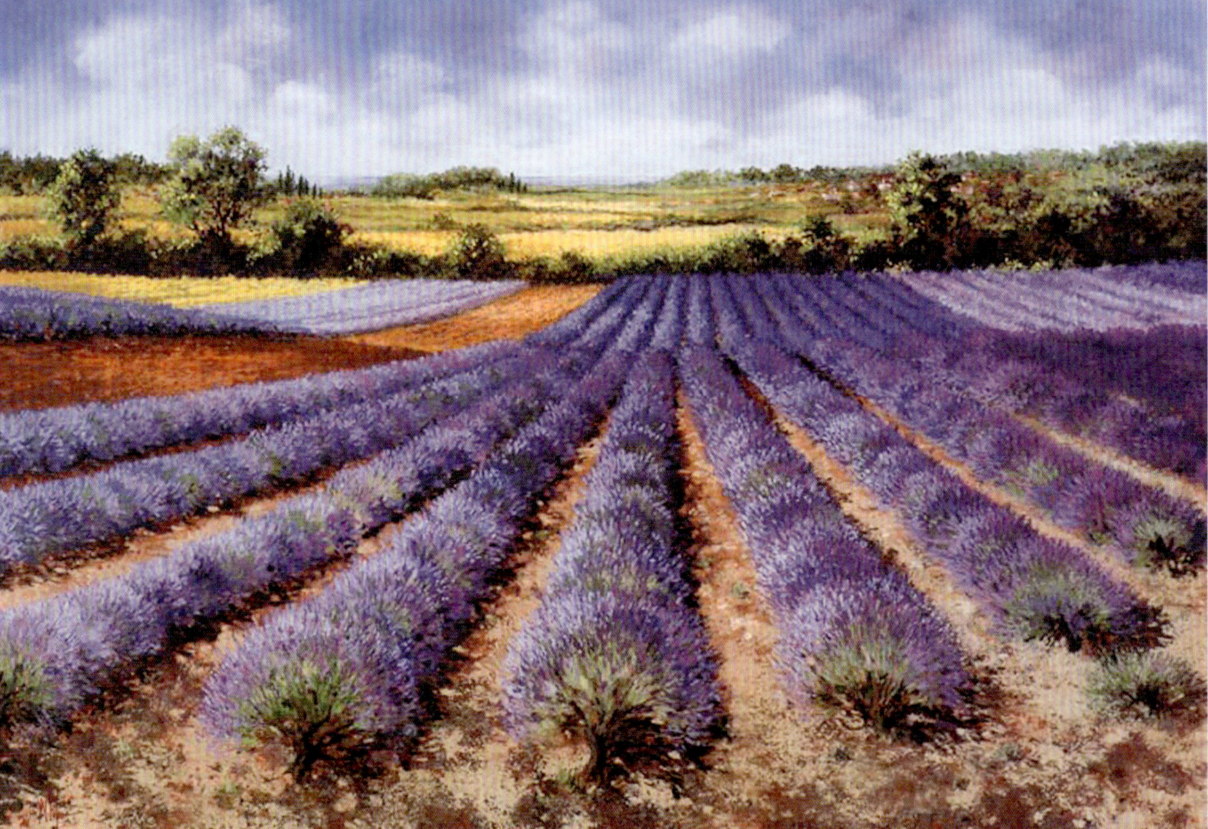

English Lavender By The Sea (2003) Pastel, Acrylic and Textures 71 x 102cm

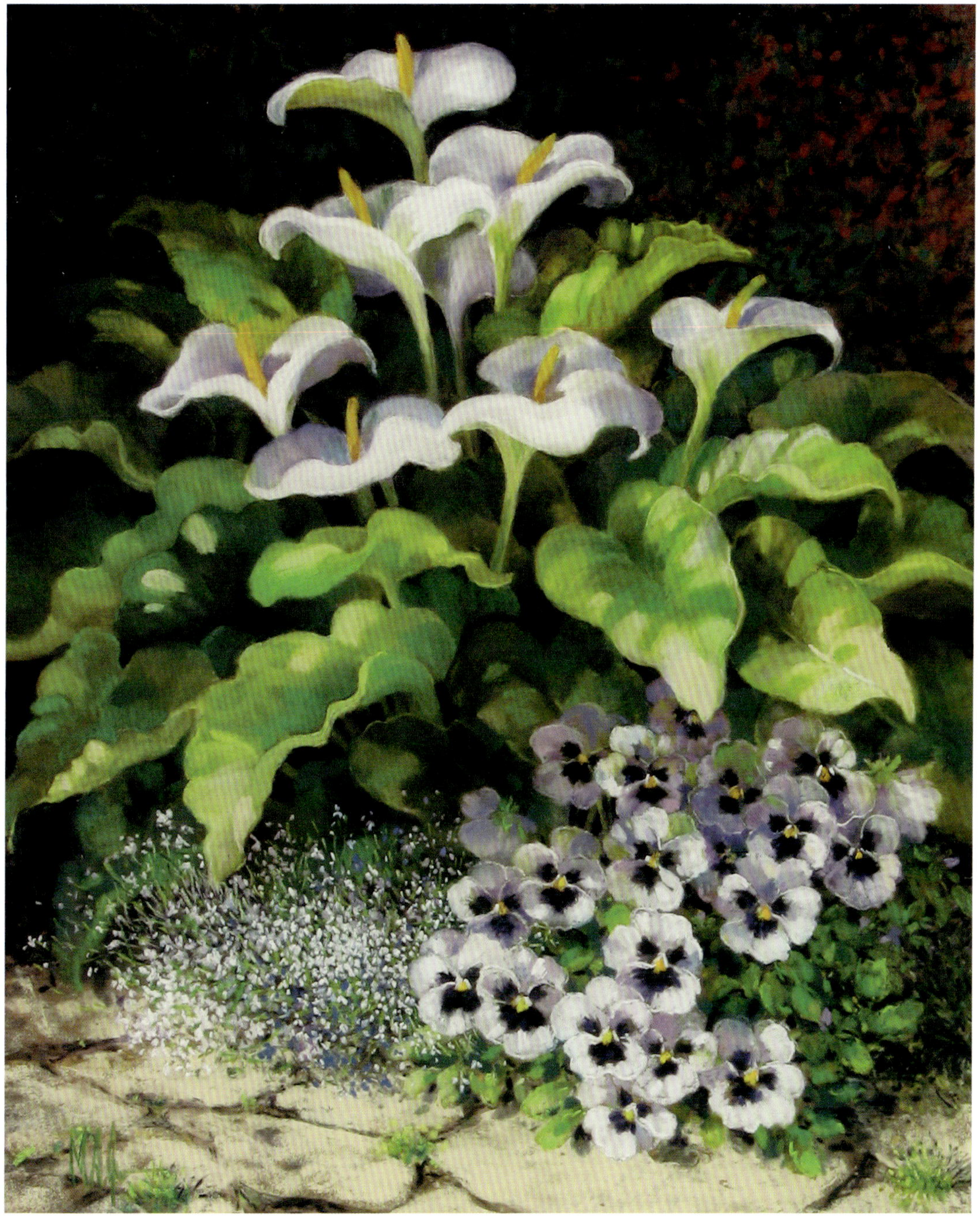

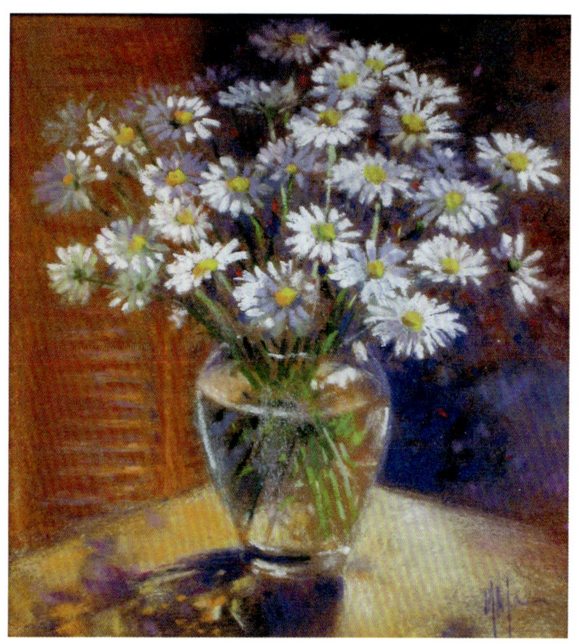

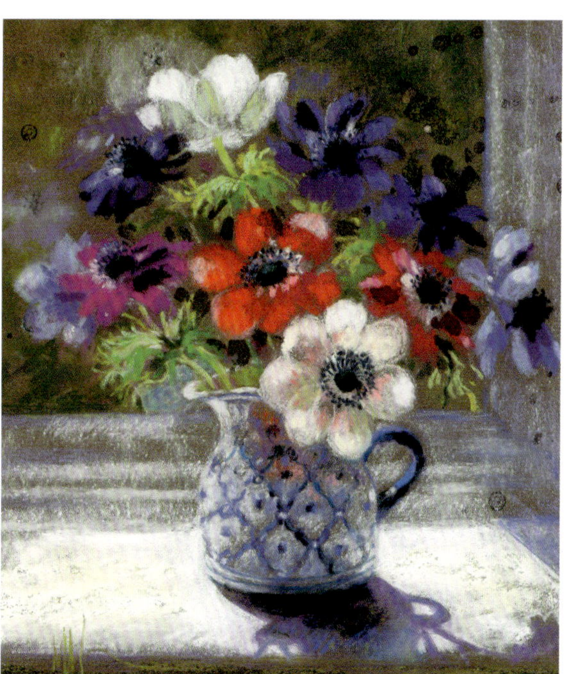

Left: *Pansies Under The Zantedeschia (2009)* Pastel 48 x 39cm; **Top Right:** *Afternoon Daisies (2009)* Pastel 22 x 20cm; **Bottom Right:** *Anemones On The Windowsill (2005)* Pastel 25 x20cm

Maureen Jordan: Behind the Scenes

More about:

Maureen...

Educated-
Design: Kingston upon Hull Art College, NDD, 1960
Pastel Painting: Self-taught
Membership of Local Art Societies-
Friend of Ipswich Art Society
Accreditation With National Art Societies -
Hesketh Hubbard, Life Drawing, London
Society of Botanical Artists
Galleries Familiar With Artist's Work-
Buckenham Galleries, Southwold, Suffolk
Francis Iles Fine Paintings, Rochester, Kent
Llewellyn Alexander [Fine Paintings], Waterloo, London
Undertakes Commissions- Yes
Website- www.maureenjordan.com

When we moved from London it took some time to find a house which had enough space for my studio, my husband's pottery and a garden for my students and me to work in. As you can see we found it, but having adjacent work spaces is not all joy however – we have different tastes in music [the speakers are in my studio]!

My working day starts with housework till 10am. Then it is either painting or tending my outside studio. My garden is very inspirational as a lot of my work is about sunlight on groups of pots and objects with flowers in the sun. For my one woman exhibition in New York I had to paint 40 pictures of flowers in terracotta pots in a very short time. Fortunately it was a very hot summer! When I am not painting or gardening, I'll be framing, delivering, stewarding or collecting pictures. At other times I'll be driving to other parts of the country giving demos or doing workshops for art societies. My considerable amount of office work is done after my evening meal sometimes into the early hours.

When painting I frequently stop for a drink, walk away from the picture and see it from a different angle when I return. Sometimes I leave a picture around in the studio for many months, and then one day I walk past it and see a mistake I had not noticed before. I changed one picture that had been a real disaster - altered it - and put it in a frame. It was the first to be sold at my private view! For this kind of work I try not to paint from photos as the camera does not pick up the colours, reflections, the flash of sunlight that I need. However, if I need to work more than one day on a picture I do photograph the group so that I can continue, as good sunlight does not come every day.

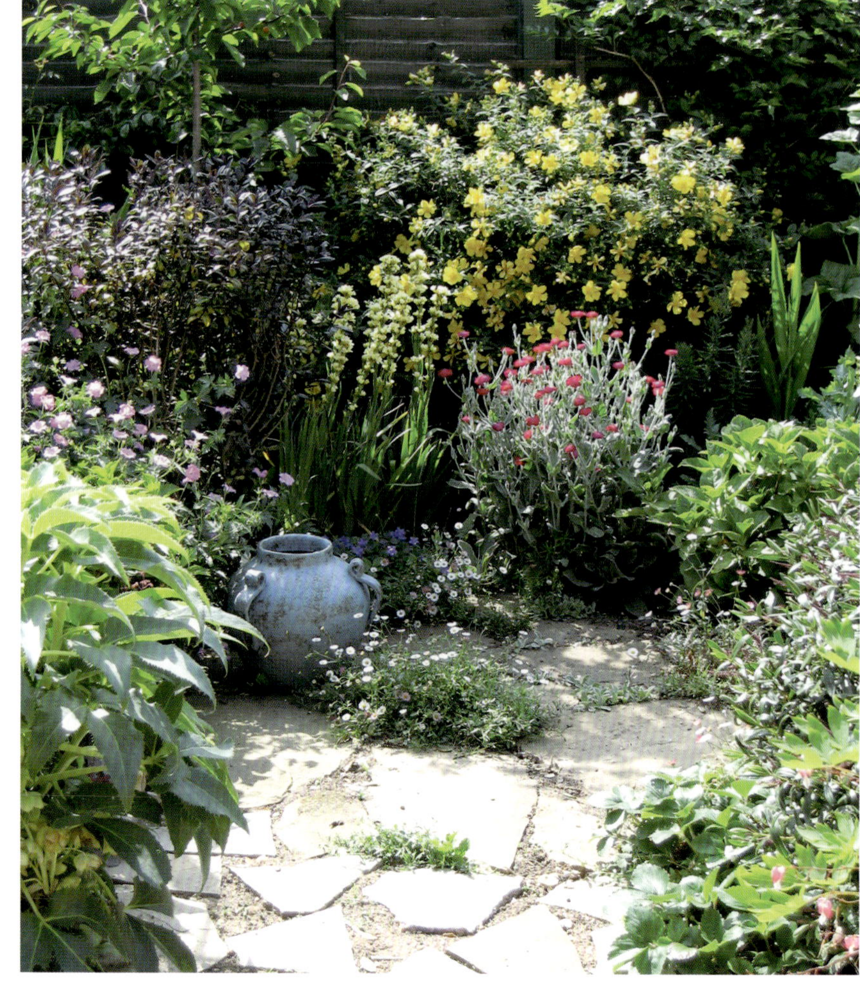

This Page: A corner of her garden where Maureen sets up groups of pots, flowers etc for her flower and garden pictures.
Opposite Page: All the equipment in Maureen's studio has to be moveable so that she can either work on more than one picture; frame or reframe her pictures; or move everything to provide more space for her students

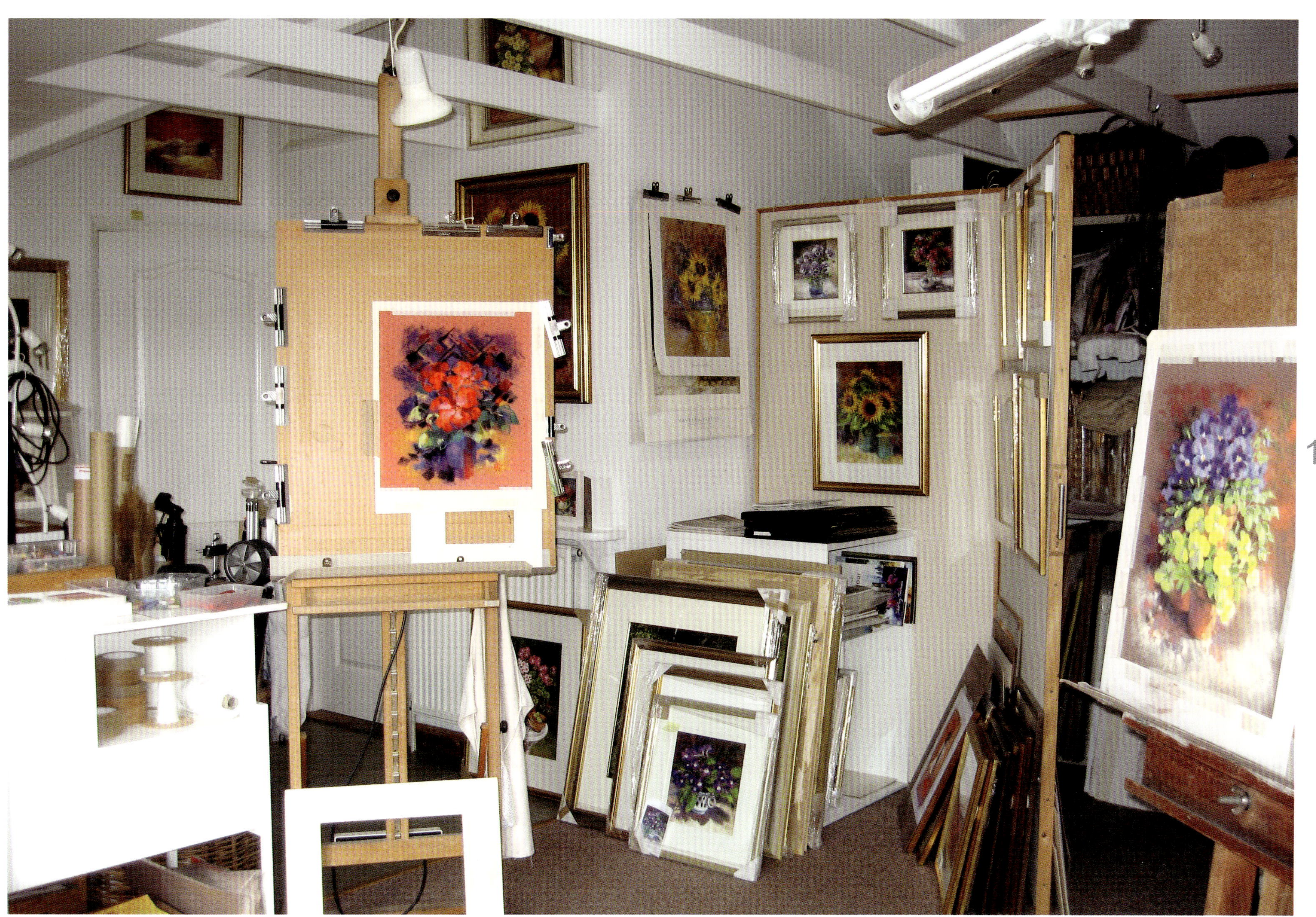

Geoff Harmer

Geoff Harmer's art works are bold and vibrant and painted with confidence using strong colours and natural compositions capturing the true essence of the scene. Whether dealing with the soft subtle textures of a tree-lined path or the stark contrast of a bright white boat lying against the quay, Geoff adapts his style and pallet accordingly, bringing the best out of the subject in front of him.
- Picturecraft Gallery, Holt, Norfolk

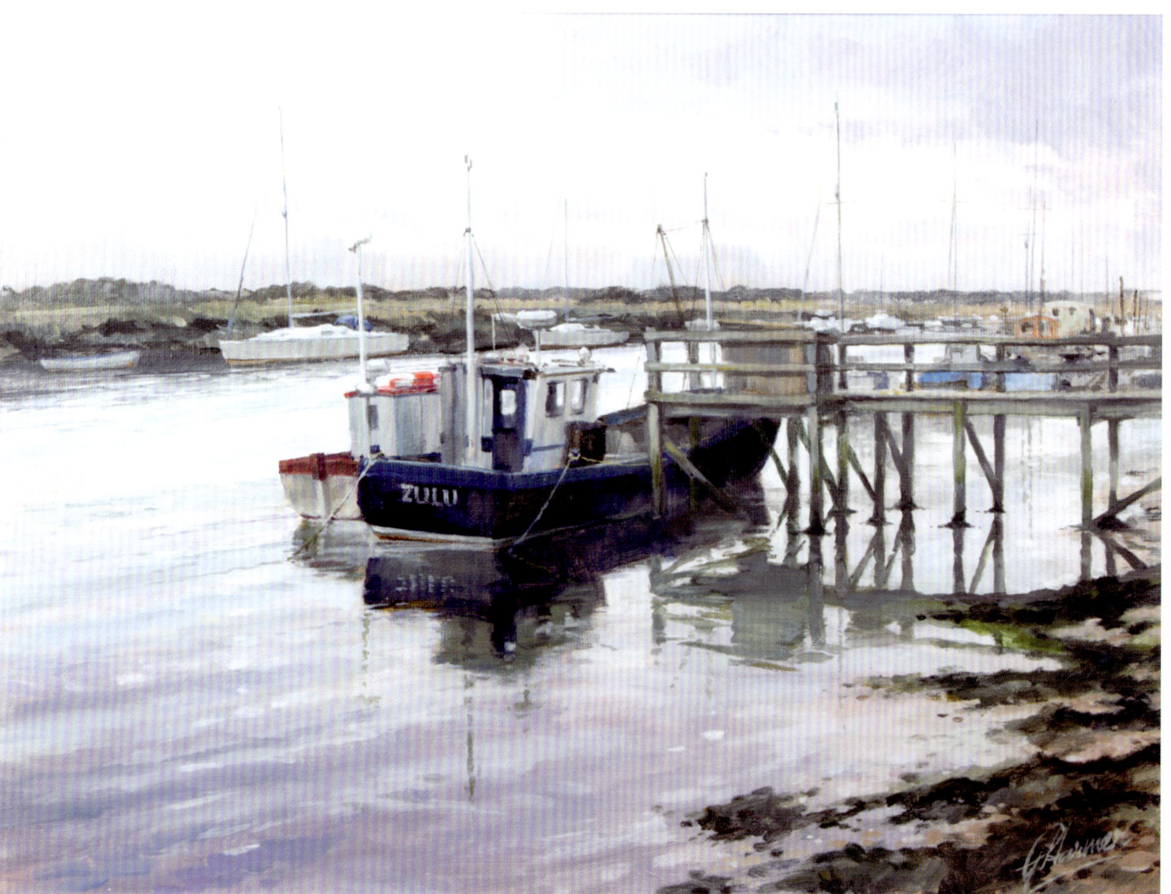

Evening Light, Southwold Harbour (2010) Oil 36 x 46cm

Geoff Harmer
Illustrator, Painter
Wickham Market, Suffolk

My inspiration has always been the sea and living near the coast of East Anglia provides an endless variety of marine subjects. My main interests are maritime history, working boats and capturing remnants of the craftsmanship of the past.

Evening Light, Southwold Harbour shows the ebbing tide flowing past the boats at rest; the reflection of the fading light fascinated me.

In *Sea Wall, Heybridge Basin* I wanted to capture the light reflecting on the mud flats, contrasting with the dark shape of the boats.

Educated- Central St Martins College of Art & Design, London
Galleries Familiar With Artist's Work-
Picturecraft Gallery, Holt, Norfolk
Kesgrave Arts, Ipswich, Suffolk
Ferini Art Gallery, Pakefield, Suffolk

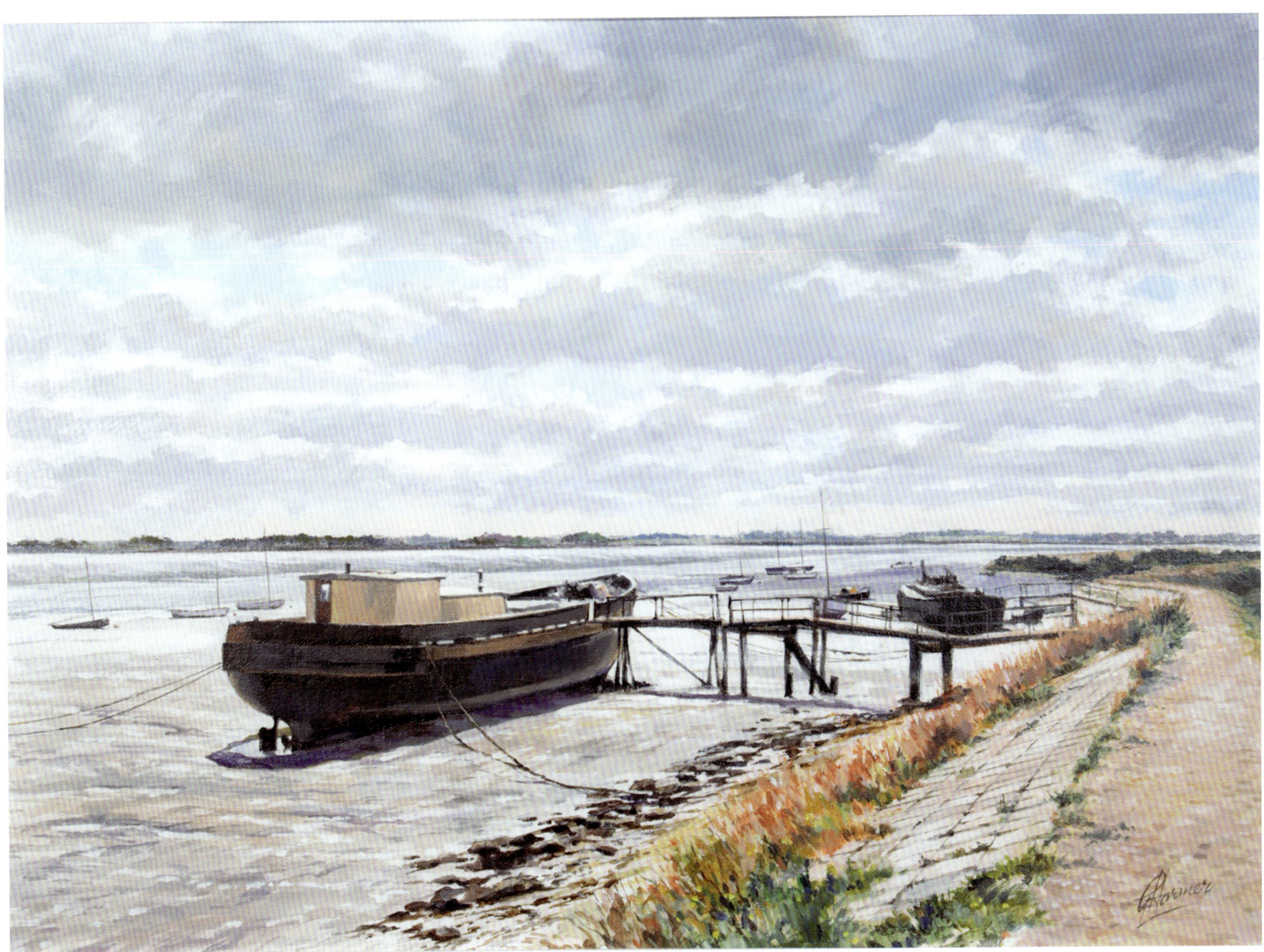

Sea Wall, Heybridge Basin (2008) Oil 46 x 61cm

Theronda Goussard Hoffman BA

Theronda Goussard Hoffman BA
Sculptor, Painter, Graphic Artist, Installation Art,
Jewellery-Maker, Legal Graffiti
Ipswich, Suffolk

I am the proud owner of Kesgrave Arts Gallery, Studio and Picture Framing. My motto in life is: I live to paint and paint to live.

I will use whatever I have to, to say whatever I want to.

I am inspired by the Suffolk coast, especially Aldeburgh.

I do say 'Aldeburgh is the Venice of Suffolk.'

I do like the art collections at the Christchurch Mansion, Ipswich.

Here I do like the landscapes of John Constable.

I do like the Dali Exhibition in County Hall on London's South Bank.

The two artists who have influenced my work are Pablo Picasso and Salvadore Dali.

My ambition is to be a great artist. My challenge is always to do greater work.

I do want people to like and understand my work.

With *Aldeburgh* my ambition is to simplify Aldeburgh and to show that by using line, I can convey the essence of Aldeburgh to the viewer. The emotional response that I would like from this piece is 'Suspension of disbelief'.

My ambition for *Fish And Chips Moments* is to typify the waiting in the queue for these world famous fish and chips. I hope people can identify with waiting in a queue for something worth waiting for.

In my third work, *Fish Fingers*, the sculpture symbolizes the eating of the fish and chips with your hands and fingers. The essence of Aldeburgh is to eat fish and chips with your hands.

Educated- Spier Artschool, Stellenbosh, South Africa 1987
Membership of Local Art Societies-
Woodbridge Art Club, Suffolk; Ipswich Art Club, Suffolk
Galleries Familiar With Artist's Work-
Aldeburgh Gallery, Aldeburgh, Suffolk
Cecil Higgs Art Gallery, Bedford, Bedfordshire
Website- www.kesgravearts.co.uk

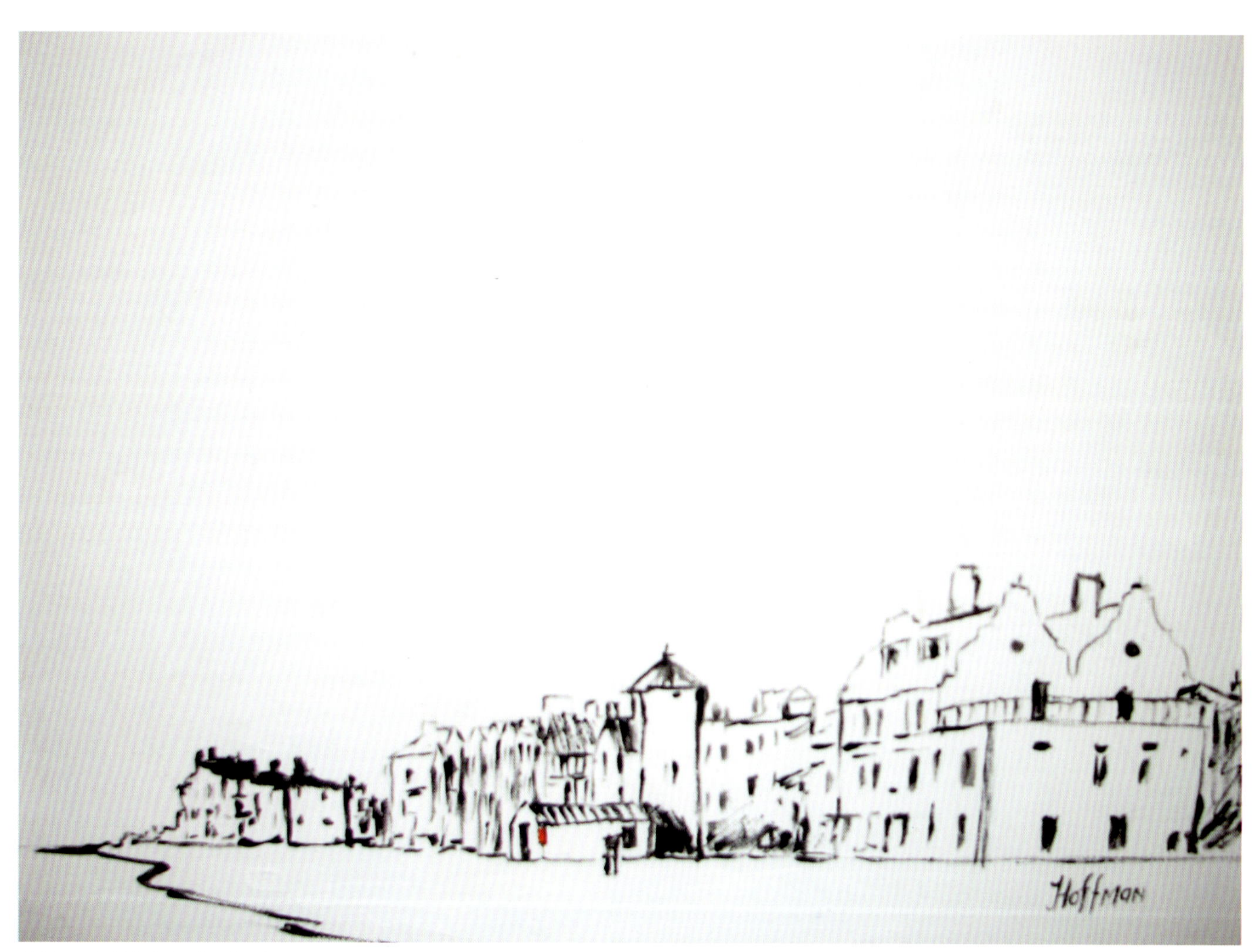

Aldeburgh (2009) Acrylic 50 x 40cm

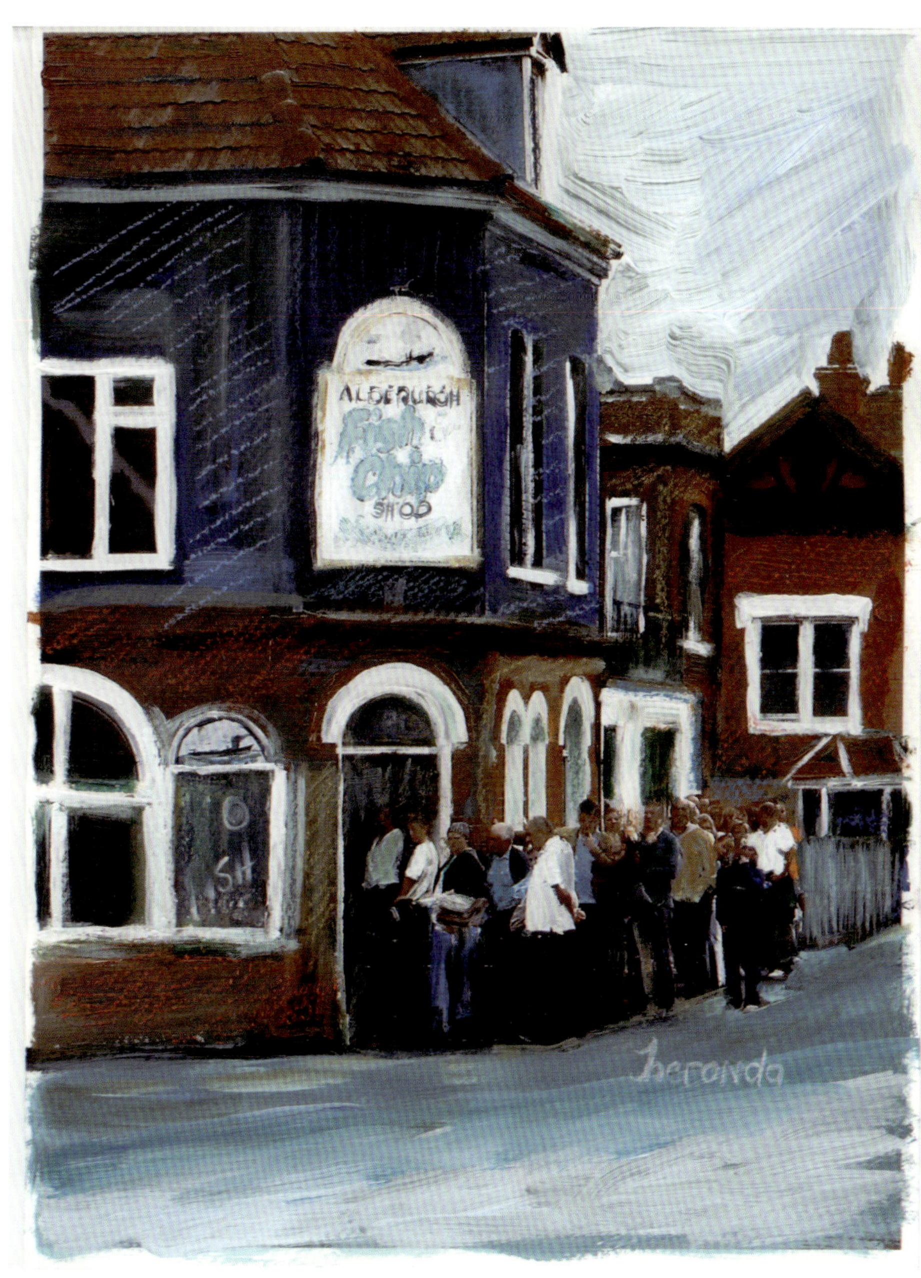

Fish and Chips Moments, Aldeburgh (2008) Mixed Media 20 x 30cm

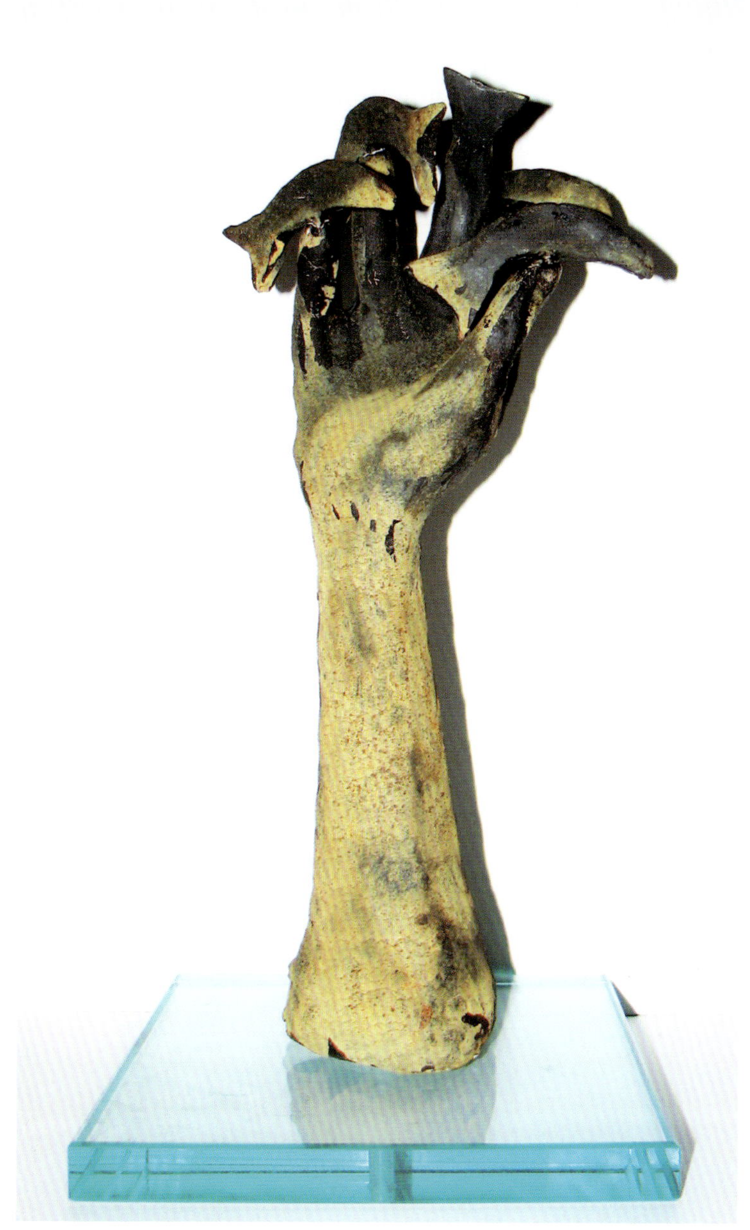

Fish Fingers (2009) Ceramic, Glass and Paint 36 x 18cm

Louise Stebbing BA (Hons)

Louise Stebbing BA (Hons)
Printmaker
Tydd Gote near Wisbech, Cambridgeshire

I returned to the Fens in 1993 after 14 years away at college and work. I love the open rural Fenland landscape with its vast skies, providing much of the inspiration for my art. I am often seen out on my bicycle with sketchbook and camera, and I often cycle the same route around the country lanes near my studio. One day I may become inspired by something I have seen for years but at this particular time the light may be hitting the subject differently or maybe my mood is different and I see the perfect subject for me.

I have been mesmerised by printmaking techniques since attending an art foundation course in Cambridge. I use a variety of techniques but recently have concentrated more on linocuts.

Country Lane is one of my most recent linocuts which began when I was out on my bicycle with my sketchbook. It was a beautiful spring morning and the blossom of the trees in the background captured my eye. I did change the atmosphere by printing a more dramatic sky; skies which we often see in the Fens.

Spring again is a recent linocut originally sketched on the same spring morning as *Country Lane*. The intense blue sky was scratched by planes and wispy clouds which I wanted to capture along with the beauty of the daffodils and blossom trees.

The inspiration for *Looking East* came from a motorcycle trip staying in a *gite* near Albi in France. The *gite* was surrounded by fantastic fields of sunflowers and vines which I sketched. Returning to my studio, I tried to capture the patchwork fields and different light in a linocut.

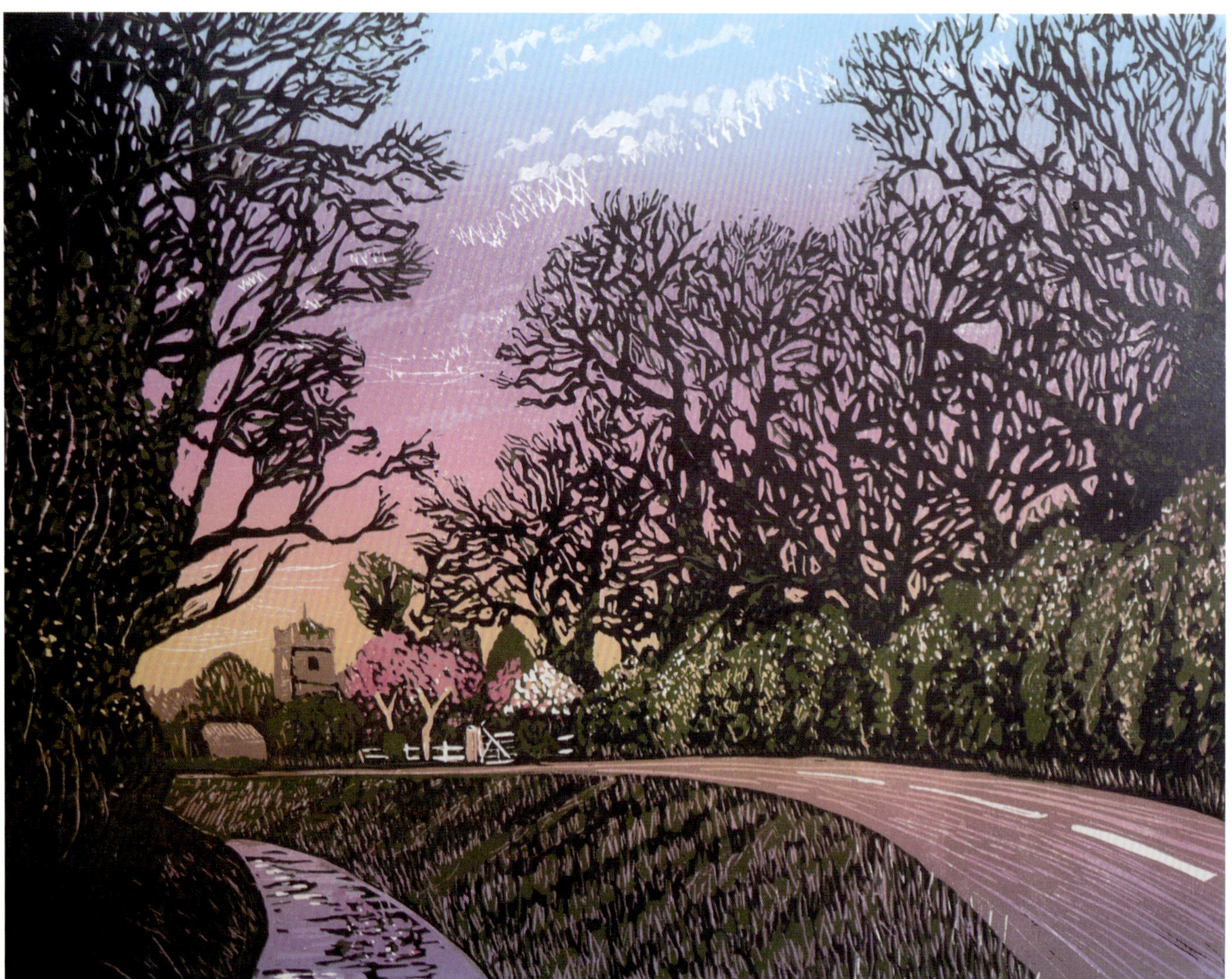

Country Lane (2010) Reduction Linocut 51 x 41cm

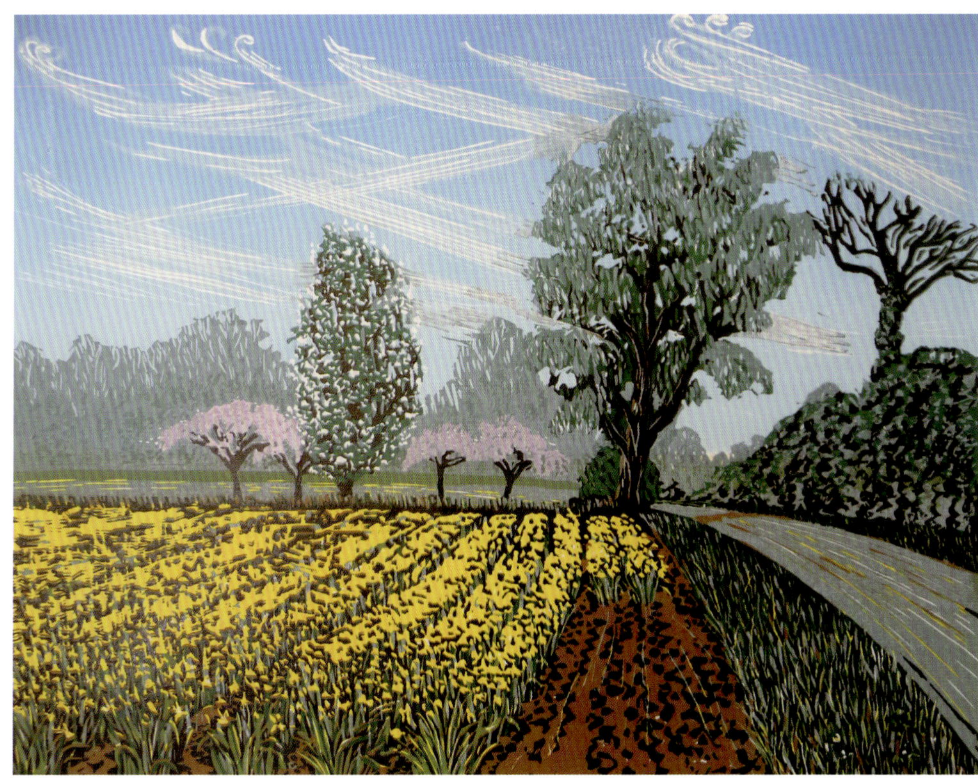

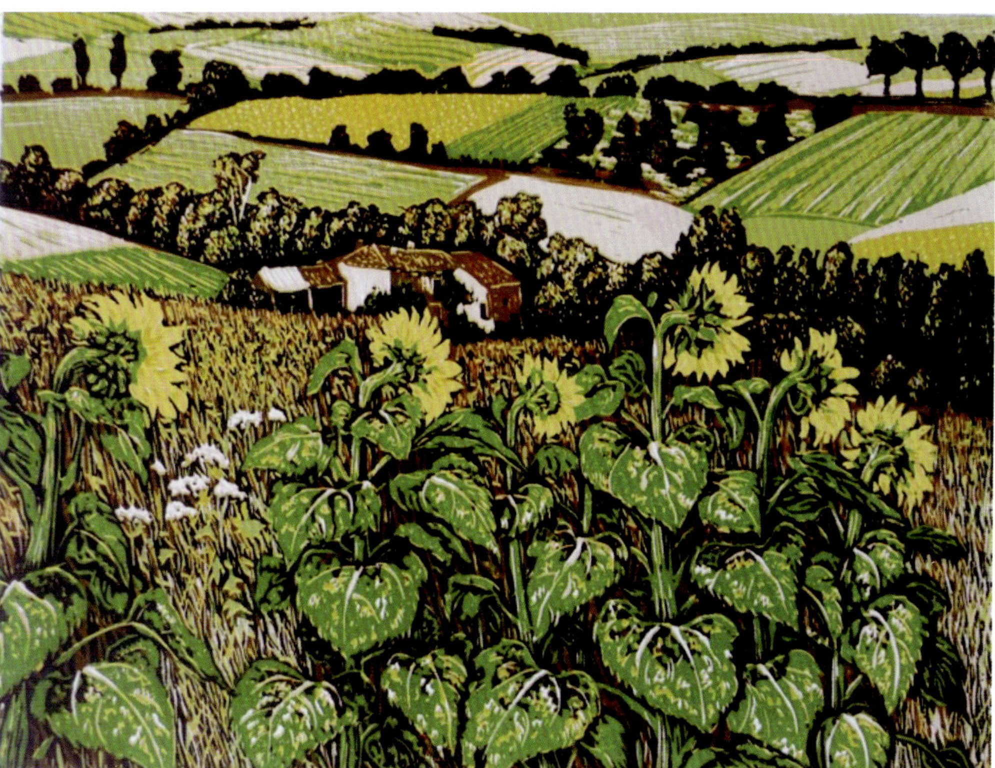

Spring (2010) Reduction Linocut 51 x 41cm

Looking East (2009) Reduction Linocut 51 x 39cm

Louise Stebbing: Behind the Scenes

More about:

Louise...

Educated-
Camberwell School of Art & Crafts London 1985
Postgraduate in Printmaking

Membership of Art Societies-
West Norfolk Artists Association

Accreditation-
Sheffield University, BA (Hons) Fine Art

Galleries Familiar With The Artist's Work-
Ropewalk Contemporary Art & Craft, Barton Upon Humber,
North Lincolnshire

Website- www.skylarkstudios.co.uk

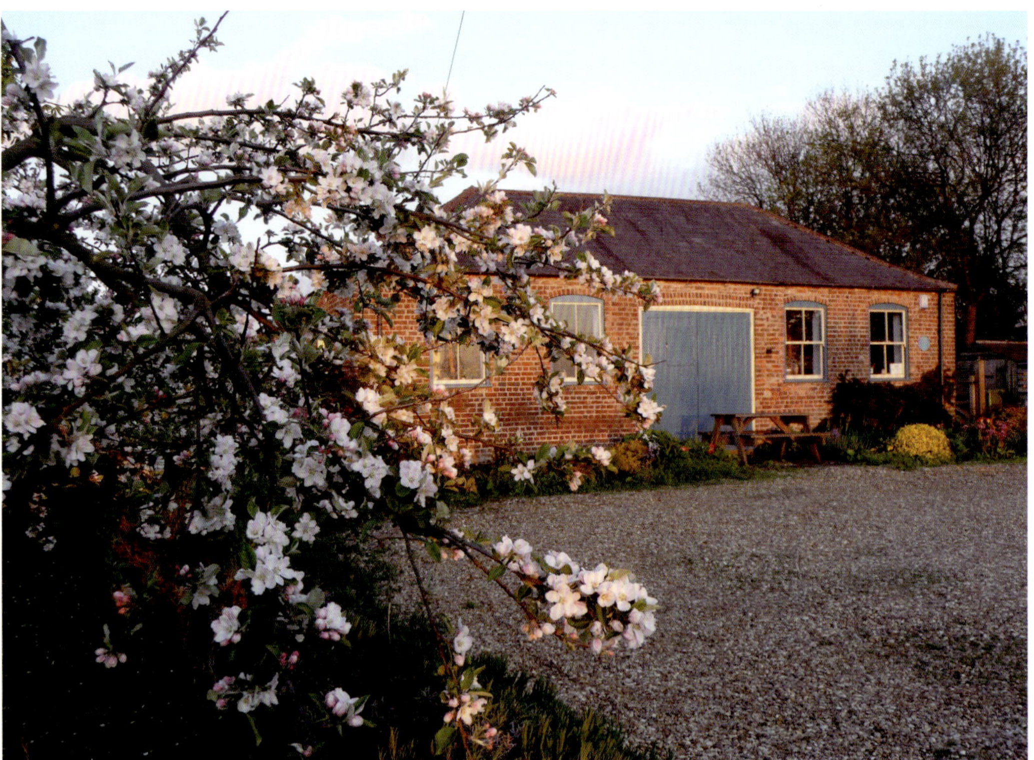

My studio is in a converted barn set in beautiful Fenland countryside. My pride and joy is my c.1840 Britannia Press that I purchased and renovated two years ago – I now use this for printing all my linocuts.

My images usually start with a sketch and I like the print to evolve as I create it – not working out too much detail in advance, but using my 30 years' experience to let the image develop in the direction it happens to take me at that particular time. I try to push the medium as far as I can, becoming really involved as I am working, constantly making decisions about the next stage.

Once I begin on a linocut I like to know I have several days free in which I will be able to continue on it. I don't like to stop once I have started. The cutting of the lino takes much longer than the printing process, so I often have to take a break when cutting out the lino, but never for long.

I usually only work on one piece at a time, becoming very engrossed in it – thinking all the time about what I'm going to do next to improve upon it.

I don't mind visitors when I'm working, but I won't be very communicative with them as my mind is on my work.

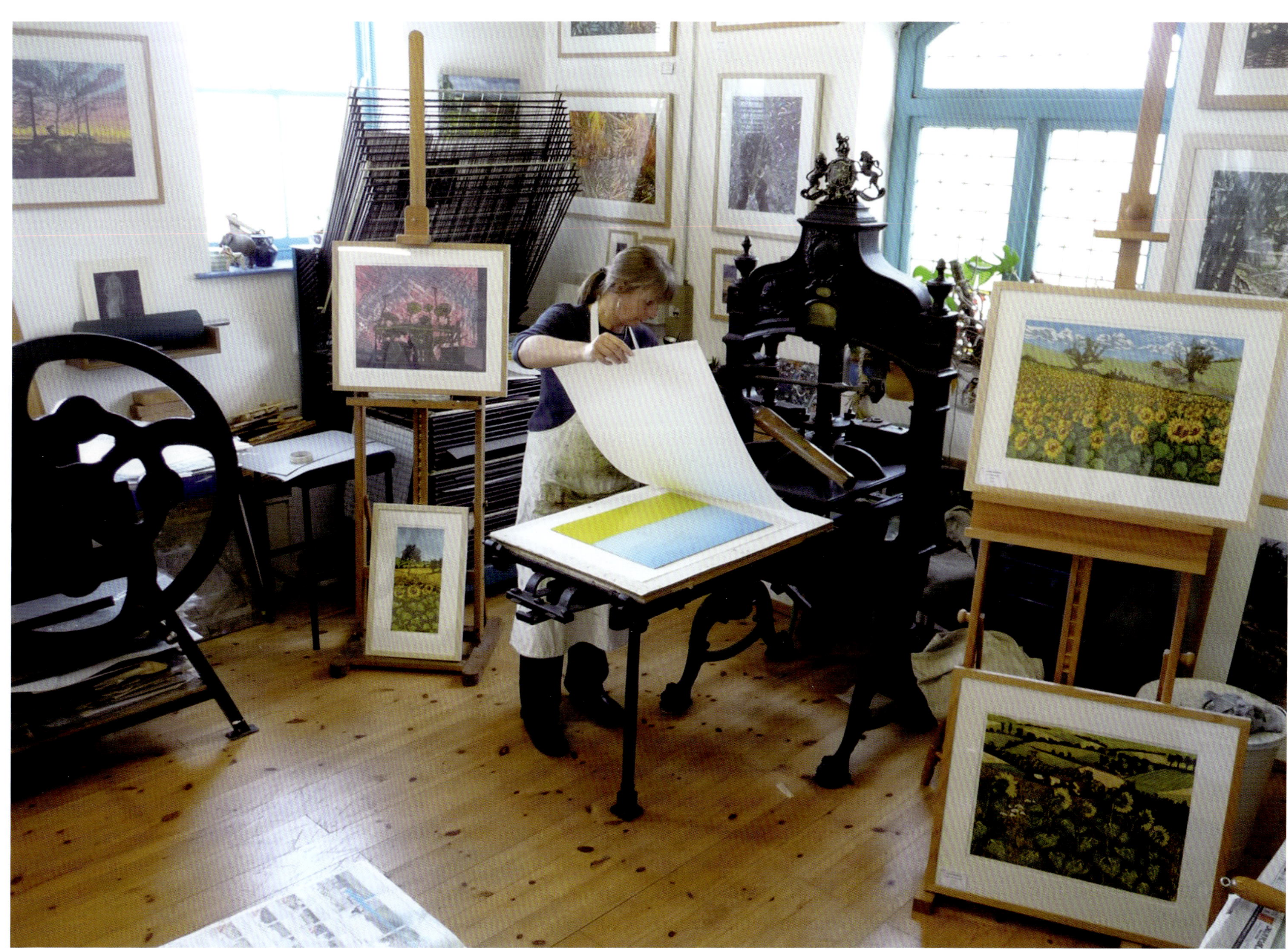
Photo Martin Stebbing

Lisa Temple-Cox

Lisa Temple-Cox
Assemblage/Mixed Media
Colchester, Essex

The environments that inspire my practice are museums and collections of medicine and anthropology; I have researched both in institutions here in the UK and in Europe. The collages and combines of Kurt Schwitters and Robert Rauschenberg have informed my art, as have surrealism and installation.

I describe my current practice as 'sheds and heads.' *Sheds* suggests my concern with installation, of art we can inhabit and immerse ourselves in: *heads*, inversely, references notions of identity rather than enclosure.

The notion of *The Double-Skinned Shed* came about through my love of sheds and other enclosed spaces. A mundane, temporary shelter, it reflects a search for permanence during a peripatetic childhood. Inhabited only by ephemera - slides of the past in another country, voices of the dead - it could reference both body and mind, flesh and imagination. All my installations have had some sense of enclosure; however the most important part of this structure might be that 'zone of the indiscernible', the gap.

Cabinet: My interests philosophically lie in exploring the realms of identity, personal history, and conscious – or unconsciousness – through the intersections of art and science.

My current visual research tends towards exploring the medical museum and the didactic moulage. I have been making experimental work inspired by methods of preserving the human body documented in the medical museum, framed by the aesthetics and discourse of the Vanitas

Last year I attended a conference in Dresden on the anatomical wax moulage. Having made a number of moulages, I found that viewers often failed to distinguish between a life mask and a death mask. In *Untitled (moulage VII)*, I explore the notion of self and identity, as expressed through the medium of the face, and the fascination exerted by the display of human remains. I want to create work that in this way both repels and attracts.

Educated- Suffolk College, Ipswich 1987
Colchester Institute, Essex, MA 2009 - 2010
Collections (Open To The Public)-
Fluxmuseum, Fort Worth, Texas, USA
Website- www.lisatemple-cox.co.uk

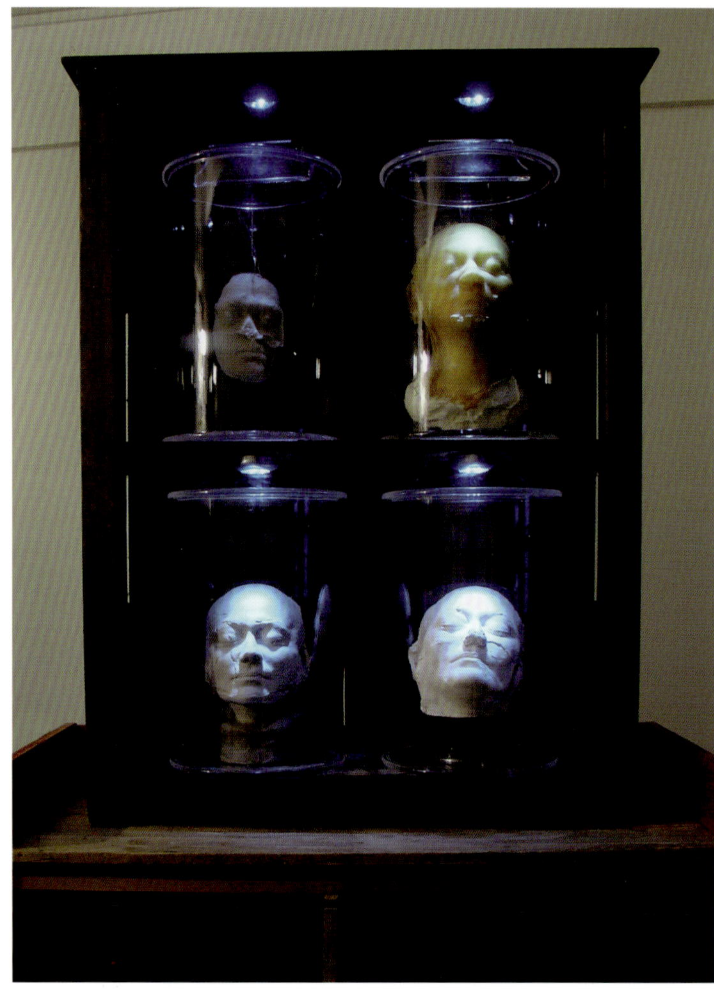

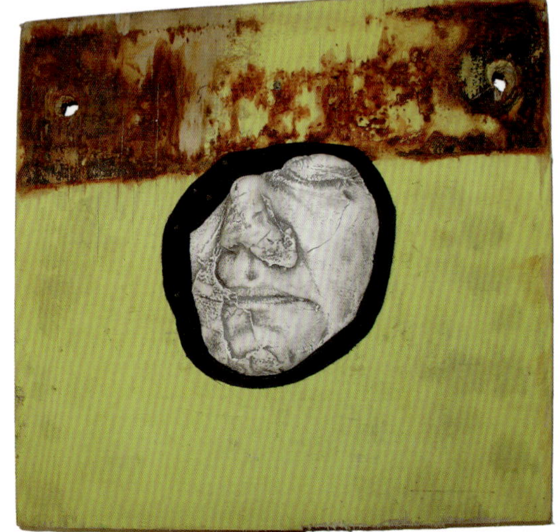

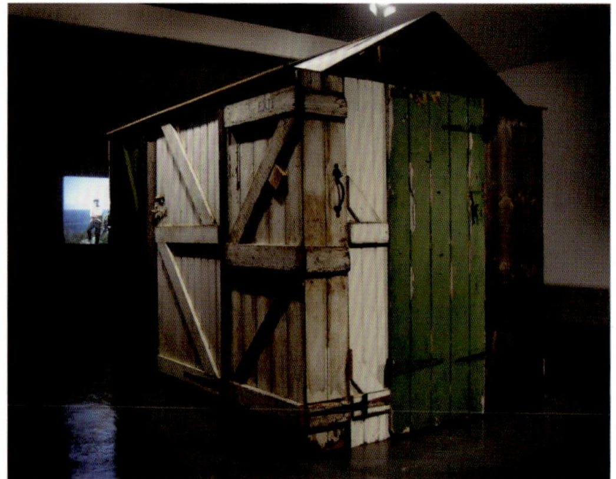

Left: *Cabinet (2010)* Wooden Cabinet, Perspex, Clay, Wax, Plaster 180 x 90x 40cm
Top Right: *Untitled (Moulage VII) (2009)* Found Wood, Fabric, Clay 25 x 30 x 5cm
Bottom Right: *The Double-Skinned Shed (2009)* Found Wood and Doors 183 x 122cm Apex Shed, Slide Projection, approx 300 x 200 x 200cm

Jayne Wurr BA (Hons)

On my first encounter with Jayne's work I was taken in by the trompe l'oeil artist. A cook's apron hanging on the wall on closer inspection was found to be made of a myriad of tiny coloured tiles. Jayne's former vocation as a textile designer is reflected in her mosaics. Her feel for fabric, its texture and how it folds makes her mosaics come alive.
- Cork Brick Gallery, Bungay, Suffolk

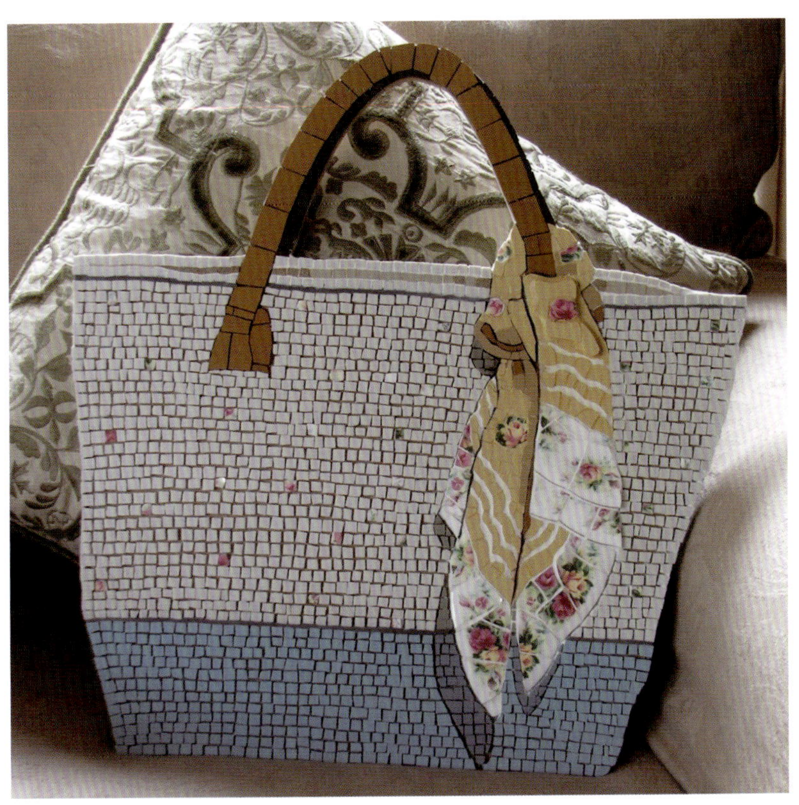

New Summer Bag (2009) Mosaic

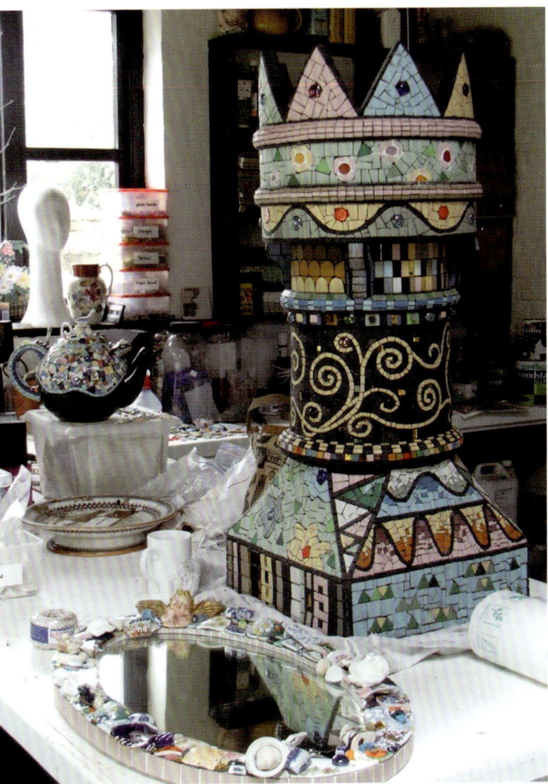

Coronation Street Meets Klimt (2010) Mosaic

Jayne Wurr BA (Hons)
Mosaic
Harleston, Norfolk

Despite its rich history, mosaic as an art form has been taken up by very few artists, seen mostly as unfashionable, yet most are overwhelmed by Gaudi's use of colour and touched by the lavish design by Ezio Frigerio of a carpet covering Rudolf Nureyev's tomb, Genevieve-des-Bois, Paris.

My mosaics are inevitably influenced by many years working as a textile designer. Surface pattern, decoration once on fabric now on ceramic, wood and glass, only a sideways step, really, but my paint brush is having a rest.

New Summer Bag was created for an exhibition in Southwold celebrating summer. I thought new summer wardrobe and came up with new bag, shoes and a summer cardi. The challenge in this piece is the scarf; to try and capture the silky softness of the fabric's folds with solid china and ceramic tiles. Mosaic is often thought of in terms of clumsy chunks of naive randomness. I try to be in control of the media rather than the other way round. I strive to break up those nasty geometric lines and squares unless they are vital to the piece.

Coronation Street Meets Klimt juxtaposes the North of England's smoky chimney and the highly decorated sophistica-tion of Gustav Klimt's rich pattern; the practical and the frivolous combined together in a place where you would least expect, photographed in the barn where I work surrounded by numerous other ongoing projects. Chimneys are a perfect structure to work on as they are so weatherproof, allowing me to take mosaic outside into the garden as sculpture. I plan other artist/chimney combos in future.

Educated-
Winchester School of Art 1977
Membership of Local Art Societies-
The Harleston and Waveney Art Trail, Norfolk
Galleries Familiar With Artist's Work-
The Southwold Gallery, Southwold, Suffolk
Cork Brick Gallery, Bungay, Suffolk
Harleston Gallery, Harleston, Norfolk

Gill Baguley

Gill's work, whether it be her organically-styled pieces or her quirky illustrative paintings, conveys skilled observation which is always well executed.
- Art-next-the-Sea, Wells-next-the-Sea, Norfolk

Gill Baguley
Painter
Kettlestone, Fakenham, Norfolk

When working on my paintings, I aim to keep my individuality and try to avoid painting what I think people want. I need to express my feelings about the world around me. I try to create work that will make viewers aware of the problems being caused by coastal erosion, but I also paint cats because they have such humour. With landscapes, I try to capture the wonderfully vibrant colours I see in the clean, unpolluted, Norfolk air.

Vincent Van Gogh is an enormous influence on my art because he had energy and the ability to see inspiration in every-day subjects. I love Picasso's humour, vitality and economy of line.

Luckily for me, I live in an ideal location and thus am most inspired by my own studio where I have wonderful light and a marvellous view of my garden with fields beyond. However, when seeking outside inspiration, I love visiting The Sainsbury Centre For Visual Arts in Norwich, Norfolk, where exhibitions are imaginatively selected and usually uncrowded, and the Tate Modern in London with its magnificent building and art collection

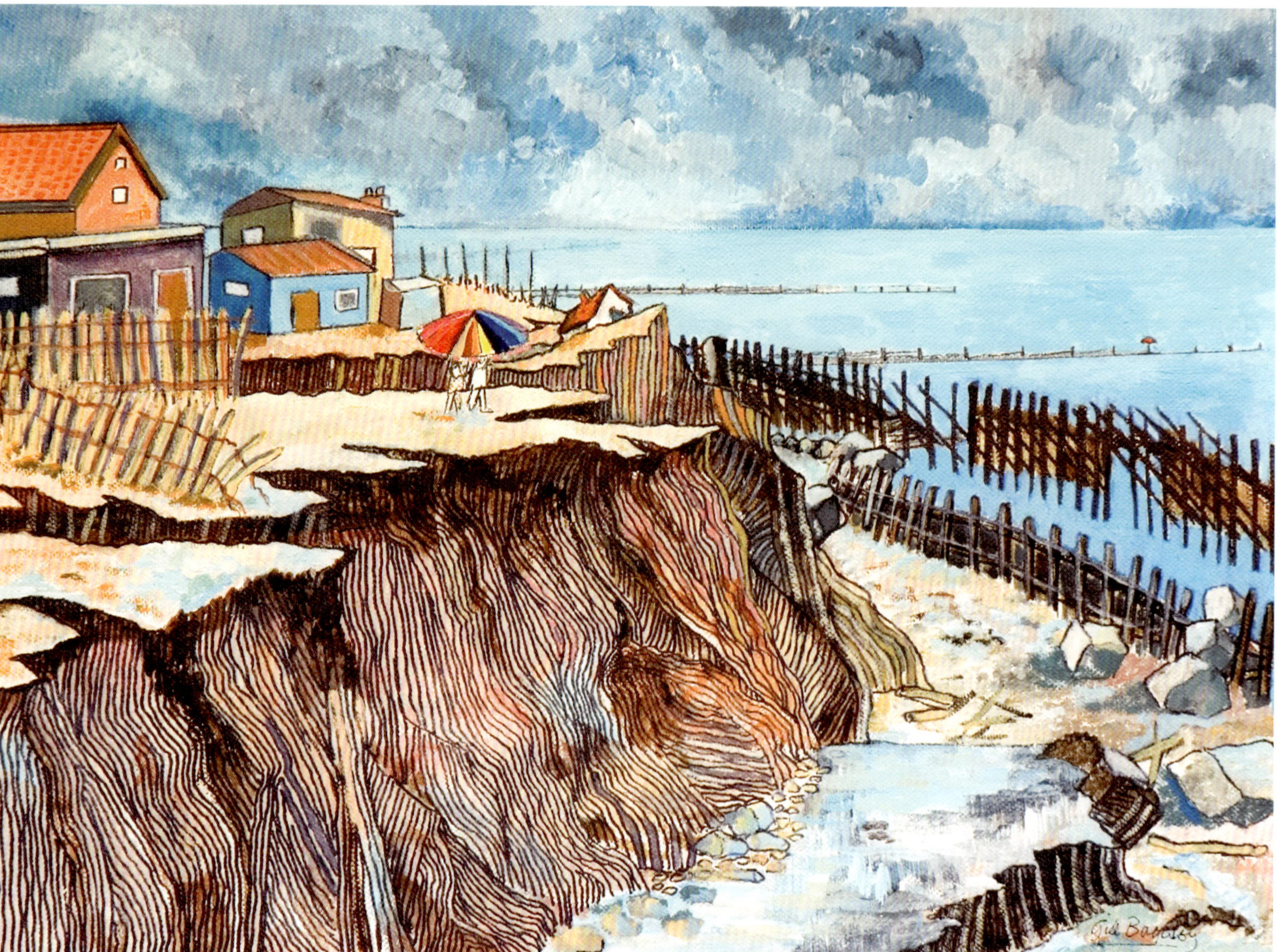

Cart Gap, Happisburgh (2007) Acrylic 30 x 40 cm

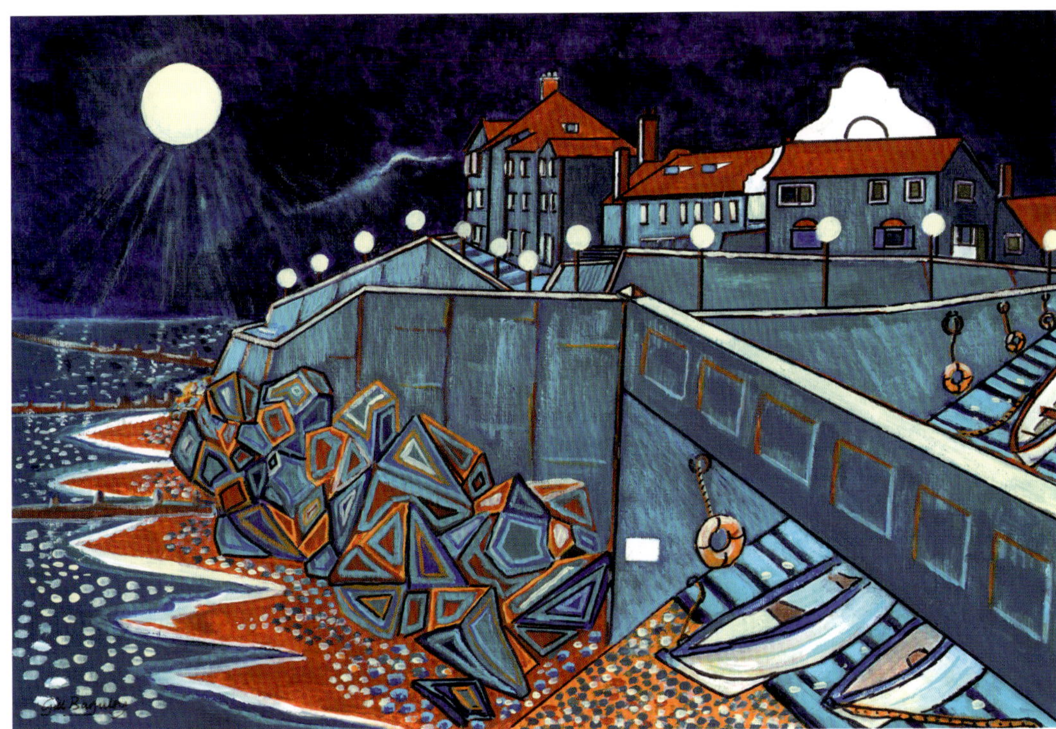

Moonstruck, Sheringham (2008) Acrylic 30 x 46 cm

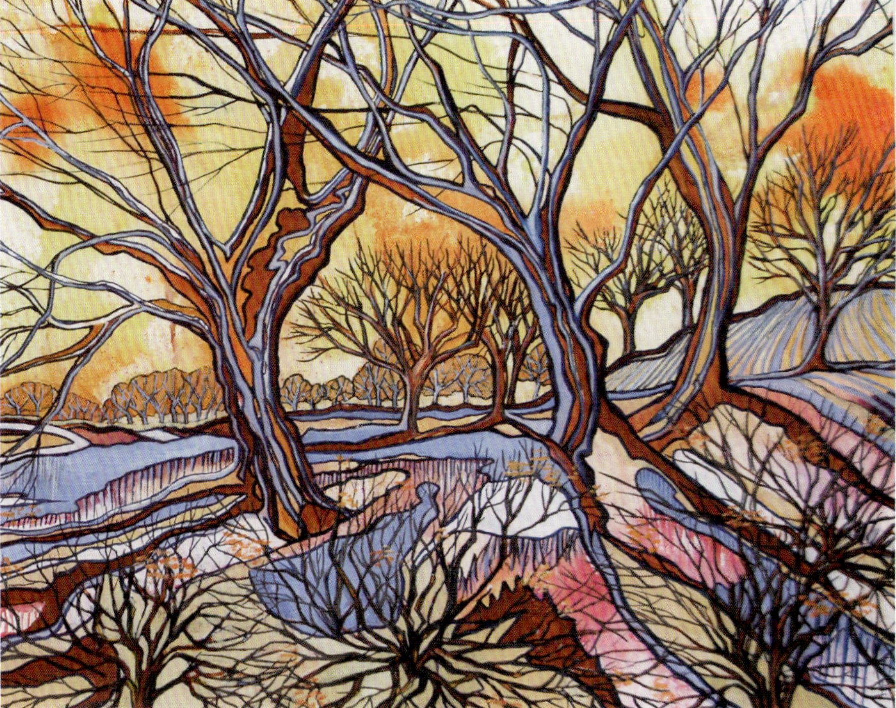

Winter Trees (2009) Acrylic Ink 60 x 56cm

Gill Baguley: Behind the Scenes

More about:

Gill....

Educated- No formal art school tuition
Galleries Familiar With Artist's Work-
Art-next-the-Sea, Wells-next-the-Sea, Norfolk
Gallery Plus, Wells-next-the-Sea, Norfolk
A Picture of Norfolk, Rackheath, Norwich, Norfolk

My studio is a spacious conservatory with a kitchen at one end and a smaller studio/garden room at the other end. It's attached to a 16th century flint cottage set in a third of an acre garden, overlooking fields at the back and the village church at the front.

Inside, the ceiling is high and the space airy. It is always warm and sunblinds have proved to be essential. I'm fairly tidy, but only because my studio is used regularly for painting groups. My work station in the corner consists of an easel, a trolley full of paints and inks, plus a table for my radio/CD player and coffee. I love music, anything from Mahler and Goretsky to Lloyd Webber, jazz, folk - anything, really. My radio is tuned either to Radio 4 or Classic FM.

I still follow the school hours pattern: start at 9.00 am, coffee at 11.00 am, snack at 12.30 pm. In winter I finish at 3.00 pm, but in the summer I'll work till 6.00 pm or even later - whilst there is light.

Food is of no interest to me - if only there were tablets! I prefer to 'graze' and love my microwave. Two gas heaters keep the temperature comfortable - the sun will do the rest.

I always have at least three canvases in progress. I flit from subject matter and medium constantly. There is usually acrylic paper mounted on boards waiting for attack from inks and brush pen. I use photographs for reference details and my head is always full of ideas. Trouble is choosing which one, but once I have made a decision I storm ahead, changing medium if I feel a block approaching, and I know that something is finished when people tell me.

I try not to labour work, so my method is to move to another piece if I'm getting frustrated. Thirty seconds is a long while for my anger to last, and I never kick the cat!

I love 'callers', as most show some interest in my work, so I rely on their reaction to the latest piece, which is invaluable to me.

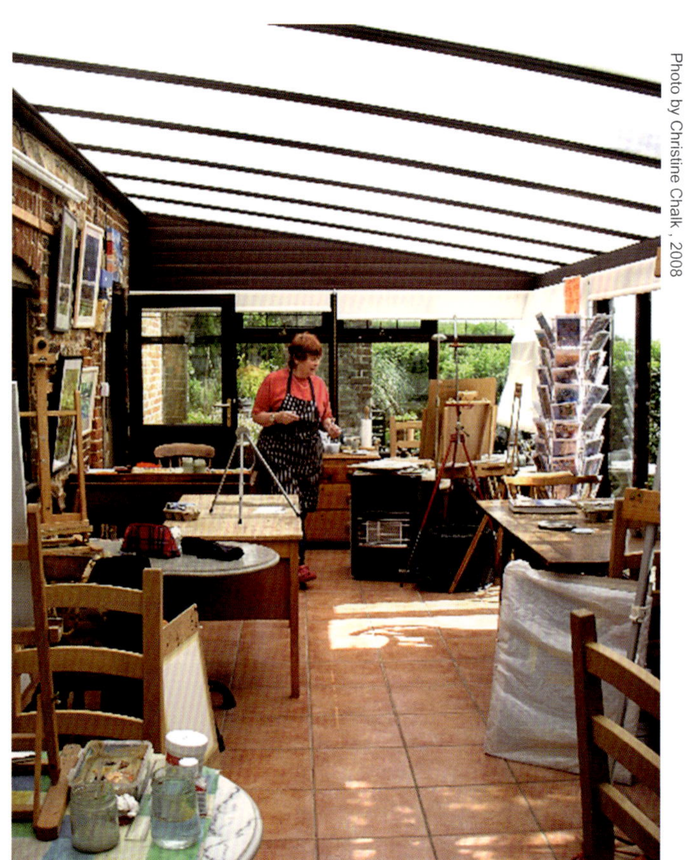

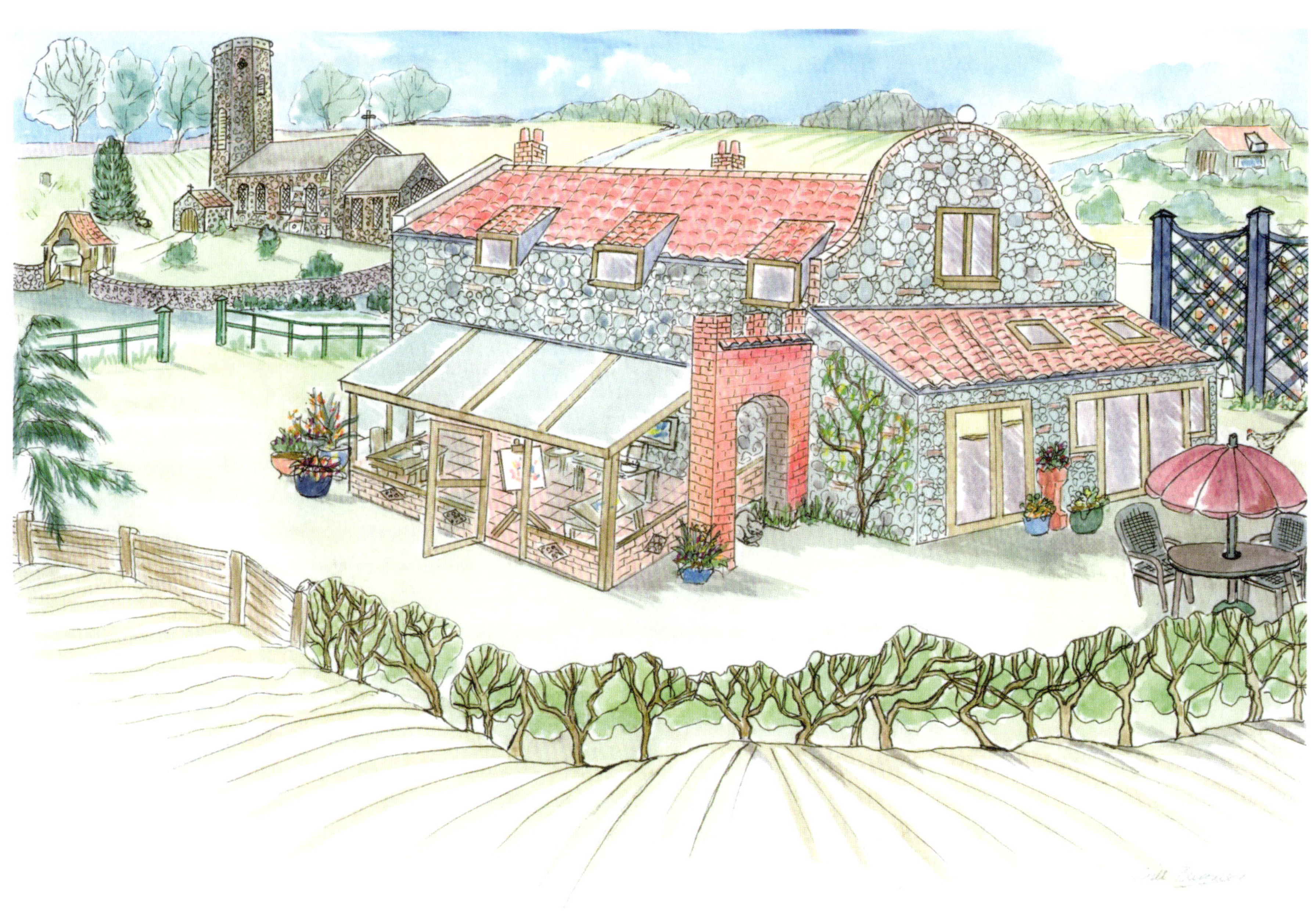

Lyn Aylward

Lyn Aylward
Painter
Thetford, Norfolk

Figurative studies provide the main focus for my work but I also particularly enjoy the challenge that portraiture brings in seeking to capture the character of a sitter. I also produce more diverse paintings and pencil work from an autobiographical perspective, which often involves subject matter derived from childhood experience and memory. I draw on influences from many artists but particularly from Chuck Close and Paula Rego. I also work to commission.

I have always been interested in the portrayal of the human figure and have recently begun working on a series of nudes. *Fold* is the largest of these works and is produced in oil on canvas. I wanted the figure to be defensive in posture and achieved this with the self-conscious folded pose used in the sitting. The feeling of unease portrayed by the sitter is further heightened by the tight framing.

Memory I: (Hunstanton) is the first painting from a series that deals with the distance of childhood memory. Shaped by my own memories of holidays spent on the East Anglian coast, the series explores the way in which we often elevate and distort particular recollections as we age. I remember seaside arcades quite vividly, with their garish colours, and wanted to portray these by using distortion of both colour and subject matter on the canvas.

The *Stephen Fry* portrait comes from a photograph by Johnny Boylan and arose from correspondence with Stephen Fry's sister, Jo. Although I much prefer to work from life, there was something about the photograph by Johnny that suggested it would make a lively study, which I hope it has achieved. I have always wanted to paint Stephen Fry and to capture something of his charm.

Membership of Local Art Societies-
Breckland Artists
Galleries Familiar With Artist's Work-
Doric Arts, Holt, Norfolk
Chimney Mill Galleries, Bury St Edmunds, Suffolk
Website-www.lynaylward.co.uk

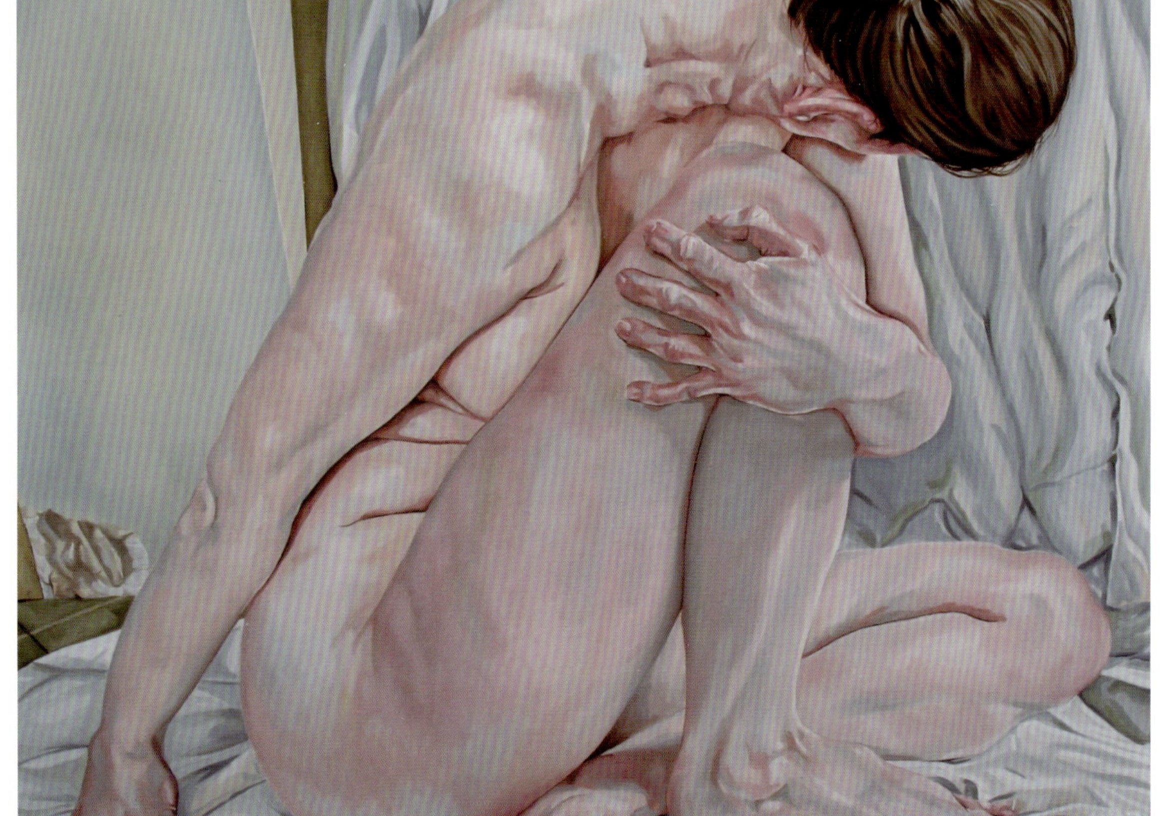

Fold (2010) Oil on Canvas 90 x 90cm

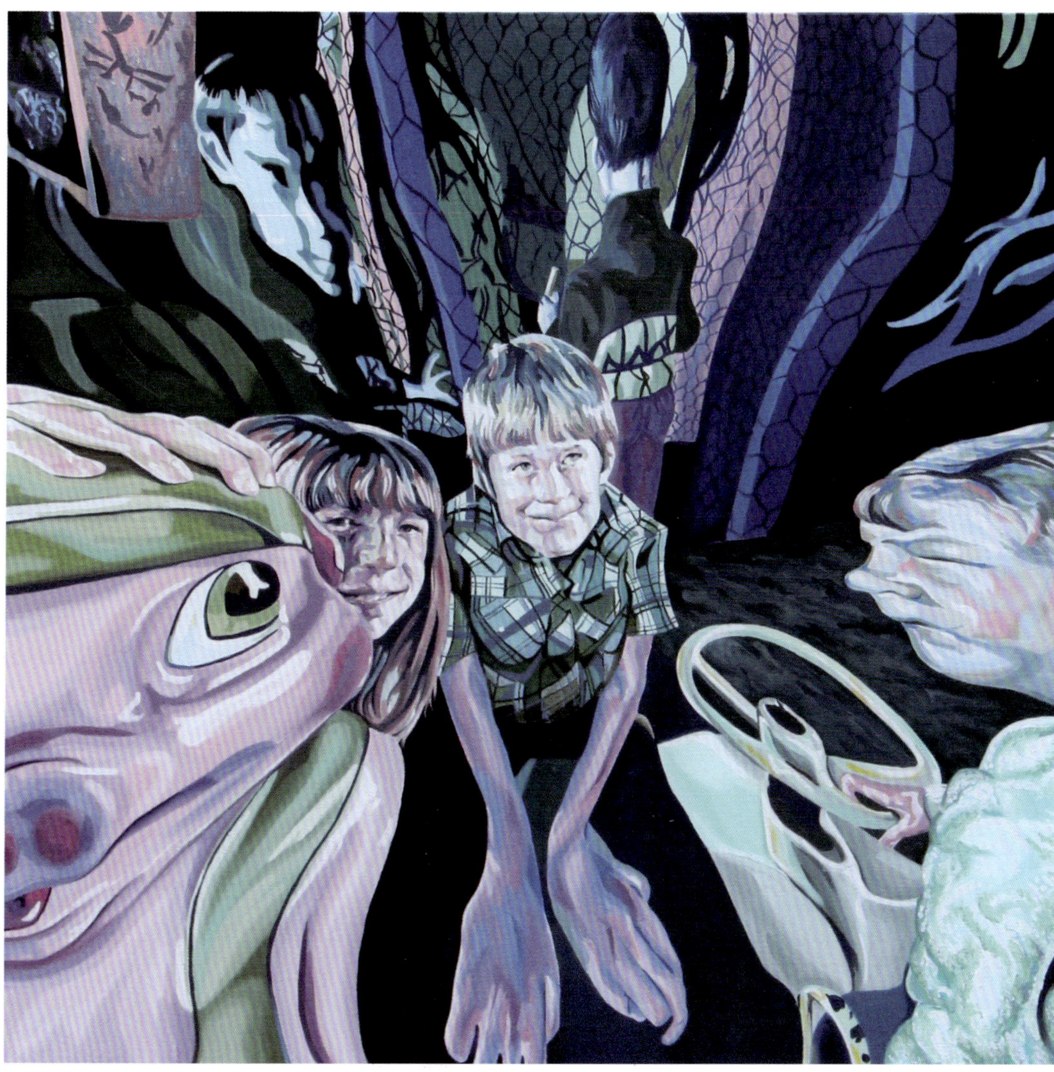

Memory I: (Hunstanton) (2009) Oil on Canvas 60 x 60cm

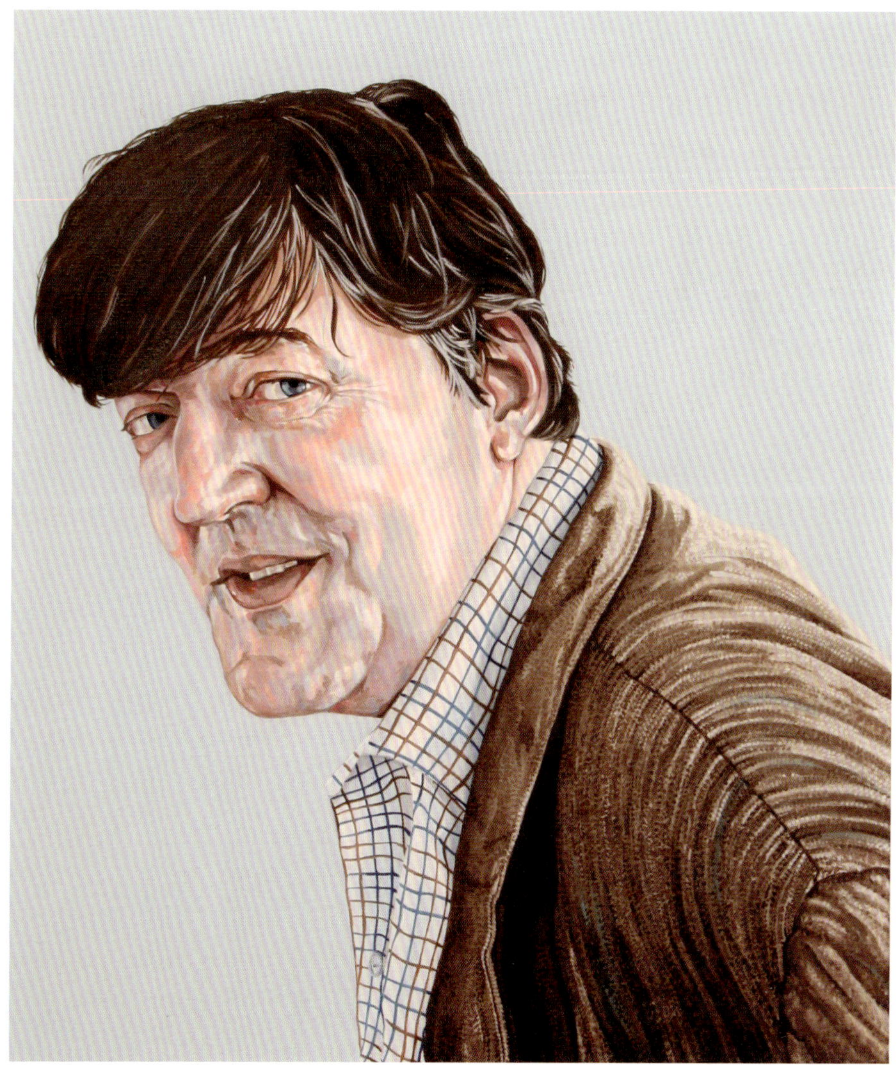

Stephen Fry (2010) Oil on Canvas 50 x 60cm

Dawn Hall

Dawn Hall's work captures the essence of our local landscape beautifully. Her large acrylic canvases use bold and dramatic brush stokes to show the energy of the sea, while her watercolours use soft and gentle hues, often depicting the light playing on water.
- Caxton Books & Fine Art, Frinton on Sea, Essex

Dawn Hall
Painter
Walton-on-the-Naze, Essex

For someone who doesn't swim very well, I spend a lot of time on the beach. The study of shadows in a wave, the detritus, the wet sand, the effects of erosion, all make for a life-long study. All this gathered information could quite easily go towards detailed realism, but I want to see passion in the brushstrokes, blobs of unexpected colour; to make people wonder why it works after viewing close up.

Wave IV could so easily have become a static representation; there is so much information to make it a true likeness. The cast shadow, the reflective colours, the shapes of the foam rivulets; I was soon engrossed in detail. When I realised what was happening I put down the brushes and picked up a credit card. No, not retail therapy, but a flexible tool for scraping on some action!

Dunes is about the tenth study of a particular spot on the eroding coastline at Walton on the Naze. I usually work in acrylics because of their fast drying textural qualities, but on this evening the colours were so soft and hazy that I felt only oils would do. It was exciting to note that the same colour mixes in both mediums produce a different ambience to a finished picture.

Brilliant Blue is another return to a familiar scene but using a new colour – I use a lot of blue! – in this case, brilliant blue. I usually work at greying and muting the paint from the tube for our English skies and seas, but this particular evening the late sun and calm sea were so vivid. Even the algae seemed luminescent. It took several mixes to feel that you should have worn your sunglasses on the walk.

Educated- No formal art school tuition
Galleries Familiar With Artist's Work-
Caxton Books &Fine Art, Frinton-on-Sea, Essex
Arna Farrington Gallery , Thorpe-le-Soken, Essex
Naze Tower Gallery, Walton-on-the-Naze, Essex
Gallery Violet, www.galleryviolet.com
Website- www.dawnhallartist.com

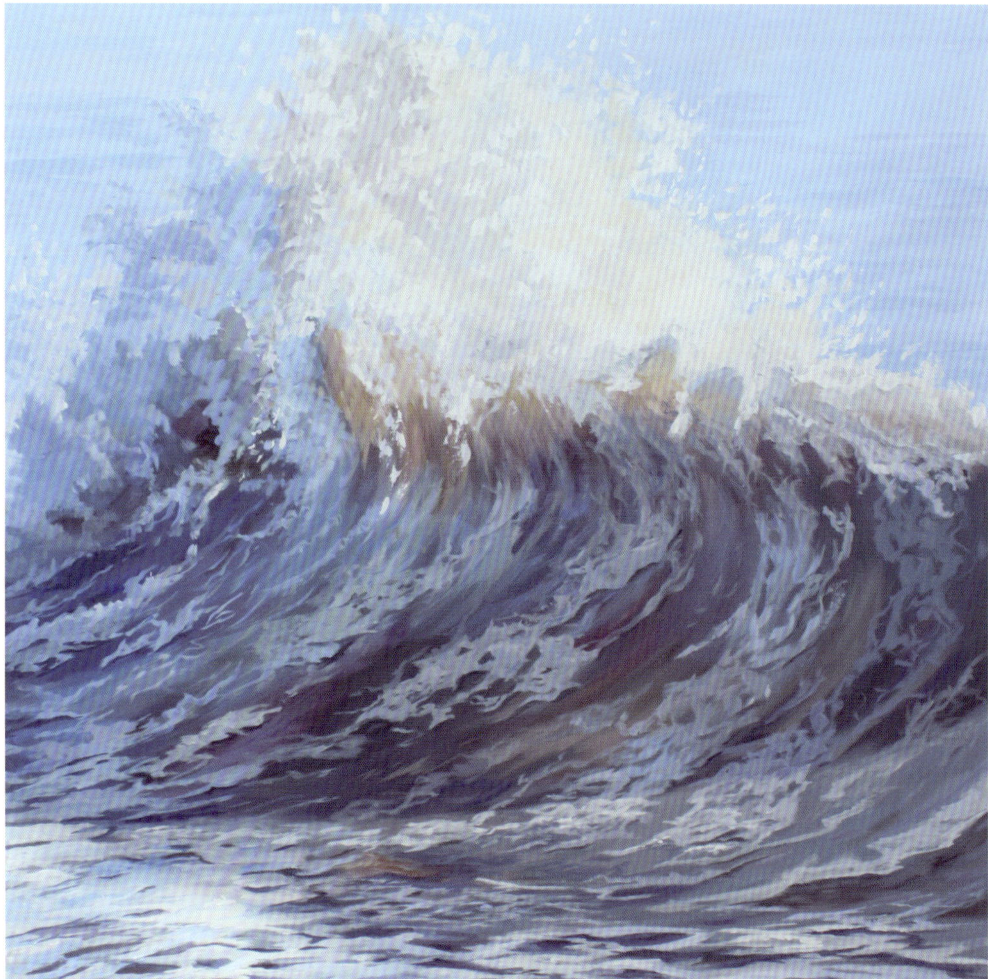

Wave IV (2010) Acrylic 100 x 100cm

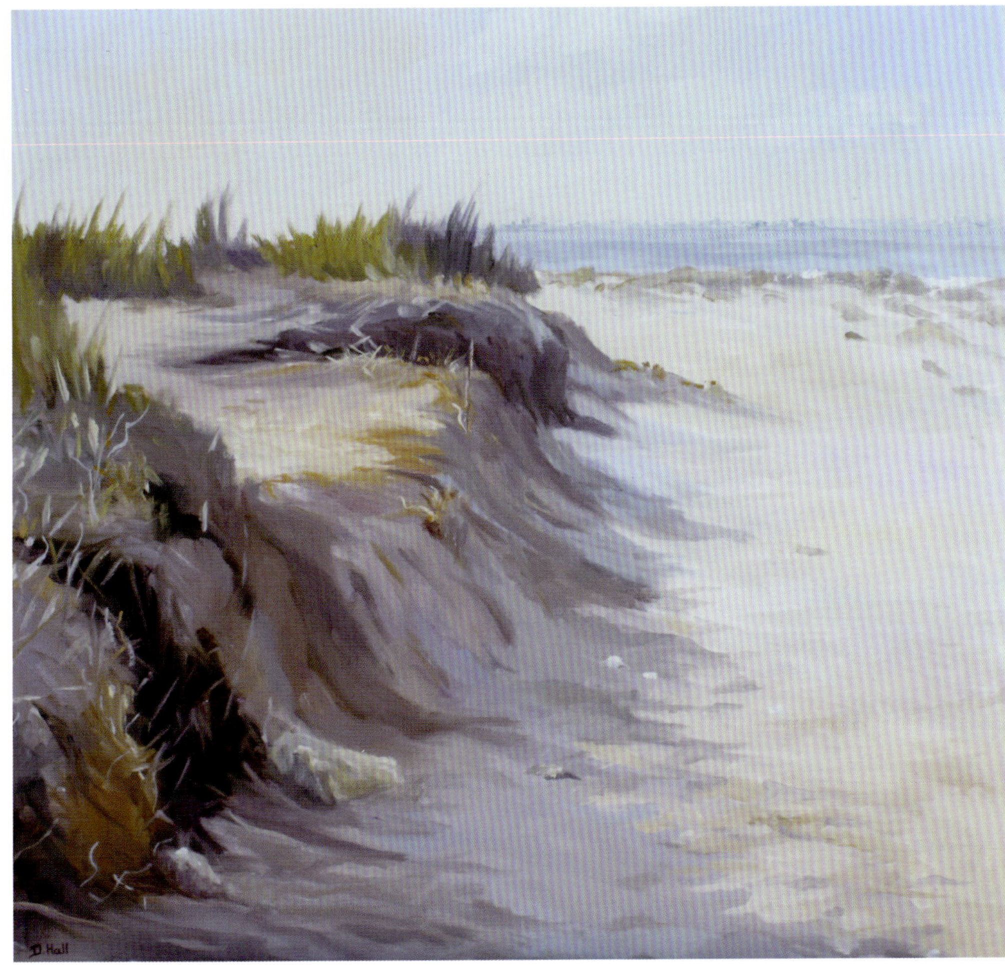

Dune (2010) Oil 50 x 50cm

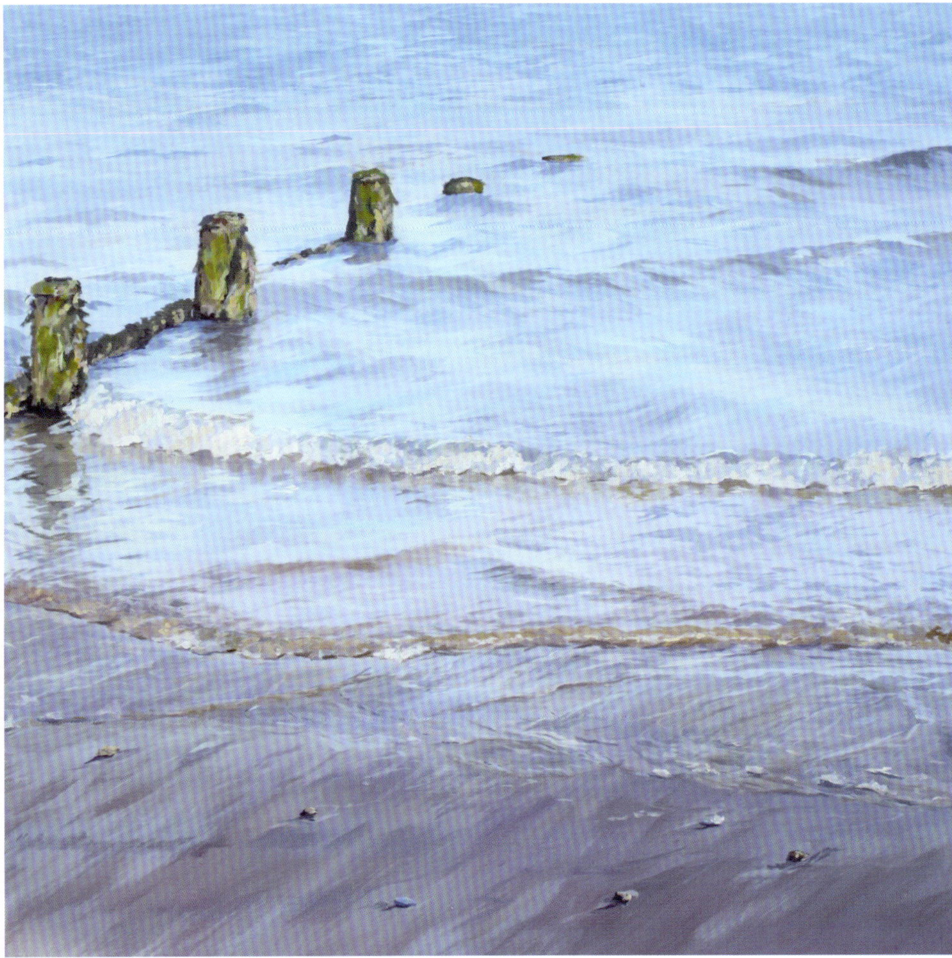

Brilliant Blue (2010) Acrylic 50 x 50cm

Philip James ROI

140

Philip James ROI
Painter
Hampton Wick, Surrey

My primary attraction was to landscape, with paintings made on site in Sussex, Dartmoor and Cumbria in the 1960s. More recently I have returned to working from the model, with figure paintings in progress each week. What I particularly enjoy is the challenge of direct observation and with this, opening up to discreet atmospheres and energies.

I gain a lot from certain artists; John Constable studies at Tate Britain and the small views by J.C Corot in The Louvre. I like to keep in touch with new art, which links me to the broader continuum of progressive work and ideas.

My art is completely integrated with my life, it is like a kind of journal and I'm constantly adding entries. I am informed by the unexpected, which stimulates invention, and by viewers' reactions. People always give me clear opinions!

Educated- Slade School of Fine Art, London
Accreditation With National Art Societies
Federation of British Artists, 2006
Galleries Familiar With Artist's Work-
Whittington Fine Art, Henley-on-Thames, London
Website- www.philipjamestudio.ndo.co.uk

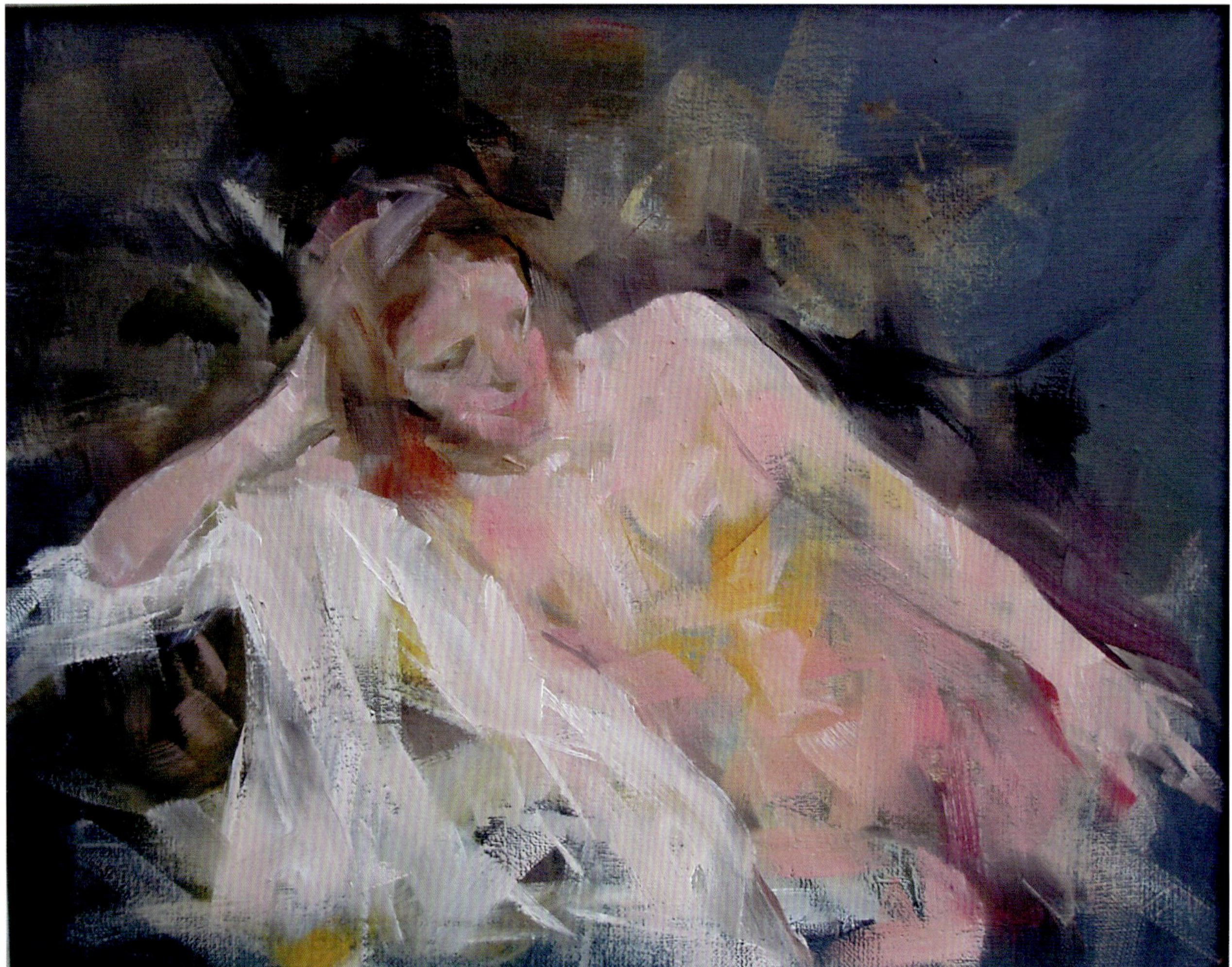

Life Model (2009) Oil 33 x 41cm

Dawn Pretty

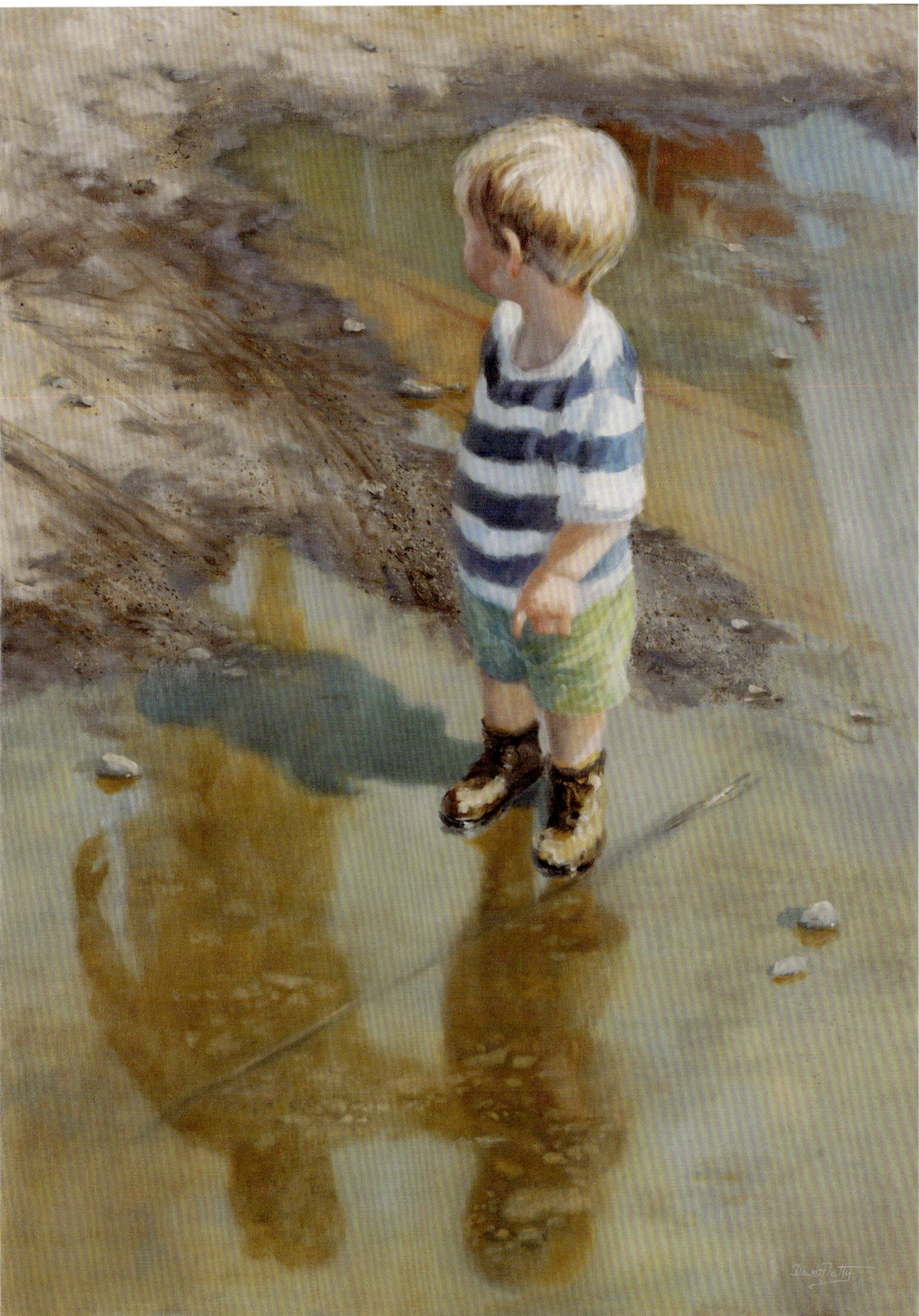

I Will Never Leave You (2006) Oil 100 x 70cm

Dawn Pretty
Painter
Halesworth, Suffolk

141

As a child I painted horses and thought my beloved farm in Rhodesia was my future. Dreaming has always been my forte, although a much maligned occupation, I identify with Beatrix Potter in saying, 'Thank God I have the seeing eye... as I lie in bed I can walk step by step on the fells and rough land seeing every stone and flower...where my old legs will never take me again.'

Loss is prevalent, loneliness cuts deep. I determined, from quite young, to bring as much good to this turbulent world as I could, seeing that the choice, in that, is at least given to us individually. Persuading inanimate paint to do something uplifting, conveying elusive qualities such as beauty and wholeness, affecting emotion, is a delicious challenge.

I am intrigued by people and reflections, that view into other dimensions, looked at but often not seen. The painting of my son William at Southwold harbour is one of many precious lost moments. I added a sense of comfort, depicting a good friend who once said, 'I will never leave you, nor forsake you.'

Educated-No formal art education
Membership of Local Art Societies-
Southwold Art Circle, Suffolk
Galleries Familiar With Artist's Work-
Buckenham Galleries, Southwold, Suffolk
The Little Gallery, Halesworth, Suffolk
Spencer Coleman Fine Art, London
Website-www.dawnpretty.com

Jeremy Rugge-Price AFAS, AAC

Jeremy Rugge-Price AFAS, AAC
Marine & Seascape Impressionist
Sudbourne, Suffolk

I am a self-taught artist. All my works are in oil and almost all of those are marine orientated. Having begun painting off the coast of Maine for many years, my main inspiration comes from the sea and the sailing ships that work upon it. In the UK I tend to paint dunes and barges. My favourite artists are Edward Seago and Matthew Alexander; these two artists have had the most influence on my work.

Pictures like *Standing Into Danger* are my favourite and they represent the fishing boats of yesteryear that braved the storm-lashed seas of the Grand Banks off the coast of Nova Scotia. Today, many of these schooners have been converted into day and weekly cruising ships around the 5000 islands of Maine. This area to me is heaven personified.

Time to Leave is a picture of Pink Sands on Harbour Island, Bahamas, where the peaceful tranquility is about to be destroyed by the approaching hurricane. As with all hurricanes, there is a moment of immense calm before the onslaught and my aim here was to reproduce that from the position I was standing on the beach.

Educated- No formal art school tuition
Accreditation With National Art Societies-
Armed Forces Art Society; Army Art Society
Galleries Familiar With Artist's Work-
Aldeburgh Contemporary Arts, Aldeburgh, Suffolk
Collections (Open To The Public)-
Mystic Marine Museum & Gallery, Mystic, USA
Website-
www.jeremyruggeprice.com
www.artlessonssuffolk.com

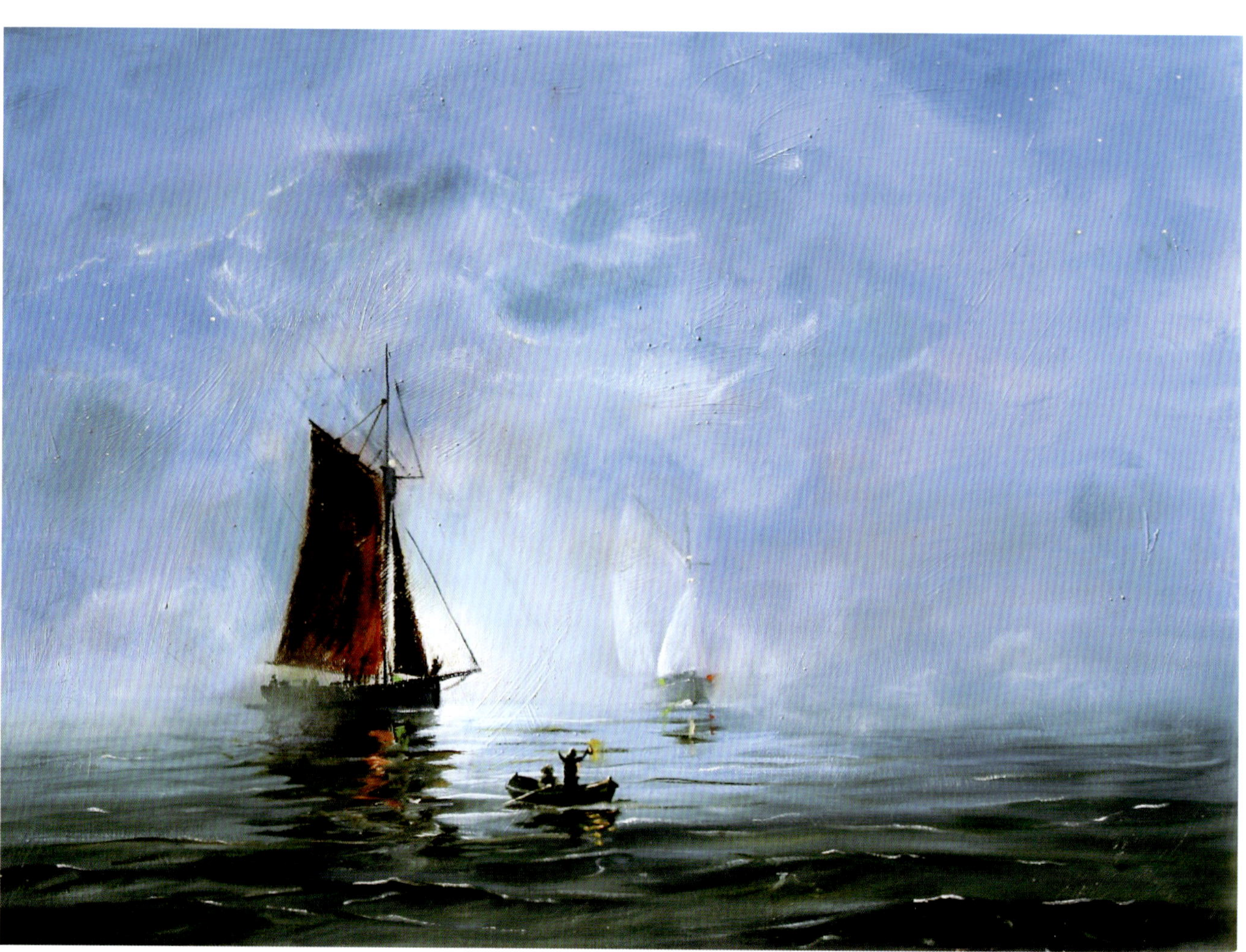

Standing Into Danger (2010) Oil 21 x 45.7cm

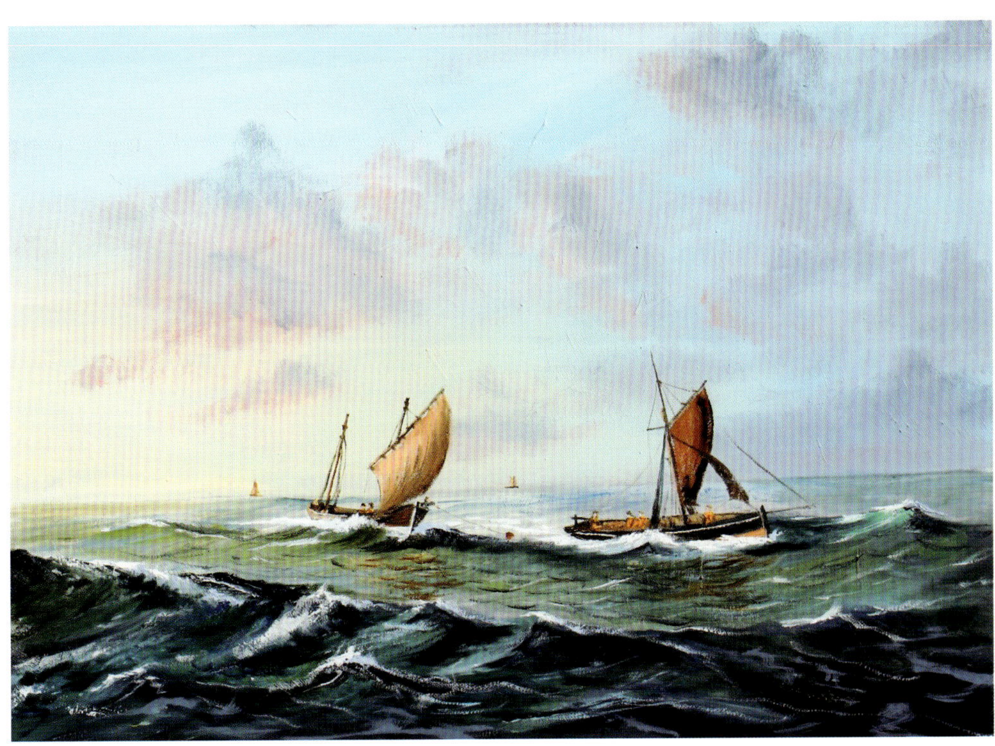

Trading The Catch (2010) Oil 121 x 45.7cm

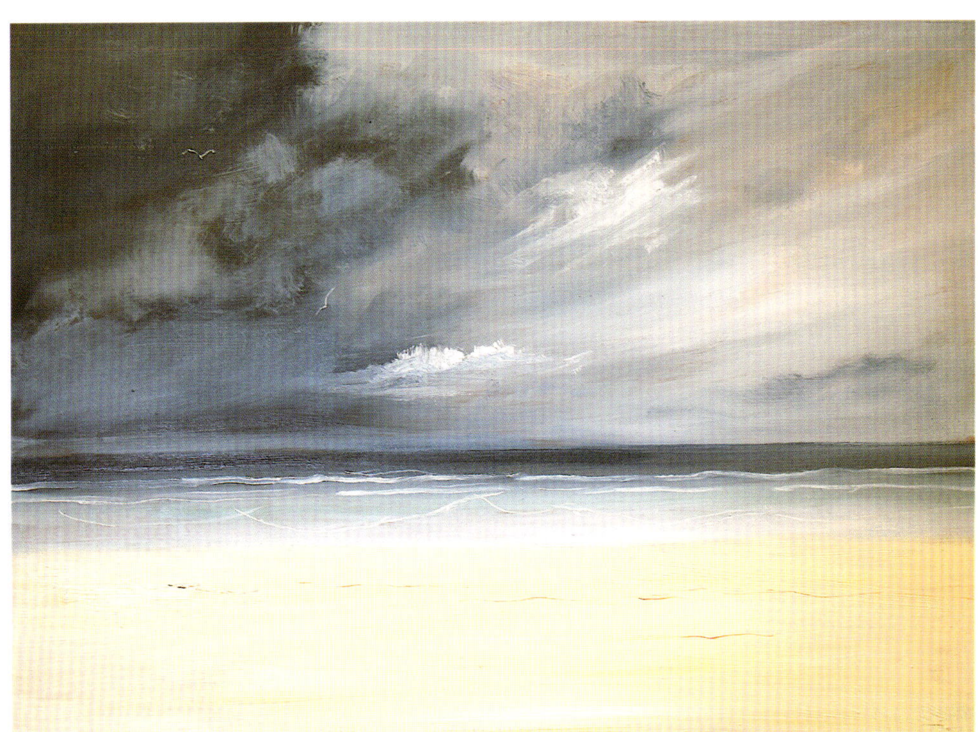

Time to Leave (2009) Oil 21 x 45.7cm

Elaine Nason

Elaine Nason makes gentle, domestic pictures, but the quiet images of subtle colour and discreet pattern also manage to contain an unusual range of feeling, often a wistful sadness mixed with an unexpected humour.
- North House Gallery, Manningtree, Essex

Elaine Nason
Painter, Printmaker
Laxfield, Suffolk

I have always been interested in the human figure and it has become my main focus in painting and printmaking. The themes I follow are usually domestic. My chief objective is to create a well-composed and harmonious image and I find it necessary to draw a great deal from direct observation.

My tastes in art are catholic but amongst artists I admire greatly are Vermeer, Cezanne, Stanley Spencer and Keith Vaughan.

The fish man called in his van with herrings and instead of being eaten - and as I love still life - they modelled for several monoprints, including *Up Jumped The Herring*. I enjoy the different processes involved in monoprinting from transfer drawing and stencils to painting directly on the plate. For this image I have used some newsprint collage as I think the neutral colour works well with the richness of the print. Monoprinting is interestingly chancy.

My neighbours Ron and Moss Fuller, a colourful couple and both artists, sat outside their cottage doors in a pose that reminded me of the little wooden figures that foretold the weather. This linoprint, *Couple At The Cottage Door*, was made using the reduction method where only one block is used, rather than one for each colour. The block is then progressively cut away as each new colour is added. I like this method as the results are more unpredictable.

In the *Drawing Day* I wanted to show how drawing is the basis of my work and how the drawn figures at the top have been translated into paint. They were made at a drawing day with friends and I wanted to convey their concentration on the model and also achieve a well-balanced composition. This picture combines my love of drawing, composition and still life

Educated- Colchester School of Art NDD 1959
Membership of Local Art Societies-
Suffolk Group
Artworks, Bury St Edmunds, Suffolk
Inside Out, Laxfield, Suffolk
Galleries Familiar With Artist's Work-
Halesworth Gallery, Halesworth, Suffolk
North House Gallery, Manningtree, Essex
Harleston Gallery, Harleston, Norfolk
Website-www.elaine-nason.co.uk

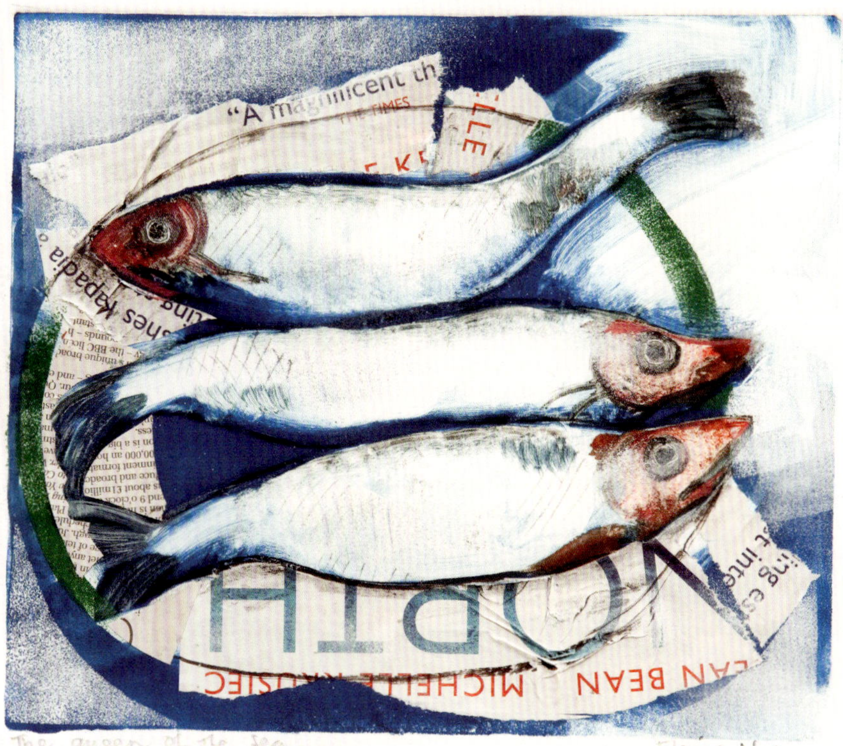

Up Jumped The Herring (2010) Monoprint 26 x 23cm

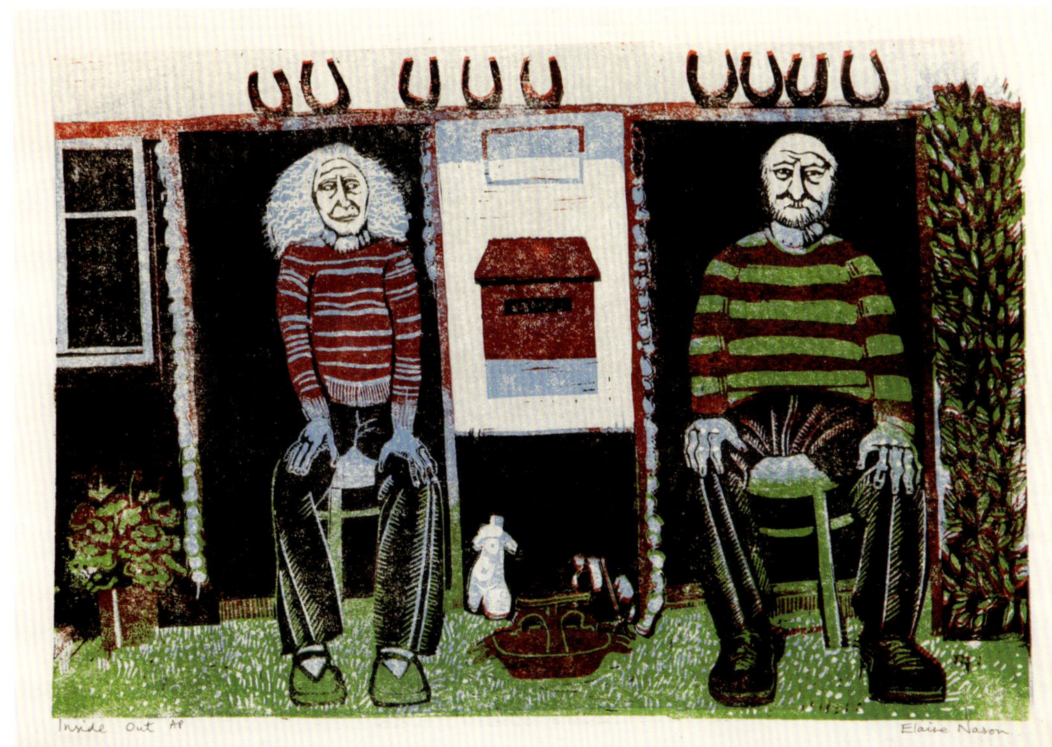

Couple At The Cottage Door (2009) Linocut 42 x 29cm

Drawing Day (2009) Oil 120 x 80cm

145

Michelle Payne

I was first introduced to Michelle Payne by my plastic surgeon shortly following my mastectomy and breast reconstruction. She had become involved with the Boudica project and was subsequently asked to head the Woman Reconstructed project. Michelle has an amazing passion for her body casting and she cast the women's breasts and torsos for the project with fantastic sensitivity and great compassion. Her life casts are so amazing and capture the life of the person she is casting.
- Anna Beckingham, Keeping Abreast

Michelle Payne
Sculptor, Painter
Beccles, Suffolk

As a full-time working lifecaster in East Anglia, there are many challenges I face on a daily basis. The first and main challenge itself is just that word, '*Life.*'

Over the years, I have helped many couples, families, grandparents who are in those awful scenarios that, due to the breakup of a marriage for instance, want to be cast with their grandchildren; or due to breast cancer and mastectomy issues, want to increase their confidence. Fortunately, I also get to enjoy the making of beautiful and sculptural embellishments for someone's bathroom or bedroom.

Silver Herring is for a series of paintings of my own. I do, however, cast fishermen's catches. If it can get to me within two days, I can cast the actual catch, and the proud fisherman can then show it was 'this big!'

I do many breastcastings, like *Poppies,* from mastectomies through to reconstruction, implants to sculptural and strategic castings. The first thing to look at funnily enough is not the obvious, it's the bonestructure and neckline of a woman.

Finally, bodybuilds. All that work, all that determination, all the procedures that take hours of strategic works. Immortalised — yes definitely. Timing is the issue of *The Body Build*, as you want to be ready for this one at your physical peak.

Educated-
Regent Academy of the Arts, London 2002
Achievements-
Award Winning Artist, Open College of the Arts
Membership of Local Art Societies-
Suffolk Open Studios
Norfolk Open Studios
Membership of National Art Societies-
Association of Lifecasters International
Galleries Familiar With Artist's Work-
Upstairs Gallery, Beccles, Suffolk
Upstairs Gallery, Great Yarmouth, Norfolk
Website- www.bigartgallery.co.uk

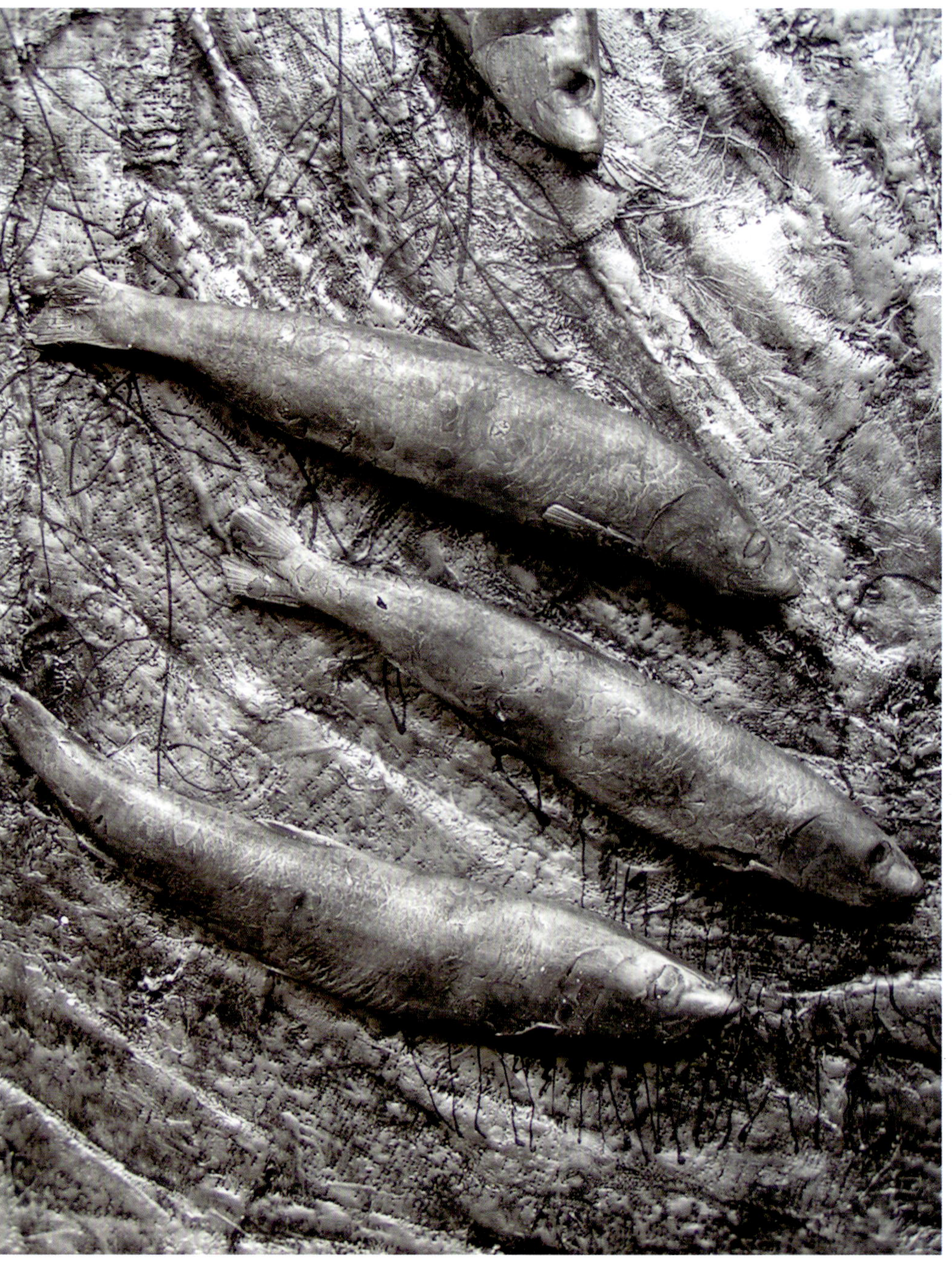

Silver Herring (2010) Gypsum and Acrylic, Life-size

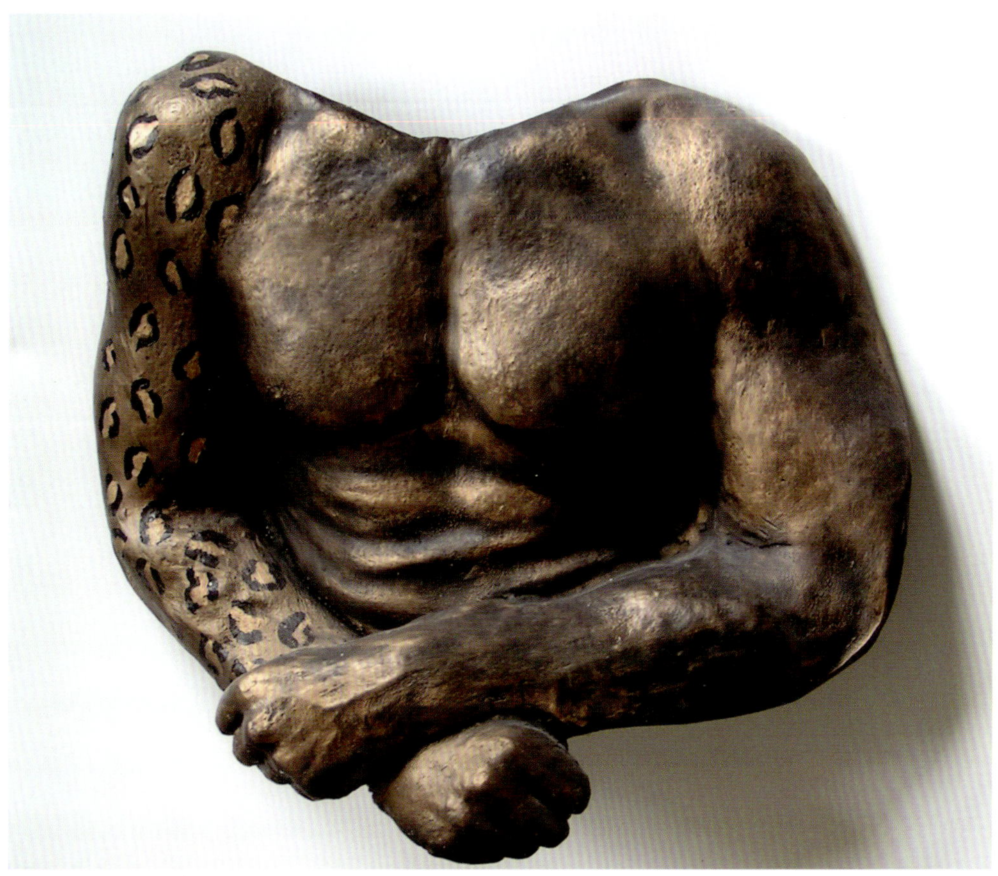

The Body Build (2009) Gypsum and Acrylic, Life-size

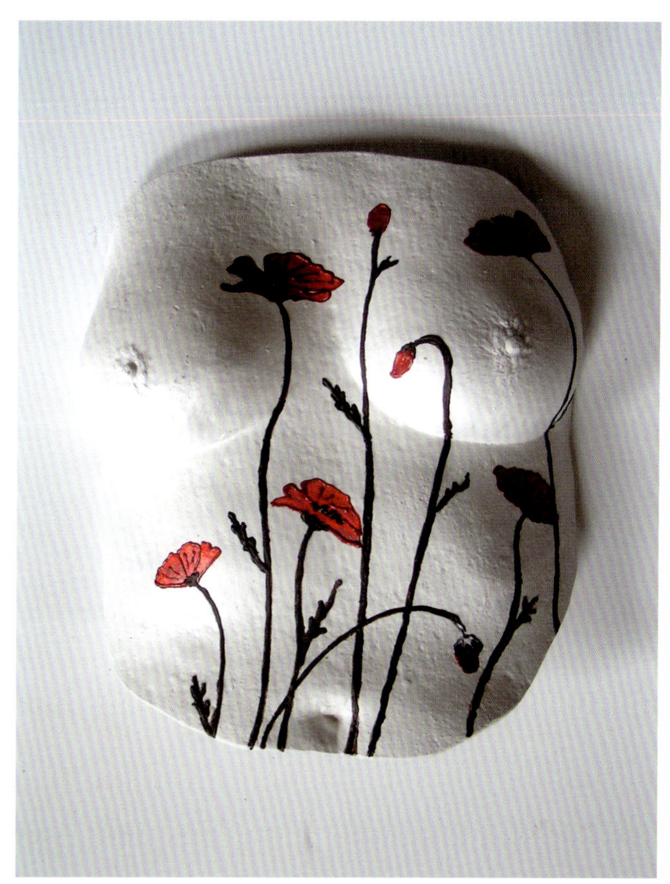

Poppies (2010) Gypsum and Acrylic, Life-size

Karen Jones BA

148

Karen Jones (BA)
Illustrator
Chelmsford, Essex

I paint with gouache, a rich, dense watercolour to create my trademark velvety flat illustrations. My style and subject matter are a mixture of the real and the other-worldly, the mysterious and the macabre.

With the inspiration of literature, history, a colour palette reminiscent of mediaeval manuscripts and the influences of artists as diverse as Caxton and Caulfield, I aim to speak of another time. I want to capture the imagination of the viewer, taking them on a journey into the world of folklore and fairytale – to discover the darker realms of the adult mind.

It is important to me that all who view my work are inspired to stop and think, to emotionally walk into my paintings.

Whether it is a gothic fairytale image or a reflection of the natural world around us, if it prompts a deeper response, I have succeeded.

Educated- London College of Printing
Galleries Familiar With Artist's Work-
Interior Angle, Chelmsford, Essex
Website- www.karenjonesillustrator.com

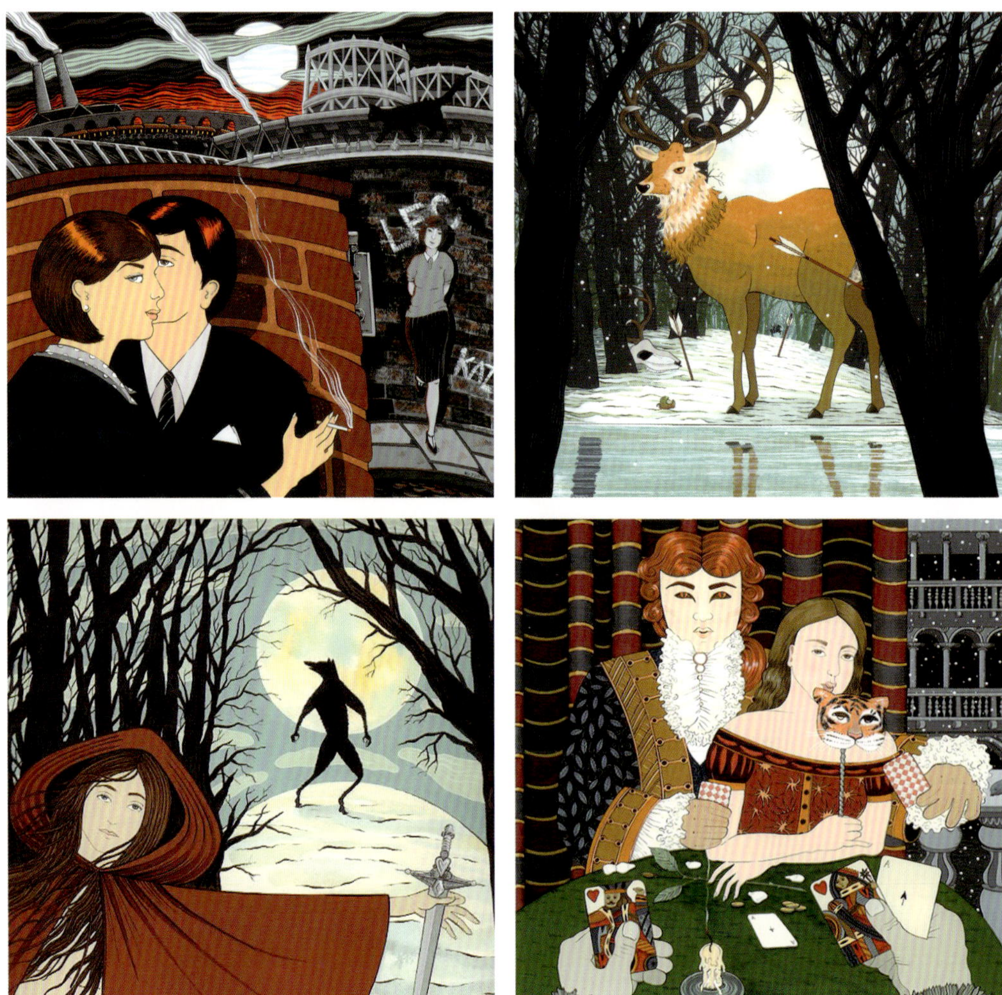

Clockwise From Top Left: *Dirty Old Town (2010)* Gouache 35 x 35cm; *Omnia Vanitas (2010)* Gouache 85 x 85cm; *My Father Said He Loved Me (2009)* Gouache 60 x 60cm; *Wolf (2009)* Gouache 30 x 30cm

Christian Figg

Notoriously elusive, and his work highly sought-after, Christian's work has a stark beauty to it. Forms are defined and redefined to the barest minimum, abstracted and yet still retaining enough to make them instantly recognisable.
- Buckenham Galleries, Southwold, Suffolk

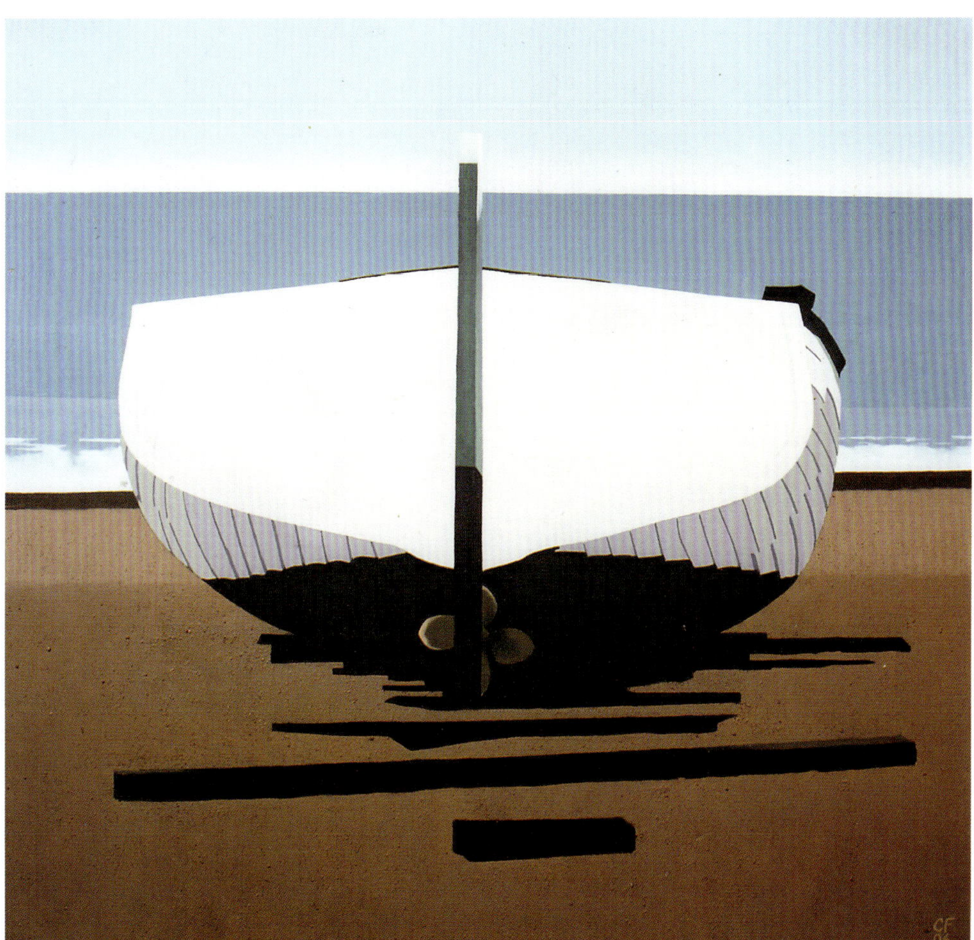

Dodger (2006) Oil on Canvas 90 x 90cm

Christian Figg
Painter
Leiston, Suffolk

I have been painting since an early age and have developed a unique personal visual language. My paintings are graphically striking, simplified in form and colour, yet subtle and are a response to the stark, raw isolation and sharp intensity of light and colour of the Suffolk coast.

My work is characterised by a sense of stillness, but with sculptural subjects and defined contrasts, dark versus light, man-made versus natural, past against present.

The painting *Dodger* shows one of the old Dunwich fishing boats sitting proud and strong on the shingle, looking out to sea. Each of the traditional open Suffolk beach boats has its own personality and story, and painting them is like painting a portrait. I approach them that way, and paint them on large canvases so that they dominate the space they are hung in. I also look for the sculptural shape of them that lends itself to abstracted forms.

Galleries Familiar With Artist's Work-
Buckenham Galleries, Southwold, Suffolk

Colin Giles MISTD

Colin Giles' earlier work included layered abstract fragments of digital photography, while recent pieces utilize his highly textured, vivid, paintings reproduced in a series of high quality, limited edition giclee prints. The multi-layered, richly-coloured compositions are reminiscent of reedbeds or swathes of flowers. The effect is bold and unusual.
- Snape Maltings Gallery, Snape, Suffolk

Colin Giles MISTD
Painter and Digital Artist
Upton, Norfolk

The main influence which drives my work is the Norfolk landscape. The shapes, colours and textures of plants and flowers seem to dominate my ideas. Although I admire the paintings of Cotman and Munnings, I do love the vibrance and freedom of Matisse. That freshness and energy are the elements I try to achieve in my work.

Experiment One and *Experiment Two* are two pieces which are variations on a theme. I began with the concept of flowers in a vase and prepared five separate canvases painted quite freely which expressed that idea. Each canvas was applied to digital software, where I experimented with superimposing several combinations of images to make an entirely new picture.

Sometimes I find exciting and unforeseen results, but more often than not images which should be rejected. This process has a high failure rate but the joys of discovery are compensation enough when I find the final piece.

I have recently become interested in photography and am absorbed with the camera as a creative medium. The work of photographers Ernst Haas and Marc Yankus were in my mind when I produced the image *Blue Rose* in which I used a double exposure. The first was slightly out of focus and the second, without moving the camera, was in focus.

Educated- London College of Printing 1963
Galleries Familiar With Artist's Work-
Snape Maltings, Saxmundham, Suffolk
Website- www.colingilesart.com

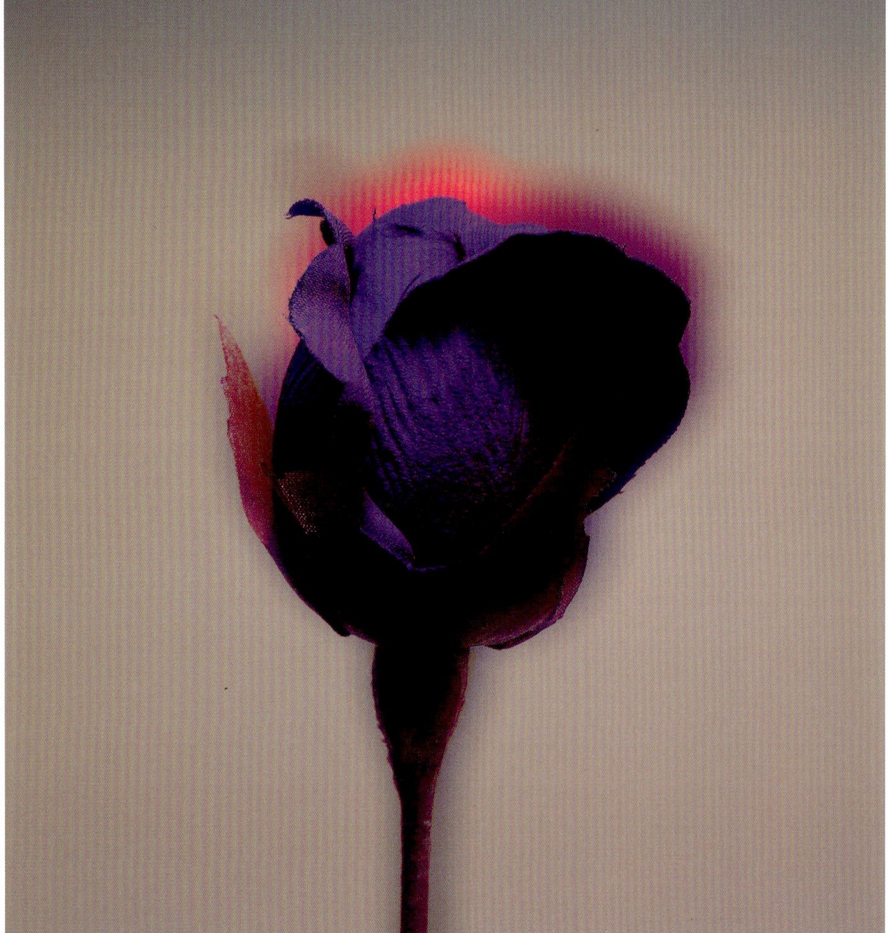

Blue Rose (2010) Acrylic and Digital Photography 28 x 28cm

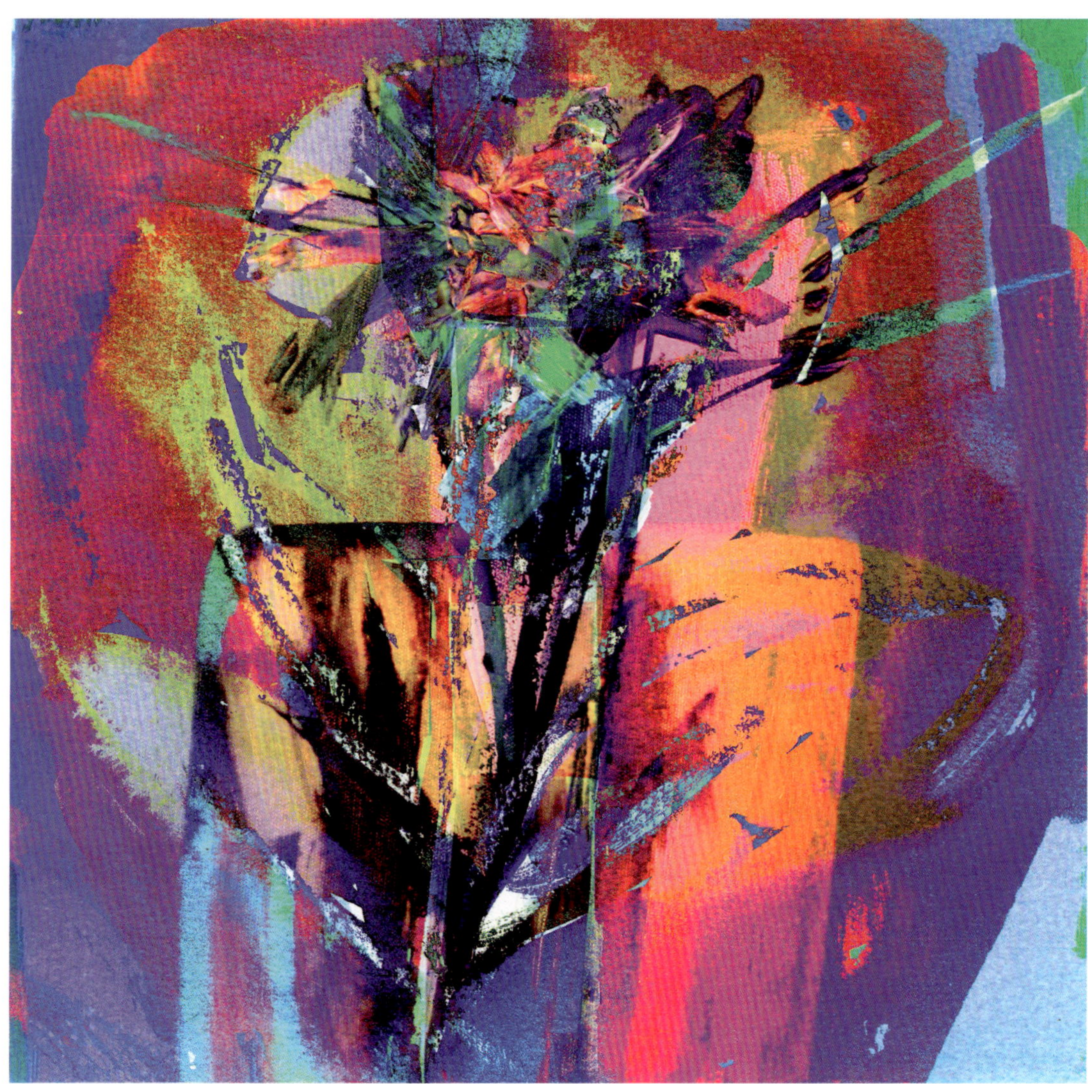

Experiment One (2009) Acrylic on Canvas and Digital Print 35 x 35cm

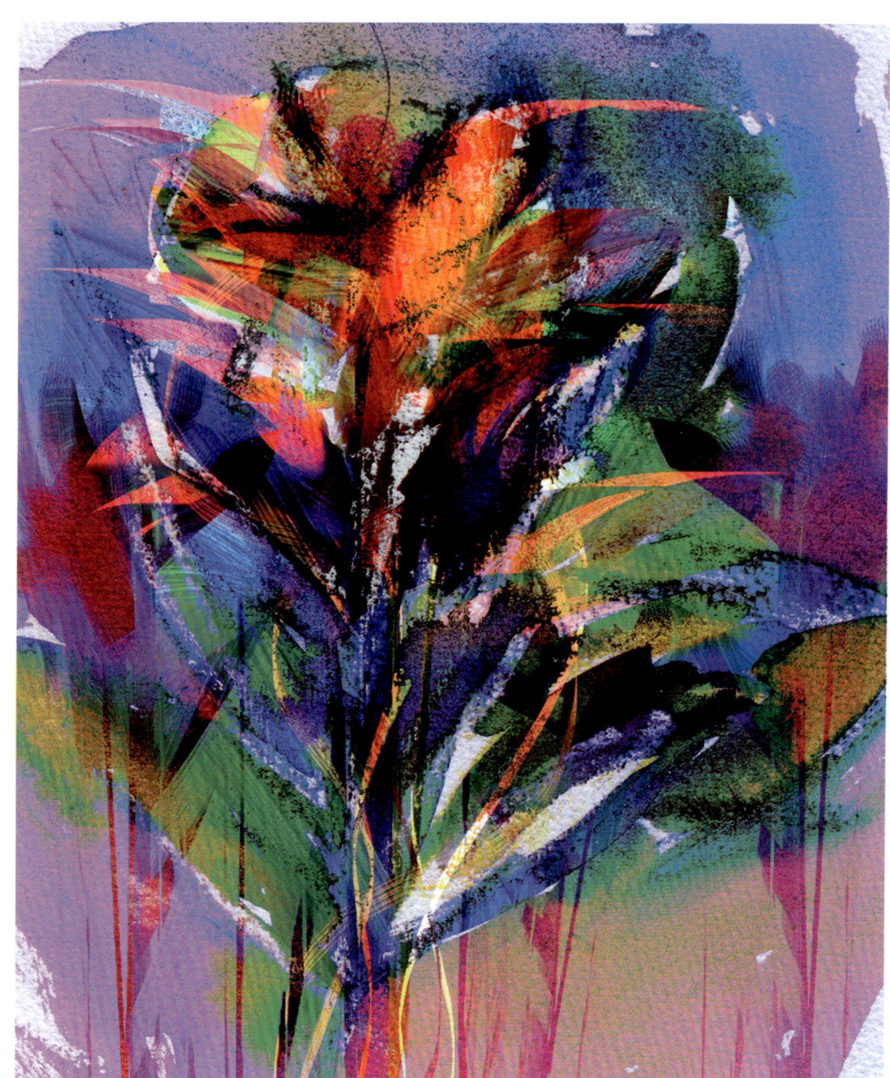

Experiment Two (2009) Acrylic on Canvas and Digital Print 43 x 35cm

Mark Ward

Mark Ward
Painter
Ubbeston Green (Near Halesworth), Suffolk

Painting is my way of dreaming myself elsewhere. I create dramas of exotic animals in tropical landscapes that take place on home-made stages. They represent places I have been to or even journeys I have yet to travel.

The life of the forest, swamp and savannah is played out by creatures made from paper, plastic, wire and string. These are happy stories, obviously artificial, where even the rhinoceros dung is colourful and shiny.

Charmed (Interval) is my homage to Rousseau, whose jungle paintings are an inspiration for me. His Snake Charmer has taken a break, leaving behind her flute, and allowing her attendant spoonbill to deputise in the central role.

The pipe-cleaner snakes all remain in an entranced state, awaiting the second act. All this takes place in the light of a paper moon and under the gaze of a wistful hornbill.

White Rhino. Usually my animals are meant to interact with other creatures in a larger landscape, but sometimes they just need their portrait painted. I had done some paper 'crinkly' elephants, and I thought the effect could work for a rhinoceros. The whole arrangement was placed on a pink base, which was heavily lit to reflect onto the white paper. Perhaps it should be called *Pink Rhino*.

Impala on Purse Hill. My wife brought home a new felt hand-bag with bobbles on it, which was crying out to be a hill with trees. It reminded me of a fifteenth century tapestry with hunting scene, so the leap from deer to impala was fairly obvious. However, because of the floppy 'tree trunks', I had to arrange the whole thing upside down. The spots around the outside represent coins for the new bag.

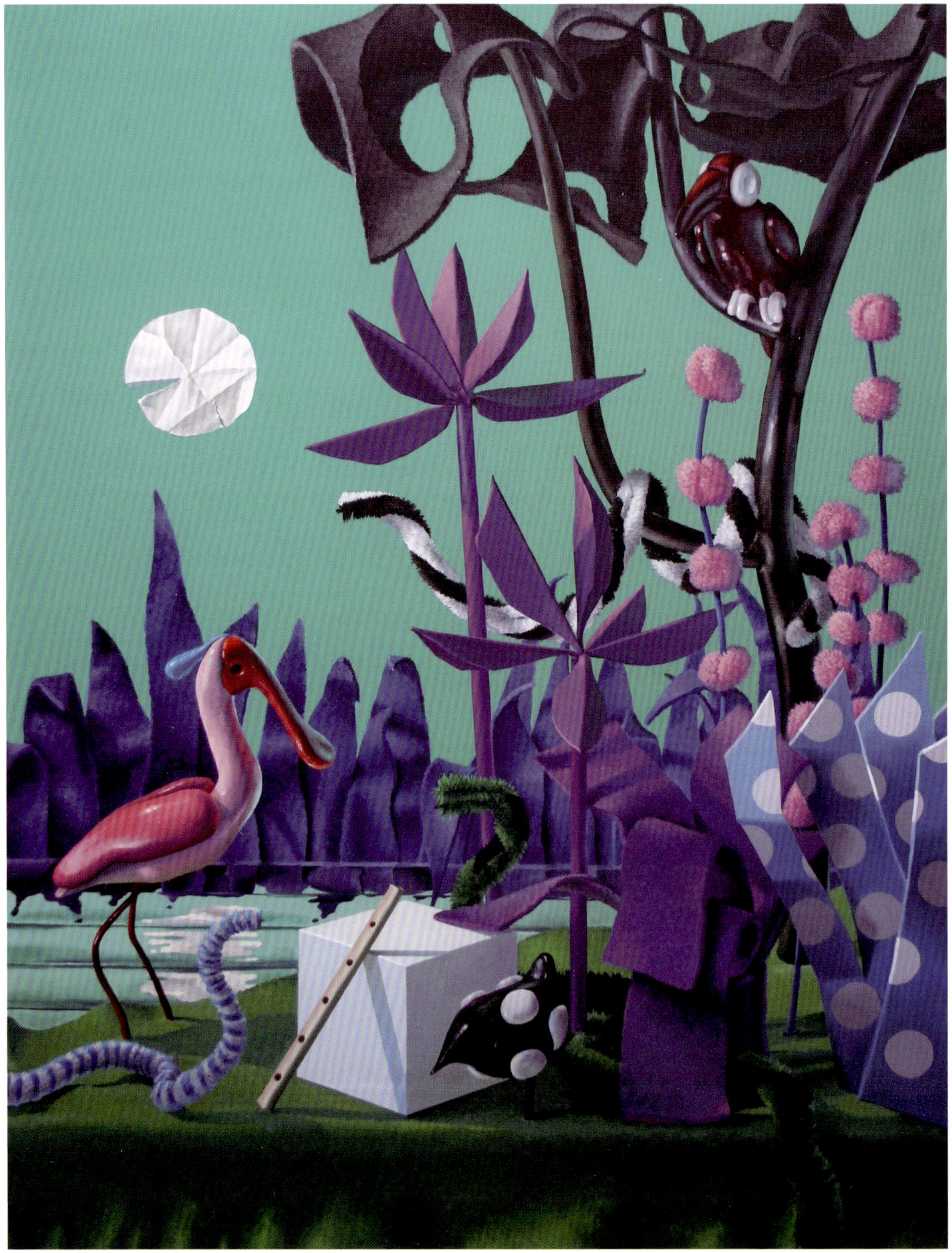

Charmed (Interval) (2008) Acrylic on Canvas 160 x 120cm

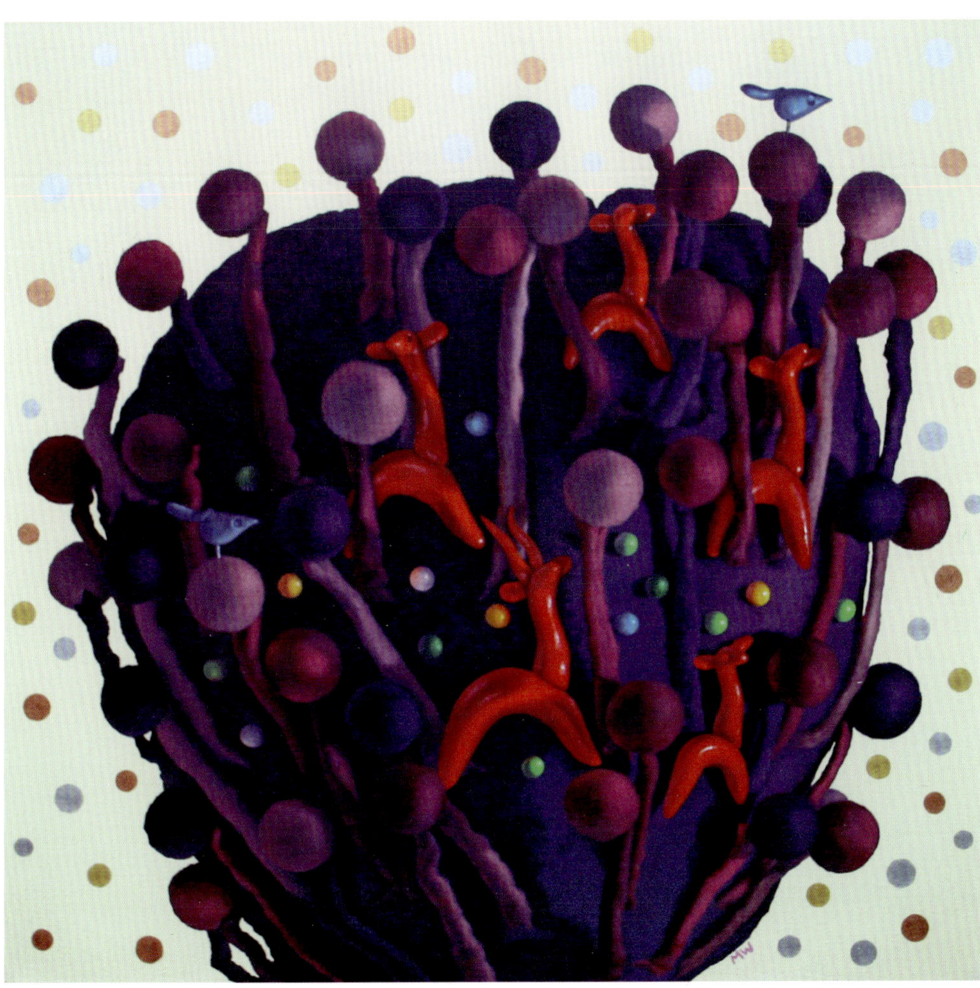

Impala on Purse Hill (2010) Acrylic on Canvas 91 x 91cm

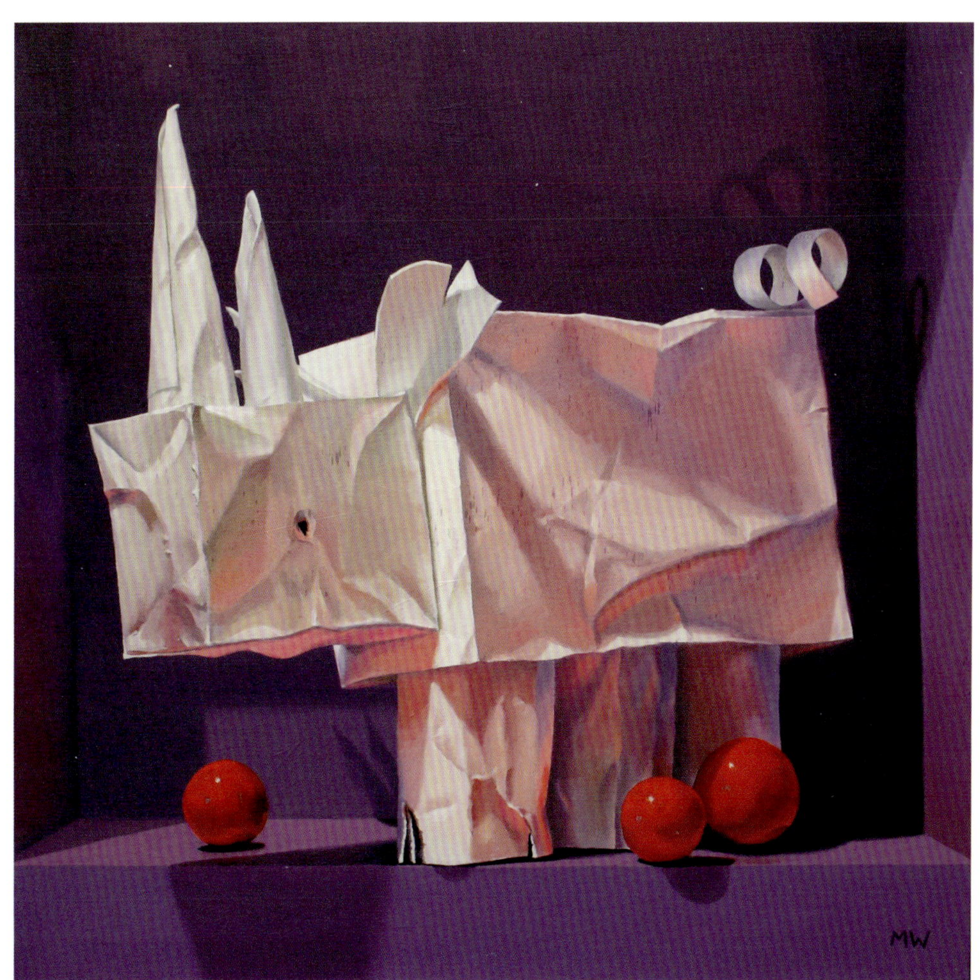

White Rhino (2010) Acrylic on Canvas 80 x 80cm

Mark Ward: Behind the Scenes

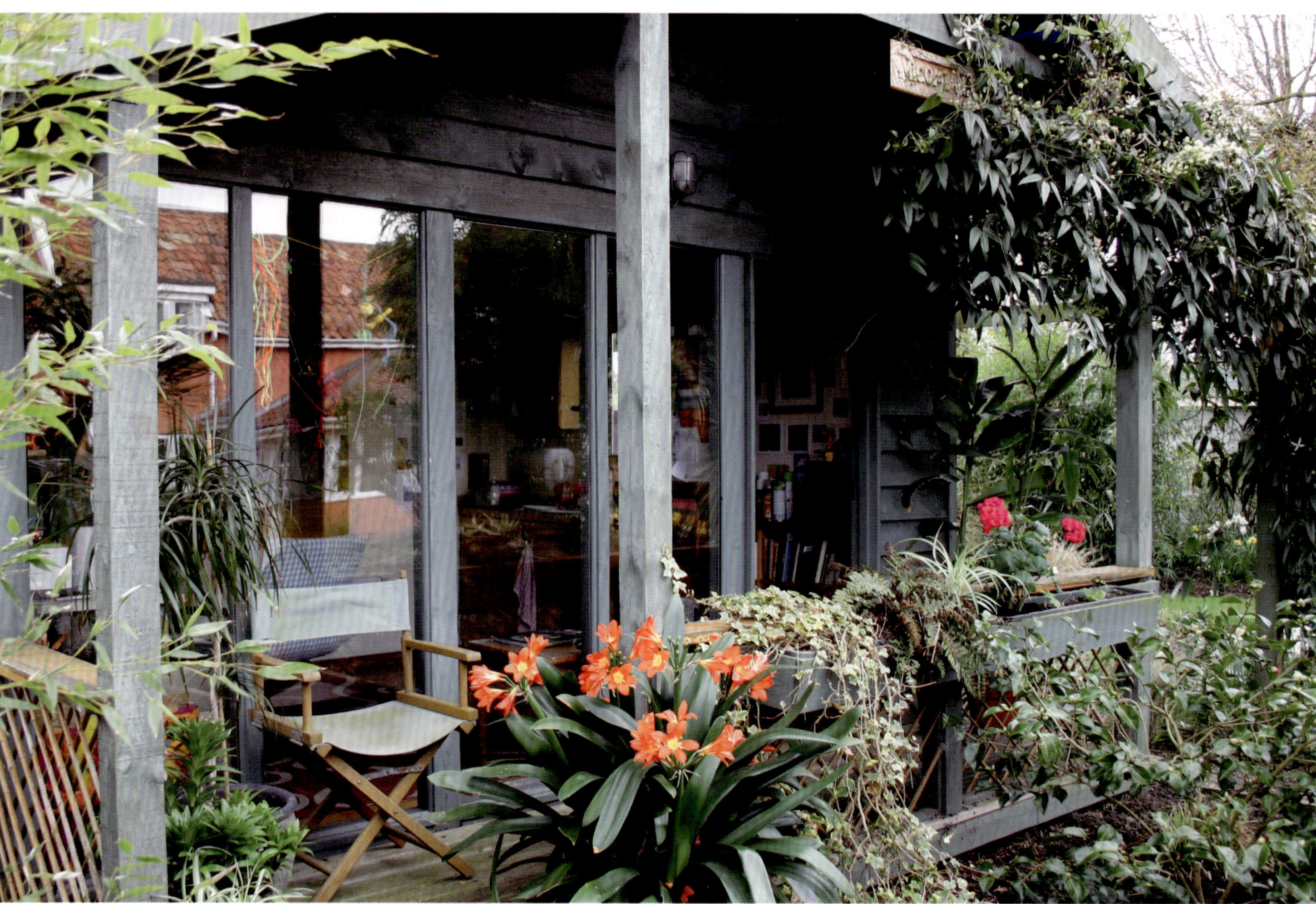

More about:

Mark....

Educated- Manchester College of Art and Design,
BA (Hons) Product Design, 1971
Galleries Familiar With Artist's Work-
Upstairs Gallery, Beccles, Suffolk
Ferini Art Gallery, Pakefield, Lowestoft, Suffolk
Art18/21, Norwich, Norfolk
Website- www.markwardart.co.uk

Building my studio was a cathartic act after many years of teaching. Its north facing glass wall overlooks a lush, tropical summer garden. The carved sign says *Migombani*; Kiswahili for *In the banana grove*.

I'm usually at work by seven, and work through until five or six, with an hour's break for lunch. This is everyday except when I'm off travelling or when the garden needs attention. Everything I paint is from observation. After constantly trying to decide where shadows should fall, I took a hint from Gainsborough and built a model. I use a sketchbook for initial thinking, but building models creates its own challenges, requiring an inventive and fun use of materials. I use a simple halogen light source, but take considerable care to achieve the right dramatic effect, with interesting shadows and colour reflections.

While my aim is usually for large and complex compositions, simpler studies of individual characters are painted in preparation. Some of these individuals have a habit of cropping up in more than one production.

Visitors to the studio are often fascinated by the shelves and drawers full of little creatures, each awaiting their next curtain call.

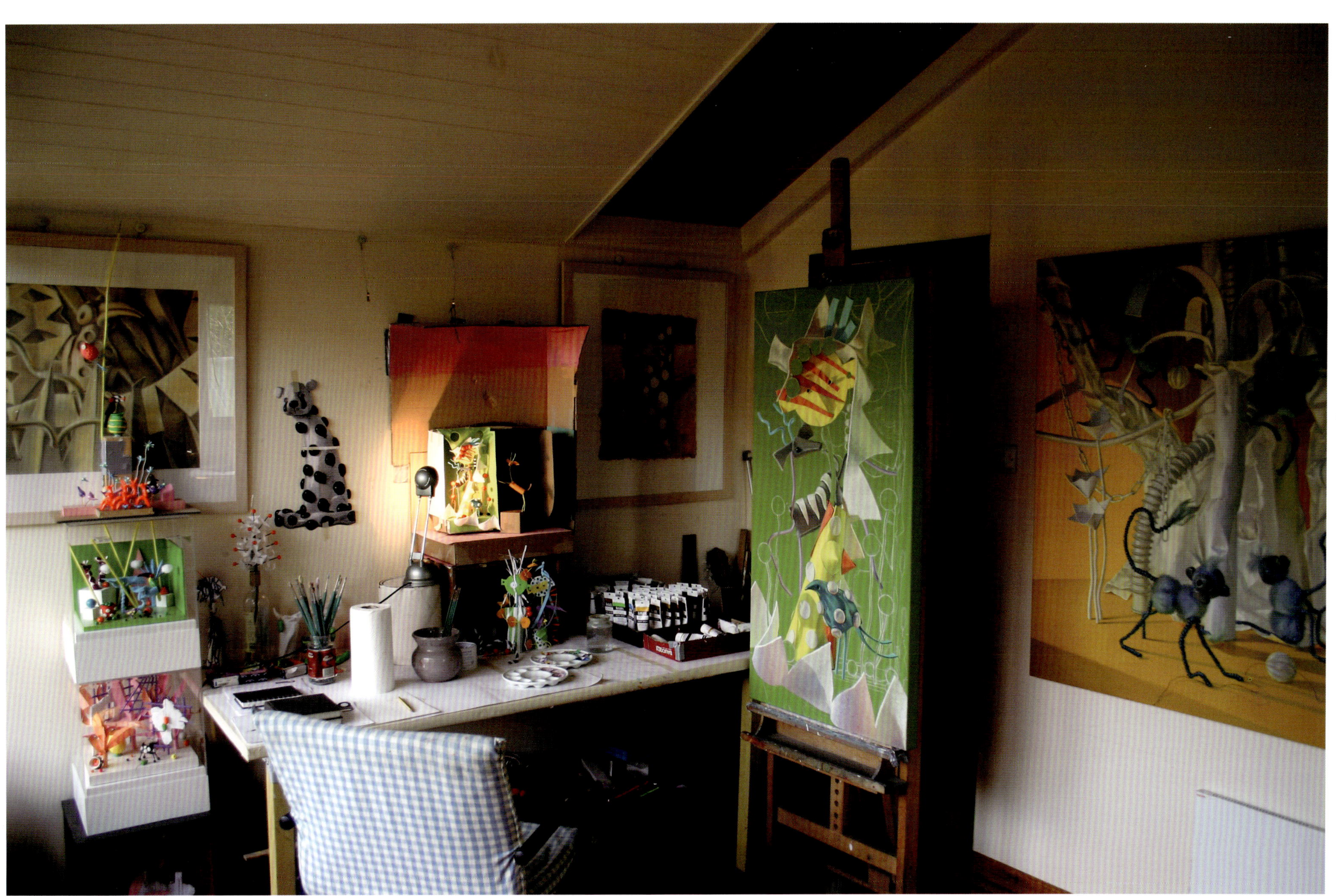

Tracey Jennings

Whether it is the delicate pen, ink and watercolour drawings or her bold, powerful, acrylic canvases, I find Tracey Jennings' work fresh and exciting. Her connections with music, both as a composer and performer, have influenced and given a unique quality and view point to her artwork. The intricacy and beauty of her flowing organic line work and her sensitive and powerful use of colour tell me that this is an exceptionally talented artist on the brink of something great.
- Mona Marnell, Glass Artist

Tracey Jennings
Mixed Media Artist
Chelmsford, Essex

As a relatively new artist I have focused on exhibiting my work in local and national exhibitions instead of galleries. My art explores a range of paint and techniques. I am inspired by nature and a deep-rooted connection with music. As an artist music inspires me to paint, as a musician art inspires me to write.

My *Beyond The Forest* collection marries rich, bold colour and textured watercolour with intricate line work. Many of these pieces have been exhibited during the past year. I am now exploring the hidden subtext within my work. Currently I am creating a collection of vibrant mixed media paintings echoed with a series of black and white pen and ink silhouette drawings inspired by music.

Educated- Anglia University, Brentwood, Essex 1998
Website- www.traceyjenningsart.com

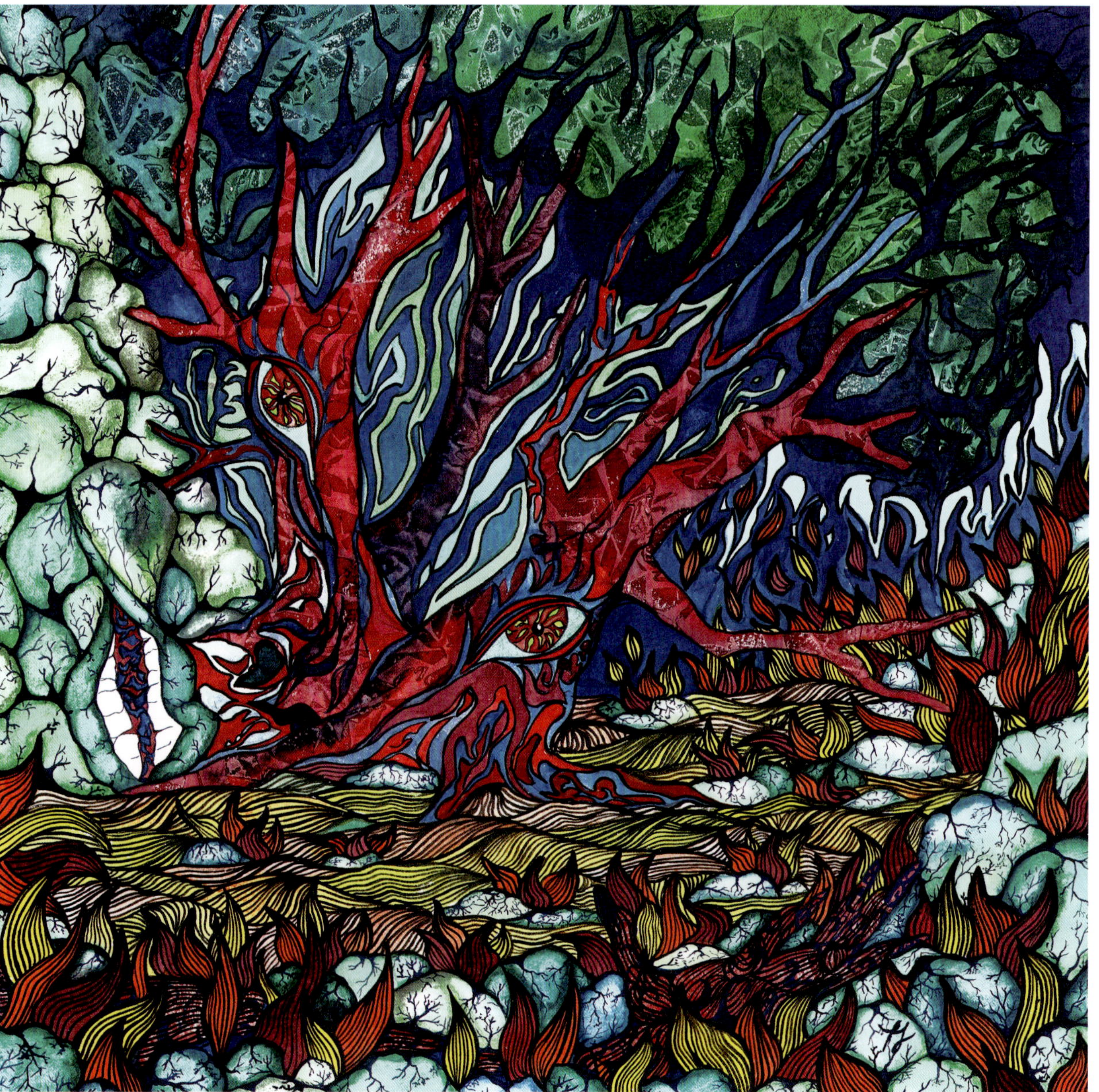

Who Can Impress The Forest, Bid The Tree, Unfix The Earth-Bound Root (2010) Watercolour 29 x 29cm

Carolyn Reeder BA (Hons)

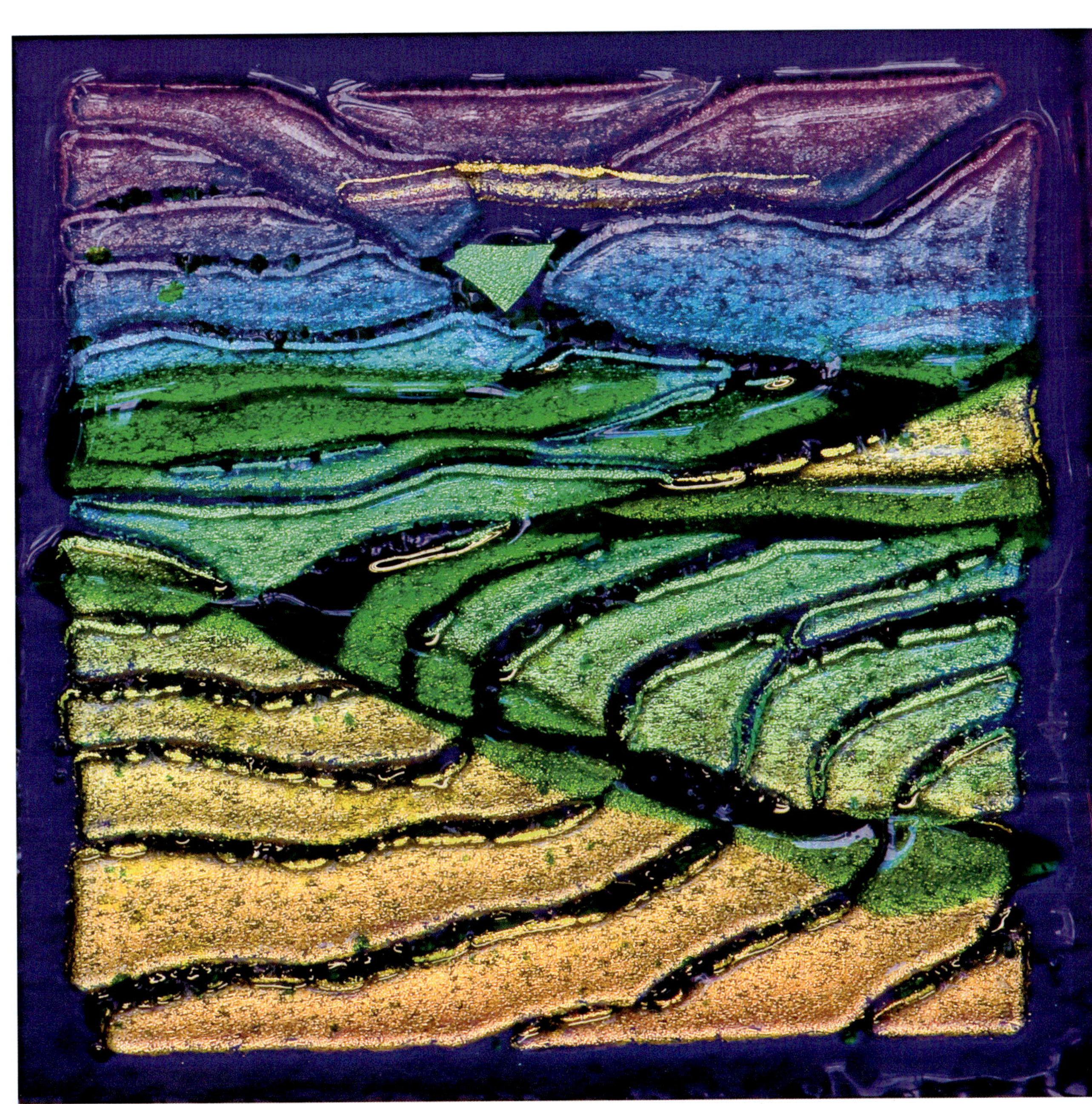

Paddy Fields (2009) Kiln Fused Dichroic Glass 35 x 25cm

Carolyn is a prolific artist whose work has grown out of a dedicated crafts base to demonstrate consistent creativity and awareness of colour and form. Carolyn's work often surprises the viewer with a fresh look and inventiveness in a range of materials and mediums, from coloured glass and paintings to textured clays. Her sculptures and pottery show an intense awareness of form and space with sensitivity to material and an inherent demonstration of the material's roots in earthiness, sensuality and longevity.
- Ferini Art Gallery, Pakefield, Suffolk

Carolyn Reeder BA (Hons)
Painter And Designer In Kiln Fused Glass
and Handbuilt Ceramics
Blundeston, Suffolk

The late artist and teacher Colin Moss helped me to develop a love of colour and texture at Ipswich Art School. This has stayed with me throughout my creative career. In addition my training in science encouraged me to experiment with different methods and materials.

Kiln fusing glass has been my greatest technical challenge. Observing the behaviour of glass and dichroic coatings in the kiln has given me scope for developing exciting design ideas. I also slump glass into handbuilt biscuit-fired molds to create unique three-dimensional pieces.

Many of my landscape and leaf designs are developed in both painting and glass and I feel that the cross-fertilisation of ideas enriches work in both media.

Paddy Fields indulges my fascination with the behaviour of the cut edges of the coated glass in this mosaic of design.

Educated- Lowestoft School of Art and Design;
Open College of the Arts
Membership of Local Art Societies- Lowestoft Art Group;
Great Yarmouth Guild of Artists and Craftsmen;
Black Dog Arts, Bungay
Galleries Familiar With Artist's Work-
Ferini Gallery, Pakefield, Suffolk
Lowestoft Arts Centre Gallery, Lowestoft, Suffolk
Abel Arts, Raveningham, Norfolk
Website- www.creeder.freeuk.com

Gillian Plummer PhD

Gillian's work is incredibly exciting to the senses as it assaults them with a realisation of just how beautiful the world we live in is.
- Gallery Violet

Gillian Plummer PhD
Creative Plant Photographer
Butley, Suffolk

Creative plant photography is a passion. Most of my work is done using a macro lens; I am a detail person.

When my eye spots something unusual, be it a distorted petal or a wonky stem, I am drawn to it. Many of my images are wild or native plants, I like the fact they are 'uncultivated' and often have important herbal medicinal qualities. Their existence in rural Suffolk is why I choose to live here.

I have a passion for poppies, I admire their flamboyance, and red is my favourite colour, hence my inspiration for *Scarlet Secrets*. This oriental poppy was battered a little by the wind and rain and as I moved closer my attention was drawn to a muddled up bunch of stamens slipping down one of the large petals.

I wanted the image to have an abstract feel, to be simple in structure and for the focus to be on the stamens cascading downwards.

In *Finger Digits* I was attracted by the bronze colour of the stems and then fascinated by all the little fingers, such detail, complexity. I had to capture it, to share my intrigue and awe.

Wanting it to be washed over by light, I got up early for several mornings to shoot it as the sun shifted around it. My intention was to capture the fingers locked inside but the boldness of the stems themselves took over.

Educated- No formal art school tuition
PhD, University of London
Membership of Local Art Societies-
Suffolk Open Studio
Accreditation With National Art Societies-
The Professional Garden Photographers' Association
Garden Media Guild
Galleries Familiar With Artist's Work-
Gallery Violet, www.galleryviolet.com; Flower Photos Creative Library, www.flowerphotos.com; The Professional Garden Photographers' Association, www.gpauk.com
Achievements-
Finalist in the 2010 'International Garden Photographer of the Year; First Prize Winner, RHS Awards, 2009, 'Garden Edibles'; Runner-up in the Garden Media Guild Awards 'Single Image of the Year' 2007; Herbology Calendar 2010, based on exhibition of Saxon herbal remedies at Sutton Hoo, National Trust 08 & 09

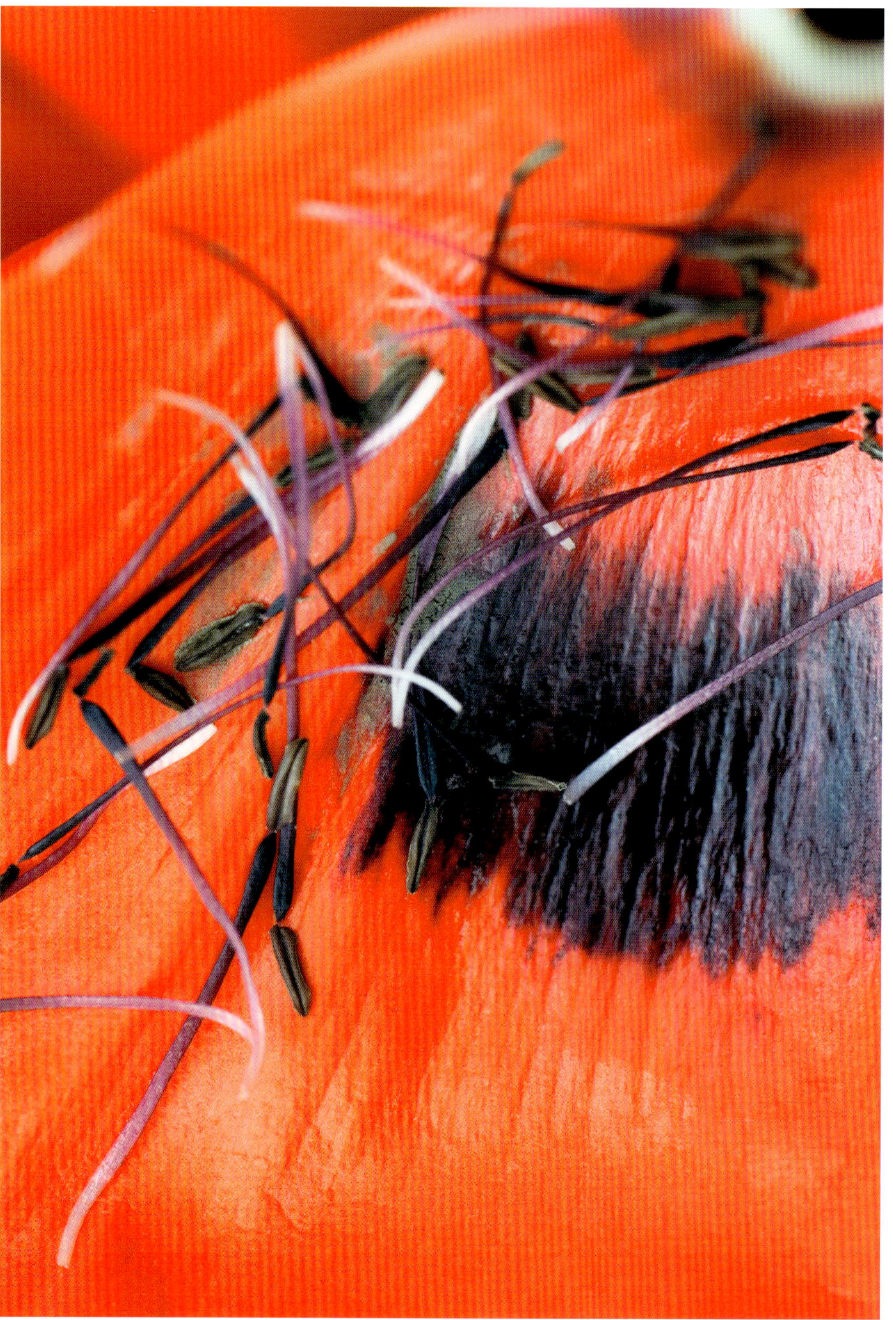

Scarlet Secrets (2009) Photograph

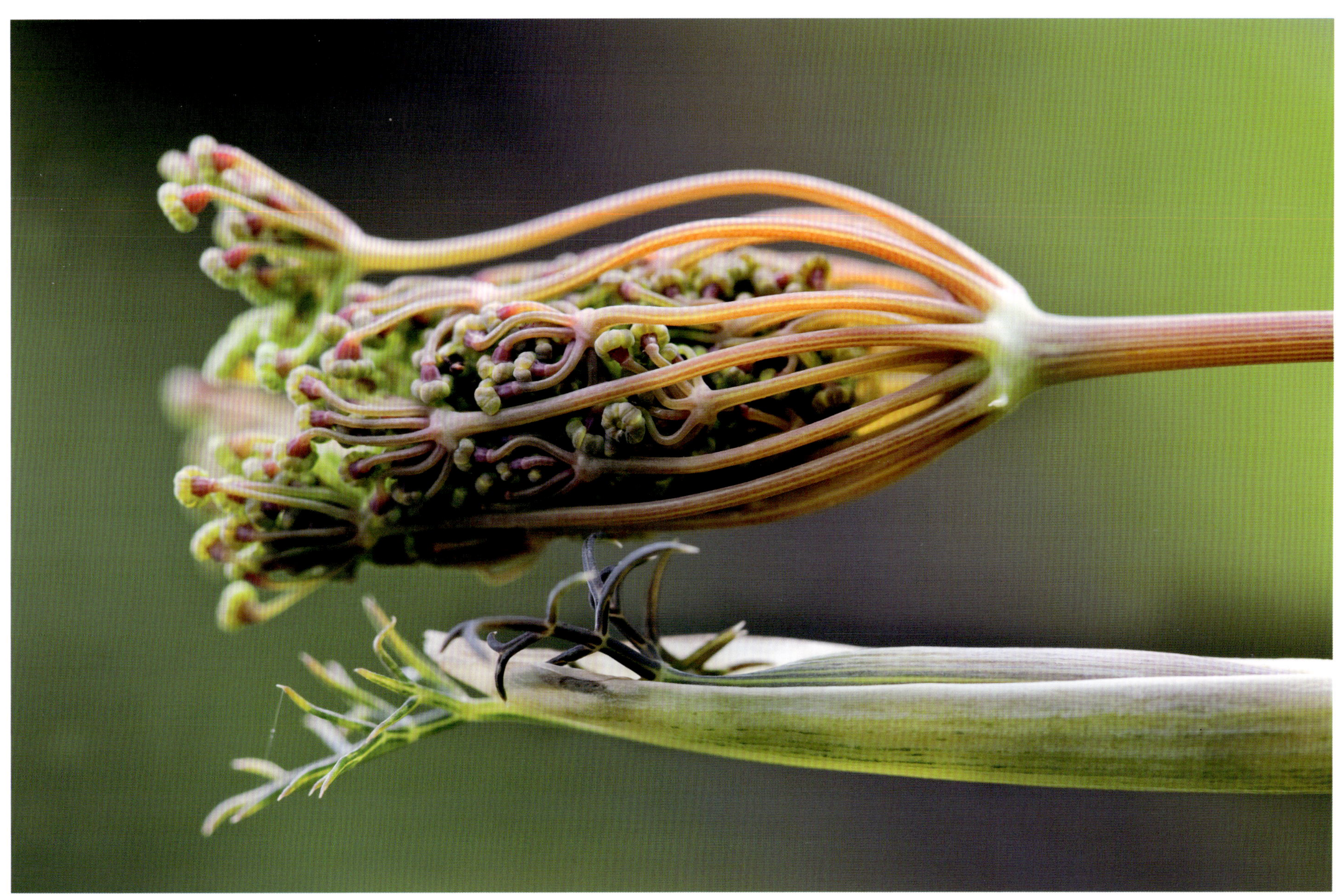

Finger Digits (2009) Photograph

Claire Louise Dowson

Claire Louise Dowson
Painter
Pakefield, Lowestoft, Suffolk

I am lucky to live at the most Easterly Point of the British Isles, which for me is more inspirational than any other place on Earth. I was born here and have returned out of choice to paint the vast seas and skies that I feel are in my blood. Influenced by the Pre-Raphaelites' use of glazes in oils, I aim to see my paintings 'glow'. Fascinated also by pattern in nature, my seas and skies each have their own identity, like a thumbprint, so I could never paint them hazily or indistinctly. However, in awe of the atmosphere that a Rothko work exudes, I may embrace more of the abstract as time goes on.

Fishing at Dawn is one of an ongoing series of sunrise paintings from my own experience of that magical early time of day when the sun seems to 'split' sea and sky, polarising light. Every sunrise is unique, changing with each passing second and those who have never seen this happen may find it hard to believe in the brilliance of my colours. However, paint on canvas can pay only small homage to the light-show played out most mornings, on the beach, two minutes from my door.

Although I have mostly painted in oils over the last seven years, I am, in fact a multi-media artist, having taught many different techniques during my teaching career. I have always used watercolour for my 'Pet Portraits', very successfully. Recently, I was introduced to some very vibrant watercolours, whose light-fastness is second to none. I am like a kiddie in a sweet shop at any art materials fair and am entranced by gorgeous colours as if I could eat them! Now, the sweet shop has come to me with these wonderful paints and I am so excited by them, it feels almost as if they paint themselves when I pick up my brush. *Historic Pakefield* is my first fairly large work in the medium and it has sold instantly. There will be lots more similar works to come as I am finding it impossible to stop painting!

Educated-
Camberwell, London (Dip. A.D.) 1963; West of England (Painting School) 1964; Keswick Hall College of Education, Norwich, Cert. Ed. (merit) 1976

Membership of Local Art Societies-
Suffolk Open Studios

Galleries Familiar With Artist's Work-
Ferini Art Gallery, Pakefield, Lowestoft, Suffolk
Upstairs Gallery, Beccles, Suffolk
Buckenham Galleries, Southwold, Suffolk

Website- www.clairelouisedowson.co.uk

Fishing at Dawn (2010) Oil on Canvas 60 x 60cm

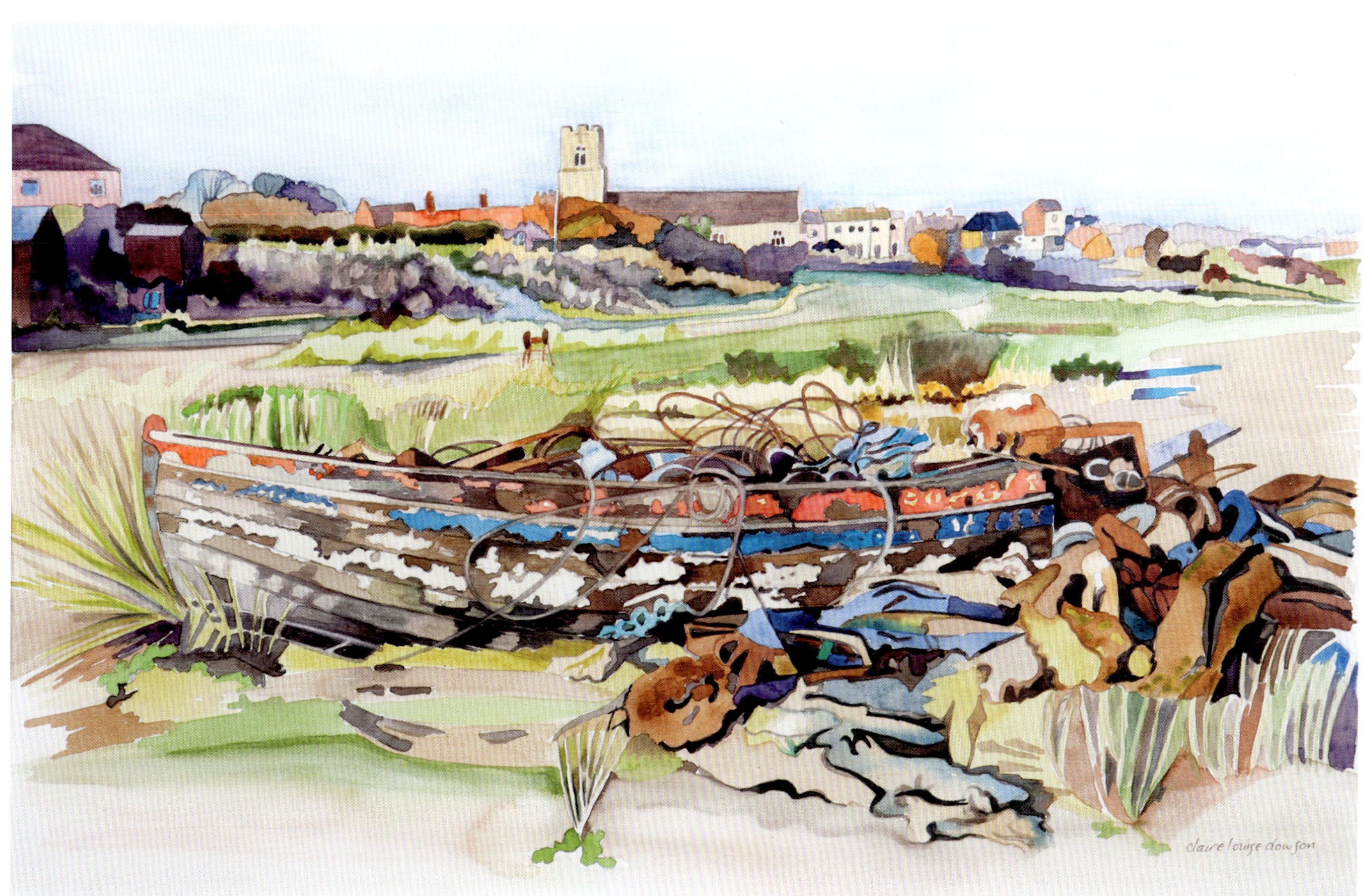

Historic Pakefield Beach (2010) Watercolour 46 x 61cm

David Page

Predominately a landscape painter of his immediate locality, David Page's work, whilst portraying the mood of this lovely part of the Waveney Valley, also acts as an important record of the social history of the area, documenting changes in the rural and built environment.
- Harleston Gallery, Harleston, Norfolk

162

David Page
Painter
Starston, Norfolk

I have lived on the Norfolk/Suffolk border now for over 25 years. My main subject has been the altering landscape, seen more in recent years as the skin of the earth than the wide vistas which still excite me, though I also paint people and things. The fields are mostly empty now, not full of folk as in Breughel's or Constable's or even in Harry Becker's time.

Spikey Ploughing describes a visual event which was only briefly there. Shortly afterwards the tractor driver ploughed round the field edges, and the image was gone. In our time, instead of people, there are large machines which carve the surface of the land, or the crops, into bas-relief.

Some Views of the Marsh was painted for Salthouse '09. Unusually for me it is a composite view. I wanted the feeling you get looking down from the sea wall across the marsh to the hills and the church, which completely fill your field of vision, though in perspective the marsh would only present a narrow strip.

Membership of Local Art Societies-
Norfolk Contemporary Art Society
Harleston & Waveney Art Trail
Galleries Familiar With Artist's Work-
Harleston Gallery, Harleston, Norfolk
Website- http://davidpageartist.wordpress.com

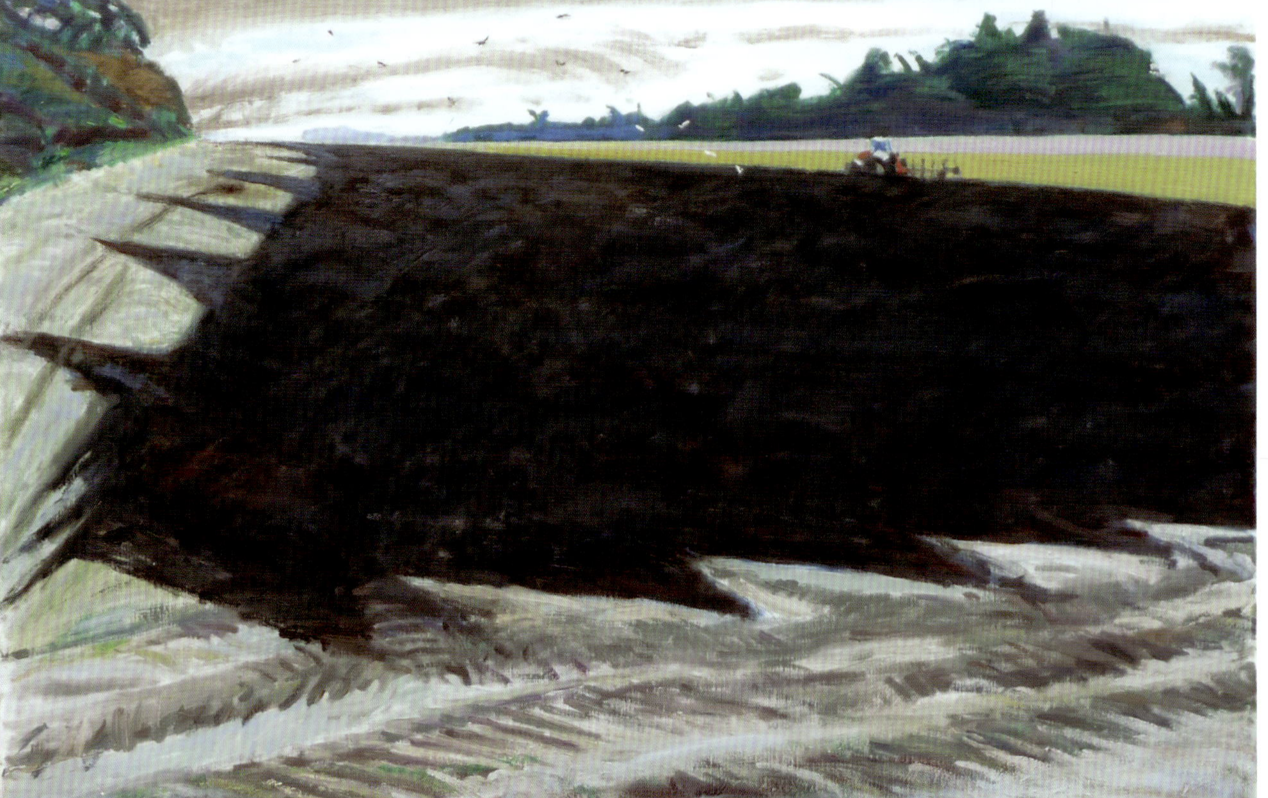

Spikey Ploughing (2009) Oil on Canvas 80 x 120cm

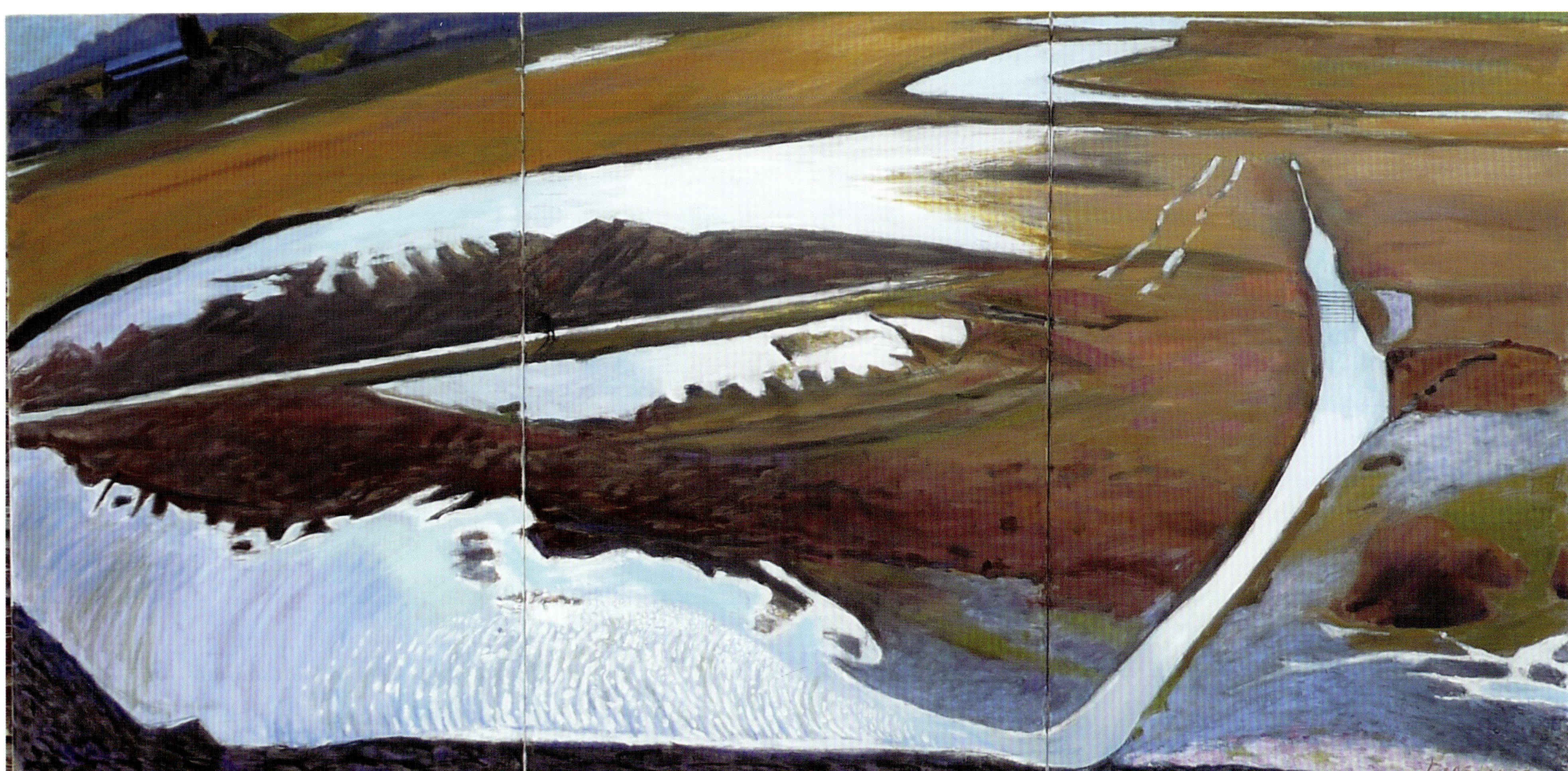

Some Views of Salthouse Marsh (2009) Oil on Canvas 120 x 240cm

Andrew Schumann

Andrew Schumann is a very cerebral artist. His work is stunning to look at, visually striking and stimulating, and interesting. But the work incorporates concepts that are not always immediately obvious, ranging from the intellectual to the emotional, from mathematical ideas to the mystery of life, and observations on the nature of our universe. It is worth seeking out the artist's own words of illumination. But in the end the works speak directly to the listening viewer.
- **King's Lynn Arts Centre, Norfolk**

Andrew Schumann
Sculptor
King's Lynn, Norfolk

As a sculptor I used to make almost exclusively cast metal works, small to large, figurative or relating to the landscape. As I became increasingly interested in processes of seeing, of pattern recognition, of feeling and touching through the eye and brain, I found the work migrating from the floor to wall, so that I now almost entirely make wall-mounted work between painting and sculpture – 3D painting – about the materials and processes of our universe.

The bead works have steadily evolved and use random numbers to produce arrays which contain patterns of spatial and colour order. The detail image of *Chaotic Symmetry 16* is life size which best shows the balance of order and chaos. Each box contains about 2,500 beads and when I look at them, in changing side or diffuse light, I feel I am looking below the surface at the universe of materials.

Recently I started a new series, using painted ¾" (2cm) discs, exploring the patterns generated by the randomness that underpins all of life. *Waves of Uncertainty* is a regular grid with random movement in all directions. A degree of stability arises from the horizontal wave lines – rather than total colour randomness – and the choice of colours: an interaction between disc position and disc colours, creating a dramatic range of brain responses.

Educated-
Cambridge University, History of Art BA 1962
Membership of Local Art Societies-
Norwich 20 Group
West Norfolk Artists Association
Galleries Familiar With Artist's Work-
Art 18/21, Norwich, Norfolk
King's Lynn Arts Centre, King's Lynn, Norfolk

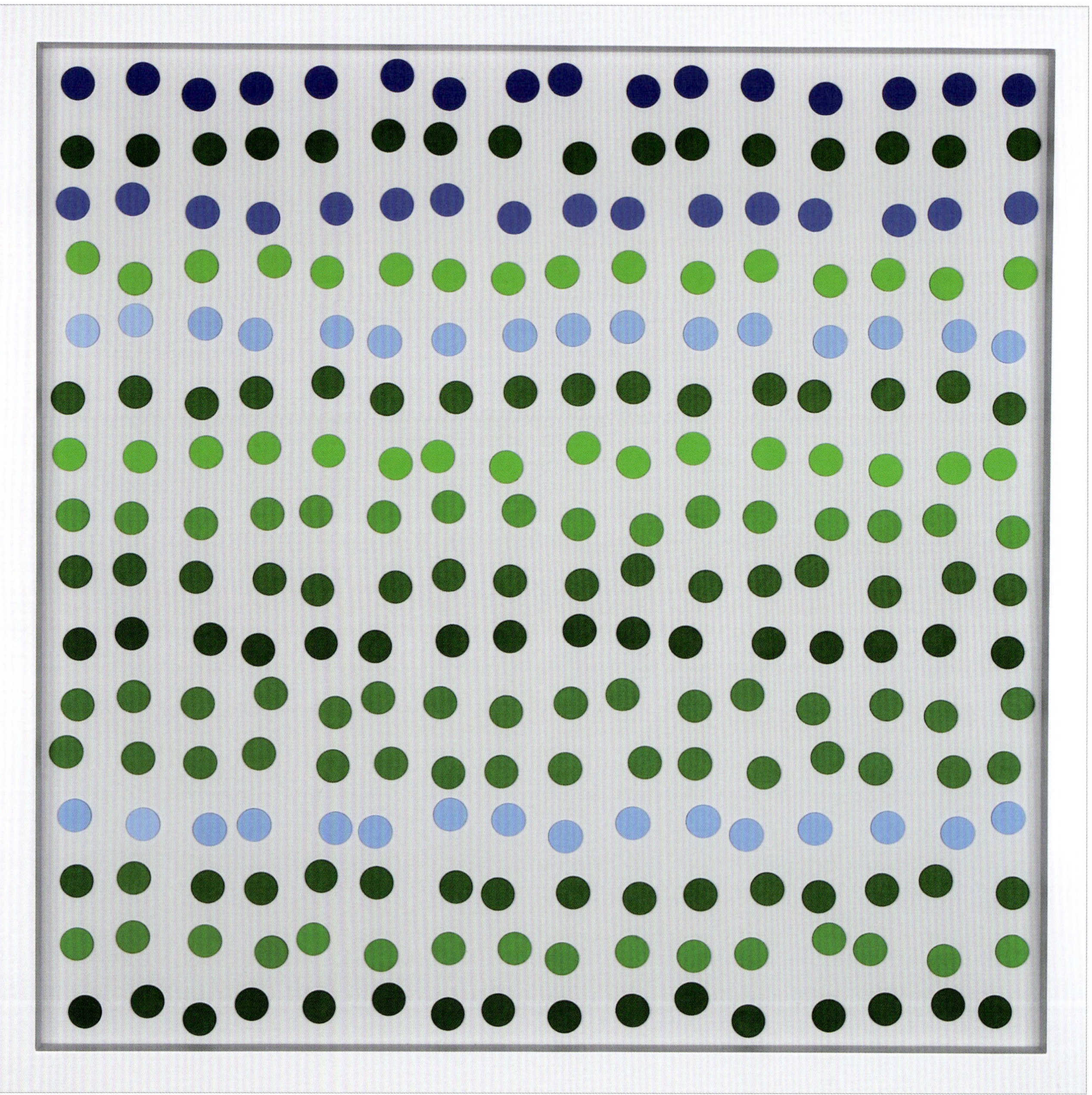

Waves of Uncertainty (2010) Painted MDF 63 x 63 x 4.5cm

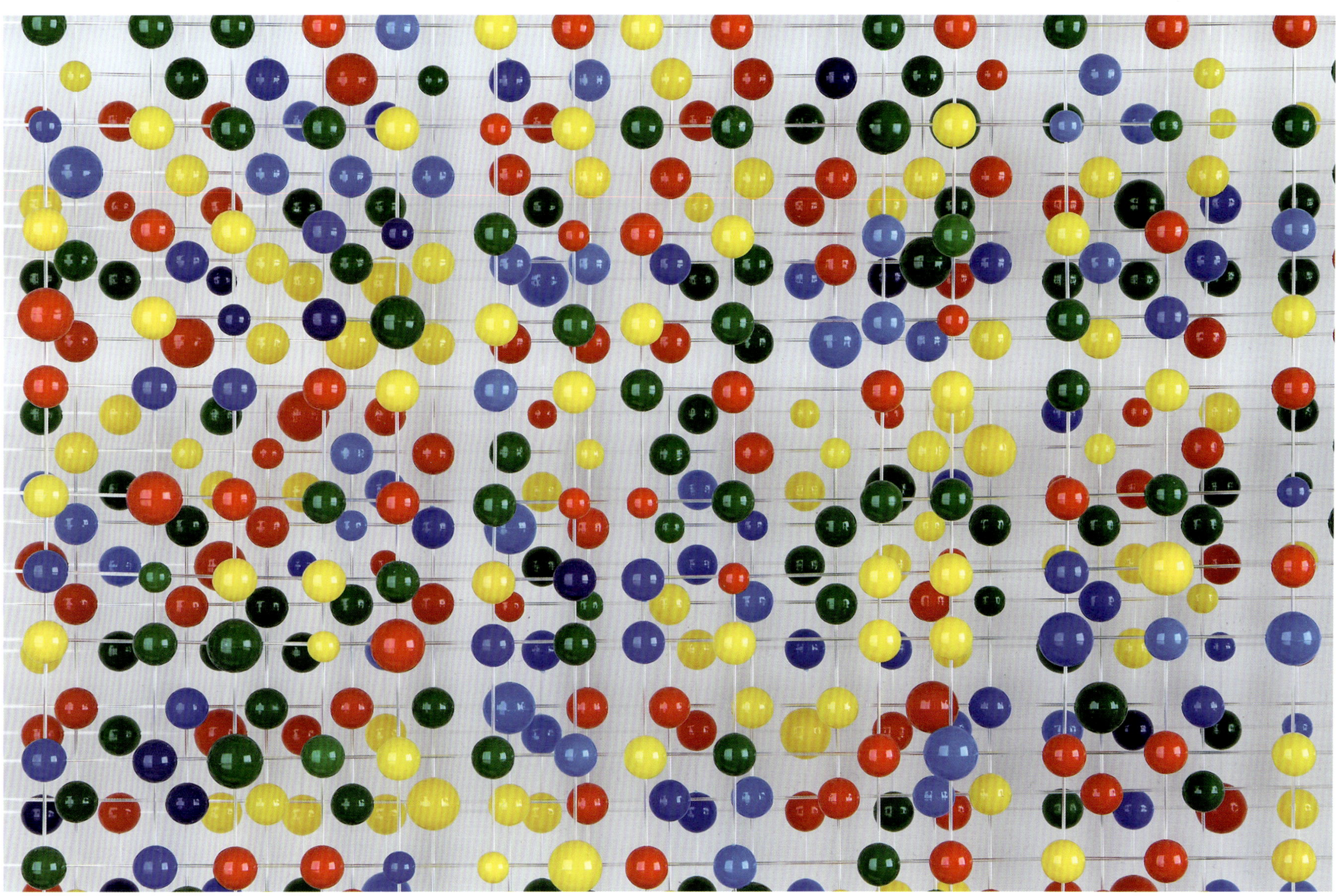

Chaotic Symmetry 16 (detail) (2009) Plastic Beads on Nylon Monofilament 67 x 67 x 9cm

Serena Hall BA (Hons)

Bold, colourful and uplifting are words that spring to mind when looking at Serena's paintings. Stand in a room full of her striking and instantly recognizable paintings, and you are transported to a world full of colour and light.
- Serena Hall Gallery, Southwold, Suffolk

Serena Hall
Painter, Mixed Media Artist
Southwold, Suffolk

My family moved to Southwold from London when I was twelve years old and overnight my bedroom window suddenly looked out onto the beach. This transition was so amazing, it would have a profound, long-lasting effect on my life. I was becoming aware of how much colour actually was in the sky, how each day created different patterns in the sand and it was this constant change that keeps me painting now. I was lucky as a child to have had family holidays in Greece, Italy and Spain and the colours and traditional crafts from these countries have also had a huge influence on the colours and pattern in my work. When I paint I am not looking to recreate a scene exactly, but to create my own unique interpretation of where I live.

Coastal Patchwork sums up everything I love about living on the coast. Also, my love of pattern and colour is clearly evident here. My still lifes are about trying to capture good moments in time; the enjoyment of living by the sea. I nearly always remember a group of friends or family gatherings when I paint a still life. It is really about capturing a memory, a moment in time.

It can be sad too, as the moments can be fleeting and it is important to remember that time spent with loved ones.

Fish for Sale is inspired by Southwold's working harbour. My mixed media work uses handmade ceramics with found and distressed wood.I use screen-printing techniques to print images from my sketchbooks, to create interesting backgrounds to my compositions.

Swimming Mackerel uses handmade ceramic fishes and screenprinted seaweed to create a work inspired by the sea. I enjoy the physical hard work that goes with making these, as I have to carry large bags of clay and cut out large sheets of wood.

In the Dunes is my favourite view of Southwold. It is the view just opposite my family home where I used to live and so it is probably the view I know the best. I never get bored of painting it as it changes all the time depending on where you are walking.

I am aware that my style of painting, which uses swatches of colour can be overpowering so I have to be aware of making sure I think about each brushstroke but not so much that it looks stilted. I want the images to look quite organic and easy on the eye, even though they are bursting with colour! I hope to always paint variations of this view, my fathers ashes are scattered here, so I feel I am always in good company.

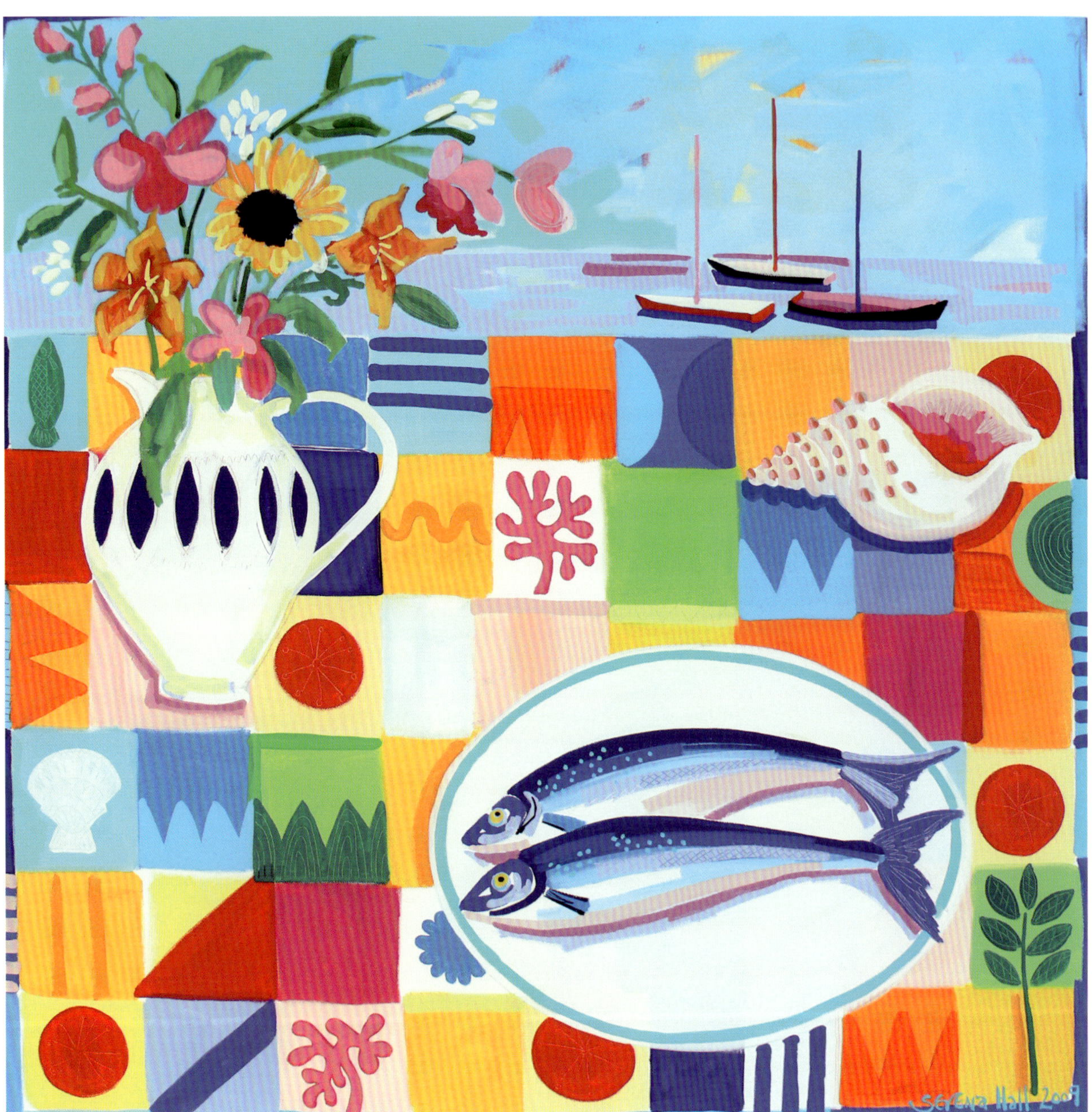

Coastal Patchwork (2009) Acrylic on Canvas 100 x 100cm

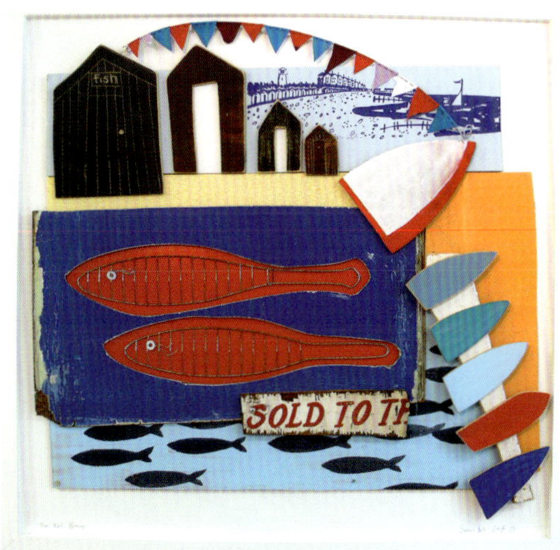

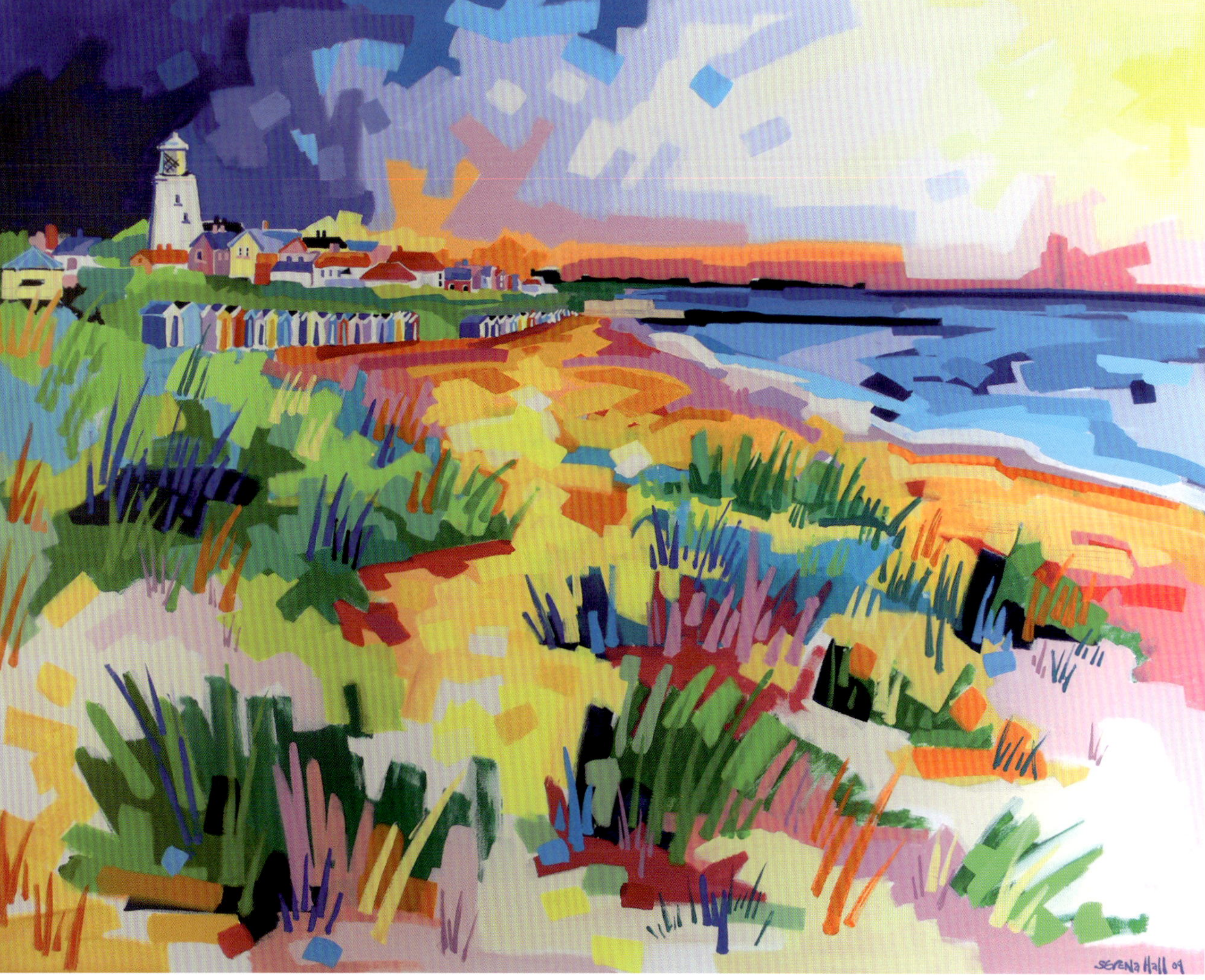

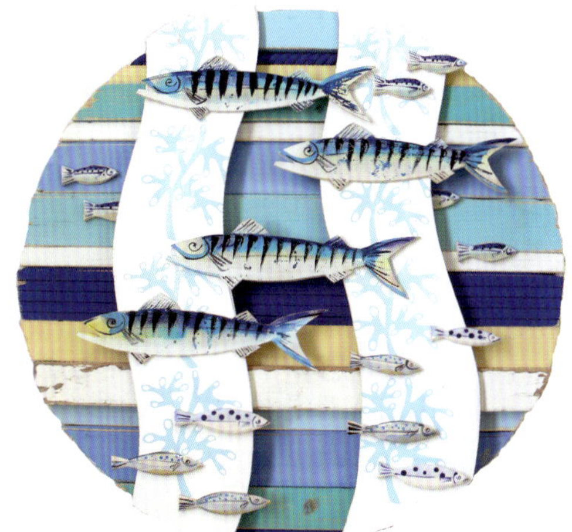

Clockwise From Top Left: *Fish for Sale* Mixed Media 100 x 100 cm; *In The Dunes (2009)* Acrylic on Canvas 122 x 152 cm; *Swimming Mackerel* Mixed Media 90cm Round

Serena Hall: Behind the Scenes

More about:

Serena....

Educated-
Edinburgh College of Art, BA (Hons) 1995
Galleries Familiar With Artist's Work-
Serena Hall Gallery, Southwold, Suffolk
Website- www.serenahallartist.com

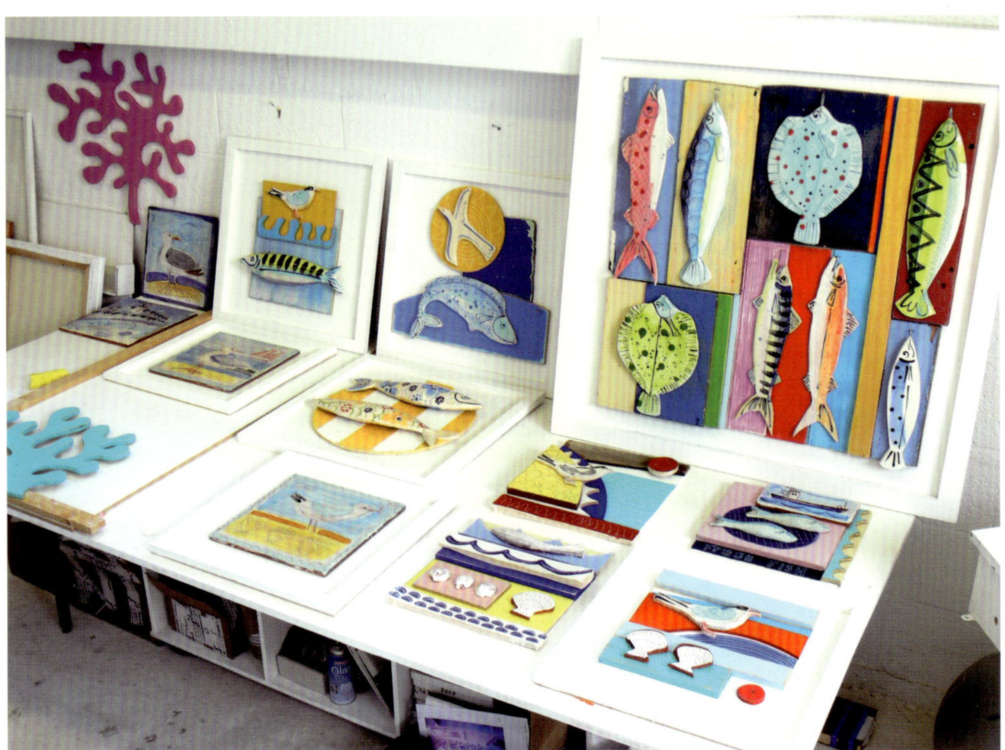

I work at least six days a week in my studio, sometimes every day for a month or more if I am really busy. It does not feel like a chore, as I know this is quite an amazing way to earn a living. I try to be in my studio by nine or ten, by the time I have done a bit of work from home. I have a smaller studio there but it's mainly for ideas and sketchbook images rather than for painting.

My current studio is the largest I have had so far, and it's great for allowing me the space to try out new ideas for my larger mixed media works and for my canvasses that are definitely getting bigger and bigger. Commissions from London tend to be for really large paintings, which I love doing, so I need the space to accommodate that.

The winter is very hard though as it gets so cold, I can wear at least three jumpers and still be freezing. I have a heater but the warmth just goes up and out of the metal ceiling. It's when your fingers go numb that it doesn't really make sense to have a big studio. As soon as it starts getting warmer I feel like I have to make up for lost time and work really hard and long hours. I switch on 80s music during the day and if I work late I enjoy classical music or Tubular Bells.

I find that I need to be more physical in the mornings so I concentrate on my mixed media work, which will include lumping clay about and cutting out huge sheets of wood, which is heavy work. Then, by the afternoon, I want to chill out and paint. This 'routine' stops me from getting into a rut and keeps me interested in what I am doing. I generally lock my studio door so that I don't keep getting interrupted but I love friends dropping in if I know they are on their way. I actually have to be very self-disciplined and work to important deadlines, so there is pressure to work hard. I look forwards to time off but it's nearly always to go to the beach, visit an art gallery or sit with a glass of wine and my sketchbook.

So, my life really is my work.

This Page: Mixed Media works
Opposite Page: Serena's painting space

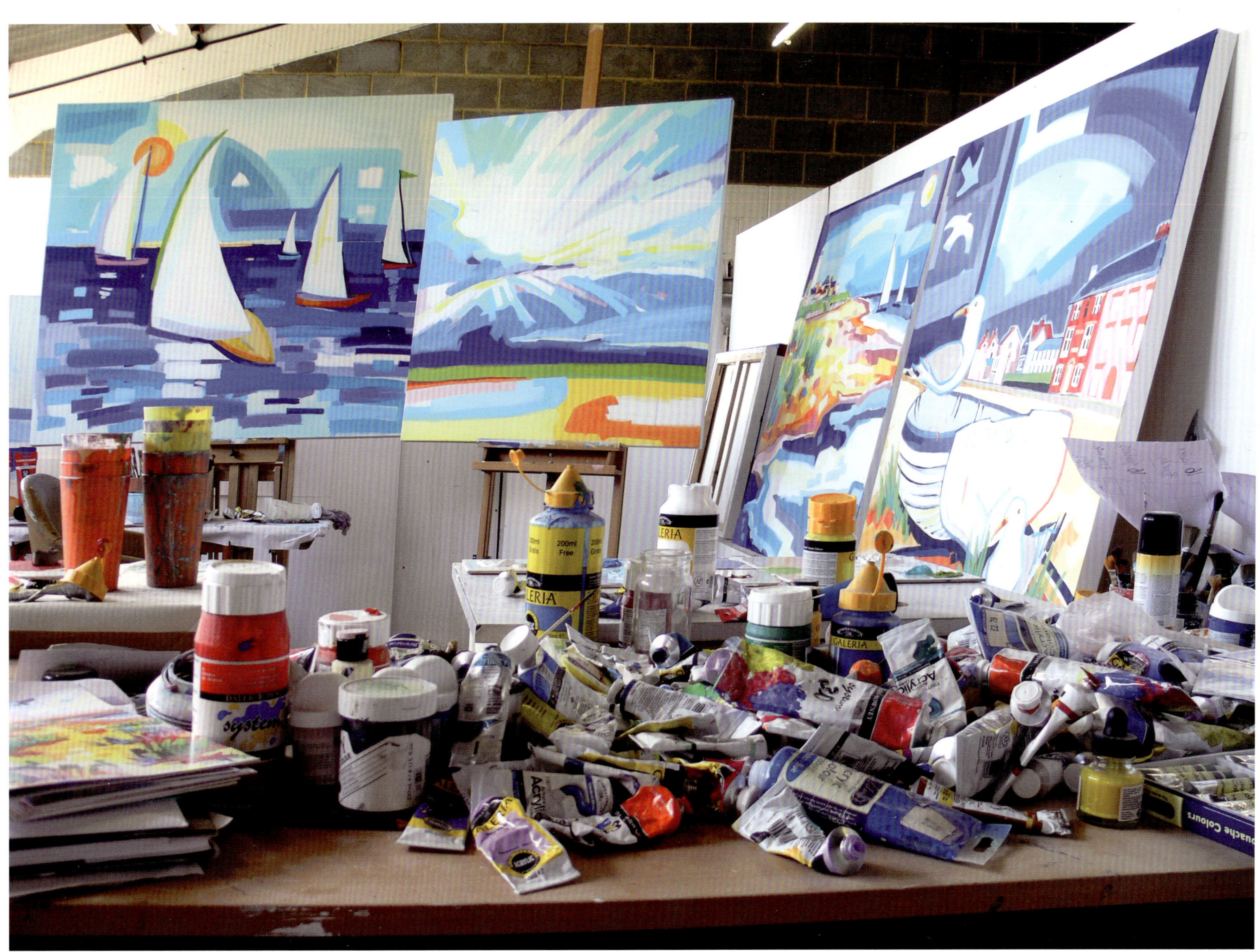

Noelle Francis

170

Noelle Francis
Painter
Bungay, Suffolk

The sea and wild natural landscapes are my main interests. During the summer months I work and paint around my Norfolk garden and the East Anglian coast.

During the winter I travel to find heat and colour in different parts of the world such as the rainforests of Borneo and South America and most recently my most inspiring ideas have come from coral reefs.

Educated-
Ravensbourne College, Kent
Cardiff School of Art, Cardiff 1965
Membership of Local Art Societies-
Black Dog Arts, Bungay, Suffolk
Galleries Familiar With Artist's Work-
Harleston Gallery, Harleston, Norfolk
Cork Brick Gallery, Bungay, Suffolk
Website- www.noellefrancis.co.uk

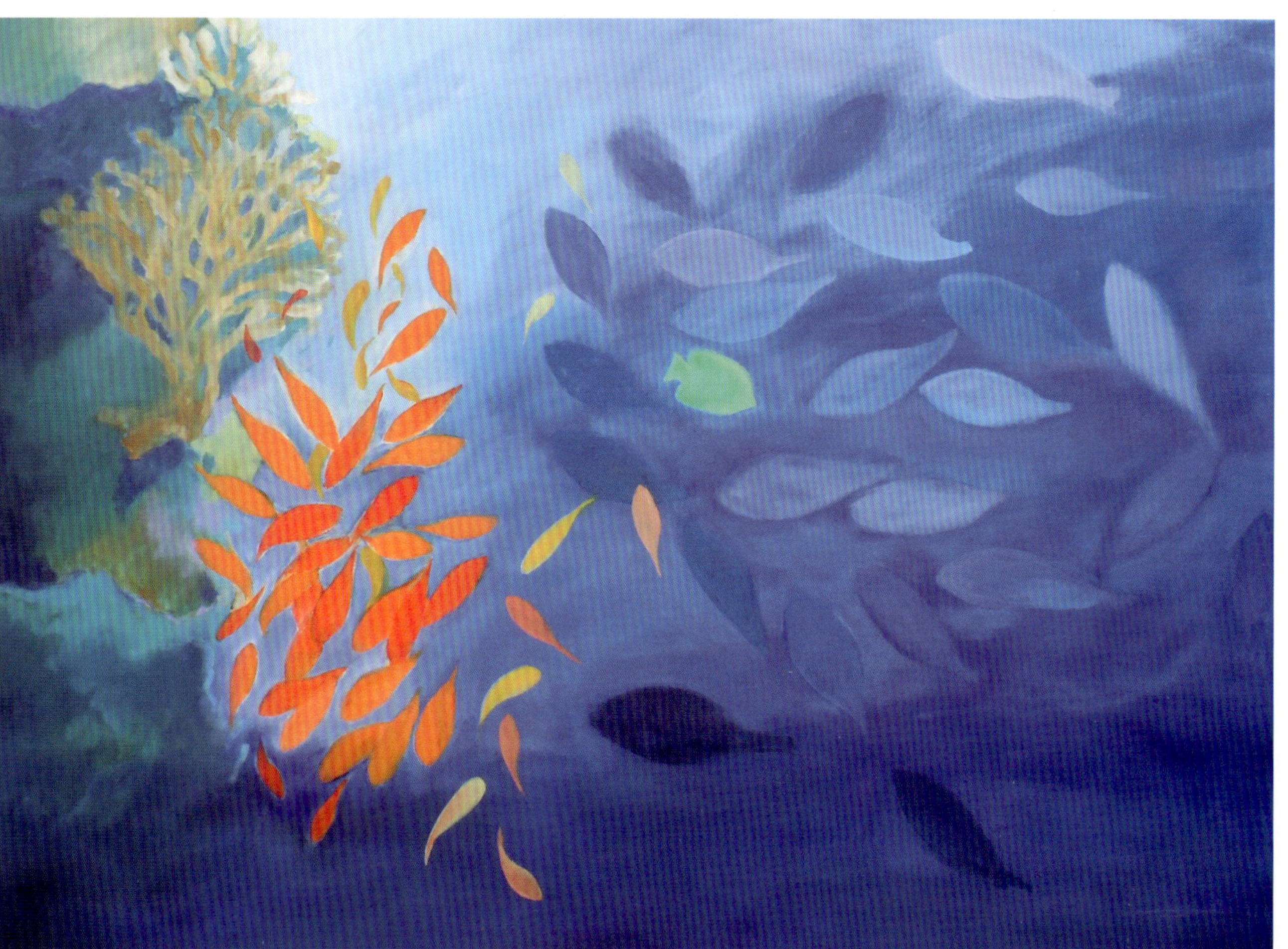

Deep Blue (2006) Oil on Canvas 121 x 92cm

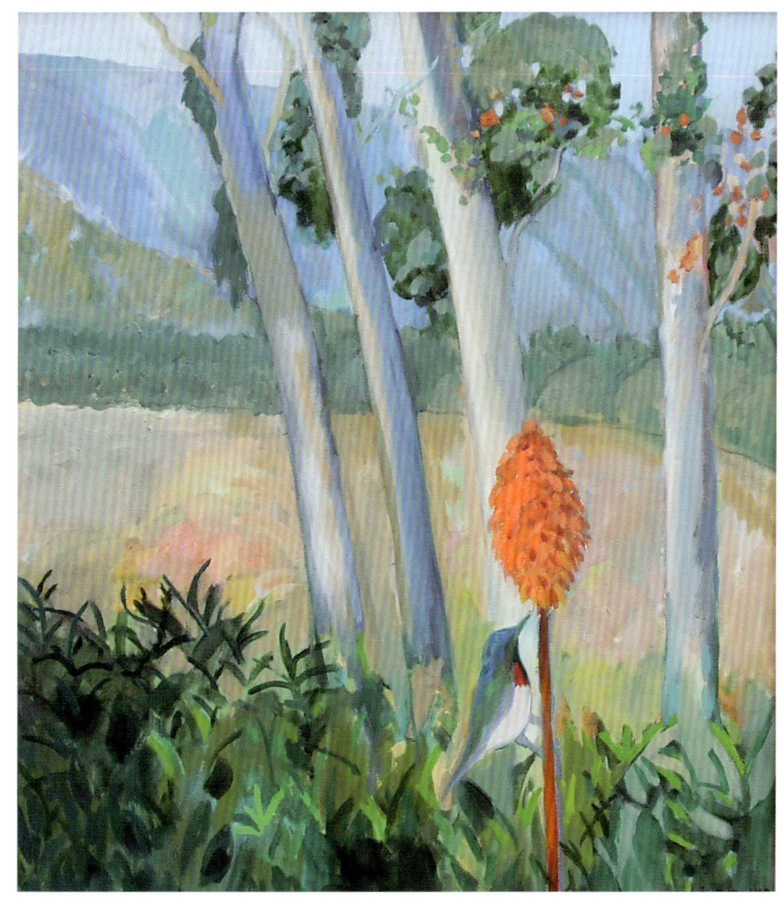

Sunbird (2008) 61 x 51cm

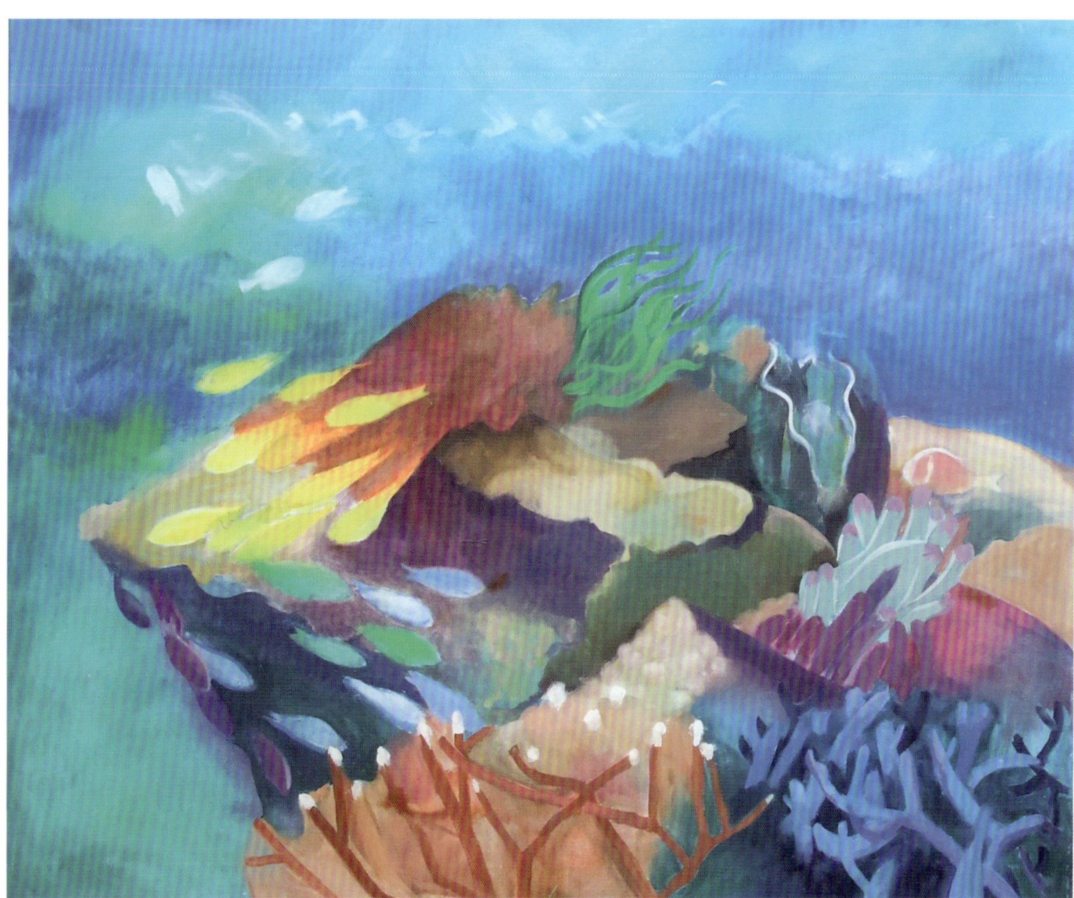

Coral (2002) Oil on Canvas 122 x 102cm

Sandi Westwood

No matter how busy Sandi makes her images - and some are extraordinarily busy, filled with a hundred or more flying, swooping, landing, perching birds - there remains an order and a stillness within each piece. Sandi's attention to detail is stunning and her work is always graceful and wonderfully peaceful in quality.
- Art-next-the-Sea, Wells-next-the-Sea, Norfolk

Sandi Westwood
Painter
Briston, Norfolk

I love my oil paint - it holds so many possibilities in the way it can be manipulated and the effects that can be achieved. I find my inspiration in the natural world but also explore hidden dimensions beyond those we see with our eyes. Sometimes a fully formed image will enter my mind but often an idea will evolve on the canvas or throughout a series of paintings.

The Eden Tree was completed over a period of two years and my interpretation of it has changed several times. I think now that it depicts man hiding from the natural beauty in the world, both real and imagined. Before it was finished I was moved to write along the top edge of the box canvas 'Plant a seed of love and watch it grow in peace and harmony'.

My large *Bird-escape* paintings have evolved over several years. I try to evoke the feeling of freedom and being drawn towards the light. *Swan Dance* and *Whooping It Up* are the most recent in the series and were inspired by my love of swans. *Whooping It Up* contains birds that have been spotted on the North Norfolk coastal marshes.

On a good day in my studio there seems to be no passage of time – it's like opening up a door in my mind to another world; everything just flows without conscious thought. I want my paintings to uplift, stir your soul or just make you smile.

Galleries Familiar With Artist's Work-
Art Next the Sea, Wells-next-the-Sea, Norfolk
Website- www.sandiwestwood.com

172

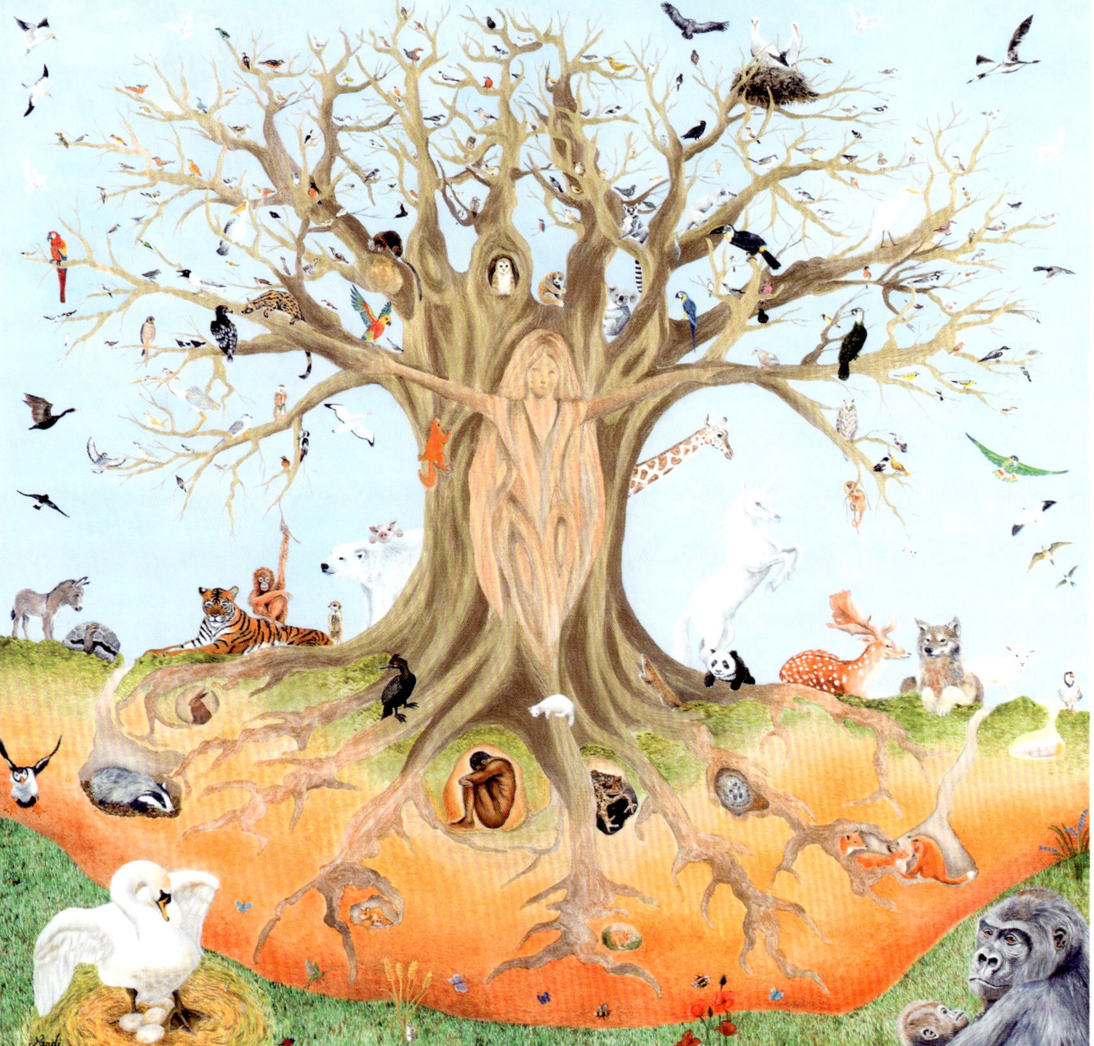

The Eden Tree (2008) 90 x 90cm

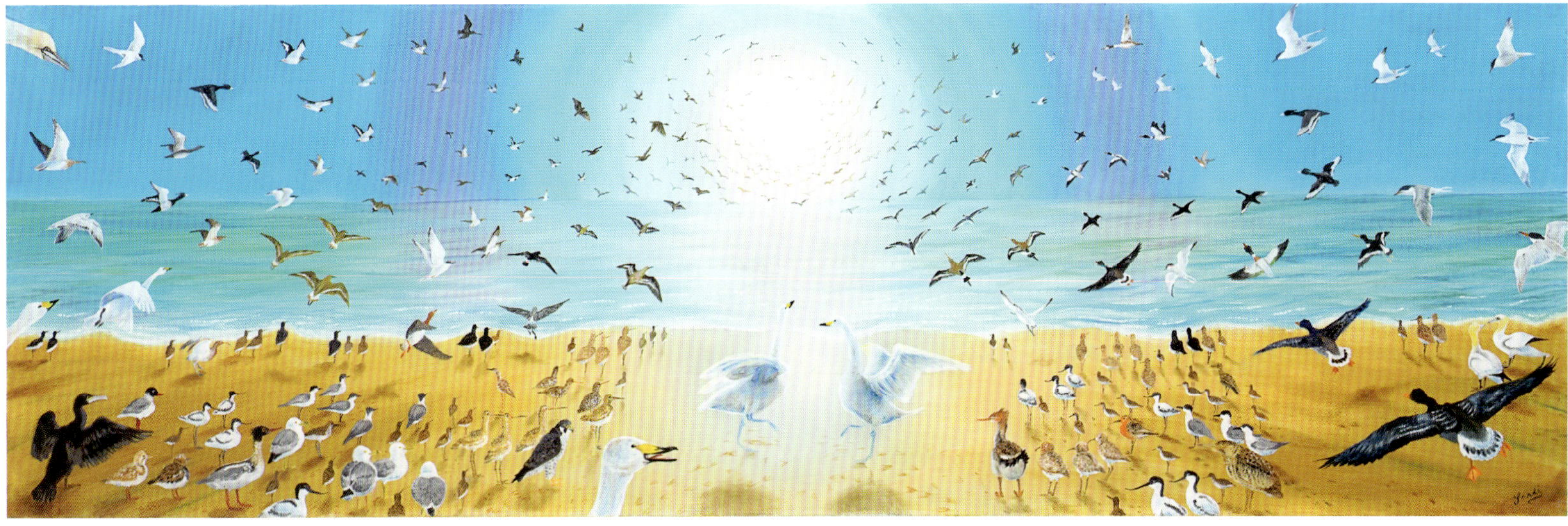

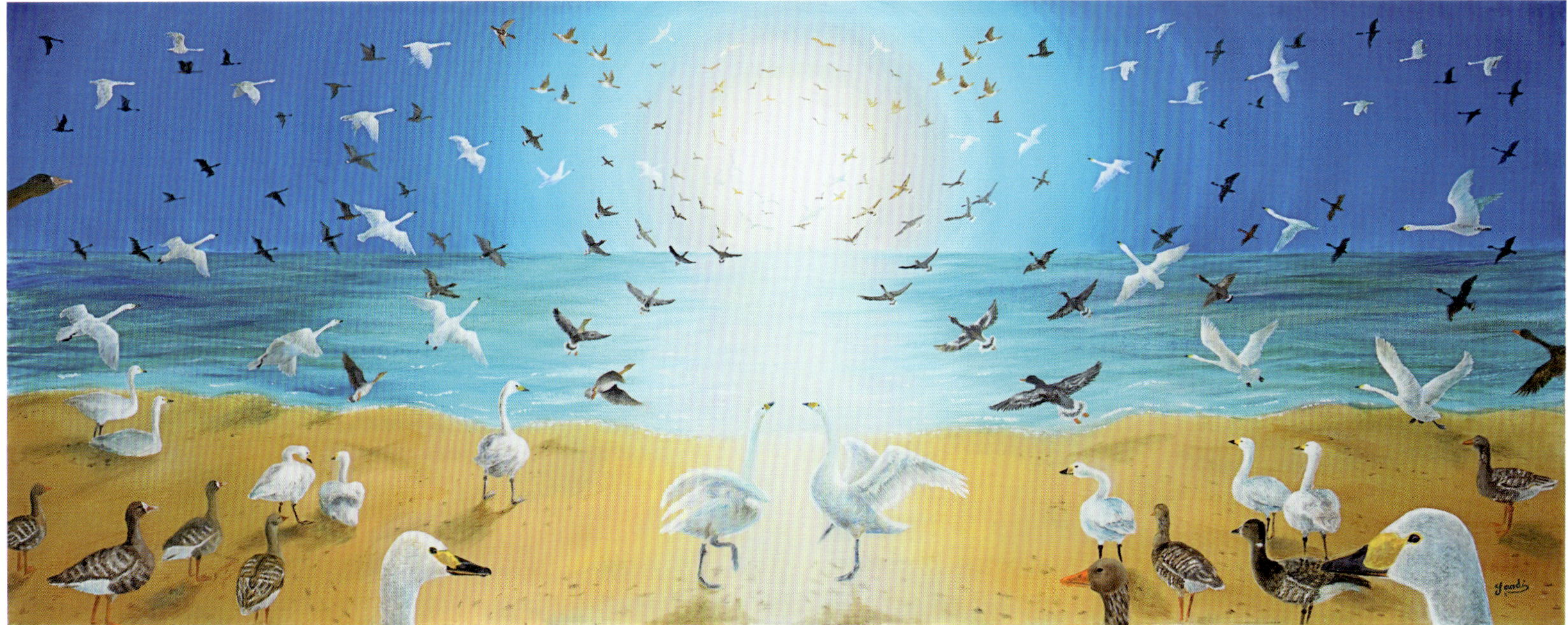

Top: *Whooping It Up (2010)* Oil 40 x 120cm
Bottom: *Swan Dance (2010)* Oil 41 x 99cm

Opinions

Abel, Doreen

The Ferini Art Gallery might have been one of the first to exhibit Doreen's paintings. Pebbles - beautifully sculptured in pastels, skilfully shaped and composed - which looked wet and real enough to touch. Almost at the same time, Doreen created beautifully-drawn seascapes with controlled subtlety of colour and shapes, conveying the power and the life of the waves and sky. Doreen's media and subject matter has diversified and extended over time into oils but there is always a strength and vitality to her work. Simultaneously her work has grown more confident and coincidentally larger canvases are often used.

- Paul Hobbs & Michaela Barber, Ferini Art Gallery, Pakefield, Suffolk

Originally tutored by her father (in her own words, he was her best and only tutor), Doreen's work encompasses her true love of the East Anglian coastline. Spending her time walking the shore, Doreen is inspired by imagery which she takes back to the studio. Here she is able to capture the freshness of breaking waves; the ripple of the water as it washes ashore. Working mainly in pastels, Doreen is able to create the most amazing feel of moisture on rock surfaces as well as the magic and power of her subject matter. Please note we do not have her work at the gallery at present (July 2010).

- Becky Munting, Buckenham Galleries, Southwold, Suffolk

Andrews, Jamie

Jamie's work never fails to ignite childlike enthusiasm. He zealously collects plasticky trinkets, charms, cracker toys, doll parts and fuzzy felts and embeds them in lashings of paint in the most intoxicating and vibrant colours. Jamie assembles narratives in boxes. Sometimes I can follow the story - a nursery rhyme or a political event perhaps - and sometimes I sense that Jamie is only revealing half the story. Behind the jolly exterior occasionally hides a dark and sinister tale. I often find myself looking at Jamie's work with a wistful sense of wonderment. When the penny drops, I feel like I'm sharing the joke with him.

- Iona Jackson, Targetfollow, Norwich, Norfolk

Aylward, Lyn

Showing portraiture for a Gallery is sometimes quite difficult but with Lyn Aylward's paintings, the portraits are so engaging that it does not matter that the viewer does not know the person in the painting. Her skill at portraying the facial expressions and character of the sitters creates instant interest. Contemporary portraiture is very much on the agenda as far as we are concerned as a Gallery, witness the interest in the BP Portrait Exhibition at the National Gallery. Lyn's very contemporary style is very much of the moment as far as contemporary art is concerned.

- Russell Boulter & Clare Walker, Doric Arts, Holt, Norfolk

A talented young artist, Lyn Aylward is certainly one to watch out for in the future; we loved her work from the start. She has an interesting colour sense and although her work is subtle, it is also strong. Lyn's portraits, possibly not always flattering, capture the essence of her subjects and her paintings reflect a keen observation of humanity at large, whether it be on holiday, walking the dog, dancing, or just watching the world go by. This work, however, does not leap light-heartedly onto the canvas and although the subject matter may be easy going, a great deal of serious thought lies behind it.

- Chimney Mill Galleries, Bury St Edmunds, Suffolk

Baddon Price, Sarah

Sarah's work is rich and vibrant, each piece is strong yet subtle. Her technique of overlaying colours gives them greater depth and texture whilst in her compositions the juxtaposition of familiar objects against backgrounds with a strong structural element, lifts the objects above the mundane but simultaneously in concord with the whole. The appeal of Sarah's work lies not just in this dichotomy, but in the way that each piece feels complete but with the power to intrigue.

- Robin Peters, The Frame Workshop, Ipswich, Suffolk

Baguley, Gill

Gill Baguley's vibrant and colourful semi-abstract paintings embrace the heart of North Norfolk. Familiar landscapes and seaside views are captured in all their glory for everyone to enjoy. She brings a rainy and windy Cromer Pier scene to life with numerous multi-coloured umbrellas, and their occupants, being blown sideways. A Wells view isn't just of beach huts; there are children having a thoroughly enjoyable time building sand castles while mum keeps a watchful eye on them and dad nods off in his deckchair. Gill's paintings always capture the very heart of the subject, often with humour, but always with an innocent honesty.

- Trevor & Joanna Woods, Gallery Plus, Wells-next-the-Sea, Norfolk

Gill paints with a very stylish printmaker's eye, defining pools of vibrant colour and line which emphasize the shapes within areas of diverging, often moody, colour with a wonderful sense of confidence. It seems she is showing the observer exactly where she intends them to look and hopefully they are rewarded with what they see. Gill's work, whether it be her organically-styled pieces or her quirky illustrative paintings, conveys skilled observation which is always well executed.

- Caroline Richmond and David Burton, Art-next-the-Sea, Wells-next-the-Sea, Norfolk

Gill Baguley's pictures capture the beauty and diversity of the North Norfolk coast and countryside in a striking and stylish way. She treats her subject matter with a colour and clarity that draws one in. Her expert composition means that her pictures, whether as originals or the high quality prints, are at home in even the most sophisticated environment, whilst the playful element that she often applies to the human participants makes the pictures come alive and encourages the eye to linger.

- Roger James, A Picture Of Norfolk, Norwich, Norfolk

Baldwin, Peter

I have long admired the work of Peter Baldwin. He paints pictures of deceptive simplicity with an underlying sophistication, not surprising in one who has lectured in art history. When writing my dictionary *Artists in Britain Since 1945*, I surveyed the work of over 14,000 artists and now find that it is individualists like Peter, often producing small and quirky images, who linger in the memory. I saw six of his paintings again in a 2009 show by the Norwich Twenty Group. They seemed as fascinating and desirable as when I first encountered his work and I am glad that he is having a London show with Duncan Campbell in September 2010.

- David Buckman, Writer and Journalist

Cordova, Gail de (BA Hons)

Richly textured landscapes mingling paint with tissue are the hallmarks of Gail de Cordova's work. Though seemingly abstract, her paintings evoke places, times, scents, breezes, seasons, memories...and one is at a loss to define exactly how these are communicated. They just are. Every work is different yet they are all unmistakably Gail's, so strong is her visual style.
- Chris Williams, Williams Art, Cambridge

Dodds, James

James Dodds is unique in his ability to paint shipping from the inside out. He makes us reassess both the tradition of marine painting from which he has emerged and the future direction the genre might take. He has in common with the so-called 'pierhead' painters and journeyman painters of previous centuries that desire to portray particular wooden vessels, but he does so in a much more intimate way, choosing to focus on the moment of construction or reconstruction when the raw strength of these great nautical skeletons is laid bare. Dodds' wooden boats are not so much represented as reconstructed on canvas, each rope and wooden joint scrupulously recorded, leading to paintings of great breadth and power.

- David Messum, Messum's Fine Art, London

James Dodds took part in the opening exhibition of Bircham Gallery in 1988, and has been a key exhibitor with us ever since. In those early days we exhibited linocuts blending the mythology of the sea with his knowledge of boatbuilding. His work grew rapidly in stature, reflecting his personal development from shipwright to professional artist with an enviable international reputation. Thematically, his work has shown a remarkable consistency - his current monumental canvases and prints are still rooted firmly in his love of the sea and the traditions of nautical life. In July 2007 James, who studied painting at the Royal College of Art, received an honorary doctorate from the University of Essex in recognition of his 'distinguished contribution to the local community as an artist and defender of our community and natural heritage.'
- Chris Harrison, Bircham Gallery, Holt, Norfolk

Dowson, Claire Louise

A recent retrospective exhibition at the Ferini Art Gallery permitted the visitor to experience the strength and continuity in Claire's work. In her earlier work could be seen the same devotion to detail, colour and strength of design that we are familiar with in her later more simplified expressions of the beach and waves. In the earlier work there was intricate pattern and texture of fabrics appliquéd onto the surface. Present throughout all Claire's paintings is that wonderful ability to interpret her vision, whether the room and its contents or the crashing patterns of the breaking waves, into a fine balance between realism and abstraction.
- Paul Hobbs & Michaela Barber, Ferini Art Gallery, Pakefield, Suffolk

Claire's work covers a multitude of mediums and subjects, from water colour animal portraits and powerful oil paintings of waves, to interesting abstract textile pieces. Her interest in pattern and texture comes through in all her pieces. Please note we do not have any work by this artist in the gallery (July 2010).
- Becky Munting, Buckenham Galleries, Southwold, Suffolk

Dowson's works have a soft harmonious feel. Whether of coastal influence in her oil paintings or to textile works and floral abundance, her approach to the balance of life is appealing to many. Seascapes show the natural beauty of the Norfolk and Suffolk coastline, not for tourism influence, but for the genuine beauty our area does give in reality, with endless skies, stormy clouds, the grey/blue soft reflection of the East Anglian area that gives calm to the viewer.
- Michelle Payne, Upstairs Gallery, Beccles, Suffolk

Farthing, Douglas (MBE, AFAS, ISWA)

Douglas' painting and drawing has a spontaneity that has come from a spirit to interpret and express the world around him. This world is very different to our safe and familiar surroundings to the point of being unknowable to most of us. Douglas records the conflict in the Middle East not just from a soldier's view but from an observer's view; the people, the land, every day life in a very poor part of the world where violence can erupt at any moment. He expresses the tension and normality of daily life of both the military and the local indigenous people.
- John Allen, Mandell's Gallery, Norwich, Norfolk

Figg, Christian

Notoriously elusive, and his work highly sought-after, we have been lucky enough to occasionally exhibit work by Christian. His work has a stark beauty to it. Forms are defined and redefined to the barest minimum, abstracted and yet still retaining enough to make them instantly recognisable. Working in a limited, muted and flat palette, Christian portrays the East Anglian coastline is an harsh representation, with no glorification in what he sees. Please note we do not have his work at the gallery at present (July 2010).
- Becky Munting, Buckenham Galleries, Southwold, Suffolk

'Christian Figg paints crisp, modern pictures of subjects with a long tradition – the coasts and landscapes of East Anglia. The sense of calm and well-being Christian's pictures evoke can only be a good thing for today's rushed lives and his works are particularly appealing because they could just as happily hang in a modern flat as they could an old-style country cottage. They are undeniably 'liveable with'; a quality which not all contemporary artists are interested in giving their works. Please note, Beecroft Art Gallery does not have any work in its collections by this artist.
- Clare Hunt, Beecroft Art Gallery, Westcliff on Sea, Essex

Francis, Noelle

Inspired by her adventurous travelling – from the rainforests of Borneo and South America to the exoticism of Morocco and underwater delights of Egypt's coral reefs – and her passion for her beautiful garden in South Norfolk, Noelle Francis has evolved a truly distinctive, highly coloured semi abstract style with which to capture her wide range of visual experiences. With their brilliant blues and golds, intense greens and scarlets, Noelle's paintings always appear to sing out in our Gallery spaces; a breath of light and colour which visitors never fail to remark upon.
- Caryl Challis, Harleston Gallery, Harleston, Norfolk

Opinions

Noelle is a much-travelled artist who regularly exhibits her rich and brilliantly coloured paintings garnered from her exploits. When at home Noelle is happy to be busy in her eye catching garden, which she tends with an artists eye for colour and form, an inspiration for more paintings that are softer and more subtle than the stronger colours from her exotic expeditions. *- Ken Skipper, Cork Brick Gallery, Bungay, Suffolk*

Freston, Tom de

Tom de Freston's work appeals deeply to me on a number of levels. It is perhaps the mixture of sincerity and humour which is the most striking. Tom has described his work as tragic-comic: 'The works' inability to achieve any of the genuine pathos of tragedy is pretty comical and the lack of genuine wit or humour in the work is pretty tragic.' For me this is one of the most insightful routes into an understanding of his intentions, although it takes a little unpicking. Often Tom's work is genuinely poignant. In the case of *Beheaded* (2010) two figures prepare to decapitate a kneeling, praying figure with a halo. The image powerfully combines images of Christian martyrdom with that of Islamic extremist al-Qaida executions. This clash of iconic religious imagery is given a further twist by the appearance of the executioner who, although poised to deliver the deadly blow, is rendered in a child-like, almost cartoon-esque, manner. The head is a large white bubble with eyes whilst the figure's left foot is painted as if by an infant. The image consequently wrong foots the viewer. It amuses for its absurdity but delivers an eternal message about power, punishment and belief. It also reveals the relationship between Tom's description of the work and the work itself: to the contrary of his statement, the painting achieves a genuine pathos, but it is created through the interplay between an absurd comedy and the considered moral and intellectual ramifications of his images.
-Henry Little, HRL Contemporary, www.hrlcontemporary.com

Fujikawa, Akiko

Akiko Fujikawa came to England decades ago and is a long-term resident of Burnham-on-Crouch, but she remains the most Japanese of print artists. Having learned the traditional woodblock method from the old Kyoto master Asano Takeji, she has remained faithful to them, in spite of the difficulties of obtaining the right materials in this country. She has also continued to work in her own very individual version of his later, deceptively naive style. Her apparently simple prints, using very few strong and contrasting flat colours, explore with some subtlety the complexities of human emotions and relationships.

-Lawrence Smith, Formerly Keeper of Japanese Antiquities, The British Museum

When I first saw the work of Akiko Fujikawa, it seemed quite different to other printmakers working in Essex, or East Anglia, and it is: a different training and technique but above all her own distinct sensibility. In 1997 I bought a woodcut *Mask 2* for Chelmsford Museum from a small show at Hylands House, Chelmsford. Akiko's colours are restrained and subtle, but see the texture too. How the soft Japanese paper interacts with the grain of each lightly-inked block. Akiko simplifies her motifs, universal like this mask, to basic components so that the print gives a jolt of recognition with surprise: so you can rearrange it like that? It becomes a collaboration between artist and viewer; each of us finds our own interpretation of its exact mood.

- Anne Lutyens-Humfrey, Formerly Keeper of Art at Chelmsford Museum, Essex

German, Jane (NDD, ATC)

Jane's work reflects her upbringing in a farming village on the Leicester/Derbyshire border. Her method of painting leaves one wondering how it is achieved; the subtle colours are muted yet luminous, with the paint worked into, rather than placed upon, the canvas. Recent works are sensual, sumptuous compositions of fruit, vegetables, pottery and fabrics, in the great tradition of the still life. The Gallery has shown Jane's work since 2002, it is sought-after and collected, especially by those who share her love of the natural world.
- Caryl Challis, Harleston Gallery, Harleston, Norfolk

Jane German's exhibition at The Cut in March 2008 with David Page was very popular; this could be explained by their figurative observation of Norfolk/Suffolk rural life. However, this unsentimental work also includes, for example, an intriguing diffusion of shape and form in the close-up of animals and demonstrates sharp visual intelligence.
- Tony Casement, The Cut, Halesworth, Suffolk

Jane has only exhibited in the gallery for a year having been introduced through the taster exhibition for the Harleston and Waveney Art Trail we hosted. We were very impressed by the quality of Jane's work, with the muted colours gently merging to build a soft pattern of shape and form. Being a country girl at heart, her farm animal subjects are painted without sentimentality but with a warmth and love of nature. In the fine detail of a cow, with its head through the hedge, you can count the hairs on its nose, showing the care and attention Jane gives to her subjects.
- Ken Skipper, Cork Brick Gallery, Bungay, Suffolk

Giles, Colin (MISTD)

Colin Giles has exhibited with us since 2006 and his work has proved a success with many of our customers. His earlier work included layered abstract fragments of digital photography, while recent pieces utilize his highly textured, vivid, paintings reproduced in a series of high quality, limited edition giclee prints. The multi-layered, richly-coloured compositions are reminiscent of reedbeds or swathes of flowers. The effect is bold and unusual. Purchasers of his work have praised it for its affordability and strong visual impact, making Colin Giles a popular addition to the Gallery.
- Snape Maltings Gallery, Snape, Suffolk

Gordon-Brown, Christophe

Christophe Gordon Brown is a cambridge-based sculptor working mostly in stone. His work is accessible through its simplicity and eye catching beauty. Once engaged you will be led in to a more complex world where form, shape, edge, light, material and texture all collude to express something more thoughtful and challenging. There is playfulness and trickery too. Follow an edge and you are unlikely to predict its ending. Accept an understanding of a piece without proper scrutiny and you will have missed a sensitivity, a care or an intent which is being presented to you to think about. His work does not mimic the natural world, rather it is a fusion of all that we make with the more eternal and enduring objects that nature scatters at our feet.
- John Bacon, Collector

Beautiful, graceful, sensuous forms are at the heart of Christophe's work. The immediate sense is of a desirable, touchable object. But there is much more to be revealed when you realise that a large chunk of sculpted marble is resting on a minute base and moves to the touch. Or that a slight incline of the head causes the shape to change dramatically, revealing a complexity of structure completely hidden at first glance. This is work of great depth which reflects Christophe's skill as a creative artist and master craftsman. The expression of complex notions gradually emerges in pared-down, beautiful simplicity. Everything, from the choice of material, the expert working of the form and the development of an object of great beauty, reflects the time, experience and care in its creation. Christophe's work can be seen in the gardens of Robinson College, Cambridge, a shopping centre in Beijing and the homes of his many collectors. He can be found working in his tiny studio in Granchester Street modelling countless forms in search of perfection and a selection of his work can be viewed on his website.
- *Chrissie Eaves-Walton, Publishing Consultant, Cambridge*

Gunn, Susan (BA Hons)

Susan Gunn's largescale abstract gesso paintings evoke both fragility and resilience, featuring cracks and fissures on the surface which evolve during the drying process. Using gesso and wax, the artist further works on the surface of her paintings to create a reflective finish in places, inviting a dialogue between viewer and object. At times visceral, at times radiating serenity, Gunn's emotive paintings evoke contemplation and display a transformative power on the spaces they inhabit. Each work displays balance and sensitivity to colour, composition and surface. Gunn's talents were duly recognised when she was awarded the Sovereign European Painting Prize in 2006. Her meditative works can be found in the public collections of the Arts Council East, the Sainsbury Centre, and Norwich Castle Museum and Art Gallery, as well as numerous private collections internationally.
- *Philippa Found, Gallery Director, ROLLO Contemporary Art, London*

Hall, Dawn

Dawn Hall's work captures the essence of our local landscape beautifully. Her large acrylic canvases use bold and dramatic brush stokes to show the energy of the sea, while her watercolours use soft and gentle hues, often depicting the light playing on water. She has gained a large following with people who love her representation of local scenes. We have a permanent exhibition of her work in the Gallery, which she regularly refreshes with new work.
- *Sally Johnson, Caxton Books & Fine Art, Frinton on Sea, Essex*

Hall, Serena

Bold, colourful and uplifting are words that spring to mind when looking at Serena's paintings. Stand in a room full of these striking and instantly recognizable paintings, and you are transported to a world full of colour and light. Her unique way of painting in colourful swatches to build up the surface composition is often remarked upon by visitors. Strong and defined areas appear in her paintings, reflecting the cut-out shapes that make up her mixed media works. Serena's mixed media pieces are also vibrant yet delicately balanced compositions in wood, metal and ceramic, which focuses on nautical themes. These are constructed in various forms and shapes, often including words and screen-printed patterns taken from her sketchbooks. Her paintings and mixed media seem to compliment one another remarkably well, with the free and confident brush marks on the ceramic parts in the mixed media pieces reminding us of those lively paintings. With their bold style, vibrant uplifting colours and charming subjects, Serena's creations are visual invitations to see beyond.
- *Marc Brown, Gallery Manager, Serena Hall Gallery, Southwold, Suffolk*

Hambling, Maggi (CBE)

Maggi Hambling's paintings of the sea show extraordinary vitality and brilliance of texture. They are amongst the best things she has done, and they are getting better and better.
- *David Scrase, Assistant Director, Collections, The Fitzwilliam Museum, Cambridge*

Suffolk born Maggi Hambling is one of today's most celebrated British artists. With close family ties to Snape and its close proximity to the coast, we are thrilled to always have a selection of Maggi's dramatic North Sea paintings for sale. Her endless passion for the sea has found expression in these tempestuous works with their highly textured, sensuous surfaces full of movement and the surging power of the sea. This energy is successfully captured in her small scale paintings, whilst her large canvases almost threaten to engulf the viewer. Challenging and inspiring, Maggi's increasingly sought-after paintings always provoke a wonderful response from visitors to the Gallery.
- *Keri Johnston, Snape Maltings, Snape, Suffolk*

Hann, Chris (Dip.AD, PGDFA London)

The sea, its people and its communities are as much a part of Chris as they are his work. It's fair to say that Chris wouldn't be the first artist to be inspired by the ocean. However, there is nothing predictable about his work. There are two exceptional qualities that distinguish Chris' paintings. Firstly, his sensitive and considered abstraction and secondly his confident and courageous use of colour - neither a typical approach to the subject matter. It's as if the meticulous execution of the painting enables him to contemplate and reflect upon his memories and experiences.
- *Iona Jackson, Targetfollow, Norwich, Norfolk*

Harmer, Geoff

Geoff Harmer staged and sold successfully during his first exhibition with us in April 2010. His art works are bold and vibrant and painted with confidence using strong colours and natural compositions capturing the true essence of the scene. Whether dealing with the soft subtle textures of a tree-lined path or the stark contrast of a bright white boat lying against the quay, Geoff adapts his style and pallet accordingly, bringing the best out of the subject in front of him. With elements of 'great' painters featuring in his works, Geoff will almost certainly make the Norfolk and Suffolk landscape his own and I very much look forward to representing him again this year.
- *Adrian Hill, Picturecraft Gallery, Holt, Norfolk*

Geoff Harmer is a versatile artist who can work just as well in oil as in watercolour. In his paintings, the use of light and colour work together to contribute to the total effect of the painting. His paintings are technically very skillful. He is an excellent draughtsman. His paintings, portraiture and coastal images are well executed and a joy to the viewer.
- *Theronda Hoffman, Kesgrave Arts, Kesgrave, Suffolk*

Opinions

Hofmann, Theronda (BA)

I have been a fan of Theronda's work since I met her in her native South Africa over ten years ago when I fell in love with her beautiful landscapes and images of everyday life. Her use of vibrant colours mirrors the effect of blinding sunlight on the land and the energy of local people - showing life in the new rainbow nation. Theronda's work in East Anglia is now inspired by the Suffolk landscape and architecture, evoking the same feelings, full of drama and energy.

- John Moore, Private Collector

Husted, Mary (BA Hons)

When Mary Husted gave a work *Dreams, Oracles, Icons* to New Hall (now Murray Edwards) in Cambridge in 1992 no one could have predicted that 15 years later, it might have resulted in such heart-warming consequences, when the work provided the trigger for bringing Mary Husted and her son together after a lifelong separation. Such a momentous occasion has also resulted in new work relating to their reunion. I hope that people will enjoy seeing and making comparisons between the two periods in the artist's life.

- Ann Jones, Southbank Centre, London

Imbued with references to visual and emotional memory, the works of Welsh artist Mary Husted emit a powerful resonance with their viewer. Mary's oeuvre consists of both abstract works and figurative pieces. Each can be seen to hold a narrative of her evolving personal history; interweaving metaphors of space, time and perception with more figurative imagery that reveal an ongoing exploration of her own identity. It is hard not to be affected by the artist's honesty or drawn into the unfurling stories hidden beneath the layers of her art.

- Amanda Rigler, New Hall Art Collection, Murray Edwards College, Cambridge

Jackson, Maz (STP SGFA)

Maz has spent a lifetime living and painting in Norfolk. Her work has a surreal and spiritual quality and is exhibited and collected worldwide. She has represented the UK at the Florence Biennale four times. Her imagery is depicted with egg tempera on gilded oak panels after the fifteenth century methods of Andrea Cennini. Her most recent work has been a superb set of woodcut images depicting the voyages of St Brendan in the sixth century. These were launched in Norwich Cathedral in May 2010.

-Richard Cobbold, Cobbold and Judd, Hintlesham, Suffolk

We have been successfully exhibiting the work for more than 25 years and it has been a pleasure to watch Maz's development into the artist of truly international standing which she is today. Maz is noted for the quality of her within her work that reflects her adherence to traditions of practice. This enables her to portray her unique imagery following the traditions of egg tempera painting. Using pure pigments and 24 carat gold on oak panels she shows a depth and richness of colour from which the imagery emerges. Each person viewing the work will perceive differently the emerging essence and messages of the painting.

- Chimney Mill Galleries, Bury St Edmunds, Suffolk

Having shown Maz's paintings for many years we are always delighted when customers view one of her pieces to explain how 15th century painting methods are achieved in a contemporary painting, using egg tempera on seasoned and gessoed oak panels often with gilding is always a pleasure. The imagery for her paintings, often quite ethereal and allegorical, also creates great interest when we exhibit her work. As a practitioner of this ancient medium and a wonderfully skilled and imaginative painter, it is not difficult for us to be enthusiastic about introducing our customers to Maz's work. She has shown at the Florence Biennale in 2003, 2005, 2007 and 2009; given the fact that you have to be invited to exhibit speaks for itself. As a Gallery, showing the work of Maz Jackson is real pleasure.

- Russell Boulter & Clare Walker, Doric Arts, Holt, Norfolk

James, Elizabeth

Elizabeth's pictures, whether watercolour, acrylic or oil are created in an expressive style that portrays the atmosphere of a place and time rather than topographical detail. She demonstrates a continuing preoccupation with the horizon, with the division between the sky and the land always a focal point of the picture. The range of colours she uses reflects very well the shades often seen around the East Anglian coast and countryside. The resulting portfolio is always of interest to our visitors and regular customers alike.

- Verena Daniels & Pat Todd, Reunion Gallery, Felixstowe, Suffolk

James, Philip (ROI)

The paintings of Philip James ROI have always had an appeal. His 'City Scapes' - oil paintings that describe the city of London so eloquently with a poetry of brush mark that both informs and delights - grabbed my attention when first introduced to this artist. You can almost smell the air of the city. James not only manages to capture 'a view' but also a 'feeling' and it is this that I believe separates him from the crowd. Contrast these works with his landscapes which employ the same unifying brush mark and you can even smell the countryside itself. A remarkable painter and one even I, collect.

- Brian J. Turner, The Turner Gallery, Exeter, Devon

Jennings, Tracey

Whether it is the delicate pen, ink and watercolour drawings or her bold, powerful,acrylic canvases - I find Tracey Jennings work fresh and exciting. Her connections with music, both as a composer and performer, have influenced and given a unique quality and view point to her artwork. Jennings' paintings and drawings engage with the viewer allowing them to discover the forms and themes within. The intricacy and beauty of her flowing organic line work and her sensitive and powerful use of colour tell me that this is an exceptionally talented artist on the brink of something great.

- Mona Marnell, Glass Artist

The work of Tracey Jennings demonstrates a pioneering engagement with the painted landscape and environment. Deploying pattern as a transformative device, it examines natural phenomena. The viewer is immersed in a wholly satisfying colour-scape, simultaneously spatial, and yet owning the surface. Visual complexity rewards repeated viewing, making the works an appropriate investment for the private and commercial buyer. Jennings' artistic progress in recent years has resulted from experimentation and clear endeavour, and she remains one to watch.

-Thadian Pillai, Thadian Pillai Studio: Art Gardens Landscape, Chelmsford, Essex

Jones, Karen (BA)

I discovered Karen's work through the Chelmsford Arts Trail two years ago. I was drawn to the subject matter immediately and so decided to delve into the thought process that lay

behind this collection of work. Having now worked with Karen, it is apparent that her great sense of humour is mirrored in each piece of her very individual work. I have never come across another artist's work showing any similarities to Karen's. Although the work is based on serious stories and historical events, it never fails to make you smile.
- Soo Turner, Interior Angle, Chelmsford, Essex

Jordan, Maureen (SBA)

Maureen Jordan's exquisite flower, garden and landscape paintings are quintessentially English. She works mainly in pastel but also experiments with watercolour, acrylic and even gold leaf to create highly detailed and delicate pieces. By mixing vibrant colour and variegated textures, Maureen creates stunning effects of abundant foliage and a glowing profusion of flowers. Her larger sweeping landscapes of Provence lavender and sunflower fields contrast with the dappled light of the smaller container gardens. Pure colour - oranges, purples, greens, yellows and crimsons - give huge vitality and show an astonishing accomplishment of careful and precise pastel work. We always have a selection of Maureen Jordan's work for sale.
- Diana Holdsworth, Llewellyn Alexander (Fine Paintings) LTD, London

Maureen has an infectious enthusiasm for her art work, and this is portrayed through her paintings. Working with soft pastels, she creates stunning flower paintings that appear so lifelike one can almost smell the flowers depicted. Using vibrant colours, her work is greatly admired and highly sought after nationally and internationally. Maureen has also created a range of works which challenges the classical depiction of flower paintings. Bold backgrounds set off the brilliant colours of flowers; this challenges the conventionally depiction of flowers in art.
- Becky Munting, Buckenham Galleries, Southwold, Suffolk

Kendrick, Chris (BA Hons)

Chris Kendrick specialises in superbly painted still lifes in oil on canvas panel. His fascination with strong light falling on glass, pewter, copper and fabric against a rich darkly painted background has been influenced by the Dutch *Stilleven* painters of the 17th C and the Spanish Masters of still life. The Mediterranean table displaying tapas, ripe peppers, figs and tomatoes, with jars of olive oil and sweet balsamic vinegar are the fine ingredients of long summer repasts. Chris Kendrick addresses these timeless themes in a modern, dramatic and contemporary style that is highly appealing to collectors of figurative painting worldwide. We always have a selection of Chris Kendrick's work for sale.
- Diana Holdsworth, Llewellyn Alexander (Fine Paintings) LTD, London

Chris Kendrick's still life works have been constantly on show in the Workshop Gallery since 2006. They attract a lot of attention from visitors who frequently comment on the illusion of depth created in his compositions and the use of vivid colour. He has an eye for realistic detail and clarity in his work, which serve to act as a distillation of visual experience, literally holding up to the light qualities in objects and materials which for the most part are taken for granted in everyday life. His use of metallic objects – particularly copper – in some recent compositions has been especially praised and has opened up new areas of exploration in his work.
- Lee Smith, Norwich Frame Workshop, Norwich, Norfolk

Knowland, Eleonora (BA Hons)

Viewers of Eleonora Knowland's work will encounter gentle, curved, canvases which reflect the volume of East Anglia's landscape. These gentle landscapes are pieced with hand stitching, as precise as that of a surgeon. Folds are made, pulling the canvases to reveal - almost like a wound - something so bright and colourful. It is as if Eleonora wants us to remember a forgotten pleasure lying beneath her soft delicate pallet of oil colour. These moments of colour are often an emerging or retreating sun framed by the huge Suffolk vista over our heads, as she writes 'freezing fog rising from frozen water-meadows in front of burning sunsets'.
- Alice Wright, Digby Gallery at the Mercury Theatre, Colchester, Essex

Eleonora has developed a unique and exciting style of painting. Her curved canvases cross the border between sculpture and painting, and it is this which is integral to her work. Inspired by the surrounding landscapes, her work captures a precise time of the day (such as *0300 Spring*, or *0730 Winter*). Stitched lines and gaps in the canvas are now appearing more in her work, and these create a structure or form in each piece. Gentle gradation of delicate hues complement the undulating canvases, with sudden bursts of brilliant vibrant colour adding dynamism to each work.
- Becky Munting, Buckenham Galleries, Southwold, Suffolk

Lawrence, Tory

Tory Lawrence started painting in 1980. Since then her work has been shown in numerous exhibitions including Thomas Williams Fine Art, Angela Flowers, Royal Academy Summer Exhibition, The Royal College of Art and the Arnolfini Gallery. In 2008 Lawrence moved from Berkshire to Suffolk, since when she has enjoyed discovering some of the secrets of this historic landscape, to which she has responded and has created many intense and beautiful oil paintings. She is a glowing, yet sensitive colourist. Art critic Andrew Lambirth writes, 'Lawrence builds up her paintings with strong touches of paint, marks made with conviction, resulting in the most gloriously animated surfaces. She draws thinly and expressively with the brush or pallet knife, or lays in the impasto with lively textures.'
- Richard Cobbold, Cobbold and Judd, Hintlesham, Suffolk

Levin, Gill (FRSA)

Gill continues to pursue her dual career of artist and jazz musician, and it could be said that her painting echoes the sounds and harmonies of her music within a visual form. Themes within her paintings are two-fold. With her structural images of decaying buildings, piers and warehouses, line and perspective determine the composition, whilst her landscapes with grasses, although structurally strong, possess a more abstract and dream like quality. She has been painting for over sixty years and her work continues to excite and stimulate the viewer.
- Caryl Challis, Harleston Gallery, Harleston, Norfolk

Gill Levin has two approaches to her painting - one factual, one imaginary. Her earlier work showed her fascination for industrial landscapes, including such monumentous structures as power stations, factories, cranes and piers. Of late, it is almost as if her 'jazz mind' has come to the fore, whereby the absence of factual details allows Gill to express herself much more broadly and freely. She concerns herself more with colours and textures within spaces rather than with objects themselves, allowing herself a great deal of 'artist's licence' in much of what she paints. Above all, the works possess a spontaneity where the pigment seemingly

flows from the brush onto board, canvas or paper. Rather like a jazz composition, the start and end results are pre-defined, but it is the journey from one to the other that can be as long and convoluted as the artist wishes to make it. Sit back, absorb and enjoy!
- Jo Banthorpe, The John Russell Contemporary Art Gallery, Ipswich, Suffolk

Lomas, Alyson (BA Hons)

New to my gallery, I think I can best describe Alyson's work as spontaneous. Despite great authority as an artist, she enjoys the process of letting the paint take its own course and form. This, combined with almost decadent use of colour at times and just enough figurative detail, gives the work real vitality and structure. I particularly like the work in diptych or triptych form where this natural approach achieves a kind of rhythm over a given number of pictures. Alyson's work will appeal to a wide audience who enjoy the visual impact of her style.
- Geoff Witts, RE+new, Woodbridge, Suffolk

Alyson's work is characterised by her use of bright and vibrant acrylic paints. Brilliant reds, gold, purple, and yellow contrast against heavy black, or purples and green compete to get the upper hand on a canvas. Her use of observational representation, combined with memories, of landscapes create interesting and sometimes challenging images. Recently she has started to introduce buildings which nestle in semi abstract fields. Through her work she tells a story of landscapes she has observed, yet enables the spectator to form their own view, thus involving them within the work fully.
- Becky Munting, Buckenham Galleries, Southwold, Suffolk

McCabe, Ruth

Ruth's pictures are very much about colour and texture. She creates a close up view of objects that almost seem to be in 3D, whilst also producing dramatic landscapes that really show differences in light and colour. With Ruth's more abstract pictures, the attention of the viewer is focused on the shapes and colour as they ponder on the message that the artist sends. The result of looking at her pictures seems to leave the viewer in a brighter mood and they leave the Gallery with a smile on their faces.
-Verena Daniels and Pat Todd, Reunion Gallery, Felixstowe, Suffolk

Inspired by walking through the Suffolk countryside, Ruth creates striking and textural pieces of art. Some of her landscape scenes are heavily textured: the ploughed fields and the water held in the furrows evoke a strong sense of time and place. In contrast, she also creates more abstract landscapes. Patterns of highly coloured grids represent the farm land you are familiar with. Again, Ruth's work develops into another style. Using predominantly shades of blue, Ruth blends and marks the paint with her hands, building up layers to create the feeling of encaustic medium rather than oils. She depicts boats left beached on the shore line. Entrails of colour lead the eye into the distance representing the retreating water. Sheep stand firmly, their rotund forms perched on thin legs, but somehow their weighty quality gives a comfort to the naïve image.
- Becky Munting, Buckenham Galleries, Southwold, Suffolk

McKechnie, Christine (NDD)

Christine McKechnie is a unique artist with the skill of a master craftsman and the imagination of an inventive artist. Her talent and energy work in tandem. She is never happier than when immersed in her own artwork, manicuring her beautiful garden and preparing culinary feasts for at least 25 people, all at the same time. Christine's effortless renditions, impeccable layering, coupled with the perfect tonality of her compositions make her work highly prized with numerous collectors.
- Doug Patterson, Artist

Christine is a new artist to Buckenham Galleries and has exhibited only once. Her work is exceptional in the quality of her collage, one has to look hard to realise the pieces are not paintings or drawing. Making images and scenes using tiny scraps of paper, her talent is remarkable. Although collage is often understated as an artistic medium, Christine takes it to another dimension.
- Becky Munting, Buckenham Galleries, Southwold, Suffolk

Morris, David (MA)

In 2008 David Morris received the Professional Photographer of the Year award for his remarkable and deeply atmospheric work. His commitment to photography is evident from the quality and sincerity of his images. He likes to work in series, and has produced moving portfolios of bar life, artisans' workshops, European cities and an Oxfordshire brewery. Landscape photography forms a major part of his work, and David is willing to go to extremes of discomfort to capture the magic of his subject, seeking the right shot at the right moment, whatever the weather, whatever the time of day or night. I regard David's work very highly: he is one of a small group of photographers that we have selected to exhibit at Bircham Gallery.
Chris Harrison, Bircham Gallery, Holt, Norfolk

On entering the gallery for the first time new visitors stop in their tracks when they see David Morris' photographs on the wall and are transfixed by the sheer quality and impact of his images. Regular visitors head eagerly to his work to see familiar views and landmarks in a completely unique light through his lens. Whether it is the pin-sharp monochrome images of Cromer pier, the brooding skies and powerful waves of the Norfolk coast, the tranquil rivers of the Broads, the atmospheric and evocative bar images in Milan or the striking vibrant colours of Normandy beach huts that catch their eye they all agree that his images are, quite simply, stunning.
- Kate Gale, The Garden House Gallery, Cromer, Norfolk

Nason, Tolly

A hundred words is not enough space to do justice to the impact of the work of Tolly Nason. When I first saw it I, quite literally, did a double-take. Tolly's work is popular with 'serious' collectors and the more casual but discerning purchasers of art, alike. Tolly has trained with some of the world's greats in the field of glass-making. Her work is beginning to be found in major public collections around the globe. Why? Her craftsmanship is impeccable. Her vision is highly original. Not just original but extremely beautiful, colourful, lively and life-enhancing are all adjectives that apply. And, into the bargain, her work represents fantastic value for money. At Sea Pictures Gallery we always ensure that we have some of her work in stock.
- Dr Alaric Pugh, Sea Pictures Gallery, Clare, Suffolk

Tolly Nason is one of the latest artists to join Buckenham Galleries. Working in the ancient method of pate de verre, Tolly creates extremely fine and delicate glass forms. Described as 'paper-like' or looking like 'sugar, these wondrous forms are her emotional response to some-

thing she has seen. Her interest in natural history is reflected in her work, whether through her small *Nauticals* and *Whimsicals* or through her striking larger works. It was the larger pieces, where Tolly recreated 14 different shapes of finch beaks, 20 times their original size, that Tolly taught herself a lot about her art, and each new project challenges her further. Delightfully refreshing, her work retains a delicate beauty.
- Becky Munting of Buckenham Galleries, Southwold, Suffolk

Nason, Elaine

Elaine Nason's paintings and prints, shown at the Gallery on a regular basis, deal with themes considered primarily feminine – works focussing on domestic incidents and predominately incorporating the human figure. Coupled with her love of pattern and form, her work reflects the expertise of the accomplished draughtswoman that she is. Subject matter and ideas from her student years continue to be reworked and developed in a fresh and exciting way.
- Caryl Challis, Harleston Gallery, Harleston, Norfolk

Elaine Nason is a Suffolk-based painter and printmaker who makes gentle, domestic pictures: still lifes or more often figures, quietly sitting, drawing or being drawn, or involved in the 'homely virtues' of washing and ironing, cooking or sewing. But the quiet images of subtle colour and discreet pattern also manage to contain an unusual range of feeling, often a wistful sadness mixed with an unexpected humour: girls choosing dresses from a rail are particularly delightful; or the figures on a railway bridge, converging in one picture and passing in another, are loaded with a sad, silent mystery but they still raise a smile or even a laugh.
- Penny Hughes-Stanton, North House Gallery, Manningtree, Essex

Newcomb, Tessa (BA Hons)

We have been showing Tessa Newcomb's delicate and lyrical paintings for a number of years. At first sight her paintings seem rooted in her native Suffolk and Norfolk countryside. However, through her unique sense of design and colour and an instinctive willingness to depart from the particular, they transport us into the elliptical and universal realm of poetry. At her best, she produces works that are both charming and decorative, that embody the spirit of place, but that still leave room for the viewer's imagination to discover, or invent, narratives of his or her own.
- Piers Feetham, Piers Feetham Gallery, London

Tessa Newcomb has been exhibiting at the Cork Brick Gallery since we opened in 1990. In this time we have watched, with affection, as she has become an acclaimed artist. The beautifully-written book by Philip Vann, illustrating some of her extensive body of work, has helped her to appeal to an even greater audience. Tessa's work is so well observed, capturing life and nature in the raw with an view that we lesser mortals miss until we are reminded by Tessa's inspiring pictures. Tessa's work is always available in the Gallery, as are signed copies of her book.
- Ken Skipper, Cork Brick Gallery, Bungay, Suffolk

Newson, Chris

I often wonder how much an artist's life experiences are reflected in their work. If you look at Chris Newson's work then yes, they are. Chris's paintings are very emotive, strong and full of colour and texture, truly three-dimensional. They show the emotion he went through following a close bereavement, the love for his wife Heidi and her work as a teacher. Other paintings show his relationship with Suffolk, golden fields and blue skies and the sometimes stormy coast, but all with Chris's inimitable use of textured paint. You can almost hear the corn rustle. An exciting artist who deserves wider appreciation, which he no doubt will receive from his upcoming exhibitions.
- The Old Printworks Gallery, Saxmundham, Suffolk

It has to be said that Chris Newson's work can be both raw and unpredictable. Painting with generous amounts of of oil, Chris at times depicts tortured characters with a jewel-like mix of colour associated with religious icons; the passion, intensity and anger being a reflection of his difficult past. But then the mood changes and you receive three small calm studies of a Suffolk landscape, so real and almost sculpted that you want to touch and connect with them. This man has got many stories to tell and it's worth keeping an eye open for his latest offerings.
- Geoff Witts, RE+new, Woodbridge, Suffolk

Nickerson, Dee

Every picture tells a story and, I believe, is in some way part autobiographical. Dee's main focus is on the female figure within a landscape, or women involved in simple solitary pursuits within the home. Dee could be classified as a 'naïve' painter – expressing innocence and credulity; ingenious. The truth is that her work is truly unique.
- Caryl Challis, Harleston Gallery, Harleston, Norfolk

At Cork Brick Gallery we are proud to have been the first gallery to exhibit Dee's paintings, for over 10 years now! Dee's pictures are distinctive in their style. Using chalk pastels and acrylics, her ladies stand, sit or busy themselves in the day to day routines of life. Dee likes to tell a story in her pictures, influenced by the weather, the seasons and the patterns and colours of nature, her landscape paintings, often from memory, have a naive quality. One of my favourite paintings is of a farm scene trying to capture every thing on the farm, not always to scale or correct perspective but like all her pictures it works, inspiring the imagination with a curious of glimpse of everyday life.
- Ken Skipper, Cork Brick Gallery, Bungay, Suffolk

Page, David

David Page has been painting since his parents gave him oil paints when he was 12. After a spell of teaching he was able to concentrate on his painting in a full time capacity, firstly in Greece and St. Ives, and for the last twenty years on the Norfolk Suffolk border. Predominately a landscape painter of his immediate locality, his work, whilst portraying the mood of this lovely part of the Waveney Valley, also acts as an important record of the social history of the area, documenting changes in the rural and built environment.
- Caryl Challis, Harleston Gallery, Harleston, Norfolk

Payne, Michelle

I was first introduced to Michelle Payne by my plastic surgeon, Elaine Sassoon, shortly following my mastectomy and breast reconstruction. She had become involved with the *Boudica* project and was subsequently asked to head the *Woman Reconstructed* project. Michelle has an amazing passion for her body casting and cast the women's breasts and torsos for the project with fantastic sensitivity and great compassion. We had all been affected

Opinions

by breast cancer and undergone radical life-saving mastectomies and incredible breast re-constructions. Michelle's life casts are so amazing and capture the life of the person she is casting. Mine will forever have pride of place on my wall as a memory of my precious life and the journey I have been through, and my cast was recently featured on the front of the fundraising calendar for breast cancer. She is truly a remarkable artist who has gone from strength to strength with both her work and her thriving business.
- Anna Beckingham, Keeping Abreast

Michelle Payne is one of the few elite lifecasters in the UK, and a member of The association of Lifecasters International. Michelle has her own artistic style - sculptural, layered works, building up layers on the canvas capturing the mood, interest and atmosphere of the surroundings. Very much in demand for her canvases and artwork, that style and attitude to her artwork steeps over into her lifecasting work. Her casts have an unique application and method that is both tactile and sculptural in its approach. Capturing the human form of her sitter in their beauty and imperfections, her signature style embodies the spirit and personality of the sitter, alongside adventurous and creative paint finishes and embellishments that finish each piece as a work of art.
- Christine Soanes, The Upstairs Gallery (Norfolk), Great Yarmouth, Norfolk

Plummer, Gillian (PhD)

Gillian's masterful use of the macro lens allows her to capture detail in a sensational way, bringing the viewer so close to the subject that the effect produced is of seeing anew those flowers and plants we may take for granted day-to-day. Her work is incredibly exciting to the senses as it assaults them with a realisation of just how beautiful the natural world we live in is. It has been an exciting time for Gillian recently – winning the RHS 'Edible' category in their Photographic Competition, being a finalist at the 'International Garden Photographer Awards' and exhibiting at Kew Gardens, all evidence of her increasingly prominent role in the world of Botanical Photography and Fine Art Photography more widely.
- Anick Purmessur, Gallery Violet, www.galleryviolet.com

Porteous-Butler, David

When you look at one of David's paintings you feel you are there. With his seascapes you can hear the sea, feel the wind and smell the fresh clean air around you. When he paints the bright and colourful Mediterranean scenes you are one of the people sitting in the café or watching the boats in warm, picturesque harbours or just enjoying the sun-drenched beaches. He achieves such wonderful results because he has a passion for the vitality of the landscape and the changing light around him. He also believes that drawing and draughtsmanship are a vital part of the artist's craft. David is truly a protégé of the great Sir Kyffin Williams R.A. who was his mentor and friend.
- Wren Gallery, Burford, Oxford

David's work conveys a strong sense of atmosphere and light. With the brilliant, sometimes blinding, light of the Mediterranean countries, one feels the heat of the day in the painting and the emotion that comes with the moment. Bold use of colour and very skilled pallet knife technique give rise to strong textural work, which can only be truly appreciated by seeing the original. Whether depicting strong sunlight or a grey wet day, his work shows the beauties of life, his figures often portraying an intimate moment of time.
- John Allen, Mandell's Gallery, Norwich, Norfolk

David produces strong, highly accomplished landscape and figurative paintings in oil. The style is impressionistic, made more so by his use of thick paint and the palette knife to achieve a rich impasto effect that brings the light and his subject matter to life. Devotees of the work of the late Sir Kyffin Williams will recognise the influence of this important and well-loved artist in David's work, which is perhaps unsurprising since David studied under him before attending the Royal College of Art and remained close to him right until his death in 2006. David's paintings are very collectable, his work appeals to young and old alike and his reputation is growing rapidly. PB, as he signs himself, is definitely a name to look out for.
- Enid Lawson Gallery, London

Pretty, Dawn

I have previously commented that to connect with a subject and be transported by what is happening on the paper or canvas, is one of the greatest pleasures. Dawn's figurative work expresses this sense, celebrating the human form, enhancing colour and accentuating life. From splashing out in batik seascapes, carefree and colourfully bold, to sensitive oil paintings of people and places.
- Mary Gundry, The Little Gallery, Halesworth, Suffolk

Reay, John (BA)

There are artists who make a lot of noise about what they do, others who quietly beaver away with humility and professionalism, gaining a loyal band of supporters. Among the latter group I place John Reay, an acknowledged master of the modern East Anglian school. His studies included Norwich School of Art, after which he chose to settle in the region that has become important to his work. John's paintings and pastels are notable for their enticing light and colour effects. I think of him primarily as a painter of beach scenes, but his unique way of depicting people engrossed in innocent outdoor activities has a wider application. His solo and mixed show appearances have included some of the most distinguished London and provincial galleries.
- David Buckman, Writer and Journalist

John has been exhibiting at the Ferini Art Gallery from its earliest days. The visitor will often recognise in his work through the splendour of light and texture, form and composition, a local scene. But whilst seeing that the figures, often mother and child, are clearly contemporary and in a contemporary setting, there is a timelessness and weight to the experience of looking. John's pictures communicate a sense of the past in the present, of emotions and qualities beyond the visual. The figures have stature, calmness and tenderness, reminding us of the delicate inter-relationship of people to landscape and vice versa.
- Paul Hobbs & Michaela Barber, Ferini Art Gallery, Pakefield, Suffolk

Renowned for his monumental figures, John continues to develop this theme. A figure reclining on a sofa with the ever-present influence of the Suffolk coast in the background, or a mother figure holding a new born baby. The difference is the choice of palette.Though the strong fragmented style and dabs of colour are still present, there are stronger colours emerging, almost like a new-found confidence. A strong sense of family and lasting are conveyed through his work.
- Becky Munting of Buckenham Galleries, Southwold, Suffolk

Reeder, Carolyn (BA)

Carolyn is a prolific artist whose work has grown out of a dedicated crafts base to demonstrate consistent creativity and awareness of colour and form. Whether in two or three dimensions, Carolyn's work often surprises the viewer with a fresh look and inventiveness in a range of materials and mediums from coloured glass and paintings to textured clays. Her sculptures and pottery show an intense awareness of form and space with sensitivity to material and an inherent demonstration of the material's roots in earthiness, sensuality and longevity. Whether in her own gallery or her classes, Carolyn provides opportunities for others to create and develop their work.

- Paul Hobbs & Michaela Barber, Ferini Art Gallery, Pakefield, Suffolk

Schumann, Andrew

Andrew Schumann is a very cerebral artist. His work is stunning to look at, visually striking and stimulating, and interesting. But the work incorporates concepts that are not always immediately obvious, ranging from the intellectual to the emotional, from mathematical ideas to the mystery of life, and observations on the nature of our universe. It is worth seeking out the artist's own words of illumination. But in the end the works speak directly to the listening viewer.

- Liz Falconbridge, King's Lynn Arts Centre, King's Lynn, Norfolk

Slattery, Nicola (BA Hons)

Nicola expresses herself both through painting in acrylics and dry point prints. The subjects are fanciful and idiosyncratic a source of an individual imagination. Will the girl with the net catch the dove? What is the girl thinking of with her reflection looking out from the pond? Her dry point prints exquisitely engraved on a Perspex sheet printed and hand coloured are smaller but none the less as evocative and curious as the paintings. Living locally, it is always exciting to see Nicola's new productions and we always have a selection of her work in stock.

- Ken Skipper, Cork Brick Gallery, Bungay, Suffolk

Smith, Beka

Beka Smith is one of the finest portrait painters I have seen come through my gallery. Her exquisitely detailed brushwork shows her talent which is a rarity in itself these days. Her break away into the alter ego series shows her capability of capturing fascinating imagery from many different angles and each one in the series reveals a sense of humour which is a great thing to be able to convey in art. All in all, her talent alongside her social charisma enables her to be one of the most communicative artists I represent.

- Jolyon Mason, Storm Fine Arts, Burnham Market, Norfolk

Spicer, Mary

Working in the beautiful Waveney valley, Mary takes her inspiration from the Suffolk landscape. Big skies and big fields make for big pictures and in these Mary excels. Acrylic, texture gel and Indian ink build up to a huge freshly ploughed field you can almost smell, or the vibrant yellow rape fields contrasted with a red barn roof in the distance. Mary's smaller paintings retain her passion for nature but with a more delicate touch often built up with scraps of paper to form a collage that gives a three-dimensional depth to the painting.

- Ken Skipper, Cork Brick Gallery, Bungay, Suffolk

Mary Spicer draws our attention to the changes that are brought about by light on the landscape. She wants to hold onto the fleeting and magical moments that barely register as being particularly important - we dismiss them from our minds because they do not conform to our idea of the scenic or romantic landscape. Working from her studio at her Norfolk home, the Artist finds herself surrounded by working fields that have a raw and primitive energy about them - they translate into visually exciting marks whilst the passing of time is represented by the layering and scraping back of paint in order to reveal the colours of the previous season.

- Jo Banthorpe, The John Russell Contemporary Art Gallery, Ipswich, Suffolk

Stebbing, Louise (BA Hons)

The work of Louise Stebbing shows a great affection for the English rural landscape. The essence of the fenlands -flat open fields, low horizons and country lanes -are beautifully captured in her vibrant prints. Louise employs the traditional method of the reduction linocut, which is seen rarely today as it is so labour intensive, but is a perfect fit to her subject matter and gives it a quality of timelessness. Her accomplished technical skills are combined with a heightened sense of colour that lifts her work above the mundane and creates a strong style that is instantly recognisable.

- Richard Hatfield, Ropewalk Contemporary Art & Craft, Barton Upon Humber,
* North Lincolnshire*

Surie, Honor (MA)

Honor acknowledges the strong influence that living on the Suffolk coast has had on her work. It is this feel for the place and the substance of her subject that forms a strong attraction to the work for people who know the area. With Honor's paintings and sculptures the medium and the subject are always in close harmony. Her life long interest in ceramics and her experience in graphic design and commercial art combine to ensure that her work always has a strong compositional focus. It's hard to distil any single aspect of her work that makes it enduringly attractive. The secret is in the combination of all the parts, including the subtle use of colour and texture which allows the viewer to feel and experience the subject and breathe the Suffolk air.

- Pat Todd, Reunion Gallery, Felixstowe, Suffolk

Well known originally for her ceramic work, Honor has turned her attention to painting in the last few years. Using acrylic in subtle muted colours, she depicts the Suffolk landscape with much authority and sensitivity. The work can be very realistic, particularly in the case of capturing light and water, but then Honor will slip into abstraction when you least expect it. Whether you are new to the charm of Suffolk or want to recall familiar landscapes, this artist's ongoing study of the area is a real and valuable reminder for us all.

- Geoff Witts, RE+new, Woodbridge, Suffolk

Honor's work at the gallery has changed from ceramics to acrylic paintings. Interestingly, her routes in ceramics do show in her paintings. Texture plays a strong part in her work. The surface of the canvas is often quite heavily scratched and marked. Her semi-abstract landscapes inspired by the Suffolk coast and countryside, beautifully rendered, are proving to be highly collectable. Please note we do not have her work at the gallery at present (July 2010).

- Becky Munting, Buckenham Galleries, Southwold, Suffolk

Opinions

Teather, Will

Will Teather is inspired by Vaudeville and black and white films. Magical realism and a collage of highbred themes bring together subjects that intrigue and leave the viewer wanting to know more.

- John Allen, Mandell's Gallery, Norwich, Norfolk

Tidman, Brüer (ARCA)

Brüer, a serious contender in contemporary art since the sixties, studied at the Royal College of Art (1961-64); his seductive colour and expressive drawing securing his place among disciples of modernism. The figure – figure in interior – his leading motif, depicts his lovers, past, present. Often erotic, always tender, one is not fixed on the subject but thrilled by the painting as a whole; his poignant drawing progressively pared, revealing the impact of colour. Brüer, brought up in Great Yarmouth, is one of the leading painters of East Anglia also exhibiting in London and abroad with work in collections including Norwich Castle Museum.

- Edna Mirecka, Chappel Galleries, Chappel, Essex

Tournay Godfrey, Delia (BA Hons)

Delia's oil paintings explore the landscape in a highly distinctive way and are appreciated for their combination of contemporary composition with a gorgeously muted palette of colours. Expanses of wall, pavement, sea or sky allow for large blocks of pure colour to fill large areas of the composition, creating a fresh, two-dimensional feel to these works. It is this and her use of figures within the landscape that make Delia's paintings so appealing. Be it walkers on a path through the reeds, shoppers intent and bustling on a crowded high street, or most powerfully perhaps, a lone figure at the edge of the sea at Aldeburgh – these wonderfully observed characters are anonymous enough for any viewer to relate to.

- Keri Johnston, Snape Maltings, Snape, Suffolk

Whether a stormy seascape, Italian landscape or simple flower studies, Delia's painting possesses calm, poetic observation coupled with sensitive technique. Attending Suffolk College as an adult, Delia's painting has an uncomplicated quality with enviable light, sure brushwork; a clear vision cleanly painted in close tones. Ken Back, deceased, became her mentor; the honesty and dedication he adhered to speaks volumes in her paintings. She is known for her small paintings of the Suffolk coast: figures capturing attitude and atmosphere; tiny people on a beach against a luminous sky, intensely felt. Delia is moving on, exploring large works emphasising her cool design and subtle palette.

- Edna Mirecka, Chappel Galleries, Chappel, Essex

Trim, Jonathan

Jonathan's atmospheric landscapes, expertly capture both the beauty of light and water in a variety of locations and the sense of emotion from being present in the moment. He possesses an outstanding ability to draw the viewer into his paintings and transport them to that place and time. Jonathan paints either on location or from his extensive sketch books and through his use of mixed media he produces work which is both powerful in colour and texture and rich in personal response.

- Alan Stratford, A2 Gallery, Wells, Somerset

Jonathan has been exhibiting at Buckenham Galleries for a number of years, and over this period of time his work has evolved and developed considerably. Initially he was working in a purely abstract style, but has now moved to expressionist landscape painting. However, it is still possible to see his abstract roots in his work. Jonathan captures a freshness and a vitality in his landscapes. The rivers, estuaries and low-lying wetlands in the surrounding landscape provide him with a constant source of inspiration. By building up layers of paint and introducing texture with sand and grit, he creates a depth to each piece. The texture heightens the overall effect of the work. Splashes of colour work to produce the feeling of lush reedbeds, or overhanging trees, or the white flash of sunlight on the surface of the water.

- Becky Munting, Buckenham Galleries, Southwold, Suffolk

Tyson, Deanna (BA, RSA)

Deanna Tyson's work can be awesome. Her inspiration comes from many cultures, though the Orient and Africa are clearly strong influences. Often in the form of a kimono, Deanna's 'honeytraps' draw us in with their beauty, then the detail of her stitched fabrics hits us with powerful words and images she wants us to consider. Injustice, bigotry, greed, cruelty and other human traits that anger her are her subject matter, her targets; soft, beautiful materials and bright colours are her palette.

- Chris Williams, Williams Art, Cambridge

Political statements and comments conveyed via handmade and painted Kimonos. Designed to shock, sometimes enrage, definitely designed to encourage discussion and maybe exploration of a theme. Multi talented as an artist, Deanna combines textiles and painting. Inventive in nature and naturally inquisitive, Deanna's natural enthusiasm is conveyed through her art. Please note we do not have any of her work in the gallery at present (July 2010).

- Becky Munting, Buckenham Galleries, Southwold, Suffolk

Ward, Mark (BA Hons)

Mark has been a Gallery artist at the Ferini Art Gallery since being seen in the Suffolk Open Studio brochure. His work, often of a large scale, literally brings into the Gallery new worlds to entice and intrigue the viewer. They look real, but then they are painted from models Mark has constructed. They feel exotic, but then Mark has travelled wide and is familiar with Africa. The visitor is at once carried into the enchanted, inspired parallel world by the colour and vibrance of pattern and design that exudes from the wall. Are they painted or could the animals and birds actually pop out from the canvas and move?

- Paul Hobbs & Michaela Barber, Ferini Art Gallery, Pakefield, Suffolk

Mark's works are bright, vivacious, colourful and three-dimensional in their approach; an inside world of characters that have journeys throughout the canvases, with each adventure being recorded alongside the flora and fauna from Ward's garden. Paper characters, East African influences and a variety of props lit, give the 3D appeal that is so popular worldwide, with Mark's works being shown both over the UK and in international galleries such as The Agora Gallery, New York and Italy's Galleria De Marchi. Mark Ward's works are instantaneously recognisable, which makes his canvases an investable collectable purchase in the arts world and to a vast collective market of our clients.

- Michelle Payne, Upstairs Gallery Beccles, Suffolk

Westwood, Sandi

No matter how busy Sandi makes her images - and some are extraordinarily busy, filled with a hundred or more flying, swooping, landing, perching birds - there remains an order and a stillness within each piece. When she concerts her talents to a single subject she attains a kind of 'Redon'-like etherial quality which conveys a beautiful golden silence. Sandi's attention to detail is stunning and her work is always graceful and wonderfully peaceful in quality.
- Caroline Richmond & David Burton, Art-next-the-Sea, Wells-next-the-Sea, Norfolk

Whelan, Brian

The enjoyable thing about showing the paintings of Brian Whelan is that they never cease to illicit a response from our clients; the highly-coloured mixed media paintings of urban landscapes and his depiction of religious story telling are thought-provoking and a feast for the eye. Contradictory perspectives, similar to a medieval painting, are always a talking point. Many of the images challenge the intellect. *The Times* calls him 'A theologically provocative maverick artist', and that really does sum up his paintings. As a Gallery, it is important that your clients are not underwhelmed when they come to visit and Brian's work certainly is not underwhelming. 'This is very strong art, not for aesthetic whimps.' Sister Wendy Beckett, Art Critic.
- Russell Boulter & Clare Walker, Doric Arts, Holt, Norfolk

White, Tony

Visitors to The Riverslade Gallery are drawn to Tony White's work and often spend some time discussing it with their companions and the Gallery staff. The bold colours and graphic shapes in Tony's work attract immediate attention, but his prints and paintings also draw the viewer in to look beyond the obvious. His work tends to invoke an emotional response, with visitors responding to the 'hidden' elements in the work and intrigued by what they personally see in the juxtaposition of shapes and colours. One of Tony's most popular prints with our visitors is his local view of Saffron Walden, although even this fairly representational work has depths to be explored.
- Carole Gray, The Riverslade Gallery, Saffron Walden, Essex

Wurr, Jayne

On my first encounter with Jayne's work I was taken in by the trompe l'oeil artist. A cook's apron hanging on the wall on closer inspection was found to be made of a myriad of tiny coloured tiles. Jayne's former vocation as a textile designer is reflected in her mosaics. Her feel for fabric, its texture and how it folds make her mosaics come alive. Food is another of Jayne's inspirations; appetising cakes and bowls of fruit would look great decorating any kitchen. Jayne's home is a delight for anyone interested in mosaic, anything with a flat surface is decorated with colourful mosaic.
- Ken Skipper, Cork Brick Gallery, Bungay, Suffolk

Galleries

A2 Gallery
78 High Street
Wells
Somerset BA5 2AJ
Tel: 01749 678482
www.a2gallery.co.uk
Jonathan Trim

A Picture of Norfolk
31 Luscombe Way
Rackheath
Norwich
Norfolk NR13 6SS
Tel: 01603 722950
www.apictureofnorfolk.com
Gill Baguley

Abel Arts
Raveningham Centre
Beccles Road
Raveningham
Norwich
Norfolk NR14 6NU
Tel: 01508 548688
Doreen Abel
Carolyn Reeder

Aldeburgh Gallery
143 High Street
Aldeburgh
Suffolk IP15 5AN
Tel: 01728 454168
www.aldeburghartsgallery.co.uk
Theronda Hoffman

Alexander Gallery
7 East Street
Brighton
East Sussex BN1 1HP
Tel: 01273 321694
www.thealxendergallery.co.uk
Pam Schomberg

Appleyard Gallery, The
14 Appleyard
Holt
Norfolk NR25 6AR
Tel: 01263 712315
www.theappleyardgallery.co.uk

Ruth McCabe
Jonathan Trim

Arna Farrington Gallery
High Street
Thorpe-le-Soken
Essex CO16 0EA
Tel: 01255 862355
www.arnaandfarrington.co.uk
Dawn Hall

Art 18/21
14 Tombland
Norwich
Norfolk NR3 1HF
Tel: 01603 763345
www.art1821.com
Peter Baldwin
Andrew Schumann
Will Teather
Mark Ward

Art-next-the-Sea
26 Staithe Street
Wells-next-the-Sea
Norfolk NE23 1AF
Tel: 01328 710722
www.artnextthesea.co.uk
Gill Baguley
Sandi Westwood

The Assembly House
Theatre Street
Norwich
Norfolk NR2 1RQ
Tel: 01603 626402
www.assemblyhousenorwich.co.uk
Will Teather

The Back2theWall Gallery
The Old Customs House
The Quay
Burnham-on-Crouch
Essex CM0 8AS
Tel: 01621 786713
www.back2thewall.co.uk
Jonathan Trim

Beecroft Art Gallery
Westcliff-on-Sea
Essex SS0 7RA
Tel: 01702 347418
www.beecroft-art-gallery.co.uk
Christian Figg

Big Blue Sky
Warham Road
Wells-next-the-Sea
Norfolk NR23 1QA
Tel: 01328 712023
www.bigbluesky.uk
Kit Wade

The Bircham Gallery
14 Market Place
Holt
Norfolk NR25 6BW
Tel: 01263 713312
www.birchamgallery.co.uk
James Dodds
David Morris

The British Museum
Great Russell Street
London WC1B 3DG
Tel: 020 73238000
www.britishmuseum.org
Akiko Fujikawa

Buckenham Galleries
81 High Street
Southwold
Suffolk IP18 6DS
Tel: 01502 725418
www.buckenham-galleries.co.uk
Alyson Lomas
Doreen Abel
Claire Louise Dowson
Christian Figg
Maureen Jordan
Eleonora Knowland
Ruth McCabe
Christine McKechnie
Tolly Nason
Dawn Pretty
John Reay
Honor Surie

Jonathan Trim
Deanna Tyson

Cambridge Contemporary Art
6 Trinity Street
Cambridge CB2 1SU
Tel: 01223 324222
www.cambridgegallery.co.uk
Nicola Slattery

Caxton Books & Fine Art
37 Connaught Avenue
Frinton-on-Sea
Essex CO13 9PN
Tel: 01255 851505
Dawn Hall

Cecil Higgs Art Gallery
Castle Lane
Bedford MK 40 3RP
www.bedford.gov.uk
01234 211222
Theronda Hoffman

Cecilia Colman Gallery
67 St John's Wood
High Street
London NU8 7NL
Tel: 020 77220686
www.ceciliacolmangallery.com
Pam Schomberg

Chappel Galleries
15 Colchester Road
Chappel
Essex CO6 2DE
Tel: 01206 240326
www.chappelgalleries.co.uk
Brüer Tidman
Delia Tournay-Godfrey

Chelmsford Museum
Oaklands Park
Moulsham Street
Chelmsford
Essex CM2 9AQ
www.chelmsford.gov.uk
Akiko Fujikawa

Chimney Mill Galleries
West Stow
Bury St Edmunds
Suffolk IP28 6ER
Tel: 01284 728234
http://chimney.easearch.info
Lyn Aylward
Maz Jackson

Christchurch Mansion
Soane Street
Ipwich
Suffolk IP4 2BE
Tel: 01473 433544
Maggi Hambling

Cobbold & Judd
Hintlesham Hall
George Street
Hintlesham
Suffolk IP8 3NS
Tel: 01206 263565/ 01473 652334
www.hintleshamhall.com
Maz Jackson
Tory Lawrence

Cork Brick Gallery
6 Earsham Street
Bungay
Suffolk NR35 1AG
Tel: 01986 894873
www.bungay-suffolk.co.uk/cork-bricks
Noelle Francis
Jane German
Tessa Newcomb
Dee Nickerson
Nicola Slattery
Mary Spicer
Jayne Wurr

Crane Kalman Gallery
178 Brompton Road
London SW3 1HQ
Tel:020 7584 7566
www.cranekalman.com
Tessa Newcomb

Crome Gallery & Frame Makers
34 Elm Hill
Norwich
Norfolk NR3 1HG
Tel: 01603 622827
www.cromegallery.co.uk
Brian Whelan

The Cut Arts Centre
8 New Cut
Halesworth
Suffolk IP19 8BY
Tel: 01986 873285
www.newcut.org
Jane German

The Darryl Nantais Gallery
59 High Street
Linton
Cambridge CB21 4HS
Tel: 01223 891289
www.nantais-gallery.co.uk
Tony White

Digby Gallery
Mercury Theatre
Balkerne Gate
Colchester
Essex CO1 1PT
Tel: 01206 577006
www.mercurytheatre.co.uk
Eleonora Knowland

Doric Arts
4 Albert Street
Holt
Norfolk NR25 6HX
Tel: 01263 711084
www.doricart.com
Lyn Aylward
Maz Jackson
Brian Whelan

Enid Lawson Gallery
11 New Cavendish Street
London W1G 9UG
Tel: 0207 9353033
www.enidlawsongallery.co.uk
David Porteous-Butler

Galleries

Ferini Art Gallery
27 - 29 All Saints Road
Pakefield
Lowestoft
Suffolk NR33 0JL
Tel: 01502 562222
www.feriniartgallery.co.uk/
Doreen Abel
Jamie Andrews
Claire Louise Dowson
Douglas Farthing
John Reay
Carolyn Reeder
Mark Ward

Firstsite Contemporary Art
4 - 6 Wyre Street
Colchester
Essex CO1 1LN
Tel: 01206 577067
www.firstsite.uk.net
Robert Priseman

The Fitzwilliam Museum
Trumpington Street
Nr Peter House
Cambridge CB2 1RB
Tel: 01223 332900
www.fitzmuseum.cam.ac.uk
Tom de Freston
Maggi Hambling

The Frame Workshop and Gallery
22 St Nicholas Street
Ipswich
Suffolk IP1 1TS
Tel: 01473 400692
www.frameworkshop.org.uk
Sarah Baddon Price

Gallery Plus
Warham Road
Wells-next-the-sea
Norfolk, NR23 1QA
Tel:01328 711609 / 07795 680674
www.gallery-plus.co.uk
Gill Baguley

The Garden House Gallery
31 Garden Street
Cromer
Norfolk NR27 9HN
Tel:01263 511234
www.garden-house-gallery.co.uk
David Morris

Gallery Violet
www.galleryviolet.com
Gillian Plummer

Halesworth Gallery
Steeple End
Halesworth
IP19 8LL Suffolk
www.halesworthgallery.co.uk
(Note: Halesworth Gallery does not
stock artists' work.
Exhibitions are 3-weekly
from May – September.)
Elaine Nason

The Harleston Gallery
3 Old Market Place
Harleston
Norfolk IP20 9BE
Tel: 01379 855366
Noelle Francis
Jane German
Gill Levin
Elaine Nason
Dee Nickerson
David Page
Jayne Wurr

The Hatfield Hines Gallery
3 Fish Hill
Holt
Norfolk NR25 6BD
Tel: 01263 713000
Mob: 07967804832
www.hatfieldhines.com
Chris Hann

Hayletts Gallery
Oakwood House
2 High Street
Maldon

Essex CM9 5PJ
Tel: 01621 851669
www.haylettsgallery.com
James Dodds
Pam Schomberg

HRL Contemporary
www.hrlcontemporary.com
Tom de Freston

i2art
26 - 28 Church Street
Saffron Walden
Essex CB10 1JQ
Tel: 01799 668211
www.i2artgallery.com
Nicola Slatter

Interior Angle
23 Wells Street
Chelmsford
Esssex CM1 1HX
Tel: 01245 593100
www.interiorangle.co.uk
Karen Jones

Jack Stephenson's Studio
Jack Stephenson works to commission
only and sometimes shows with the
Suffolk Group. He can be contacted on:
jackstephenson@metronet.co.uk

The John Russell Contemporary Art Gallery
4-6 Wherry Lane
Ipswich
Suffolk IP4 1LG
Tel: 01473 212051
www.artone.co.uk
Gill Levin
Mary Spicer

Kesgrave Arts
83 Main Road
Kesgrave, Ipswich
Suffolk IP5 1AF
Tel:01473 333553
www.kesgravearts.co.uk
Geoff Harmer
Theronda Hoffman

Kettle's Yard
Castle Street
Cambridge CB3 0AQ
Tel: 01223 748100
www.kettlesyard.co.uk
Tom de Freston

King's Lynn Arts Centre
King Street
King's Lynn
Norfolk PE30 1HA
Tel: 01553 779095
www.kingslynnarts.co.uk
Andrew Schumann

Lesley Craze Gallery
33 - 35a Clerkenwell Green
London EC1R 0DU
Tel: 020 76080393
www.lesleycrazegallery.co.uk
Eleonora Knowland

The Little Gallery
5 Market Place
Halesworth
Suffolk IP19 8BA
Tel:01986 875367
www.marygundry.com
Dawn Pretty

Llewellyn Alexander (Fine Paintings)
124 The Cut
Waterloo
London SE1 8LN
Tel: 020 7620 1322
www.llewellynalexander.com
Maureen Jordan
Chris Kendrick

Lowestoft Arts Centre Gallery
13 St Peters Street
Triangle Market Place
Lowestoft
Suffolk NR32 1QA
Tel: 01502 500004
www.lowestoft-arts.org
Carolyn Reeder

Mandell's Gallery
Elm Hill
Norwich NR3 1HN
Tel: 01603 626892
www.mandellsgallery.co.uk
Douglas Farthing
David Porteous-Butler
Will Teather

Messum's Fine Art
8 Cork Street
LondonW1S
Tel: 020 74375545
www.messums.com
James Dodds

Naze Tower
The Naze
Old Hall Lane
Walton-on-the-Naze
Essex CO14 8LE
Tel: 01255 852519/ 860151
www.nazetower.co.uk
Dawn Hall

New Hall Art Collection
Murray Edwards College
University of Cambridge
Cambridge CB3 0DF
Tel: 01223 769404
www-art.newhall.cam.ac.uk
Mary Husted

North House Gallery
The Walls
Manningtree
Essex CO11 1AS
Tel: 01206 392717
www.northhousegallery.co.uk
Elaine Nason

Norwich Castle Museum & Art Gallery
Castle Meadow
Norwich
Norfolk
Tel: 01603 493625
Susan Gunn
Brüer Tidman

Norwich Frame Workshop
1 St Benedicts
Norwich NE2 4PE
Tel: 01603 616779
www.norwichonline.co.uk
Chris Kendrick

The Old Printworks
27 High Street
Saxmundham
Suffolk IP17 1AF
Tel:01728 602026
Chris Newson

Picturecraft Gallery
23 Lee's Yard
Holt
Norfolk NR25 6HS
Tel: 01263 711040,
www.picturecraftgallery.com
Geoff Harmer

Piers Feetham Fine Art
475 Fullham Road
London SW6 1HL
Tel: 020 7381 3031
www.piersfeethamgallery.com
Tessa Newcomb

The Pin Mill Gallery
Pin Mill Lane
Chelmondiston
Suffolk IP9 1JN
Tel: 01473 780130
www.wildraspberryonline.co.uk/pinmillgallery/index.php
Sarah Baddon Price

Primavera
10 King's Parade
Cambridge CB2 1SJ
Tel: 01223 357708
www.primaverauk.com
Tolly Nason
Deanna Tyson

Galleries

RE+new Gallery
63a The Thoroughfare
Woodbridge
Suffolk IP12 1AA
Tel: 01394 386314
Alyson Lomas
Chris Newson
Honor Surie

Reunion Gallery
36 Gainsborough Road
Felixstowe
Suffolk IP11 7HR
Tel: 01394 273366
www.reuniongallery.co.uk
Elizabeth James
Ruth McCabe
Honor Surie

Riverslade Gallery
5 Jubilee Court
Hill Street
Saffron Walden
Suffolk CB10 1EH
Tel: 07523893671
Tony White

ROLLO Gallery
51 Cleveland Street
London W1T 4JH
Tel: 020 75800020
www.rolloart.com
Susan Gunn

Ropewalk Contemporary Art & Craft
Multkiln Road
Barton Upon Humber
North Lincolnshire DN18 5JT
Tel: 01652 660380
www.the-ropewalk.co.uk
Louise Stebbing

Sainsbury Centre For Visual Arts
University of East Anglia
Norwich NE4 7TJ
Tel: 01603 593199
www.scva.org.uk
Susan Gunn

Saint Giles Street Gallery
51 St Giles Street
Norwich NR2 1JR
Tel: 01603 663333
www.sgsgallery.com
Brian Whelan

Sea Pictures Gallery
Well Lane
Clare
Suffolk CO10 8NH
Tel: 01787 279024
www.seapicturesgallery.com
Tolly Nason

Serena Hall Gallery
16 Queen Street
Southwold
Suffolk
Tel:01502 723887
www.serenahallgallery.co.uk/
Serena Hall

School House Gallery
The School House,
Wighton, Nr Wells Next The Sea,
Norfolk NR23 1AL
Tel: 01328 820457
Brüer Tidman

Sheringham Little Theatre Gallery
2 Station Road
Sheringham
Norfolk NR26 8RE
Tel: 01263 822347
www.sheringhamlittletheatre.com
Gill Baguley

Snape Maltings Gallery
Snape, nr Aldeburgh
Suffolk IP17 1SR
Tel: 01728 688303
www.snapemaltings.co.uk
Colin Giles
Maggi Hambling
Delia Tournay-Godfrey

Southwold Gallery
64a High Street
Southwold
Suffolk IP18 6DN
Tel: 01502 723888
www.southwoldgallery.co.uk
Chris Kendrick
Gill Levin
Dee Nickerson
Jayne Wurr

Storm Fine Arts
Fern Cottage
Market Place
Burnham Market
Norfolk PE31 8HD
Tel : 07736 241 762
www.stormfinearts.com
Beka Smith

Strand Gallery
164 High Street
Aldeburgh
Suffolk IP15 5AQ
Tel: 01728 454695
www.strandgallery.co.uk
Tessa Newcomb
Delia Tournay-Godfrey

Targetfollow
Riverside House
11-13 Riverside Road
Norwich
Norfolk NR1 1SQ
Tel: 01603 218368 or 07733 264367
www.targetfollow-arts.co.uk
Jamie Andrews
Chris Hann

Thompson's Gallery (London)
15 New Cavendish Street
London W1G 9UB
T +44 (0) 20 79353595
www.thompsonsgallery.co.uk
Brian Whelan

Thompson's Gallery (Suffolk)
175 High St.
 Aldeburgh
Suffolk IP15 5AN
Tel: 01728 453743
www.thompsonsgallery.com/Aldeburgh
Jennifer Mackay Windle
John Reay

The Town Hall Galleries
Cornhill
Ipswich
Suffolk IP1 1DH
Tel: 01473 432863
www.townhallgalleries.org.uk
Tory Lawrence

The Turner Gallery
88 Queen Street
Exeter
Devon EX4 3RP
Tel:01392 273673
www.bibleproject.co.uk
Philip James

The University of Essex
Wivenhoe Park, Colchester
Essex CO4 3SQ
Tel: 01206 873333
Robert Priseman

The Upstairs Gallery (Norfolk)
Main Cross Road
Great Yarmouth
NR30 3NZ
Tel: 01493 857574
www.bigartgallery.co.uk
Michelle Payne

The Upstairs Gallery (Suffolk)
Exchange Square
Beccles
Suffolk NR34 9HH
Tel: 01502 717191
www.bigartgallery.co.uk
Claire Louise Dowson
Michelle Payne
Mark Ward

Wildwood Gallery
40 Churchgate Street
Bury St Edmunds, Suffolk IP33 1RG
01284 752 938
www.wildwoodgallery.co.uk/

Williams Art
5 Dales Brewery
Gwydir Street
Cambridge CB1 2LJ
Tel: 01223 311687
www.williamsart.co.uk
Gail de Cordova
Deanna Tyson

Wittington Fine Art
26 Hart Street
Henley-on-Thames
Oxfordshire RG9 2AU
Tel: 01491 410787
www.wittingtonfineart.com
Philip James

Wren Gallery
Bear Court, 34 Lower High Street
Burford
Oxen, OX18 4RR
www.wrenfineart.com
David Porteous-Butler

Index

A

A Picture of Norfolk 134, 174, 186
A2 Gallery 50 184, 186
Abel Arts 157, 186
Abel, Doreen **114**, 174
Abington, Cambridgeshire 32
AFAS Armed Forces Art Society 56
Aldeburgh Contemporary Arts 142
Aldeburgh Gallery 124, 186
Alexander Gallery 20 186
Andrews, Jamie **82**, 174
Andrews, Michael 88
Anglia University 156
Anglian Potters 20
Anteros Art Centre 81
Anteros Arts Foundation 81
Appleyard Gallery 50, 186
Appleyard Gallery, The 62
Archant Collection 92
Armed Forces Art Society 142
Army Art Society 142
Arna Farrington Gallery 138, 186
Art 18/21 81, 154, 164, 186
Art Institute of Boston 53
Art-next-the-Sea 132, 174, 185, 186
Artists, Cambridgeshire 23, 28, 32, 64-69, 126,
Artists, Essex 10, 20, 24, 50, 86-89, 130, 138,
    148, 156,
Artists, Norfolk 12, 18, 22, 34, 40, 46, 58, 72-79,
    81, 90-95, 102, 122, 131-133, 136, 150, 162-
    165, 172
Artists, Suffolk 6, 14, 42, 48, 52-55, 60-63, 70, 80,
    82, 96-101, 106-119, 124, 141-147, 149, 152,
    157-161, 166-171
Arts Club, The 36
Arts Council, The 92, 108
Artworks 48, 100, 144
Asano, Takeji 24
Assembly House, The 186
Association of Lifecasters International 146
Auerbach, Frank 88
Australian National Gallery, Australia 8
Australian National University 30
Aylward, Lyn **136**, 174

B

Back2theWall Gallery, The 50, 186
Bacon, Francis 88
Baddon Price, Sarah **60**, 174
Baguley, Gill **132**, 174

Baldwin, Peter **12**, 174
Barlow Lyde & Gilbert 58
Barnes-Graham, Wilhelmina 86
Bath Academy of Art 16
Bawden, Edward 86
Beccles, Suffolk 114, 146
Bedfordshire County Council 58
Beecroft Art Gallery 175, 186
Big Blue Sky 78, 186
Bircham Gallery 10, 40, 175, 180, 186
Bishops Art Prize 92
Black Dog Arts 157 170
Blundeston, Suffolk 157
Borough Road College 78
Bowey, Olwyn 96
Boyd, Arthur 34
BP Portrait Awards 38
Bradford Metropolitan Museum 16
Braintree Museum 20, 26
Breckland Artists 136
Brighton Polytechnic 52
Briston, Norfolk 172
British Museum, The 6, 8, 24, 26 176, 186
Broughton House Gallery 68
Buckenham Galleries 23, 32, 48, 50, 62, 98,
    100, 108, 112, 114, 120, 141, 149, 160,
    174, 175, 179, 180, 181, 182, 183, 184,
    186
Buckman, David 110, 174, 182
Bungay, Suffolk 170
Burnham on Crouch, Essex 24
Bury St. Edmunds Art Society 18
Butetown Artists, Cardiff Bay, Wales 30
Butley, Suffolk 158

C

C21 Shop 78
Cam-creative 32
CAMBA (Cambridge Artists) 32
Camberwell School of Art 8, 128, 160
Cambridge 64, 68
Cambridge Art Movement 23, 68
Cambridge Contemporary Art 58, 187
Cambridge Design Collective 23
Cambridge Open Studios 23, 32, 86
Cambridge University 66, 164
Cambridgeshire Artists See Artists, Cambridgeshire
Cardiff School of Art 170
Carter, Angela 81
Castle Museum, Norwich 8

Caxton Books & Fine Art 138, 177, 187
Cecil Higgs Art Gallery 124, 187
Cecilia Colman Gallery 20, 187
Central St Martins College of Art & Design 40, 122
Cezanne, Paul 24
Chappel Galleries 72, 74, 116, 184, 187
Chelmsford Museum 26, 176, 187
Chelmsford, Essex 148, 156
Chelsea College of Art and Design 81
Chelsea School of Art 94
Chimney Mill Galleries 18, 136, 174, 178, 187
Christ's College, Cambridge 66
Christchurch Mansion 6, 8, 187
Close, Chuck 136
Cobbold and Judd 18, 106, 178, 179, 187
Colbourn, Lilian 78
Colchester Art Society 10
Colchester Institute, School of Art and Design 20,
    100, 130, 144
Colchester, Essex 20, 130
Commander of the British Empire 8
Constable, John 6
Contemporary Art Society 94
Coper, Hans 20
Cordova, Gail de **68**, 175
Cork Brick Gallery 16, 46, 52, 58, 76, 131, 170,
    176, 181, 183, 185, 187
Corpus Christi College 88
Cotman, John Sell 78
Council Borough Collection of Ipswich 106
Council For National Academic Awards 104
Council of Europe 108
Coventry Art School 58
Crane Kalman Gallery 16, 187
Cranfield University 88
Crittall Windows 20
Crome Gallery & Frame Makers 36, 187
Cromer, Norfolk 40
Curwen Print Study Centre 86
Cut, The 46, 176, 187

D

Darryl Nantais Gallery 86, 187
Darwin, Charles 32
Derby Museums and Art Gallery 88
Delaney, Mary 48
Digby Gallery, Colchester, Essex 100, 179, 187
Ditchingham, Suffolk 52
Dodds, James **10**, 175
Doncaster Art Gallery 112

Doric Arts 18, 34, 36, 136, 174, 178, 185, 187
Dowson, Claire Louise **160**, 175

E
Eardley, Joan 52
East Anglian Art Fund 36, 92
East Anglian School of Painting 8
East Harling, Norfolk 18
East Suffolk Design and Fine Art Society 53
Eaves-Walton, Chrissie 177
Edinburgh College of Art 168
Enid Lawson Gallery 42, 44, 182, 187
Essex Artists. *See* Artists, Essex
Exeter College of Art and Design 68
Eye, Suffolk 100

F
Farthing, Douglas **54**, 175
Federation of British Artists 140
Feddon, Mary 14, 76
Fens, The 18
Ferini Art Gallery 56, 84, 112, 114, 122, 154, 157, 160,
    174, 175, 182, 183, 184, 188
Figg, Christian **149**, 175
Firstsite Contemporary Art 88, 188
Fitzwilliam College 38
Fitzwilliam Museum, The 6, 8, 64, 66, 177, 188
Flint Gallery 78
Flower Photos Creative Library 158
Fluxmuseum, USA 130
Frame Workshop, The 60, 174, 188
Framlingham, Suffolk 108
Francis Iles Fine Paintings, Rochester, Kent 120
Francis, Noelle **170**, 175
Freston, Tom de **64**, 176
Friedrich, Casper David 88
Friend of Ipswich Art Society 120
Frost, Terry 86
Fry Art Gallery, Saffron Walden 86
Fujikawa, Akiko **24**, 176
Fulbourn, Cambridgeshire 23

G
Galleries. *See* by individual name
Galley@Horning, The 40
Gallery Plus 134, 174, 188
Gallery Violet 138, 158, 182, 188
Garcia Marquez, Gabriel 81
Garden House Gallery, The 40, 180, 188
Garden Media Guild 158

German, Jane **46**, 176
Giles, Colin **150**, 176
Goldsmith's College 96
Gordon-Brown, Christophe **28**, 176
Goussard Hoffman, Theronda *See* Hoffmann
Goya, Francisco de 88
Great Yarmouth College of Art & Design 76
Great Yarmouth Guild of Artists and Craftsmen 157
Great Yarmouth, Norfolk 72
Gresham, Norfolk 78
Guggenheim, The 88
Gulbenkian Foundation, Portugal 8
Gunn, Susan **90**, 177

H
Halesworth Gallery 144, 188
Halesworth, Suffolk 141
Hall, Dawn **138**, 177
Hall, Serena **166**, 177
Hambling, Maggi **6**, 177
Hampton Wick, Surrey 140
Hann, Chris **102**, 177
Hanworth, Norfolk 34
Harleston & Waveney Art Trail, The 46, 94, 131, 162
Harleston & Waveney Art Trail Collective, The 76
Harleston Gallery 46, 94, 131, 144, 162, 170, 175, 176,
    179, 181, 188
Harleston, Norfolk 58, 76, 131
Harmer, Geoff **122**, 177
Hatfield Hines Gallery, The 104, 188
Hayletts Gallery 10, 20, 188
Heem, Jan de 22
Hepworth, Barbara 86
Hereford College, Oxford, Oxfordshire 94
Hesketh Hubbard 120
Hodgkin, Howard 78
Hoffman, Theronda Goussard **124**, 178
Howard, Ken 96
HRL Contemporary 64, 66, 176, 188
Husted, Mary **30**, 178

I
i2art 58, 68, 188
Ice House Gallery 26
Imperial College of Science, The 74
Inside Out 144
Interior Angle 148, 179, 188
Ipswich Art Club 124
Ipswich Borough Council 98
Ipswich Performing Arts School 70

Ipswich School of Art 8
Ipswich, Suffolk 60, 116, 118, 124
ISWA International Society of War Artists 56

J
Jackson, Maz **18**, 178
James, Elizabeth **80**, 178
James, Philip **140**, 178
JD Wetherspoon plc 58
Jennings, Tracey **156**, 178
John Lewis Partnership 94
John Russell Gallery, The 52, 94, 183, 188
Jones, Karen **148**, 178
Jordan, Maureen **118**, 179

K
Kalf, Willem 22
Keeping Abreast 146, 182
Kendrick, Chris **22**, 179
Kesgrave Arts 122, 177, 188
Keswick Hall College of Education 160
Kettle's Yard 66, 189
Kettlestone, Fakenham 132
King's Lynn Arts Centre 164, 183, 189
King's Lynn, Norfolk 164
Kingston School of Art 48
Kingston upon Hull Art College 120
Klimt, Gustav 20
Knowland, Eleonora **100**, 179

L
Lanyon, Peter 78
Lawrence, Tory **106**, 179
Laxfield, Suffolk 144
Leeds University (Huddersfield Polytechnic) 50
Leicester Collection for Schools 58
Leigh Art Trail 50
Leigh-on-Sea 50
Leiston, Suffolk 53, 149
Lesley Craze Gallery 100, 189
Levin, Gill **94**, 179
Levy Plumb Visual Arts Residency 66
Lillford, Ralph 78
Little Gallery, The 141, 182, 189
Liverpool University 108
Llewellyn Alexander (Fine Paintings) 22, 118, 179, 189
Lomas, Alyson **108**, 180
London College of Printing 148, 150
Loughborough College of Art and Design 28, 46
Lowestoft Art Group 157

Index

Lowestoft Arts Centre Gallery 157, 189
Lowestoft School of Art and Design 157
Lowestoft, Suffolk 54, 82, 110
Lucas Industries 88

M
Mackay Windle, Jennifer **53**
Manchester College of Art and Design 154
Mandell's Gallery, Norwich, Norfolk 44, 54, 56, 81,
    175, 182, 184, 189
Mannington & Wolterton Estate, The 81
Matisse, Henri 24, 68
McCabe, Ruth **62**, 180
McKechnie, Christine **48**, 180
Messum's Fine Art, London 10, 175, 189
MFU Mutual 88
Middleton, Suffolk 96
Milden, Suffolk 42
Monet, Claude 42
Moore, Henry 86
Morris, David **40**, 180
Murray Edwards College, Cambridge 178
Museo della Carta e della Filigrana, Italy 86
Museum of Art, Detroit, USA 18
Musee D'Orsay, Paris, France 42
Musée de la Main, Switzerland 8
Museum of Modern Art, New York 6
Mystic Marine Museum & Gallery, Mystic, USA 142

N
Nason, Elaine **144**, 181
Nason, Tolly **32**, 180
National Army Museum 56
National Gallery, The 6, 64
National Portrait Gallery 8, 76
Naze Tower Gallery 138, 189
Needham, Norfolk 94
New Hall Art Collection, Murray Edwards College 30,
    178, 189
Newcastle University 23
Newcomb, Mary 14
Newcomb, Tessa **14**, 181
Newport, Essex 86
Newport Museum and Art Gallery 30
Newson, Chris **70**, 181
Nicholson, Ben 24
Nicholson, Winifed 14
Nickerson, Dee **76**, 181
Nine Artists 100
Nishijima, Katsuyuki 26

Norfolk Artists . *See* Artists, Norfolk
Norfolk Contemporary Art Society 36, 46, 52, 58, 92,
    94, 162
Norfolk Institute of Art & Design 22
Norfolk Open Studios 146
North House Gallery 144, 181, 189
North Norfolk Organisation for Visual Arts (NOVA) 78
Northern College 88
Norwich Castle 74.
Norwich 20 Group 94, 164
Norwich Art School, Norwich, Norfolk 112
Norwich Assembly House 81
Norwich Castle 92, 189
Norwich Frame Workshop 22, 179, 189
Norwich, Norfolk 22 81, 90, 102
Norwich School of Art and Design *See* Norwich
    University College of the Arts
Norwich Twenty Group 18, 52
Norwich University College of the Arts 12, 18, 80, 81,
    92, 98
NYArts Gallery Collection, Beijing, China 18

O
Officer of the British Empire 8
Old Printworks Gallery, The 70, 181, 189
Open College of the Arts 157
Outpost 92

P
Page, David **162**, 181
Palace House 23
Paris, France 14
Pastel Guild of Europe 53
Payne, Michelle **146**, 181
Picasso, Pablo 24
Picturecraft Gallery 122, 177, 189
Piers Feetham Gallery 14, 16, 181, 189
Pilchuck Glass School, Seattle, USA 32
Pin Mill Gallery, The 60, 189
Pissaro, Camille 42
Plummer, Gillian **158**, 182
Porteous-Butler, David **42**, 182
Portsmouth Museum and Art Gallery 104
Potter, Mary 14
Poussin 64, 88
Pretty, Dawn **141**, 182
Primavera 23, 32, 189
Princeton University, USA 32
Priseman, Robert **88**
Professional Garden Photographers' Association 158

Professional Photographer of the Year Magazine 40

Q
Queen Elizabeth II Law Courts 58

R
Rauschenberg, Robert 78
Ravensbourne College, Kent 170
RE+new, Woodbridge, Suffolk 70, 98, 108, 180,
181, 183, 190
Reay, John **110**, 182
Reeder, Carolyn **157**, 183
Regent Academy of the Arts 146
Rego, Paula 136
Rembrandt 6, 64
Rendham, Suffolk 106
Reunion Gallery 62, 80, 98, 178, 180, 183, 190
Rhode Island School of Design, USA 32
Rickshore House 26
Rijkers Art Collection, Netherlands 74
Riverslade Gallery, The 86, 185, 190
Rodin, Auguste 6
Rodin Museum, Paris 6
ROLLO Contemporary Art, London 90, 92, 177, 190
Ropewalk Contemporary Art & Craft 126, 183, 190
Rothenstein, Michael 86
Rothko, Mark 6, 160
Royal Academy of Arts 36
Royal Collection, Windsor Castle 88
Royal College of Art 10, 74
Royal Society of Arts, The 23, 94
Rugge-Price, Jeremy **142**

S
Sainsbury Centre for Visual Arts, Norwich 90, 92, 190
Saint Giles Street Gallery 190
Salthouse 11, 12
Saxmundham, Suffolk 6, 70
Schomberg, Pam **20**
School House Gallery 74, 190
Schumann, Andrew **164**, 183
Schwitters, Kurt 24
Scrase, David 6
Sea Pictures Gallery 32, 180, 190
Second Floor Studios and Arts 38
Serena Hall Gallery 166, 177, 190
Sheffield Hallam University 88
Sheffield University 128
Sheringham Little Theatre Gallery 190
Sheringham, Norfolk 12

Sisley, Alfred 42
Slade School of Fine Art 8, 104, 140
Slattery, Nicola **58**, 183
Sligo School of Art, Ireland 20
Slough Picture Collection, Middlesex 94
Smith, Beka **38**, 183
Snape Maltings Gallery 8, 116, 150, 176,
    177, 184, 190
Society of Botanical Artists 120
Society of Designer Craftsman 20, 23
Society of East Anglian Watercolourists 86
Society of Egg Tempera Painters 18
Society of Graphic Fine Art 18
Society of Graphics Art 48
South Glamorgan Institute of Higher Education 30
Southbank Centre 178
Southolt, Suffolk 48
Southwold Art Circle 62, 96, 141
Southwold Gallery 22, 76, 94, 131, 190
Southwold, Suffolk 14, 166
Sovereign Art Foundation, The 92
Sovereign European Painting Prize 92
Spencer Coleman Fine Art, London 141
Spencer, Stanley 76
Spicer, Mary **52**, 183
Spier Artschool, Stellenbosh, South Africa 124
St Giles Street Gallery 36
St Martins School of Art 108
    See also Central St Martins College of Art & Design
Starston, Norfolk 46, 162
Stebbing, Louise **126**, 183
Stephenson, Jack **96**, 188
Storm Fine Arts 38, 183, 190
Stowmarket, Suffolk 80
Strand Gallery 16, 116, 190
Sudbourne, Suffolk 142
Suffolk Artists. *See* Artists, Suffolk
Suffolk College (University of East Anglia) 116
Suffolk College, Ipswich 130
Suffolk Crafts 20
Suffolk Group, The 961, 44
Suffolk Open Studios 48, 62, 80, 146, 158, 160
Surie, Honor **98**, 183

T
Targetfollow 82, 102, 174, 177, 190
Tate Collection 8
Teather, Will **81**, 184
Temple-Cox, Lisa **130**
Thadian Pillai Studio 178

Thetford, Norfolk 136
Thompson's Gallery (London) 36, 190
Thompson's Gallery (Suffolk) 53, 112, 191
Tidman, Brüer **72**, 184
Tindle, David 96
Titian, Tiziano Vecellio 6, 64
Tournay-Godfrey, Delia **116**, 184
Town Hall Galleries, The 106, 191
Tress, David 52
Trevisan International Art 18
Trim, Jonathan **50**, 184
Tuddenham Parish Council 98
Turner Gallery, The , Exeter 140, 178, 191
Twombly, Cy 6
Tydd Gote near Wisbech, Cambridgeshire 126
Tyson, Deanna **23**, 184

U
Ubbeston Green (Near Halesworth), Suffolk 152
University College London 104
University of East Anglia, Norwich 116
University of Essex, The 10, 74, 191
University of Essex Art Gallery, The 88
University of Glamorgan Art Collection, Wales 30
University of Hull, The 88
University of Kent, The 88
University of London 158
University of West of England,The 38
Upstairs Gallery, Suffolk 146, 152, 160,
    175, 184, 191
Upstairs Gallery, Norfolk 146, 182, 191
Upton, Norfolk 150

V
Vale of Glamorgan, South Wales 30
Vallien, Bertil 32
Van Gogh, Vincent 6
Van Rijn, Rembrandt *See* Rembrandt
Vann, Philip 16
Venice, Italy 14
Vermeer, Johannes 88
Victoria and Albert Museum, London 8

W
Wade, Kit **78**
Walton-on-the-Naze, Essex 138
Ward, Mark **152**, 184
Warhol, Andy 88
Wayper, Dr Leslie 38
Welsh Group, The 30

Welsh National Library 44
Wenhaston, Suffolk 14, 62
West Norfolk Artists Association 128, 164
West of England (Painting School) 160
Westwood, Sandi **172**, 185
Whelan, Brian **34**, 185
White, Tony **86**, 185
Whitworth Art Gallery, Manchester 16
Wickham Market, Suffolk 122
Wildwood Gallery 36, 191
Williams Art 23, 68, 175, 184, 191
Williams, Sir Kyffiin 42
Wimbledon School of Art 16
Winchester School of Art 32, 60, 108, 131
Wittington Fine Art 140, 191
Willingham, Cambridgeshire 32
Wivenhoe, Essex 10, 88
Wolverhampton Art Gallery 88
Women's Arts Association, Wales 30
Woodbridge Art Club 124
Woodbridge, Suffolk 98
Wren Gallery 44, 182, 191
Wurr, Jayne **131**, 185

Y
Yale Center for British Art, USA 8

Previous book in this series:

The Artist in Our Midst: Suffolk & Norfolk

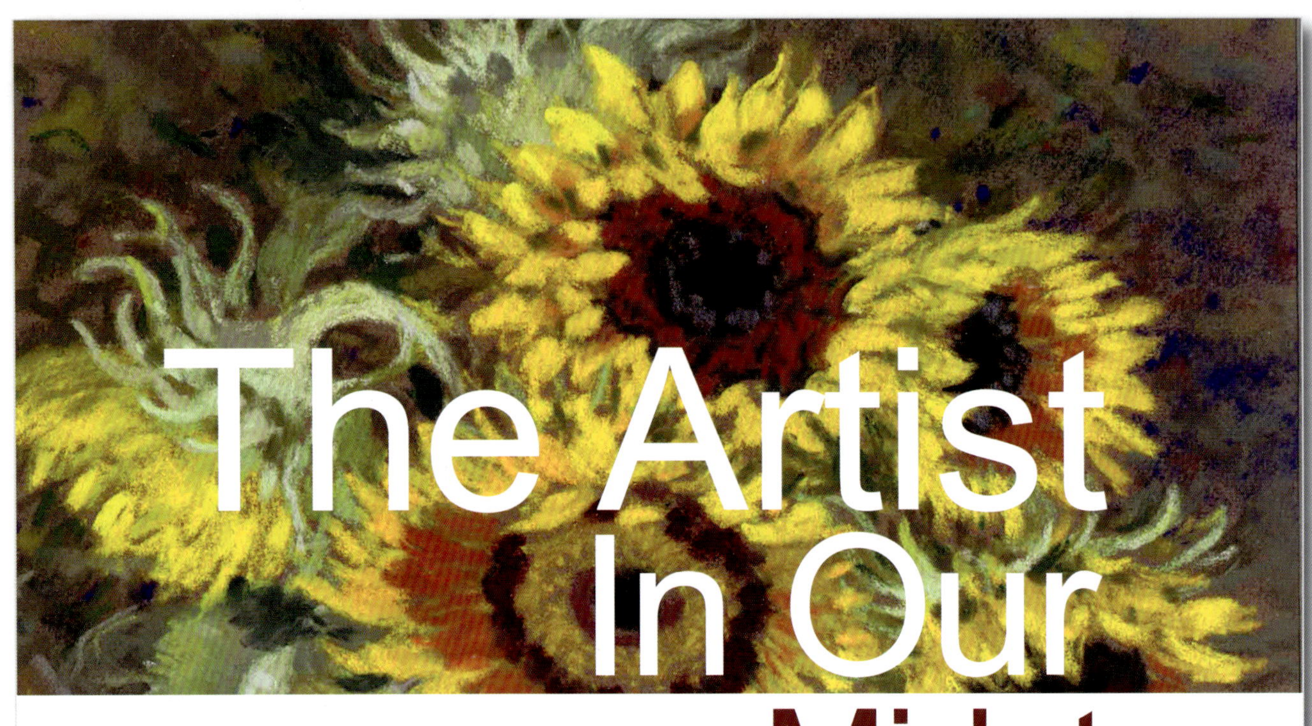

A beautiful book containing 88 colour images by
48 leading Norfolk and Suffolk contemporary artists
£14.99
Tel: 01502 710427
www.greenpebble.co.uk